The Encyclopedia of

THE HORSE

The Encyclopedia of
THE

Edited by Lieutenant-Colonel C. E. G. Hope and G. N. Jackson

HORSE

Advisory Editor: William Steinkraus

PEERAGE BOOKS

First published in Great Britain by Ebury Press and Pelham Books Ltd

This edition published by Peerage Books
59 Grosvenor Street
London W1

ISBN 0 907408 18 4

This book was designed and produced
by The Rainbird Publishing Group Ltd
36 Park Street
London W1

Printed in Hong Kong

Editors' Note

The late Lieut Colonel Charles Evelyn Graham Hope (1900–71) was a retired cavalry officer turned equestrian writer and editor who gave his readers the benefit of wide knowledge of his subject, allied to a rare integrity and a passionate concern for the welfare of the horse. His loss was felt keenly in the horse world. From the beginning he conceived of this encyclopedia as an international work and contributors were commissioned, as far as possible, from the appropriate countries to write with authority on breeds and equestrian activities. We are grateful for the help and enthusiasm of all those who offered extra assistance in compiling this book and who sent information and photographs to us. This book could not have been produced without their support.

How to use this book

As a work of reference, this book is arranged in a single, alphabetical sequence: **Breton and Breton Heavy Draught** and **Bridles** follow **Breeding,** and a cross-reference to the first is found under **Corlay Horse.** Where it is thought that the reader may gain useful additional information from reading other entries, these are indicated within articles by small capitals. To provide consistency, British spellings have been adopted for breeds and technical terms. Place-names are given as currently used in the country concerned, except for a few cities (Munich, Prague, etc.) where the English spelling is more widely known. Transliterations from Cyrillic and Arabic scripts have presented problems; cross-references will be found to guide the reader from variants in spelling to the appropriate article.

Contributors

HCA Harlan C. Abbey. American journalist: author, *Showing Your Horse.*

AA Anthony Amaral. Writer on Western American subjects, natural history and horses; author, *Comanche, Movie Horses,* etc.

MEA Max E. Ammann. Editor-in-chief of weekly. Contributor to European and American equestrian magazines.

HA Prof. Hugo Araki. Professor and Director of Computer Centre at Kyoto Sangyo University, Japan. Captain, Japanese Olympic Equestrian Team 1968.

KAA Kenneth Ashurst Austin, F.R.G.S. Sometime Tutor in Australian history, Trinity College, University of Melbourne. Author, *The Voyage of the Investigator, The Lights of Cobb and Co.,* etc.

CGEB Captain C. G. E. Barclay. Joint Master, Puckridge Hounds from 1947.

MBe Mona Bennett, Executive Officer, Riding Clubs' Committee, British Horse Society.

LFB Lida Fleitmann Bloodgood. American horsewoman, ex-M.F.H. and show rider; author, *Comments on Hacks and Hunters, The Horse in Art, Hoofs in the Distance, The Saddle of Queens,* and (with Major Piero Santini) *The Horseman's Dictionary.*

EB Eduardo Botta. Equestrian editor, *La Nación* (Buenos Aires) and Director, *El Caballo.*

RAB R. A. Brown. Secretary, Coaching Club, London Harness Horse Parade. Former Secretary, British Horse Society, Hackney Horse Society, etc.; author, *Horse Brasses, History of the Coaching Club.*

MB Michael Bullen. Former British Olympic Three-Day-Event rider; Managing Director, J. A. Peden Ltd, horse transportation company.

JCa Judith Campbell. Author, *The Queen Rides, Police Horses, Princess Anne and her Horses,* etc.

JC Brigadier J. Clabby, C.B.E., M.R.C.V.S. Chief Executive Officer, The Animal Health Trust.

JLC Jennifer Loriston-Clarke (née Bullen). Noted British show rider.

MC Michael Clayton. Broadcaster; author, *A Hunting We Will Go, Hickstead: The First Twelve Years,* etc.

WSC Colonel W. S. Codrington, T.D., M.R.C.V.S. Veterinary surgeon; author, *Know Your Horse.*

CC Christopher Coldrey. Editor, *Horse and Hound, Southern Africa;* equestrian broadcaster.

LC L. Constance, M.R.C.V.S. Veterinary surgeon.

RC Ramon Coto. Director of Publicity, Oriental Park, Cuba; turf writer, Cuba, Puerto Rico and the United States.

HKC Helen K. Crabtree. Instructor, trainer and judge; author, *Saddle Seat Equitation.*

GHC Colonel G. H. Critchley. Horseman and judge of horses; Chairman, Riding Establishments Act Committee, British Horse Society.

CJC Charles J. Cronan. Breeder of Saddlebred, Standard bred and Thoroughbred horses. Executive Secretary, American Saddle Horse Breeders' Association.

ZD Zita Denholm. Editor, *A Race of Horsemen,* contributor to horse journals; founder, pony club movement in Queensland; historian in Australian pastoral development.

AD Anthony Dent. Breeder of ponies; author, *The Purebred Exmoor Pony, Donkey, The Story of the Ass,* and (with D. Machin Goodall) *The Foals of Epona;* contributor to horse journals; translator from German and French.

ND Neil Dougall. Contributor to *Horse and Hound, Stud and Stable, Riding* etc.; author, *Stallions: their Management and Handling;* breeder and stud manager.

PD Colonel Paul Downing. Editor, *The Carriage Journal.*

EHE Captain E. Hartley Edwards. Editor, *Riding;* author, *Saddlery, Horseman's Guide, Owning a Pony.*

GE George Ennor. A racing correspondent, *The Sporting Life.*

HE H. Epstein. Professor of Animal Breeding, Hebrew University of Jerusalem; author, *Domestic Animals of China, The Origin of the Domestic Animals of Africa, Domestic Animals of Nepal.*

GWE Gerald W. Evans. Secretary, The Hunters' Improvement and National Light Horse Breeding Society.

WSF W. Sidney Felton, Lawyer and Trustee; amateur horseman, author, judge and a founder of the U.S. Pony Club, Inc.

LF Louise Firouz. Hippologist and breeder of Caspian ponies.

JEF Judith E. Forbis. Breeder of Arabs; contributor to *Arab Horse Journal, Your Pony, Arabian Horse News* etc.; author, *Hoofbeats Along the Tigris,* etc.

CF C. Formston, F.R.C.V.S. Professor of Surgery and Vice-Principal, Royal Veterinary College, London.

JF Jean Froissard, Écuyer-Professeur, F.F.S.E., equestrian journalist; contributor to magazines in Britain, France and the United States; instructor; author of books on equitation, jumping and dressage.

JRCG Brigadier Jack R. C. Gannon, C.B.E., M.V.O. Polo correspondent to *The Field;* Hon. Secretary, Hurlingham Polo Association since 1945; committee member, Indian Polo Association 1913–32.

LG Leslie Gardiner. Author, traveller and Italophile. Contributor to *The Light Horse, The Horseman's Year,* etc.

JG John Gaselee. British freelance journalist and broadcaster specializing in insurance.

DMG Daphne Machin Goodall. Member, wild horse specialist group, Survival Service Commission, authority on horse breeds; author, *Horses of the World, Huntsmen of a Golden Age, History of Horse Breeding,* etc.

SG Susanne Grubb. Journalist, commentator and P.R. Account Executive. Former Belvoir Pony Club member.

HG Colonel Humphrey Guinness. Member of three British international polo squads; member of Olympic Army Team 1936.

JKH John Kenneth Habgood. Writer on horses, dogs, wildlife and the North Yorkshire countryside.

AHa Alison Hardcastle. Stud owner, breeder of Arabs and Anglo-Arabs. Judge and council member, British Arab Horse Society.

FH Frederick Harper, Extension Associate in Horse Management, Rutgers University, College of Agriculture and Environmental Science (U.S.A.).

JH Joseph Hefter. Fellow of The Company of Military Historians; secretary, Military History Institute.

TH Theo Herbert. Historian; author of books on horses and hunting; correspondent to *New Zealand Horse and Pony;* founder member and instructor, New Zealand Horse and Pony Club.

JHew James Hewat. Master of Bloodhounds; owner, road coach 'Harrier'; driving/riding instructor; contributor to *Horse and Hound,* etc.

MH Michael Hickman. Past professional show-jumping course builder to the British Show Jumping Association, judge, consultant, etc.

DH Duncan Holden. Master of Dannevirke Hunt 1945–54. Former chief examiner, N.Z. Pony Club. Co-founder N.Z. Horse Society and President 1962–5.

CEGH Lt-Col C. E. G. Hope. Founder editor, *Pony* and *The Light Horse;* author, *The Horse Trials Story,* etc.

AH Anna Hulbert. Art historian and restorer.

II Dr Ivan Iorov. Senior scientific worker on horse breeding, Research Institute of Animal Breeding, Kostinbrod, Bulgaria.

GNJ G. N. Jackson, C.M.G., M.B.E., Horseman and breeder; author of *Effective Horsemanship.*

ADHJ A. D. H. Jones. Clerk, The Saddler's Company.

DJ Dave Jones. Horseman, trainer; author, *Practical Western Horsemanship.*

LTJ Linda Tellington Jones. Director, Pacific Coast Equestrian Institute; judge and organizer of competitive trail rides.

WEJ William E. Jones, D.V.M., Ph.D.

Assistant Professor, College of Veterinary Medicine, Michigan State University. Author (with Ralph Bogart), *Genetics of the Horse.*

RJ Rudi Jurkschat. Circus equestrian trainer and horseman.

SK Sonia Kelly. Writer on equine subjects; author, *The Connemara Pony.*

RK Ruth Kitching. Hon. Consultant Secretary, Cleveland Bay Horse Society and Editor of the Stud Book and Magazine; breeder of Cleveland Bays.

FIDL Flor Isava de Laferriere. Venezuelan horsewoman.

GBL George B. Lalonde. Executive Secretary, Pony of the Americas Club, Inc.

GL Gloria Lanigan. Judge and lecturer; contributor to *Hoofs and Horns, Arab Horse News,* etc. Australian horsewoman and stud manager.

ML Muriel Anne Lennox. Horsewoman. Editor, *Canadian Horse;* formerly co-publisher, show horse magazine *The Corinthian;* director, Canadian Dressage Owners and Riders Association.

PL Countess Lewenhaupt (née Penelope Molteno); former horse trials rider. Now lives in Sweden and breeds Arabs and New Forest ponies.

MAL Mary Aiken Littauer. Archaeologist specializing in horses and horse gear.

VSL Captain Vladimir S. Littauer. American horseman, riding instructor; author of *Be a Better Horseman, Commonsense Horsemanship, The Development of Modern Riding, Schooling Your Horse,* etc.

CL Christopher Lofting. Editor-publisher, *Rodeo Magazine;* former staff member of *Life* magazine.

PMM Pamela Macgregor-Morris. Horsewoman and breeder; equitation correspondent of *The Times;* regular contributor to *Horse and Hound, The Chronicle of the Horse* (U.S.A.), *L'Anné Hippique* (Switzerland), etc.; author of 21 books.

RMacW Rosalie MacWilliam. Founder director and registrar, American Paso Fino Horse Association; contributor to *Western Horseman, The Chronicle of the Horse,* etc.

JHM J. H. Mason, Joint Secretary, The Animal Health Trust.

POM Pedro Oscar Mayorga. Member of the Argentine Olympic Jumping Team 1956; F.E.I. bureau member 1956–64 and second Vice President since 1964.

TM Tony Morris. Editor, *Bloodstock Breeders Review.*

RM Roger Mortimer. Racing journalist; author, *The Derby, The Jockey Club, Twenty Great Horses;* editor, *Encyclopedia of Flat Racing.*

GM Genevieve Murphy. Equestrian correspondent of the *Observer;* editor, *Pony Club Annual;* contributor to *The Light Horse,* etc.

PN Peter Nagy. Hungarian librarian and equestrian correspondent.

PNe Premysl Neumann. Czechoslovak equestrian writer; racing, riding and breeding correspondent of *Lidová demokracie* and *Jazdectvo (Equitation).*

WOF Wendy O'Flaherty, Ph.D. Lecturer at School of Oriental and African Studies, University of London; studied dressage at the Moscow Hippodrome.

RO Richard Onslow. Author, *The Heath and the Turf.*

GTP Dr G. T. Peacock, M.B., Ch.B.

FTP Frank T. Phelps. Racing writer for newspapers in Lexington, Kentucky.

AP Colonel Alois Podhajsky. Former Director, Spanish Riding School of Vienna. Author, *The Complete Training of Horse and Rider, My Horses, My Teachers, My Dancing White Horses, The Spanish Riding School of Vienna, The Riding Teacher,* etc.

VP Prof. Vladimir Popov. Chief of Horse Breeding Section, Research Institute of Animal Breeding, Academy of Agricultural Sciences, Kostinbrod, Bulgaria.

TP Tony Power. Hunting correspondent, *Irish Field.*

DR David Reid. Horseman; involved in administration of British Junior Three-Day-Event Championship; council member, Hunters' Improvement and National Light Horse Breeding Society.

GR German Rieckehoff. President, Puerto Rican Equestrian Federation; member Puerto Rican Olympic Committee.

TR Tom Ryder. Internationally known coachman and authority on Hackneys; author of *The High Stepper, On the Box Seat.*

ES Étienne Saurel. French horseman; Président d'Honneur de l'Association d' Éleveurs de Chevaux Camargue; author *Histoire de L'Équitation; Pratique de l'Équitation d'après les Maîtres Français, Le Cheval, Équitation et Sports Hippiques,* etc.

AHS A. H. Saxon, Ph.D. Associate Professor, Dept of Speech and Theatre, City College of the City University of New York; author, *Enter Foot and Horse.*

ESch Erika Schiele. Journalist; author, *The Arab Horse in Europe, Horse Buying, Riding Horse Management, Allah's Favourites,* etc.

EFS Elizabeth Friedlaender-Searle. Co-founder, American Vaulting Association and co-editor, *Vaulting News*; author, *Vaulting, The Art of Gymnastics on the Moving Horse.*

MNS Mrs M. N. Serrell. Member, American Horse Shows Association Dressage Committee; recognized dressage judge; competitor; President, The American Dressage Institute.

GGS George Gaylord Simpson. Vertebrate palaeontologist; former Curator, Chairman and Dean, American Museum of Natural History, Professor at Harvard and Columbia Universities; now Professor at University of Arizona and President, the Simroe Foundation; author, *Horses, Life of the Past, The Meaning of Evolution, The Major Features of Evolution,* etc.

WS Wouter Slob. Ex-cavalry officer. Founder, Royal Dutch Riding Clubs Association and chief instructor; founder, Netherlands Warmblood Association; contributor to periodicals in Holland, Germany, Great Britain, etc., author of 25 books on horses, riding, driving, etc.

TJS T. J. Sophian, B.A. (Oxon), Barrister; author, *Horses and the Law.*

GS Glenda Spooner, D.B.H.S. Chairman, The 'Ponies of Britain'; author, *Handbook of Showing, Instructions in Ponymastership.*

SS Sylvia Stanier. Teacher of equitation, writer and artist.

RS Randy Steffen. Artist and writer of Sioux ancestry; authority on the American West and Plains Indians; Fellow of The Company of Military Historians.

MAS M. A. Stoneridge. American journalist; author, *A Horse of Your Own* and *Great Horses of Our Time.*

HJS Helen J. Stubblefield. Secretary, Galiceño Horse Breeders Association, Inc.

RSS R. S. Summerhays. Horseman; writer on equestrian and equine subjects; former Editor, *Riding;* past President, National Pony and Arab Horse Societies; author, *Summerhays' Encyclopaedia for Horsemen, The Problem Horse, Elements of Riding, Elements of Hunting,* etc.

MMT Mrs M. M. Taylor. Breeder of Welsh crossbred ponies (U.S.A.).

PT Patrick Tenison. Horseman and breeder in Jamaica.

WWT William W. Thomson, M.R.C.V.S. Journalist; technical adviser to the British Horse Society's Combined Training Committee.

CCT Charles Chenevix-Trench. Author, *History of Horsemanship* and several works of history and biography.

DRT Diana R. Tuke. Horsewoman, journalist and equestrian correspondent. Author, *Bit by Bit, Stitch by Stitch, Horse by Horse,* etc.

RT Major Robin Tuke. Formerly of The Buffs (Royal East Kent Regiment); freelance journalist.

SAW Stella Archer Walker. Writer on equestrian art and literature of the horse; author, *Horses of Renown, Long Live the Horse, Sporting Art: England 1700–1900,* etc.

MHW Maudie Hunter-Warfel. Founder, National Foundation for Happy Horsemanship for the Handicapped, Inc.

SW Sanders Watney. President, The Coaching Club; President, The British Driving Society; holder of B.H.S. Medal of Honour.

BW Benton Watson. P.R. Assistant, American Quarter Horse Association.

GWe Geoffrey Webster. Deputy Director, Racing Information Bureau.

EW Elisabeth Weiland. Journalist and photographer specializing in horses and animal behaviour; author, *Pferdezucht in der Schweiz.*

FWCW Lt-Col F. W. C. Weldon, M.V.O., M.B.E., M.C. Director, Badminton Horse Trials. Captain, British Three-Day-Event Team, 1954–64.

GW George Wheatley. Riding instructor; author, *Schooling A Young Horse, Stable Management for the Owner Groom, Keep your Own Pony, The Pony Rider's Book,* etc.

SWi Sheila Willcox. Leading British three-day-event team rider from 1956. Author, *Three Days Running.*

PW Peter Willett, F.S.A. Racing and breeding correspondent, *Sporting Chronicle.* Breeding correspondent, *Horse and Hound.* Author, *An Introduction to the Thoroughbred, The Thoroughbred.*

DW Dorian Williams. Horseman; Master of Foxhounds; broadcaster; Chairman, the National Equestrian Centre; author, *The Horseman's Year, The Horseman's Companion, Show Jumping,* etc.

MW Michael Williams, Point-to-point correspondent, *Sporting Life;* Editor, *Pony* and *The Light Horse;* author, *The Continuing Story of Point-to-Pointing.*

MoW Moyra Williams, B.Litt (Oxon), D.Phil (Oxon). Author, *Horse Psychology, Adventures Unbridled, A Breed of Horses.*

WHW W. H. Woods. Secretary, Suffolk Horse Society.

Acknowledgments and Notes on Illustrations

The producers of this book wish to express their grateful thanks to Professor C. Formston, F.R.C.V.S. and Mr L. Constance, F.R.C.V.S. for technical advice, Miss Marion Murphy and the staff of *Pony* and *The Light Horse*, Mr K. R. Stevens of *Hoofs and Horns*, Miss L. Malden, Mr Sanders Watney, to all contributors and many others who suggested sources of information and illustrations, and also all those who are indicated by the following list of illustrations, especially the governing bodies and staffs of the libraries and museums and the individual owners of photographs. Every effort has been made to trace the primary sources of illustrations; in one or two cases where it has not been possible, the producers wish to apologize if the acknowledgment proves to be inadequate; in no case is such inadequacy intentional and if any owner of copyright who has remained untraced will communicate with the producers a reasonable fee will be paid and the required acknowledgment made in future editions of the book.

Colour illustrations

Drawings

The drawings throughout the book, unless otherwise noted, are by Annabel Milne. The drawings on page 270 are based on ones by E. Trumler after H. Ebhardt.
The maps, diagrams and drawings on pages xi, xii, xiii, 81, 122–3, 145, 166, 234–5 and 268 are by Howard Dyke.

Monochrome photographs

Tuke (as 77a,b,c,d)

88 Brumbies. *Photo: Australian News and Information Bureau*

89 **a.** Calgary Stampede. *Photo: Canadian Government Travel Bureau*
b. Budyonny. *Photo: V/O Prodintorg; A. Storch*

90 East Bulgarian. *Photo: Vl. Popov*

91 **a.** Byerley Turk. *Photo: John R. Freeman Ltd, courtesy Fores' Gallery*
b. Calgary Stampede. *Photo: Canadian Government Travel Bureau*

92 Racing in Edmonton, Alberta. *Information Canada Photothèque. Photo: Chris Lund*

97 Cape Horse. *Photo: Natal Mounted Reserve Comrades' Association, courtesy D. Child*

98 **a.** Captain Federico Caprilli. *Photo: L. F. Bloodgood*
b. Cylinder seal of 'Darius the Great King', 6th-5th century B.C. *British Museum*

99 **a.** Slidecar. *Ulster Museum*
b. Travois. *Museum of the American Indian, Heye Foundation*

100 Bas-relief of the Elamite army, 7th century B.C. *British Museum*

101 **a.** Curricle. *Photo: Pony/Light Horse*
b. Highflier phaeton. Fairman Rogers, *Manual of Coaching*, 1900. *British Museum*

102 Caspian pony. *Photo: Carlos A. Casal, Jr*

103 Packhorses on Newton Moor, Yorkshire. *Photo: Tindale's of Whitby*

104 Relief of horse and attendant, 7th century A.D. *University of Philadelphia Museum*

105 Chinese polo, watercolour on silk, 15th century. *Crown Copyright, Victoria and Albert Museum*

106 **a,b,c,** 107. Ponies in Mongolia. *Photos: H. Epstein*

108 Circus horses. *Photo: H. Alder*

110 Cleveland Bay. *Photo: Childe Photography*

113 Clydesdale. *Photo: Leslie Lane*

114 *The Edinburgh to London Stage*, painting by J. C. Maggs, 1856. *Photo: Richard Green*

115 Cob. *Photo: Leslie Lane*

117 Comtois. *Photo: Photostore*

121 Hamburg Derby arena. *Photo: London Express News and Feature Service*

124 **a.** Cutting horse in training. *Photo: Dave Jones*
b. Cattle drafting. *Photo: Australian News and Information Service; W. Pedersen*

125 **a.** Kladruber horses. *Photo: P. Neumann*
b. Hayrakes. *Photo: E. Preston*

126 **a.** Danubian. *Photo: Vl. Popov*
b. Darley Arabian. *Photo: The Mansell Collection*

127 Hickstead Derby Bank. *Photo: Rex Coleman*

128 **a.** Diomed. *Photo: The Mansell Collection*
b. Epsom Derby, 1896. *Photo: The Mansell Collection*
c. Epsom Derby, 1968. *Photo: Syndication International*

129 Engraving, *The Great Horse*, by Albrecht Dürer, 1505. *British Museum*

131 Don. *Photo: Sally Anne Thompson*

133 **a,b.** Dressage. *Photos: Elisabeth Weiland, Zollikon*

134 **a.** Hackney. *Photo: Leslie Lane*
b. Pair of Oldenburgs. *Photo: Freudy Photos*

135 Tandem. *Photo: John H. Berry*

136 Hungarian driving team. *Photo: Hung Art; A. Alapfy*

138 Dülmen. *Photo: Klaus Zeeb, courtesy L. Malden.*

139 **a.** Dutch Warmblood. *Photo: Heemskerk Duker, courtesy W. Slob*
b. Gondola. *Photo: Hook, courtesy Vl. Popov*

140 Egyptian dancing horse. *Photo: J. E. Forbis*

142 Dr Rainer Klimke riding Mehmed D. *Photo: Elisabeth Weiland, Zollikon*

143 Sheila Willcox riding Fair and Square. *Photo: Monty*

146 Falabella. *Photo: Pony/Light Horse*

148 Finnish mare. *Photo: L. Malden*

149 Newmarket, 1767. *Photo: The Mansell Collection*

150 Mahmoud. *Photo: W. W. Rouch & Co. Ltd*

151 Longchamp, 1900. *Photo: Giraudon*

152 **a.** Gran Premio, Milan, 1971. *Photo: Agenzia Giornalistical Italia*
b. Anilin. *Photo: Konyevodstva Museum*

154 Melbourne Cup, 1970. *Photo: Australian News and Information Bureau; T. Rowe*

155 *Iroquois*, painting by J. Flatman, 1882. *The National Museum of Racing, Inc., Saratoga Springs, N.Y.*

156 Forward Seat. *Photo: Jane M. Dillon*

157 Curre Hunt. *Photo: Jim Meads*

158 Cadre Noir. *Photo: J. Decker; © SPADEM Paris 1973*

159 Haras du Pin. *Photo: Photostore*

160 **a.** Vincennes, 1971. *Photo: A.P.R.H.*
b. French Trotter. *Photo: Photostore*

161 **a.** Friesian. *Photo: W. Slob*
b. Galiceño. *Photo: Galiceño Horse Breeders Assn Inc.*
c. Galloway. *Photo by courtesy of the Manx Museum*

162 **a.** Gelderland. *Photo: W. Slob*
b. East Friesian. *Photo: H. Sting, courtesy L. Malden*

163 Marbach National Stud. *Photo: Erika Schiele*

165 **a.** Grand Liverpool Steeplechase, 1839. *Photo: The Mansell Collection*
b. Grand National Steeplechase, 1968. *Photo: Syndication International*

167 Old English Black. F. Street, *The History of the Shire Horse*, 1883. *British Museum*

168 Highland ponies. *Photo: Leslie Lane*

172 Groningen. *Photo: W. Slob*

173 Hack. *Photo: Leslie Lane*

174 Eastertide. *Photo: W. W. Rouch & Co. Ltd*

175 Hackney. *Photo: Leslie Lane*

178 Clydesdales. *Photo: Lee Weatherley*

179 Painting by George Catlin. *Photo: The Mansell Collection*

181 Engraving by Riedinger, 1730. *British Museum*

182 *The Polish Rider*, painting by Rembrandt van Rijn. *Copyright The Frick Collection, New York*

183 **a,b.** Horse Trials. *Photos: Cyril E. Diamond*

184 **a.** Burghley, 1971. *Photo: Leslie Lane*
b. Huçul. *Photo: L. Malden*

185 Harness racing. *Photo: Hung Art, A. Alapfy*

189 Hunter. *Photo: Leslie Lane*

190 191 Hunting. *Photos: Jim Meads*

192 Music from George Turbervile, *The Booke of Falconrie, 1575. British Museum*

193 Galway Blazers. *Photo: Irish Tourist Board*

194 **a.** Hurdling. *Photo: Syndication International*
b. Hunting. *Photo: Jim Meads*

195 Iceland. *Photo: Icelandic Photo and Press Service*

196 **a.** Baluchi. *Photo: Baluchistan Government*
b. Kathiawari. *Photo: Gujarat State Dept of Animal Husbandry*
c. Spiti. *Photo: Indian Ministry of Food & Agriculture, courtesy L. Malden*

197 **a.** Bhutia. *Photo: Dr P. Bhattacharya, courtesy L. Malden*
b. Canal horse. *Photo: Syndication International*

199 Iomud. *Photo: V/O Prodintorg; A. Storch*

201 Irish Draught. *Photo: I. Ruthven*

202 **a,b,c.** Japanese horses. *Photos: Y. Nishikawa*

204 Bridget Parker riding Cornish Gold. *Photo: United Press International*

205 **a.** Danish warriors, detail from English ms. of Prudentius, *Psychomachia*, 11th century. *British Museum*
b. Jutland. *Photo: G. Halling Nielsen, courtesy L. Malden*

206 **a.** Kabardin. *Photo: Novosti*
b. Karabair. *Photo: Sally Anne Thompson*

207 **a.** Karabakh, **b.** Kazakh. *Photos: V/O Prodintorg; A. Storch*

208 **a.** Kentucky Derby, 1971. *Photo: Caufield & Shook, Inc., courtesy Churchill Downs, Inc.*
b. Knabstrup. *Photo: G. Halling Nielsen, courtesy L. Malden*

209 **a.** Konik. *Photo: Sally Anne Thompson*
b. Kulan. *Photo: D. Darlow*
c. Kustanair. *Photo: V/O Prodintorg; A. Storch*
d. La Guérinière. Engraving after Toquet, from Jules Théodore Pellier, *Le Langage Équestre*, 1889. *British Museum*

211 Latvian. *Photo: V/O Prodintorg; A. Storch*

213 **a.** Moroccan Barb, **b.** Moroccan Arab. *Photos: Photostore*
c. Lipizzaners. *Photo: Sally Anne Thompson*

214 Londoners welcome the Earl of Derby after Richard II's surrender of the crown; early 15th-century French ms. *British Museum. Photo: courtesy George Weidenfeld & Nicolson Ltd.*

215 Lithuanian Heavy Horse. *Photo: V/O Prodintorg; A. Storch*

216 Lokai. *Photo: V/O Prodintorg; A. Storch*

217 **a.** Veterinary checkpoint. *Photo: Western Horseman*
b. Exmoor, September 1965. *Photo: Jim Meads*

219 Mangalarga. *Photo: Daphne Machin Goodall*

220 Maryland Hunt Cup, 1969. *Photo: Winants Bros. Inc.*

221 Masuren. *Photo: Centralna Agencja Fotograficzna, Poland*

223 Charreada. *Photo: Janet March-Penney*

225 **a.** Mongolian pony. *Photo: H. Epstein*
b. Anon. Chinese drawing of Mongol archer on horseback, Ming Dynasty, 15th or 16th century. *Crown Copyright, Victoria and Albert Museum*

227 Roy Rogers and Trigger. *Photo:* A. Amaral

228 **a,b,c.** Ponies. *Photos: Leslie Lane*

229 Dales pony. *Photo: Pony/Light Horse*

230 **a.** New Forest pony. *Photo: Spectrum; H. E. Lomax*
b. Dartmoor pony. *Photo: Leslie Lane*
c. Exmoor ponies. *Photo: Exmoor Pony Society*
231 **a.** Connemara ponies. *Photo: Jack H. Coote*
b. Welsh Mountain pony. *Photo: Leslie Lane*
232 **a.** Kokburi. *Photo: V/O Prodintorg; A. Storch*
b. Basuto Mounted Policeman. *Photo: Lesotho Mounted Police, courtesy D. Child*
233 Royal Canadian Mounted Police. *Photo: Canadian Government Travel Bureau*
236 **a.** Centaur. Richard Berenger, *The History and Art of Horsemanship*, 1771. *British Museum*
b. Pegasus on silver tetradrachm. *British Museum*
237 Marengo. Select proof of engraving of painting by James Ward, R.A., published by R. Ackermann, 1824. *Photo: The Mansell Collection*
238 National Horse Show. *Photo: Bryan & Corrigan, Inc.*
239 Welsh Mountain ponies. *Photo: Leslie Lane*
240 **a,b.** Nepalese ponies. *Photos: H. Epstein*
241 Engraving. William Cavendish, Duke of Newcastle, *A General System of Horsemanship*, 1743. *British Museum*
242 **a.** Kirgiz, **b.** New Kirgiz. *Photos: V/O Prodintorg; A. Storch*
243 Show Jumping. *Photo: High Commissioner for New Zealand*
244 **a.** Nonius 50. *Photo: P. Neumann*
b. Anglo-Norman. *Photo: Photostore*
c. Selle Français stallion, Soleil Levant, Haras du Pin. *Photo: Photostore*
245 North Swedish horse. *Photo: Royal Veterinary College, Stockholm*
246 Oldenburg. *Photo: G. Halling Nielsen, courtesy L. Malden*
247 Detail from black-figured Panathenaic amphora, Kuban group, early 4th century B.C. *British Museum*
248 William Steinkraus riding Snowbound. *Photo: Associated Press*
249 Jim Day riding Canadian Club. *Photo: E. D. Lacey*
250 **a.** G. Mancinelli riding Ambassador. *Photo: E. D. Lacey*
b. Richard Meade riding Laurieston. *Photo: Syndication International*
c. Detail from Standard of Ur. *British Museum*
251 Orlov Trotters. *Photo: V/O Prodintorg; A. Storch*
253 **a.** Paso Fino. *Photo from collection of Mary Slater*
b. Passo Corese. *Photo: Leslie Gardiner*
254 Part of Altai barrow treasure, 3rd-1st century B.C. *Hermitage Museum, Leningrad. Photo: John Massey Stewart*
256 Peruvian Paso Horse. *Photo: José Musante*
257 Pinzgauer. *Photo: Charles Fennell*
258 **a.** Pleven. *Photo: Vl. Popov*
b. Engraving. Antoine de Pluvinel, *L'Instruction du Roy*, 1627. *London Library, Photo: John R. Freeman Ltd.*
259 Point-to-Point. *Photo: John H. Berry*
260 **a,b.** Poitevin. *Photos: Photostore*
265 **a.** Wielkopolski. *Photo: Z. Raczkowska*
b. Hindu women playing polo. Painting after a 16th-century miniature. *Photo: The Mansell Collection*
266 Polo, North Kashmir, 1889. *Illustrated London News*
267 **a,b.** Polo. *Photos: Pony/Light Horse*
269 **a.** Polo Crosse. *Photo: Australian News and Information Bureau: A. Ozolins*
b. Polo Pony. *Photo: El Caballo*
272 **a.** Mérens. *Photo: Dépot d'Etalons de Tarbes, France*
b. Pottok. *Photo: Photostore*
273 **a.** Pony Express. Print from drawing by G. H. Andrews. *Photo: The Mansell Collection*
b. Pony of the Americas. *Photo: Mrs E. S. Buntin, Jr*
274 Pony Trekking. *Photo: British Tourist Authority*
275 **a.** Lusitano. *Photo: Sally Anne Thompson*
b. Lascaux. *Photo: Caisse Nationale des Monuments Historiques.*
c. Lascaux. *Photo: French Government Tourist Office*
277 **a.** Quarter Horse. *Photo: Western Horseman*
b. Quarter Horse. *Photo: Country Life (N.S.W.) Newspapers Pty Ltd.*
278 Bullfighting. *Photo: Portuguese State Office*
279 Rhenish Belgian draught horse. *Photo: G. Halling Nielsen, courtesy L. Malden*
282 Carol Hoffman riding Salem. *Photo: Leslie Lane*
283 **a.** Russ. *Photo: G. Cornelius*
b. Russian Trotter. *Photo: Novosti; A. Shagin*
c. Russian Heavy Draught. *Photo: Novosti*
284 Sable Island ponies. *Information Canada Photothèque. Photo: Bob Brooks*
285 Cathy Noble riding Ridgefield Genius Again. *Photo: Shirley Paulette*
287 Schleswig. *Photo: Foto Tiedemann*
288 Shires. *Photo: Lee Weatherley*
289 **a.** Col Harry Llewellyn riding Foxhunter. *Photo: W. W. Rouch & Co. Ltd*
b. Marion (Coakes) Mould riding Stroller. *Photo: Monty*
c. Capt. Billy Ringrose riding Loch an Easpaig. *Photo: Leslie Lane*
290 **a.** Capt. R. d'Inzeo riding Merano. *Photo: Leslie Lane*
b. Hans Günter Winkler riding Torphy. *Photo: E. D. Lacey*
292 **a.** Frank Chapot riding Anakonda. *Photo: Leslie Lane*
b. Nelson Pessoa riding Gran Geste. *Photo: Leslie Lane*
293 *Queen Isabella of Bourbon*, painting by Diego Rodriguez da Silva y Velásquez. *Museo del Prado, Madrid*
294 Skyros pony. *Photo: Pony/Light Horse*
295 **a.** Bryanston Equitation Centre. *Photo: Fotosport; J. Ker*
b. Soviet Heavy Draught. *Photo: V/O Prodintorg; A. Storch*
c. *Hispanus Alter*, engraving by Stradanus (Jan van Straet). *British Museum. Photo: John R. Freeman Ltd*
296 Quadrille, *Photo: Herz Color Verlag*
301 **a.** Equestrian version of Richard III, performed London, 1856. *Collection A. H. Saxon*
b. Mosaic hunting scene from Carthage, *c.* 500 A.D. *British Museum*
302 Albatross and S. Dancer. *Photo: U.S. Trotting Association; Ed Keys*
303 Plate IV from *The First Steeplechase on Record*, engraved by J. Harris after H. Alken, 1839. *Photo: The Mansell Collection*
305 Grand Pardubice. *Photo: P. Neumann*
306 Strelets. *Photo: V/O Prodintorg; A. Storch*
307 Ninna Stoor riding Casanova. *Photo: Foto-Eilert*
308 Racing, St Moritz, 1971. *Photo: Elisabeth Weiland, Zollikon*
310 Tennessee Walking Horse. *Photo: W. W. Harlin Sr*
313 **a.** *St Simon*, painting by B. Cam Norton, 1884. *Photo: The Mansell Collection*
b. *Flying Childers at the Winning Post*, from an engraving of 1882. *Photo: The Mansell Collection*
314 **a.** Florida Downs. *Photo: U.S. Travel Service*
b. Donatello II. *Photo: W. W. Rouch & Co. Ltd*
315 Timor. *Photo: L. Malden*
316 Toric. *Photo: V/O Prodintorg; A. Storch*
317 Trait du Nord. *Photo: Photostore*
319 Ethan Allen and Mate and Dexter. Lithograph by Nathaniel Currier and James Ives, 1867. *Yale University Art Gallery, The Mabel Brady Garvan Collection*
321 E. Guerin riding Native Dancer. *Photo: Bob Coglianese*
322 Racing. *Photo: U.S. Travel Service*
323 Bronco riding. *Photo: U.S. Travel Service*
324 Neal Shapiro riding Sloopy. *Photo: E. D. Lacey*
325 Yakut. *Photo: V/O Prodintorg; A. Storch*
326 **a.** Troika racing. *Photo: Novosti; M. Ozersky*
b. Tskhenburti. *Photo: Novosti; F. Grinberg, E. Pesov*
327 Vaulting. *Photo: G. Kesselboch*
328 **a.** Viatka. **b.** Vladimir. *Photos: V/O Prodintorg; A. Storch*
329 Detail from *The Battle of Issus*, mosaic from Pompeii. *Museo Nazionale, Naples. Photo: The Mansell Collection*
330 *Officer of the Imperial Guard*, painting by Théodore Géricault, *c.* 1812. *Louvre. Photo: Giraudon*
331 Cossacks. *Photo: Novosti*
332 R.S.P.C.A. official. *Photo: Will Green*
333 'Balanced ride' saddle. *Photo: Dave Jones*
334 Polo in Jamaica. *Photo: Jamaica Tourist Board*
335 Yorkshire Coach Horse. *Yorkshire Coach Horse Society Stud Book. Photo: John R. Freeman Ltd*
336 **a.** *E. zebra. Photo: South African Embassy*
b. *E. burchelli. Photo: Daphne Machin Goodall*
c. Stuffed specimen of true quagga. *Inst. voor Tax. Zoöl, Amsterdam.*

Horses of the World

Canada
- □ Appaloosa
- Arab
- Canadian Pacer
- Quarter Horse
- Thoroughbred
- ◆ Sable Island

U.S.A.
- □ American Cleveland Bay
- American Hackney
- Appaloosa
- Arab
- Morgan
- Mustang
- Palomino
- Paso Fino
- Quarter Horse
- Saddlebred
- Standardbred
- Tennessee Walking Horse
- Thoroughbred
- Wyoming 'wild' horses
- ■ American Clydesdale
- American Belgian
- American Percheron
- ◆ American Hackney Pony
- Assateague
- Chincoteague
- Galiceño

Mexico
- □ Arab
- Charro Horse

Puerto Rico
- □ Andalusian
- Paso Fino
- Thoroughbred

West Indies
- □ Arab
- Paso Fino
- Quarter Horse
- Thoroughbred
- ◆ Haiti Pony

Venezuela
- □ Arab
- Criollo
- Thoroughbred

Brazil
- □ Arab
- Bahia
- Campolino
- Crioulo Brazileiro
- Curraleiro
- Guarapuavano
- Mangalarga
- Mimoseano
- Sertanejo
- Thoroughbred

Chile
- □ Arab
- Thoroughbred

Peru
- □ Arab
- Peruvian Stepping Horse
- Thoroughbred
- ◆ Costeño
- Criollo
- Morochuco
- Serrano

Argentina
- □ Anglo-Argentine Polo Pony
- Arab
- Criollo
- Thoroughbred
- ■ Percheron
- ◆ Falabella

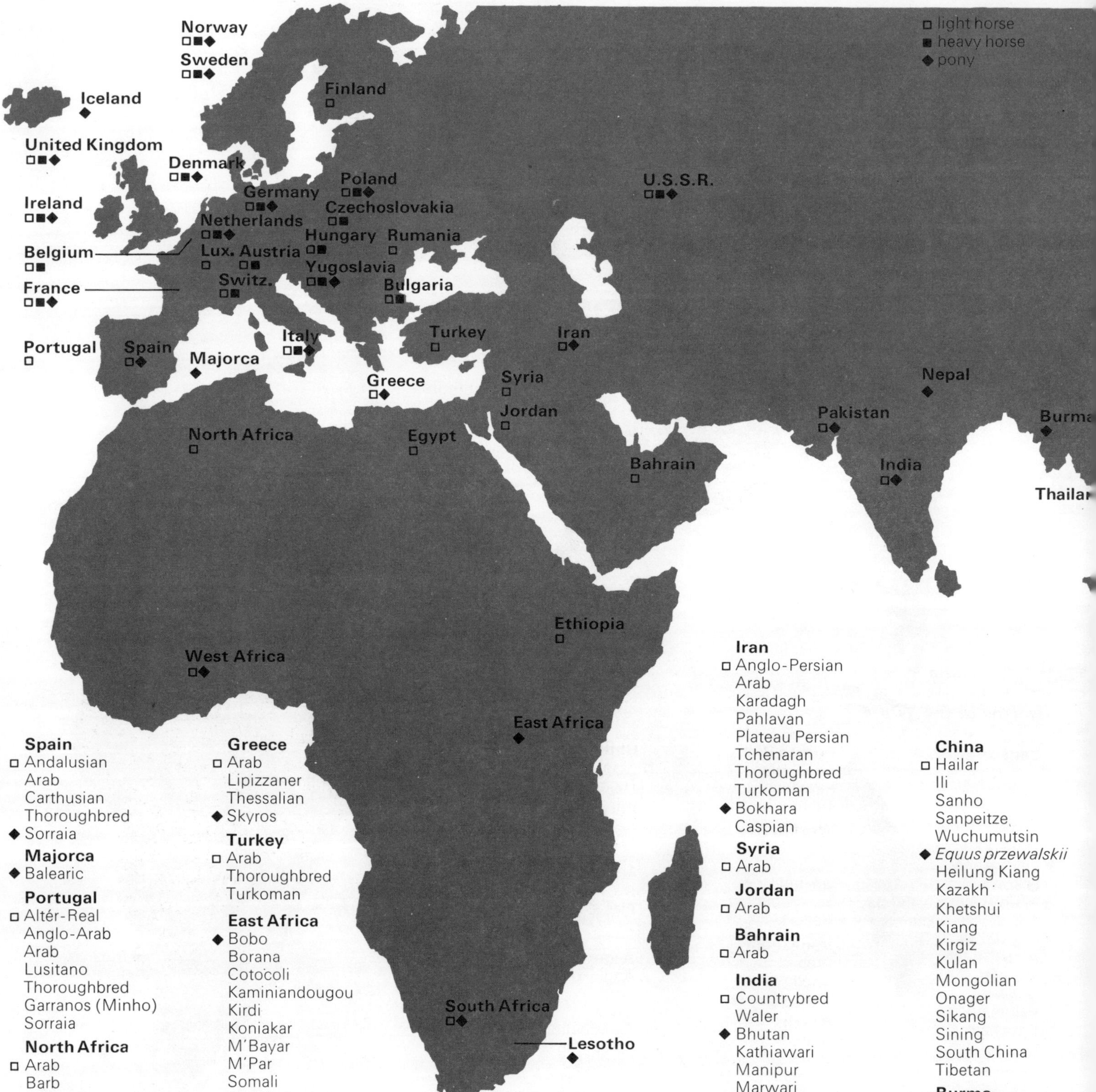

Spain
□ Andalusian
Arab
Carthusian
Thoroughbred
◆ Sorraia

Majorca
◆ Balearic

Portugal
□ Altér-Real
Anglo-Arab
Arab
Lusitano
Thoroughbred
Garranos (Minho)
Sorraia

North Africa
□ Arab
Barb
Dongola

West Africa
□ Barouéli
Bélédougou
Djerma
Foutanké
Fula
Hausa
Hodh
Sahel
Senegal
◆ African Wild Ass

Greece
□ Arab
Lipizzaner
Thessalian
◆ Skyros

Turkey
□ Arab
Thoroughbred
Turkoman

East Africa
◆ Bobo
Borana
Cotocoli
Kaminiandougou
Kirdi
Koniakar
M'Bayar
M'Par
Somali
Songhaï
Southern
Torodi
Western Sudan
Zebra

South Africa
□ Arab
Saddlebred
Thoroughbred
◆ Quagga
Welsh
Zebra

Egypt
□ Arab

Ethiopia
□ Galla

Lesotho
◆ Basuto

Iran
□ Anglo-Persian
Arab
Karadagh
Pahlavan
Plateau Persian
Tchenaran
Thoroughbred
Turkoman
◆ Bokhara
Caspian

Syria
□ Arab

Jordan
□ Arab

Bahrain
□ Arab

India
□ Countrybred
Waler
◆ Bhutan
Kathiawari
Manipur
Marwari
Mongolian
Spiti
Yarkand

Pakistan
□ Countrybred
◆ Bachuli
Kabuli

Nepal
◆ Bhotia
Tarai
Tibetan

China
□ Hailar
Ili
Sanho
Sanpeitze
Wuchumutsin
◆ *Equus przewalskii*
Heilung Kiang
Kazakh
Khetshui
Kiang
Kirgiz
Kulan
Mongolian
Onager
Sikang
Sining
South China
Tibetan

Burma
◆ Burma Pony

Thailand
◆ Thai Pony

Vietnam
◆ Vietnamese Pony

Indonesia
◆ Batak
Gayoe
Sandalwood
Timor

Iceland
◆ Iceland Ponies

United Kingdom
□ Anglo-Arab
Arab
Cleveland Bay
Hackney
Hunter
Thoroughbred
■ Clydesdale
Percheron
Shire
Suffolk
Welsh Cob
◆ Dales
Dartmoor
Exmoor
Fell
Hackney
Highland
New Forest
Shetland
Welsh
Welsh Mountain

Ireland
□ Arab
Hunter
Thoroughbred
■ Irish Draught
◆ Connemara

Australia
□ Arab
Brumby
Palomino
Quarter Horse
Saddlebred
Thoroughbred
Waler
■ Clydesdale
◆ Australian

Norway
□ Trotter
■ Gudbrandsdal Dølehest
◆ Fjord

Sweden
□ Arab
North Swedish
Swedish Halfbred
Thoroughbred
Trotter
■ Ardennais
◆ Connemara
Fjord
Iceland
New Forest
Russ (Gotland, Viking)
Shetland
Welsh

Denmark
□ Arab
Knabstrup
■ Frederiksborg
Jutland
◆ Fjord

Finland
□ Finnish Horse

France
□ Anglo-Arab
Anglo-Norman
Arab
Norman
Selle Français
Tarbais
Thoroughbred
Trotter
■ Ardennais
Auxois
Boulonnais
Breton
Comtois
Percheron
Poitevin Mulassier
Trait du Nord
◆ Barthais
Camargue
Corsican
Landais
Mérens
Pottok

Luxembourg
□ Arab

New Zealand
□ Arab
Quarter Horse
Standardbred
Thoroughbred
■ Clydesdale
◆ New Zealand

Belgium
□ Arab
Thoroughbred
■ Ardennais
Brabant

Netherlands
□ Arab
Dutch Warmblood
Gelderland
■ Friesian
Groningen
◆ Fjord
Haflinger
Iceland

Germany
□ Arab
Bavarian Warmblood
Brandenburg
East Friesian
Haflinger
Hanoverian
Masuren
Mecklenburg
Rhineland
Rottaler
Thoroughbred
Trakehner
Trotter
Württemberg
■ Holstein
Oldenburg
Schleswig
Schwarzwald
◆ Dülmen

Austria
□ Arab
Haflinger
Lipizzaner
■ Pinzgauer Noriker

Switzerland
□ Arab
Swiss Warmblood
■ Freiberger (Franches-Montagnes)

Italy
□ Arab
Calabrese
Maremma
Murgese
Salerno
Sardinian
Thoroughbred
Trotter
■ Italian Heavy Draught
◆ Avelignese

Yugoslavia
□ Arab
Lipizzaner
■ Pinzgauer Noriker
◆ Bosnian Pony

Rumania
□ Arab

Bulgaria
□ Arab
East Bulgarian
Pleven
■ Danubian
Russian Heavy Draught

Poland
□ Anglo-Arab
Arab
Ermland (Stuhm)
Masuren
Mierzyn
Posen
Sokolsky
Tarpan
Thoroughbred
■ Ardennes
Gudbrandsdal
◆ Huçul
Konik
Panje

U.S.S.R.
□ Akhal Teke
Altai
Arab
Budyonny
Don
Iomud
Kabardin
Karabair
Karabakh
Kustanair
Kuznetsky
Lokai
Metis Trotter
Narimsky
New Kirgiz
Orlov Trotter
Priobsky
Russian Trotter
Tersky
Toric
Tushinsky
Tuvinsky
Zemaituka
■ Latvian Harness
Lithuanian Heavy Draught
Pechora
Russian Heavy Draught
Soviet Heavy Draught
Vladimir Heavy Draught
Voronezh
◆ Adayevsky
Bashkirsky
Kazakh
Viatka
Yakut

Czechoslovakia
□ Anglo-Arab
Arab
Kladruber
Lipizzaner
Nonius
Thoroughbred
■ Pinzgauer Noriker

Hungary
□ Arab
Furioso
Gidran
Lipizzaner
Muraköz
Nonius
North Star
Shagya
Thoroughbred
■ Pinzgauer Noriker

Horse and Pony Societies

International

Fédération Équestre Internationale
Chevalier H. de Menten de Horne
Avenue Hamoir 38, 1180 Brussels, Belgium

International League for the Protection of Horses
4 Bloomsbury Square, London WC1A 2RP
England

International Pony Breeders' Association
Professor Mitchell
Royal Dick Veterinary College, Edinburgh
Scotland

World Arabian Horse Organization
Major J. D. Gray
Woodpeckers, Nightingale Road, Ash, Aldershot
Hampshire

National Equestrian Federations
Affiliated to the Fédération Équestre Internationale

Algeria
Fédération Algérienne des Sports Équestres
Rue Didouche Mourad 21, Algiers

Argentina
Federación Ecuestre Argentina
Rodriquez Peña 1934 – Planta Baja, Buenos Aires

Australia
The Equestrian Federation of Australia
Royal Show Grounds, Epsom Road, Ascot Vale 2

Austria
Österreichische Campagnereiter Gesellschaft
Haus des Sports, Prinz Eugenstrasse 12
Vienna IV

Belgium
Fédération Royale Belge des Sports Équestres
Avenue Hamoir 38, 1180 Brussels

Bolivia
Federación Boliviana de Deportes Ecuestres
Casilla 329, La Paz

Brazil
Confederação Brasileira de Hipismo
Rua Sete de Setembre 81, Sala 302
Rio de Janeiro

Bulgaria
Comité Suprème de Culture Physique et des Sports
Boulevard Tolbukhin 18, Sofia

Canada
The Canadian Horse Shows Association
57 Bloor Street West, Toronto, Ontario

Chile
Federación Nacional de Deportes Ecuestres
Calle Compania 1630, Santiago de Chile

Colombia
Association Colombienne des Sports Equestres
Calle 13 no 8–39 – Oficina 609, Bogota

Cuba
Federación Ecuestre Cubana
Comité Olimpico Cubana
Hotel Habana Libre, Havana

Czechoslovakia
Fédération Équestre Tchécoslovaque
Na Porici 12, Prague 11

Denmark
Dansk Rideforbund
Vestre Paradisvej 51, Holte

Ecuador
Federación Ecuatoriana de Deportes Ecuestres
Apartado 410, Quito

Finland
Suomen Ratsastajainliitto
Paasitie 9 B 2, Helsinki 83

France
Fédération Française des Sports Équestres
Faubourg St Honoré 164, 75 Paris VIIIe

German Democratic Republic
Deutsche Pferdesport Verband der Deutschen Demokratischen Republik
Nationale Reiterliche Vereinigung
Storkowerstrasse 118, Berlin 1055

German Federal Republic
Deutsche Reiterliche Vereinigung
Adenauerallee 174, 53 Bonn

Greece
Association Hellénique d'Athlétisme Amateur
Avenue Panepistimioy 25, Athens

Guatemala
Federación de Ecuestre de Guatemala
Apartado Postal 1525, Guatemala C.A.

Hungary
Fédération Hongroise d'Équitation
Holda Utca 1, Budapest V

Iran (Persia)
The Iranian Equestrian Federation
Iranian Olympic Committee
Kakke Verzesh, Teheran

Republic of Ireland
The National Equestrian Federation of Ireland
Ball's Bridge, Dublin

Israel
The Israeli Horse Society
P.O. Box 14111, Tel Aviv

Italy
Federazione Italiana Sport Equestri
Palazzo delle Federazioni
Viale Tiziano 70, Rome

Japan
Fédération Équestre Japonaise
Kanda Surugadai 4–6, Chiyoda-ku, Tokyo

Korea
Korean Equestrian Federation
19 Mukyo-Dong
K.A.A.A. Building, Room 611, Seoul

Lebanon
Fédération Libanaise des Sports Équestres
B.P. 5035, Beirut

Libya
Fédération Nationale Libyenne Équestre
Maidan Abi Setta
P.O. Box 4507, Tripoli

Luxembourg
Fédération Luxembourgeoise des Sports Équestres
Route de Thionville 90, Luxembourg

Mexico
Federación Ecuestre Mexicana
Insurgentes Sur no 222 Desp. 405
Mexico 7 D.F.

Morocco
Fédération Royale Marocaine des Sports Équestres
Garde Royale, Rabat

Netherlands
Nederlandse Hippische Sportbond
Waalsdorperlaan 29a
Wassenaar (Post Den Haag)

New Zealand
The New Zealand Horse Society
P.O. Box 13, Hastings

Norway
Norges Rytterforbund
Postboks 204 L, Oslo

Peru
Federación Peruana de Deportes Ecuestres
Estadio Nacional, Puerta 29, Lima

Poland
Polski Zwiazek Jezdziecki
Sienkiewicza 12, Warsaw

Portugal
Federação Equestre Portuguesa
Rua de San Pedro de Alcantara 79
Lisbon 2

Puerto Rico
Federación Puertorriqueña de Deportes Ecuestres
Apartado de Correos 4959, San Juan

Rhodesia
The Rhodesian Horse Society
P.O. Box 2415, Salisbury

Rumania
Federatia Romina de Calarie
Vasile Conta 16, Bucharest

Senegal
Fédération Sénégalaise des Sports Équestres
Avenue William Ponty 16, Dakar

South Africa
South African National Equestrian Federation
17 Tulip Avenue
Sunridge Park, Port Elizabeth

Spain
Federación Nacional Hipica
Montesquinza 8, Madrid 4

Sweden
Svenska Ridsportens Centralförbund
Östermalmsgatan 80
Stockholm Ö.

Switzerland
Fédération Suisse des Sports Équestres
Comité Central: Bahnhofstrasse 36, Zurich
Section Concours Hippiques: Blankweg 70
3072 Ostermundigen

Tunisia
Fédération Tunisienne de Tir et d' Équitation
Stand National de Tir El Ouardia
Sidi Belhassen, Tunis

Turkey
Fédération Équestre Turque
Ucyol-Mazlak, Istanbul

United Arab Republic
Fédération Équestre de la République Arabe Unie
13 Sharia Kasr-el-Nil, Cairo

United Kingdom
The British Horse Society
National Equestrian Centre
Stoneleigh, Kenilworth, Warwickshire

Uruguay
Federación Uruguaya de Deportes Ecuestres
Avenida Agraciada 1546, Montevideo

U.S.A.
American Horse Shows Association
527 Madison Avenue, New York, NY 10022

U.S.S.R.
Fédération Équestre d'U.R.S.S.
Skaternyi Pereulok 4, Moscow

Venezuela
Federación Venezolana de Deportes Ecuestres
Apartado 3588, Caracas

Yugoslavia
Fédération Équestre Yougoslave
27 General Zdanov Street, Belgrade

Societies in the United Kingdom

Arab Horse Society
Loughmoe, Shelley Close, Itchen Abbas, Winchester, Hampshire

Association of British Riding Schools
Warwick Cottage Stables, Hurst Lane,
Headley, Epsom, Surrey

British Driving Society
L. H. Candler, Esq.
10 Morley Avenue, New Milton, Hampshire

British Equine Veterinary Association
N. Nico, Esq. M.R.C.V.S.
20 Tangier Road, Guildford, Surrey

British Horse Society
J. E. Blackmore, Esq.
National Equestrian Centre, Stoneleigh,
Kenilworth, Warwickshire, CV8 2LR

British Palomino Society
Mrs P. Howell
Kingsettle Stud, Cholderton, Salisbury,
Wiltshire

British Percheron Horse Society
A. E. Vyse, Esq.
Owen Webb House, Gresham Road,
Cambridge CB1 2EP

British Show Hack & Cob Association
J. E. Blackmore Esq.
National Equestrian Centre, Stoneleigh,
Kenilworth, Warwickshire, CV8 2LR

British Show Jumping Association
Major M. Dewey
National Equestrian Centre, Stoneleigh,
Kenilworth, Warwickshire, CV8 2LR

British Show Pony Society
Captain R. Grellis
Smale Farm, Wisborough Green, Sussex

British Spotted Horse Society
Miss J. Eddie,
Nash End, Bisley, Stroud, Gloucestershire
GL6 7AJ

British Veterinary Association
7 Mansfield Street, Portland Place,
London W1M 0AT

Cleveland Bay Horse Society
R. F. H. Stephenson, Esq.
20 Castlegate, York

Clydesdale Horse Society
R. Jarvis, Esq.
19 Hillington Gardens, Glasgow SW2

Dales Pony Society
Cleveland House, Hutton Gate,
Guisborough, Yorkshire

Dartmoor Pony Society
Lower Hisley, Lustleigh,
Newton Abbot, Devon

Donkey Show Society
Mrs W. Greenway
Prouts Farm, Hawkley, Nr Liss, Hampshire

English Connemara Pony Society
Mrs Barthop
The Quinta, Bentley, Farnham, Surrey

Exmoor Pony Society
Mrs J. Watts
Quarry Cottage, Sampford Brett, Williton,
Somerset

Fell Pony Society
Miss P. Crossland
Packway, Windermere, Westmorland

Hackney Horse Society
Major G. Worboys
35 Belgrave Square, London SW1X 8QB

Highland Pony Society
51–53 High Street, Dunblane, Perthshire

Horses and Ponies Protection Association
1 Station Parade, Balham, London SW12 9AZ

Hunters' Improvement and National Light
Horse Breeding Society
G. W. Evans, Esq.
17 Devonshire Street, London W1N 2BQ

Hurlingham Polo Association
Brig. J. R. C. Gannon, C.B.E., M.V.O.
204 Idol Lane, London EC3

Jockey Club
Newmarket, Suffolk
or 42 Portman Square, London W1H 9FH

London Harness Horse Parade Society
R. A. Brown, Esq.
65 Medfield Street, London SW15

Masters of Foxhounds Association
Lt-Col J. E. S. Chamberlayne
The Elm, Chipping Norton, Oxfordshire OX7 5NS

National Master Farriers', Blacksmiths' and
Agricultural Engineers' Association
B. Marshall, Esq.
48 Spencer Place, Leeds LS7 4BR, Yorkshire

National Pony Society
Cmdr B. H. Brown, R.N. (Ret'd)
Stoke Lodge, 85 Cliddesden Road,
Basingstoke, Hampshire

New Forest Pony and Cattle Breeding Society
Miss D. MacNair
Beacon Corner, Burley, Ringwood, Hampshire

Ponies of Britain
Mrs G. Spooner
Brookside Farm, Ascot, Berkshire

Racehorse Owners' Association
Col F. M. Beale
26 Charing Cross Road, London WC2H 0DG

Riding for the Disabled Association
Miss C. M. L. Haynes
British Horse Society
National Equestrian Centre, Stoneleigh,
Kenilworth, Warwickshire CV8 2LR

Royal Society for the Prevention of
Cruelty to Animals
105 Jermyn Street, London SW1Y 6EG

Saddlers Company
Saddlers Hall, Gutter Lane,
Cheapside, London EC2 V6BR

Shetland Pony Stud Book Society
D. M. Patterson, Esq.
8 Whinfield Road, Montrose, Angus

Shire Horse Society
R. W. Bird, Esq.
12 Priestgate, Peterborough

Society of Master Saddlers, Ltd
9 St Thomas Street, London SE1

Suffolk Horse Society
W. J. Woods, Esq.
6 Church Street, Woodbridge, Suffolk

Thoroughbred Breeders' Association
26 Bloomsbury Way, London WC1A 2SP

Weatherby & Sons
41 Portman Square, London W1H 9FH

Welsh Pony and Cob Society
T. E. Roberts, Esq.
32 North Parade, Aberystwyth, Cardiganshire

Societies in the Republic of Ireland

Connemara Pony Breeders' Society
J. Killeen, Esq.
4 Nuns' Island, Galway, Eire

Societies in the U.S.A.

American Association of Equine Practitioners
Route 5, 14 Hillcrest Circle, Golden, CO 80401

American Dressage Institute
Daniels Road, Saratoga Springs, NY 12866

American Hackney Horse Society
527 Madison Avenue, New York, NY 10022

American Horse Council
1776 K Street NW, Washington DC 20006

American Horse Shows Association
527 Madison Avenue, New York, NY 10022

American Humane Association
P.O. Box 1266, Denver, CO 80201

American Masters of Foxhounds Association
112 Water Street, Boston, MA 02109

American Morgan Horse Association
P.O. Box 17157, West Hartford, CT 06117

American Mustang Association
P.O. Box 9249, Phoenix, AZ 85020

American Paint Horse Association
P.O. Box 12487, Fort Worth, TX 76116

American Paso Fino Pleasure Horse
Association, Inc.
501 Wood, Pittsburgh, PA 15222

American Quarter Horse Association
P.O. Box 200, Amarillo, TX 79105

American Saddle Horse Breeders' Association
929 S. Fourth Street, Louisville, KY 40203

American Society for the Prevention of
Cruelty to Animals
441 E. 92nd Street, New York, NY 10028

American Veterinary Medical Association
600 S. Michigan Ave., Chicago, IL 60605

The Appaloosa Horse Club
P.O. Box 403, Moscow, ID 93843

Arabian Horse Registry of America, Inc.
One Executive Park, 7801 Belleview Avenue
Englewood, CO 80110

Churchill Downs, Inc.
P.O. Box 8427, Louisville, KY 40208

Cross-Bred Pony Registry
1108 Jackson Street, Omaha, NE 68102

Galiceño Horse Breeders Association
708 People's Bank Building, Tyler, TX 75701

Happy Horsemanship for the Handicapped, Inc.
The National Foundation for the Handicapped,
Inc.
Box 462, Malvern PA 19355

International Rodeo Association
P.O. Box 615, Pauls Valley, OK 73075

The Jockey Club
300 Park Avenue, New York, NY 10022

Morven Park International Equestrian Institute
Route 2, Box 8, Leesburg, VA 22075

National Appaloosa Pony, Inc.
P.O. Box 297, Rochester, IN 46957

National Cutting Horse Association
806 First National Bank Building, Midland,
TX 79701

National Steeplechase and Hunt Association
6407 Wilson Boulevard, Arlington, VA 22205

Palomino Horse Breeders of America
P.O. Box 249, Mineral Wells, TX 76067

Pinto Horse Association of America
8245 Hillside Avenue, Alta Loma, CA 91701

Pony of the Americas Club
P.O. Box 1447, Mason City, IA 50401

Rodeo Cowboys Association
2929 West 19th Avenue, Denver, CO 80204

Standard Jack and Jennet Registry of America
Route 7, Todd Road, Lexington, KY 40502

Tennessee Walking Horse Breeders Association
P.O. Box 286, Lewisburg, TN 37091

U.S. Trotting Association (Standardbred)
750 Michigan Avenue, Columbus, OH 43215

U.S. Trotting Pony Association
P.O. Box 1250, Lafayette, IN 47902

Welsh Pony Society of America
202 N. Church Street, West Chester, PA 19380

Colour plates pages 17–36

17
Turkoman (Turkmen). Bred on the Turkoman Steppes in northern Iran adjoining the U.S.S.R., this is a hardy desert horse, noted for its strength and endurance.

18
Above Kladrub (see Czechoslovakia). The famous white Kladrub horses were bred as coach horses for the imperial court in Vienna. Today they are popular competitors in international driving events.
Below Carthusian. The horses bred by Terry are descended from the pure Andalusian horses selectively bred by Carthusian monks.

19
Thoroughbred. *Above* Trademark, now at stud at Tarbes, in the French Pyrenees. *Below* Nijinsky, winner of the 1970 Epsom Derby, is a fine example of a racehorse bred in Canada.

20
Above Shagya Arab. Bred first at Bábolna in Hungary, the Shagya strain of Arab has spread all over Europe. It was once a popular cavalry horse.
Below North Star (see Hungary). This English Thoroughbred/Hungarian warmblood cross is an excellent saddle horse suitable for jumping and dressage. It is sometimes also used for light draught work.

21
Above Hanoverian. Once a famous coach horse, the Hanoverian is now one of the most popular European breeds for show jumping and horse trials.
Below Holstein. Originally from the marshes surrounding the lower Elbe and nearby rivers, the Holstein became a heavy coach and artillery horse; it is also a strong, heavyweight saddle horse and sometimes a good show jumper.

22
Above Trakehner (East Prussian). One of the oldest warmblood breeds in Germany, the Trakehner is known today as an elegant saddle horse, particularly suitable for dressage and show jumping.
Below Camargue. This tough and agile horse from the Rhône delta on the Mediterranean is ridden by local herdsmen; it is potentially an excellent saddle horse.

23
Lipizzaner. Famous today for its performances at the Spanish Riding School of Vienna, the Lipizzaner is descended from horses bred in Spain under Moorish occupation. The Lipizzaner has harmonious conformation and graceful movements.

24
Above Appaloosa. With its distinctive coloured spots, concentrated on white hind quarters, the Appaloosa is a popular saddle horse in the United States; it is also used for circus work.
Below Pinto (Paint Horse). A colour type rather than a breed, the Pinto is found all over the world but is especially popular in North America.

25
Above Palomino. A colour type rather than a breed, the Palomino is especially popular in the United States, where it is used as a saddle horse and for parades.
Below Morgan. Tracing back to one foundation sire, usually known as Justin Morgan, this American breed is an ideal general-purpose saddle horse and a fast roadster.

26
Above Don. Once used by the Tsarist cavalry, the Russian Don is now a useful saddle and harness horse.
Below Tersky. First developed in the northern Caucasus and widely used to improve other breeds in the U.S.S.R., the Tersky is a good-natured, intelligent and hardy saddle horse.

27
Akhal Teke. Supreme among Russian sporting horses, the Akhal Teke has superb natural gaits.

28
Above Karadagh. From the northwest of Iran, the elegant Karadagh is now feared to be dying out.
Below Plateau Persian. Descended from various Persian strains dating back to the Achamaenian Empire in the sixth century B.C., the Plateau Persian is a tough, surefooted mountain horse.

29
Above Pinzgauer Noriker (South German Heavy Horse). Usually brown or chestnut but often spotted, this hardy, surefooted heavy horse is well suited to the mountains.
Below Suffolk Horse. The Suffolk 'Punch', always chestnut, is the only clean-legged British native draught horse. It is very gentle and economical to keep.

30
Above Shire Horse. Descended from the medieval Great Horse, the English Shire is the largest and heaviest purebred horse in the world.
Below Breton Heavy Draught Horse. Noted for improving other draught breeds, the Breton is exceedingly adaptable and hardy.

31
Percheron. Native to the hills of Perche, the Percheron has been exported to many countries and is particularly popular in England. It is always grey or black, clean-legged, energetic, strong and hardy. *Above* A French Percheron stallion at Haras du Pin, Normandy. *Below* an English Percheron stallion.

32
Above Haflinger. Originally bred in the district of Hafling, this useful and hardworking Austrian breed can carry or pull loads up and down the steepest mountain slopes.
Below Russ (Gotland). Native to the Swedish island of Gotland, the hardy Russ is an excellent trotter and a good jumper.

33
Fjord. The Norwegian Fjord pony, with black dorsal stripe and characteristic stiff mane, traditionally hogged, is a useful general-purpose animal for hill-farm work.

34
Above Iceland. Descended from ponies brought over by Norse settlers, the hardy Iceland ponies are of every colour, including piebald and skewbald.
Below Knabstrup. This scarce Danish breed of spotted horses, dating from the Napoleonic Wars, has been used a good deal for circus work.

35
Above Basuto. Used in the Boer War, the Basuto pony is surefooted, courageous and tough.
Below Ass, Domestic. First tamed to work before the horse, the ass, now found all over the world, is probably of multiple wild ancestry. It does best where the climate is hot and dry and is used primarily as a pack animal.

36
Above Mustangs. The feral horses of the American West, descended from horses introduced by the Spanish *conquistadores,* now have to be protected by law.
Below Criollos (see Argentina, Peru). These close-coupled, sturdy South American ponies are also derived from horses brought by Spanish settlers. Having undergone rigorous natural selection for about three hundred years of wild life, they are remarkably hardy: the two horses which carried Professor A. F. Tschiffely on his famous ride from Buenos Aires to Washington in 1925–7 were Criollos.

Terry
Terry
Terry
Terry
Terry

58

Aachen

Germany's official international horse show, held in Aachen early in July each year, is renowned as the toughest in the world. The courses, built by Hans ('Mickey') Brinckmann, himself a leading international rider before World War II, are big and solid, carrying enormous spreads, and it takes an Olympic-type horse to win the Grand Prix. Despite the fact that it is harder to win here than at any other show in Europe, Aachen is the most popular show in the world and it often attracts 15–20 full international teams, many of them from the Communist countries. The NATIONS' CUP is therefore a marathon contest and the form produced is a reliable guide to the performances of the top teams. Prize money is high and so riders are always anxious to compete.

Dressage competitions are held in their own arena, whose grandstands are packed with the cognoscenti from 8 a.m. daily. The winners parade in the main arena and give demonstrations. There are also numerous driving competitions, and they too attract a large international entry.

The showground, built after World War II, just outside the town where Charlemagne had his palace, is admirably appointed with permanent stabling, sand exercise arenas and jumping paddocks for warming-up. There is a large covered grandstand and even more extensive uncovered accommodation. On the final Sunday the ground is packed to capacity (estimated to exceed 50,000). It is traditional for all the spectators to wave white handkerchiefs at the departing gladiators in an unusual and impressive farewell parade. PMM

Abats le Sultan see Mounted Games

Accoutrements

Early Times to 500 B.C.: domestication of the horse, probably for meat, probably began on the steppes north of the Black Sea sometime during the third millennium B.C. Whether horses were ridden there for herding is unknown, although it seems likely. But no gear has survived and, if it existed, it must have been of perishable material such as ropes or thongs.

The horse's earliest accoutrements are from the civilized lands of the Near East, where it did not appear in any quantity until the early part of the second millennium B.C., and where it was used primarily in draught. At first it was harnessed and controlled as the first draught equids had been, the *hemippus*, or native Syrian onager, or the African ass, which may have reached Mesopotamia in the third millennium B.C. These had been driven like oxen, the earliest traction animals, in paired draught under a yoke, and with a nose ring for control.
BRIDLING AND BITTING: although the pole-and-yoke hitch continued right through Roman times, by about 1700 B.C. sparse but undeniable figured evidence of paired lines indicates either noseband or bit control. Earliest material evidence of the latter comes from fourteenth-century B.C. Gaza. One document is a bronze bit with plain bar mouthpiece and wheel-shaped cheekpieces with spikes on their inner surfaces. The other is a flat elongated bronze cheekpiece, also spiked. This type was held in place at right angles to the horse's mouth by divided cheekstraps. The mouthpiece ends passed through holes in the middle of the cheekpieces, and terminated in loops, to which reins may have been attached directly or by means of larger wire loops. This type usually had a jointed mouthpiece, either twisted or plain. The spikes usually found on the inside of these cheekpieces indicate emphasis on directional control, hence their use as driving bits. Sometimes a low-placed noseband was the means of control. The horses of Thutmosis IV of Egypt (1425–1408 B.C.) were apparently bridled thus.

The most elaborate Oriental bits are from Luristan in western Iran, and are usually dated to the tenth-seventh centuries B.C. These have straight mouthpieces, the ends of which pass through cheekpieces cast in a variety of forms: horses, mouflons, monsters, gods, demons. They also were held in place by divided cheekstraps and were spiked.

The chariot horse dominated the civilized world through the second millennium B.C., but early in the first millennium B.C. it began to be replaced by the ridden one. With the new emphasis on riding, bits changed. Each canon of a jointed snaffle was often

Accoutrements. *Top:* Fourteenth-century B.C. bar bit, with wheel-shaped and spiked cheek-pieces, found at Gaza
Above: Bronze bit with horses from Luristan, Western Iran, *c.* 900–700 B.C.
Below: Near-Eastern bit with rough mouthpiece, probably dating from the sixth century B.C.

cast rigidly with its cheekpiece, instead of passing freely through it. Spikes on the inner surfaces of the cheekpieces were replaced by 'warts' on the mouthpieces. Directional control had become easier, with the weight of the rider's body to assist it, but braking power had declined when the footboards of a chariot were abandoned for the back of a stirrupless horse, and this was frequently compensated by severer mouthpieces.

Mycenaean Greek bits reflect contemporary Levantine practice in their wheel-shaped or bar cheekpieces. Other early European bits, Hungarian ones of the fifteenth or fourteenth centuries B.C., are usually of antler tines, mounted like Oriental ones, with a divided cheekstrap, but had a soft mouthpiece made of rope, rawhide, or gut. Their prototypes are found in Bronze Age Anatolia, whence they journeyed west. This simple bit continued in popular use even after metal ones were adopted by those who could afford them.

Greek bits of the seventh and sixth centuries B.C. had cheekpieces in the shape of bars or arcs, mounted on divided cheek-straps. They most frequently had jointed mouthpieces. A separate studded 'burr' was used, rather than studding the cheekpiece. It is usually shown on chariot horses, and may have been a way of adapting a riding bit to driving.

Early Italic bronze bits of the ninth-seventh centuries B.C. have mostly jointed mouthpieces, the ends of which pass through decorative cheekpieces. These are often in the form of horses, and were mounted on divided cheekstraps. The majority have been found in pairs, indicating driving use. The cheeks are unstudded and the mouthpieces mild.

BLINKERS: the earliest known blinkers are fourteenth-century B.C. Egyptian. Although the ones found are of bark overlaid with gold leaf, the fact that some of them simulate scale armour probably indicates that they originated as protection against projectiles. Blinkers were possibly in uninterrupted use, for quantities of carved ivory ones of the eight and seventh centuries B.C. have been found in Assyria. These, although presumably of Syrian origin, often bear Egyptian motifs. Similar bronze or ivory blinkers of *c.* 600 B.C. have been found in Cyprus.

BREASTPLATES: breastplates are depicted on ridden horses on ninth-eighth-century B.C. Assyrian reliefs, and bronze ones have been found in Cyprus associated with seventh-century B.C. chariot horses.

HEAD PROTECTION: the ninth-seventh-century B.C. Levant has yielded many bronze or ivory protective or decorative frontlets of spatular or elongated triangular shape, which hung down the face and were sometimes hinged so as to extend back over the poll. A bronze cap helmet, covering the poll and the upper third of the neck, is attested in Egyptian art from the fourteenth century B.C., and by an actual eighth- or seventh-century B.C. example from northwest Iran.

RIDING PADS: mounted troops first appeared in ninth-century B.C. Assyria. They never used saddles, but by the seventh century B.C. rode on animal skins or quilted cloths, held in place merely by breastbands. By the sixth century B.C., Persians and Ionian Greeks were also using riding cloths.

TRAPPERS: Egyptian chariot horses wore trappers made of pieces of coloured leather, and sometimes perhaps of bronze scales. No scales themselves have been found in Egypt, but such are listed in documents from fifteenth-century B.C. Nuzi in Mesopotamia, where actual plates have also been found. Oxhide and plate trappers are seen on Assyrian reliefs of the eighth and seventh centuries B.C., and plates presumed to be from horse armour have been found. MAL

Reference: J. K. Anderson, *Ancient Greek Horsemanship*, Berkeley, 1961. V. G. Childe, 'Wheeled Vehicles' in Singer, Holmyard and Hall, *A History of Technology I*, Oxford, 1954. V. Karageorghis, 'Horse Burials on the Island of Salamis', *Archaeology 18*, 1965. M. A. Littauer, 'Bits and Pieces', *Antiquity XLIII*, 1969. J. J. Orchard, *Equestrian Bridle-Harness Ornaments*, Aberdeen, 1967. J. A. H. Potratz, *Die Trensen des alten Orient*, Rome, 1966.

Late Classical Times to Early Middle Ages: except for certain technical advances in China, every important development over this period, in terms of Western Europe known as the Dark Ages, affected riding rather than driving, and was due to a gradual breakdown of certain material aspects of that Graeco-Roman culture which had spread over the entire Western world in the wake of the Roman imperial armies. Civilian life within the secure confines of the Empire with its stable conditions of law and order, its high standard of civil engineering and its state-run system of posts and rest-houses on the great trunk roads, which was the same everywhere between Carlisle and Constantinople, permitted a great volume of wheeled traffic over long distances.

But during the fourth century of the Christian era this security was passing away, and with it the reliability of public services of all kinds. Private carriages (mostly mule-drawn) which had reached the peak of efficiency practicable within the limits of the 'antique' system of traction (see above and Carriages of Antiquity) required a measure of servicing which the well-to-do traveller found less and less often available; not even the curricles of the imperial postal service were able to function under conditions where a fresh team, proper fodder, and bedding for man and horse would not be forthcoming as a matter of course at a fixed point at the end of the day's stage. The same journeys continued to be made, on public as well as on private business, if no longer for pleasure; but now they had to be made on horseback, which made improvisation in the matters mentioned above easier, as well as the negotiation of the roads themselves. The thousands of miles of uniformly designed and constructed *pavé* that traversed Europe from end to end were no longer regularly repaired: a horse could skirt round the potholes that would shake a carriage to pieces after prolonged jolting over them. More important, many bridges once broken (or burned down: many were of wood) in the course of military operations were simply not rebuilt, and were replaced by fords which might or might not be at the same site as the bridge. Horses could pass fords unsuitable for wheeled vehicles; at the worst, they could swim the river.

At the same time cavalry became increasingly important in the Roman army, having once been merely ancillary to the legion, which was an armoured infantry formation. The supremacy of cavalry advanced more rapidly and from an earlier date in the East than in the West. From the first moment of the Roman confrontation with the Persians—that is, the time between 60 and 70 B.C. when the Romans had taken over Syria and advanced to the head-waters of the Tigris—the legions of the eastern front found themselves opposed all the time to an enemy consisting overwhelmingly of mounted troops; substantially of mounted archers. A legion, as originally constituted, was unable to cope with such an enemy in open warfare for lack of mobility. It proved necessary to raise more and more mounted troops for service as auxiliaries and eventually to change the establishment of the legion so that the proportion of foot-marching troops in it was drastically reduced.

Military demands alone made the development of an effective saddle imperative, in the West as much as in the East. Artistic conservatism prevents this appearing in equestrian portraiture, but by the beginning of the second century A.D. the Roman military saddle was a solid leather structure. It was not held in place by a girth in our sense but by a roller that passed overall, invariably also by a breastplate and a form of crupper; but it was still essentially a pad or pilch, with no tree. The antique bridle with Y-forked cheekpieces was still in use, but side by side with it a pattern in which the 'side' members crossed X-wise over the nose of the horse. At the same period the curb bit with more or less high port appears, often with disks at both ends of the mouthpiece. Joints on bridle, breastplate and crupper were covered by metal trappings, mostly in the form of rosettes. Buckles were still unknown.

There was in fact no pressing reason why a 'true' saddle, built on a tree consisting of two arches joined by bars should be developed, so long as stirrups were not in use, the only effective method of attaching stirrup leathers being to the bars. Invasions of Europe by mounted Asiatic nomads whose chief weapon was the bow continued throughout the period as they had done since the first SCYTHIAN raids, but none of these, until the time of the Huns, used stirrups. Even so, the use of stirrups was not adopted in the West until Charlemagne's wars against the Avars of what is now Hungary, and there is no evidence of their general use on the Continent until the ninth century. In Britain this comes slightly later, and the earliest found are of Viking design.

Accoutrements. This Anglo-Saxon manuscript indicates that as late as the eleventh century A.D. stirrups were not necessarily used even by warriors.

Even in Britain, the practice of riding with stirrups seems to have spread slowly, for about the year 1000, when northern and eastern England had been settled by stirrup-using Scandinavians for more than a century, pictures drawn in Canterbury in Kent show hunting parties and warriors riding on 'modern'-looking saddles but without stirrups. The stirrup was adopted by the Scandinavians through their contact with the steppe peoples in the region of the Vistula river.

Two other innovations radically affecting harness came into northwest Europe through similar channels, not before A.D. 800 at the earliest. The Vikings of the east, the Varangians who exploited the trade routes between the Baltic, the Black Sea and the Caspian, traded with Arabs returning from territories newly won over to Islam, such as Bokhara and Samarkand. From these regions the Arabs brought with them the *hame collar*, an invention of the Turkic peoples which, in conjunction with shafts, made it possible for one horse to draw carts that hitherto could only have been moved by two bullocks. The alternative to this, the *breast collar*, seems to

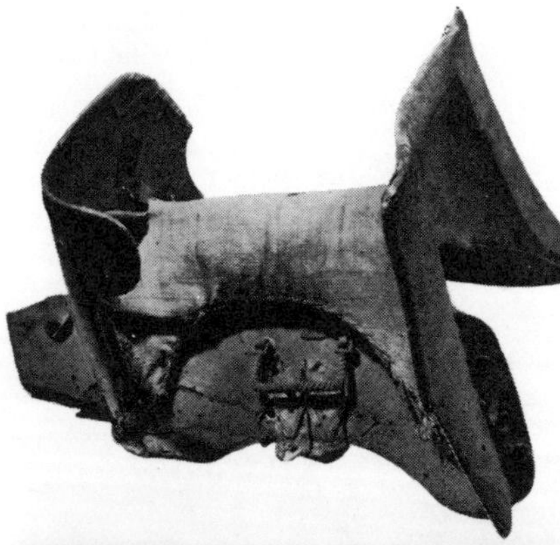

Accoutrements. *Top:* The saddle used at the funeral of Henry V in 1422
Above: The same kind of saddle, used by a contemporary horseman, from a carving in Henry V's chapel, Westminster Abbey
Below right: Saddle from *Le Maneige Royal* (1623) by Antoine de Pluvinel

have been devised in the North, probably by adapting reindeer harness. It was probably used first for harnessing horses to sleighs, with traces. The combination of traces with either kind of draught collar brought about an enormous revolution in harness work, having more than twice the efficiency of the old yoke-and-pole gear to which the entire transport system of the ancient world had been tied. Added to this, improved types of wagon, with free-turning fore-axles that had at least a 30-degree lock, and rear wheels larger than the front pair, now came into use in the West. They had long existed, outside the boundaries of the old Empire, but until after the barbarian invasions were not in use west of the Rhine. In Charlemagne's empire a system of roads and bridges began to be built up, approaching, though distantly, that of the Romans, but the vehicles that plied on it, and the harness by which they were drawn, were superior to those of classical times and contained the germ of future roadgoing coaches and carriages.

Other Oriental influences came into play long before the period of the Crusades, largely by way of the Moorish emirates in Spain. The Arabs before the time of Mohammed had been largely a camel-borne people, and as they increasingly adopted the horse for warfare they applied to it the *haqma* or camel-bridle (hackamore), a much lighter and more delicate contrivance than any previously used in Europe. The Bedouin camel-saddle, with its pronounced peak both at pommel and cantle, was adapted by them for use on the horse and accounts in part for the design of the medieval saddle, which both for war and for peace was very deep-seated, so much so that its use alone made the characteristic seat with almost straight leg inevitable. AD

Later Middle Ages and Renaissance:
THE SADDLE: the stirrup, previously used in the Far East for some centuries, reached Europe about the eighth century. (The first dated representation in the West is on the altar frontal of Sant'Ambrogio, Milan, A.D. 835.) It revolutionized the art of riding, and consequently methods of warfare. The soft saddle of earlier times gave place to a rigid structure, enabling the rider to keep his seat when charging an opponent with a lance. During the period of the Crusades the pommel and cantle increased in height until, by the fourteenth century, they partly encircled the rider on a war saddle. For ordinary riding, however, the pommel and cantle were low.

A rare surviving example of a war saddle is that of Henry V in Westminster Abbey. A pair of shaped boards lies along each side of the horse's spine, joined by two iron arches to which pommel and cantle are attached. Embroidered padding covered the top; there must also have been stuffing underneath. The rider sat high above the horse's back, well-situated to wield a sword or lance.

Developments in warfare required a more agile horse; the saddle now tended towards a deeper seat, giving more contact with the horse, such as that illustrated by Antoine de PLUVINEL.

While the Western knight, who used a lance, rode long, the archer-horseman of Asia had shorter stirrups. This style reached eastern Europe. Short stirrups were also used in Spain, for *gineta* horsemanship, in conjunction with the Moorish ring-curb. The saddle was usually secured by a woven girth, and by a breeching-shaped crupper and a breastplate. The whole was often sumptuously decorated: a number of riding-saddles survive, of carved ivory or bone, and the trappings and caparisons were frequently embroidered and studded with enamelled bosses and coats of arms.

THE BRIDLE: both the snaffle and curb were known to the Romans, but the latter appears to have been little used until after c. A.D. 1000 as warhorses gradually became heavier and greater collection was required. It commonly took the form of a pelham, with one pair of reins plain and one decorated. The mouthpiece was usually plain and jointed, or with a high, Eastern-style port. Sometimes there were two bars, one above another, hanging low in the mouth. A much greater variety of ingenious and unpleasant bits was developed in the Renaissance, but enlightened writers agreed that only three should normally be used: the 'plain canon', a tapered, jointed mouthpiece; the 'scach', a roughened version for harder mouths; and the 'melon', thick and rounded for sensitive horses. There was often a 'water chene' for mouthing. The curb-chain was of large, smooth links, or even of leather.

While the snaffle remained in use for many purposes, the schooled horse of the Renaissance was expected to wear a single-rein curb. However, in order not to spoil his mouth, his training was begun in a *cavesson*. This sometimes had a metal or chain noseband, but Thomas Blundeville, in 1580, recommends the Neopolitan type, of plaited cord. Next, 'false reins' were attached to the top eyes of the bit to form a pelham, and finally the horse graduated to a single curb.

Accoutrements. *Below:* The 'cannone', 'scaccia' and 'melone' bits illustrated by Federico Grisone in *Ordini di Cavalcare* (1550)
Below right: The form and shell-like flutings of this complete war harness for man and horse, made for a member of the Freiburg family, *c.* 1475–85, are characteristic of German Gothic armour at its best.

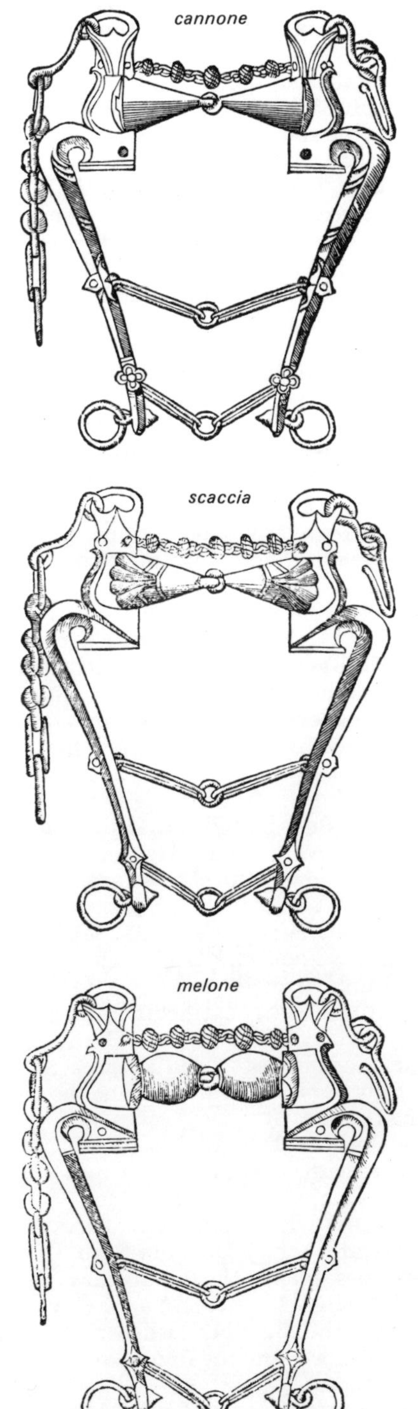

Many gadgets are described by Renaissance writers for difficult horses, some with modern equivalents. The standing martingale was used during schooling, and the 'musroll' served as a drop noseband (sometimes metal-studded.) Various types of trammel were used to teach a horse to amble. Pillars appeared in the riding-school *c.* 1600.

HORSE ARMOUR: as weapons developed, and horses were bred larger to carry the more heavily armoured rider, they themselves were given some protection. By the end of the thirteenth century flowing caparisons are often represented; a variety of materials may have been placed underneath. In the fifteenth century steel plate bards for horses begin to appear. Early examples are rare: one of the finest is that of von Freiburg, *c.* 1475–85, in the Wallace Collection, London. This weighs 71 lb 11½ oz, including the saddle (rider's suit 76 lb 13½ oz) as it is a light field-armour, fluted for strength. The more solid bards of the sixteenth century were more unwieldy; they remained in use into the seventeenth century, when the sport of jousting lost its popularity. A complete bard consists of a *chanfron* on the horse's face, a *crinet* of hinged plates down his mane (usually with mail under his neck), a *peytreil* protecting the chest and a *crupper* over the croup, with *flanchards* below the saddle on each side. AH

After the Renaissance: in the first half of the seventeenth century the only horsemanship to be taken seriously was the *manège* riding of the Great Horse. To collect this ponderous creature a severe curb-bit was necessary (see Later Middle Ages and Renaissance above). As jousting was no longer fashionable, the exaggerated heights of pommel and cantle were reduced until the saddle resembled the modern Western saddle. The weight was spread over a large, stiff saddlecloth; the seat sloped from front to rear; a moderately high pommel and cantle fixed the rider firmly in the centre of his saddle. The rider's thighs were wedged between pads fore and aft.

The English Duke of NEWCASTLE introduced in mid-century a bearing-rein to give the rider a two-to-one mechanical advantage in turning a horse's head 'though he be as stiff-necked as a bull'. It had a vogue, but it was a faulty device since it unduly constricted a horse and made it difficult for it to learn to canter with the inner leg leading.

Though *manège* riders did not realize it, the Great Horse was on its way out. The future lay with racing and foxhunting. For these, especially from about 1680 onwards when the enclosing of fields made it necessary for the hunter to jump hedges or fences, the saddles and bits of the Duke of Newcastle were positively dangerous—let anyone who questions this try jumping in a Western saddle (see Western Tack): he will be fortunate if he escapes emasculation.

There were in the seventeenth century saddles other than these used for the *manège*: a flat 'travelling pad'; a large, plain, Scottish saddle; 'light and nimble' saddles used for hunting and racing. From these there evolved a general-purpose saddle, flat in the seat, with straight-cut panels, which resembled the modern 'show-ring saddle'. It was a gradual process, and one cannot say exactly when the old type gave away to the new; but David Morier's picture, *Horses at Wilton House*, shows both in use in the mid-eighteenth century.

Medieval and Renaissance horsemen did

not always use the curb bit. Fourteenth-century pictures show snaffles in use for hunting and the tournament. In a well-known picture of a race through Florence in the fifteenth century, most of the jockeys are using snaffles. One can safely assume that seventeenth-century horsemen often used the snaffle for racing and hunting, or combined it with a curb to make a double bridle. De LA GUÉRINIÈRE, the famous French riding master, noted that an English hunter should gallop 'as he would without a rider', clear indication that for hunting a snaffle or mild double bridle was usual. The latter seems to have been more common for racing until the end of the eighteenth century, when Samuel Chifney, the Prince of Wales's jockey, popularized the snaffle. (He could pull a horse as well with one as with the other, and His Royal Highness had to be warned that, if he continued to employ Chifney, 'no gentleman would start with him'.) Throughout the nineteenth century

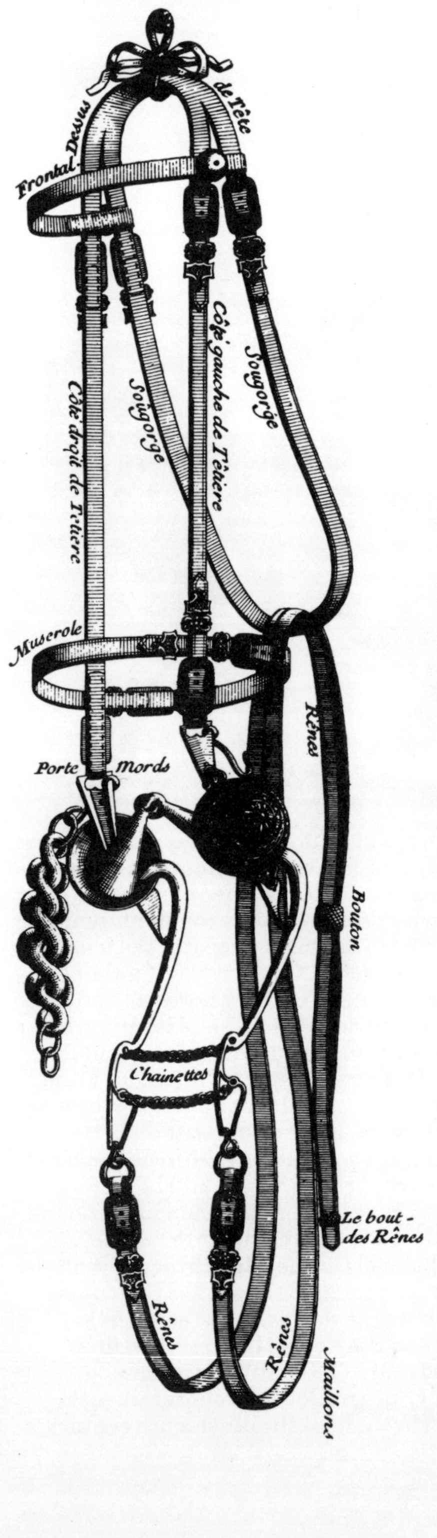

Accoutrements. Bridle with simple cannon bit, shown by La Guérinière in his *Ecole de Cavalerie* (1733)

bitting was very much as it is today. For hunting and hacking riders used the snaffle, double bridle or various forms of pelham according to taste; for flat racing, the snaffle; for steeplechasing, the double bridle gradually gave way to the snaffle. The saddle for all purposes resembled a rather straight-cut modern hunting or polo-saddle.

For military purposes something different was required, designed to carry about 18 stone (252 lb or 114 kg) of trooper, arms and equipment. It must spread this great weight over as wide an area as possible of dorsal muscle and ribs, and keep it off the spine of a horse which has lost condition in a hard campaign. It must encourage a tired rider to sit up in the centre of his saddle instead of flopping about, giving his horse a sore back. So the British cavalry saddle, from the Napoleonic wars until the present day, had a steel (originally a beechwood) frame with high, wide front- and rear-arch, to which was laced the detachable seat. The weight was well distributed over long, wide side-bars, padded with numnah pads which could easily be altered in shape to fit any back. Under it was a four-fold blanket, which could be folded in different ways to relieve pressure. An adjustable V-attachment enabled the girth to be moved forward or back, to fit a peculiar conformation or avoid a girth gall. It is a first-class saddle for long-distance riding, and very little can happen to it which an ingenious rider cannot repair with jack-knife, screwdriver and a strip of rawhide. The British officer's saddle (known as the Colonial Pattern) and most Continental military saddles (e.g. the German) are more orthodox in design, larger and stronger adaptations of the ordinary civilian saddle.

Similarly the cavalry thought that civilian bits would not do. For ceremonial parades, and, more questionably, for hand-to-hand combat a greater degree of collection was required than could be given by these. So the military bit was at first the Hanoverian, a very severe pelham-type curb with a high port and long cheek pieces; then the Universal Bit, also a form of pelham which, according to how it is fitted, can be very mild or severe.

In the eighteenth century the breastplate, crupper and breeching dropped almost out of use for normal purposes; and in the nineteenth the martingale, standing and running, was devised. The tendency in the twentieth century has been for greater simplicity in bits and great specialization in saddles. There are few horses now which will not go in a snaffle, double bridle, pelham or Kimblewick. Saddle seats tend to be deeper than those of our fathers, and the panels (except in the dressage saddle) are cut to suit the forward seat. There are featherweight saddles for racing, and saddles with kneepads to help keep the show jumper in the plate. CCT

Reference: William Cavendish, Duke of Newcastle, *A General System of Horsemanship*, 1743. G. Tylden, *Horses and Saddlery of the British Army*, London, 1965. Charles Chenevix Trench, *A History of Horsemanship*, London, 1970.

Actor, Horse as see Stage, Horse on the, Motion Pictures, Horse in

Adayevsky see U.S.S.R., Kazakh

Africa

The horses of Africa are classed into three groups: (1) Oriental, (2) Barb and Dongola, (3) Ponies.

The Oriental group comprises horses derived from southwest Asia and resembling the Arab in type and conformation. Horses of this type are found mainly in the coastal plains of Libya, Tunisia, Algeria and Morocco, and are occasionally seen among the horses of Tuareg and other desert tribes. They average 14 hands (1·42 m) in height, and are of a harmonious conformation and high-spirited elegant appearance, with compact forequarters and square well-set hindquarters. The head is short, with a wide square forehead, straight profile, short alert ears, and lively eyes. Horses of Oriental type reached Egypt first during the sixteenth century B.C. But the majority of the recent Oriental horses of Africa doubtless originate from later importations, especially from the horses introduced in the course of the Arab invasions of the seventh and eleventh centuries A.D.

The Barb and Dongola horses are closely allied. They are generally distinguished by a rather coarse head with a convex profile, light body, long legs and a sloping croup. They are derived, at least partly, from the Iberian peninsula where horses of this type were common during the Iron Age and medieval times. The Barb is bred in the hills and mountains of Libya, Tunisia, Algeria and Morocco where several local types are recognized. In West Africa it is represented by several breeds, such as the Hodh, Sahel, Senegal (River), Foutanké, Bélédougou (Banamba) and Barouéli.

The Dongola is nearly extinct in its original home, but is still bred in Chad, Bornu and Sokoto, and in West Africa is represented by the Fula horse of Cameroun, and the Hausa and Djerma.

Like the Barb, the Dongola has been much crossed with Oriental stock. Crossbred types of Dongola and Oriental derivation are found in Ethiopia and Eritrea (Ethiopian Galla horse). Dongola-Barb crossbred types, such as the Bandiagara (Gondo or Macina), Mossi and Yagha (Liptako), occur in the Niger bend where the Barb from the north and the Dongolawi from the east meet.

The pony breeds of East and West Africa are descended from Oriental, Barb and Don-

Above: **Africa.** Northern Nigerian tribesmen in traditional costume

Far right: **Ageing.** A Longitudinal section of an incisor tooth. B Cross-sections of the same tooth at different ages: (1) at five to six years (2) at eight to nine years (3) at eleven to twelve years (4) at thirteen to fourteen years

gola stocks in various proportions. Their small size is due to the unfavourable climatic conditions south of the Sahara and near the equator. These breeds include the Somali, Borana (Galla), Western Sudan (Kordofani), Kirdi (Lake, Chari, Logone, Sara), Cotocoli (Togo), Torodi, Songhaï, Pony of the South, Kaminiandougou, Bobo (Minianka), Koniakar, M'Bayar, and M'Par (Cayar).

The Basuto pony of Lesotho, now nearly extinct, is descended mainly from horses of Oriental type (Arab and Thoroughbred) imported into South Africa during the nineteenth century. See also Southern Africa. Large parts of Africa are closed to horses by the tsetse fly. HE

Ageing

The permanent dentition of the horse consists of six incisor teeth, two canines or tushes and twelve molar or cheek teeth in each jaw. The incisors and first three cheek teeth are preceded by temporary or milk teeth.

The canine teeth are usually confined to the male although they are quite often seen in rudimentary form in the mare. The incisors are designated in pairs: centrals, laterals and corners; it is to these teeth that reference is made when assessing the animal's age. This is possible because the temporary teeth erupt and are replaced by permanent teeth at fairly regular intervals. When all the permanent incisor teeth have fully erupted the horse is said to have a full mouth; from then on the age is estimated from the changes that occur in the tables (wearing surfaces of the lower incisor teeth) and the angles at which they meet those of the upper jaw (see drawings overleaf).

Up to and including seven years the age of a horse can be estimated with some accuracy. After seven years this method of ageing is less precise and therefore horses over seven years old are often described as 'aged'.

At birth, or within two weeks, the foal has two central incisors in each jaw. The laterals appear at 4–6 weeks and the corners erupt at 6–9 months.

At one year all the temporary teeth are well up but the corners are shell-like and only in wear along their anterior borders. At this time care must be taken to differentiate between temporary and permanent incisors, otherwise, particularly in ponies, a yearling may be mistaken for a five-year-old. All the temporary teeth are in wear by two years and at approximately two and a half years the two centrals are displaced by permanent teeth that grow level with the others at three years.

At three and a half years the lateral permanent teeth erupt and at four and a half years the two corners are replaced by permanent teeth and the canines or tushes will have made their appearance. The permanent incisors are much larger than their whiter and more spatulate predecessors and are readily distinguished by two vertical grooves on the front of the upper teeth and one on the lower. The infundibulum (mark on the table of each permanent tooth) is also much more clearly defined.

At five years the corner teeth are level with their neighbours but they are not in full wear until the horse is nearly six years old.

At seven years the cavity of the mark has disappeared from the centrals and laterals but their rings of enamel may still persist. A seven-year-old hook may have developed

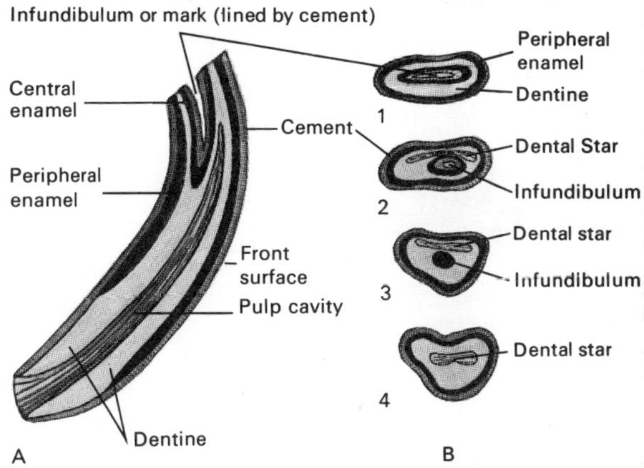

on the posterior part of the upper corner teeth due to incomplete apposition with their opposite numbers in the lower jaw.

At eight years the mark is still evident in the corner teeth. The centrals will be more triangular in shape and in these a secondary mark (dental star) will have appeared anterior in position to the previous mark. This is due to the wearing down of the tooth and the exposure of the pulp cavity. It has no enamel ring. The upper corner teeth will have lost their hooks.

At nine years the dental star will appear on the lateral teeth, the tables of which are now becoming triangular. An indistinct enamel ring may still be visible on the corners.

At ten years the dental star will be present in all the lower incisors and a groove (Galvayne's groove) emerges from the gum of the upper corner incisor. It generally grows downwards and at fifteen years reaches halfway down the tooth. It extends along the whole length of the tooth at about twenty years.

After ten years the incisors become more and more triangular in shape and the angle between the lower and upper teeth becomes more acute. At the same time the gums recede and the teeth appear longer.

In assessing age one must take into account the fact that Thoroughbreds are more likely to be born early in the year and other breeds later. For this reason all Thoroughbreds in the Northern Hemisphere are dated from 1 January and all others from 1 May. CF

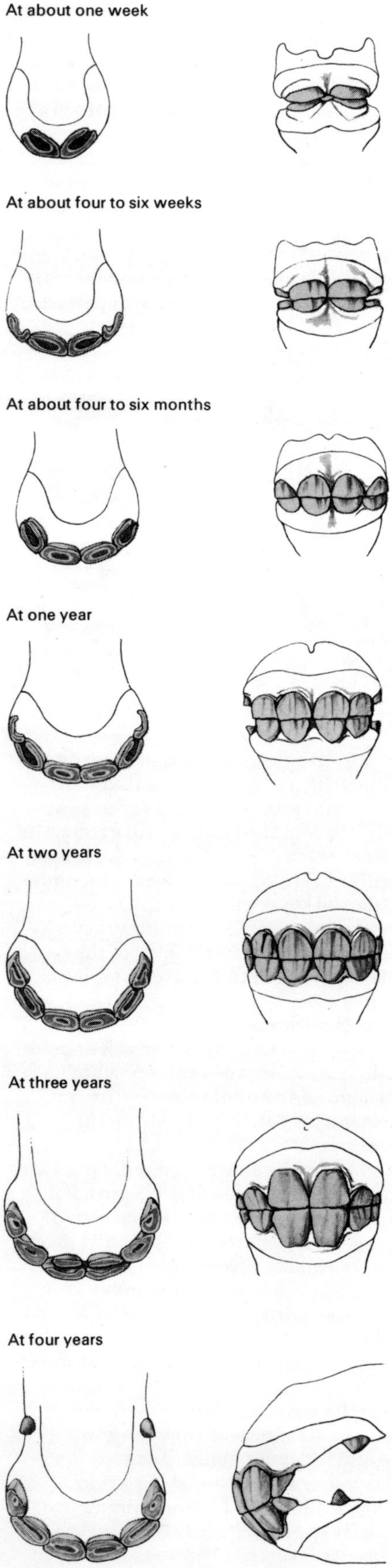

Age (Longevity)

The lifespan of a horse depends on the care it receives and work it does. Inheritance also influences this. A horse of five years supposedly equals a man of 20; a horse of 10 a man of 40. After this the difference lessens, a horse of 12 corresponding to a man of 50 and a horse of 30 to a man of 80. The greatest recorded age is held to date by Old Billy, an English barge horse belonging to the Manchester-Irwell Navigation Company, who died at 62. LFB

Age of a Thoroughbred

The age of an ordinary horse or pony is taken from 1 May of the year in which it was foaled. The age of a Thoroughbred is judged as from 1 January in the northern hemisphere; in the southern hemisphere, 1 August. Therefore, according to British and U.S. rulings, a horse born in late December is a year old from the racing point of view on 1 January immediately following its birth, and hence most breedings are arranged with early spring foals in mind. DRT

Agriculture

The first use of the horse, even among people who practised arable farming, was for purposes of war, hunting, ceremonial and, more particularly, religious ritual, though the last-named was often practised directly in aid of husbandry, and the horse taken to embody the Spirit of the Corn. Thus the Bronze Age rock pictures of northern Europe showing horses yoked to the plough do not represent the day-to-day work of the farm; they are only there to draw the symbolical first furrow of the season, after which the oxen take over. Horse taming first arose among peoples who practised hardly any crop-husbandry but were simply stock-breeders, and the first economic use of the horse was therefore as herdsman's mount, the beginning of a long story which ends with the cowboy, the vaquero, the Australian stockman and the Cumberland shepherd on his Fell pony.

Even in Europe today, where agriculture is nearing the end of its animal-traction phase, the horse working on the land is exceptional in the entire Mediterranean zone. Where ploughing is not done by oxen, it is done by mules. One could draw a line midway across France, north of which horses work in the plough, and south of it only oxen or mules. In any case the horse is unsuitable for cultivation of the most valued Mediterranean crops, grapes. The mule and the ass, treading carefully with narrow hoofs on a narrow track, are the most suitable animals for working in the Mediterranean vineyards.

Even in systems of agriculture where ploughing was done exclusively by oxen, as in Anglo-Saxon England, harrowing was done by horses, and in some parts of the British Isles virtually without harness;

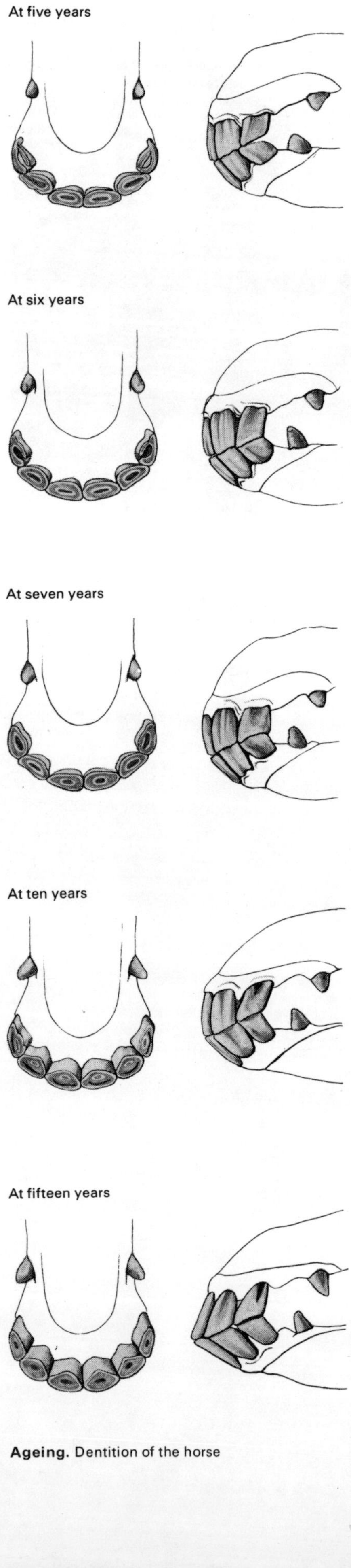

Ageing. Dentition of the horse

Agriculture. In fourteenth-century England horses were used to draw harrows *(below)*, while oxen were used for ploughing. Horse ploughing *(centre)* was introduced to Europe by the Vikings. *Bottom:* This 33-horse team combine harvester was photographed in the State of Washington in 1902.

there was a headcollar of hair rope, and the harrow, which consisted only of a couple of thorn bushes, was simply tied to the tail. This method was still practised in Ireland during the lifetime of Edmund Spenser (*c.* 1598). In some parts of Europe the role of the horse is indispensable but strictly limited: on the Isle of Skyros in the Aegean the island ponies are only used after the grain harvest, where they tread out the corn before it is winnowed. The horse's role as the agricultural maid-of-all work probably arose by a widening of some originally quite narrow function such as this. In medieval England, we see in the Luttrell Psalter (1340) a team of oxen in the plough but a team of horses in the harvest cart. It was only gradually that this specialization was broken up. Farmers everywhere were reluctant to abandon the working ox because it was cheaper to feed than a working horse, and could be 'finished' as far-from-baby-beef at seven years old. The process was almost complete in East Yorkshire by the 1640s; according to Henry Best of Elmswell's *Farming Book*, the calendar of a progressive yeoman, he had six teams of plough horses which also went in the wagon, and only one team of draught oxen. But there were still ox-ploughs in Sussex in the present century.

Horse ploughing as the usual practice first arose in Scandinavia in the Viking Age. The Norseman spent the summer plundering the coasts of Europe. But before he left he had to do the spring ploughing, and when the cruise was over he still had to get in the harvest. If the 'Viking season' was not to be unduly curtailed, he must get through these chores quicker than the pace of oxen would allow. By this example the practice spread along the Continental coastline between Jutland and Brittany, and the distribution of heavy breeds of horse for agricultural use follows this pattern, from the JUTLAND breed itself to the powerful Breton draught horse by way of the ARDENNAIS, the BOULONNAIS, and most of all the Norman plough horse which bears the same relation to the Anglo-Norman as the Irish Draught mares do to Irish Hunters. The same pattern is observable in Britain; the coasts most exposed to Viking invasion produced the most massive work horses: Suffolk, Lincolnshire (the home of the Old English Black, ancestor of the Shire), the Clyde valley, vulnerable to the raiding Norsemen from their bases in the Western isles, and Cleveland in Yorkshire where the famous bay horses once worked in the plough.

The great technical advances of the late eighteenth century, with early reaping and mowing machines, improved harrows and hoes, rollers, drills and special kinds of plough, all depended on the motive power of such horses as the SHIRE. The limit to the size of team that could be used was set, in practice, by the width of English field gates, allowing a maximum of three horses abreast. But in the American prairie states, Canada and Australia, enormous teams up to a dozen abreast drew harvesting machines. and gang ploughs of a size that only became usable in Britain after mechanization. Thus in these wide arable lands the economic use of the heavy draught horse has persisted much later, and has enabled the British breeder of Shires or CLYDESDALES to maintain a nucleus of first-class horses primarily for overseas export. AD

A.H.C. see American Horse Council

A.H.S.A. see American Horse Shows Association

Aids

The various means the rider employs to train and guide his horse include *natural aids*, such as the legs, hands, body, weight and voice, and *artificial aids* such as spurs and whip. Other classifications are *upper* and *lower* aids (hands and legs), *lateral* and *diagonal* aids (combinations of hand and leg aids on the same side of the horse or opposite sides).

Properly combining several simultaneously applied aids in order to prompt a movement, *coordination of the aids*, is beyond the rider's competence till he acquires the *independence of the aids*, whereby each of them is able to act independently of all others: legs from hands, hand from hand, leg from leg. Since, however, all and any leg and hand action must derive from the poise and balance of the upper body, the first premise is a good *seat* giving the rider *steadiness*.

Note that in equitation, where by definition all is movement and movement is all, steadiness does not signify total absence of it, but absence of any useless or counterproductive movement, voluntary or involuntary. The rider must be so joined to his horse in motion that he always accompanies, never precedes or lags behind it. In sum, the aids, their independence and coordination are contingent on seat and consequent steadiness, plus, more intangibly, *equestrian tact,* i.e. a sense of measure and timing.

In early training, lateral aids, which are more clearly understood by the horse, are used. Once it has understood, if the movement at hand requires it, the trainer changes over to the diagonal aids. The lateral aids are also used to cope with resistances because, unlike the diagonal aids, they do not offer the horse support on either hand or leg to bolster his defence.

The hands (upper aids) control pace, speed and direction by *acting, resisting* or *yielding*.

They *act* when slowing down, halting, reining back, changing direction or positioning part or all of the horse, by finger pressure on the reins, reinforced, if necessary, by a vertical raising of the wrists and/or the use of the body weight. Backward traction on the reins is not used as an aid under any circumstances.

They *resist* when, though ceasing to act, they do not yield and maintain the previously established rein tension; or when they oppose the horse's resistance. The force of opposition is strictly equal, never superior to that of the resistance; hands yield as soon as the horse does.

They *yield* when they cease either to act or resist; this yielding may vary in explicitness from a simple slackening of the fingers to totally slack reins.

The hands can act *simultaneously* or *singly:* simultaneously to obtain a change of pace, a halt, a rein back, or collection; singly when concerned with direction or position.

When acting singly, there is a distinction between the *active* hand and the *passive* hand which, yielding and/or resisting, contributes to, sustains or limits the effect of the acting hand.

The hands make use of five *rein effects*. The first two act on the forehand, the last three act by *opposing* shoulders to haunches and therefore are called *effects of opposition*.
(1) the *opening rein* has a natural action upon the horse. It draws its nose in the direction to be taken; the head and neck being so orientated, barrel and quarters will follow their direction;
(2) the *neck rein* acts on the base of the neck, nudging it in the intended direction;
(3) the (right) *direct rein of opposition* prompts a turn to the right by shifting the haunches to the left. The right rein acts in a direction parallel to the horse's axis.
(4) the (right) *counter-rein of opposition in front of the withers* prompts a turn to the left by shifting the shoulders to the left, the haunches to the right; right rein to the left, in such a way that an imaginary extension of it would pass in front of the withers.
(5) The (right) *counter-rein of opposition behind the withers* or 'intermediate' rein between third and fourth effect, acts on the right shoulder and haunch, the entire horse being pushed left; right rein to the left, but here in such a way that an imaginary extension of it would pass behind the withers.

The success of all rein effects depends on the quality of the forward movement; for, as the late Commandant Jean Licart would say, 'the hands indicate, the legs oblige'. Depending on the art and science of both horse and rider, they may be infinitely shaded in their subtlety.

The *legs* (lower aids) produce primarily the forward movement and shift or hold the haunches. They too act, resist, or yield.

They *act simultaneously* and slightly behind the girth in prompting, maintaining or increasing the forward movement, emphasis going anywhere from a mere throbbing of the calf inside the boot, via a pressure or touch of the leg, to a prick or outright attack by the spur.

They *act singly*, at the girth, from back to front, to increase the forward movement or, at the normal place, by pressure perpendicular to its body, to prompt the horse to bend;

or slightly behind the normal place and from front to back, to shift the haunches to the side opposite this 'action of the single leg'.

They *resist singly* when they firmly bar a shift of the haunches.

They *yield singly or simultaneously* when, without ceasing to be in contact, they relax all pressure.

The *body weight*, as an aid, is more complementary than determining while the position of the rider's body influences the horse/rider balance; his movement to change to a more effective position affects the overall balance too, entailing an occasional contrast or even conflict in transit. The cautious rider should therefore use his distribution of weight rather more as a means not to disturb than to change his horse's balance. His position should, to quote General Decarpentry, 'give an illusion of immutability . . . ' by being 'vertical at the halt and adjusted to the direction, speed and body inclination of the horse, in movement'. JF

Aintree

Aintree, just north of Liverpool, Lancashire, England, is famous for the GRAND NATIONAL. When first run in 1837 the race was known as the Grand Liverpool Steeplechase. Flat races are also run at Aintree and the course has given its name to a type of breastplate, the Aintree or racing girth. DRT

Airs, Classical

Airs, Classical. Courbette in hand at the Spanish Riding School of Vienna

Classical equitation aims at the development and perfection of the natural movements of the horse. Exercises on the ground, as demanded at DRESSAGE TESTS, range from walk, trot, and canter on a single track, through lateral work when the horse moves forward and sideways, to *piaffe* and *passage* in which riding becomes art. The airs above the ground, developed from the natural leaps of the horse, are the *levade* and *pesade*, the horse rising on its deeply bent haunches with its forelegs folded under its chest, and the *capriole*, a horizontal leap with the hind legs kicking vigorously. When not striking with its hind legs the horse performs a *ballotade*. In the *courbette* it leaps several times on its hind legs without touching the ground with its forelegs. A single leap on the hind legs is called a *croupade*. *Mezair* and half *courbettes* are now obsolete.

In the sixteenth to eighteenth centuries these airs belonged to the training of a school horse and were used in jousts and tournaments. Today they are practised only at the SPANISH RIDING SCHOOL OF VIENNA. AP

Akhal Teke, Akhal Tekin

The Russian Akhal Teke is in much demand as a jumper, due to its elastic and powerful spring, but has a tendency to be obstinate and to refuse. Nevertheless, this breed is supreme among Russian sporting horses; an Akhal Teke stallion (Absent) won the Grand Prix de Dressage at the Rome Olympics in 1960. It has a light head, with large, wide-set eyes and very long neck, set on high up. The body is long, muscular, and usually slender, occasionally with an insufficiently developed chest cage and a tendency to develop a tender back. The legs are long and dry, with clearly exaggerated sinews. It usually has a small, silky mane, a short tail, and an absence of 'feather'; some have no mane or forelock at all. The hoofs are rather large but regularly formed, often with low heels. Average height at withers for stallions is about 15·1 hands (1·54 m), for mares about 15 hands (1·52 m); bone below the knee for stallions is 7½ in (19 cm), for mares 7 in (18·1 cm). The breed has superb natural movement, a very distinctive, soft and elastic walk and a flowing movement at trot and canter, as if sliding over the ground; the body does not swing, but the leg is moved from the lower joints. The Akhal Teke is bred in Turkmen, Kazakhstan, Uzbekistan, and Kirghiz, as well as at the Tersky stud in the Northern Caucasus. See Turkoman, U.S.S.R. WOF

Albinism

The congenital absence of pigment from the skin and other tissues. The horse with an absence of pigment in the iris of the eye is often described as 'wall-eyed'. CF

Alcock Arabian

The Alcock Arabian, a grey Arab stallion, has the distinction of being the forefather of all grey THOROUGHBREDS. Imported with the Holdernesse Turk to England via Constantinople by Sir Robert Sutton and probably first known as Sutton's Arabian, he changed hands several times during the next eighteen years or so and was called the Pelham or Ancaster Arabian and probably also the Akaster Turk. He was owned by the Duke of Ancaster in 1722–4. Alcock was neither his first nor last owner, but somehow that is the name by which he became known. His son Crab can be found at the end of most famous pedigrees, like that of The Tetrarch. DRT

Altai see U.S.S.R.

Altér see Spain, Brazil

Altér-Real see Portugal

Amateur and Professional

A professional is a person who derives financial gain from horses in any way, whether by buying and selling, riding for hire, instructing in equitation, or lending his name to commercial products, for reward, in order to stimulate sales.

For some years the Olympic Games committee, and others, have been levelling charges of 'shamateurism' at the leading show-jumping riders of many nations. To some extent the **FÉDÉRATION ÉQUESTRE INTERNATIONALE** and the affiliated national federations have been able to counter the charge by contending that, in show jumping, the prize money (often substantial in recent years) is credited to the horse, rather than to the rider. Those riders who have been able to prove that their ostensible means of livelihood was derived from any source other than horses (from agriculture, for example) have experienced no difficulty in obtaining an amateur licence. Many federations claim that there is no longer any object in differentiating between the two, and wish that the distinction might be abolished. In fact, only the knowledge that they will be barred from competing in the **OLYMPIC GAMES**, still regarded as the highest honour which the sport has to offer, prevents many riders from renouncing their amateur status. As it is, only two professional licences are granted annually to show-jumping riders in Britain, though in racing under both codes the amateurs are heavily outnumbered by the professionals. There is also a substantial professional element in North American show-jumping circles; but the U.S. and Canadian Olympic teams are perhaps the most genuinely amateur squads in the world. PMM

Amble see Gaits

American Dressage Institute

The American Dressage Institute is a non-profit organization founded in 1967 to 'encourage, train and educate American horsemen in the art of classical riding from the level of elementary dressage to Grand Prix, and to provide exhibitions of these techniques and skills before the general public in order to expand the knowledge of and interest in classical equitation'. It is supported by individual memberships and about 20 affiliated associations throughout the United States and maintains a permanent staff of instructors and horses. The facilities are located on the campus of Skidmore College. Applicants must be 18 years old or over with some basic knowledge of dressage. The office is at Daniels Road, Saratoga Springs, N.Y. 12866. MNS

American Horse Council

The A.H.C. is a national trade association representing over one million American horsemen. Its major purposes are to advise government officials about legislation affecting horse owners and riders, and to foster and expand scientific research relating to the horse. Its members include individuals and some 40–50 organizations (breeders, racetrack operators, pleasure riders, foxhunters, etc.). Among services provided to members are a tax reference service, programs on horse health and the establishment of riding trails. Its office is at 1776 K Street N.W., Washington, D.C. 20006, U.S.A. HCA

American Horse Shows Association

The ruling body of most horse shows in the United States was founded in 1917 in New York City, by sportsmen and delegates from 50 major horse shows. It now has about 13,000 members and sanctions nearly 700 horse shows each year. Its rule book is probably used by another 1,000 non-member shows. The A.H.S.A. (527 Madison Ave, New York, N.Y.) assigns dates to all recognized shows, licenses judges, stewards and technical delegates, maintains records, adjusts disputes, promotes riding and international competition, and protects the welfare of show horses by conducting tests for narcotics and inspections for cruelty. HCA

American Indians see Horsemanship, American Indian

American Saddle Seat Equitation see Saddle Seat Equitation

American Stagecoach

The American stagecoach was a four-wheeled horse-drawn vehicle, usually enclosed, and slung on leather thoroughbraces. There were numerous manufacturers of this peculiarly American vehicle, but the best known was Abbot-Downing Company of Concord, New Hampshire, whose colourful coaches saw service in South Africa and Australia (see Australian Stagecoach) as well as all parts of North America.

From about 1825 to the end of the horse-drawn era there were four basic types of American coaches. The lightest was termed the *light hotel coach*, distinguished by the absence of brakes, a panelled front boot, and a rear luggage boot without leather covering. The *heavy mail coach*, fitted with brakes operated by the driver with a foot lever, had the same type of body with graceful compound curves as the lighter town version, but was furnished with heavy leather panels for the front boot on the driver's box, and a full leather covering for the rear luggage boot. The leather thoroughbraces for both types were slung from iron-braced jacks on front and rear bolsters. The third distinct type was the *stage wagon*, whose body was squared, and lacked the beauty and curved panelling of the first two coaches. The body of the *stage wagon* was partially enclosed by uncurved panelling. Leather or canvas curtains protected the passengers from the weather, just as similar curtains completely enclosed both the light hotel coach and the heavy mail coach. The leather thoroughbraces were attached by a different method on the *stage wagon*, and the *mud wagon*, the fourth type: simple wooden members, bolted to the reaches of the undercarriage, afforded fastening of the thoroughbraces by U-

American Stagecoach. Heavy Concord Coach made by the Abbot-Downing Company of Concord, New Hampshire

bolts at each end of the heavy leathers. The body of the *mud wagon* was square in design, and had a minimum of panelling. Protection of passengers from dust and rain was afforded by long canvas or leather curtains which were rolled up and secured in good weather.

Each of the above types had several variations, but all were constructed of the best hardwoods and in a manner that allowed many to survive in excellent condition to the present day. All but the *light hotel coach* were designed to be drawn by either four or six horses, depending on the terrain through which they ran. The light coach was often pulled by a single team. See also Coaching and colour plate, page 264. RS

Americas, Pony of the see Pony of the Americas

Anaesthetics Act, Animals (United Kingdom)

In order to protect animals from unnecessary suffering an Act was passed in 1919, and later amended, to ensure that operations were not performed on animals without the use of anaesthetics. In 1954 the Act required that all operations involving either the bone structure or sensitive tissues must be performed under an anaesthetic and in 1964 an amendment was passed that included castration. Failure to comply with the Act, whether the person is a registered veterinary surgeon, practitioner or a layman, can lead to a fine of up to £50 or prison. DRT

Anatomy see Conformation

Andalusian

Spain was famous for the horses of the province of Andalusia from antiquity to the Middle Ages. This breed developed during the 700 years of Moorish dominion, when the native horses of Spain were crossed with BARBS brought in by the Moors. NORIKER blood may also have been used. See Carthusian, Spain. DMG

Anglo-Arab

In Britain: a horse defined by the Arab Horse Society as being an animal in whose pedigree exists no strain of blood other than Thoroughbred or Arab. It may be the product of an Arab stallion on a Thoroughbred mare or vice versa, or any further crosses of this blood; in Britain the percentage of either is irrelevant. To be eligible for the Anglo-Arab Stud book the Thoroughbred ancestry must be registered in the General Stud Book and the Arab in the Arab Horse Stud Book. Anglo-Arabs bred overseas may, subject to the recommendation of Council, be accepted in the A.H.S.B. provided that their pedigrees are approved by a Society recognized by the Arab Horse Society. The requirements of other countries are not necessarily the same. The Anglo-Arab is rapidly increasing in popularity, registrations rising from 49 in 1965 to 113 in 1970. At the Arab Horse Society's annual show in 1965 entries numbered 77 and rose to 120 in 1970.

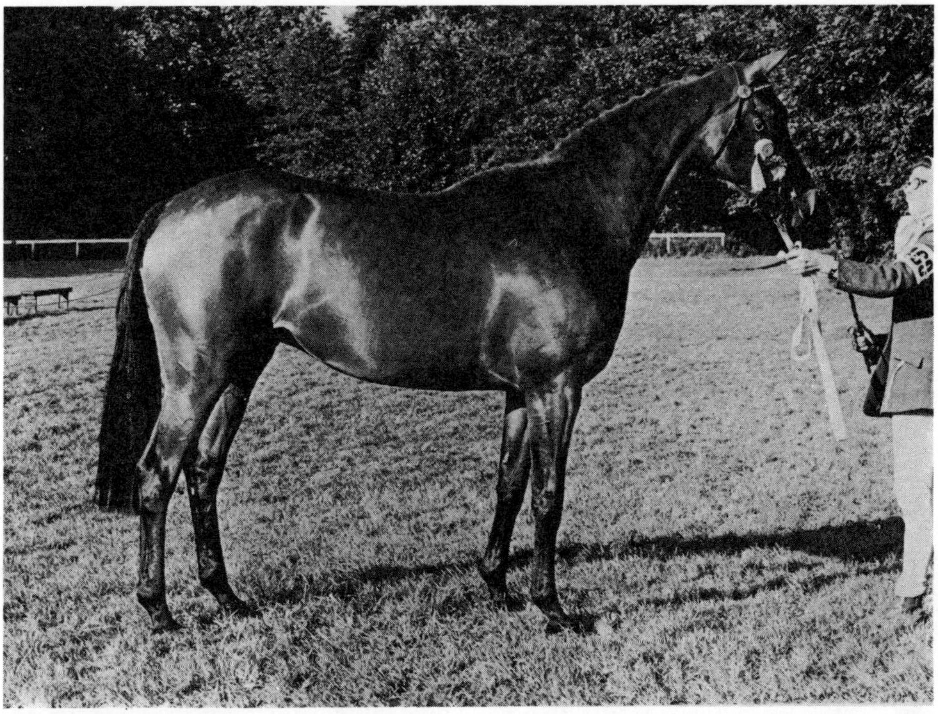

Anglo-Arab. British-bred mare Scindian Enchantress

No standard of type has been laid down for this composite breed, now acknowledged as a breed in its own right, and it is judged in hand, as a riding horse, and under saddle as either hack, or hunter, depending on the quality, conformation and size of the individual animal. However, a type is fast emerging, and discriminating breeders are producing Anglo-Arabs of uniformly correct make and shape, with tremendous size and scope combined with great elegance and good bone. The real merit of the Anglo-Arab lies in the fact that it commonly inherits the best of both worlds: the additional speed and substance of its Thoroughbred forebears together with the soundness and stamina, the natural balance and pride of bearing and the extreme sweetness of temperament of the Arabian, thus producing the ideal all-purpose saddle horse. The most popular method of breeding is that of Arab stallion on Thoroughbred mare, which has frequently been found to produce progeny of greater size than either parent. Crossing an Arabian mare to a Thoroughbred stallion is less usual as the progeny is likely to be smaller and of less monetary value than a purebred from the same mare. Numerous permutations are obviously possible but less commonly practised, probably because the outcome is considered to be less predictable.

Results of the Arab Horse Society's annual versatility contest for the Lady Yule Memorial Trophy show that Anglo-Arabs are to be found in the forefront of all spheres of competitive equestrian sport, and marks contributing to the final total have been won in jumping and show classes, dressage competitions, combined training and hunter trials. Between 1960 and 1970 many well-known and successful horses such as Desert Storm, Grey Cylla, Royal Constellation, Colcannon, Dolphin Play, Twyford Gallant and Scindian Enchantress did much to increase the breed's popularity and enhance its value. AHa

In France: Anglo-Arab stallions are found especially at the National Studs at Tarbes and Pau, in the southwest of France near the Pyrenees, and at Pompadour national stud in Limousin (these studs correspond to the principal breeding zones: for the Anglo-Arab of the southwest, Tarbes, Gers and western Pyrenean regions; for the Anglo-Arab of Limousin, the regions round Limoges and Brive, in central France west of the Auvergne Mountains). Anglo-Arabs of the southwest or Pyrenees are of a lighter type and often run in races which are reserved for them. They were extensively used by the French light cavalry up to World War II. Anglo-Arabs from Limousin are generally larger and more muscular. Both are often very good natural jumpers. Anglo-Arabs are generally excellent horses for various saddle uses. Although they are now bred in many countries, the climate and soil in these regions of France suit them particularly well, and France probably produces the best Anglo-Arabs.

Anglo-Arab. Natural ability for jumping and good paces make this breed popular for show jumping, eventing and dressage. These mares are French.

In early days invasions and exchanges brought Oriental blood to the native equine population of southwestern France. Later these already improved horses (Navarrins and Bigourdans, from the provinces of Navarre and Bigorre respectively), crossed with Arab, English and above all Anglo-Arab blood, produced the *demi-sang du midi* (halfbred of the southwest) or Tarbais, whose breeding zone stretches along the Spanish frontier region. The Limousin, which some people believe was tempered with Oriental blood from horses left behind by the Moors defeated at Poitiers (732), was thought highly of at the French court in the eighteenth century, and also by Napoleon. After the Napoleonic wars the need to reconstitute breeding stock according to the fashion for purebred horses (English or Arab) stimulated imports, and attempts to cross the two breeds began in about 1820. But credit for the systematic creation of the breed, starting in 1836, goes to the director of studs, E. Gayot, then at Pompadour. It came from the stallions Massoud (Arab) and Aslan (Turk) and from the three English Thoroughbred mares, Dair, Common Mare and Selim Mare. The method of alternate crossing, which avoids the predominance of any one breed and ensures that the characteristics of the Arab do not disappear with time, has proved to be the best. Since 1942 Anglo-Arabs, once separated into purebred Anglo-Arab (50 per cent of each race) and halfbred, have been included in the same stud book, that of the Anglo-Arab. This horse must have a minimum of 25 per cent Arab blood.

The Anglo-Arab is a large Arab, measuring 14·3–16·2 hands (1·49–1·70 m) and sometimes more. As with the English Thoroughbred, there is no standard type. It has inherited many of the qualities of its forebears —docility, courage, hardiness, balance, and natural ability for jumping, showy paces, intelligence, and the superior size, speed and power of the English Thoroughbred—all qualities making it suitable for racing, show jumping, dressage, hunting and, formerly, war. Its coat is usually bay or chestnut, the head is delicate, the nose usually straight, the eyes open and expressive. It has a wide forehead, mobile ears, well-set neck, deep chest, very oblique shoulder, short back, long and horizontal rump. Its limbs are sound and, although the cannons are sometimes light of bone below the knee, the bone is dense and of good quality. A solid frame enables it to carry weight. Among Anglo-Arabs the most notable in different spheres of activity have been Aiglonne (ridden by Captain Chevallier), Field Trials Olympic Champion in London in 1948, Harpagon (ridden by Col Jousseaume), who won several medals for dressage in different Olympic Games, and Rempart (ridden by Col Wattel, *Écuyer en Chef* of the Cadre Noir of Saumur, 1921–29, and generally considered the finest French dressage rider of the century). ES

Anglo-Norman

see Norman, Anglo-Norman and French Saddle Horse

Anglo-Persian and Pahlavan

These are bred primarily by H.I.M. the Shah in his stables at Farahabad on the outskirts of Teheran. Both breeds have retained the best qualities of their respective ancestors and have performed well in mountains, on the racetrack and in jumping competitions. Although the Anglo-Persian, bred in much the same way as the ANGLO-ARAB, is self-explanatory, the origins of the Pahlavan merit a closer look. In the early 1950s, Abdofazl Atabai, in charge of the Imperial Stables, created what is now known as the Pahlavan by crossing Thoroughbred, Plateau Persian and imported Arab stock. The result, after years of selection, is a tall (15·2–16 hands or 1·57–1·65 m), elegant and strong horse combining the soundness and grace of the Plateau Persian and Arab with the height and jumping abilities of the Thoroughbred. Kambiz Atabai, who inherited his father's position at the Imperial Stables, has continued the selection and breeding of Pahlavans and they are now a fully established breed in Iran. LF

Animal Health Trust see Equine Research Station

Antiquity, Horses in

The last word has not yet been written on the types and breeds of horses and ponies in ancient times. Indeed, a great deal of research still has to be done to establish origin, habitat and subsequent breeding centres in Europe, central Asia and China. Dr Nobis of Kiel (following Prof. Herre) believes that prehistoric *Equus przewalskii* produced three types of descendants: *Equus przewalskii przewalskii Poliakov* (the present-day ASIATIC WILD HORSE; *Equus przewalskii gmelini Antonius* (the TARPAN of forest and steppe varieties); and *Equus przewalskii silvaticus*, a heavier form which may have become extinct in the diluvial period and for this reason is sometimes called the 'diluvial' horse. Miklós Jankovich (after H. Ebhardt 1961), on the other hand, in *Pferde, Reiter, Völkerstürme* (1968), translated as *They Rode Into Europe*, shows four types: Pony type I, Pony type II, Horse type III and Horse type IV (see Pony).

Lady Wentworth, who founded the famous Crabbet Stud, believed the Arabian horse to be a breed by itself with no evolution in common with other breeds. This, we know, was, on historical, geographical and evolutionary grounds, mistaken and is mentioned here only because some lovers of the Arabian horse have almost made a cult of the 'purity' of the breed. In fact, it is generally considered that the Arab, the Oriental horse of the steppes, is descended from the steppe Tarpan which once roamed the plains of southern Russia, west of the Urals, while the heavy draught horse evolved from the 'diluvial' horse.

Although a complete evolutionary scale of fossil skeletons of *Equus* has been found in the western United States, it is doubtful if the claim by Dr George Gaylord Simpson and others, that horses *migrated* across the Bering Straits to populate the Old World before becoming extinct in the New, can be really valid. Horses apparently do not migrate, as we understand the word. Wild herds have a well-defined territory. Certainly colts cast out from a herd by the ruling stallion will wander considerable distances until they have been able to entice mares of their own. This being so, the question arises as to how *Equus* did populate the Old World. Since the zebra *(Equus zebra)*, onager *(Equus hemionus onager)* and ass *(Equus asinus)* evolved in the Old World, there seems to be no reason why the horse should not have done so too. It seems probable that small segregated herds or groups of horses were formed in very early prehistoric times throughout the Old World but it is unlikely that the horse population was extravagantly numerous, in spite of the claims made for the remains found at Solutré in France. Early man may have had small semi-domesticated herds which moved with him and in this way the nomad herdsman of the earliest historical times came to exist. Around 5000 B.C. some became settled farmers on the more fertile lands of Mesopotamia and Europe. Within the segregated groups of horses already mentioned, environment, climate, food, etc. would gradually contribute to characteristics differentiating one herd from another: the mountain horse would differ from the steppe horse, as it does today.

One hitherto unexplained characteristic separates the horse from the pony. Ponies are not small horses; nor do draught horses have pony characteristics. An almost indefinable quality appears to be associated with the poll, the area between the eyes and from the eyes to the ears. Ponies have very small ears; horses, on the other hand, have by comparison long ears.

The argument as to whether domesticated horses were first ridden or driven is pointless since both must have developed in different places. To carry a man a horse must have a strong back, while a weak-backed horse can be driven provided the right harness exists (see Carriages of Antiquity). The early reindeer people (*c.* 5000 B.C.) rode and drove their reindeer to sleds. The Yakuts and Urjandraiers followed this custom once they had domesticated the local species of *Equus*. It may be assumed that forest and mountain ponies would have stronger backs than steppe or desert horses; forests and mountains are also more suitable for riding, while flat country is more suitable for draught transport. The earliest record of chariot animals, in this case the ONAGER (although the ox was already domesticated for draught) comes from Sumer (*c.* 3500 B.C.). According to some authorities, the scarcity of horses was responsible for mule breeding. Rarity also, made the horse valuable and revered, to be used only by kings and of especial religious significance (see Myth and Legend, Horse in). Once the horse became established in southern Asia, breeding centres developed. Particular areas are known: the Altai mountains, Chorezem, Ferghana, the Euphrates and

Horses in Antiquity. Silver rein-ring from the pole of a chariot with onager in electrum, from Ur, *c.* 2500 B.C.

Tigris valleys, Cilicia and Lydia; in Europe, the Karst, Ardennes and the Sorraia river valley in the Iberian peninsula. Other areas may come to light. Following breeding areas, we find breeding centres or studs: the most famous in antiquity was Nisea (Nish in Ferghana) whence the 'heavenly' horses were obtained for Chinese studs *c.* 150 B.C. The present-day KARABAIR is bred at Dzhizak in the same area. Merv and Nisa, where the Parthians had a centre, are near Ashkabad, breeding centre of the modern AKHAL TEKE of Turkmen; Bactrian horses were famous in the cavalry of Darius, while the Chatti of a millennium earlier, who had a mountain pony breed, had to send to Babylonia for chariot horses. The kings of Akkad and Mari had horses brought from Charsamna (Harsamna), thought to be east of the Cilician Gates. Constantine I sent 200 Cappadocian horses to Yemeni princes in A.D. 400—the first record of horses in southern Arabia. See also Pazyryk Burials.

Because of its rarity the horse of antiquity was greatly valued and cherished. The Moslems consider that horses came after man in the ranks of creation. As kingdoms grew and expanded more and more horses were wanted, at first, for war chariots (although racing was also popular) and later for cavalry. The Assyrians bred a lighter horse than the Persians; the Chinese court went thousands of miles and fought two wars to obtain good animals from across the Tien-Shan mountains. The ancient Greeks preferred Thessalian and Thracian horses, which were generally white. There were a number of recognized breeds in the first millennium B.C. In central Europe during the following millennium there were herds of wild horses in many forests. There are records of horses in old Saxony (indicated by the white horse on the rulers' coats-of-arms) from the eighth century A.D. when the Franks demanded a tribute of 300 from the Saxons of north Germany. The Senner stud, now extinct, dated from the tenth century. Earlier still, there are Roman records of several distinct types of horses used by the German tribes in the Rhineland area, and Caesar mentions in *De Bello Gallico* the horses of the Ardennes, the ancestors of the present-day heavy BRABANT and RHINELAND. In the Iberian peninsula both the wild SORRAIA and the now domesticated MINHO are ancient types; they later provided the foundation stock for New World exports, leading to the CRIOLLO. Undoubtedly France also had wild, semi-wild and semi-domesticated breeds. For British native breeds see Mountain and Moorland.

In Asia Minor (*c.* 63 B.C.) the Corduène bred horses near Lake Van Gölu; Lord Oxford's Bloody-Shouldered Arabian (A.D. 1719) was a horse of the 'Gordeen' breed. Karakemish was an international horse market 3,000 years ago, and from nearby Aleppo many Syrian Oriental horses were exported to Britain in the seventeenth and eighteenth centuries to help found the THOROUGHBRED racehorse breed. Abidin estimates that only 100 years ago, over one hundred so-called Arabian strains could be named (see Arab). DMG

Reference: *Der Alte Orient*, band 38 I. Abidin, *Pferdezucht und Pferderassen im osmanischen Reiche*, Berlin, 1918; D. M. Goodall, *Horses of the World*, London, 1965; D. M. Goodall, *History of Horse Breeding*, London, 1973; Miklós Jankovich, *They Rode Into Europe*, London, 1971.

Appaloosa

This breed has distinctive round or irregular coloured spots concentrated on white hindquarters, striped hoofs, wispy tail and mane, and a characteristic white sclera encircling the eye.

Horses of similar markings are seen in ancient Chinese and Persian Art, but the development of the Appaloosa breed is attributed to the Nez Percé Indians of the northwestern United States, a fertile region including parts of Oregon, Washington, and Idaho, drained by the Palouse River. 'Appaloosa' is a corruption of 'Palouse Horse' or 'Palousy'. The horses are said to have reached the Nez Percé from Mexico, where a number were brought by Cortes from Spain in the sixteenth century. Others made their way to South America. Their ancestors probably came to Spain from Central Asia. The forehand may be of any colour, blending into a region of white over the hindquarters that is spotted in the same colour as the forehand. White Appaloosas may have spots of another colour over the entire body. There are many variations of the six basic patterns: frost, leopard, marble, snowflake, spotted blanket, and white blanket. Mottled skin is visible around the nostrils, lips and genitalia. The vertically striped hoofs are said to be more resilient than ordinary hoofs and to help account for the breed's remarkable endurance.

The modern Appaloosa weighs 950–1,175 lb (435–560 kg) and is 14–15·3 hands (1·42–1·62 m) high, although there is no maximum height limit. Crosses with other breeds have resulted in a horse with the overall appearance of a wellbred cow-pony, rather large-boned for its size, with a short straight back, strong limbs, and a tractable disposition. After a period of decline, the Appaloosa became increasingly popular due to its striking appearance combined with handiness, speed, and stamina. But not until the founding in 1938 of the Appaloosa Horse Club, Inc. (Moscow, Idaho) and of the Appaloosa Horse Club of Canada, was it recognized as an official breed. MAS

Appointments

The term 'appointments' refers to saddlery and harness worn by horses or ponies when working. In the show ring marks are awarded for the care of appointments in the general turnout, where it is taken into consideration in judging certain classes. DRT

Apprentices see Careers with Horses

Arab Horse

Origin: the origin and domestication of the horse in general and of the Arab Horse in particular have always been of great interest. But whereas we know a good deal about the horse in the Old Orient, i.e. in Asia Minor, Persia and the countries of the Fertile Crescent along the big river valleys of the Euphrates and Tigris, the Orontes, Jordan and Nile, our knowledge of the ancient horse in Arabia proper is scanty. Here we rely upon different, often contradictory, theories and upon the legends of the Bedouin.

Although scientists have long held the view that the wild ancestor of the domesticated horse was either the TARPAN or Przevalski's Horse (see Asiatic Wild Horse) or both, in recent times some researchers have become convinced that four prototypes of wild horses existed (see Ponies), among them an Oriental type. This would give a credible explanation for the development of such elegant, graceful and speedy animals as the 'drinkers of the wind'. Comparing the aristocratic Arabs, pictured over 3000 years ago in early Egyptian art, with the completely different clumsy, stocky northern horses shown in prehistoric European rock drawings and cave paintings, it is hard to discover a relationship between them except that they are all horses.

Because of the insufficiency of archaeological material, there are various theories about the area where this Oriental prototype lived as an indigenous wild horse. Obviously it was neither in Egypt nor Assyria, nor Babylonia, nor the old Turan (now Turkestan). Hitherto, it was held that wild horses never existed in those Asiatic and African zones that began to dry out at the end of the Ice Age and finally became steppes and deserts. Some finds in the late 1950s, however, revealed that such ideas may have to be revised in the future. Digs in Japan, West Iran, and in the South Libyan Acacus mountains of the Fezzan have yielded fossil bones and rock drawings of wild horses of unmistakable Arab type (M. Schaefer, *Wie werde ich Pferdekenner*, Munich, 1971). This puts the ideas of authors such as Upton, Seydel, Raswan and Lady Wentworth in a rather new light: they maintained that some thousand years ago, living conditions suitable for wild horses probably developed in Central or South Arabia, a conviction that corresponds with the belief of the Bedouin Arabs.

One must distinguish between the old Bedouin tradition and the later Islamic version blending the creation of the horse with religious allegory. According to the Bedouin tradition, the horse lived wild in the Nejd or Yemen until it was caught and tamed by their forefathers. This happened in approximately 3000 B.C., in the time of Baz, the great-great-grandson of Noah who owned the wild mare Baz. Mohammed, recognizing very soon the great value of efficient cavalry, especially after his defeat at Mount Ohod in A.D. 625 by superior mounted forces, placed great emphasis on the horse. Allah was believed to have created the horse out of a handful of South Wind, saying: 'Thy name shall be Arabian, and virtue bound into the hair of thy forelock, and plunder on thy back. I have preferred thee above all beasts of burden, inasmuch as I have made thy master thy friend. I have given thee the power of flight without wings, be it in onslaught or in retreat. I will set men on thy back, that shall honour and praise me and sing Halleluja to My name.' Ishmael, son of Abraham and ancestor of the Bedouin, was said to have been the first man to ride a horse, an Arab horse. Other personalities from ancient Israel were connected by Islamic tradition with the horse, including King David and his son Solomon (see Myth and Legend, Horse in).

The opponents of the wild horse theory claim that no horse bones have been found in Arabia. That is true but inconclusive. To look for bones on the ground would be useless in Arabia. Steppe and desert soon efface all human and animal traces and restore the primordial state with the help of wind, sand and the extreme climate. Discoveries below the ground presuppose special digs, but none has been made in Central Arabia, only a few in the Fertile Crescent, in Yemen, Hadramaut and East Arabia.

Arab Horse. *Left:* Rock inscriptions with horse and camel, found in the Nejd by Professor J. Euting in 1883
Below: Bedouin riding equipment is simple: a halter with chain as noseband, a single rope as rein, and a leather or woollen pad, girthed with a web, as saddle. The chain around the horse's neck is intended to avert the evil eye.

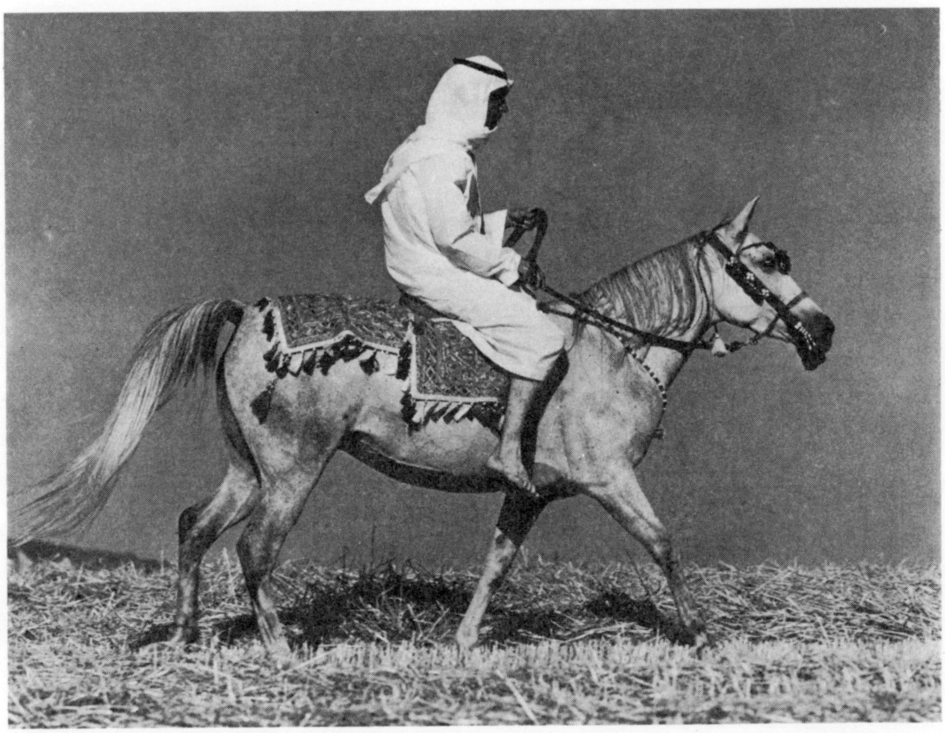

First Use of the Horse in Arabia: in the Semitic languages the word 'arab' originally signified 'steppe' or 'dry, waste area'. Historians and geographers of Antiquity and the Middle Ages used the terms Arabia and Arab rather vaguely, applying them to all the adjacent regions, sometimes as far as Asia Minor, and to any nomadic tribe. The much-quoted Strabo (63 B.C.–A.D. 20) wrote that Arabia had no horses. But he based his statement on the report of Aelius Gallus, who campaigned in the Yemen (25–24 B.C.), and told Strabo that he had not seen any horses there. From this, Strabo concluded that there were no horses in the whole of Arabia.

The northern boundary of Arabia proper is, strictly speaking, the 30th degree of latitude, i.e. the line from Kuwait to Aqaba. European exploration of the area south of this line took place comparatively recently. The first Westerner to cross it from the Persian Gulf to the Red Sea was the British Captain G. F. Sadlier, who, in trying to negotiate with the Egyptian Ibrahim Pasha on behalf of the East India Company in 1818–19, had to go to Medina and thus unintentionally became the 'discoverer' of Nejd. But he was interested neither in the Bedouin nor in their horses. The next Europeans to enter Nejd appeared decades later. Only a few of them were interested in horses: Palgrave (1863), Guarmani (1863–4), Lady Anne and Wilfrid Blunt (1880–1), Baron Nolde (1892–3) and Musil (1908–10, 1915). The old culture zones of the kingdoms in Hadramaut and Yemen attracted more explorers, and people out to buy horses for Europe and America preferred places in Syria and Iraq, less difficult and dangerous to reach.

Since the Bedouin do 'not write, neither read', we have no exact historical evidence of the first use of horses in Central Arabia. There is no doubt that the tribes bred them long before Mohammed's time. An Assyrian inscription reports that King Sargon II (721–705 B.C.) received horses as tribute from King Itamar of Saba (now Yemen). Euting (1883–4) discovered near Taima a vast number of rock inscriptions with animals, including horses of the finest Arab type. The work of the former Banu Thamud tribe, these inscriptions have been dated at about A.D. 300. Furthermore, famous pre-Islamic poets such as Tofail el-Kail, Zeid el-Kail, Nabirah, Antara and Imru' -al-Qays glorified their high-spirited, pure horses. The assertion that horse breeding started with Mohammed cannot be true. Horse breeding as well as camel breeding was the preserve of the Nejdi Bedouin. Mohammed was a townsman from Mecca, no more a horse-breeding centre than the rest of the hot and humid Tihama. But, convinced of the necessity of horses for his purposes, he sent messengers to the Bedouin tribes to buy horses, paying with slaves. Furthermore, he encouraged the faithful to expand their long-established horse breeding by promising them heavenly rewards: 'As many grains of barley as thou givest thy horse, so many sins shall be forgiven thee!' Without the existence of a large and well-established breeding stock, Mohammed's successors could hardly have conquered the whole dry zone between Tripoli and Egypt in the West and Persia in the East within the short time of 18 years (A.D. 633–651). Whatever the Arab horse's origin may be, whenever and wherever its first use took place, it is a well-established fact that the wandering Bedouin of Central Arabia bred the best, most versatile and most beautiful horse in the world.

Bedouin Life, the Camel and the Horse: without knowing the Bedouin way of life, it is impossible to understand their horse and their breeding system. The extremely hard living conditions of the desert, which ruthlessly stamped out all weaklings and let only the fittest survive developed all the characteristic attributes of the Bedouin: courage, generosity, tenacity, sternness, incredible frugality and patience, constant vigilance, dignity, and a sometimes overweening pride. As he wandered from pasture to pasture, always on the move in an implacable environment, the Bedouin's life was a continual struggle, and hunger and thirst were constant companions. Alone he was lost: so families and clans united into tribes under the leadership of a sheikh. There was no written code, but the unwritten law of the desert was respected by everybody.

The main precepts of this law were the subordination of each individual to the well-being of the tribe, generous hospitality, even towards an enemy, as soon as he had touched the tentrope, and the obligations of the blood feud. Secret theft was a crime, but robbery with the sword was legitimate, procuring property, fame and glory.

The camel was the most useful animal and property of the Bedouin. It provided them with wool, leather, ropes, fuel, meat and milk, thus giving them absolute freedom and independence to move in the desert at will. The camel was the foundation of life; the horse was pride and honour. It was with the help of the horse that property could be protected and augmented. Robbery of camels and horses was the noblest way to increase property, provided the principles of honour were observed.

Characteristics of the Arab Horse: origin, soil, use and selection developed special characteristics which distinguish the Arab from all other breeds, also from the ordinary Oriental horse in the neighbouring countries, so often sold abroad as a 'pure Arab'. The Arab has much in common with its Bedouin owner; strength, calm, stamina, patience, intelligence, high spirits, alertness, leanness, and noble appearance. The

Arab Horse. The Arab has a comparatively small and fine head, arched neck, and stands erect with tail carried high. For detailed characteristics of type and conformation, see text.

Arab is hot, but quiet, full of energy and well-mannered, never shy or nervous.

DETAILED CHARACTERISTICS OF TYPE AND CONFORMATION: **Head:** comparatively small from poll to muzzle; small muzzle; large, fine-edged nostrils; low and wide-set, prominent, expressive, large eyes; deep jowls, wide between the branches; straight or preferably dished profile with prominent forehead *(jibbah)*; small, curved, well-shaped ears; large free windpipe; altogether lean and well chiselled.

Neck: long; light; arched; very flexible; fine and clean throat; set high; running well into good withers.

Trunk: well-muscled, long, sloping shoulders; broad, muscular chest; deep girth; well-sprung ribs; short back; broad, strong loins; long, level croup; long, muscular, round quarters; high-set, high-carried tail.

Legs: straight, of regular formation; large, strong, clearly-defined knees and hocks; flat, very dense bone; short cannons; prominent, dry tendons; moderately long, sloping pasterns; round, hard, smooth hoofs with clean heels.

Colours: solid, bright, strong colours, except legs and face; black not desirable; dark skin; fine, silky mane and tail; fine hair; satiny coat with a metallic sheen.

Heights: 14·1–15·1 hands (1·44–1·55 m).

GAITS (according to conformation, training and use): **Walk:** long, free, regular, covering much ground.

Trot: smart, free, swinging; not used in the desert.

Gallop: easy, smooth, balanced, extended, untiring.

OTHER ATTRIBUTES: dry, noble, harmonious, balanced appearance; speed joined with stamina; surefootedness; remarkable skill and adaptability; soundness, freedom from respiratory troubles and ringbone; vitality; longevity; very quick recovery; fertility; prepotency.

The characteristics described above are the ideal. No horse had them all, at least not in perfection. The usual criticism of too fine joints, short, straight shoulders, short croup and therefore short trunk and high-standing legs (resulting in bad gaits and action) normally affect the ordinary Oriental more than the genuine Arab. It is nowhere possible to breed only the highest quality, but the exigencies of desert life destroyed all weaklings with serious faults.

Two faults, however, are found in the true Arab: (1) occasional cow hocks, normally only a minor fault resulting from too early use and not affecting performance; (2) small size, caused by the aridity of the climate, extremes of temperature, ruthless selection by performance, frequent starvation, and dry, concentrated, not entirely vegetable feed. Nevertheless, the desert horse could carry a man both far and fast. Besides camel's milk, the feed consisted of fresh herbage only in winter and early spring, at other times of dried dates, locusts, meat, and, if the owner could afford it, some barley. Thus the Arab was fined down to a minimum of substance.

Use and Breeding System: from earliest times, Arab mares were ridden and used as hunters and war mares. Stallions served only as stud horses. Since the tribes needed only a few colts, most were sold to horse dealers.

The main breeding principles were selection according to performance and purity of blood. Convinced that they owned the best breed in the world, the Bedouin wished to maintain it. In their eyes, even the smallest drop of alien blood would only spoil, never improve. They did not tolerate the slightest uncertainty, being fanatical about bloodlines and genealogies. The *asil,* the pure mare, alone could carry them to victory. Before raids they even sewed up the vaginas of their mares to prevent any *mésalliance*, especially as they believed in telegony: an *asil* mare once covered by a non-*asil* stallion was for ever lost to her *asil* class and demoted to the status *kadish* (impure). The same happened to captured or stolen mares with the faintest suspicion, the tiniest gap or unknown ancestor in their pedigrees; in the case of a stallion, he was in no circumstances used for mating, no matter how perfect his conformation.

Mares were sometimes taken hundreds of miles for a proper mating, which always took place before witnesses. To improve their bloodlines, the Bedouin long practised inbreeding. In this way they fixed the type, consolidated the breed and established its prepotency.

Kuhaylan or *Kuhaylan Ajuz*, meaning the ancient pure breed, was the generic term for the *asil* Arab. From this Kuhaylan stock, all the many strains, substrains and families derived, according to the individual taste of breeders or the characteristics of a celebrated animal. The wellknown story that all pure Arabs are direct descendants of five mares of the Prophet is said to be a coffeehouse legend for strangers. The most celebrated strains, all divided into many substrains, are Kuhaylan, Hamdani, Hadban, Shuwayman, Wadnan, Saqlawi, 'Abayyan, Dahman, Milwah, Mu'wajj, Rishan, Tuwaysan, Mu'niqi, Jilfan, Abu' Urqub, Kubayshan, Mukhallad, Rabdan, Sa'dan, Samhan. As long as pure breeding within the strain was practised, separate distinguishable characteristics were established; strain-mixing effaced them. The foal always had the strain of his dam. The pedigrees were handed down orally from father to son. Since horses personified the honour not only of their owners but of the whole tribe, no Bedouin ever lied about pedigrees.

Exceptional dryness about 300 years ago caused large tribes to migrate north from Nejd for better pastures: the Shammar into Mesopotamia, the Anazeh into the Syrian desert. While the Anazeh subtribes Fed'an, Sba'a, 'Amarat, Weld'Ali and Ruala remained famous for their excellent, pure horses, some of the Shammar yielded to the temptation of breeding for size by crossing their stock with the horses of Turkoman and Kurdish tribes. According to Raswen, this changed the Mu'niqi strain into an angular type.

Present Situation: twentieth-century civilization and technology and the pacification and gradual settlement of the tribes have signified the end of the celebrated war mare. Horse breeding still exists, but merely for the racetracks. Some studs are owned by princes and kings. But few still attach importance to purity. Apart from the horses of the Saud family, Sheikh Isa bîn Sulman Al Khalifa, the ruler of Bahrain, owns the only large collection (about 500) of the original desert-type horses remaining in the world today.

International Cooperation: because of variations in taste, breeding targets, use, feeding, environment, bloodlines and other factors, the countries outside Arabia have developed different standards, rules and definitions for desert-breds, purebreds, partbreds, and Anglo-Arabs. Thus a number of horses and their descendants are registered in some studbooks as purebreds and in others as partbreds. Rules for admittance to studbooks differ too. For example, the American Registry does not admit Russian purebreds from Tersk, but the peak price ($150,000) was paid for the stallion Naborr, bred there. This stallion is only registered in the United States because he was previously used in Poland and was registered in the Polish Arabian Studbook. There are also considerable differences in the use of stallions. While some countries with strict animal breeding laws allow only stallions with a government licence after inspection to be used as sires, with mandatory performance tests, other countries have no restrictions at all.

Satisfactory solutions of the many problems can only be found through international cooperation. Preliminary steps were taken during the First International Conference of Arab Horse Societies in 1967 in London, followed by a second one in 1970 and a third in Seville in Spain in 1972. In 1970 the World Arabian Horse Organization (W.A.H.O.) was established with the following members: Australasia, Belgium, Bulgaria, Denmark, Hungary, Israel, the Netherlands, North America, Poland, Portugal, South Africa, Spain, Sweden, United Arab Republic, United Kingdom, U.S.S.R., West Germany. ESch

A summary of the position of Arab breeding, in the most important countries follows (in alphabetical order by country or area):

Africa, North: pure Arab breeding is mainly concentrated in State-owned studs: Sidi Thabet (Tunisia), Tiaret (Algiers),

Tripoli (Libya), Meknes, Temara (Morocco); Barbs and crosses are also bred. Egypt is the only Arabic-speaking country to publish a studbook: Volume 1 in 1948, Volume 2 in 1967. It contains only the purebreds of the El Zahraa National Stud. Members of the Egyptian royal family and Lady Blunt provided the foundation stock, descended predominantly from the desert horses of Abbas Pasha I (1848–54). The extraordinary quality and type of the El Zahraa Arabs has promoted their worldwide export. Hamdan Stables is the only private stud with a printed studbook. Arab races are held in all North African countries. ESch

Africa, South: numerous studs with purebreds and partbreds are united in The Arab Horse Breeders' Society, formed in 1949. The stock is based mostly on imports from Britain and Egypt. All horses are registered in the South African Studbook. A special Arab Studbook was published in 1972. Because of the huge distances only triennial National Championship shows are possible. ESch

Australia and New Zealand: Arab breeding, built on imports from England, has been flourishing in eastern Australia since 1922. Except for two government studs in New South Wales (established in 1949) and Queensland (established in 1958), all studs are privately owned and registered in the studbook of The Arab Horse Society of Australia. The great Royal Shows at Brisbane, Sydney and Melbourne have special Arab classes. Purebreds, partbreds, and Anglo-Arabs are popular for range work, dressage and show jumping, as well as for harness and trail use. Increasing interest in the breed has resulted in the foundation of the New Zealand Arab Horse Society with its own studbook. ESch

Austria: the famous military stud at Radautz in the Carpathian mountains, founded in 1792 and dissolved in 1919, had large purebred and partbred sections. Today in Austria there are a few breeders of partbreds, as well as breeders of purebreds such as August Eutermoser at Enns, with a pure Egyptian herd. An Arab Horse Society was founded in 1972. ESch

Belgium: since 1966 there has been one stud with purebreds at Vlimmeren, some miles east of Antwerp. ESch

Bulgaria: Oriental blood was infused after the Turkish occupation in 1389. The National stud at Kabijuk near Kolarovgrad, founded in 1864, was repeatedly dissolved and re-established. The foundation stallions Pamuk and Bebe, farewell presents of the Turkish Sultan Abdul Hamid II, and the Polish Kontur established precious sire lines. Further imports followed from Hungary and Poland. Kabijuk breeds partbred Arabs and halfbreds to improve local horses. Among the 180 brood mares are 40 Arabs. ESch

Central and South America: several studs with purebreds and partbreds exist in Mexico, Brazil, Chile and the Argentine with foundation stock from Arabia, England, Germany and the U.S.A. Most of the studs are in the Argentine, where Arabs are often used as ranch horses. ESch

Czechoslovakia: to meet the demands of the Slovak stallion depots, the Czechoslovak Republic, founded after World War I, had to establish a national breeding centre, which began in 1921 at Topolčianky near Nitra. At first, Arabs and LIPIZZANERS were bred, soon followed by HUÇULS, all well-suited to mountainous terrain. The Arab foundation stock consisted of three partbred stallions, 21 partbred and seven purebred mares. After World War II a fourth section of jumping and dressage horses was added. The farm now houses 400 head,

Arab Horse. *Above:* Purebred Arab stallion, Alaa el Din, at the Egyptian National Stud Farm, El Zahraa
Below left: Aethon, supreme champion Arab exhibit and champion Arab stallion of the 1971 Sydney Royal Show, Australia

among them 115 brood mares: 50 Arabs, 25 Lipizzaners, 20 Huçuls, 20 Thoroughbreds and halfbreds. The Topolčianky Arab is of a noble, harmonious type. It is planned to build up a purebred section. See also Czechoslovakia. ESch

Denmark: apart from Arabs imported by the Royal Frederiksborg Stud in about 1850, the importance of Arab blood for light horses was not realized until 1945, when the Danish Federation of Light-horse Breeders received some fine old Arab stallions from the Schumann circus. Proper Arab breeding dates only from 1962, when mares were imported from England and Germany. Increasing interest in the Arab led to further imports. K. Nyegaard, owner of more than 100 horses, installed a large breeding and riding centre to demonstrate the versatility of the Arab. The Danish Society for Arab Horse Breeding *(Dansk Selskab for Arabisk Hesteavl)* was founded in 1967 and published the first studbook for purebreds in 1968. ESch

France: of three recorded early attempts at pure Arab breeding, only one survived: the Pompadour National Stud, set up in 1761 by King Louis XV. First expeditions to Syria in 1779 and 1790 returned with 32 stallions. Recognizing the superiority of the Arab war horses during his Egyptian campaign, Napoleon intensified imports: 222 stallions and 31 mares were imported from the Middle East alone between 1800 and 1850, and used at different places, especially at Pau and Tarbes (in the Pyrenees). The demand for larger size inspired Gayot, the ingenious manager of Pompadour from 1843, to create the ANGLO-ARAB by crossing the THOROUGHBRED mare with the purebred Arab stallion, later permitting also an Anglo-Arab sire and dam. Arabs and Anglo-Arabs were and are used as racehorses, Anglo-Arabs also becoming a favourite mount of the French cavalry. Since World War II the Anglo-Arab has been used extensively for show jumping, winning even Olympic honours. State-owned purebred Arab stallions and the majority of Anglo-Arabs are assigned to the stallion depots at Pompadour, Pau, Tarbes and Ajaccio (Corsica). Recently, purebred Arab breeding has increased; several new private studs have been started, recruiting their foundation stock partly from the Netherlands, Poland, Spain and Egypt. The breeders' association is the *Syndicat des Éleveurs et Amateurs du Cheval Arabe.* The studbook is kept by the Ministry of Agriculture. ESch

Germany: pure Arab breeding dates back to 1817, when King Wilhelm I of Württemberg began his stud at Weil with top desert horses. Murana I founded the oldest surviving female purebred family in Europe. Bairactar, a sire for 21 years, had an unequalled influence on European horses, mainly through his descendant Amurath Weil 1881. The King purchased further desert Arabs year after year. He bred like the Bedouin, establishing consistent families by rigorous selection and inbreeding; thus, for a century, Weil was the most important European Arab centre with a worldwide influence. The Great Depression compelled the royal family to leave it to the State of Württemberg in 1932. Since then the heritage of Weil has really been continued at the Marbach National Stud.

World War II ended all private breeding. First attempts after 1945 resulted in some studs, multiplying gradually through the activities of the breeders' society, *Gesellschaft der Züchter und Freunde des arabischen Pferdes e V*, established in 1949. *The Arab Horse in Europe* (1967) by Erika Schiele caused such extraordinary interest that numerous imports were arranged from Bulgaria, Czechoslovakia, Britain, Egypt, Hungary, Lebanon, Rumania, Sweden, Spain, the U.S.A., the U.S.S.R. and Yugoslavia. Differences of opinion produced a second association with a separate registry in 1970, the *Araber Stutbuch Deutschland e V.*

In East Germany, Arab breeding is restricted to the Zoological Garden at Rostock, using Polish bloodlines. ESch

Great Britain: the THOROUGHBRED racehorse as it is known today owes its very existence to the three Arabian sires, the BYERLEY TURK imported in 1689, the DARLEY ARABIAN in 1705 and the GODOLPHIN ARABIAN in 1728.

As the popularity of horseracing increased with the inevitable demand for more speed, a larger horse was developed; the demand for Arab blood decreased and the purebred Arab as a progenitor of racehorses ceased to exist. Interest in the breed dwindled over the intervening years and it is probable that this decline would have continued in the twentieth century had it not been for the foresight and energy of Wilfrid Scawen Blunt and his wife Lady Anne Blunt, who between 1878 and 1881 visited the great horse-breeding tribes of the Arabian deserts and bought many stallions and mares which were ultimately to form the Crabbet Stud in Sussex, England. Even then, and for many years, general interest in the breed was slight until a small body of enthusiasts formed the Arab Horse Society in 1918.

It can be said that the worldwide growth in the popularity of Arabs dates from the 1960s. Imports of horses from the Arabian desert itself virtually ceased, but there was an ever-growing demand for them by horse-breeding countries throughout the world. Relying almost entirely on their own resources and greatly helped by an energetic Society, a large number of Arab studs started throughout Britain and a considerable export was fostered, the country being recognized as the fountainhead to which went those requiring stock. This happy state has continued to the present; although

Arab Horse. *Top:* Grojec, a purebred stallion bred in Poland and imported to England *Above:* Skowronek, bred at the Janow Podlaski stud in Poland in 1908 and imported to England by Lady Wentworth, has had an important influence on the breed and on children's show ponies.

a few Arabs have been imported, they have been greatly exceeded by exports. Those imported have been mainly purebred mares and stallions bred in Poland. Although most of these arrived in the latter half of the twentieth century, a grey stallion, Skowronek, whose blood has had a marked and very advantageous effect on the breed, was bred there in 1908 and imported to England. Arab blood remains of the greatest importance to horse breeding. RSS

Greece: there is no Arab horse breeding, but races for Arabs are held at Athens with horses imported from Egypt and the Lebanon. ESch

Holland: see Netherlands.

Hungary: Oriental blood, introduced in the sixteenth century by the Turkish conquerors, nicked well with the tough Hungarian steppe horses. After the disastrous losses of the Napoleonic wars, European studs turned mostly to Oriental sires. While most mated them with native mares, a few magnates such as Count Hunyady and Baron Fechtig bought mares too and built up pure Arab herds. Fechtig employed some excellent agents, purchasing unique treasures from the desert. The stallions Tajar, Ebchan, El Bedavy, Siglavy Gidran and the mare Tiffle left indelible traces. Unfortunately Arab breeding was discontinued after the deaths of Hunyady and Fechtig.

The Bábolna National Stud, 20 miles east of Györ, founded in 1789 as a military stud, has remained the real pillar of Hungarian Arab breeding. From 1816 Bábolna covered local mares with Oriental stallions. Pure Arab breeding did not start until 1836, when the commandants acquired sufficient Arabs in the Orient. Among them the grey Shagya became the foundation sire of the best Arab lines under the Austro-Hungarian monarchy. The influx of fresh desert blood lasted till 1931, when the Bedouin stallion Kuhaylan Zaid arrived. Bábolna also permanently exchanged horses with other good European studs. World War II and subsequent uncertainly entailed an unwarrantedly rigorous cut in the stock, from which the stud did not recover until 1962. Now it is flourishing again, especially after several imports of purebred Egyptian stallions and mares since 1968. The studbook differentiates 'pure-blood' Arabs, tracing exclusively to desert horses, and *Araberrasse* (Arab breed), in whose pedigrees are found tiny portions of alien blood at the beginning of the nineteenth century. Genetically they are virtually purebred, since no further alien blood has been added. ESch

Iran: see separate entry on Persian Arab.

Ireland: the Arab in Ireland comes under the jurisdiction of the Arab Horse Society (of Great Britain) with an Irish Committee formed in 1970 for local organization in Eire. Fewer than 20 purebred Arabian stallions and very few studs exist in Ireland, and partbreds outnumber purebreds by at least ten to one; however, there are signs of increasing interest in the Arabian breed. One purebred stallion, Naseel (Raftan/Naxina), bred in 1936 by Lady Yule and owned by Mrs S. A. Nicholson of Kells, Co. Meath, proved an outstanding influence as a sire of quality children's ponies, including such British champions as the renowned Pretty Polly and My Pretty Maid. SAW

Italy: the use of Arab blood is concentrated essentially in Sardinia and Sicily, where it has transmitted an Oriental look to the native horses. In Sicily, Baron Grimaldi di Niscia founded a stud for purebreds and Anglo-Arabs in 1882 at Catania. ESch

Luxembourg: two small studs with purebreds are registered in Germany, one of them with stock from Jordan and Egypt. ESch

Mexico: see Central and South America.

Netherlands: the pioneer of Arab breeding was the late H. Hoyer, who imported the stallion Houbaran from England in 1930 and launched vigorous publicity. In 1935 he founded *Het Arabische Paardenstamboek,* which put on its first show in 1939. It was Houbaran who encouraged Dr H. C. Houtappel to install the largest and most successful stud, Rodania, beginning in 1937 with the stallion Rythal, bred by Lady Wentworth. In 1969 part of the stud moved to Sussex, England.

In 1952 the *Paardenstamboek* published its first studbook for purebreds, with about 100 entries, mostly English imports or their descendants. Since October 1970 a magazine has appeared with news and articles. Recent and growing interest in the breed led to imports from Britain, Germany, Hungary,

Poland, Spain and the U.S.S.R. In August 1971 the first purebred show was held with an attendance of 110 animals. Only stallions with a government licence are admitted as sires. The stallion list for 1971 contains 36 purebreds, 14 partbreds and two Arabs. Arab stallions are frequently used to improve the very popular HAFLINGERS. ESch

New Zealand: see Australia and New Zealand.

Poland: the lack of good sires and Polish delight in elegant horseflesh prompted some wealthy noblemen from the beginning of the nineteenth century to acquire suitable

breeding material from the Orient, mainly stallions to improve Polish mares. Slawuta and Gumniska, the studs belonging to the Princes Sanguszko, imported 73 stallions and nine mares before 1914. Obviously, purebreeding was not intended, especially as seven mares were barren and the rest left only one colt and two fillies. Other famous studs, such as Bialocerkiew (Count Branicki) and Antoniny (Count Potocki, breeder of Skowronek), showed the same picture, except two: the Sawran stud of Count Rzewuski, who returned from Arabia with 81 stallions and 33 mares of priceless value (unfortunately the stud was dispersed after 1831); and the Jarzowce stud of Count Dzieduszycki, who purchased from the Bedouin in 1845 seven stallions and the mares Gazella, Mlecha, and Sahara, all of the purest blood and highest quality, as were their descendants; his successors mixed them later with other stock. By careful selection and by favouring prepotent stallions of outstanding type through many generations, Poles bred Arabs that won gold medals for their quality, beauty and 'purity' at World Expositions in Paris. The Slawuta, Antoniny and Bialocerkiew studs became victims of the Revolution in 1917. Private Arab breeding ceased after World War II.

The State did not begin breeding Arabs until 1919 at Janow Podlaski, with stock from Radautz and private farms. Excellent breeding and stock-rearing systems soon made the stud first-rate. On 5 October 1939 Janow was captured by the Russian Army. It was rebuilt by the Germans and evacuated to Holstein when the Russian offensive approached. At home again since 1946, Janow has become world famous. Michalow, the second National Arab stud, was founded in 1953. The studbook (P.A.S.B.), kept by the Ministry of Agriculture, has been regularly published since 1926. International Arab auctions have been held at Janow since 1970. Training and testing on the racetrack for two years, obligatory for all Arab colts and fillies at two years old, have been essential in producing a horse capable of high performance, in demand all over the world. ESch

Portugal: the National Stud at Fonte Boa began a purebred section at the beginning of this century with Arabs from Syria, North Africa and France, adding later stock from Spain and Crabbet Park, England. The associated stallion depot keeps Arabs and Anglo-Arabs available to breeders without fee; they are generally used to produce Anglo-Arabs. G. Gyão at Reguengos de Monsaraz, the only enthusiastic pure Arab breeder, started in 1961 with Spanish Arabs and in 1968 won all the gold and silver medals at the Feria International del Campo in Madrid. ESch

Rumania: with 35 Arabs from the former Radautz stock, Rumania began a new stud at the old place in 1920. Forced to flee in 1940, it moved several times. The centre of Arab breeding is now the Mangalia National Stud on the Black Sea coast, founded in 1929 with Bábolna Arabs and infused with new blood from Poland in 1937 and 1955. Mangalia has about 15 purebred and 85 'Arab breed' mares. Among the 1,300 State-owned sires are 360 Arab stallions. There is no private breeding. ESch

South America: see Central and South America.

Spain: the desert horses imported by Queen Isabella II in 1850 were the first entries in the Spanish Arab Studbook, set up in 1885, kept and published since by the Ministry of War. Intensive Arab breeding began in 1905 with stock from Poland and Syria at the Yeguada Militar, the Andalusian Army Stud. In the course of time many private studs arose, in 1970 uniting to form the *Asociación Española de Criadores de Caballos Arabes*. The Andalusian climate and feed stamped the Arabs there with a dry desert look. ESch

Sweden: from time to time during the last two centuries Arab stallions were imported into Sweden either as riding horses or to cross with and improve local breeds. Purebred Arab breeding in Sweden started in the late 1950s, with the import of the grey Marbach-bred stallion Jager, then the chestnut Kariba, bred in Scotland from Crabbet Park bloodlines. Jager was used mainly on the SWEDISH HALFBRED mares and Kariba mainly on pony mares, but Kariba in particular aroused such admiration that many people started importing mares and stallions from England and Poland. During the 1960s the numbers increased enormously, both by breeding and by further imports; in 1971 there were over 300 registered purebred Arabs in Sweden and 22 stallions standing at public stud. In 1970 the first imports came from the U.S.A. and included a yearling colt and five foals. A flourishing Arab Horse Society rigidly controls registrations and organizes a show every second year. The quality of Swedish stock is emphasized by the export of many stallions and mares to the United States and West Germany. PL

Arab Horse. *Far left:* Gwarny, the present senior stallion at Janow Podlaski, Poland, is the sole surviving male of the Bairactar line from old Weil. *Below:* Egyptian purebreds from El Zahraa are highly valued in the United States. This stallion, Rashad Ibn Nazeer, was exported to New Mexico.

Switzerland: there are several owners of Arabs, like the Swiss National Circus Knie, but no proper breeding except at the private stud at Origlio (Ticino). Since 1942 the Avenches National Stud has successfully infused Arab blood into the Freiberger breed. ESch

U.S.A.: in 1908 the Arabian Horse Club of America was established, now called The Arabian Horse Registry of America, Inc. The club published its first studbook in 1909, and ever since there have been permanent imports from Europe, mostly Britain and Poland, from Egypt, the Near East and Saudi Arabia. Meanwhile the Arab has conquered the whole continent with California as its main centre. From 1960 to 1970 the breed experienced a real explosion: more Arabs were registered in 1970 than in the first 50 years of the registry's history. Some figures illustrate this (see table). ESch

Year	*Registered purebreds*	*Registered owners*
1909	71	11
1960	16,657	6,609
1970	62,173	21,116

Live purebreds in U.S.A.:	approx. 50,000
Among them in California:	approx. 10,000
Studfarms:	only private ones
Foundation of first breeders' association:	1944 in California
First Arab show:	1945 in California
Setting up of an Arabian Division within the A.H.S.A. (American Horse Shows Association):	1949
Publication of Arabian Rules:	in the 1950 Rule Book
Foundation of the International Arabian Horse Association (holding association of the breeders' clubs):	1950
Number of clubs united in this association in 1970:	110
Setting up of National Arabian Championship Classes:	1957
First Arabian Horse race:	1959 at Laurel, Maryland
Pari-mutuel races:	since 1967, now at 10 places
First Arabian International Cutting Horse Jubilee:	1970 at Filer, Idaho
Peak price:	$150,000 for stallion Naborr in 1969
Arabs are used for:	pleasure riding, hunting, jumping, dressage, trail riding, ranch work, parades, in harness

U.S.S.R.: in latter centuries Oriental stallions were highly esteemed by tsars and noblemen, e.g. the Arab Smetanka, ancestor of the ORLOV TROTTER. The Revolution swept their studs away. With what remained and 17 Hungarian Arabs, the Soviet State founded in 1921 the Tersk stud in the Caucasus, developing from this mixture the TERSKY breed. Pure Arab breeding began in 1930 with stock from Bábolna and France, increased by Arabs from Crabbet Park, England, in 1936. The Polish stud Janow Podlaski was incorporated in 1939; there was later some booty from Germany. After 1945 permanent blood exchange with Poland took place. President Nasser presented two stallions from El Zahraa and 19 Arabs were bought from Egyptian racing stables in 1968. Tersk owns 250 purebreds, among them 80 brood mares. Tersk also breeds AKHAL TEKE horses. International auctions began in 1970. All Arabs are tested on the racetrack. The first Studbook, published in 1965, is kept by the Ministry of Agriculture. There is no private breeding. See also U.S.S.R. ESch

Yugoslavia: early Oriental influence through the Turkish occupation existed from 1389. Before World War II several noblemen, particularly Prince Odelscalchi, owned pure Arab studs. The State has bred Arabs since 1895 at Borike near Sarajevo with horses from Syria and Bábolna, and later added stock from Poland and in 1970 from Marbach. Today Borike is the breeding centre for Arabs ('Arab breed') and Bosnian horses. There are no private studs. ESch

Archers, Mounted see Warfare

Ardennais

Ardennais. A champion stallion

A descendant of the snub-nosed prehistoric horse of Solutré, native to the Ardennes, the Ardennais is the dean of French horses. Demand both in France and from overseas has made it even more popular today than the PERCHERON or BOULONNAIS. It derives its energy from Oriental blood, its increased size (maximum 15·2½ hands or 1·60 m) from Belgian blood from the time that it was a popular coach horse (14·1 hands or 1·45 m), first in the royal armies, then in the imperial armies. Its strength, calm and extreme gentleness explain the popularity of this horse and of horses bred from it. It is compactly built, has short legs, and a large frame. Its coat is bay, chestnut, roan or strawberry roan. Losses from wars have inevitably resulted in the importation of Belgian and Dutch stallions. ES

Argentina

Argentina is at present going through a period of transition between the production of horses in large numbers without considering quality very much, and the breeding of few but good horses while searching for the right type for each purpose. The wide, fertile prairies, world-famous for the numbers of cattle raised on them, are just right for breeding horses. People in Argentina, especially in the army, which is in charge of practically all equestrian development, believe that this country could become the main source of horses and mules and an ambitious and bold plan to produce high-quality horses ideal for sports is now being put into practice. The policy is directed by the technical wing of the Argentine army, the *Comando de Remonta y Veterinaria*, which helps and orientates its 1,300 registered horse breeders. Anticipating the needs of national security, equestrian sports and agriculture, the plan will be carried out in two stages (short- and medium-term). In addition to official and private action, a large sum of money raised from the racecourses is being invested. Argentina is the second largest producer of Thoroughbreds in the world; the only reason that she is not one of the largest exporters is that their qualities, for instance adaptability to any climate, are not widely known. Prices are relatively low, as breeding in Argentina is very cheap.

The polo pony, on the other hand, is known worldwide. There is no player with a five-goal handicap or better who does not want to ride Argentinian polo ponies. They are fast, gentle and have wonderful mouths, qualities improved even more by a training from accumulated experience found only in Argentina. Thoroughbreds and polo ponies do not need assistance, so developmental efforts are concentrated on crossbreds for sports and Percherons which produce the best mares for mules, essential for work in the mountains.

There is a group of breeders of the Criollo, a very useful horse for farm work, about 15·1 hands (1·55 m) high. Some enthusiastic ranchers have as many as 300 Criollos on their *haciendas*.

Argentina has about forty racecourses, most of which lose money except those in Buenos Aires and San Isidro, which make enough to keep the others going. Every year about 2,000 two-year-olds are sold by auction.

Today (1972) Argentina has five polo players with a 10-goal handicap, unprecedented in the history of polo, so it is easy to understand how this country has won all possible titles for this sport. There is virtually no threat to this position since people on the ranches begin to play at an early age; they are already veterans at 18.

Riding is practised fairly intensively and at a reasonable level of skill. The best riders are as good as any in the world; Argentina would shine more in international competition if the owners of the best horses were not tempted by large sums of money to sell them off.

Other sporting activities, rather less important, include *pato*, a kind of mounted basket-ball, trotting, mostly popular in the provinces of Buenos Aires and Cordoba, and rather informal hunting. There is an annual long-distance ride for Criollo breeders: 15 days over a 750-km (470 mile) route; the horse must carry 110 kg (242 lb or 17 stone) and must receive no treatment nor food not found on the way. It is a method of selecting the best horses under working conditions and the winners are valuable for breeding. EB

Armour see Accoutrements, Warfare

Art, Horse in

For centuries the agriculture, transport, military manoeuvre and recreation of most nations owed their animation in great measure to the horse. It is not remarkable, therefore, that in the art of the world genus *Equus* plays an important and frequent role.

By 2000 B.C. the Egyptians in models and on pottery vases were showing stallions harnessed to chariots on the military, religious and ceremonial occasions of the Pharaohs. These horses trot with identical rhythmic action and balanced uniformity, decked in matching head plumes. In the great kingdoms of the Middle East—Assyria, Babylon and Persia—hunting from chariots was the recreation of the powerful rulers in the ninth century B.C., recorded in such carvings, formalized but also dramatic in conception, as the magnificent Assyrian stone relief *The Lion Hunt of King Assurnasirpal*.

In the art of the Far East the horse also appeared through the ages in designs of battles, hunts and ceremonial cavalcades. The representations of the rounded, strong Chinese horse in terra cottas of the Han Dynasty (206 B.C.–A.D. 220) and the T'ang Dynasty (618–906 A.D.) became also mortuary ornaments and ally natural form with a curious humanity.

The ancient Greeks, next to the human figure, used the horse as their most constant subject. Equine quality and elegance began to make their mark in the ridden as well as the chariot horses appearing on their black and red figured vase paintings and pottery funeral vessels. Though the laws of symmetrical design were strictly followed in representations of the aristocrat of the day in his quadriga, the horses began to suggest a nervous tension and liveliness. Equestrian art broke away from formality to attain an apex of classical achievement in the Parthenon Frieze of the Acropolis, dated from the middle of the fifth century B.C., depicting the procession of the Athenians on foot, mounted and in chariots. The horses appear magnificently as individuals, many ridden but without reins and bridles. Eyes, nostrils, veins, hoofs and manes are depicted in precise and varying detail, and also suggested in the composition are equine dignity and strength allied to a continuing mobility. In this frieze lies the quintessence of Hellenic art in the marriage of truth with beauty. This same attention to detail exists in the four horses on the façade of St Mark's, Venice (see colour plate page 93) where the texture of the skin of the horses varies in different parts of the body. Controversy has always existed over this equestrian group allegedly by the Greek sculptor Lysippos and said to have been brought from Chios to Constantinople in the fifth century A.D. Though always referred to as bronze they are actually cast from an amalgam of copper, silver and gold. More recent research suggests the work may be a Roman copy of a Greek sculpture of the fourth to third centuries, but whatever their origin the group possesses an unusual lightness and elegance.

By the Roman era the horse had become synonymous with military power, often symbolized artistically by immense size. The enormous bronze statue of the second century A.D. of the Emperor Marcus Aurelius on the Capitol in Rome epitomizes every equestrian statue of the great. Colossal and impressive, this mountain of a horse dominates the Roman world and was to be copied throughout the ages. It served as inspiration over 1200 years later for both Andrea del Verrocchio's figure of Colleoni in Venice and Donatello's memorial statue of Gattamelata in Padua. This same symbolism appears in Etienne-Maurice Falconet's bronze equestrian monument of Peter the Great in Leningrad, commissioned by Empress Catherine II, a work of brilliant technique as the horse rears up on a granite plinth with forelegs unsupported.

In pictures with a religious motif the horse made constant appearances, as in the medieval nativity scenes where the Magi ride either light-boned Arabian hacks or roman-nosed chargers of Flemish blood. The legend of the Charity of St Martin dating from the thirteenth century was used in many contrasting media: in Icelandic tapestries, Italian woodcarvings, Dutch oil paintings and French models in china; in each case the typical young cavalier and riding horse of the day are portrayed to provide a valuable documentary

The Horse in Art. Part of the Panathenaic procession from the north frieze of the Parthenon, fifth century B.C.

The Horse in Art. *Above: The Vision of St Eustace,* painting by Antonio Pisano (called Pisanello), *c.* 1440
Top right: The Infante Balthasar Carlos on Horseback, painting by Velásquez, *c.* 1634
Centre right: Portrait of Pieter Schout on Horseback, painting by Thomas de Keyser, 1660
Bottom right: The Derby at Epsom, painting by Théodore Géricault, 1821
Far right: La Cirque, painting by Georges Seurat, 1891

of equestrian fashion through the ages, showing horseflesh, clothes, saddlery and riding style. Almost equally frequent were the many versions of the Vision of St Eustace, headed by the outstanding painting *c.* 1440 by Antonio Pisano (called Pisanello) with its finely accoutred chestnut horse and rider and delicate animals of the chase.

In Renaissance art the splendour of fine horses and elegant horsemanship became a status symbol; with the influence of the popular Italian schools of *haute école*, riders of noble birth were painted monotonously *en levade*, whether Titian's armoured Charles V in the Battle of Mühlberg (1548), the portraits by Van Dyck of Charles I on dun chargers of Neapolitan breeding, or Velásquez' equestrian portrait of the little Infante Don Balthasar Carlos. In each of these pictures the skilled pose of the rider plays an integral part in its composition. Less flamboyant in style but of outstanding merit is the *Portrait of Pieter Schout* painted in 1660 by the Amsterdam artist Thomas de Keyser (1597–1667). In contrasting vein in many pictures of the Low Countries by such artists as Wouwerman, Cuyp, Potter and others the horse appears in tranquil rural compositions which were to contrast with the Teutonic portrayals of the horse in hawking and stag-hunting scenes by Joannes Stradanus (1523–1605) and Johann Elias Ridinger (1698–1767). The ceremonial ritual of the chase as enjoyed by Louis XIV and Louis XV and their courtiers is recorded by François Desportes (1661–1743) and Jean-Baptiste Oudry (1686–1755) with romantic savagery and with the horse taking a paramount role.

Such Flemish and Dutch painters as Jan Fyt, Jan Wyck and Pieter Tillemans, who came to England at the end of the seventeenth century, were instrumental in founding the British School of sporting art. This *genre* of animal painting dominated by the horse remains unique and had no counterpart in any other country. Though many of these sporting painters possessed Continental names and forebears—Tillemans, the Sartorius family, the Alken family, Herring, Barraud—and such early exponents as Francis Barlow (1626–1702) and John Wootton (*c.* 1677–1765) respectively were directly influenced byBohemian-born Wenceslaus Hollar and Wyck, the style of painting quickly shed all foreign nuances and became almost aggressively English. Such artists as James Seymour, James Ward, Sawrey Gilpin, Henry Alken Sr, Ben Marshall, James Pollard and John Ferneley Sr between 1725 and 1860 produced some splendid pictures not only of famous hunts, renowned horses and the brief heyday of the coaching era but above all of the English country way of life; in this lies their greatness.

Outstanding among these British artists and one of the world's greatest painters of the horse is self-taught, versatile George Stubbs (1724–1806). His *Anatomy of the Horse,* published in 1766 with engravings by his own hand, stamped him as a draughtsman of exceptional talent and exquisite accuracy; his studies of mares and foals, of the Thoroughbred racehorse, equestrian portraits and such great sporting occasions as *The Grosvenor Hunt* (see colour plate, pages 94–5) bear the quality of genius in their understanding of conformation and perceptive composition. In the middle of the nineteenth century sporting art in the British vein was to be introduced into the United States of America by such British emigrés as Edward Troye (1808–1874) and Arthur Fitzwilliam Tait (1819–1905), who influenced Henry Stull's numerous pictures of the American racehorse. Frederic Remington, born in New York State in 1851, besides painting steeplechase scenes won considerable acclaim for his pictures of life in the Wild West. In recent years such artists of first-class talent as Smithson Broadhead and Milton Monasco, painting in the conventional tradition, have made the modern Thoroughbred their subject. The greatest artist of the horse to emerge from the New World has undoubtedly been Henry Haseltine (1877–1962), who achieved international fame with his bronze equestrian statues, portraits and splendid polo groups, and war memorial commissions like the moving *Les Revenants*.

Such French artists as Jacques Louis David (1748–1825) in his Napoleonic pictures, Eugène Delacroix (1798–1863), the

major exponent of the French Romantic movement, and Carle and Horace Vernet (1758–1836 and 1789–1863) all used the strong decorative elements of equine conformation to bring action and panache to their works. Théodore Géricault (1791–1824), a dedicated horseman, brought both a practical attention to detail and a flair for presenting the speed and excitement of the galloping horse to such works as *The Derby at Epsom*, 1821. Working at this time and in the same style should be mentioned two Polish artists of the horse. Piotr Michalowski (1800–1855?) painted military subjects, equestrian portraits and riding scenes with great perception and expertise. His compatriot Josef Kossak (1824–1899) in quieter vein used the agricultural horse as an important subject. German artists of the horse working at the same time include Franz Krüger, Wilhelm von Kobell, who specialized in military subjects, and the prolific Adolf Schreyer, who frequently used Oriental breeds as models for his works.

At the end of the nineteenth century, breaking away from the conventional equestrian scene, Henri de Toulouse-Lautrec (1864–1901), influenced by the simple clarity of Japanese prints, produced vivid pictures of the horse in clear simple outline. Such French Impressionists as Edgar Degas and Edouard Manet found inspiration on the racecourse, Georges Seurat in the circus; Paul Gauguin painted the native ponies of Tahiti; and Pierre Auguste Renoir produced one equestrian masterpiece, *L'Amazone*, with its proud simpering mama and plump son riding in the Bois de Boulogne.

Joseph Crawhall and Robert Bevan, both born in the 1860s, escaped from the English traditional sporting scene to paint the horse in Impressionist style. Sir Alfred Munnings, P.R.A. (1879–1959), England's greatest horse artist since Stubbs, possessed a brilliant colour sense plus an inherent understanding of equine character and quality which led him to become an inspired painter of the Thoroughbred and English racing and hunting scenes. Lionel Edwards painted conventional but immensely talented pictures of English field sports in the twentieth century, but John Skeaping, R.A., born in 1907, fulfilled the demand for a new look in his impressions of the equestrian scene in his mobile bronzes and fluent gouache paintings.

It is remarkable in an era dedicated to sophisticated mechanical devices that the horse still contributes an important element in the works of so many artists. Pablo Picasso (b. 1881) in *Homme et Cheval* and in the devastating *Guernica*, Marc Chagall (b. 1887) in the folklore fantasies of his native Russia, Franz Marc (1880–1916) in Cubist form in his red and blue horses, Raoul Dufy (1877–1953) in simple, gay racing scenes, and Marino Marini in his many bronzes, all return to equine form to suggest the wonder, horror and excitement of the modern age. See also Prehistoric Art, Horse in. SAW

Artillery see Warfare

Asiatic Wild Horse

Equus przewalskii przewalskii Poliakov, the Asiatic or Mongolian Wild Horse, discovered by Col. N. M. Przevalski in 1881, inhabits an area in the Tachin Schara Nuru mountains (mountains of the yellow horses) of 44° latitude and 94° longitude. A few very small herds are said still to exist although the horses have been driven very near to extinction by man's predatory habits in hunting and encroaching upon the few waterholes. These unique wild horses are on the danger list of the Survival Service Commission, and the Chinese, Mongolian and Russian Governments have now outlawed hunting. There are today about 200 specimens in zoos in Europe and the U.S.A. where they are carefully bred. Prague Zoo has the largest herd in captivity and the Studbook is organized by Dr Jiri Volf. It is hoped eventually to return some specimens to their natural habitat. The Russian Government is considering creating another reserve where the wild horse can continue to breed undisturbed. DMG

Reference: Dr Erna Mohr, *The Asiatic Wild Horse*, London, 1971.

A.S.P.C.A. see Welfare Associations

Ass, African Wild

This is the principal, perhaps the only, wild ancestor of the domestic ass; there are two extant races, of which the Nubian most resembles the domestic. Formerly both races inhabited the whole of North Africa from the Atlantic to the Indian Ocean, right up to the Mediterranean shore. Now the Nubian is only found far inland, in such deserts as those of the Fezzan, southern Algeria. It is only 12 hands high (1·22 m), and is distinguished by a black stripe on the shoulder.

Further southeast, towards the Horn of Africa, the Somali Ass is found. This is much taller, up to 14 hands (1·42 m), reddish-grey, without dorsal or shoulder stripes. It has zebra-like stripes on the legs. The boundary between the two races runs through Ethiopia, where it is estimated a total wild stock of some 500 survives. AD

Ass, Asiatic Wild

This falls into two groups, the ONAGERS of Western Asia and the kiangs and kulans of Central and East Central Asia. All survive wild in much greater numbers than the African species. They have dorsal stripes but no shoulder or leg stripes. The kulan (dzigetai) of Transcaspia, Turkmenia, Turkestan, North China, Mongolia and southern Siberia, is 12·2 hands (1·27 m) or taller, with pale dun underparts, and reddish-yellow back and sides. Many local races are recognized, the most westerly of them shading imperceptibly into the most easterly of the onagers. The kiang of Tibet is much larger, about 14 hands (1·42 m), with very coarse head, pale underparts, bright brown back and sides. All these species have longer ears than horses but shorter than those of 'true' asses. AD

Ass, Domestic

The ass was first domesticated at least 5,000 years ago, certainly before horses were tamed to work. It is widely supposed that all domestic asses are of unmixed African, specifically Nubian ancestry, but early Greek pictures of asses show the zebra-striped legs characteristic of the Somali, not of the Nubian, race, and the Sulaib Bedouin who have no horses or camels maintained as late as the 1930s that the vigour of their very superior strain of pack and riding asses was kept up by frequent crosses with wild male onagers from the desert. Therefore it is quite likely that asses, especially in Asia, are of multiple wild ancestry, as horses have recently been proved to be. What is indisputable is that the original centre or centres of domestication lay wholly within Africa, and within the habitat of the Nubian race, either in Libya or in the southern part of the Eastern Desert of Egypt. Thence the use of asses spread across Sinai into Asia, and via Asia Minor into Europe, largely as an essential part of the vine-growing (as opposed to merely wine-drinking) habit; the ass was the handiest animal for cultivation of the vineyard, for harvesting the vintage and for operating the earliest types of wine-press. It spread across western Europe as far as Britain and Gaul with the Roman conquest, and did not become common in eastern Europe north of the Balkans until much later. It is ill-adapted to a wet cold climate, hence it has never been of great economic importance outside the Mediterranean, the sole exception being the Poitevin region of Atlantic France, where the secret of breeding giant jacks (which are not exposed to winter weather) for covering mares to produce mules, has long been exploited (see Poitevin Mulassier). The same climatic limitations apply outside Europe. The ass has spread to the temperate and warm regions of all continents, notably America, but only does really well where the climate is hot and dry. It is used primarily as a pack animal, secondarily as a riding mount, only in the third place in harness. AD

Assateague see Chincoteague

Below: **Asiatic Wild Horse.** *Equus przewalskii* at the Prague Zoo

Bottom: **Domestic Ass.** The rear donkey in this tandem shows primitive leg stripes as well as the more common dorsal stripe.

Assyria

One of the great military empires of the ancient Orient, that of the Assyrians had its centre at the upper end of the Tigris and Euphrates basin, and thus lay between the territory of the HITTITES and the Persians, from both of which it borrowed much. Assyrian art of the great period has a realistic style and is carried out in a medium (low relief) which allows details of the musculature of the horse to appear. These very abundant sculptures are the first pictures showing unmistakably grain-fed horses in hard condition. Notably in the monumental art of the ninth century B.C., but also earlier and later, we see chariot teams in battle, in state processions, and out hunting (possibly from the chariot in flat terrain like Mesopotamia) and also ridden horses. The first really effective cavalry, including mounted archers, in Assyria seems to have emerged in the ninth century. Before that there were various makeshift devices, such as a 'Gretna Green' system in which the archer was almost seated on the withers, while the 'driver' sat behind him and handled the reins. A great variety of equine types is shown, many of pony size not larger than the modern CASPIAN but many much larger, especially the ridden horses which come up to near 16 hands (1·65 m). Almost all are of pleasing conformation by our standards, with clear tendons and flat bone. Styles of dressing manes and tails were elaborate, and we have pictures of Assyrian grooms and troopers performing stable duties which only differ from our own in the frequency with which horses are washed. The earliest pictures of mules in harness (a pair to a very heavy wagon) also come from Assyria. AD

Auction Sales

In considering auction sales of horses in Britain, the name of Tattersalls inevitably springs to mind. With an annual turnover now in the region of £9 million, they are without serious rivals. The quite recently formed Doncaster Bloodstock Sales have done some good business in recent years, and many promising jumpers and point-to-pointers are disposed of at Botterills Ascot Bloodstock Sales; these firms, though, are not in the same league as Tattersalls. Robert J. Goff and Co. do a fine trade in Ireland but even so many Irish breeders prefer to send their stock to Newmarket to be sold by Tattersalls.

Tattersalls was founded in 1766 by a Yorkshireman, Richard Tattersall, who acquired premises at Hyde Park Corner, London. His twice-weekly sales became a *rendezvous* for the fashionable world. Carriages, hounds and dogs were sold there as well as horses. In 1865 the premises moved a mile westwards to Knightsbridge Green where sales of hunters, hacks, ponies, carriages and saddlery were held till 1939. After World War II the Knightsbridge premises were sold, the sale yard and boxes were demolished and the famous Rotunda with the statue of the Fox removed to Newmarket but Tattersalls still maintain a London office at Knightsbridge Green.

Assyria. Bas-reliefs from Nineveh (seventh century B.C.) show King Ashurbanipal hunting lion

Towards the end of the eighteenth century Tattersalls were holding sales in Newmarket High Street, a practice continuing till 1860 when land behind Queensbury House was rented. In 1870 the sales were transferred to Park Paddocks and have stayed there ever since. In 1965 the new luxurious, up-to-date sales ring with ample seating accommodation and central heating was used for the first time.

From 1838 to 1958 Tattersalls, except during the war years, always held their main yearling sale at Doncaster during St Leger week. The custom was discontinued when Tattersalls were unable to accept the new terms offered by the Doncaster Corporation. The latter were certainly the losers as St Leger week has never been quite the same since.

Nowadays 20,000-guinea yearlings are a commonplace. In 1890 when Baron de Hirsch bid 5,500 guineas for the Hampton Court yearling filly La Flèche, it was considered a truly fantastic sum. Mr Edmund Tattersall was sufficiently moved to call from the rostrum for 'Three cheers for the Baron and success for the Royal Stud'. There was a sensation, too, in 1900 when Mr Robert Sievier bid 10,000 guineas for the yearling filly Sceptre at a sale of the late Duke of Westminster's bloodstock. Both these fillies were bargains. La Flèche won the One Thousand Guineas, the Oaks and the Gold Cup and was terribly unlucky not to win the Derby, too. Sceptre won every Classic except the Derby.

The chief sales now conducted by Tattersalls are the six-day October sale of yearlings at the beginning of that month; the four-day Houghton Sale of yearlings a fortnight later, a shorter catalogue than at the previous sale but of more consistently high quality; the six-day 'Mixed' Sale at the end of October when many horses in training are offered; and finally the six-day December Sale, a feature of which is the many well-bred brood mares and fillies out of training that pass through the ring. This sale is

Auction Sales. A colt being auctioned at the Newmarket Houghton Sales

always attended by a crowd of overseas buyers and it was in December 1967 that the two-year-old Vaguely Noble, destined to win the Prix de l'Arc de Triomphe the following year, was sold for 136,000 guineas. At the Houghton Sales in 1971 a yearling filly by Native Prince out of Review was sold for 117,000 guineas. RM

There are two major auction-sale concerns in North America: Fasig-Tipton Co., Inc., and its corporate affiliates in Florida, California and Kentucky, and Keeneland Sales.

Fasig-Tipton can trace its history through several reorganizations and metamorphoses to the late nineteenth century. But in its modern form it was the creation largely of its former President, now Chairman of the Board, Humphrey S. Finney, who organized a group of Virginia breeders to revive the dying concern at the end of World War II.

Wartime transportation restrictions and Fasig-Tipton's financial problems led to the formation in 1944 of the Breeders' Sales Co., originally a cooperative of Kentucky breeders. This was later reorganized as the Keeneland Sales Division of the Keeneland Association, which also operates Keeneland Race Course where the Keeneland Sales pavilion is located.

Keeneland conducts auctions almost exclusively at its Lexington, Ky., headquarters. The Summer Yearling Sales there in late July is one of the two leading North American auctions for horses of that age. The Fall Yearling Sales in September and the Fall Breeding-Stock Sales in November are the largest such auctions on the continent, with over 1,000 head in each.

Fasig-Tipton conducts the other major yearling auction on the continent, the Saratoga Yearling Sales at Saratoga Springs, N.Y., in early August. Through associations with various local breeding organizations, Fasig-Tipton and its affiliates also hold other major auctions, including the Hialeah Two-Year-Old Sales in Florida, Del Mar (now Hollywood) Yearling Sales in California, Maryland Fall Sales at Timonium and Woodbine Yearling Sales in Canada. Fasig-Tipton also holds auctions of horses of racing age during the New York racing season. FTP

Auge Horse see Percheron

Australia

Australia has no native horses or ponies. Settled by Europeans in 1788, it was soon importing stock to facilitate transport and settlement and to assist exploration. The earliest imports recorded are THOROUGHBREDS, a TIMOR pony (1803) and CLEVELAND BAYS (1825). There is no documented claim to the introduction of the first CLYDESDALES, but they were certainly in evidence by 1830. The expansionist period of settlement up to about 1900 was the heyday of practical horse breeding. Draught horses opened agricultural land, hauled wool clips and provisions, and, in the cities, did heavy delivery work. Racing grew as a sport and with it the Thoroughbred industry. The Thoroughbred in dilution influenced light draught animals and ponies but most importantly produced the Waler.

The Waler (the New South Wales horse in the jargon of the Indian market buyers) was the dominantly Thoroughbred, 15-hand (1·52 m) animal considered the most suitable type for stock horses, general personal transport, light harness work and army remounts. It was a type rather than a breed, remarkable for stamina rather than for speed. Between 1850 and 1930 numbers were exported annually to India as remounts (see India and Pakistan). Numbers of animals bred for both saddle and draught work declined in the period 1920–45, though there was no parallel drop in racing. By 1939 in the more populated parts of the country horses were more used for pleasure riding than for necessary transport, though in country areas the drover, the musterer, the boundary rider and the occasional mailman still used them of necessity. In 1940 the Australian Light Horse regiments were mechanized.

The earliest organized public racing in the country took place in Sydney near the end of the eighteenth century, but the nature of the settlement and settlers ensured that wherever a township or centre of population sprang up a racecourse usually followed. The 'picnic' race meeting with grassfed mounts paddocked and trained under committee supervision is the characteristically Australian racing occasion. On metropolitan tracks the event is much more like its overseas parallel.

A typically Australian horse sport is campdrafting, which came from needs of drovers and stockmen to separate large mobs of cattle into component groups: cattle to be sold from cattle to be retained, breeding cows from those to be fattened, etc. On large runs this operation often took place away from established yards, or with the use of only rudimentary yards. The horse that could separate individual beasts from their mobs, efficiently 'draft' them off to another location or mob and prevent their breaking back to the original mob was the 'camp' horse. 'Campdrafting' as a competitive sport is a stylized form of this operation. Originally the most highly prized camp horses were Thoroughbreds of the Waler type, but the Quarter horse is now influencing this sport extensively. It is usually conducted at rodeos together with buckjumping (bucking) and bullock riding, both of which are becoming Americanized in style and presentation.

In the years since 1945 the introduction of overseas equestrian competitions has radically widened the scope of Australian riding. Show jumping, combined training and dressage have all been introduced and added to traditional gymkhanas, in hand and saddle classes and riding competitions. Probably the most significant educational factor in the period has been the growth of the pony club movement since the first club was formed in Victoria in 1948, while the winning of a Gold Medal by the Australian three-day event team in the 1960 Olympic Games gave a considerable fillip to Combined Training.

Polo crosse, introduced in 1938, joined polo, which had been played back in the nineteenth century; endurance riding appeared in 1966; other competitions of specifically American derivation, cutting horse, trail horse, etc., have appeared sporadically since 1969. Hunting was early introduced as a sport, originally for a quarry of native animals, e.g. the kangaroo, but subsequently for introduced fox. Hunt clubs operate in some of the capital cities and in some rural areas in the southern states, though many of them organize drags on most occasions. ZD

Reference: D. Martin, *Australia Astride*, Sydney, 1959; M. I. Clarke, *Care of the Australian Horse and Pony*, Adelaide, 1966; Z. White (ed.), *A Race of Horsemen*, Brisbane, 1963; *Hoofs and Horns*, the magazine of Australian riding, Adelaide, monthly, 1945 ff.

Breeds: throughout Australia numerous studs breed horses and ponies of the highest quality to fulfil the diverse requirements of the racetrack, show ring, pony club, camp draft, rodeo, polo, three-day-event or stock work on a sheep or cattle station.

One distinctive type of horse developed here is the Australian Stock Horse or Waler, which performs creditably in all of the above categories. These horses were originally bred by colonial graziers and stockmen as agile working stock horses with great endurance. Station mares and cobs of good substance, sound conformation and proven working ability were put to Thoroughbred stallions, with an occasional dash of Arab blood. Usually 14·2–16 hands (1·47–1·65 m) high, they have a long rein, light forehand, prominent withers, strong back, deep, well ribbed up trunk, good hindquarters and excellent legs. Their sound saddle-horse conformation combined with a kind but alert temperament makes them very versatile mounts.

Traditionally, the THOROUGHBRED has been the backbone of the horse industry in Australia. Most of the successful English, French, American, Italian and New Zealand bloodlines are represented as well as the famed Colonial lines whose descendants have proved themselves here and overseas.

Harness racing is well established. The first STANDARDBRED Daniel Boone was imported from the U.S.A. in 1869; today there are studs representing many of the world's best trotting bloodlines. Australian-bred trotters have recently been highly successful in the U.S.A. and other countries.

ARABS have made their presence felt since the end of the eighteenth century when many desert-bred animals came via India and had a strong influence on the early general horse population as well as the Colonial racing stock. Over 100 purebred Arab sires are listed in the Australian Thoroughbred Stud Book. In the last decade there has been an unprecedented interest in breeding Arabs with many new imports so that the principal British, American, Polish, Egyptian and Russian bloodlines (as well as the Australian lines descended from desert-bred importations) are now present. Consequently, the standard of Arabs seen in the show ring today is excellent. There are many studs breeding purebred, partbred and Anglo-Arabs in substantial numbers. Since its inception in 1957 The Arab Horse Society of Australasia has recorded over 6,000 registrations.

Another breed gaining popularity is the American QUARTER HORSE. First imported in 1954, it took over ten years to establish itself. Now there is a keen demand and large shipments are imported. The special events provided for the breed at shows and rodeos, a progressive upgrading system and excellent promotion by the Australian Quarter Horse Association have assured the success of the breed and there are now over 2,000 registered Quarter Horses.

With the help of the Australian Palomino Horse Breeders Association, PALOMINOS are becoming more prominent in the show ring and there are now some splendid types being bred that combine good conformation with the correct colour.

Australia. *Below:* View Bank Caesar, a champion Australian Pony stallion
Bottom: A typical Waler used by the New South Wales Mounted Police. During World War I more than 120,000 Walers were exported to the Allied Armies in India, Africa, Palestine and Europe.

Australia. The Grand Parade of livestock, horses and riders at the Sydney Royal Agricultural Show

The Australian Pony Stud Book Society was formed in 1931 and under its guidance a keen interest in pony breeding has been maintained. There is strong competition at shows in led, saddle and harness classes, partly due to the high quality of the various imported ponies that founded the early studs. The breeds represented include Welsh Mountain, Welsh, Shetland, Highland, New Forest, Connemara, Hackney and the Australian Pony. Little known outside Australia, the last resembles a high-caste miniature Arab. Arabs did in fact influence its development but the foundation sire was the beautiful Welsh Mountain pony Grey Light imported in 1911. Height 12–14 hands (1·22–1·42 m), these ponies have an Arab head with small ears, fine gullet, long arched neck, well-laid shoulders, prominent withers, short back and loins, deep barrel, rounded, strong hindquarters, fine clean legs and gay tail carriage. Because the forehand resembles that of a much larger horse they have a long smooth stride and provide a delightful ride for a child or small adult.

The heavy draught breeds have unfortunately declined in numbers but there are still a few Clydesdale studs and some of the larger shows provide classes for them. A few individual studs also breed the American SADDLEBRED, ANDALUSIAN, HOLSTEIN, HACKNEY HORSE, PERCHERON and APPALOOSA. GL

Australian Noseband

An Australian noseband keeps the bit well up in the horse's mouth and also applies pressure to the nose, acting as a check to over-strong racehorses. A strap of rubber passes from between the horse's ears, where it is attached to the headpiece of the bridle, down the bridge of the nose and splits to end in two rubber rings that act as bit guards. DRT

Australian Pony see Australia

Australian Stagecoach

The Australian Stagecoach was developed for long-distance travel in the Australian Outback. Early coach lines in Australia operated over rough tracks. Often the driver simply picked the firmest ground through open, unfenced country, the 'natural road'. At first, steel-sprung English coaches were used, but they were too heavy and too rigidly sprung to traverse such tracks without frequently suffering damage.

Similar conditions had existed in some parts of the United States, but in 1827 Lewis Downing of Concord, New Hampshire, probably assisted by Joseph Stephens Abbot, built a coach in which a rounded body was suspended on leather straps several layers thick, called 'thoroughbraces'. These were hung from tall iron brackets known as 'jacks', which were mounted on a light but strong hickory undercarriage. This new flexible suspension proved very satisfactory on rough roads. Speeds of 15 mph or more could be maintained between stages. By the time of the Californian Gold Rushes in 1849, Abbot and Downing's Concord 'Jack' coaches were in use on most long-distance lines in the United States (see American Stagecoach).

During the Australian Gold Rushes, four young Americans — Freeman Cobb, John Murray Peck, James Swanton, and J. B. Lamber — came to Victoria and founded the famous firm of Cobb and Co in 1853. They had had coaching experience, and during that year they imported Concord coaches and stage wagons (vehicles with a simple low-slung body supported on thoroughbraces), and used them to operate a coach line between Melbourne and the Bendigo diggings. Superior organization and the revolutionary Concord coach helped the partners and their successors to prosper, until by the 1880s Cobb and Co's network in New South Wales and Queensland extended over 6,000 miles, probably the longest system in the world.

In 1862 Cobb and Co established a coachbuilding factory at Bathurst, New South Wales, and some years later another at Brisbane, Queensland. By 1886, most of the Company's routes were between towns in the dry inland, and in that year Cobb and Co transferred all its coachbuilding activities to Charleville, Queensland, 500 miles from the coast, in a unique attempt to season timber and build vehicles in the same climatic conditions in which they would be

used. At these factories the typically Australian stagecoach was evolved.

The high jacks and the rounded body of the Concord coach were dispensed with. A severely rectangular flat-floored body was slung on practically straight thoroughbraces, like the Concord wagon. The interior was finished with Spartan severity; windows had no glass, and there were no doors: canvas blinds which could be rolled up were substituted. A boot consisting of a hinged platform suspended by chains at the rear of the body provided for luggage, and more could be carried on the roof, around which ran a low iron railing. The coach reached its final form in the models built at Charleville, which incorporated such refinements as a canvas apron to protect outside passengers from wind and rain, a folding hood over the driver's seat, and powerful acetylene lamps.

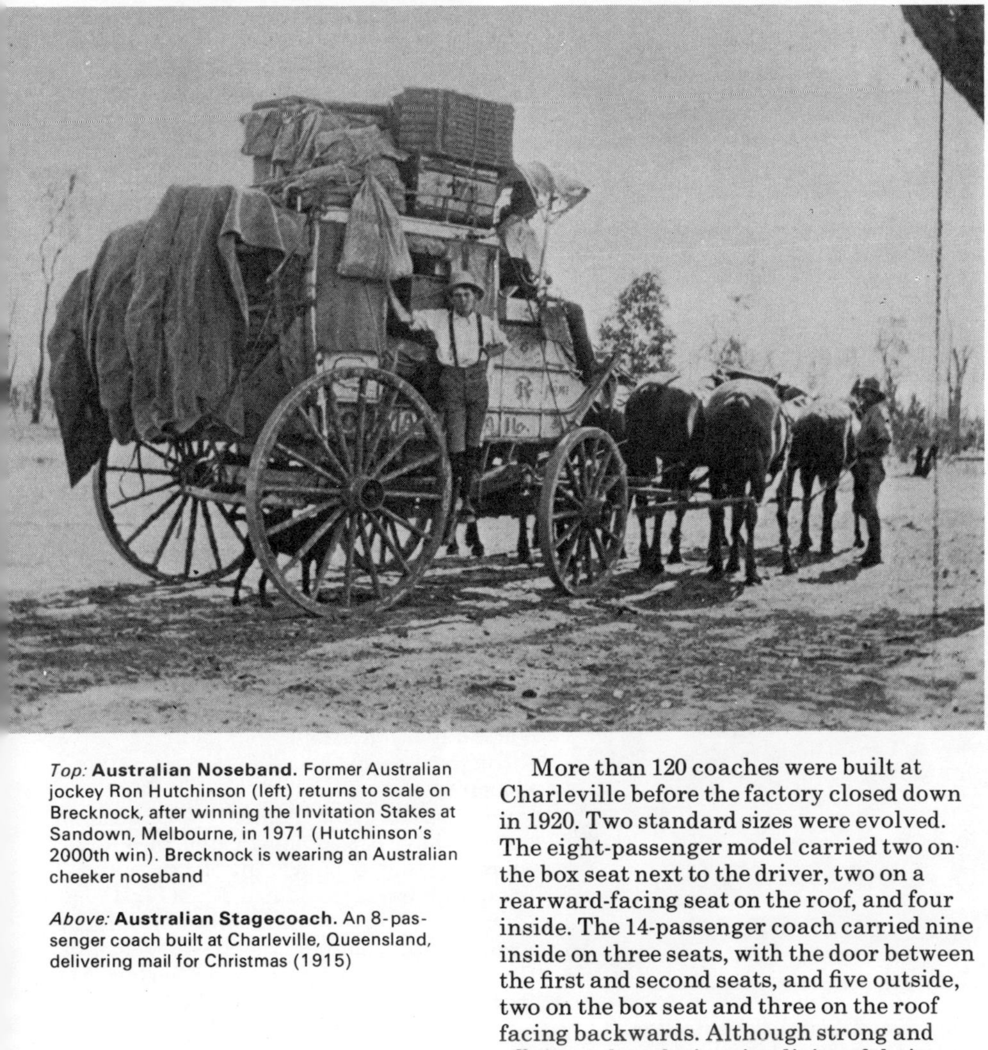

Top: **Australian Noseband.** Former Australian jockey Ron Hutchinson (left) returns to scale on Brecknock, after winning the Invitation Stakes at Sandown, Melbourne, in 1971 (Hutchinson's 2000th win). Brecknock is wearing an Australian cheeker noseband

Above: **Australian Stagecoach.** An 8-passenger coach built at Charleville, Queensland, delivering mail for Christmas (1915)

More than 120 coaches were built at Charleville before the factory closed down in 1920. Two standard sizes were evolved. The eight-passenger model carried two on the box seat next to the driver, two on a rearward-facing seat on the roof, and four inside. The 14-passenger coach carried nine inside on three seats, with the door between the first and second seats, and five outside, two on the box seat and three on the roof facing backwards. Although strong and efficient, the relative simplicity of their design made these coaches very economical to build. The original Concords imported by Cobb in 1853 had cost U.S. $3,000 each; the 14-passenger Charleville-built coach sold for £210 sterling sixty years later.

Australian coaches at first were drawn by teams harnessed in pairs or *spans*. A six-horse team used three spans—*leaders*, *swings*, and *wheelers*. After the late 1860s, Cobb and Co adopted a system of harnessing five- or seven-horse teams, with three horses in the lead, and two or four horses 'in the pole' according to the size of the coach. One horse, the middle leader, or *body horse*, whose traces were connected to a swingle bar hooked directly to the end of the pole, now played the major part in steering the coach, greatly improving the driver's control. Also, he could now reach all the horses with the whip. A special 'coacher' type of horse was bred until 1914, and teams were carefully matched for strength, pace, and on important routes for colour as well. KAA

Reference: For an extensive bibliography, see K. A. Austin, *The Lights of Cobb and Co*, 1967.

Austria

In 1950 there were about 283,000 horses in Austria. Figures for 1971 indicate only 58,875, an unfortunate decrease for a country which has been involved with horses throughout its history. The oldest breed is the PINZGAUER (Noriker), taking its name from the Roman province *Noricum*. The breed may have descended, in part, from horses used by the Roman tribunes or knights. An ancient breed of pack ponies descended from an even earlier primitive mountain breed, may also have played a part in producing the Noriker. The LIPIZZANER bred at Piber, near Graz, is of ancient lineage. Horses of the old Karst breed were probably used as models for the famous Parthenon Friezes now in the British Museum. This is one of Europe's oldest warmblood breeds since Karst, near Trieste, was valued by the Greeks as a horse-breeding district. Later the Karst became the Great Horse of Austrian medieval chivalry, and in the sixteenth century the lighter Genet blood, based on the Barb, from Spain, plus the heavier VILLANOS was introduced to Lipizza. Thus the Lipizzaner breed was born. In times of war the stud at Piber has changed hands several times and the horses have had to be evacuated. In 1809, it was captured by the French, in 1918 by the Italians, in 1943 after German occupation the stud was overrun by Soviet forces. The American General George Patton saved a large herd of mares at the end of the 1939-45 war.

The name of the capital, Vienna, conjures up the names of Emperor Franz Joseph of Austria-Hungary and his beautiful Empress Elizabeth, both passionate lovers of horses. The Empress in particular adored fox-hunting and was frequently in England and Ireland for the season, until her tragic assassination in 1898. The SPANISH RIDING SCHOOL OF VIENNA moved into its present quarters in 1735. The close connection between the Austrian and Spanish courts

Top: **Austria.** Lipizzaners graze at Piber, near Graz.

Above: **Auxois**

led to Spanish and Andalusian stallions being used in the Imperial Studs of Austria, thus originating the famous Neapolitan parade horse. The Augsburg artist and engraver Johann Jakob Ridinger has shown us the exact requirements of a horseman of the eighteenth century. His excellent engravings depict all the School movements as well as horses of Neapolitan strain. DMG

Auxois

An ancient breed, formerly used for coach and draught work in the plateaux of the northeast of Burgundy, the Auxois was crossed in the nineteenth century with PERCHERON and BOULONNAIS stallions. This crossing was later abandoned in favour of Belgian and mainly ARDENNAIS blood. The purebred Auxois today is a powerful horse of 15·2½ hands (1·60 m) minimum, with a short, arched neck. Its coat is bay, strawberry or roan. Greys and blacks are excluded from the studbook. ES

Avelignese

This small and stocky Italian pack and draught horse or more correctly pony, as its average height is 14·2 hands (1·47 m), is now chiefly bred in the Trento, in the Veneto, Tuscany and more rarely in central Italy. Supposedly descended from the old Avellinum-Haflinger (see Italy), it is related to the HAFLINGER of Austria. It is reputed to have a fair amount of Oriental blood from the stallion El Bedavi, brought to Austria from Arabia, although the present stock shows little sign of this. With its short, somewhat heavy neck, short legs and powerful quarters, great strength in proportion to its size, courage, docility and longevity, it is becoming popular even in foreign countries. It is invariably chestnut with white markings and a light mane and tail somewhat similar to those of the PALOMINO. LFB

B

Babylonia

During its early history, about the fifth millennium B.C., Babylonia was subdivided into Akkad and Sumer, These and Chaldea (of the Bible). The Sumerians domesticated the ONAGER *c.* 3000 B.C. and possibly the ass for pack transport. Their culture influenced the ASSYRIANS and there was constant intercommunication among neighbouring states through trade and war. The horse possibly appeared, as a rare occurrence, in Babylonia from the north (Akkad) *c.* 2300 B.C. but may not have been domesticated, although there is extant an engraving of a rider and, possibly, a horse from Susa, Elam I & II (turn of the fourth to third millennium). The French anthropologist De Mecquenem is of the opinion that the date is even earlier. At first equines were harnessed like oxen with a yoke, later a type of half-collar or neckband was invented (see Carriages of Antiquity). In the earliest stages of domestication the nose ring was used on the onager (see the royal standard of Sumer *c.* 2500 B.C. in the British Museum). It is not always easy to differentiate between the species and many are referred to simply as 'equine'.

Later terminology refers to 'mule', sometimes to 'bastard'. Salonen refers to the ancient 'Sulgi song': 'a horse on the (caravan) road with waving tail'. But the horse is clearly a rare animal and only to be used by kings.

Around the middle of the second millennium the two-wheeled chariot was beginning to be replaced by a new invention, cavalry. As the Hittite empire declined, Babylonia became the centre for breeding for which it was ideally situated, with the flat fertile plain watered by the lower Tigris and Euphrates (now southern Iraq). The Hittite king Hattusili III wrote to the ruler of Babylonia begging him to send horses. 'Send me horses . . . well-made colts. The stallions thy father hath sent me were of good stock, now they are old . . . It is very cold in Hatti and old horses do not live long. Send me, brother, young stallions for there are enough old nags in my land'. Although white horses played a considerable rôle, especially for cult and religious purposes, in ancient Europe and Mesopotamia, Babylonia seems to be more or less exempt from the white horse cult. There is, however, one letter from the time of Samsuilunas in which the addressee is asked to supply two white horses, but there is no trace of their use for religious purposes. An ancient text gives colours: white (grey), coloured, brown, chestnut. Generally the only names given to horses denoted colours or physical attributions. There was great care in feeding and exercising. The kings of Babylonia, Assyria, Hatti and Syria sent horses as well as their daughters to the Egyptian Pharoahs in return for presents of gold.

As to the type of horse used, Wiesner is certain that the chariot horse was descended from the TARPAN of the south Russian steppes. There is no connection with the Przevalski horse. They were small horses and thus were more suitable for driving than riding. It is probable that the rulers of New Babylonia (*c.* 620 B.C.) were able to import well-bred horses from Ferghana and Nisea. See Mesopotamia. DMG

Reference: J. Weisner, *Fahren und Reiten in Alteuropa und im alten Orient*, Leipzig, 1939. A. Salonen, *Hippologica Accadica*, Wiesbaden, 1956. E. Weidner, *Weisse Pferde im alten Orient, Bib. Orient.* ix, No 5/6, 1952. Daphne Machin Goodall, *The History of Horse Breeding*, London, 1973.

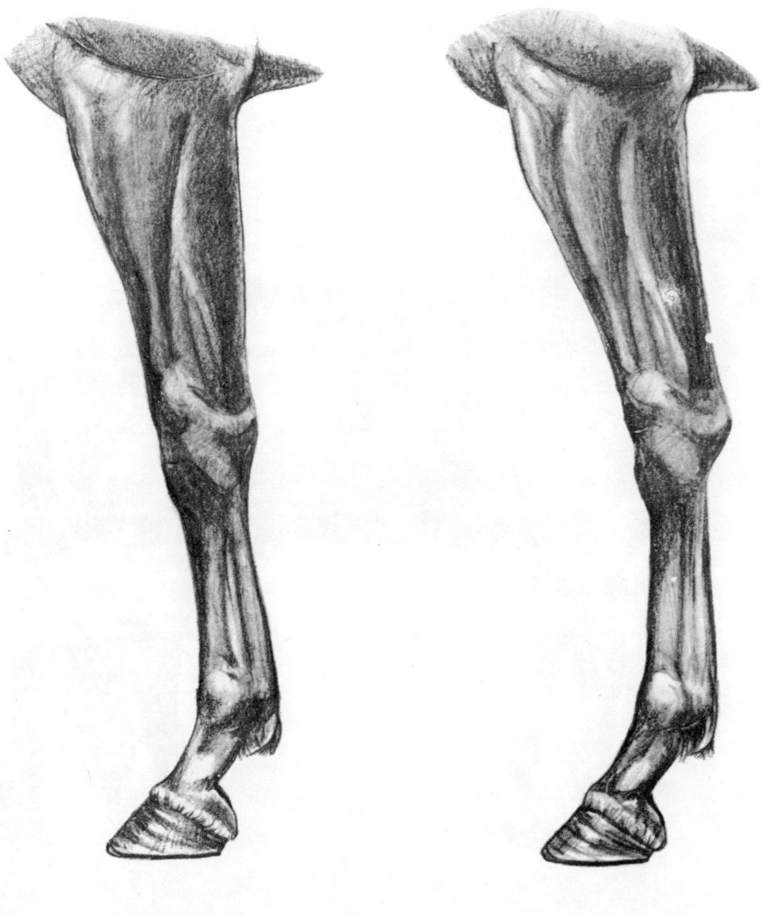

Back at the Knee. *Left:* Normal fore leg *Right:* Fore leg back at the knee

Back at the Knee (Calf Knee)

The anterior line of the knee is concave. Opposite to OVER AT THE KNEE. CF

Badminton

Badminton, the Cotswold home of the Dukes of Beaufort in Gloucestershire, England, was famous for its connection with sports long before the Badminton Three-Day Horse Trials. The kennels of the Duke of Beaufort's Foxhounds (dating from 1720) are near the house. The game of badminton was first played there in 1851. It gave its name to *The Badminton Library*, a series of sporting books published by Longmans from the late 1870s to early 1900s. The HORSE TRIALS, held each spring, began in 1949. DRT

Bahamas see West Indies

Bahia see Brazil

Bahrain

One of the largest single collections of Arabian horses in the world belongs to H. H. Sheikh Isa bîn Sulman al Khalifa, ruler of Bahrain. Members of the great horse-breeding Anazeh confederation, the Al Khalifa, went to Bahrain some two centuries ago taking with them many of Arabia's finest steeds which they have maintained in purity to this day. The majority of Arabians round the globe trace in some measure to the horses of Abbas Pasha I, Viceroy of Egypt from 1848 to 1854, who in turn derived much of his priceless collection from Bahrain. The precious strains of Dahman Shahwan, Duhaym al Najib and Kuhaylan Jellabi, among others, were fanatically preserved by the Al Khalifa. Stallions are chosen only from the Dahman, Jellabi, Krushan, Shawaf, Wadnan and Mlolshan families. However, there are some 22 strains preserved in tail female lines. Sheikh Isa's royal stud consists of approximately 500

Arabians. Racing is a favourite sport and most horses are tried on the track. No trip to the Arab world in search of Arabian horses is complete without a visit to Bahrain. See also Arab. JEF

Baiga see Horse Sports under U.S.S.R.

Bakhtiari see Plateau Persian

Balearic
An ancient breed found in Majorca, especially in the Palma district; it takes its name from the group of islands. Its main characteristics are slender legs, graceful carriage and arched neck, short, thick and crowned by an upright mane. Colours range from light to dark brown. The head, with ears carried towards the rear rather than pricked forward, has a markedly Roman nose. DRT

Ballotade see Airs, Classical

Banbury see Bits and Bitting

Barb see Libyan

Barberi, I
These riderless races, run annually for centuries during the Roman carnival, were known as *I Barberi* because the horses were chiefly BARBS or ARABS. The horses, entirely loose, wore only a network of pear-shaped goads on their flanks and their owners' colours in head-plumes. Starting at the Piazza del Popolo, where they were released by colourfully attired attendants called *barbaresche*, they galloped down the Corso between cheering crowds until stopped by a sheet drawn across a now non-existent street near the Piazza Venezia.

Introduced to Rome by the Venetian Pope Paul II in the fifteenth century, the races were run less for monetary reasons than for the honour of winning the *pali*, a silk banner similar to those from which the famous PALIO of Siena derives its name. At first popular only among the masses, during the eighteenth and nineteenth centuries the races became fashionable among the aristocracy, and Roman princes spent fortunes on breeding horses branded with their heraldic crests for these races. In 1882 the races were prohibited by royal degree after a fatal accident among the crowd occurred under the eyes of Queen Margherita, who was watching from a balcony of Palazzo Fiano. They were continued for a short while in the Piazza del Popolo, enclosed by hoardings, and later in the Piazza di Siena, but eventually died out. LFB

Bardot see Jennet

Barême
The French term for the three tables of jumping faults established by the FÉDÉRATION ÉQUESTRE INTERNATIONALE and used for all competitions conducted under F.E.I. rules. Under Table A a knockdown equals 4 faults, the first refusal or disobedience 3 faults and the second 6. Under Table B a knockdown equals 10 seconds, under Table C penalties range from as little as 3 seconds to as much as 17 depending upon the length of the course.

Bars
A toothless space in the mouth, between the incisors and molars, where the bit rests. See Bits and Bitting

Barthais Pony see French Ponies

Bashkirsky
This Russian breed has been improved by crossing with Russian riding horses (BUDYONNY and DON) in the south and with harness horses (Trotters and Ardennes) in the west and north. Like the KAZAKH, it yields much milk, but stands higher on its legs and has a better-developed front. The mountain type is smaller than the steppe type and is more suitable for riding. Bay, chestnut, and dun are the prevalent colours. This is a hardy, calm, good-natured horse. Average height at withers for the mountain type is 13·1¼ hands (1·35 m), for the steppe type 13·1½ hands (1·37 m); bone below the knee for the mountain 7 in (17·8 cm), for the steppe 7 in (17·1 cm). WOF

Basque Pony see French Ponies

Bashkirsky

Basseri see Persian Horse, Plateau Persian

Basuto

The Basuto Pony owes its origin to the Dutch East India Co. which imported Arabs and Barbs from Java to the Cape in 1653; these horses also became the founders of the CAPE HORSE. Arabs, Barbs and Persians continued to arrive in South Africa until about 1811, although between 1770 and 1790 English THOROUGHBREDS were imported too.

The familiar type of Basuto dates from about 1830: a quality head proclaiming its good breeding in the past is coupled with longish back, small thickset body, short legs, very hard hoofs and a toughness and self-reliance that normally denotes a wild horse. This remarkably surefooted and fearless pony can gallop up and down hills where any ordinary horse and rider would think twice of walking. Endurance too is characteristic; they are capable of doing 60–80 miles in a day with 13–14 stone (182–206 lb or 83–94 kg) on their backs. They were used as troop horses in the Boer War, as well as for racing and polo. See colour plate, page 35. DRT

Batak

A native of Sumatra, the Batak or Deli pony takes its name from the hills of Batak and the port of Deli from which it is exported to Singapore. A strong infusion of Arab blood has left its mark in handsome, well-bred heads set on high crested necks. Small, they stand only 11·3 hands (1·19 m) though some reach 12·1–12·2 hands (1·24–1·27 m).

The Gayoe pony from northern Sumatra is stouter than the Batak, with heavier hindquarters and shorter, thicker legs. It lacks the fiery nature and speed of the Batak for it has less Arab blood. See also Indonesia. DRT

Baucher, François

François Baucher, horseman and instructor of equitation, was born in 1796 at Versailles. While working for an uncle in Turin, he acquired a love and knowledge of horses. After the fall of the Empire he toured the famous riding schools in order to study their various methods before setting up his own school in Harve. Before long his fame had spread and at the request of some amateurs in Rouen he set up a second school there and for the next 12 years spent winter and spring in Rouen and summer and autumn in Harve. Eventually he sold out and went to Paris where he joined Jules Pellier with whom he wrote his *Dialogues sur Equitation.* For ten years he trained horses for the Champs-Elysées Circus. In later years he travelled in Italy in the circus and teaching. Returning to France in 1849, he gave a series of lectures to some officers among whom was Lt (later General) L'Hotte, who became the greatest French master of military equitation.

Baucher developed three distinct 'manners' of riding during his riding life. His teaching was much challenged by the Comte D'AURE and his followers; d'Aure in the end had the greater influence on the riding world. Nevertheless, Baucher's principles are still practised today in Portugal by the great maestro Nuno Oliviera and his pupils.

Baucher died in Paris in 1873. He wrote several works on equitation including *Dictionnaire raisonné d'Equitation* (1833) and *Méthode d'Equitation basée sur de nouveaux principes* (1842), and gave his name to a bit. DRT

Beberbeck

Beberbeck Stud, near Kassel, West Germany, was founded in 1720, originally to breed palomino horses. It ceased to exist in 1930 although horses are still bred in Kurhessen and are entered in the stud book, where about 2,000 mares are registered. Stallions in private hands have increased. DMG

Bedding

Wheat straw is the best; it absorbs moisture well and lasts longest. Long straw is better if obtainable than short, combined straw. *Oat straw* is soft and quickly becomes saturated. It is not recommended because horses like its taste and may eat it. *Barley straw* should not be used. The awns irritate the skin and, if eaten, may cause colic. *Peat* is heavy to work. Damp patches should be dug out daily and replaced with fresh peat, otherwise it may cause foot trouble. *Wood shavings* are becoming increasingly used as they are comparatively cheap. They must be clean and free from oil, paint, screws, nails, pieces of paper or other foreign bodies. They act as a deodorant. Remove wet patches daily or maggots may breed; shavings also tend to become heated and cause foot troubles. *Sawdust* may overheat if damp patches are not frequently removed. It should also be free from foreign bodies. Replace the whole bed at least once a fortnight. It can be used with a layer of straw on top which forms a thicker, more comfortable bed. *Bracken* should be gathered when green and dried slowly or it tends to crumble into powder. It is sometimes used in Scotland but not recommended. Green bracken should not be used as it is poisonous if eaten. *Sand* is sometimes used in tropical countries. It is not good as it causes sand colic if eaten. It may be used under a fairly thick layer of straw. *Deep litter* is not advised unless managed properly. Pick up droppings, remove damp, soggy straw and put on a fresh layer. Remove the whole bed about once a month. It may be economical and warm but entails very hard work when digging out and removing the whole bed periodically. GW

Beetewk see Bitjug under Voronezh Harness Horse

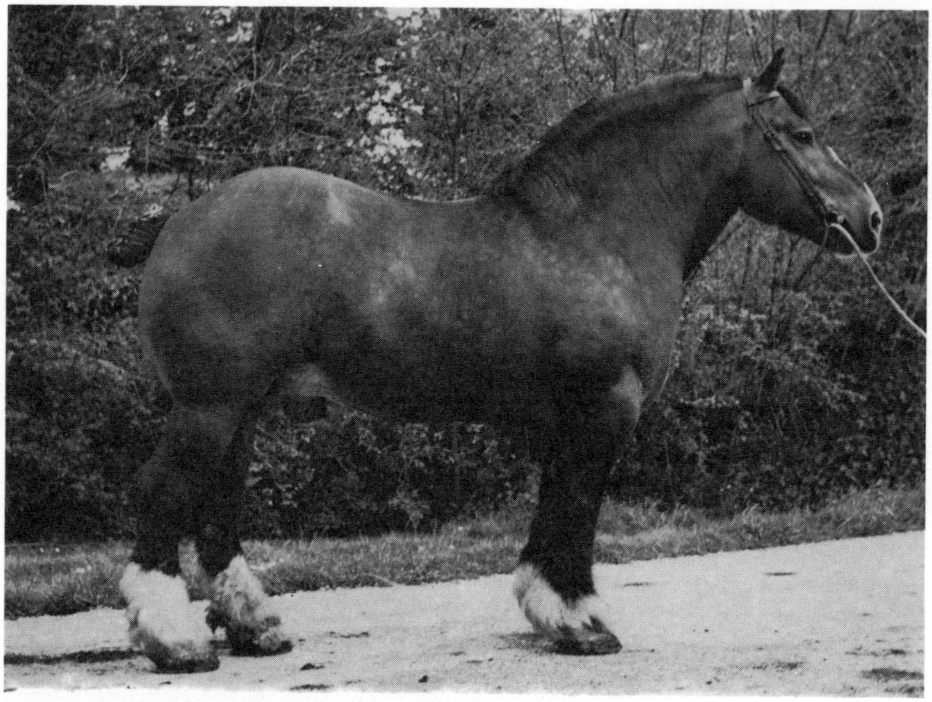

Belgium. A Brabant stallion

B.E.F. see British Equestrian Federation

Belgium

Although horse breeding in modern Belgium is very much on the decline, in earlier times the opposite was the case, especially in the breeding of the heavy horse. Some experts think that the heavy working horse of Belgium is a descendant of the large horse of the Quaternary period and more recently of the ARDENNES horse. Both soil and climate are ideal for rearing horses of a heavier stamp. Caesar noted and used these horses, while from the eleventh to the sixteenth century the provinces of Flanders and Brabant were both noted for breeding a heavy type of war horse. During this period a number of Flanders horses were imported into Britain and these helped to lay the foundations for both the SHIRE and CLYDESDALE heavy draught horse breeds. Even the SUFFOLK PUNCH, bred up from the native cob, may well have had 'Flanders' blood. It should, however, be understood that whereas the heavy Brabant horse became known as a breed the Flanders horse was not. During the seventeenth and eighteenth centuries introductions of French, Dutch, Holstein and Danish horses were made but cross-breeding was unsuccessful. Belgian farmers preferred their traditional method of breeding their particular heavy horse, which was now in demand throughout Europe for agriculture and particularly as draught power for industrial transport.

Germany developed the RHINELAND or Rhenish from the Belgian horse. North America has regularly imported Belgian horses, since heavy horses especially can be used where mechanized power is impracticable. Ninety per cent of the equine population of Belgium consisted of heavy draught horses of which the Brabant, the present-day Belgian horse, is the heaviest and most widely used. The heavy, rich and rather damp diluvial soil was inclined to make the horses soft with lymphatic joints, but the modern Belgian horse has outgrown these faults and is a strong, short-backed, heavily-muscled animal on powerful short legs. Several types are bred according to locality and the colour is generally roan with black points, and chestnut.

A few THOROUGHBRED horses and trotters are also bred in Belgium from imported stock. Pony breeds are entirely imported. DMG

Berrichon, Berry Horse see Percheron

Betting

Betting takes place in Great Britain on every horse race in which there are two or more runners, most of it with bookmakers and the remaining small proportion with the TOTALISATOR. The backer can invest a sum ranging from 5p to £10,000, though there are now few such large individual bets. There are three means of betting: in cash with a bookmaker or totalisator on course; via a credit account on or off course or in cash in an off-course betting office. Credit accounts are settled weekly, cash bets after each race. There is an endless variety of bets available from a straightforward win only to an accumulator (in which all the horses must win) involving any number of horses. There are also 'yankees', 'round robins' and many others which vary up and down the country. Most betting is done on a win only basis; horses can also be backed 'each way' (to be placed). Most off-course bookmaker bets are settled at starting price, which is decided by on course experts according to the odds available. A tax of $2\frac{1}{2}$ per cent on betting was introduced in 1966; this was increased to 5 per cent in 1968 and to 6 per cent (off-course only) in 1970. GE

In North America there are no legal bookmakers (except in Nevada, where all forms of gambling are legal under state supervision); all legal wagering is done on the track through the pari-mutuels, except for the New York off-track betting system.

Bets may be made in sums of $2 and up; various tracks provide facilities for wagers of $5, $10, $50 and sometimes $100. A backer may buy as many tickets in any denominations as he wishes. All betting is for cash, and wagers are paid as soon as each result is official. Horses may be backed to win (finish first), place (finish first or second) or show (finish first, second or third). Some tracks also offer a 'combination' ticket, in values of $6, $15 and $30, which backs a horse to win, place and show. Some of the multiple-wagering opportunities, including

Exactas, Perfectas and Quinellas, are offered in minimum betting denominations other than $2: the betting unit may be $3 or $5, or multiples thereof, depending on the policy of the individual track.

In 1971 legal off-track betting was introduced in New York State, although to mid-1972 shops had been opened only in New York City. Monies bet through these shops on New York races are tabulated through the track betting machinery, and track odds are paid. This off-track betting organization permits credit betting by telephone after customers have deposited money, but such credit accounts are available only to residents of the state. The off-track betting organization also accepts wagers on occasional major out-of-state races; separate pools, with no direct relation to the on-track odds, are conducted in such cases.

All betting pools are subject to a deduction ('take') which is split between the track and the state, or in some cases the city or county, where the track is located. The terms and division of the 'take' varies from state to state.

In Canada, especially in its major racing province of Ontario, 'messenger services' have been established to accept wagers off the track and transmit the bets to the track. Track officials are trying to outlaw such services on the ground that the money deposited often never reaches the track, which is thus deprived of that portion of its betting handle and income. FTP

B.H.S. see British Horse Society

Bitiug, Bitjug see Voronezh Harness Horse

Bits and Bitting

Bits are many and varied and fall into three principal groups: snaffle, double and Pelham. Each group shows many variations. **Snaffle:** this is the most important and probably the most numerous, found in a variety of materials and mouthpieces. Materials used are metal, rubber, vulcanite, nylon and even leather (as a covering); mouthpieces include straight bar, mullen (straight with a slight curve), single and double-jointed, and many more such as chain, roller and gag. The cheekpieces too vary: a bit can have a plain ring or an eggbutt side, or a long cheek as in the Fulmer snaffle; the mouthpiece itself with a metal bit can be smooth, plain or twisted, ridged, or even square, the latter very sharp as it cuts into the bars. The thickness varies too, some bits having very thin mouthpieces, others fat ones. Thin bits can cut if used roughly; these include most of the racing snaffles. Fat mouthpieces, such as the German mouthpieces, rubber and nylon, or vulcanite, are far kinder as they rest over a greater area of the mouth and do not cut nearly so easily. Of the snaffles for the ordinary rider an eggbutt-sided jointed plain snaffle is probably the most useful. The eggbutt sides prevent the corners of the mouth being chafed as can happen with a ring bit. **Double:** as its name implies, this consists of two bits: a Weymouth, which is a curb bit, and a bridoon (bradoon) which is a snaffle. Other forms of curb bits are found, the most common being the Banbury, a curb bit with revolving cheekpieces. The construction and action of a curb bit differ from those of a snaffle. The snaffle acts on the horse's lips, tongue, and to some extent the bars, while the curb not only acts on these parts, but also through the curb chain, on the curb (chin) groove, and to some extent the poll and, if the port of the bit is high, the roof of the mouth as well. The object of the curb bit is to obtain a degree of flexion by inducing the horse to relax its jaw. A curb bit is shaped like an 'H', the sides of the 'H' forming the cheeks of the bit. The rings at the top are attached to the headpiece of the bridle while the reins are fixed to the lower rings. The cross bar of the 'H' forms the mouthpiece, which can be straight, mullen or Cambridge, the last like a humpbacked bridge, in other words 'ported'. The port varies in size and height from a low rounded curve, giving comfortable room for the tongue, to a high square-shaped one that acts on the roof of the mouth by levering the mouth open. The former is kind, the latter cruel. Attached to the top rings are two curb hooks from which the curb chain is hung. These chains vary: some are single-linked, others double. They may also be made of leather or elastic. The curb chain passes behind the horse's jaw so that it lies flat in the curb groove just above the lower lip. When the curb rein is brought into action the lower end of the curb bit moves back towards the rider's hands and tightens the chain.

The best double for the average rider is called a 'Tom Thumb'. This is a simple Weymouth curb bit with a low port, smooth mouthpiece and short cheeks; the longer the cheek the greater the leverage on the curb chain, so a short cheek is mild in its action. The bridoon should have a smooth jointed mouthpiece and not be too thin. **Pelham:** the Pelham is a combination of the curb and snaffle in one mouthpiece. Two reins are normally used, the bridoon rein being fixed to rings adjoining the mouthpiece. All kinds of mouthpieces and materials are found. Many horses go well in a Pelham, but nonetheless, it is very hard to obtain a definite action from either rein if the reins are used together. For this reason a Pelham that is recommended is the Kimblewick, which employs only one rein and has single large 'D' rings running from above the mouthpiece to the bottom of the cheek. Normally the rider's hands, if held high, bring the bridoon action into play, but

Bits and Bitting. (1) A German eggbutt jointed snaffle. (2) A short-cheek slidemouth Weymouth and wire-ring jointed bridoon. For a similar mullen slidemouth Pelham, see Bridles. (3) A mullen slidemouth Weymouth. (4) A Kimblewick (Pelham)

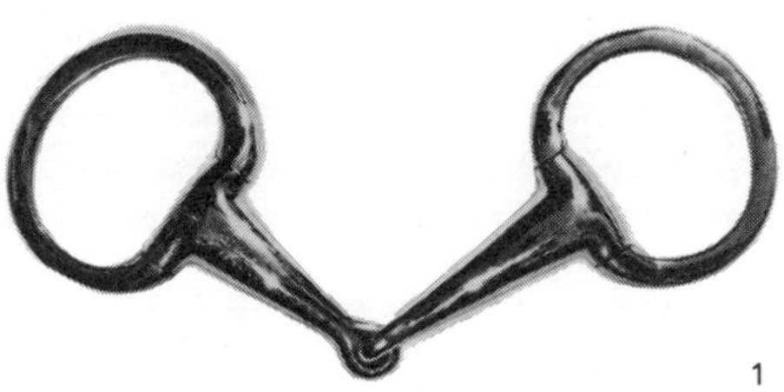

1

2

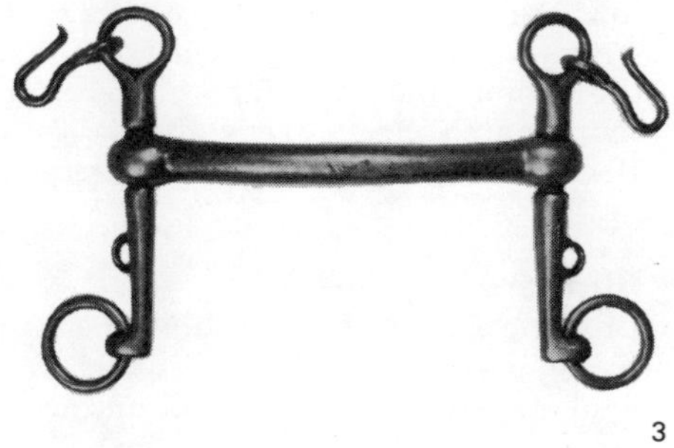

3

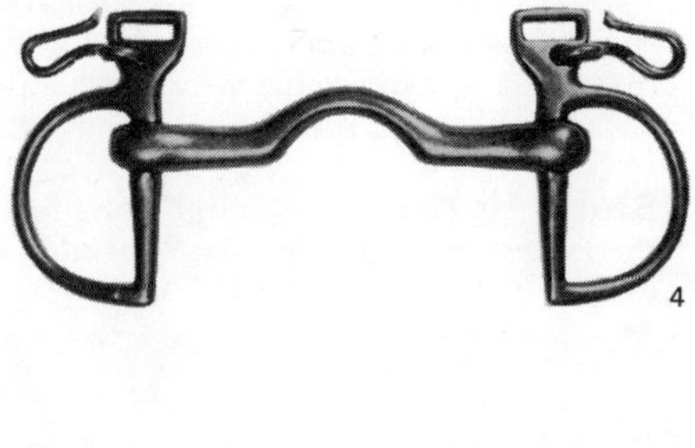

4

on lowering the hands the curb. It is a good bit in experienced hands.

When choosing a suitable bit for a horse, comfort and control are of paramount importance. Comfort is desirable for the horse; control for the rider as he must at all times be master. While a rider uses his seat and legs to create impulsion and forward movement, he regulates them with his hands by means of contact with the horse's mouth through the bit, by way of the reins. Horses' mouths are very sensitive and can vary a great deal: some are long, others short; some have fat, fleshy lips with well covered bars, others have thin lips which are lightly covered and easily damaged.

When bitting a horse attention should be paid to the teeth. They can cause trouble when fitting a bit for they are placed so that they sometimes get in the way. The teeth that cause most trouble are the tushes, spike-like teeth found normally in stallions and geldings, and sometimes in mares, which are situated directly behind the front teeth, reducing the space on the bars available for a bit. The bit should be adjusted well behind them. The other troublesome teeth are wolf teeth: if these are present, they are directly in front of the molars, and the horse bites on them each time it closes its mouth on the bit. Like human wisdom teeth, they are best out but must be removed by a veterinary surgeon. The molars get sharp and must be filed at least once a year by a veterinary surgeon, or they will cut the tongue and cheeks, making the horse fretful as well as making it uncomfortable for it to eat hard food. Bits and bitting is a complex and lengthy subject which needs detailed study, but the basic principle is to ensure that the bridle fits and does not pinch or rub. When the leather part of the bridle has been placed over the horse's head, there should be room for two fingers under all the straps and the width of a hand when placed sideways under the throatlatch. The bit (or bits if a double is used) must be adjusted so as to touch the corners of the horse's lips without stretching or wrinkling them. Comfort is the keynote and a mild bit is often better than a harsh one. For Driving Bits, see Driving Harness. See also Accoutrements. DRT

Blinkers

Blinkers are used to prevent a horse seeing to the side or rear. Driving blinkers (or winkers) are fixed to the bridle and are made of leather often with a crest or embellishment on the outside (see Driving Harness). Those used in racing and other forms of riding (but not competitive work, for which they are banned) are in the form of a hood with leather cups that act as shields. DRT

Blood Horse a term usually applied to the THOROUGHBRED. See also Warmblood. CF

Blue Grass

Among the best known of the *Poa* genus, range and pasture grasses most widely found in temperate and cool regions, is the blue grass of Kentucky, one of the principal horse-breeding centres in the United States, where the limestone soil and water produces a rich, dark, bluish-green, fine-leaved perennial foliage that is reputed to build sound bones. Because of its prevalence there, Kentucky is called 'The Blue Grass State'.

The Blue Grass Stakes is a $1\frac{1}{8}$-mile (1·9 km) race for three-year-old Thoroughbreds, run at the Keeneland racetrack in Lexington, Kentucky, since 1911. It may be a preview of the KENTUCKY DERBY, which it precedes. Past winners include Arts and Letters (1969), Forward Pass (1968), Northern Dancer (1964), Chateaugay (1963), Round Table (1957), Bimelech (1940), and Bull Lea (1938). MAS

Blue Riband

'Blue Riband' or 'Blue Ribbon' (after the colour of the rosette or ribbon awarded for first prize) is applied to the highest honour in any competition. The GRAND NATIONAL is often called the Blue Riband of steeplechasing in Great Britain, and the DERBY is the Blue Riband of flat racing. DRT

Bog Spavin

A chronic distension of the capsule of the true hock joint, occurring at its antero-internal aspect. This frequently co-exists with articular THOROUGHPIN. CF

Bokhara

The work horse or pony described by Capt. Hayes as coming from the Samarkand district of Turkestan is quite distinct from both the CASPIAN and TURKOMAN in being stocky and coarse. It is probably a direct descendant of the coarse Scythian horse (remains of two kinds of Scythian horses have been found in PAZYRYK, one tall and

Below: **Blinkers.** Racing blinkers

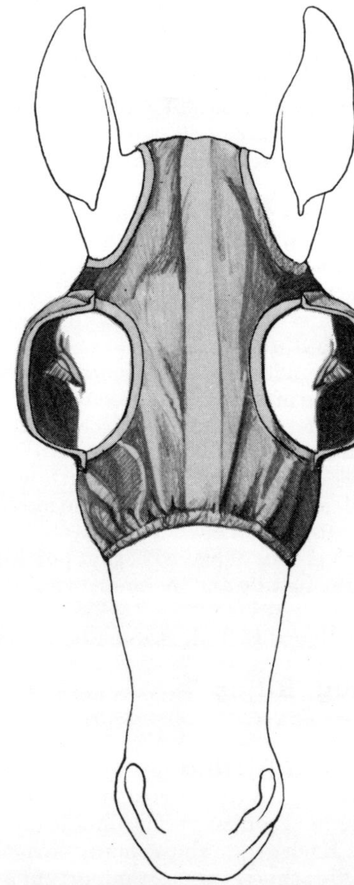

Bottom: **Blue Grass.** Thoroughbreds graze in the Blue Grass region of Kentucky.

Below: **Bog Spavin** (arrowed), shown here with Capped Hock

Bottom right: **Boulonnais.** A team of stallions

light, the other short and stocky) and, as such, is a distinct breed going back at least 2,000 years. LF
Reference: Capt. M. H. Hayes. *The Points of the Horse*, London, 1896, 7th rev. ed. 1969

Bolter

A term used to describe a horse that refuses to respond to the bit. Sometimes this is due to pain, either from pressure of the bit on the wolf's teeth or the bars (see Bits and Bitting), causing the animal to cross its jaw. Occasionally in an animal that has been ridden by a person with heavy hands the bars are dead to any sensation. WSC

Bolting

In its anxiety to eat its food a horse may swallow it so quickly that it does not masticate it properly. This habit, known as bolting, is not only uneconomical but predisposes to indigestion or even choking because the food mass is not sufficiently moistened by the saliva before it is swallowed. To prevent this, mix chaff with dry feeds of oats, etc. so that the animal has to chew the mass more. Small and frequent feeds should be given. WSC

Bone

A term referring to the span of bone and tendons immediately below the knee. WSC

Boot, Brushing

A horse that is apt to strike itself (see Brushing) when working should wear some form of brushing boot to prevent injury. They come in several forms designed to protect the legs, especially round the area of the fetlock joints, and are usually made of felt but can also be made of leather; two simpler forms are the Yorkshire boot, a piece of rugging fastened by a tape round above the fetlock joint and then folded over to give a double thickness of material, and a rubber ring fastened round the leg just above the fetlock joint. See also Clothing, Horse. DRT

Bosnian

This native mountain pony of Yugoslavia and chief representative of Balkan pony types is something like the HUÇUL, although not quite so compact. It is probably descended from the primitive wild forms of the TARPAN. Much Arab blood has now been introduced. It is bred in Herzegovina, Montenegro and Macedonia. DMG

Boulonnais

Born in the border country on the northern coast of France, the Boulonnais has received a double portion of foreign blood: Arab from Caesar's time, and northern European blood in the Middle Ages which gave it weight and power. During the Crusades there were new imports of Arabs, then crossings with ANDALUSIANS which themselves had much Oriental blood. Since the seventeenth century there have been two varieties: the small, less than 16 hands (1·65 m), the *mareyeur* (horse of the tide), a lively type used for the carts which carried freshly caught fish from the coast to Paris, and the large, 16 hands and over (1·60–1·70 m) much

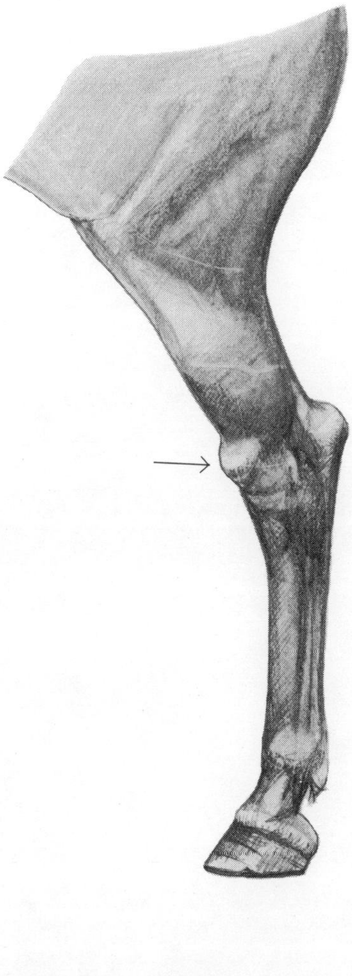

in demand today. The Oriental contribution to this distinguished horse is still more apparent than in the Percheron. The Boulonnais has a short head, straight or concave nose, small ears and mouth, fine skin, silky coat and bushy mane. Much appreciated in other countries, the Boulonnais has been called the noblest draught horse. The coat is grey, sometimes bay or chestnut. ES

Brabant, Brabançon see Belgium

Braiding see Plaiting

Brandenburg Horse see Germany

Brasses see Horse Brasses

Brazil

Brazil is one of the leading countries of South America in breeding horses of quality. These are descended from the Spanish Altér in central Brazil, and the ANDALUSIAN in the southern part of the country. The modern southern breeds are the Campolino, Mangalarga and the Crioulo Brazileiro, similar to the Criollo of South America generally. In 1819, the Emperor Dom João VII imported stallions from Portugal to stand at the royal stud at Cachoeira do Campo. Although the modern Campolino has Andalusian characteristics, traces of THOROUGHBRED, PERCHERON and ORLOV which were later introduced may be seen in some horses. It is a muscular but lightly built horse with strong legs, has stamina and can stay long distances.

Both Altér and Andalusian stallions were sent to the stud of Baron Alfenas in the State of Minas Gerais, in 1812 by Dom João. They were crossed with local mares and so laid the foundations for the Mangalarga breed. This horse is of good conformation but stands only at 14–15 hands (1·42–1·52 m). It has a useful turn of speed with a peculiar high-stepping gait which adds to its elegance.

The Crioulo Brazileiro, the best type of horse in Brazil, is an excellent cavalry horse, ranch horse, plays polo and when big enough makes a good show jumper. Its origin goes back to 1535 when Pedro de Mendoza, the Spanish explorer, founded Buenos Aires and Santissima Trinidade. He brought about 72 horses with him and when it became necessary to retire from Buenos Aires, some 44 horses were turned loose on the pampas. These were the ancestors of the feral Argentine Criollo.

Other native breeds are the Guarapuavano, which is disappearing, the Mimoseano, Bahia and Curraleiro and the Sertanejo from the extreme north. Thoroughbreds are also bred for the races, which are very popular in Brazil. DMG

Breaking

Breaking, the education of a horse for the purpose for which it is required, should not be confused with schooling, which properly refers to further training of a horse already broken. Although the breaking of horses has advanced over the past thousand years, the Romans, Persians, North Africans and American Indians all contributed points still of interest today.

A horse which has been correctly handled from birth is a more responsive animal when the day to break it arrives, usually when it is three or four years old. The importance of correct handling in its early years cannot be overstressed. It should be accustomed to wearing a halter and being led from a few weeks old and the early sight of saddlery or harness will be of help as when it is accustomed to the equipment it will accept it without fear. After the halter the first stage is to get the horse to accept the girth passing round its body and after this the bit should be placed gently in its mouth. Later, side reins are added and it will grow used to the attachment to the girth or roller or 'dumb jockey' of mouth to body and manual control coming into play. All this takes place in the stable. Then the horse will be led out and walked around.

The next stage is the lungeing rein which accustoms the horse to go to and from its trainer on command. Many trainers then use two long reins and drive the horse from the ground at the walk and slow trot, halting and walking on to verbal command.

Next comes the saddle or collar depending upon whether the horse is to be broken for riding or harness work. With the saddle this is carefully fitted on to the horse and after it has become accustomed to the feel, the rider, under the trainer's command, should quietly and gently lie over the horse's back while the horse is held and then led round by the trainer. Once this has been accepted the horse will usually take quite calmly to the rider mounting and sitting upright in the normal way. It is most advantageous to talk gently and reassuringly to the horse all the time.

The horse is now led out bearing the rider; much care should be taken to ensure that the rider does not touch the horse's mouth at this stage. The trainer leads the horse and controls it throughout. He will now put the horse back on the lunge to work at a walk, trot and canter carrying its rider.

Next the rider gives a feel from the reins which are now attached to the bit as well as the side reins while the trainer continues to use the lunge. The rider uses the reins in response to the trainer's commands. As the horse becomes more responsive to the bit and bridle reins, so the trainer will begin to release the side reins. As the animal continues to improve the trainer will now work it without the lunge rein in an enclosed schooling area.

The horse has already learned to respond to hand aids and to move from an applied

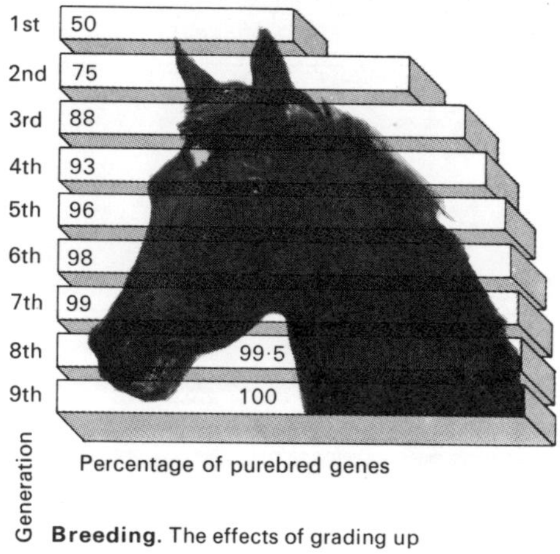

Breeding. The effects of grading up

pressure; now the rider's leg aids must be correctly responded to. A foal has a natural instinct to go to its dam and rub against her to relieve any discomfort. It now has to learn to move away from the leg and not, as is its instinct, to lean into it. Once the young horse has learned to obey the aids and to go well for his rider its breaking days are over and needs only advanced schooling.

The breaking of a horse to harness is a slightly different matter. A large number of trainers prefer to break young horses to the saddle first and have a quiet response before introducing the animal to harness. The fact that sixty years ago many horses were bound to do nothing but collar work meant a rather different system and as there is a marked revival of interest in driving it is becoming necessary to break increasing numbers of horses to harness. At first the same method is used as for the riding horse but the stage of introducing the saddle and rider is replaced for the harness horse by the introduction of the collar. A well-fitting collar is of primary importance.

The harness horse must learn to receive orders that cannot be applied directly to its body as they are to the riding horse. The voice, the rein and the whip are the aids used in driving and the proper use of these aid is vital. After long reining it is useful to attach traces to an old tractor tyre or a log so that the animal becomes accustomed to pulling against a weight. It must learn to lean into a collar and take the weight of a vehicle behind it. At the turn of the century it was usually possible to start the young horse beside a senior 'schoolmaster' horse in double harness. This is often not possible today and training must be started without help from a schooled horse. The majority of horses take well to harness provided that the trainer is experienced in this type of work. See also Long-reining, Lungeing. JHEW

Breaking Tackle see Tackle, Breaking

Breeding

A horse breeder must have as a goal the type of horse he wants to produce, and to be successful he must consistently work towards its accomplishment. He may wish to produce a heavy harness horse with a gentle disposition, a fleet-footed racehorse, or a spotted riding horse for ladies. The final product can be judged good or bad only in relation to his original goal: a draught horse cannot be judged to be poor because it is not fleet-footed any more than a racehorse can be judged poor because it cannot pull a heavy load.

The successful breeder will choose goals which not only reflect particular characteristics of colour, or temperament, but also those that augment the usefulness of the horse for whatever task it is developed: good eyesight, strong legs, disease resistance, etc.

Successful progress towards achieving breeding goals requires a system. Breeders of purebred horses use either: (1) a continuous *outbreeding*, using unrelated stallions, or (2) *inbreeding*, using stallions related to the mares. Breeders who do not limit their program to a single breed use either a system of *grading up*, in which the mares, generation after generation, are bred to stallions of one breed; or a system of *crossbreeding* in which relatively purebred mares of one type are bred to purebred stallions of another type, often with a change of breed from one generation to another.

In the beginning a purebred breeder can generally make good progress by breeding to unrelated stallions with the desired characteristics. However, if he is consistent in his goals, he will find within a few generations that the stallions in his own herd have more of the desired characteristics than any other stallions he can find. At this point some type of inbreeding, often defined as the mating of animals more closely related than the average of the breed, generally follows.

Successful inbreeding will be determined by (1) the soundness of the breeding animals, (2) the effectiveness of selection, and (3) the rate of inbreeding. The more sound or free from flaw the breeding stock, the better chance the new generation will also be sound; but just as the desirable traits are concentrated into prepotency, so any unsoundness contributes to an increased weakness in the next generation. To be successful, inbreeding must be accompanied by a selection process in each generation which places those horses with the most desirable traits in an active role in the breeding program, at the same time eliminating any evident unsoundness. If inbreeding is practised gradually over the years successful selection becomes possible, otherwise unsoundness is likely to be coupled with desirable traits within the same animals. Inbreeding usually takes the form of *linebreeding*, an attempt to obtain as much blood of a particular stallion or mare in a herd as possible while at the same time limiting the amount of inbreeding. Inbreeding with successful selection will result in herd improvement, but when inbreeding of 25 to 50 per cent is reached, some loss of vigour usually occurs.

Grading up is a sound practice used by many non-purebred breeders: non-registered mares are bred to registered stallions of only one breed for a number of generations. A breeder generally begins with mares containing at least 50 per cent of the blood of the breed to which they will be later crossed. Fillies in each generation will have an increasing amount of purebred blood as shown in the accompanying chart. Within six generations the mares of the herd will carry over 98 per cent purebred genes.

Since purebred breeding tends to result in inbreeding, and inbreeding results in a lack of vigour, some breeders conduct a continual crossbreeding program. Quality stock can result from crossbreeding if good purebred animals of different breeds are used. Hybrid vigour can be maintained if breed A is first crossed with breed B, then their offspring crossed to breed C.

Selection within the breeding program involves two important considerations: the horses with the most desirable traits of the breed should be saved for breeding, but those with unsoundnesses must be eliminated. Problems arise when the better traits and a severe unsoundness occur in the same individual. Here the breeder's judgment and experience must help him to decide which animals to cull.

There are three methods of selection: *tandem: minimum culling level*, and *index*. In the tandem method a breeder concentrates on one trait at a time, selecting only for the first trait until it reaches a satisfactory level within his herd, then concentrating on selection for a second trait, and so on. In the minimum culling level, a minimum standard is established for each trait. Any horse not measuring up to any one of the minimum standards is culled. With the index method a value or index is placed on each trait and these are totalled, giving a composite score for each animal. Animals with the lowest score are culled.

A number of aids can be used in selection apart from the animal's appearance, which usually gives only a partial picture of its true constitution. A pedigree reveals how an animal should develop, production records tell how it actually performs and a progeny test tells how well traits will be transmitted to offspring. All of these techniques should be used.

Once a breeder has decided upon a set of definite goals, progress towards them may be slow or rapid depending upon a number of factors. The number of traits involved is important; the more traits under consideration, the slower the progress. Rate of progress is also determined by the breeder's steadfastness of purpose. Changing goals with fads over the years severely hampers any sort of real progress. Rate of production within the herd is an important consideration as well as the size of the herd. If selection is to be effective, a sufficient number of animals must be available from which to select. Persistent disease problems within a herd can also reduce the number of animals or, more seriously, may mask desirable traits so that good animals are culled.

Often a horse's external appearance does not accurately reflect its true genetic nature. Variations in the environment and feeding conditions are the usual causes of this discrepancy; occasionally one trait may mask another. This discrepancy can have a tremendous slowing effect upon progress made in the breeding program.

The level of performance also strongly influences the rate of progress made toward the goals. It is easy to improve a poor herd by crossing to excellent stallions, but progress is much slower with an excellent herd, because it is difficult to find a stallion that will upgrade it to any great extent. WEJ

Reference: W. E. Jones and R. Bogart, *Genetics of the Horse*, East Lansing, Michigan, 1971.

Breeding, Hunter

Horses suitable for the various forms of the chase have been bred in England and Ireland for many centuries. Anglo-Norman sportsmen hunted the wolf, bear and boar and later the hart, stag, hind, roebuck and hare. The fox was not hunted until less than two hundred and fifty years ago.

Two centuries ago, halfbred horses were in great demand. They were delightful animals to ride, according to the nineteenth-century writer Nimrod (Charles Apperley): 'When in his best form, he was a truly shaped and powerful animal, possessing prodigious strength, with a fine command of frame, considerable length of neck, a slight curve in his crest, which was always high and firm and the head beautifully put on. In addition to the very great pains taken with his mouth in the bitting, and an excellent education in the school or at the bar, he was what was termed a complete snaffle-bridle horse, and a standing as well as flying leaper'. This slow, steady animal was a cross between the not quite thoroughbred horse and the common draught mare.

A century later, the increased speed of hounds and the fast coaches required horses 'pretty well-bred on each side of the head'.

Hunter Breeding. Miss Diana Tuke's Thoroughbred Hunter Galavant, sired by premium stallion Galmont, at the Stowell Park Hunter Trials, Gloucestershire. The stone wall is typical of Cotswold hunting country.

'Mares of *this* variety put to through-bred stallions, and *their produce crossed with pure blood*, create the sort of animal that comes *now* under the denomination of the half-bred English hunter, or cock-tail'. Melton Mowbray produced the best hunters, 'in no place upon earth is condition attended to with so much care, or managed with such skill'. One stable at Quorndon Hall, then the centre of the Quorn hounds, held twenty-eight horses and was so arranged that a visitor standing in the centre could see each individual animal: 'and, being furnished with seats, and lighted by powerful lamps, forms a high treat to the eye of the sportsman on a winter's evening'.

The style, the type of hunter and its *condition* have long since vanished from the hunting scene. Thoroughbred stallions are used to breed hunters, show-jumpers and event horses under the auspices of the HUNTERS' IMPROVEMENT AND NATIONAL LIGHT HORSE BREEDING SOCIETY. These stallions are often not of the type, stamina nor condition of those used decades ago and the mares they are put to are of every size, shape and character. Some, being threequarter-bred, have the characteristics of the true brood mare: when bloodlines are carefully selected, the progeny may result in very good horses indeed. The best make their mark not especially as hunters but as chasers and Olympic Trials horses. Ireland, long famous for the quality of her horses, used to import mares from Eastern Europe. Ireland also bred the native Irish draught mare, which came from the not very large Irish warhorse with Spanish blood. Crosses of Thoroughbred, halfbred and draught-bred produced a strong, tireless, short-legged horse, sound in wind and limb. It makes an excellent jumper but takes time to develop. DMG

Breeding, Pony

There are nine breeds of ponies indigenous to the British Isles: Connemara (Ireland), Dales (from the valleys of the Pennine range in northern England), Dartmoor (Devon), Exmoor (Somerset), Fell (mainly from west of the Pennine range), Highland (Scotland), New Forest (Hampshire), Shetland (Orkney and Shetland), Welsh (Wales). Many are now also bred in private studs all over the British Isles. They can be divided into (1) *Large type:* Connemara, Dales, Fell, Highland, New Forest; (2) *Welsh:* subdivided into Welsh Cobs, evolved from the original Welsh Mountain ponies, registered in Section D of the Welsh Stud Book; Welsh Ponies of Cob Type, also evolved from the Welsh Mountain, not exceeding 13·2 hands (1·37 m), registered in Section C; and Welsh Ponies, also upgraded from the Welsh Mountain, not exceeding 13·2 hands (1·37 m) but lighter in type than the Welsh Ponies of Cob Type, registered in Section B; (3) *Small Type:* Dartmoor, Exmoor, Shetland, Welsh Mountain.

All these ponies have been known since prehistoric times (see Ponies) and have played an important part in Great Britain through the centuries. Despite exploitation by meat racketeers during and after World War II, causing thousands of ponies to go to slaughterhouses when meat was short, breeders wisely retained a nucleus of their best mares. The scarcity of stallions led to various undesirable crossings with other blood, as indeed had occurred in the past. But in the main every breed has retained its own characteristics, and today if there is any crossbreeding the progeny is not entered in the studbooks proper for several generations. Demand, especially overseas, for fully registered ponies is increasing.

Thanks largely to an organization founded in 1952 because of the drift to the slaughterhouses, now internationally known and respected as the 'Ponies of Britain', a campaign was launched to publicize British native ponies and those upgraded from them through Thoroughbred and Arab blood. Much-needed publicity was afforded them and they are now recognized not only for their own virtues but as the foundation stock of all ponies (and many horses) upgraded from them.

Today riding of all kinds has increased enormously. The breeding and owning of children's ponies for pleasure or business has never been greater. Few breeders, however, make a worthwhile profit because of ever-rising costs. There is certainly a demand for British native breeds, and also for ponies of higher performance upgraded by Thoroughbred and/or Arab blood for the show ring, show jumping, hunter trials and events, and for everyday riding, especially with the Pony Club. Demand from overseas as well has increased both the quality and the price, but overseas buyers should remember that the Ponies Act 1969 now prohibits the export of any pony exceeding 12·2 hands (1·27 m) but not exceeding 14·2 hands (1·47 m) for less than £100, or any pony 12·2 hands or under for less than £70. The minimum export value for a Shetland pony is £40. Studs have been founded in Holland, Belgium, France, Scandinavia, Italy, South Africa and Australia, while breeders in the United States are very large customers. Overseas breeders, however, realize that they must import from Britain from time to time to replenish their stock or they lose the famous characterisitics of hardiness, good bone and feet, sagacity and equable temperaments.

One of the greatest assets of the native breeds is their essential use as the foundation for breeding larger and better animals without losing the pony characteristics. Crossing the Large Type native breeds with the Small, however, is not a success. Shetlands should never be crossed with any other breed. To obtain small ponies with quality, Welsh and Dartmoor crossed with Arab have proved successful. Thoroughbred crossed with any of the breeds except Shetland produces animals with a high degree of performance. Possibly the most successful policy of all is the crossing of native/Arab/Thoroughbred in varying proportions. Ponies with these three bloods have enjoyed great success in all fields. The proportion of the three bloods is dictated by the type and size of animal wanted. See also Mountain and Moorland, Riding Ponies. GS

In the United States, especially in the East, the biggest demand is for show ponies of hunter type. Classes for hunter ponies are usually divided into 13 hands (1·32 m) and below, and over 13 hands, not to exceed 14·2 hands (1·47 m). The most popular cross to achieve height is Welsh with Thoroughbred or *vice versa* which usually produces 14·0–14·1 hand (1·42–1·44 m) ponies of quality and ability. The Welsh/Arabian cross produces a fine pony but one that is often the wrong size for the market. Welsh/Arabian crosses below 13 hands, however, are in great demand. Major shows offer breeding classes for crossbreds suitable for children's show ponies. There is also a crossbred registry.

American hunter ponies must show under saddle and over fences, with the main emphasis on the latter. They are judged on their style of jumping, way of moving and manners as well as conformation. A show will usually offer one class under saddle, perhaps three or four classes over fences and a model class. The championship is decided on an accumulation of points earned in each class. MMT

Breeding, Thoroughbred

Breeders of Thoroughbreds have one advantage over breeders of some farm animals and other commercially valuable creatures. It is that Thoroughbreds of both sexes are called upon to perform the primary function of the breed, to race, so that breeders in making their mating plans are able to take short cuts denied to the breeders of, say, certain breeds of cattle in which the males may be valued for beef production or the females for milk yield and the primary function is not attributable to both sexes. A successful racehorse of either sex must have many of the genes required for good performance; the mating of two successful racehorses brings the reasonable prospect of offspring with the aptitude to race. Indeed Thoroughbred progress for nearly three centuries has been based on the principle of mating the best to the best. Breeders of many other commercially valuable creatures have had to place greater reliance on the lengthier processes of the progeny test.

This advantage for breeders is offset by the disadvantage that the Thoroughbred, in order to achieve success on the racecourse, must be a perfect physical machine and have no debilitating mental or temperamental flaws. The racehorse is exposed to very severe physical, mental and temperamental pressures. In this respect it differs from any other commercially valuable creature which depends on the maximum development of a single quality and is not exposed to the same pressures, physical or otherwise. The all-round excellence required in the Thoroughbred precludes the intensive inbreeding which can bring rapid movement in single-quality creatures. Moreover the intensive inbreeding which may be applied successfully to animals required in a particular environment is inapplicable to the Thoroughbred, which is called upon to race, and to breed, in conditions of the widest climatic and geographical diversity. Few other commercially valuable creatures can match its adaptability, for Thoroughbreds of the highest international standard have been bred in conditions as diverse as Canada and Russia, with their long winters of uninterrupted frost, the semi-tropical regions of Florida, the temperate regions of Great Britain, Ireland, France and New Zealand, and the semi-desert regions of California and South Africa. This adaptability has been preserved by the maintenance of genetic variability over periods of twenty or thirty generations since the foundation of the breed.

In spite of this general variability, Thoroughbred bloodlines developed in particular regions tend to evolve characteristics determined by such environmental factors as climate, soil and feeding, and, probably the most important of all, the pattern of racing practised in the countries concerned. The various patterns place contrasting emphasis on such qualities as precocity and later physical maturity, speed and stamina. After generations of separate development bloodlines from different regions and countries may be united and so produce superior individuals through the phenomenon of hybrid vigour or, as it has been called in the context of the Thoroughbred, the international outcross. Horses like the Canadian-bred Nijinsky, winner of the English TRIPLE CROWN in 1970, are examples of the international outcross in action.

Breeders in Great Britain and Ireland face special and unique problems as a result of the varied racing systems of those countries and their consequent diversity of aims. British and Irish breeders have to supply a market for four basic types of Thoroughbred: (1) precociously fast animals capable of winning as two-year-olds and over the sprint distances of five and six furlongs (1,000 m and 1,209 m) thereafter; (2) classic animals capable of excelling over distances from one mile to one and three-quarter miles (1,609 m to 2,816 m) as three-year-olds; (3) stayers capable of excelling over distances of one and a half miles to two and a half miles (2414 m to 4023 m) as three-year-olds and thereafter; (4) jumpers capable of winning over hurdles and fences from four years of age upwards.

Although many animals are bred for dual purposes and there are many intermediate types, the joint breeding industries of Great Britain and Ireland are stratified in a manner unexampled elsewhere. No other country has specialized breeding of horses for hurdling and steeplechasing; in the United States, where annual production of about 23,000 foals is numerically about three times as great as the combined production of Great Britain and Ireland, breeders have the practically single-minded aim of breeding horses of tremendous speed and precocity, able to excel over distances from three furlongs to one mile (603–1,609 m) as two-year-olds, but not required to stay more than one and a quarter miles (2,011 m) as three-year-olds and thereafter.

Since the resources of the British and Irish breeding industries are split among so many different objectives, it is not to be wondered at that their products in any particular category are sometimes inferior to the products of specialized industries abroad. Figures published in Weatherby's Statistical Supplement for 1970 showed that returns made to the General Stud Book, the genealogical record for the Thoroughbreds of Great Britain and Ireland, accounted for 12,457 mares covered the previous year. These mares produced 6,381 living foals in the home countries and 278 abroad. To obtain a true picture of total production of horses for racing in Great Britain and Ireland it is necessary to add production, estimated at not less than 1,000, of non-Thoroughbred or 'halfbred' horses. Non-Thoroughbreds account for about 12 per cent of all horses registered for racing, mostly but not exclusively for jumping. At present there are no properly authenticated breeding records of non-Thoroughbred racehorses, but, by a decision of the racing authorities in 1971, a Register of Non-Thoroughbred Mares is to be set up and breeding records kept to the same standards as the General Stud Book.

There are about 7,000 breeders of Thoroughbreds in Great Britain and Ireland. The large majority (nearly 90 per cent) of them own three mares or fewer. At the other end of the scale, only about ten breeders in the two countries own more than 30 mares. Most of the really big concentrations of mares are in the hands of private breeders, whose studs are stocked with animals of the highest class, and who use the best stallions with the aim of breeding horses capable of winning the Classic and other important races.

At least half of the total production of racehorses in Great Britain and Ireland is in the hands of commercial breeders who supply the market for foals, yearlings and, in the case of jumpers, more mature horses. In 1970, 2,345 yearlings were sold at public auction, mostly at Newmarket, Doncaster and Dublin. There is a subtle difference in the objectives of private and commercial breeders, for, whereas the private breeder aims solely to produce winners, the commercial breeder has his eye firmly on the price realized in the sale ring, and has to follow the often capricious dictates of fashion. Private breeders have been the mainstay of Classic production in the past and are likely to remain so.

Soaring demand and soaring prices on a worldwide scale have resulted in soaring production of Thoroughbreds. During the 1960s production in Great Britain and Ireland increased by about a third, but at the same time factors like the syndication of top-class stallions for sums up to £2 million put the most fashionable stock out of the reach of all but the richest private breeders and the commercial breeders with access to large capital resources. Nevertheless the Thoroughbred refused to be confined within the straitjacket of big business and horses like Brigadier Gerard, a brilliant performer on the international scene, continued to show that good Thoroughbreds can be bred from slender resources and kept the hopes of small breeders alive. PW

While most Thoroughbred breeders in North America concentrate on racing precocity, there remain a few who attempt to produce classic stock on the Anglo-Irish model. The increasing successes of runners bred in North America but raced in Europe, where opportunities for such stock are much greater than at home, bespeaks the international status of such breeders.

European successes and the relative ease of modern horse transportation have accelerated the international traffic in horses.

Thoroughbred Breeding. Mr and Mrs J. Hislop's Brigadier Gerard, out of La Paiva by Queen's Hussar, is a very much better racehorse than his pedigree might have suggested, although descended in the female line from Pretty Polly, who won the 100 Guineas, Oaks and St Leger in 1904. Having won 17 out of his 18 races, he was nominated Racehorse of the Year by the British Press in 1972 and was at stud in 1973.

Breton. *Below:* Breton heavy draught mares
Bottom: A *Postier Breton* team

Not only have owners from Europe, Japan, South America and other distant parts of the world become important buyers at North American auctions, but breeders from Europe and, in particular, Japan have begun to establish branches of their home breeding farms in North America, in order to gain ready access to American blood.

In the United States, Kentucky remains the chief centre of Thoroughbred breeding, as it has been since the late nineteenth century. But recently its pre-eminence has been seriously challenged, especially by Florida, California and Maryland. Every state except Alaska produces some Thoroughbreds.

Canadian Thoroughbred production is concentrated in Ontario, although there are also breeding farms from Quebec to British Columbia, particularly in Alberta and Manitoba. Mexican Thoroughbred breeding is concentrated around the capital, Mexico City. FTP

Breton and Breton Heavy Draught

The five *départements* of Brittany have the densest equine population in France. Saddle and draught horses have co-existed since the time of the primitive indigenous horse, ancestor of the *bidet*, a pacer much in demand in the Middle Ages, and the strong and hardy *sommier*. The Corlay horse, 14·3–15·1 hands (1·50–1·55 m), crossed with ARAB and THOROUGHBRED, a saddle or light coach horse, is now rare. The *Postier Breton*, a coach or light draught horse of 15·1 hands (about 1·55 m), crossed in the nineteenth century with the NORFOLK TROTTER, is very representative of the local breed, and was formerly famous for use with light artillery.

The Breton heavy draught horse, enlarged in the nineteenth and twentieth centuries by PERCHERON, ARDENNAIS or BOULONNAIS blood, has the special characteristics of the Breton: strength for a relatively limited weight (minimum 1,212 lb or 550 kg), lively gaits and hardiness. Noted for improving other breeds of draught horses, the Breton adapts to all climates. Its head is rather concave and expressive, neck strong and arched, body wide and short, limbs very muscular. The strawberry roan coat is much in demand, the black rare. The common studbook (common to both the Breton and Breton Heavy Draught) has been closed since 1951. ES

Bridles

Bridles fall into five main divisions. The simplest form is the *snaffle*, employing a single mouthpiece which may be either jointed at the centre or half-moon shaped (mullen mouth). The latter, particularly when made of rubber, or to a lesser extent of vulcanite, is the mildest of all bitting arrangements, as the 'nutcracker' action of the jointed bit is absent. The action of the snaffle may be upward against the corners of the lips, when the head is held low, or directly across the 'bars' of the lower jaw when the head is raised and the nose is held slightly in advance of the vertical.

The *gag* bridle is an accentuated form of snaffle aimed at raising the head; this is achieved by rounding the leather cheekpieces and passing them through holes at top and bottom of the bit ring, the rein being attached directly to the cheekpiece where

Bridles. (1) Adjustable drop noseband and egg-butt snaffle. (2) Short-cheek slidemouth Weymouth and wire-ring bridoon with double-link curb chain. (3) Kimblewick (Pelham). (4) With a Pelham, no definite action results from either rein.

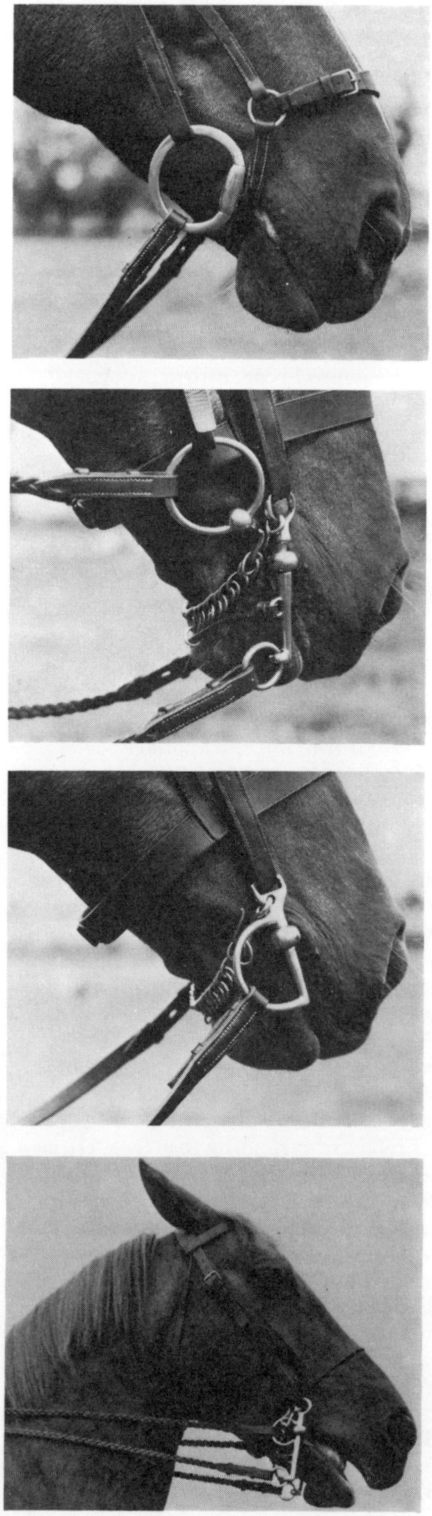

it emerges from the lower hole. Pressure on the rein, therefore, results in a strong upward action of the bit against the corners of the mouth and a corresponding elevation of the horse's head.

The *Weymouth* or *double* bridle employs both snaffle (to raise the head) and a curb bit with curb chain which has the ability to lower the head and to retract the nose according to the pressures applied. The mouthpiece of the curb bit, by being made with a central port, allowing room for the tongue, bears directly upon the bars, while the downward pressure thus induced is assisted by a corresponding pressure on the poll made possible by the movement of the eye, to which the cheekpiece is attached, on the cheekpiece itself and thence, through the head strap, onto the poll. The curb chain, tightening in the curb groove, causes a retraction of the nose and assists flexion in the lower jaw. The severity of the curb depends upon the length of the curb cheek, a long curb having greater leverage than a short one.

A *Pelham* bit endeavours to produce the same action as that of a double but employs a single mouthpiece and a cheek fitted with bit rings. Snaffle action occurs in response to pressure on the top (snaffle) rein and curb action when the lower rein is operated. Since many Pelhams are made with mullen mouths pressure is put on the tongue rather than the bars, as is the case with the double bridle, and is consequently less definite. Other types of mouthpiece, ported or jointed, may be used in Pelham bits and the action is then altered accordingly. Bitless describes various types of bridle that act upon the nose and do not employ pressures on the mouth itself through the agency of a bit. See also Nosebands, Accoutrements, Bits and Bitting. EHE

British Equestrian Federation

A body formed in 1972 representing both the BRITISH HORSE SOCIETY and BRITISH SHOW JUMPING ASSOCIATION whose aim is to co-ordinate the policy interests of common concern to both these bodies in dealing with the FÉDÉRATION ÉQUESTRE INTERNATIONALE and other national federations.

British Horse Society

The B.H.S., the national organization responsible for equitation, guarding the interests of horses and riders, promoting the art of riding and encouraging the care and welfare of ponies, is the national representative on the FÉDÉRATION ÉQUESTRE INTERNATIONALE; it runs the ROYAL INTERNATIONAL HORSE SHOW, controls and regulates HORSE TRIALS and DRESSAGE, and, with the co-operation of the BRITISH SHOW JUMPING ASSOCIATION, selects and trains the teams to represent Great Britain in all international and Olympic competitions. It is the parent body of the PONY CLUB and of the affiliated RIDING SCHOOLS. It operates through its council and a number of committees: Combined Training, Dressage, Riding Clubs, Horse and Pony Breeds, Shows, Riding Establishments Act, Horsemanship and Examinations, Development, Royal International Horse Show, British Equestrian Team. It was formed in 1947 by an amalgamation of two separate societies, the National Horse Association, which broadly represented the interests of the ordinary rider and of riding schools, and the Institute of the Horse, which concentrated on advanced equitation. It holds examinations every year for Instructors' and Assistant Instructors' Certificates, and for Fellowships of the British Horse Society, of which two are awarded each year, and inspects riding schools which apply for its approval certificates. Its headquarters are The National Equestrian Centre, Stoneleigh, Kenilworth, Warwickshire, CV8 2LR. CEGH

British Show Jumping Association

In 1921 a number of show-jumping riders including Tommy Glencross, Fred Foster, Frank Alison, Phil Blackmore, Sam Marsh and Tom Taylor, decided that this Association should be formed. It came into being within a year with Col V. D. S. Williams and Col 'Taffy' Walwyn as joint secretaries. The original membership was 100 and the annual income £200.

The Association quickly grew and by the late 1920s was accepted as the governing body for show jumping in Britain. Towards the end of the 1930s, thanks to the lack of success by British riders (other than cavalry officers) in the international field, largely due to important differences between B.S.J.A. rules and those of the FÉDÉRATION ÉQUESTRE INTERNATIONALE, British show jumping was at a low ebb. After World War II, however, Col Sir Michael Ansell became Chairman of the B.S.J.A. and revolutionized the sport so that British riders now have a reputation second to none. There are now 10,000 members of the Association. DW

Broken Wind

This condition can occur in any horse in an acute or chronic form but is more common in ponies. It is recognized by a prolonged low, dry cough and a double flank movement on expiration. A disease of domestication, it is associated with poorly ventilated stables and dusty hay. The changes that occur in the lungs are irreversible but the condition can be alleviated by an outdoor environment and judicious feeding. CF

Bronco, Bronc see Mustang

Brumby

The Australian Brumby is descended from imported horses turned loose on the ranges

Above: **Brumby.** Descended from animals imported in the nineteenth century, these semi-wild horses are found in many remote parts of Australia.

Above right: **Bucking.** A bronc 'crow-hops' at the Calgary Stampede.

Below right: **Budyonny**

during and after the great Gold Rush of 1851. There they bred indiscriminately and through lack of selection and inferior grazing they deteriorated to 'scrub' horses, became very numerous, and in 1962 culling by mechanized methods was resorted to, landrovers and helicopters being used to shoot down many animals. The Brumby is said to be difficult to tame, although why this should be so is hard to understand: in South America horses are often kept in a semi-wild state on the steppe lands and ranches and when rounded up and trained they make useful ranch ponies. DMG

Brushing

Injury in the region of the fetlock joint caused by the inner branch of the shoe of the opposite foot. See Feet and Shoeing. CF

B.S.J.A. see British Show Jumping Association

Buckaroo, Buckeroo

This is the colloquial name for the Australian cowboy or herdsman (chiefly of sheep) in the Outback. The name comes from their renown as 'bronco-busters' of completely untrained horses, especially of the WALERS which share with the American bronco the dubious reputation of being the only genuine buckjumpers (see Bucking): they land stiff-legged between each jump and combine or alternate their bucks with a rear, a manoeuvre known as 'sun-fishing'. LFB

Buckhounds, Buckhunting see Staghunting and Buckhunting

Bucking

A horse that wishes to rid itself of an unwanted rider normally rears, 'crow-hops' (makes a stiff-legged jump) or kicks. What is wanted in a rodeo arena, however, is for the animal to combine the stiff-legged jumping with high kicking. In order to accentuate this, the horse is fitted with a flank strap, a leather strap fleece-lined to prevent injury, approximately where a belt would fit on a man. Despite charges of cruelty, if properly fitted it does not cause pain but encourages the animal to kick high in the air.

The modern rodeo stock contractor must pay a high price for a horse that bucks consistently well. There is no such thing as a bucking breed: any horse that does well in the arena can qualify. A good bucker needs strength and substance to take the strain, but must not be too heavy. The best are usually crossbred, combining the strength of the draught horse breeds with the courage and agility of the lighter breeds. Today stock contractors are attempting to breed an aptitude for bucking into their animals; before long a new breed, known as the bucking horse, may emerge. CL

Buckskin see Colours and Markings

Budyonny

The Budyonny is used for riding, sport, cavalry, transport, harness and farm work. Budyonny stallions have been extremely valuable in developing and improving the KAZAKH, KIRGIZ, DON, and other Russian breeds. There are three types: massive, Eastern, and middle. All have a strong constitution, well-developed muscles, a rather massive structure but the appearance of a true riding horse, and an energetic but calm temperament. The head is medium-sized and dry, with a straight or slightly concave profile. The neck is long and set on high; often it is curved. The withers are high, the back relatively short, wide and even, the loins wide, medium long, and muscular. The croup is usually long, the shoulder long and slanting, the ribs long and rounded, the legs dry with good bone and clearly outlined tendons. The pasterns are medium long, usually properly slanted. The hoof is medium large, regularly formed, with sturdy, good bone. Faults that tend to occur in this breed are spreading fore legs, clumsiness, and hind legs that are too straight. Chestnut is the most prevalent colour, but brown, bay and black are also common; greys almost never occur.

Average height at withers for stallions is 15·2½ hands (1·61 m), for mares 15·2 hands (1·57 m); bone below the knee for stallions 8½ in (21·8 cm) for mares 7¾ in (19·8 cm).

The Budyonny shows good, productive, regular movement in all paces and jumps well. The stallions have been successful in international dressage, and Budyonny horses have covered 1,200 m (¾ mile) in 1 min

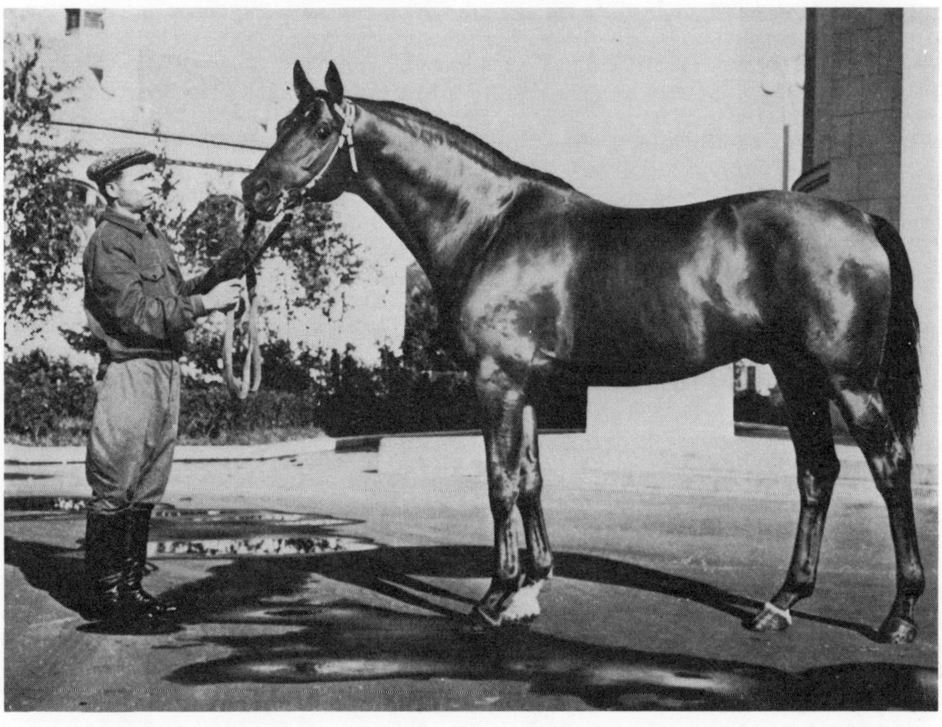

14 sec, 8,000 m (5 miles) in 11 min 30 sec.

The Budyonny is now bred in the southern parts of Russia, in the Ukraine, and in the Kazakh and Kirgiz republics of the Soviet Union. Don and English Thoroughbreds were crossed with local steppe horses, especially the Kazakh and Kirgiz, to produce the Budyonny named after the great Soviet cavalry leader of the Civil War. Don-Kazakh crosses, though hardy, were prone to certain faults in the legs, and the low-set neck and insufficient withers made them uncomfortable to ride. Kazakh-Thoroughbred crosses, on the other hand, moved freely and gracefully but were not sufficiently hardy or fertile. Don mares put to Thoroughbred stallions produced better crosses than vice versa. By 1948 the breed was fully developed and recognized. WOF

Bulgaria

The Bulgarians settled in the Balkan peninsula from the plain of the Russian Volga river 1300 years ago. Their life was closely linked with the use of the horse: as transport during almost uninterrupted periods of wars and migrations, as a source of meat and milk, and, later, in agriculture as a draught animal. The horse was therefore appreciated and treated with great affection by the Bulgarians; no Bulgarian was considered genuine unless he was a clever horseman. The flag of the ancient Bulgarians, consisting of horses' taiis, also indicated the importance of horses.

During Bulgaria's long history, horse breeding played an important role in the country's development. Systematic improvements were started only after Bulgaria was freed from Turkish rule (1878), which had lasted over five centuries. The first studs were organized at the end of the nineteenth century with horses imported from Austria-Hungary, Russia and other countries. Arab and partly Thoroughbred and halfbred stallions were used to improve the Bulgarian breeds at an early stage. During the last forty years the use of Arab stallions has decreased and improvement has been based mostly upon different halfbred stallions, in certain districts the RUSSIAN HEAVY DRAUGHT, HUÇUL and KABARDIN breeds serving this purpose. Breeding in Bulgaria for many years created three local halfbred breeds: the EAST BULGARIAN, PLEVEN and Danubian, all fine draught horses. Pleven and East Bulgarian horses are also excellent riding horses.

By the end of 1970 there were some 170,000 horses in Bulgaria, a decline of over 65 per cent since World War II as a result of fast development of cooperatives which led to the increased mechanization of agriculture. The halfbreds predominate but there are also pure Arabs, Russian Heavy Draught horses and other breeds. The horses with the highest reproductive performance (some 5,000 mares and 450 stallions) are

Bulgaria. In this photograph, taken in Czechoslovakia, the two horses on the left, Soleika and Narvik, are East Bulgarian.

reared at six state studs, nine stallion studs and many agricultural state and cooperative farms. Most horses are used in agriculture and forestry; the number in this category is decreasing although the rate has now slowed down. The demand for riding horses, however, increases every year. Amateur riding and pony trekking around seaside and mountain health resorts are very popular. Horses are raced at the Central Racecourse in Sofia and at several regional racecourses. There are also modern stadia for competitive sports, one in Sofia and about twenty in the provinces run by the Bulgarian Athletics and Sports Union. Many horses, mostly halfbred, have been exported from Bulgaria to various western European and other countries over the last 10–15 years. Breeding is directed entirely by the Ministry of Agriculture and Food Industry and its provincial units, assisted by workers using the latest scientific methods. Scientific work on horse breeding is concentrated at the Central Research Institute of Animal Breeding at Kostinbrod and the Department of Horse Breeding at the Higher Agricultural Institute. VP, II

Bullfighting see Rejoneador

Burghley

The site, in Northamptonshire, England, of the Burghley Horse Trials, started in 1961 at the Marquess of Exeter's seat. These trials are always held in late summer and are now considered on a par with the BADMINTON Horse Trials held in the spring. It has become almost traditional for the top riders to start with Badminton and finish with Burghley each year. The first winner in 1961 was Miss Annelei Drummond-Hay riding Merely-a-Monarch; in 1971 the winner was H.R.H. the Princess Anne riding Doublet. See Horse Trials. JHew

Burma Pony

The Burma pony, akin in type to the Manipuri, is chiefly bred in the Shan Hills of East Burma. It was used for polo by British officers stationed in Burma at the end of the nineteenth century. Average height is about 13 hands (1·32 m). It was described thus by Captain Hayes: 'The body of the Burma pony has great depth in comparison with its length. For a saddle pony, he has a nice head and neck and fair shoulders; but his croup is too drooping. He is much better "topped" than he is below his elbows and stifles. His forearms and gaskins are poor, and he has sickle hocks'. CEGH

Reference: Capt. M. H. Hayes, *The Points of the Horse*, London, 1893, 7th revised ed. 1969.

Burro see Ass, Domestic

Buttero

The buttero is a mounted herdsman of the Roman *Campagna* and Roman and Tuscan *Maremma*, corresponding to the American COWBOY, Argentine and Brazilian GAUCHO or Mexican VAQUERO. The name *buttero* comes from the Greek *boter* ('sticker of bulls') for he carries a long stick with which to round up cattle and horses. He is usually accompanied by a white Maremmana sheep dog and mounted on a MAREMMANA horse which is bridle-wise and has the same easy lope as the American cowpony. His tack is also similar to that of the cowboy: a heavy saddle (*bardella*) with a horn around which he winds his lasso. The buttero's most characteristic features are a wide black sombrero, goatskin 'chaps' and a great black cape. Like the Western cowboy, he is fast disappearing, but he has been immortalized in the paintings of the Anglo-American artist R. Henry Coleman. LFB

Buying and Selling

The buying and selling of horses is still very largely in the hands of the horse dealers. Every horse dealer of any standing will have a number of 'spotters' in various parts of the country, and he will have a very fair knowledge of the horses exhibited in the shows, run in the point-to-points, and hunted with the packs of hounds of his district, and running, unbroken, in the local fields. Those who slip through the net are bought and sold privately, but where any sizeable sum of money is concerned there is generally at least one horse dealer who is going to take his percentage of the profits.

Every advantage is to be gained from recourse to a reputable dealer. If he has a reputation he will guard it jealously. He will stand by the horse he sells, and if it proves to be unsuitable he will take it back and supply another in its place. There is no such guarantee if a horse is bought from a private individual, or even when purchased at auction, unless it can be proved that it does not fulfil its conditions of warranty.

It is some safeguard to have the intended purchase examined by a veterinary surgeon, as there is then little likelihood of buying an unsound horse. With a veterinary surgeon and a horse dealer on the side of the buyer, the margin of error is narrowed still further. Buying a horse or pony at auction is not a practice to be recommended to the novice owner; even the most experienced horsemen have been known to make expensive mistakes when buying a horse under the hammer. See also Auction Sales. PMM

Buzkashi see Mounted Games

Byerley Turk

An Eastern horse captured at the siege of Buda from the Turks, brought to England by Capt Byerley who rode him at the Battle of the Boyne and through all the wars of King William in Ireland. He was never raced but proved an excellent sire although he covered few mares. One of his most famous descendants was Herod, bred in 1758. The ancestry of the Byerley Turk is obscure; there were hundreds of different strains of horses in the Near East and many were exported from Aleppo during the seventeenth and eighteenth centuries. This stallion is renowned as the eldest of the three principal sires who helped to found the English THOROUGHBRED. DMG

Cabuli Pony see Kabuli Pony under India and Pakistan

Cadre Noir see France, Equitation in

Café-au-lait Horses French name for ISABELLAS

Calabrese see Italy

Calf Roping see Rodeo

Calgary Stampede

The largest of the three top RODEOS (the Pendleton (Oregon) Round-Up, the Cheyenne (Wyoming) Frontier Days and the Calgary (Alberta, Canada) Stampede) is the Calgary Exhibition and Stampede; one of the richest and best-attended rodeos, it offers racing, a funfair and fireworks as well. CL

Calico see Colours and Markings

Calkins (Caulkins, Caulks)

In order to raise the heel of a shoe, or to prevent slipping, the heel of the shoe is turned down to form a wedge or calkin.

Below: **Byerley Turk.** The eldest of the three famous founders of the Thoroughbred, the Byerley Turk's male line descends to the present through Herod.

Bottom: **Calgary Stampede.** Chuckwagon racing is one of Calgary's most exciting events. In each race four wagons compete, each accompanied by four outriders.

Where only one calkin is required on the outside heel, the inside heel is built up into a wedge to balance. For riding horses safety studs have largely replaced calkins to prevent slipping. See Feet and Shoeing. DRT

Camargue

The Camargue horse lives in the marshes of the Rhône delta on the Mediterranean and its environs. The origin of the breed is very ancient. It was mentioned at the beginning of the Christian era and many experts believe it to be descended from the prehistoric horse of Solutré. What is certain is that, in spite of crossings over the centuries, often with BARBS, its habitat and free life in *manades* (herds) have given it special characteristics, including exceptional hardiness. It is a small horse of 13·1–14·1 hands (1·35–1·45 m) with a brownish coat at birth which lightens to grey. Of primitive appearance, it has a rough coat, a straight, square head, a short, strong neck, often sloping rump and strong limbs. Camargues are ridden by *gardians*, the local cowboys, to herd the many black bulls, the region's principal wealth. Mainly because of the independence of the breeders, the Camargue has only been officially recognized as a breed since 1967. The breeders are now grouped in an association and admit a minimum of discipline and the breed is encouraged by the State Administration. The first horses bought by the State Stud Administration and trained in a conventional way have confirmed that the Camargue is potentially an excellent saddle horse. ES

Campdrafting see Australia, Cutting Horse

Campolino see Brazil

Canada

Canada could well be a 'sleeping giant' within the realm of international equestrian competition. Relative newcomers to horse sports, Canadians began to take an active interest in the early 1960s. Since then the number of horses has risen from 200,000 to somewhere between 800,000 and 1,000,000.

Growth in any of the many areas of pleasure and recreational horse activities has been almost entirely due to the efforts of one or two people. Before E. P. Taylor took an active interest in Thoroughbred horse-racing, tracks, facilities and the calibre of the Canadian-bred Thoroughbred left much to be desired. Today Canadian Thoroughbred tracks are second to none and Woodbine Racetrack just north of Toronto is outstanding. Windfields Farm and Mr Taylor also provided Canadians with the outstanding homegrown product Northern Dancer, leading sire for North America in 1971 and sire of the famous Nijinsky.

Under the leadership of the late Anatole Pieregorodski, Canada brought home its first Olympic medal in 1956, won by the three-day-event team of Jim Elder on Collean, John Rumble on Kilroy and Brian Herbinson on Tara. Pieregorodski's death in 1961 dealt a sad blow to Canada's Olympic aspirations. It was not until 1968 that Canada was able to field a complete equestrian team in all three Olympic disciplines. On the last day of the Mexico Games Jim Elder, Tom Gayford and Jim Day won the Grand Prix des Nations and brought home Canada's only gold medal. This win provided the necessary incentive for much-

Canada. Racing at the Northland Race Track, Edmonton, Alberta

Colour plate: **Horse in Art.** The 'bronze' horses at St Mark's Cathedral, Venice, were thought to be by the Greek sculptor Lysippos but were possibly a Roman copy of a Greek sculpture. *Overleaf:* **Horse in Art.** *The Grosvenor Hunt,* painting by George Stubbs, R.A.

needed investment in Canadian horses and horse shows. Individual and corporate donations to the sport have been a tremendous boon.

Today, Canada's strength is in young riders. Of the fourteen medallists at the 1971 Pan American Games in Cali, Columbia, all but four were under thirty. The two people most responsible for fostering this present reserve of young horsemen were Lou Mikucki and Landon Bladen. One of Mikucki's greatest achievements was in establishing Canada's first truly international junior competition, an event which attracts youngsters from all over the world and offers Canadian riders the type of competition they will find on European circuits. Mrs Bladen headed the Pony Club movement which now has a membership of over 3,000 with branches across the country.

Dressage has recently gained increasing popularity, inspired primarily by the young Canadian dressage competitor Christilot Hanson.

Standardbred racing is extraordinarily popular with Canadian racing fans. Most of the harness race meetings are held at night, under the lights. In 1970 Canada boasted the leading harness driver in North America, Herve Fillion, who in 1971 broke his own record by winning 543 races and grossing $1,915,945 in purses. In 1971 the Canadian horse Fresh Yankee became the first North American-bred Standardbred to earn more than $1,000,000 in prize money.

The Quarter Horse population is increasing; by the beginning of 1972 registered Quarter Horses numbered slightly fewer than 20,000.

With mechanized farming and the trend toward urban living, the draught horse population has decreased drastically in the last fifty years. In the early days the Clydesdale was numerically the most important breed; Percherons and Belgian Ardennes began to be popular in the early 1920s. Since 1966 many draught mares have been crossbred with Thoroughbreds to develop a good, strong field hunter. ML

Canadian Pacer see Saddlebred Horse

Cape Cart see Carriages, History of

Cape Horse

The South African Cape Horse, a popular breed in the early nineteenth century and distinguished in the Boer War, was derived from horses imported by the Dutch East India Company in the seventeenth century, with later additions of ARAB, BARB and THOROUGHBRED blood. It has declined since the end of the nineteenth century and is now represented by its descendant the BASUTO PONY.

Capped Elbow

An inflammatory distension of the subcutaneous bursa at the point of the elbow, sometimes called a 'shoe boil' because it is often caused by bruising by the inner branch of the shoe when the horse is lying down. CF

Capped Hock

An inflammatory swelling at the point of the hock, due to injury to its subcutaneous bursa. CF

Caprilli, Federico

Captain Federico Caprilli was born in April 1868 in Leghorn. After attending the Rome and the Modena Military academies, he was posted as a second lieutenant to the Pied-

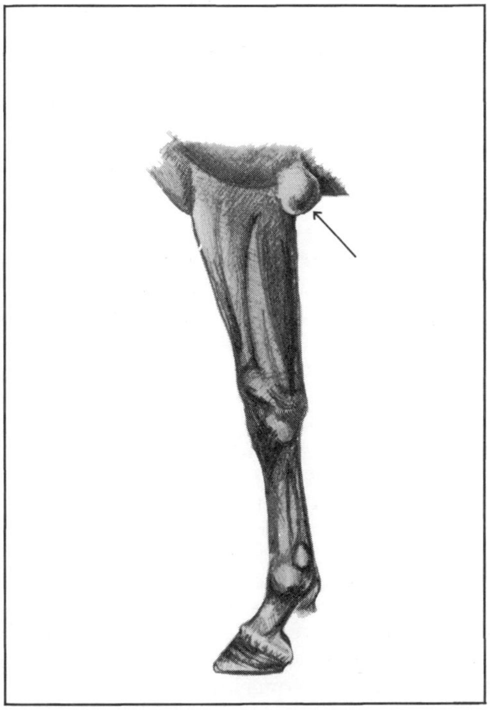

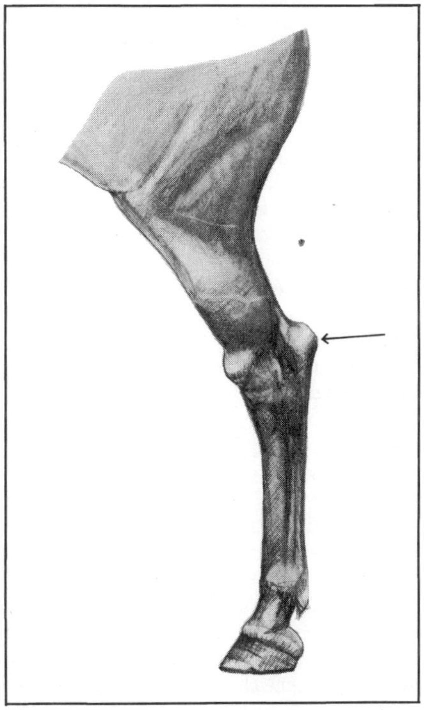

Top: **Cape Horse.** A Boer War volunteer with his troop horse

Above left: **Capped Elbow** (arrowed), shown here with Windgall
Above right: **Capped Hock** (arrowed), shown here with Bog Spavin

Colour plate: **Accoutrements.** The armour shown on this French equestrian model (*c.* 1640) is more solid than the earlier field-armour shown on page 41.

mont regiment at Saluzzo and later transferred to the Genoa Cavalry regiment stationed at Gallarate, near Turin.

After several years at PINEROLO, the Cavalry School founded by King Louis XV, he was nominated Instructor at TOR DI QUINTO in 1894. He next succeeded Cesare Paderni as instructor at Pinerolo and abolished the classical school of riding then in fashion, which he considered totally unsuited to cross-country riding. After various private experiments he formally introduced, against much official opposition, the FORWARD SEAT, negotiating for the first time the famous *Scivalone* (slide) at Tor di Quinto in this position, and proving his theories by winning innumerable competitions as well as the Army Horse Championship, riding his Irish horse 'Pouf' in this manner. By 1907 the Forward Seat was officially adopted by the entire Italian cavalry.

Purely a cavalry man possessed of no literary abilities, Caprilli wrote only a few notes on the Forward Seat which appeared in the Italian *Revista di Cavalleria* in 1901. These were interpreted to the English-speaking world by his friend and pupil, Major Piero SANTINI, in his books and lectures. The notes themselves were translated verbatim by Santini but did not appear in book form until after his death.

Caprilli died at Turin in December 1907 while riding his horse at a walk, probably from a heart attack or possibly as a result of a previous injury to his head. LFB

Caprilli. The birth of the Forward Seat: Captain Federico Caprilli jumping in 1906

Capriole see Airs, Classical

Careers with Horses

Although only the chosen few occupy the most coveted positions in the horse world, such as a leading National Hunt or flat race jockey, or rider of a string of top-class show jumpers complete with a deep-pursed owner to pay the bills, there are many rewarding careers with horses which provide a life rich in everything but financial gain.

Those who have not grown up in a horse-minded family need not be at a disadvantage when it comes to embracing a career with horses. There are plenty of good riding schools where the rudiments of horse lore may be acquired, and a couple of years spent as a working pupil (see Working Pupil Scheme) under a good instructor is an adequate grounding for the qualifying examinations which will enable those who pass them to derive their living from the horse. The racing stables attract the more adventurous young people, most of whom have some preliminary knowledge of horses and riding and aspire to become jockeys after serving their apprenticeship. But there is little scope for girls in racing stables. It is the riding school which provides the better opportunities for girls, who may later decide to take up work in hunting stables, in private stables with hunters or show horses, or to remain in riding schools as instructors or stable managers. Breeding studs provide another outlet; lightweight riders are always in demand for breaking high-class children's ponies.

The BRITISH HORSE SOCIETY insists on candidates for their examinations being 17½ years old, and recommends that a good general education is the best foundation for a career with horses, where responsibility and the ability to make sound decisions quickly are all-important. Students may then study for their instructor's certificate, horsemaster's certificate, stable manager's or equitation certificate.

Hunt service demands long hours and hard work, but for those who love the chase and all that goes with it this is a rewarding life. Here, again, there is more opportunity for boys than for girls, and so far the few women huntsmen have served only in an amateur capacity, though female whippers-in are not unknown in the less fashionable hunting countries.

Stud work is fascinating for those whose interest lies in breeding; though few women are really capable of handling a stallion during the covering season, they are frequently better with the mares and foals than many men. Long-reining and backing yearlings is another job that can be well done by a capable girl, although by and large the Thoroughbred studs rely very largely on male labour, and girls are more acceptable to the numerous pony studs that exist throughout Great Britain and increasingly overseas.

Few aspire no higher than being a groom, but the right sort of groom who knows his job and is conscientious is always in demand. Those who like to travel are well suited by situations with international show jumpers, dressage horses or three-day event horses, and British grooms are often

Carriages of Antiquity. 'Darius the Great King' hunted lion from a chariot with spoked wheels (sixth-fifth century B.C.).

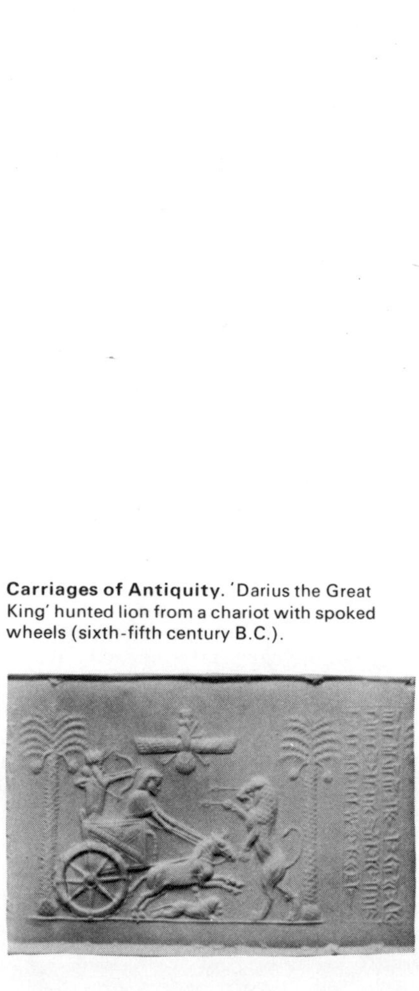

sought by stables in continental Europe and in the United States.

The main requirements are knowledge, experience and common sense learned in a correct school, plus the ability to work hard and to put the horses' needs first. There is no substitute for a sound basic training under an old-time horsemaster, and those who employ young people with horses invariably prefer this background to any number of letters after the name, which are sometimes awarded on theoretical knowledge rather than on its practical application. PMM

In the United States, careers with horses occupy a smaller proportion of the total work force than in Great Britain. There are, therefore, fewer job opportunities but greater financial rewards.

There is a shortage of competent farriers and also of veterinarians for large animals. Training for careers in these fields is provided by a few specialized organizations but mainly by state universities. Cornell and the University of Pennsylvania offer perhaps the most prestigious diplomas in veterinary science, with an increasing number of young women among the graduates.

Apart from stable work, jobs with horses can be found mostly in instruction: at riding academies, boarding stables and summer camps, the latter being of special interest since such work does not impair a rider's amateur status. Racing stables have begun to accept women as grooms, assistant trainers, and as jockeys. Show stables have long provided job opportunities for women. The American horse show world includes many professional riders, who far outnumber the amateurs in Open classes.

Most other careers with horses fall into the category of self-employment, such as horse-dealing and rodeo riding (in which trick riding and barrel racing are the domain of girl riders). MAS

Caribbean Islands see West Indies

Carriages of Antiquity

Evidence of drawn vehicles has been found by archaeologists as far back as the Mesolithic period. It is believed that primitive sliding vehicles or sleds of skins or tree bark were used very early; they are still used in Lapland, northern Asia and Sumer, and have also been found in Egypt, Assyria and Sumer. American Indians developed the travois, drawn by dogs before they acquired the horse. A similar vehicle, the slide car, was used in Ireland and parts of Scotland from early times.

Little is known of the transition of the sliding vehicle to one that rolled. The earliest evidence of the use of wheels is a sketch of a sled on wheels in account tablets of the Inanna temple at Brech in Sumer (about 3500 B.C.), indicating that wheels may have evolved from rollers put under a sled. Remains of actual wheeled vehicles have been found in royal tombs at Ur, Susa and Kish (3000–2000 B.C.). Models and pictures of the same period have been found in Assyria, north Syria, the Indus valley, Turkmenia, Georgia, south Russia, China, the Balkans, Sardinia, Spain, Scandinavia and the British Isles.

The oldest known wheels are 'tripartite disks', three flat pieces of wood fitted together to form a circle and held in place by two wooden battens fixed across them. Through the middle plank ran the axle arm, secured on the outside of the wheel hub by a linchpin. It is not known whether the axles were rigidly fixed to the vehicle or

Carriages of Antiquity. *Below:* A turf slide-car with straw-harnessed mountain pony, Glendun, Co. Antrim, *c.* 1900
Bottom: Cheyenne Indian travois at Lame Deer, Montana.

Carriages of Antiquity. The Elamite army hasten into battle (seventh century B.C.).

revolved with the wheels. This type of wheel was widely used: it has been found from Asia Minor to northern Europe. A later improvement was the addition of a wooden rim studded with nails for protection.

The much lighter spoked wheel first appears pictorially in northern Mesopotamia in about 2000 B.C. and was rapidly developed for war chariots in Egypt from about 1600 B.C. China had spoked wheels from about 1300 B.C., Sweden about 1000 B.C. and Central Europe a little later.

It is thought that paired draught animals antedate the single animal because draught animals, usually oxen, had in most places been used in pairs in ploughs. The four-wheeled chariots shown on the Standard of Ur (see Onager) are drawn by yoked pairs of onagers. Yokes were unsuitable, however, for equines, and so additional harness consisting of girths and broad breastbands were added. Unfortunately, as the breastband was attached to the top of the yoke it pressed against the animal's throat and made it difficult for it to breathe and therefore restricted the weight it could pull. Oddly enough an efficient horse harness did not exist until about the beginning of the tenth century A.D. when the horse collar was invented. Apparently only oxen and onagers were used for draught work until about 2000 B.C. when the horse began to be used by the HITTITES. It was generally associated with the fast new lightweight war chariots with spoked wheels while carts and wagons were still generally drawn by oxen. See also Accoutrements. PD

Reference: Dr V. Gordon Childe, 'Rotary Motion and Wheeled Vehicles' in *A History of Technology*, Vol. 1, London, 1954.
Johann Christian Ginzrot, *Die Wagen und Führwerker der Griechen und Homer und Anderen Alten Völker,* Munich, 1817.
Ezra M. Stratton, *The World on Wheels*, New York, 1817.
E. M. Jope, 'Vehicles and Harness' in *A History of Technology*, Vol. 1, London, 1954.

Carriages, History of

Man made much use of the saddle and pack horse before the carriage came into general use. The earliest carriage in perfect condition to be found today is the State Chariot of Tutankhamen (1361–1352 B.C.) in the Cairo Museum. The Romans used many heavy four-wheeled wagons as well as their chariots, but these were not adopted by other nations. The first recorded carriage to be built in Great Britain was by William Rippon for the second Earl of Rutland in 1555. Rippon is also recorded as having supplied carriages to Mary, Queen of Scots, in 1556 and to Queen Elizabeth I of England in 1564. There is no record of any of these carriages being in existence today. The oldest existing carriage in Britain, believed to have been built in 1672, is in the Maidstone Museum in Kent.

The true age of horsedrawn vehicles can be said to have arrived in the eighteenth century. The State Coach in the Royal Mews is dated 1762 and a detailed price list survives to show what it cost. The Royal Mail coaches, soon joined by the road coaches, really started the carriage era (see Coaching). The old and rigid whip springs gave way to improved types of suspension; the more delicately adapted C-springs were increasingly used.

The other carriage of importance to the innkeeper who stabled the coach horses at stages and provided accommodation for passengers, was the post chaise, a four-wheeled two-door vehicle invariably his property. It was built upon a perch with a full connection between the front and back axles. The body was C-sprung, giving a fairly easy journey for its passengers. The lamps were attached to the front of the body in a fairly high position. There was no box seat as the vehicles were driven by a post boy riding the near horse and hand-controlling the off horse. Although they were expensive to hire there was a great call for post chaises and some British inns still have the old front notice 'Post Horses for Hire'. Not a single example of an innkeeper's post chaise survives today though there are one or two private post chaises still in existence originally built for wealthy private families.

The demand for horsedrawn carriages continued to increase and many different types of vehicle were built. It became fashionable to be an owner/driver and by the late eighteenth century many young men were skilled whips. Demanding true skill in driving, the high phaeton was a popular vehicle of this period. It eventually reached such improbable heights that many artists and cartoonists of the period took pleasure in depicting gentle ladies being helped out of first floor windows to reach the box and join the gentleman sitting some 20 ft (6 m) above his horses, but in apparent control. It is of interest to note that the high-flier phaeton, so popular when driven by the Prince of Wales, was later replaced in popularity as His Royal Highness became older by the pony phaeton, a long, low vehicle.

In the late 1830s the spread of railways put an end to the use of coaches for public transport. The fashionable revival at the end of the nineteenth century was only a sporting pastime and therefore the participants rarely needed to drive in all weathers like their predecessors. The carriage builder was not affected, however, until the arrival of the car as large numbers of private carriages continued to be required. The invention of the elliptic spring by Elliot in 1804 introduced a form of springing never surpassed even today. It replaced C-springing almost entirely as it gave a much more even ride and was used on every type of vehicle from the wagon to the gig. Over the years the general construction of carriages continued to improve; in the 1880s the solid rubber tyre which made for quiet running came into existence. Since then no form of improvement in carriage building has been found.

The names of different types have often come from the name of the builder or the place in which they were made. Many modifications were made to suit individual owners and there was much variety among vehicles of similar type. Carriages of different types appeared throughout the world but it was generally accepted that French and British carriage builders were the masters of their craft. Queen Victoria had a carriage built as a gift for the Emperor of China and although the ultimate fate of this vehicle is not known he is believed to have travelled in it once only.

In North America the most famous indigenous vehicle built was the Western coach (see American Stagecoach); the Cape cart of South Africa and the AUSTRALIAN STAGECOACH were local variations. After the visit of Buffalo Bill's Circus Western coach style driving was tried by some people in Britain but it was found to be unsuitable for British horses (the Cow Pony of the Wild West was a much smaller animal than British harness horses). The Cape cart type of driving has rarely been used in Britain.

A difficult vehicle to drive is the curricle, popular in the early part of the eighteenth century, as the horses, a pair, carry a steel bar over their pads and have to move exactly in stride. The most useful and most popular vehicle for general purposes was the two-wheeled dogcart or gig. As a light single-horse vehicle they were superb. For public use in cities before the coming of the motor taxicab, the Hansom cab, often known as 'the gondola of London' was of great importance. Two-wheeled and forward-facing, with the driver sitting high up behind, it was an ideal vehicle for city travel. Hansoms were nearly all destroyed to make room for the motor taxi and are now rare and much sought after. The four-wheeled brougham in public service, often referred to as a 'fly', continued to be used rather later, particularly in country districts. They seated four people and carried large quantities of luggage to and from the railway stations and were therefore in greater demand than the Hansom.

By the 1920s the use of the horsedrawn carriage was, apart from tradesmen's vehicles, fast disappearing, but interest in driving for pleasure began to revive about the middle 1950s. The founding of the British Driving Society in 1957 has done a great deal to encourage driving in Britain. Many people now collect and restore horse-drawn vehicles of all types. Several firms do extensive rebuilding, and even building from scratch, carriage painting and lining, signwriting and decorating vehicles in the manner of the old craftsmen. See also Carriages of Antiquity, Coaching, Driving. JHEW

Carriages. *Below:* A curricle and pair of Cleveland Bays in the Royal Mews, London
Bottom: The highflier phaeton, popular in the late eighteenth century

Carrousel

An equestrian choreography carried out at the various paces as a spectacle. It excludes the *haute-école* movements pertaining to *quadrilles, reprises, pas de deux* or *pas de trois*, terms not to be confused with *carrousel.*

The original *carrousels* were series of equestrian games, largely stylized stagings of mock battles, running at the ring, etc., including 'horse ballets', like the one directed in 1612 by PLUVINEL on the Place Royale, now the Place des Vosges, to celebrate the Spanish double alliance; or the famous one dreamed up in 1662 by King Louis XIV, staged on the quadrangle between the Louvre and the Tuileries, called to this day La Place du Carrousel. The monarch himself rode in it, Perrault described and Sylvestre engraved it. An early example of the modern, non-martial version is Van Meyten's 1743 representation of 'The Empress Maria Theresa's Great Ladies' Carrousel at the Spanish Court Riding School in Vienna'. *Carrousels* are still officially performed there and at Saumur. JF

Caspian Pony

Carthusian

The present breed of Carthusian horses owes the purity of the strain to the efforts of Carthusian monks. The origin of this breed is similar to that of the ANDALUSIAN but in the seventeenth and eighteenth century decadence set in when heavy stallions from Denmark, Holland and Naples were crossed with the hard but beautifully proportioned smaller Andalusian mares of Asiatic and African origin, in an effort to breed bigger animals. The religious orders breeding horses, particularly the Carthusians of Jerez, remained true to selective breeding of the pure Andalusian. The private studs of Terry and Salvatierra have lines to the original Carthusian horses. DMG

Caspian Pony

The Caspian Pony, really a miniature horse, is thought to be the last remaining example of Iran's native wild horse, the ancient miniature horse used by the Mesopotamians in the third millennium B.C. and coveted by the Achamaenians and Sassanians for ceremonial purposes from the fifth century B.C. to the seventh century A.D. Thought to be extinct for at least 1000 years, a few specimens were found grazing on the shores of the Caspian Sea and pulling carts in the coastal towns in the spring of 1965. Extensive osteological work, blood studies and comparative bone studies have been carried out and, although much work remains, the great similarity of size, head structure and slimness of bone has made researchers optimistic about tracing a connection between the modern Caspian and ancient miniature horse.

Although bones of wild horses have been found in Mesolithic cave remains near Kermanshah in ancient Media, the area described as the homeland of the small horse by Greek writers, no miniature horses are to be found there now. Records indicate, however, that some time during the last millennium tribes from Kermanshah were exiled to Kalar Dasht on the northern slopes of the Elborz mountains near the Caspian Sea and that these tribes brought 'ponies' with them. Through this lucky chance the tiny horse of the past was given an opportunity for survival.

The Caspian stands at 9·2–11·2 hands (0·96–1·16 m). It has an extremely broad forehead, large eye, slim muzzle, arched neck, short back, high-set tail and very slim legs with oval hoofs. Colours are grey, bay and chestnut, bay being predominant. It is estimated that there are no more than 50 specimens left. LF

Cast

A situation in which a recumbent animal gets into a position from which it cannot rise. The usual cause is rolling: the horse may be too close to a wall when rolling over, or get its hind legs fast underneath a projecting object such as a manger. A rope should be put around the limbs and the horse pulled back the way it originally went. A special roller with an arch at the withers will often be the best way to prevent a horse from rolling over. WSC

Cataract

An opacity of the lens of the eye or of its capsule that interferes with the passage of light. It is regarded as hereditary but may result from injury or a previous attack of PERIODIC OPHTHALMIA. CF

Cattle Cutting, Cattle Drafting

see Cutting Horse

Cavalletti

Cavalletti (rarely used singular *cavalletto*) were first thought of by Captain Urbertalli of the Italian Cavalry School, PINEROLO. Later they were described and their use explained by Major Piero SANTINI, who introduced CAPRILLI's Forward Seat to the English-speaking world.

When properly constructed, *cavalletti* consist of thick round rails on triangular supports raised exactly 12 in (31 cm) from the ground and placed at regular intervals from each other. In proportion to the space at the horseman's disposition, the more *cavalletti* that can be erected in a *manège* or schooling ground the better, because they can be arranged in groups of six or more along the longest side of the arena, some at 3 ft (1 m) intervals allowing only one stride of the horse between the *cavalletti*, and others at 6 ft (2 m) intervals allowing two strides. These present two long grills which the horse cannot attempt to jump but must negotiate slowly on an in-and-out principle. The work can of course be varied by raising every other rail, then every third rail or per-

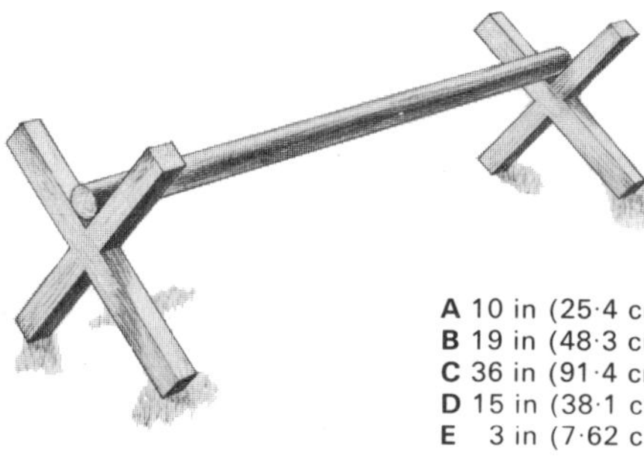

A 10 in (25·4 cm)
B 19 in (48·3 cm)
C 36 in (91·4 cm)
D 15 in (38·1 cm)
E 3 in (7·62 cm)

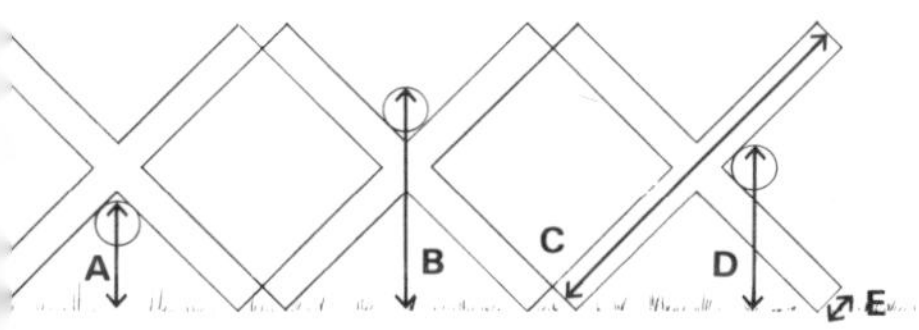

Above: **Cavalletti**

Below: **Chapman Horse.** This photograph, taken during the making of a film in North Yorkshire, in the heart of Cleveland breeding country, shows a string of packhorses as used by the chapmen

haps the two at each end of the grill. The greater the weight of the *cavalletti* bars the better. Light rails are to be avoided as horses do not respect them and, as is the case with all barriers high and low, nothing is more dangerous than a light rail knocking around loose between a horse's legs.

Cavalletti are intended to be used not with a horse on a lunge nor, as frequently seen today, merely as a series of low jumps to be rushed at and galloped over at speed. They are intended for training a mounted colt at a walk or trot, as a deliberate exercise to teach the horse to place its feet exactly right. To accomplish this the rhythm must always be slow. This in its turn quietens even the most nervous and excitable horses and riders.

Their special purpose is to force the horse to lower its head if it carries it too high, because it must see exactly where it is putting its feet in order to avoid stumbling. Likewise when trotting, although the horse must naturally lift its feet slightly more than it would do normally, thereby increasing elasticity, this is accomplished without unnecessary 'collection' or 'bending at the poll'. LFB

Cavalry see Warfare, Horse in

Cave Paintings see Prehistoric Art, Horse in

Cavendish, William, Duke of Newcastle see Newcastle, William Cavendish, Duke of

Cayuse
The name *cayuse* is sometimes applied to the American horse of the West; not necessarily a wild horse. This is also the name of a tribe of Indians living in the plateau regions of the Northwest, but there seems to be no connection between this tribe and the term as applied to the western American horse. RS

C.C.I., C.C.I.O. see Concours

C.D.I., C.D.I.O. see Concours

Chambon see Martingales

Chapman Horse
'Chapman horse' was the old name for the CLEVELAND BAY, derived from its use as a packhorse by English chapmen or travelling merchants of the seventeenth and eighteenth centuries. It is reputed to have carried tremendous burdens. William Youatt (1776–1847) tells of 700-lb (320-kg) loads carried 60 miles in 24 hours, the journey performed four times a week. Its powerful loins and quarters, and celebrated ability to 'walk five miles in the hour and trot sixteen', have been inherited by the present-day Cleveland Bay. RK

Chariot Horses see Warfare, Horse in

Charro Horse see Mexico

Charrolais see Norman, Anglo-Norman and French Saddle Horse

C.H.I., C.H.I.O. see Concours

Chifney (Chiffney)
A circular bit with either (a) a plain mouth, when it is an ordinary colt lead bit, or (b) a reversed half-circle mouth, when it is known as an anti-rear bit. Both owe their origin to Samuel Chifney (1753–1807), who rode Skyscraper to victory in the 1789 Derby and was the first jockey to ride a 'waiting' race and finish with a rush. DRT

China
The early Chinese association with horses was somewhat unhappy. The nomad tribes who plagued the western provinces of the Middle Kingdom at some time during the second millennium B.C.—there is a rock drawing of a mounted archer in Ladakh dating from about 1200 B.C.—began riding ponies which they had already domesticated and which were descended from the Central

China. *Above:* This seventh-century A.D. relief of horse and groom shows a remarkably modern-looking saddle with stirrups.
Far right: A fifteenth-century A.D. Chinese game of polo

Asian variety of wild horse known as Przevalski's (see Asiatic Wild Horse). They were archers, and the combination of the horse's mobility with an efficient missile weapon made them most formidable warriors. The horse, they discovered, made raiding into the settled districts a profitable and pleasurable pastime.

Pride or conservatism made the Chinese slow to follow the barbarians' example. Their armies were of infantry, supported by a few two- and four-horse chariots. The robes of civilized man were unsuitable for riding. The crossbow, which the Chinese invented in the fourth century B.C., was man's most accurate and powerful missile weapon before the rifle, but could not be bent and loaded on horseback. For several centuries they had to suffer the arrows of these outrageous Huns, building in the third century B.C. the Great Wall to keep out raiders, or at least to obstruct their triumphant return laden with plunder. No doubt a lazy or intrepid Chinese occasionally clambered up on a pony before then, but it was not until the third century B.C. that the vigorous, semi-barbarian Chin dynasty put their frontier forces on horseback and adopted for their cavalry the tactics and the clothing, trousers and hooded tunics, of the nomads. No doubt many of the Chin cavalry were in fact barbarian mercenaries.

If the Chinese were slow to adopt an alien culture, they were alert to improve on it. In 128 B.C. an imperial mission journeyed to Ferghana, near modern Samarkand, and returned with tales of 'heavenly horses' descended from the wild TARPAN of the Ukraine, selectively bred and grain-fed for centuries, far larger and faster than the Huns' shaggy ponies. Possibly they brought back some of these wonderful creatures: certainly they brought alfalfa, or lucerne, a good horse fodder. A later expedition to Ferghana was accompanied by two horse-trainers, whose scarcity value is attested by their emoluments and status, those of military governors. This expedition, after prodigious exertions, returned safely with a score of heavenly stallions, besides ponies of baser breed. A century later Ferghana horses were reported in the Imperial Park, used presumably as a stud farm.

In China proper the horse was still a comparative rarity, reserved for the rich, the elite of the army and the imperial courier service. To encourage horse breeding, in the third century A.D. families were compelled to keep a horse, provided free, with its fodder, by the government. In the seventh century A.D. the T'ang Emperors established in the arid steppes of the interior vast stud farms, holding 300,000 horses at seven acres to the horse.

The rich hunted with horse, hawk and hound as early as the first century B.C., the favourite quarry being hare and pheasant. POLO, introduced probably by the Kitan Tartars, was played before the emperor as early as A.D. 710. It became something of a court craze, and even ladies were taught to play on donkeys. An emperor of the tenth century was reproved by one of his ministers for lowering himself so far as to gallop in public after a little ball, jostled by subjects with no regard for rank or dignity.

But Chinese horse culture was essentially that of the nomad tribes who numbered their horses by the million and taught boys to shoot from the saddle as soon as they were old enough to sit astride a sheep. The Chinese, always realists, admitted that their horses, in words inscribed on a tomb, 'cannot vie with [the Huns'] horses in climbing rocky heights or fording mountain torrents, nor our horsemen with theirs in galloping over steep paths and shooting arrows while in rapid motion.' They taught their horses to amble, sure sign of equestrian decadence, for the amble is of all paces the most comfortable for the rider but the most exhausting for the horse. A school mathematics problem of the Han period suggests, almost incredibly, that 190 Li (6 km or $3\frac{3}{4}$ miles) was a good day's ride.

It was almost certainly the nomads who invented the stirrup. This is shown unmistakably for the first time on a fifth-century pottery jug from Korea, then under Kitan influence; and is first mentioned in writing, as a Hun invention, by a Chinese officer serving on the western frontier in A.D. 477. It was perhaps man's most important technical invention since the bit. For long-distance travel the trot is by far the best pace, fast and tiring neither for horse nor man provided there are stirrups, but uncomfortable for both without stirrups. Moreover, as any polo-player knows, one can hit with more force and accuracy standing in the stirrups than sitting down in the saddle, and probably this applied also to mounted archery. Stirrups, too, made possible hand-to-hand fighting on horseback: without them, a rider would be too apprehensive of falling off to put much weight behind a spear- or sword-stroke.

The horse-nomads were of many tribes: Huns, Kitans, Turks, Mongols, Tartars. The wide steppes of Central Asia seemed to spawn them for centuries, swarming out to east, south and west, terrorizing and subjugating more civilized peoples. North of the Yellow River China was conquered in turn by Kitans in the eleventh, Mongols in the thirteenth and Tartars (or Manchus) in the seventeenth centuries. It is unlikely that nomad horse culture differed much from tribe to tribe or from one century to another. What medieval Europeans wrote about Mongols or Turks would have applied more or less to Huns a thousand years earlier. Squat, bowlegged from a life in the saddle, with long, unkempt hair and shrill voices, their hideous appearance seemed to confirm legends of demonic ancestry. 'Their indolence refused to cultivate the earth, and their restless spirit despised the confines of a solitary life'. Put in language less sonorous than Gibbon's, the barren steppes forced on them a nomadic life of ceaseless wandering in search of water and grazing. They moved hardly a yard except on horseback. They drank mares' milk, fermented so as to be slightly intoxicating; they ate cheese made from it. Slabs of horsemeat or mutton they pressed under the saddle to squeeze out the blood and carried round, half-dried and stinking, as an active-service ration. Their stench almost turned the stomachs of Crusaders who met them. They organized vast drives for game, the horde closing in from a circle fifty miles wide: excellent training for extended cavalry operations. Some carried sword and spear, but the short, powerful, recurved bow was their main weapon: on a campaign each man carried one or two spare bows and three quivers of arrows. Some wore mail, but most wore cuirasses made of overlapping strips of horse-hide, stiffened with bitumen. They swam their ponies across rivers, floating their saddles and other gear wrapped in waterproof leather groundsheets. Except for the horses of the special courier service, their ponies, grass-fed, could not have been great individual performers; they achieved mobility by the *remuda* system, each man having four or five horses which he rode for a few hours in turn. Their herdsmen, to catch horses, used not a lasso, but a long, slender bamboo, like a salmon-rod, with a noose at the end. Their saddle was high-arched, deep and padded, resting on a large numnah, thick and stiff to spread the weight. They rode rather short, in the easy, natural style of Asia, their ponies not bent or collected by any curb, but moving along at a steady, easy pace, controlled by a plain snaffle.

It was these people and their descendants who were the horsemen of China. The Chinese proper despised physical exertion, and after two centuries of civilization even the Manchus thought hunting and polo beneath them. Their horses were, by the nineteenth century, wonderful performers for their size, like miniature hunters, not very fast, but

handy and able to carry a beefy European up and down the polo ground or round a point-to-point course. Today China is the only great power to maintain a large force of horsed cavalry, three divisions, presumably for use in the rough country along that eternally troublesome western frontier. CCT

Reference: A. D. H. Bivar, 'The Stirrup and its Origins', *Oriental Art*, N.S. 1, No. 2, (1955), 3.7; Edward Gibbon, *Decline and Fall of the Roman Empire*; Marco Polo, *The Travels*; H. A. Giles, *The Civilization of China*, London, 1911; Charles Chenevix Trench, *A History of Horsemanship*, London, 1970; K. Scott Latourette, *The Chinese, their History and Culture*, London, 1934.

Breeds: with the exception of the south-eastern provinces where the buffalo is the principal draught animal, horses are bred in nearly every part of China. The greatest concentration of horses is in Inner Mongolia and the adjacent provinces of Sinkiang, Ningsia and Heilung Kiang. Indeed, most Chinese horses are derived from the north, especially Mongolia. The most important market used to be held outside the Great Frontier Gate, which afforded entry and exit through the Great Wall. Here horse

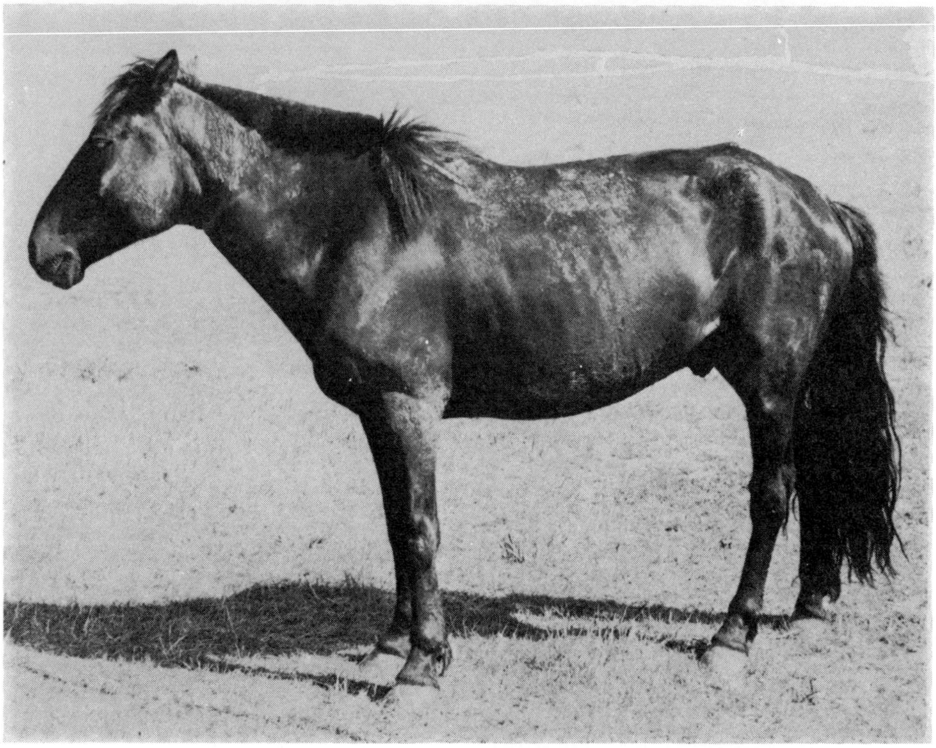

dealers from as far south as Hunan province would buy Mongolian ponies.

The domestic horse was introduced into northern China from the west. It first appeared in northeastern China during the period of the Neolithic Lung-Shan culture in the first half of the second millennium B.C.

The horses of China are classed into seven major types and six local breeds. Each of the main types includes several local varieties. The ponies of Inner Mongolia stand 12·2–13 hands (1·27–1·32 m) at the withers and weigh 550–660 lb (250–300 kg). They vary considerably in conformation, especially in cranial type. Generally they are distinguished by a long, rather heavy head. The majority are well-muscled, thick-set and of compact build. In the grassland zone of Inner Mongolia ponies of a fairly refined type are encountered; in some the head is reminiscent of an Arab's. In the scrubland and semi-desert areas of the Gobi the ponies often have coarse heads and necks, and resemble the wild *Equus przewalskii*. Mongolian ponies are used for riding, pack work, draught, milk and meat. They can carry a pack of 175–220 lb (80–100 kg) or draw a load of 1750–2200 lb (800–1000 kg) over a distance of 25–37 miles (40–60 km) per day. The mares are milked for three months after foaling. The yield is approximately 400–485 lb (180–200 kg) per lactation in addition to that taken by the foal. The milk is fermented into koumiss, and from this a fairly strong alcoholic spirit may be distilled.

A variety of the Mongolian pony is bred in the northwestern part of Heilung Kiang province contiguous with the breeding area of Mongolian ponies in northeastern Inner Mongolia. The Heilung Kiang pony has a large head with a slightly convex profile. On stud farms stallions are now being selected for more refined heads.

In western Manchuria and the adjacent eastern part of Inner Mongolia three closely related breeds are produced: the Sanho, Hailar and Sanpeitze. They are 14–15 hands (1·42–1·52 m) high and weigh 880–990 lb (400–500 kg). All of them are descended from crossbreds of stallions imported from Russia in Tsarist or recent times and local Mongolian mares. In the fertile grassland southwest of the breeding region of the Hailar horse in Inner Mongolia, an improved type of Mongolian horse, standing 13–14 hands (1·32–1·42 m) at the withers and weighing 640–660 lb (290–300 kg), has been bred since ancient times. It is called Wuchumutsin (Wuchuminsin) from a small town in its breeding area.

In the western and northwestern parts of Sinkiang, bordering on Kazakhstan, Kirgiziya and Tadzhikistan, U.S.S.R., the small, hardy rather coarse-headed KAZAKH and KIRGIZ ponies are found. They differ mainly in size, the Kazakh standing about 2 in (5 cm) higher at the withers than the Kirgiz. Another riding and pack horse, the Ili, has been developed in Sinkiang from local ponies of Mongolian type and imported Russian horses. It has a height of 14·2–15 hands (1·47–1·52 m) and weighs 770–880 lb (350–400 kg). At one time the Ili was ram-headed, but the modern breeding standard prefers a straight profile.

The Tibetan pony or Nanfan, bred in the grassy areas of the tableland, is 12·2–14 hands (1·27–1·42 m) high and weighs 660–990 lb (300–400 kg). In the eastern part of Tsinghai and in southwest Kansu the Sining, a 13-hand (1·32 m) saddle and pack pony, weighing 770–820 lb (350–410 kg), is used along the pack trails into Tibet. In northeastern Tsinghai the Tatung pony, of similar size to the Sining, is used for pack work on mountain paths. The Khetshui pony is bred in southeast Tsinghai, western Kansu and northern Szechwan. It stands 13–13·2 hands (1·32–1·37 m) high and weighs 660–880 lb (300–400 kg), being larger and stronger than the Mongolian. The Sikang or Hsiangcheng pony of eastern Tibet and western Szechwan is 12 hands (1·22 m), light-muscled but of strong constitution, endurance, surefootedness on steep mountain paths and climbing ability at high altitudes. In South China 10–12-hand (1·02–1·22 m) ponies are bred in moderate numbers in hill and mountain areas. They are surefooted and suitable for mountain work and are variously called Szechwan, Yunnan, Kweichow, Lichwan or Kienyang. HE

Chincoteague

The origin of these small ponies, named after islands off the Atlantic coast of the state of Virginia, is obscure. Legend has it that a boat carrying Moorish ponies from North Africa to Peru was wrecked off the Virginia coast in the sixteenth century. Some of the ponies swam ashore to the islands of Assateague and Chincoteague, where their descendants survived practically unnoticed for many years. Since their discovery, they have improved in appearance and conformation, partly, it is rumoured, through a recent introduction of Welsh pony stallions to the herds which still roam wild. Every year on Chincoteague island there is a 'penning', or roundup, of the pony yearlings, followed by a public auction sale.

Most Chincoteagues and Assateagues are pintos, although they also appear in all the pony colours, including jet black. Due to their wild life and their rather stubborn character, they are not easy to train. Carefully handled, however, they can become gentle and well-mannered, and their small size makes them a child's pony that is growing in popularity. MAS

China. *Above left:* Mongolian riding pony, Inner Mongolia
Below left: Wuchumutsin stallion, Inner Mongolia
Below: Heilung Kiang pony stallion, Manchuria

Chivalry and the Tournament

The focus of chivalry was the mounted knight. During the eleventh and twelfth centuries, when the cult was developing in Europe, he was so immeasurably superior to the foot soldier that he could look on war as a game, played for honour and profit. When no war was available, both could be won with less trouble and discomfort in tournaments. With these was linked the pursuit of 'courtly love', or polite adultery. A knight selected some married lady, preferably of a rank slightly higher than his own, and by his prowess in the tournament won her amatory favours. Not unnaturally, the Church disapproved of tournaments, but could not stop them.

The earliest tournaments were savage little battles, with sharpened weapons, between gangs of knights more or less equal in numbers. Gradually these became single combats, more and more formalized, with strict rules such as a ban on striking an opponent's horse. There was a regular class of 'knight errant', perambulating tournament experts who made a good profit from the horses and armour of defeated knights.

Late in the thirteenth century the English longbow made its dramatic appearance. The archer, not the knight, became master of the battlefield. Because horses could not ride through the arrow hail, knights, encased in heavier and heavier plate armour, had perforce to fight on foot. Only in the tournament did the ideal of chivalry, the mounted knight, survive. But because it now had to carry some 30 stone (420 lb or 190 kg), the charger of the late fifteenth century was a ponderous monster who could scarcely be spurred into an earthshaking trot. The tournament became more and more artificial. Only blunted weapons were used, and to avoid dangerous collisions, knights 'fought' across a stout barrier. The object of a charge was to topple your opponent off his horse; or, at least, break your lance on him to prove you had struck him fair and square. To facilitate this, lances were made light and brittle, and some tournament saddles had no cantle so that one could roll off unhurt.

By the sixteenth century tournaments had lost all contact with military reality: they were simply a costly and not very dangerous spectator sport. CCT

Reference: Ruth C. Harvey, *Moriz von Craun and the Chivalric World*, Oxford, 1961; *Studies in Mediaeval History presented to F. M. Powicke,* Oxford, 1948; C. Oman, *The Art of War in the Middle Ages,* Oxford, 1884; Charles Chenevix Trench, *A History of Horsemanship,* London, 1970.

Chuck Wagon Race see Rodeo

Cinch see Western Tack

Circus. Liberty Horses

Circus, Horses in the

Circus horses fall, broadly speaking, into three distinct groups: the High School horse, the Liberty horse and the vaulting horse, or resinback. The High School horse, often thoroughbred or nearly so, is trained to a fairly high standard according to the competence of the practitioner to give a smooth and elegant display of High School airs. The Liberty horse, which also attains a high standard of training while performing without any physical contact with the trainer, works as one of a group of perhaps a dozen matched companions, often Arabs, bedecked with coloured harness and ostrich-feather plumes. The resinback or 'jockey horse' is a steady, dependable, broad-backed and often somewhat plebian animal which canters round the ring while riders stand on its back and leap on and off.

The Thoroughbred makes the best Liberty horse but is more difficult to train and, being longer, takes up more space in the ring. Arabs are thus found in Liberty acts more often. They are small, supple and manoeuvrable, and more of them can be fitted into the circus ring. Stallions are preferable to mares as they invariably show themselves better.

Training is achieved by cues and by voice, with constant repetition. The early work is carried out individually on the lunge. Gradually the group is put together after the horses have learned to stop, go, and change direction across the centre of the ring. The next stage is the teaching of pirouettes. Even though they may never be used in the routine they are an essential part of training, for they make the horse supple and teach it to use itself.

It is important never to frighten a horse. It must have respect for its trainer, or it will not be obedient, but it must never be afraid. The tone of voice is more important than the actual words that are used, and thus all over the world the same words are often used, whatever the nationality of the trainer. For instance, if he wants the horses to change direction he says: 'Changéeee!', prolonging the final syllable so that the word is easily identified and understood by the horse.

An offshoot of the Liberty act is the *da capo*, when the entire group leaves the ring and some of them return, singly, to perform some particular movement on their own, still at liberty. The movements chosen are those for which each particular animal has shown some especial aptitude during training: a *piaffe*, perhaps, with bells strapped to its fetlocks, or a *capriole*, or walking on the hind legs. This last is not easy for Arabs, because of the conformation of their hindquarters. The extent of the training demonstrated will depend on the ambition and ability of the trainer and the competence of the raw material on which he has to work. Another variation of the Liberty act is a mixed group of horses and ponies performing in the ring together, often working in opposite directions in concentric circles, as in a *carrousel.* A mixed group is interesting for the public; there is endless fascination in seeing them alternate, large animal followed by small, and then regain their place according to type, six horses followed by six ponies.

Big Thoroughbreds are the most favoured for High School work, chiefly because they are more impressive and show their action much more spectacularly than do the little Arabs or the Lipizzaners. But, because their bodies are longer, they are more difficult to train, for their hind legs need to be brought under them, and the whole process of attaining collection and impulsion is more difficult than in the shorter-backed, closer-coupled Arabs, which have a natural balance and need far less in the way of training. Arabs are also far more placid; the temperament of some Thoroughbreds makes them more difficult though they are infinitely more rewarding.

The resinback is generally fairly closely related to the carthorse; its main requirements are a wide back, a quiet temperament and a comfortable canter, without too much action behind the saddle, whose rhythm it is able to maintain without changes of tempo. It must also be fairly imperturbable, for 'jockey' acts are often noisy and, quite apart from all the leaping on and off which it must endure with equanimity, may also include a clown who will run behind it holding on to its tail, hang upside down, suspended by one foot, in the region of its belly, and generally disregard its dignity in an effort to raise a laugh. A good jockey horse is completely unflappable and has long since ceased to wonder at the absurdity of man, being content to plod round the ring indefinitely at the same unbroken canter, heedless of everything that goes on around it.

Liberty horses can usually be ridden; this is important not only so that they can double as riding horses in any act, such as a cowboy or Foreign Legion display, that may require it, but also so that the stable boys may ride them to the station on the nights when the circus moves on to another town. But the High School horses, and their riders, are the aristocrats of the ring. Their accoutrements are elaborate, their standard of training is often high, though sometimes less so now than in the past, when some of the greatest riders such as François BAUCHER and Henri Cuyer were of their number, and their riders are beautifully turned out in period costume.

In comparison with racehorses, hunters and almost every other type of horse, circus horses do very little work. Apart from their training sessions in the morning, when they may be in the ring for half an hour, their working periods are confined to ten minutes or so, twice a day, and three times on Saturdays. In consequence they tend to live to a ripe old age. A great many are still working when they are over twenty years old, and their legs are as clean as those of many horses only half their age. They are never shod, so their feet are hard and good, and they are well fed and well strapped in order that they may look their best in the ring. RJ

City Livery Companies

There are 84 Livery Companies in the City of London, mostly of great antiquity, some of whose origins cannot accurately be traced. Over thirty have their own hall; new ones are still being built to replace some of those lost in World War II. The companies were originally trade and religious guilds, mainly concerned with the standards and conditions of work within their respective trades, often with wide jurisdiction, as well as with the welfare of their members. They have had to revise their objectives considerably since the Industrial Revolution. Many, however, still maintain an active link with their parent trade and give assistance in education and many charitable ventures. They also still value and maintain their traditionally high reputation for generous hospitality.

Companies of equestrian interest are the Worshipful Companies of 'Saddlers', 'Farriers', 'Loriners' and 'Coachmakers and Coach Harness-makers'. ADHJ

Classical Seat see La Guérinière

Classic Races

There are five English Classic races: the 2000 Guineas, the 1000 Guineas, the Derby, the Oaks and the St Leger. The 1000 Guineas and the Oaks are for fillies only. Fillies may run in the 2000 Guineas, the Derby and the St Leger. Geldings are barred. All the Classic races are for three-year-olds. The 2000 and 1000 Guineas are run over the Rowley Mile (1·6 km) at Newmarket; the Derby and the Oaks $1\frac{1}{2}$ miles (2·4 km) at Epsom; the St Leger over a distance rather greater than $1\frac{3}{4}$ miles (2·9 km) at Doncaster. The St Leger is the oldest, founded in 1776. The Oaks was founded in 1779, the Derby in 1780, the 2000 Guineas in 1809 and the 1000 in 1814. No horse has ever won all five but Sceptre won all bar the Derby in 1902. In 1868 Formosa dead-heated for the 2000 Guineas and won the 1000 Guineas, Oaks and St Leger. See Flat Racing. RM

The United States classics, which only roughly parallel their English models, are the KENTUCKY DERBY (founded 1875), $1\frac{1}{4}$ miles (2·0 km), at Churchill Downs on the first Saturday in May, the Preakness Stakes (1873), $1\frac{3}{16}$ miles (1·9 km), at Pimlico two weeks later, the Belmont Stakes (1867), $1\frac{1}{2}$ miles (2·4 km), three weeks after that, and the Coaching Club American Oaks (1917), $1\frac{1}{2}$ miles (2·4 km), the following week, also at Belmont. The latter is limited to fillies, which may also compete in the other three classics but rarely do so. There is no barrier against geldings in the Derby, Preakness or Belmont.

No exact American equivalent of the 1000 Guineas exists, but the Kentucky Oaks, $1\frac{1}{16}$ miles (1·7 km) at Churchill Downs on the day before the Derby, is probably the most prestigious filly race before the Coaching Club American Oaks.

Eight horses have won the 'Triple Crown' of Kentucky Derby, Preakness and Belmont, the most recent being Citation (1948). No Coaching Club American Oaks winner has ever won one of the other classics. FTP

Claybank Dun see Colours and Markings

Cleaning Clothes

An essential aspect of any stable is cleanliness. This goes for rugs, blankets, bandages, boots and kneecaps, in fact anything worn by the horse, besides the rider's clothes.

New Zealand rugs can be cleaned by laying them face down on clean concrete and playing the stable hose on the canvas; once wet, scrub them hard with a clean stable broom. Turn over and repeat on the wool lining. Rinse well and throw a good bucketful of disinfectant over both sides and then hang over a gate to drip dry.

Airborne (string) rugs can be washed either at home in the sink or in a machine and hung outside to dry—so too, can summer sheets of cotton or linen. Wool and jute rugs and blankets can either be cleaned or washed in a washing machine. If you use a launderette they can be dried there too. Set the machine at cool wash. Before washing rugs brush them clean with a stiff brush; in fact this should be done throughout the winter. Rollers are best washed at home and scrubbed with plain water with a little disinfectant added.

Boots and kneecaps, like rollers, are best brushed and scrubbed over with disinfectant and water, taking care not to get them too wet. All leather straps should then be oiled and soaped well.

The rider's breeches and jodhpurs are best washed before getting too dirty. Coats should be well brushed and cleaned when required. Nylon jodhpurs soak well and scrub clean very easily, then drip dry. DRT

Cleaning Tack

Buying and repairing tack is so expensive that regular cleaning is essential. Daily inspection reveals incipient wear, e.g. stitching on bridles, buckles and billets, and signs of wear on stirrup leathers, girth straps, etc. Sponge tack daily with glycerine saddle soap; once or twice weekly take it to pieces completely and clean thoroughly. Apply neatsfoot oil monthly to all leather; use sparingly, rubbing it in with the fingers. Never use a mineral oil. Polish bits and stirrup irons daily.

Requirements: saddle-soap, bridle-hook, wash leather, sponge, new dandy brush (kept especially for serge saddle linings), pieces of clean rag, stable rubber, glycerine soap, bar of soft soap, metal-cleaning pads, neatsfoot oil, bucket (warm water).

Method: undo the bridle, hanging its parts on the bridle-hook. Having stripped the saddle on the saddle-horse, hang up leathers and girth. Place irons and bit(s) in water.

Sponge all mud off saddle, hold pommel downwards over the bucket. 'Jockey marks' can be removed by scraping with twisted horsehair, well soaped. Clean thoroughly under the flaps, and the lining if of leather. Then dry and stand saddle on the saddle-horse for soaping with a nearly dry sponge; if too wet it lathers. Soap all leather thoroughly, rubbing well in. If a leather lining is not thoroughly soaped, sweat and grease will harden it, causing saddle galls. Similarly with a leather girth: keep a strip of flannel the same length, soaked in neatsfoot oil, inside a folded leather girth.

Sponge grease and dirt off a linen lining, without wetting it too much. Brush a serge lining thoroughly with the dandy brush. Polish the irons with metal-cleaning pads and a clean rag. Reassemble the clean saddle, run up irons on leathers; cover with a stable rubber.

Similarly, wash, dry and soap thoroughly all leather parts of the bridle. Polish the dried bit(s) and reassemble.

Never wash nylon girths with detergent; use soft soap and warm water. When storing tack, first rub castor oil or dubbin into the flesh side of all leather. Never stand leather too near any direct heat. GW

Clench, Clinch

Clench, Clinch the protruding shank of a nail holding the shoe on the hoof. See Feet and Shoeing

Cleveland Bay

The origins of the Cleveland Bay, one of Britain's oldest native breeds, are obscure, but it has been recognized as a distinct breed for more than two hundred years. Colour is invariably bay with black points, any white other than a small white star being regarded as evidence of crossbreeding and entailing rejection from the Stud Book. Usual height is 16·0–16·2 hands (1·65–1·72 m), often not attained before five or six years of age. There should be 8½–9½ in (21·6–24·1 cm) of flat bone below the knee and legs as free from superfluous hair as those of the THOROUGHBRED (with whom it shares some Oriental ancestors). The breed has a unique combination of activity and strength and transmits these qualities, as well as its bay colour, to its offspring when it is crossed with other breeds. It takes its name from the Cleveland district of North Yorkshire where it was once the all-purpose farm horse: strong enough to plough, active enough to take the family gig to church or market, and a bold, surefooted (though not

Cleveland Bay. Stallion, Mulgrave Supreme

very fast) hunter. During the nineteenth century it was exported all over the world as an 'improver' to grade up native breeds; today it is in increasing demand to cross with the Thoroughbred, the first cross producing good hunters up to weight and notable as great jumpers, and the second cross with blood producing big high quality horses which can gallop and are proving well suited to the comparatively new sport of COMBINED TRAINING. This constant use for crossing means that the pure breed will remain small in numbers, but it undoubtedly has a part to play in the production of the modern saddle horse, especially where size and jumping prowess are important. Pure-bred geldings are used for harness work, though for this purpose too the first cross with the Thoroughbred is often preferred. RK

Clipping

If horses with a thick winter coat are given hard and/or fast work (e.g. hunting), they tend to sweat and lose condition. It is also much harder to dry and groom them thoroughly and to remove all the mud and sweat. They may therefore be clipped. If a horse is *clipped right out*, the whole coat is removed, including that of the legs. The mane can be left on for plaiting or may be hogged, which helps to make a thick neck look thinner. In a *hunter clip* hair is left on the legs from the thigh downwards to protect the horse against thorns and scratches while hunting. It can be either with or without a saddle mark (the hair left on in the shape of the saddle). Horses that are clipped right out or hunter clipped are kept stabled and in winter should only be turned out in a New Zealand rug.

In a *trace clip* the horse is clipped under the neck and level to where the traces of a cart would go. The belly is clipped; the top of the neck, the back along the croup to the tail and the legs from the level of the thigh are not clipped. A trace-clipped horse can be turned out in mild weather in winter, as its loins, the most vulnerable part, are protected from cold and damp by the coat. In a *blanket clip* the neck and back to the level where a blanket thrown over the horse would reach, together with the legs, are left unclipped: practical if a horse is to be turned out but perhaps not very beautiful. GW

Clothing, Horse

The general purpose of clothing, the items worn by the horse in stables or when travelling, is to replace the natural coat removed from the horse by clipping. Customary clothing for a clipped stabled horse in winter is an 8-lb (3·62-kg) striped wool blanket over which is placed a *night* or *stable rug* made of jute or sail canvas lined with wool blanketing. The rugs may be kept in place by either a body roller made of leather, web or jute, or by surcingles sewn on to the top rug. The *body roller* may take two forms. The first, and more commonplace, is made with two stuffed pads lying on either side of the spine to prevent continual pressure on that part. The second employs a metal hoop, joining the two pads, and is more effective in ensuring that the spine is entirely free from pressure. Such rollers are also called 'anti-cast' since the hoop prevents the horse from rolling over on its back and being trapped in a corner of the box in that position. Also used in stable and when travelling is the cellular cotton-mesh anti-sweat sheet. The sheet operates on the same principle as the 'string' vest: the mesh, when covered by a top rug, creates air pockets next to the body which act as a form of insulation against cold and heat. The sheet assists a horse to cool off after exercise without risk of becoming chilled and will prevent heavy 'breaking out' after periods of exceptional stress such as hunting or racing. To replace the stable rug, when travelling or attending events, a wool *day rug* is employed. These are available in a variety of colours and bindings and may be embroidered with the owner's initials. The method used to keep the rug in place is the same as that employed on the stable rug. For travelling a *tail guard* is frequently included. Made of either soft leather or cloth, this fastens round the top 12 in (30·50 cm) of the tail and is secured by a strap fastened to the rear of the body roller. It prevents the tail being rubbed by a horse leaning against the back of the horsebox stall or the rear ramp of a trailer.

Bandages and protective *boots* may also be considered as horse clothing. For travelling and stable use, wool bandages are put on over a layer of gamgee tissue or felt and extend from below the knee or hock as far down as the coronary band above the hoof. They act as a protection against knocks and also retain warmth in the lower limbs. Exercise bandages, used to support the legs, are made from a narrower cotton flex or elasticated material and extend only to a point above the fetlock joint. To absorb concussion when jumping or galloping and to ensure that no restriction of the circulation occurs the bandage must be put on over an initial covering of cotton wool or something similar.

Boots are largely protective and supporting. One of the most common is the *brushing boot*, either of leather or felt, used on a horse whose conformation is such that there is a danger of its striking the inside of one leg with the shoe of the other when in movement. The *over-reach boot* is used for jumping and is usually a bell shape of latex rubber fitted over the hoof to protect the heels of the fore legs from a blow which might be caused by the toe of a hind shoe. There are, however, boots designed specifically for travelling, in particular the *kneecap* and the *hock boot.* The latter may also be fitted in the stable.

A recent innovation in horse clothing is a quilted rug of nylon, claimed to be an efficient insulator and to do away with the necessity of providing an under-blanket. Rugs of this type, specially waterproofed, can also be used on clipped horses put out during the daytime in winter and kept on the 'combined' method. Usually, however, horses kept in this manner are supplied with *New Zealand rugs* made of strong, waterproof canvas, wool-lined on the top half only. Such rugs must employ leg straps or at least a fillet string passing between the hind legs or round the lower part of the quarters to prevent the rug being blown over the back in windy weather. In addition a surcingle is necessary or, preferably, an arrangement of three soft leather straps fastened to each side of the rug and culminating in one passing between the fore legs and secured at the breast. The latter method is that employed on the true New Zealand rug.

Racing clothing, normal stable wear apart, consists of a rectangular *quarter sheet*, of wool or worsted cloth extending from the withers to just beyond the croup, and a similar sheet used in the paddock (a 'paddock sheet') while parading before a race. The first is used under the saddle during exercising and requires no special form of fastening. The paddock sheet is secured by a narrow width roller of matching material to which is fastened a breast strap. Both are fitted with fillet strings. Other items in the clothing of a racehorse are a *cap*, enveloping head and ears, used for exercise, and a *hood*, covering the whole neck as well as the head, which may be used for travelling or in the stable.

For summer use, on show animals etc., cotton or linen *summer sheets* shaped like a stable rug, are used to keep the coat clean.

Headcollars may also be considered as part of horse clothing. Essentially, the headcollar is made of leather and is used to tie up a horse in the box for grooming, when travelling or when led to and from the paddock. It may also be used to show young, unbroken stock in show ring classes.

Halters are cheaper, more simple versions of headcollars, usually made of hemp or cotton. A lead rope is incorporated and most halters can be adjusted for size by manipulating the knot lying behind the cheek bones. EHE

While horse clothing in the United States is basically the same as described above, the terminology may differ. For example, 'over-reach boots' are normally referred to as *bell boots*, although their form and function are the same. No distinction is made between 'night' and 'day' rugs, which are generally called *blankets*. A well-equipped American horse is generally furnished with little more than a wool-lined *stable blanket,*

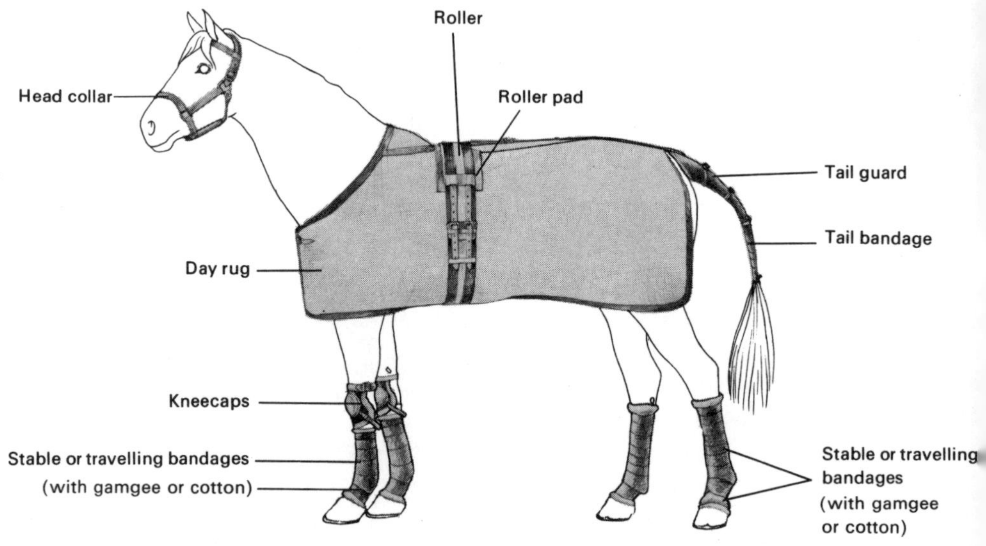

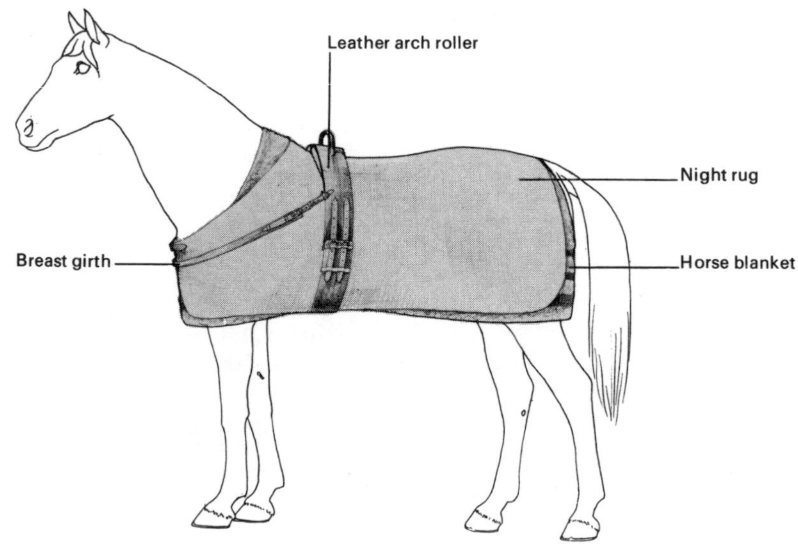

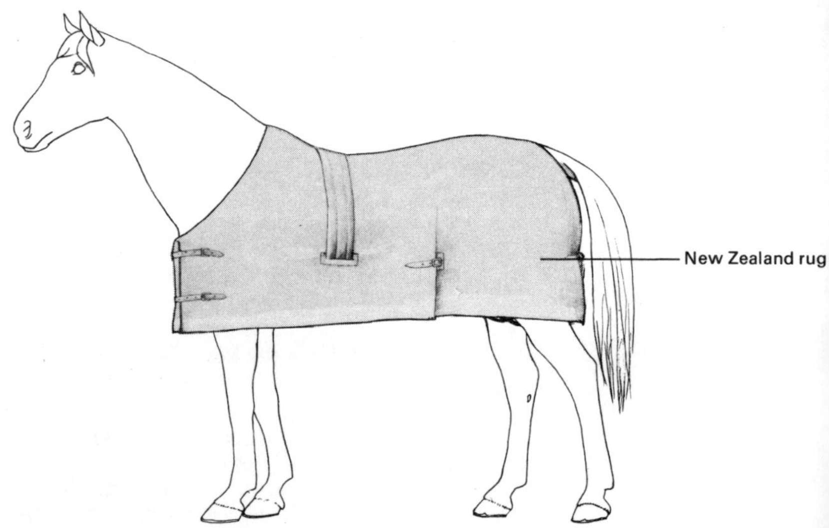

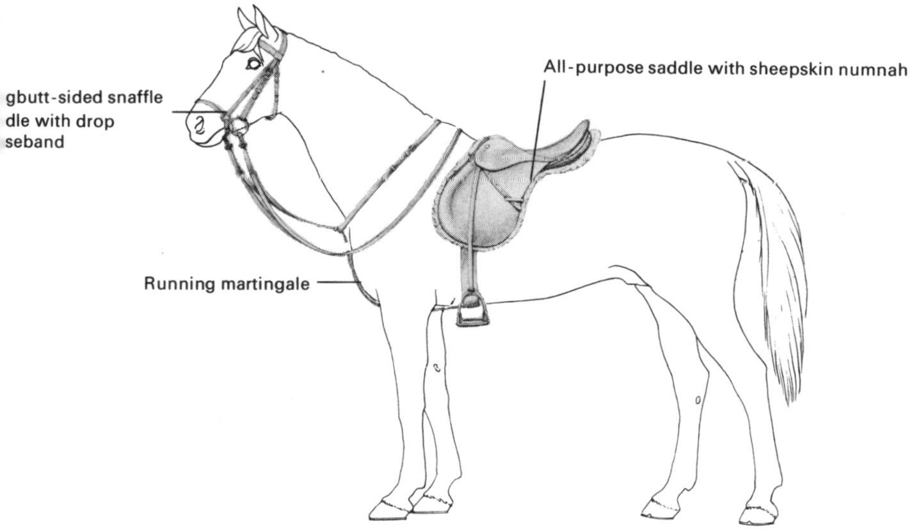

placed either under or over a cotton *stable sheet* (the sheet alone being worn in the summer), a *cooler*, which is a large, square, lightweight wool blanket worn during 'cooling-out' after exercise, and possibly an even lighter version, called a *breezer*, in very hot weather. *Quarter sheets, caps* and *hoods* are seldom seen in American racing stables, where the usual clothing of a racehorse is practically the same as that of a hunter or jumper. MAS

Clydesdale

When road surfaces in Britain were improved about the middle of the eighteenth century the packhorse gave place to shoulder haulage and thus the Clydesdale horse evolved in the county of Lanarkshire, then known as Clydesdale. Similar to the SHIRE HORSE in size and weight, this famous breed from Scotland also has a wealth of hair ('feather') largely covering the feet and legs and splashed about the underbody. Of these two great heavy draught horses the Clydesdale is the more active and shows rather more quality in type. Both have a world-wide reputation. RSS

Left and above: **Horse Clothing**

Below right: **Clydesdale.** A champion stallion. Often similar in colouring to Shires, Clydesdales usually have less hair on the legs and are lighter in build.

Coaching

The word 'coach' is thought to be derived from the town of Kotze in Hungary, where coaches are believed to have originated during the sixteenth century. Because of the bad state of the roads, they were not extensively used in England until the seventeenth century, and then only in towns, and on country roads in summer only, as they were large, heavy vehicles quite unlike the carriages known now as coaches. It was not therefore until the latter years of the eighteenth century, when the great engineers Telford and Macadam had improved road surfaces, that coaches were more generally used, and were built as lighter and more graceful vehicles.

In 1784, the Postmaster-General, John Palmer, made transport history by running the first mail coach from Bath to London—the journey of approximately one hundred miles being achieved in the fantastic time of 15 hours. (Mails had previously been carried by post boys on horseback, a slow and unreliable method, since they were frequently held up by highwaymen, with whom some postboys may have been in league.) From this time on, the mail coach became a feature of the British way of life, and by 1820, when road surfaces had been further improved, the Golden Age of coaching had begun.

Mail coaches belonged to the Postmaster-General, who arranged with contractors to provide the horses, the teams being changed every ten miles or so along the road. These contractors were usually innkeepers of some of the great coaching inns situated in the city of London near the Post Office at St Martin-le-Grand. Such names as Sherman of the 'Bull and Mouth', St Martin's Lane, and Chaplin of the 'Swan with Two Necks', Lad Lane, were among the many contractors. The main contractor usually horsed the mail himself for the first two or three stages out of London, subcontracting the later stages. The horsing of a coach over a long distance was a very highly organized and complex business; the fact that over two thousand horses were stabled at Hounslow, the first change for all coaches travelling west out of London, gives some idea of the large scale and complexity of the undertaking.

A guard, wearing the royal livery of scarlet and gold, was employed by the Post Office. He was responsible both for time keeping and for the safety of the mails and sat alone on a single seat at the back, armed with a blunderbuss, with his feet over the trapdoor of the hind boot in which were stored the mails. He also carried a horn with which to alert both inn and tollgate keepers of the arrival of the coach, as well as to warn other road users of its approach. Apart from tunes played to amuse both the passengers and himself, there were various 'code' tunes for the movements of the coach for the guard to sound, such as: 'pulling up'; 'passing near (and/or off) side'; 'turning left, and/or right'; 'clear the road'. In addition to the mails, these coaches could carry eight passengers —four inside, and four on top—and the fares varied from 5d a mile inside, to 3d outside; an 'outsider' was a person who could not afford the inside fare.

All mail coaches started from the General Post Office at 8.30 p.m. nightly and ran through the night to their destinations, averaging 10–12 mph. Tollgates had to be opened for them as the mail travelled free, and nothing was allowed to stop them. Time keeping was also so good that in country districts clocks were set by the passing of the mail coach. Fog, snow, and floods were some of the hazards but even in bad conditions the mails had to be got through, and if necessary, the guards would abandon their coaches and, riding one of the horses, would themselves carry the mailbags to their destinations. The fastest coach was the Devonport, known as the 'Quicksilver', the only mail coach to acquire a name; it averaged a speed of as much as twelve miles per hour.

Following the institution of mail coaches, proprietors were quick to follow by putting road, or stage, coaches on all the major routes in England. Unlike the mails, however, which were always painted in royal colours—maroon bodies, with scarlet wheels and undercarriage, and the royal cipher painted on the door panels—the road coaches were painted gaily in a variety of colours, and with the names of their various stopping places on their bodies, together with paintings of inn-signs etc. All road coaches had names, usually with a sporting flavour, such as 'Tally-Ho'; 'Comet'; 'Red Rover', and they copied the mail coaches by having guards in scarlet livery to sound the horn, and to look after the passengers and luggage. As they travelled by day, and had short stops for meals, they were slightly slower than the mails, and their fares were also cheaper, but they had accommodation for more passengers: twelve, as opposed to the mail's four, on top, but like the mails, room for only four inside.

During the Georgian era, driving was very popular with the sporting fraternity and it became fashionable for young 'bloods' to persuade the professional coachmen into allowing them to 'have a handfull' for a few stages. This was forbidden for safety reasons, but it resulted in the private coach, or drag, being developed, and in the art of four-in-hand driving being continued. Drags were always painted sombrely, and in the owner's family colours, with his crest or monogram painted on the doors and hind boot. They were used for driving to race-meetings, where they formed a perfect stand, and for other social occasions connected with the fashionable driving clubs.

Coaching. The Edinburgh to London stage, painted by J. C. Maggs, 1856

Whereas the mail coach had only a single seat at the back for the guard, road coaches had accommodation for four people; drags had seating for only two, occupied by two grooms wearing livery to match the colouring of the vehicle.

When the first railway opened in 1836, the coaches began to disappear; by 1845 all the main routes had been taken over and the vast coaching industry collapsed. Roads and roadside inns were no longer used to any great extent, coach proprietors faced bankruptcy and coachmen were reduced to driving pair-horse buses and cabs. In remote parts of England where the railways had not penetrated, some coaches lingered on, even into the twentieth century, but the Golden Age of coaching had gone. For many years the roads were virtually unused, but in the latter part of the nineteenth century, a revival of coaching took place.

Day road coaches were put on some of their old routes in the summer by coaching enthusiasts, the best remembered being an American, Mr Alfred Vanderbilt, who ran his 'Viking' and 'Venture' coaches between London and Brighton right up to the outbreak of World War I. Mr Vanderbilt was also an elected member of the COACHING CLUB, the last of many driving clubs, but still in existence today. SW

Coaching Club

The Coaching Club was founded in 1871 in England by Lt-Col Henry Armytage, to provide an association for those people interested in coaching who were unable to join the Four-in-Hand Club, formed in 1856, which was very exclusive and had a very limited membership. The Coaching Club's first President was the 8th Duke of Beaufort, in honour of whom a livery, consisting of a Beaufort blue driving coat with buff-coloured waistcoat and gold buttons engraved 'C.C.', was designed. The tradition of wearing cornflowers, previously the custom of mail coachmen and guards when parading on the king's birthday, was also brought back into use. SW

Cob

The term, which has no literal continental European equivalent (perhaps the French *bidet* is the nearest), was not applied to horses before the eighteenth century. It denotes something compact, solid, rounded in contour. A summary definition is 'a short-legged horse having the head and neck of a pony'. Welsh Cobs apart, they are hardly a distinct breed. The type can arise out of a cross between, say, an Arab stallion and a Highland mare, or a Suffolk stallion and an Arab mare, but it would hardly do so consistently in repeated pairings of the same parents. English regions where the cob type has been notably bred are East Anglia and Devon. Cobs of the riding type are a by-product of hunter breeding, since a proportion of foals by Thoroughbred stallions out of hunter mares of unknown ancestry will grow into cobs. The type existed before the word; it was called a 'rouncy' (Fr. *roncin*, Lat. *runcinus*) and in feudal times was the mount of the squire in war and of the reeve (estate steward) in peace. Size: 14·2–15·2 hands (1·47–1·57 m). AD

Coldblood see Warmblood

Colic

A term used to cover all forms of abdominal pain but usually attributable to disturbances of the stomach and intestines. It is almost peculiar to the horse and could be connected with its inability to vomit. Most cases arise from errors in management and feeding, but young horses are subject to *verminous colic,* caused when wandering worm larvae block blood vessels and thereby cut off the blood supply to a part of the bowel. CF

Collected Paces see Movements

Colours and Markings

When describing horses the coat colour is the main feature. Markings are the areas of white on the head, body and limbs. It is necessary for identification purposes that colours and markings, natural or adventitious, should be accurately described. It is for this reason that terms like 'stocking' and 'sock' are now outmoded in deference to a more reliable delineated area on an outlined diagram, a method used for the registration of Thoroughbreds. Coat colour at birth may not be permanent and so care must be taken in assessing the colour of any horse under one year old.

Body Colours: The principal body colours are black, brown, bay and chestnut; in cases of doubt, the colour of the muzzle is the deciding factor. The term 'whole coloured' denotes no hairs of any other colour on the body, head or limbs.

Bay: shades varying from dull red approaching brown to a yellowish colour approaching chestnut, with a black mane and tail and almost invariably black on the limbs.

Bay Roan: see Roan (below).

Bay–Brown: the predominating colour is brown, with bay muzzle, black limbs, mane and tail.

Black: black pigment is general throughout the coat, limbs, mane and tail, with no pattern factor present other than white markings.

Black–Brown: the predominant colour is black, with muzzle and sometimes flanks brown or tan.

Blue Dun: see Dun (below).

Blue Roan: see Roan (below).

Brown: there is a mixture of black and brown pigment in the coat, with black limbs, mane and tail.

Buckskin: an American term describing two shades, one slightly lighter than and one darker than a pumpkin.

Calico: an American term describing a parti-coloured horse (see Pinto below).

Chestnut: yellow-coloured hair in different degrees of intensity. A 'true' chestnut has a chestnut mane and tail which may be lighter or darker than the body colour. Lighter-coloured chestnuts may have flaxen manes and tails.

Claybank Dun: a uniform reddish-yellow colour with slightly darker mane and tail, as opposed to the Palomino (see below) which has a lighter mane and tail.

Cream: the body coat is cream-coloured,

Cob. A present-day show cob, Jonathan, ridden by Roy Trigg

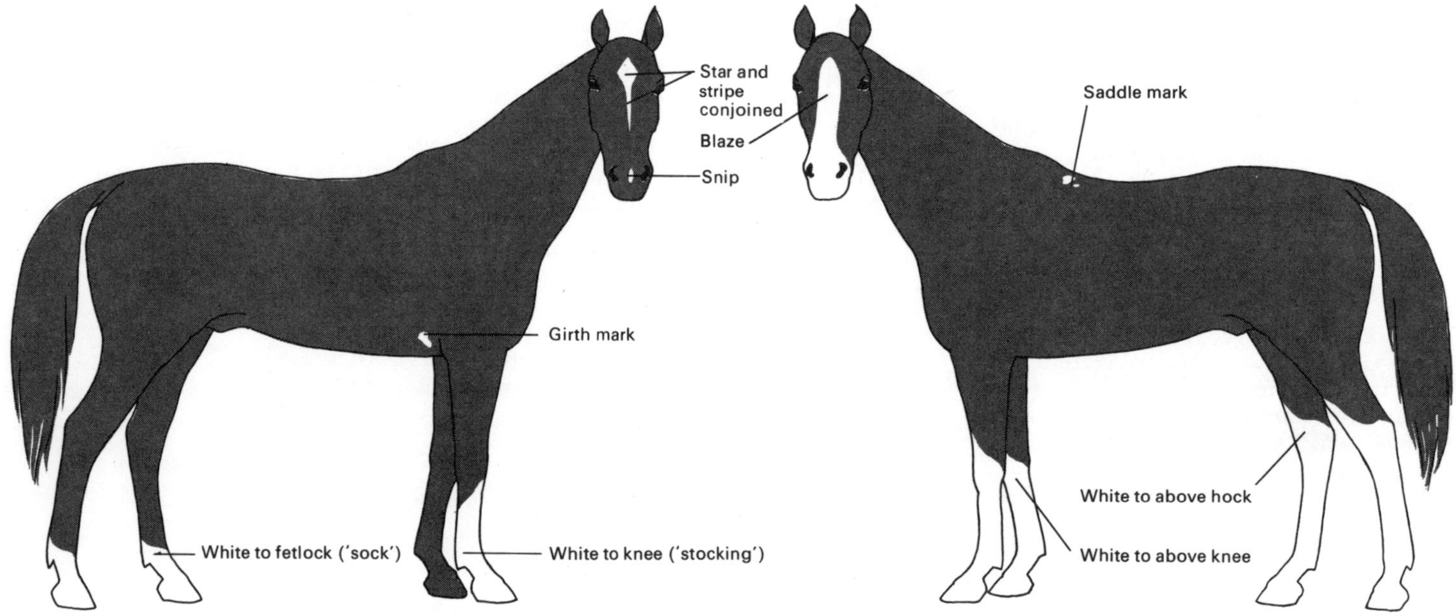

Colours and Markings. The markings of the horse. The terms 'sock' and 'stocking' are not officially used since they do not define the area of the markings with sufficient accuracy.

with unpigmented skin. The iris is deficient in pigment and is often devoid of it, giving the eye a pinkish or bluish appearance. See also separate entry on Albinism.

Dun: in a *blue dun* the body colour is a dilute black evenly distributed. The mane and tail are black. There may be a dorsal band (list) and/or a withers stripe. The skin is black. In a *yellow dun* there is a diffuse yellow pigment in the hair. They may be a dorsal band, withers stripe, and bars on the legs. The striping is usually associated with black pigment on the head and limbs. The skin is black.

Grey: the body coat is a varying mosaic of black and white hairs, with black skin. With increasing age the coat grows lighter. The many variations should all be described by the general term 'grey'. The *flea-bitten grey* may contain three colours or the two basic colours.

Palomino: rich golden colour, varying to pale yellow or dark cream with flaxen mane and tail.

Piebald: see Pinto (below).

Pinto: a term used in North America to describe all parti-coloured horses (also known as *calicos*), in Britain differentiated as *piebalds* (where the body coat consists of large irregular patches of black and white with generally well-defined lines of demarcation between the two colours) or *skewbalds* (where the body coat consists of large irregular patches of white and of any definite colour except black, with generally well-defined lines of demarcation between the colours). *Odd-coloured* horses have large irregular patches of more than two colours, which may merge into each other at the edge of the patches. In the *tobiano*, believed to possess the more dominant gene and more common on the western and southwestern plains of the United States, where they were much used by American Indians, the basic colour is white, with large patches of black or brown; the head and neck are usually dark, the legs white from the knees down. In the *overo*, more common in South America, the basic colouring is usually dark, often roan, with 'lightning streaks'. The eyes may be dark or blue 'glass' or 'wall' eyes, in either type. APPALOOSAS have spotted coats but are distinct from pintos in that the white is concentrated over the loins and hips with scattered dark spots on the body.

Roan: a sprinkling of hairs of one colour on another basic colour; roans are distinguished by the ground or body colours, all of which are permanent. In *blue roans* the body colour is black or black-brown, with an admixture of white hair, which gives a blue tinge. On the limbs from the knees and hocks down the black hairs usually predominate. In *bay* or *red roans* the body colour is bay or bay-brown with an admixture of white hairs, giving a reddish tinge. On the limbs from the knees and hocks down the black hairs usually predominate. In *strawberry* or *chestnut roans* the body colour is chestnut with an admixture of white hairs.

Skewbald: see Pinto (above).

Sorrel: an American term describing a variety of chestnut-reddish-brown.

Strawberry Roan: see Roan (above).

Yellow Dun: see Dun (above).

Markings: all certificates of identification should be accompanied by a diagram on which the markings are indicated accurately.

Head markings include the *star*, any white markings on the forehead, the *stripe*, a narrow white marking down the face, not wider than the flat anterior surface of the nasal bones, the *blaze*, a white marking covering almost the whole of the forehead between the eyes and extending beyond the width of the nasal bones and usually to the muzzle, the *white face*, where the white covers the forehead and front of the face, extending laterally towards the mouth, the *snip*, an isolated white marking situated between or in the regions of the nostrils, and the *white muzzle*, where the white embraces both lips and extends to the region of the nostrils. *Wall eye* describes a lack of pigment in the iris, either partial or complete, which gives a pinkish-white or bluish-white appearance to the eye.

Body marks include *zebra marks*, striping on the limbs, neck, withers or quarters. In describing a horse the presence of differently coloured hairs in *mane* and *tail* should be specified. *Whorls*, small areas where the hairs adopt a special pattern around a centre spot, are also important for identification.

White markings on the *limbs* should be accurately defined, e.g. *white heel, white coronet, white to below the fetlock,* etc. Patches where the pigment of the skin is absent should be described as *flesh marks*. There are many *acquired marks* that are permanent, e.g. *saddle marks, bridle marks, collar marks, girth marks, tattoos,* etc. Wherever these occur they should be described.

The U.S. Jockey Club recognizes only black, dark bay or brown, bay, chestnut, grey and roan as coat colours, and requires very specific descriptions of markings, distinguishing, for example, between nine types of star. CF

Reference: *Colours and Markings of Horses,* a report of the Sub-Committee of the Royal College of Veterinary Surgeons, London, 1965; *Method of Identifying the Thoroughbred,* published by the U.S. Jockey Club, 1967.

Colt
An immature male horse over one year old.

Colt Foal
A male foal under one year old. CF

Combined Driving
see Driving Competitions

Combined Training
Combined Training competitions, also called HORSE TRIALS or THREE-DAY EVENTS, are an all-round test of horse and horsemanship. Whether a horse trial takes place all on one day or is spread out over two or more days, it always consists of three tests: dressage, cross-country and show jumping, the marks for which are cumulative. In theory, the relative influence of the tests should be in the ratio dressage 3: cross-country 12: show jumping 1.

Cross-country obstacles are always fixed and solid (they do not knock down as do those in show jumping) so that errors of jumping, which are severely penalized, are confined to refusals and falls. Ability to negotiate such obstacles is obviously essential, but speed and stamina are also critical, whether in novice horse trials, where the distance may be as little as 1 mile (1,500 m) with 15–20 obstacles or in a full-scale international three-day event, where the test includes a $2\frac{1}{4}$-mile (3,600 m) steeplechase as well as a cross-country course up to 5 miles (8,000 m) long with 30–35 obstacles.

Success in horse trials will chiefly depend on the strength and courage of the horse, closely coupled with the spirit and tact of the rider. FWCW

Competitive Trail Riding
see Long Distance Riding

Comtois
Named after Franche-Comté, a hilly border *département* on the French/Swiss frontier,

Comtois. A mare and foal on the French-Swiss border

the ancient Comtois horse is said to have been imported by the Burgundians, who gave their name to Burgundy and were defeated by the Franks in the sixth century. Valued as a stud animal by the Emperor Charles V (of Austria and Spain), it was also much used by the armies of Louis XIV of France. This light draught horse of 14·3–15·3 hands (1·50–1·60 m), reared in a mountainous and rugged country, is strong and hardy and has short but lively gaits. It is usually bay and has a straight neck, square head and good withers. In spite of sometimes being cow-hocked, its surefootedness and good balance predispose it to use in the mountains. ES

Concord Coach

A coach with a flexible suspension built for rough roads in Concord, New Hampshire. See American Stagecoach, Australian Stagecoach.

Concours Hippiques

Under the rules of the FÉDÉRATION ÉQUESTRE INTERNATIONALE there are four categories of horse show for each of the equestrian disciplines. The lowest level is for national competitions in which only competitors from that nation take part: the Concours National (CN). On the next level, two nations compete in Concours d'Amitié (CA). If more than two take part the term Concours International (CI) is used. The single most important show in the country, for which the organizing country bears financial responsibility, and at which the NATIONS' CUP of the host country is contested, is called the Concours International Officiel (CIO). These categories apply to each of the four disciplines: jumping, dressage, eventing, driving (see chart).

Conformation

Horse: conformation refers to the make and shape of a horse and varies according to the breed and uses to which it is put. However, all horses and ponies have some points of conformation in common: a straight back, neither roach nor sway; a neat head with clear big eyes and neck set on to good clean shoulders; well-sprung ribs and a good girth allowing heart room; strong hindquarters with a well-placed tail; strong hocks, flat knees, short, flat cannon bones, good joints; strong, not brittle, 'open' hoofs with well-formed frogs; the legs should be placed 'square', not seeming to appear 'out of one hole'.

A harness or draught horse will have straighter shoulders than a well-made saddle horse, whose shoulders should slope to good marked withers with a rather longer neck. Harness horses must have very good hard bone and joints and both types must stand square, covering as much ground as possible. The action of both must be level and straight, so that at the walk the hind foot overtakes the imprint of the fore foot. The saddle horse has an easy gliding trot with the foot not far from the ground, whereas the harness horse is allowed more action. This becomes rather exaggerated in the show hackney. The stride of the draught horse is active but not high, enabling it to put weight into its collar. The action of the mountain or moorland pony (when not bred out) may resemble a paddle, an essential gait when covering marsh or moorland; mountain ponies may also have a shorter stride.

The conformation for breeding stock takes into account the points favoured for the particular breed. In addition, a stallion should be of masculine type, with a well-marked (shaped) head, clear eye and good coat; he should represent the breed and appear to be capable of reproducing himself. Sometimes the stallion is so 'well done' that he appears to be top-heavy and fat is mistaken for muscle; he must be free from hereditary faults, have proved himself (on the racecourse etc.) and be good-tempered with character. The mare should have a roomy barrel and possess the general qualities of a matron, i.e. 'motherliness', a kind eye and gentle manners; she should be a good doer but not gross. Gross mares rarely make good mothers or raise good foals. She should also have an assurance of good health and have no disease nor hereditary faults. A filly which looks like a gelding and

Conformation. *Far right, above:* The anatomy of the horse
Far right, below: The principal organs of the horse

		Jumping Concours de Saut	*Dressage Concours de Dressage*	*Eventing Concours Complet*	*Driving Concours d' Attelage*
Concours Hippiques	Concours National (CN)	Concours de Saut National (CSN)	Concours de Dressage National (CDN)	Concours Complet National (CCN)	Concours d' Attelage (CAN)
	Concours d'Amitié (CA)	Concours de Saut d'Amitié (CSA)	Concours de Dressage d'Amitié (CDA)	Concours Complet d'Amitié (CCA)	Concours d' Attelage d' Amitié (CAA)
	Concours International (CI)	Concours de Saut International (CSI)	Concours de Dressage International (CDI)	Concours Complet International (CCI)	Concours d' Attelage International (CAI)
	Concours International Officiel (CIO)	Concours de Saut International Officiel (CSIO)	Concours de Dressage International Officiel (CDIO)	Concours Complet International Officiel (CCIO)	Concours d' Attelage International Officiel (CAIO)

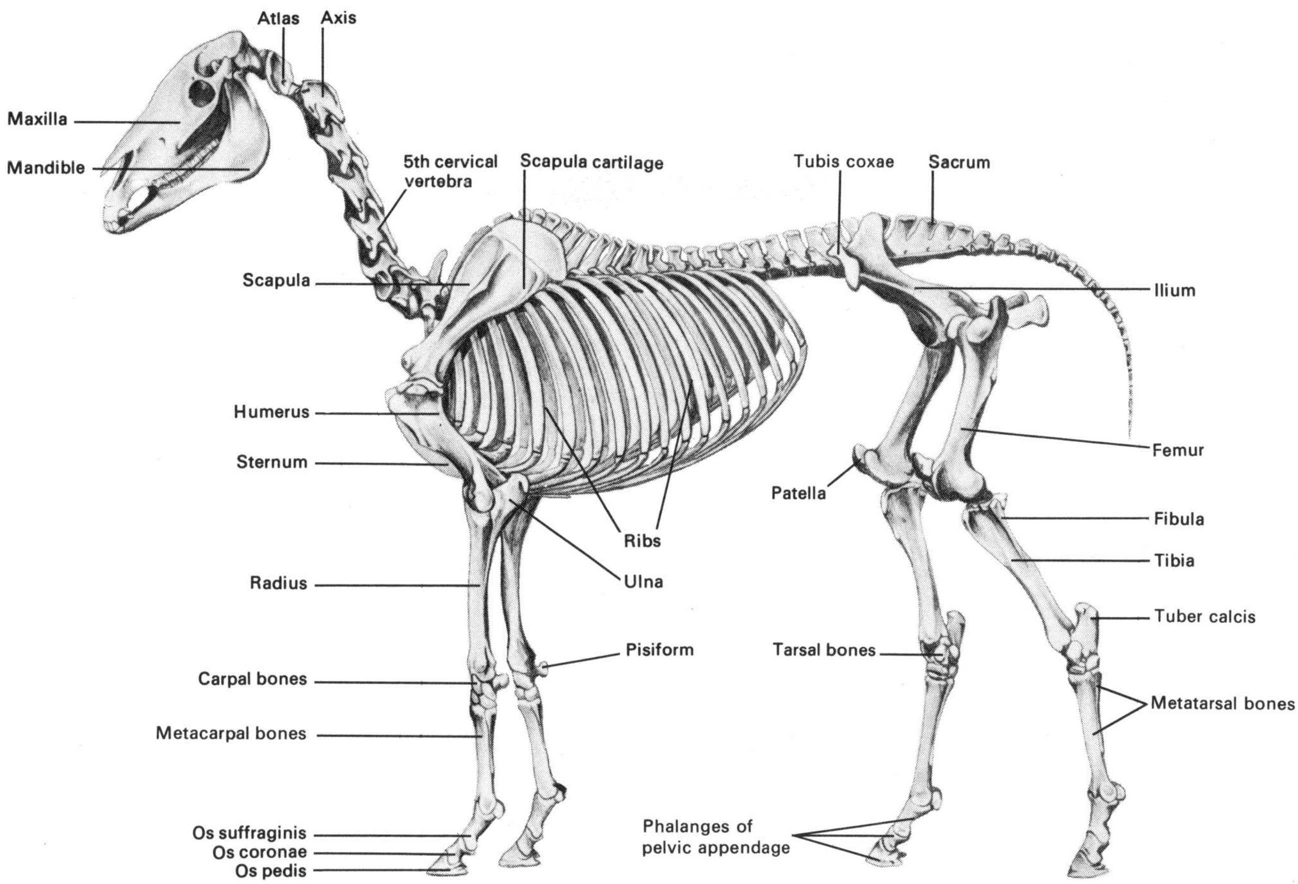
Atlas
Axis
Maxilla
Mandible
5th cervical vertebra
Scapula cartilage
Tubis coxae
Sacrum
Scapula
Ilium
Humerus
Sternum
Femur
Patella
Fibula
Ribs
Tibia
Ulna
Radius
Tuber calcis
Pisiform
Tarsal bones
Carpal bones
Metatarsal bones
Metacarpal bones
Phalanges of pelvic appendage
Os suffraginis
Os coronae
Os pedis

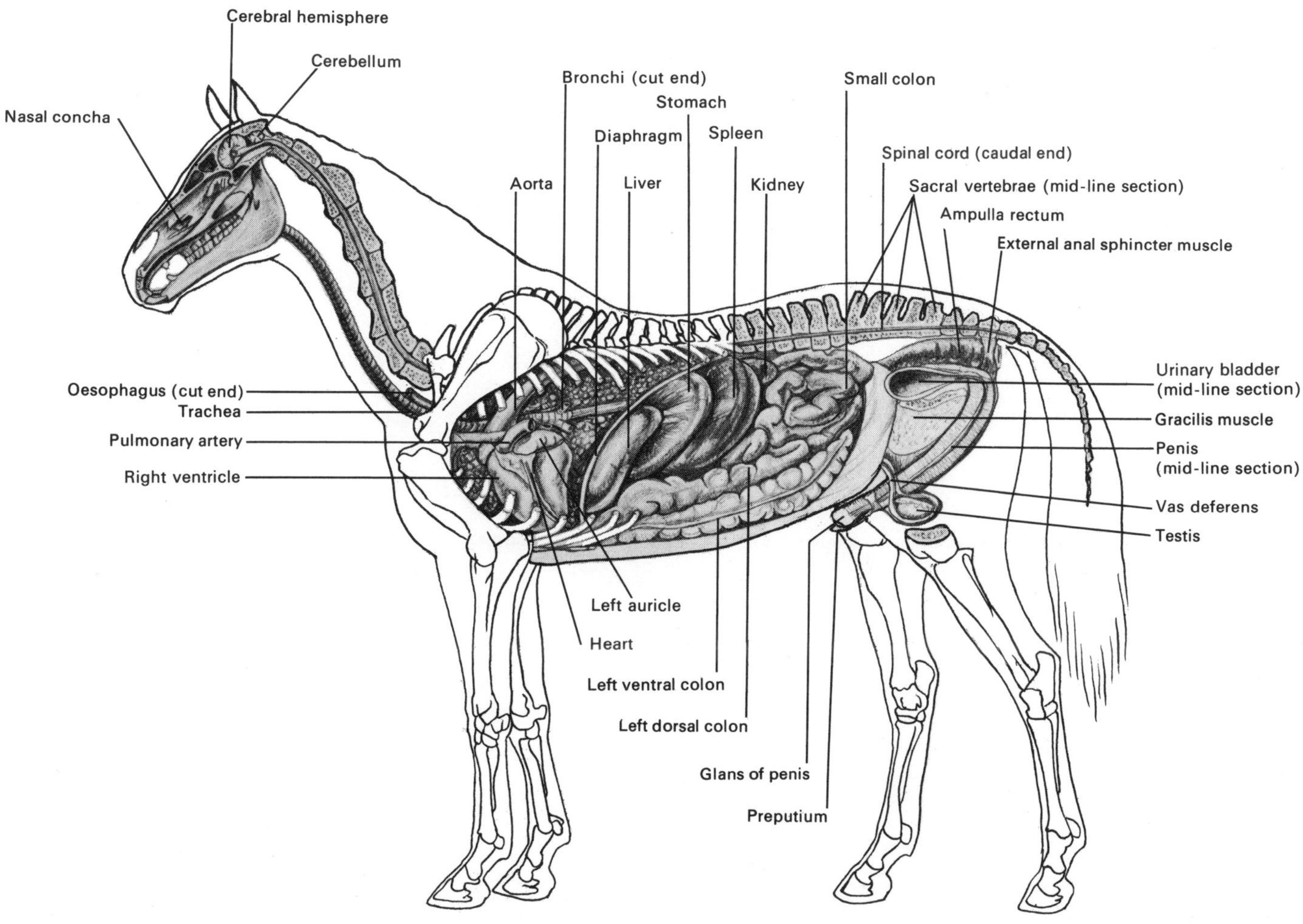
Cerebral hemisphere
Cerebellum
Nasal concha
Bronchi (cut end)
Small colon
Stomach
Diaphragm
Spleen
Spinal cord (caudal end)
Aorta
Liver
Kidney
Sacral vertebrae (mid-line section)
Ampulla rectum
External anal sphincter muscle
Urinary bladder (mid-line section)
Oesophagus (cut end)
Trachea
Gracilis muscle
Pulmonary artery
Penis (mid-line section)
Right ventricle
Vas deferens
Testis
Left auricle
Heart
Left ventral colon
Left dorsal colon
Glans of penis
Preputium

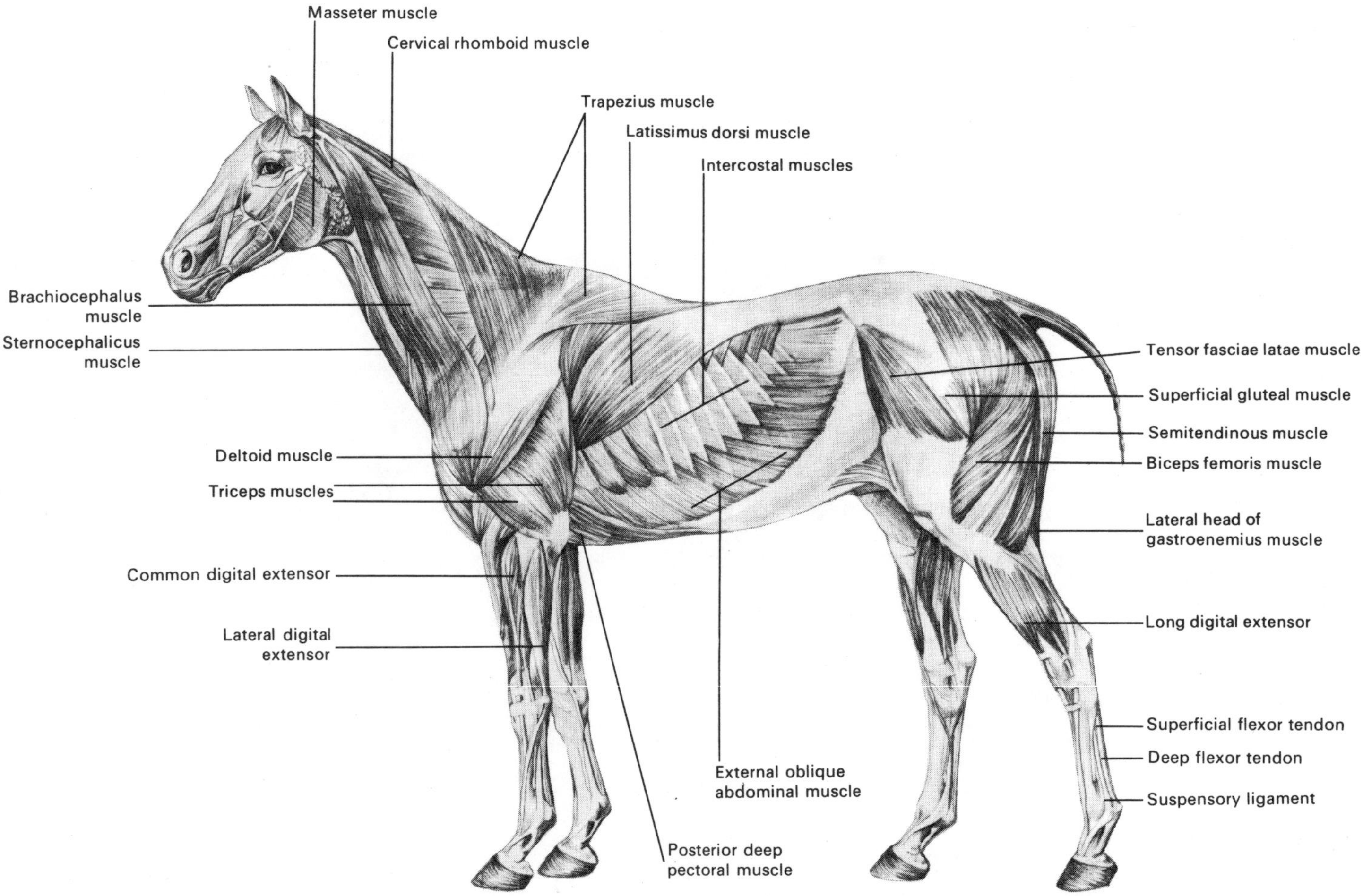
Masseter muscle
Cervical rhomboid muscle
Trapezius muscle
Latissimus dorsi muscle
Intercostal muscles
Brachiocephalus muscle
Sternocephalicus muscle
Tensor fasciae latae muscle
Superficial gluteal muscle
Semitendinous muscle
Biceps femoris muscle
Deltoid muscle
Triceps muscles
Lateral head of gastroenemius muscle
Common digital extensor
Long digital extensor
Lateral digital extensor
Superficial flexor tendon
Deep flexor tendon
External oblique abdominal muscle
Suspensory ligament
Posterior deep pectoral muscle

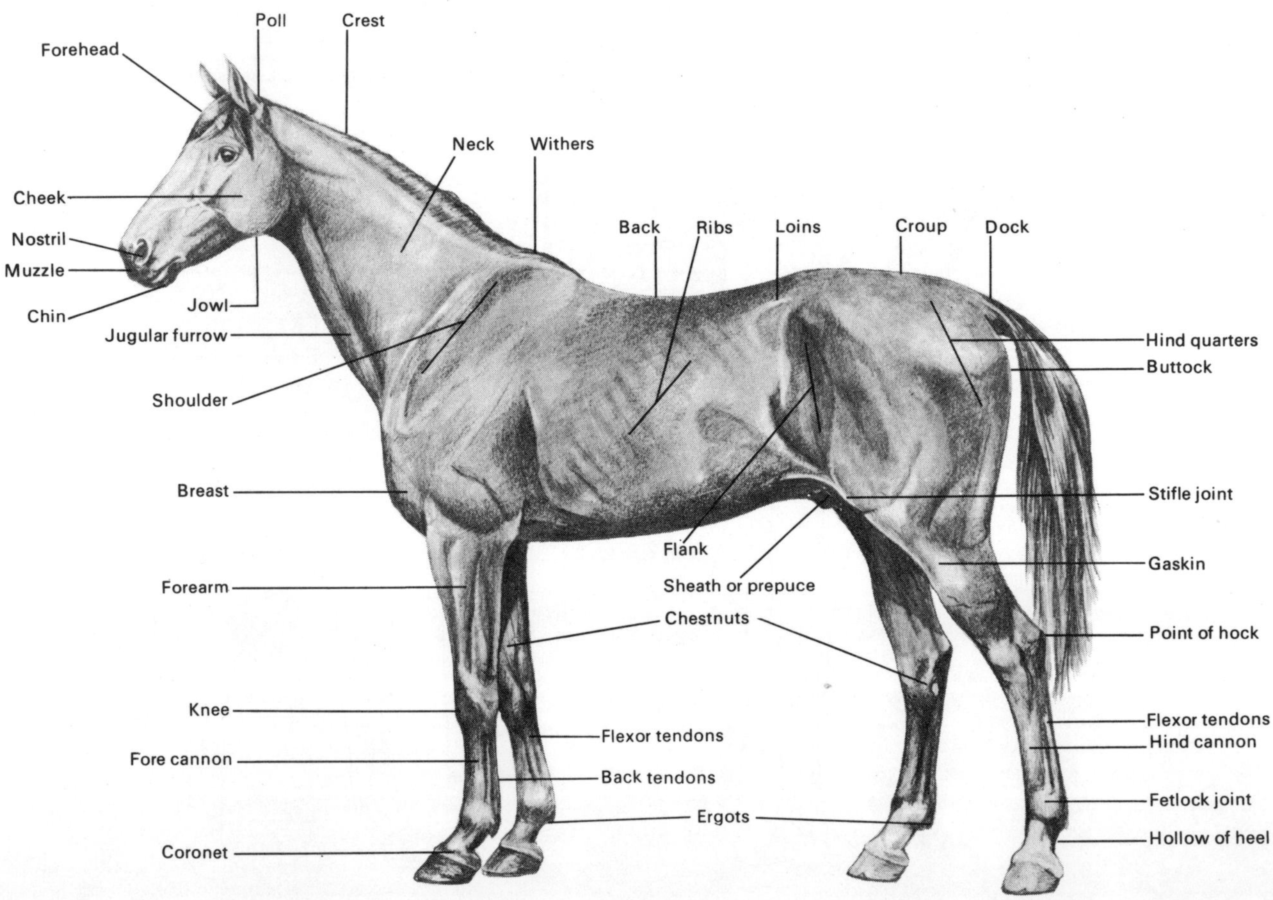
Poll
Crest
Forehead
Neck
Withers
Cheek
Back
Ribs
Loins
Croup
Dock
Nostril
Muzzle
Chin
Jowl
Jugular furrow
Hind quarters
Buttock
Shoulder
Breast
Stifle joint
Flank
Gaskin
Forearm
Sheath or prepuce
Chestnuts
Point of hock
Knee
Flexor tendons
Flexor tendons
Hind cannon
Fore cannon
Back tendons
Fetlock joint
Ergots
Hollow of heel
Coronet

a colt with a feminine expression are not suitable for breeding. All good horses are a good colour.

Donkey: the general conformation of the horse also applies to the donkey. In addition there are essential asinine characteristics, such as long ears, although over-long ears are not desired, a well-formed 'wise' face and head with clear, intelligent eyes. The croup and stifle should not be weak or flabby and as far as possible the hocks should be well-defined; neither sickle nor cow hocks are to be encouraged. The gait should be straight and active and not fumbling. The coat should be well-sprung and healthy to the touch. It is essential that donkeys are well-mannered and do not kick or bite. DMG

Connemara Pony see Mountain and Moorland Ponies

Corlay Horse see Breton and Breton Heavy Draught

Corn

A bruise of the sensitive tissues of the sole in the angle between the bar and the wall at the inside heel of the front feet. It is caused by pressure from lodged stones or, more frequently, by the shoes being left on for too long. CF

Corsican Pony see French Ponies

Cossacks

After the absolute domination of the Tartar khans over the rulers of Muscovy had ceased, the southern parts of European Russia, without defensible boundaries, were still open to raiding and cattle-lifting from the Tartar tribes of the Crimea, and increasingly from the Turks along the coasts of the Black Sea.

A certain measure of protection was afforded by outlaws, many of them runaway serfs, from central Russia, who had adopted a roving way of life in imitation of the Tartar raiders together with their particular styles of horsemanship, weapons and saddlery. Cossack and Kazakh are the same word, meaning nomadic herdsman. The Tsars treated with the Cossack communities in the first instance to ensure that their raids were directed towards the Turks and not inwards towards Muscovy. They became virtually self-governing military communities, stock-breeders but not in the first place horse-breeders: up to the early eighteenth century they considered it more honourable to steal horses than to breed them. The Russian expansion across Siberia to the Pacific was made possible by the victories of Cossack cavalry, and Cossack colonies were also established in the new territories. So although there is a Cossack (essentially Tartar or Turkish) style of horsemanship and horse-mastership, there is hardly such a thing as a Cossack horse, since the colonists were mounted on whatever horse was native to the region they colonized. Nevertheless Cossack skill in breeding, breaking and training has contributed much to the development of many noted Russian breeds. See Kazakh. AD

Counter-Canter see Movements

Courbette see Airs, Classical

Course Building

Show Jumping: comparatively few of the millions who watch show jumping on television realize that their enjoyment of the spectacle or disappointment at a dull finish depends entirely on the judgment of one person, the course builder or Clerk of the Course. In his hands rests the success or failure of every competition, for his assessment of certain data and his correct interpretation of this assessment into fences, heights, spreads and distances not only make or mar the competition as a spectacle, but also make or mar the enjoyment of rider and horse and can easily ruin a horse's courage for life.

Horses are graded according to the amount of prize money won. Lower grades consist of horses just embarking on a show-jumping career, together with others which have not been able to win enough money to reach a higher grade, either because of their own or their riders' shortcomings. The quality and capabilities of top-grade horses vary from the Olympic class through up and coming youngsters to horses which are reaching the end of their show-jumping careers. The course builder must know the capabilities and current form of individuals in the top grade if he is to build a course which will be fair to each type of contestant and enjoyable to all.

He must also consider the time allotted

Conformation. *Far left, above:* The muscles of the horse
Far left, below: The points of the horse

Below: **Course Building.** A traditional show ring, that of the Hamburg Derby, which began in 1920

for the competition. A mathematical calculation based on the number of starters and the length of the course will give the number of clear rounds which can be catered for within the time given for the competition. Provided the show organizers have been sensible and correct in accepting the number of entries for the allotted time, the course builder should aim to get the correct number of clear rounds in order to use up that time exactly, after allowing time for competitors to walk the course and receive their prizes. If the organizers miscalculate the number of starters in relation to the allotted time, the course builder should never penalize the competitors by building a course that is too severe in order to keep an unreasonable time schedule. He must instead help the show organizers to replan the timetable so that the jumping competition can take place over a fair and reasonable course.

Having studied quality, numbers and time, the course builder must make a plan that will fully and fairly test horse and rider, setting problems which will be enjoyable and beneficial for both to overcome, and at the same time produce exciting entertainment for spectators. Four ingredients, mixed judiciously together, are at his disposal: (1) the track or route the horse and rider have to follow from start to finish; (2) the number of fences to be negotiated along the route; (3) the constitution and construction of each fence; (4) the varying distances that can be imposed between them.

Novice horses and riders require a course and fences which will encourage both in their efforts to reach proficiency at show jumping. Plenty of room should therefore be left between fences and distance problems should not be employed. For more experienced horses and riders distance between fences may be reduced to three or four strides, which will make it necessary for the horse and rider to be more accurate in approaching and negotiating each obstacle. Distances should not be the means of setting a trap or insoluble problem; they should only be used to illustrate the degree of control and obedience achieved. By the judicious use of distances between fences the course builder dealing with top-class horses can build fences which, although big, are pleasant to jump.

The course builder must have a thorough knowledge of a horse's capabilities at all stages of training and experience so that he knows what constitutes a pleasant or unpleasant obstacle or course. He must also know from personal riding experience exactly what an obstacle looks like both to horse and to rider. An innate sympathy for the horse is absolutely essential. Lack of sympathy and incomplete knowledge in a course builder can not only ruin show-jumping competitions for spectators but, more important, it can quickly ruin a nation's chances of success in international competitions. MH

Cross country: the way in which the designer sets about planning a cross-country course depends very much upon its purpose and the standard of horse and rider for which it is catering. Although maximum heights are laid down for all standards from Pony Club to the Olympic Games, they reflect very little on the severity of any given course. The maximum height for novice fences under the British Horse Society's rules is 3 ft 6 in (1·07 m) and the limit for fences in the Olympic Games held under FÉDÉRATION ÉQUESTRE INTERNATIONALE rules is only 5 in (0·13 m) higher. It seems a very small difference to separate the beginner from the internationally experienced, but in practice it can be very important indeed. It is, however, absolutely vital that the course designer should know exactly what he is attempting to achieve and appreciate the standard of severity required to test, without overfacing, the horses and riders who are going to jump over his fences. This

Two steps down, stone wall
'Quarry'

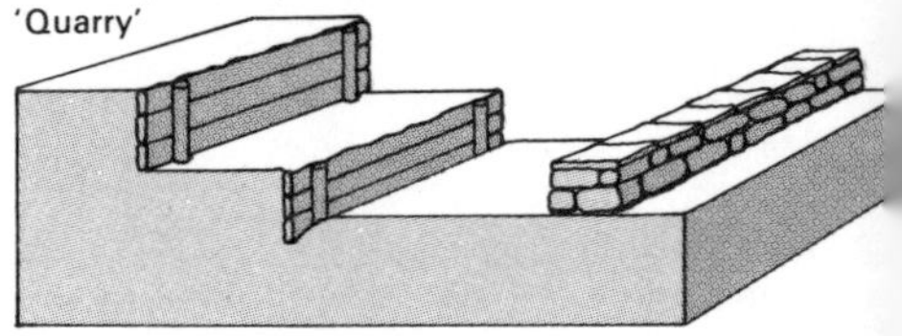

Post and rails, ditch, post and rails
'Coffin'

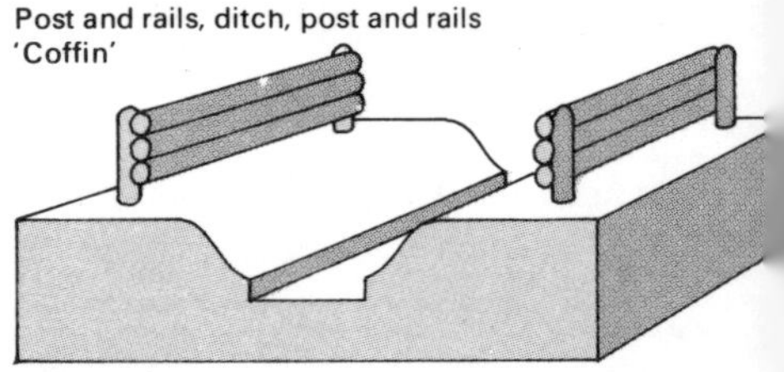

Parallel rails and hedge

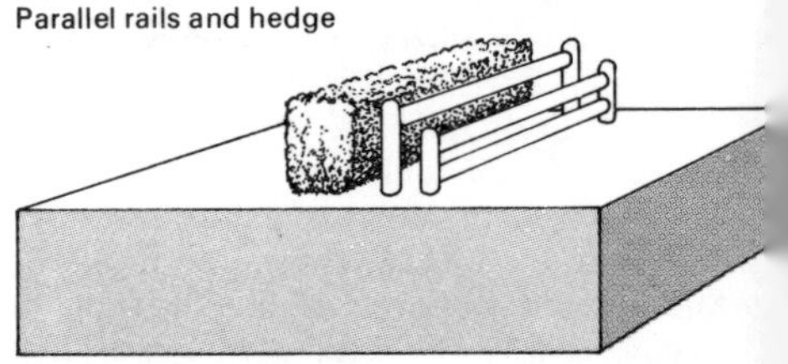

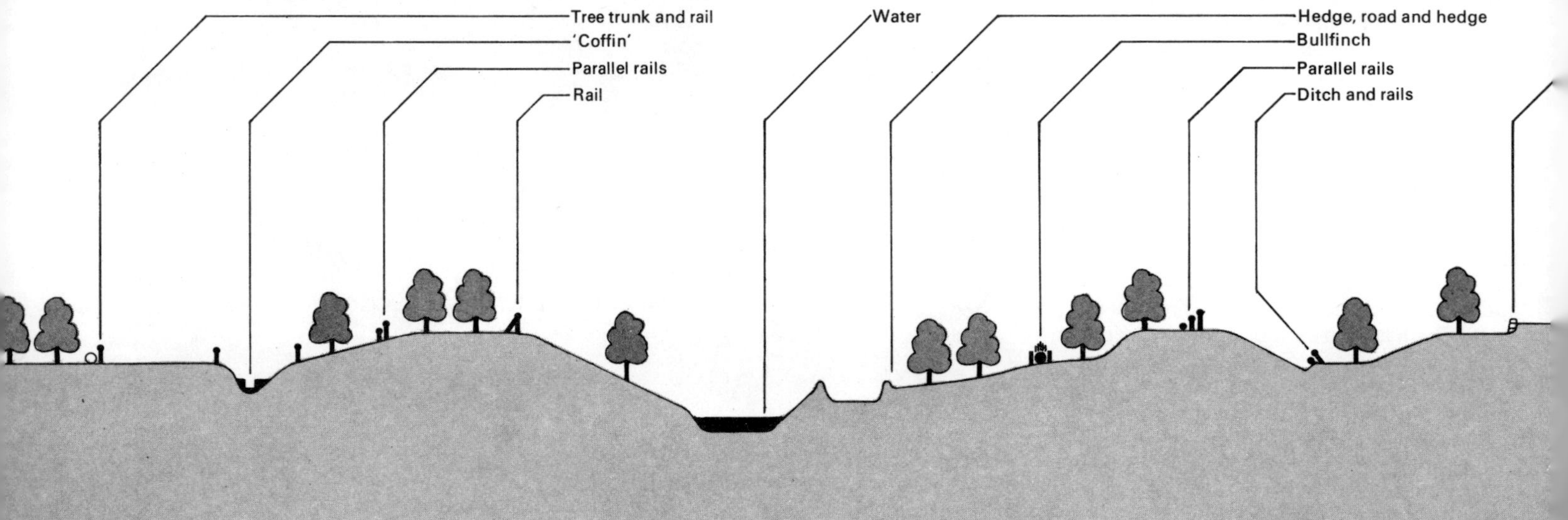

is something only experience can teach.

Generally, the smaller the course the more difficult it is to introduce variation and interest, for many of the bigger and more interesting fences are not satisfactory when reduced in scale. For this reason many course designers tend to make novice courses rather too difficult.

The designer generally starts by walking round the course with the owner of the land to decide the suitability of the site and to learn exactly what land may be used and what may not, at the same time looking for any interesting features and the state of the going. The latter varies with the time of the year, but at this stage the designer looks for any ground that should be avoided. The presence of rushes and patches of rather darker coloured grass should always arouse suspicion, and it should be axiomatic that any doubtful going, however conveniently situated, should be excluded. Having thoroughly familiarized himself with the ground it becomes possible for the designer to link up the various features into a continuous course. At this stage it is important to decide the situation of the start and finish, which for a timed competition must be together. Next the length of the course must be considered and a rough measurement can be taken from a 25 in to the mile map, which subsequently will be confirmed by measuring on the ground with a 'wheel'. There will always be a number of features on which it is easy to think up individual fences. If there are no natural fence lines to add to these, the designer's ingenuity is considerably taxed. On the other hand if there are natural fences he is often little better off, for most sites have the same type of fence enclosing every field. Repetitive thorn hedges with ditches or drystone walls become an embarrassment. With either natural or artificial fences the greater the variation the greater the appreciation. All materials used in construction should be really imposing and strong. WWT

Cowboy

The ranch cowboy in America, whose life and customs have been influenced directly by the Spanish herders since the sixteenth century, is the mainstay of present horse and cattle handling in the western territories of both the United States and Canada. Clothing, equipment and methods of handling stock have been passed down and refined from the Spanish and Mexican VAQUEROS. RS

The descendant of the ranch cowboy, the modern RODEO cowboy is like a professional athlete, but is completely on his own, without organized teams, salaries, insurance, team doctors or guarantees of any kind. He pays his own expenses, including entrance fees, out of what he wins. Most cowboys would not want it any other way since they like the independence of their way of life. A top cowboy can win $40,000 a year or more. Some earn even more by endorsing various products. Although only a handful of the thousands who compete each year can make a living from rodeo alone, its appeal is so strong that young men from farms and ranches all over the United States and Canada continue to 'go down the road'. CL

Cow Hocks

The joints of the hock are inclined towards each other. CF

Cow Pony see Cutting Horse

Crib Biting

Grasping the top of a door or the edge of the manger with the incisor teeth and swallowing air, leading to tympany and indigestion. Incisor teeth show irregular wear. See Vices. CF

Criollo see Argentina, Brazil, Peru

Crioulo Brazileiro see Brazil

Crossbreeding see Breeding

Course Building. Cross-country obstacles are of various types, built according to the terrain and available local materials.

Diagonal rail

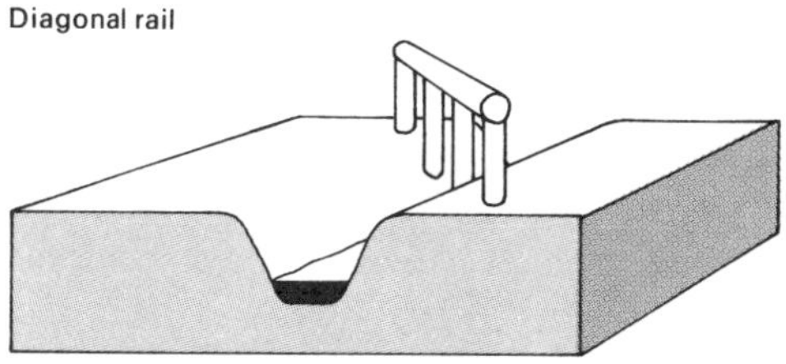

Crossed rails over ditch
'Cross question'

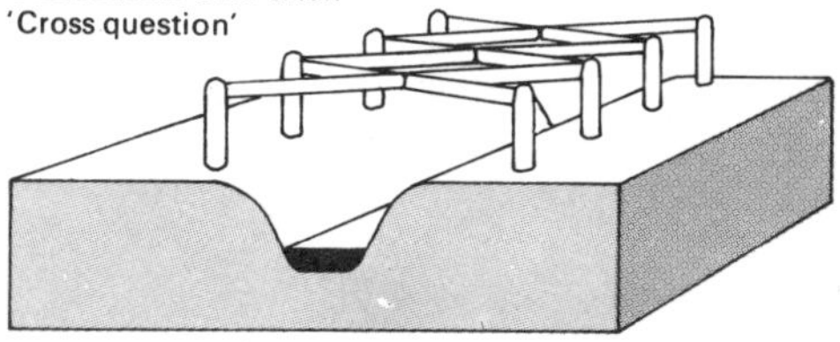

Stack of logs
'Woodpile'

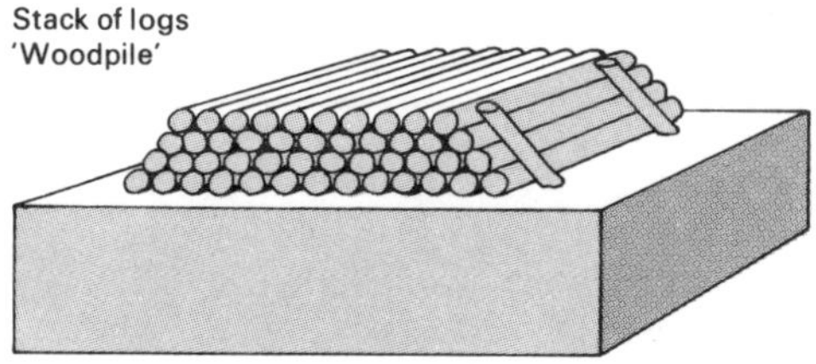

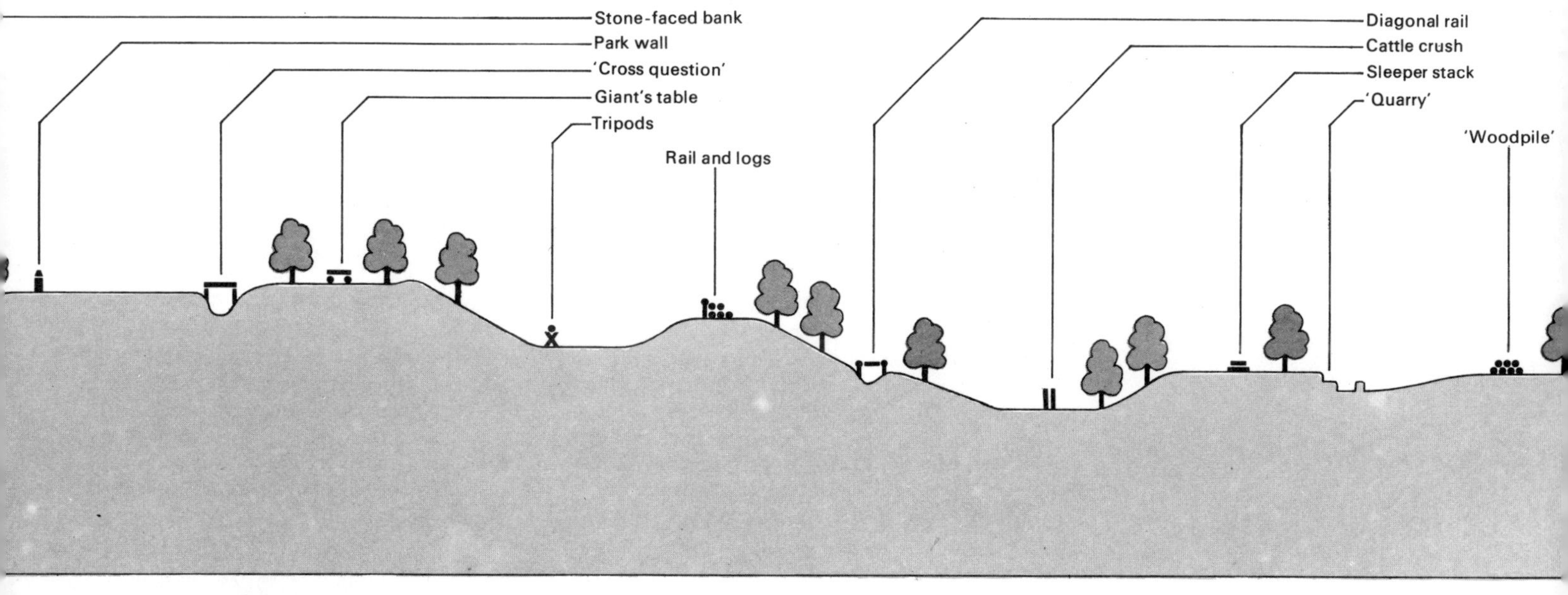

Cross-Country Events see Horse Trials, Combined Training, Course Building

Croupade see Airs, Classical

C.S.I., C.S.I.O. see Concours

Cuba see West Indies

Curb
A prominence about a hand's breadth below the point of the hock, conspicuous when the horse is viewed from the side. This is caused by sprain of the calcaneo-metatarsal ligament. CF

Curraleiro see Brazil

Cutting Horse
When cattle ranching started in the western United States, there were few fences and pens in which to hold and sort the cattle. They were herded, gathered and separated on the open range; horses were necessary for this work and the best of the cow horses could ease into a herd, drive the desired cow out and hold her out. A herd would be held

Cutting Horse. *Top:* An American cutting horse in training whirls to block the calf to keep it from getting back to the herd.
Above: A bullock breaks away from the mob during drafting in the Kimberleys, the far northern region of Western Australia.

on the gathering grounds and a 'cut' (herd of desired cows) would be started. Some riders would hold the main herd; others would station themselves to hold the 'cut'. A rider on a cutting horse would ease into the main herd, select a cow and drive her out to the 'cut', blocking her attempts to go back to the herd.

Today many people enjoy riding and showing cutting horses, and the sport has moved from the cattle ranges to show arenas with competition rules. The cutting horse is ridden quietly into the herd (slowly enough not to disturb the cattle but decisively enough to 'make the cut'), the cow is eased out and driven towards the centre of the arena. 'Turnback' men drive the cow back towards the cutting horse to make more action than normal, for in competition the rider has only $2\frac{1}{2}$ minutes to show what his horse can do. He is not allowed to rein or cue the horse in any way. Points are deducted for cueing, poor work, allowing the cow to get to the back fence and losing the cow. DJ

Czechoslovakia
The largest and most celebrated stud in Czechoslovakia is that at Kladruby-on-Elbe, founded in the middle of the sixteenth century by Emperor Maximilian II, who brought a number of Spanish horses to Bohemia and stabled them in the grounds of a deer park at Kladruby. In 1756 the castle and stables were burned down and all documents destroyed. The Emperor Joseph II (Maria Theresa's son) rebuilt them and in 1770 a new phase began which has continued uninterrupted to the present. The famous white Kladrub horses of the Generale and Generalissimo family are bred there. The first strain was founded in 1787 by Generale, the second some years later by his son Generalissimo. They have a pronounced head, noble stature and majestic walk. They were formerly bred mainly as coach horses for the imperial court in Vienna. Nowadays the Kladrub white horses are slightly reduced in numbers, but teams of 10, 8, 6 and 4 often take part in international events. Kladruby now breeds mainly halfbred horses of the Furioso, Alarm and Gidran families; there are on average 500–550 horses there at any one time.

Of other studs where horses are bred for sport, the best-known is the former military stud at Albertovec in Silesia, now controlled by the Ministry of Agriculture. Others are at Tlumačov in Moravia, Šamorín and Motěšice in Slovakia. The well-known Topolčianky stud is also in Slovakia. Arab horses are bred here. A small number of mountain horses, Fird (Fjord), Nonius and Anglo-Arab horses are bred for sport. An international auction of riding horses from all Czechoslovak studs is held annually at Topolčianky.

English Thoroughbreds are bred at Napajedla in Moravia. This stud was founded by the amateur rider Count Aristide Baltazzi in 1887; the first stallion bred there was the English Derby winner of 1876, Kisbér. There are now about 50–60 brood mares there. Horses are also bred by many of the state farms and agricultural cooperatives, as well as by a number of private breeders and riding clubs. Most of the horses bred in Czechoslovakia are warmbloods; they are suitable for riding and light draught work. In Moravia crosses with English Thoroughbreds are favoured, and in Slovakia Arab or Anglo-Arab crosses predominate. English Thoroughbred horses are also bred at Xaverov, near Prague, where the stallions Court Gift and Royal David, imported from England, are currently standing.

Today there are over 45,000 horses in Czechoslovakia. Twenty years ago there were nearly 600,000. Competitive riding in Czechoslovakia is controlled by the Czechoslovak Horse Riding Federation to which both the Czech and Slovak Federations belong. Every year national championships are held in all events. There are currently about 150 riding clubs in the Czech Republic and another 40 in the Slovak Republic. The number of registered riders totals 7,000, with about 1,200 registered horses including about 400 first-rate competition horses. See also Grand Pardubice.

Arab: the Arab has a long and rich tradition in Czechoslovakia, or rather in Slovakia. Its introduction can be traced to the period of the Turkish wars when Turks gained the favour of Hungarian princes through the excellence of their Arab horses, which in turn greatly improved the progeny of the local mares.

The State stud at Topolčianky in Slovakia —about 150 km (95 miles) northeast of Bratislava, the capital of Slovakia—was founded in 1921, and today is the only one in Czechoslovakia where pure Arabs are bred. This stud extends over six estates, between 220 and 480 m (720–1,575 ft) above sea level. The area consists of 940 hectares (2,323 acres) of fields and meadows, woods, gardens and vineyards. In 1921 stallions were bought from Radovec and Bábolna in Hungary and from Poland. Those from Radovec were stallions of the Shagya and Dahoman families, those from Bábolna were also Shagya, and from Poland came Aghil Aga and Jasmak. The descendants of the Shagya strain from Radovec are typical Arabs, of impressive stature, long swinging walk and good performance, mostly grey in colour. There is little difference between the Radovec and Bábolna strains.

The descendants of Polish stallions form another numbered strain of Arab horses, but they are mostly brown in colour. Currently the stallions standing at Topolčianky are Dahoman (born 1954), Shagya XXI (1950), Koheilen (1961) and Rasim II (1958). All of them are Czech bred. The only foreign stallion is Siglavy from Bábolna. There are 25 Arab brood mares, 15 of Shagya strain, three Koheilen, four Orestes, two Saqlawi (Siglavy) and one Rasim. During its fifty years the Topolčianky stud has produced hundreds of Arabs, many of which have been sold to other countries, including the United States and West Germany. PNe

Dahoman a strain of ARAB

Da-Kyu see Mounted Games, Polo.

Dales Pony see Mountain and Moorland

Danubian Horse

The Danubian Horse was developed from the NONIUS breed at the Georgi Dimitrov State Agricultural Farm near Pleven over four or five decades. Nonius stallions and mares were imported from Hungary, Yugoslavia and Czechoslovakia. By crossing

Czechoslovakia. *Below:* A team of thirteen Kladruber horses
Bottom: Horsedrawn hayrakes

purebred Nonius stallions with Anglo-Arab mares of the Gidran strain a horse was created of solid and compact conformation, without coarseness. The Danubian is black or dark chestnut and about 15·2½ hands (1·60 m) high. It is a draught horse, able to pull heavy loads (up to 13 tons) at a good speed. Some Danubian horses of the lighter type are also used for riding and competitive sports, certain crosses with Thoroughbred stallions producing good jumpers. This breed is found in the Danube region and in the southern Bulgarian plains. VP, II

Darashouri see Persian Horse, Plateau Persian

Darley Arabian
This horse of Eastern origin was imported by Mr Darley, brother of Mr Brewster Darley of Buttercranbe (now called Aldby Park) near York. He was foaled around 1702, was a bay horse with a blaze and three white socks and stood about 15 hands (1·52 m). Wootton painted an excellent picture of him. He proved to be a more important sire than either the BYERLEY TURK or the GODOLPHIN BARB. The Darley Arabian sired the two brothers Flying Childers and Bartlett's Childers, out of the famous mare Betty Leedes. His great-great-grandson was Eclipse, of whom it was said: 'Eclipse first, the rest nowhere'. See Thoroughbred. DMG

Below: **Danubian**

Bottom: **Darley Arabian.** One of the three famous foundation sires of the Thoroughbred, one of his sons was Flying Childers. Another was Bulle Rock, the first Thoroughbred to go to America.

Dartmoor see Mountain and Moorland

d'Aure
Comte Antoine Henri Philippe Léon d'Aure (1799–1863) was a noted French master of equitation during the reigns of Louis XVIII and Charles X. He was the last *Écuyer en Chef* of the Royal Equestrian School of Versailles (dissolved in 1830) and the first (1847) *Écuyer en Chef* of the famous *Cadre Noir* of Saumur (see France).

Although in the first chapter of his book, *Traité d'Équitation*, he pays tribute to BAUCHER, three years his senior, his own teachings were in fact the antithesis of Baucher's, for d'Aure considered excessive dressage, outside the circus, entirely fallacious and positively harmful to cavalry, foreshadowing in a sense the theories evolved more than a century later and in more concrete form by CAPRILLI and SANTINI.

He attempted to combine at Saumur the good points of both the German and the English schools by avoiding the excessive over-collection of the former and the slapdash style of the latter. However, unlike Caprilli or Santini, d'Aure established no fixed theories. In the end it was Baucher who recommended the use of the plain snaffle bit while d'Aure selected as his successor at Saumur an exponent of dressage. LFB

de la Guérinière, François Robichon see La Guérinière, François Robichon de

Deli see Batak

Demi-sang see Norman, Anglo-Norman and French Saddle Horse

Denmark
The horse population of Denmark has decreased since World War II and is said now to number about 35,000. The FJORD PONY breed, which originated in Norway, predominates and is in great demand by small fruit and vegetable growers.

In 1562, under King Frederick II (1559–88), Denmark was the leading breeder and supplier of school horses to the courts of Continental Europe. In the eighteenth century the Frederiksborg horse was used as an 'improver' in many studs; in some parts of the Jutland peninsula it was used on the old medium-heavy JUTLAND breed to get more activity. From the middle of the seventeenth century to the end of the eighteenth the Frederiksborg was admired, according to Count Wrangel, writing in 1908, for 'elegant conformation, his lively and kindly temperament and his strong, sweeping and high action'. The stud was dissolved in 1839. The modern Frederiksborg has little, if any, connection with the old breed. But it is a very good light draught/harness horse, generally chestnut in colour.

One of the most important breeds was and still is the Jutland, whose ancestors supplied knights with war horses. In 1862 the imported dark chestnut stallion Oppenheim LXII influenced the breed enormously. He has often been described erroneously as a SHIRE, but according to Danish breeders was a SUFFOLK PUNCH; this is more likely since Oppenheim, a horse dealer operating from Hamburg, had bought and imported Suffolk Punches into Germany for the Mecklenburg Stud. DMG

Reference: Count C. G. Wrangel, *Die Rassen des Pferdes*, Stuttgart, 1908–9.

Derby (Jumping)

The prototype show-jumping Derby was held in Hamburg and was so successful that the formula of cross-country show jumping over a long course incorporating such permanent obstacles as banks, sunken fences, water ditches and stone walls has been adopted elsewhere with considerable enthusiasm. The most noteworthy examples are the W. D. and H. O. Wills British Jumping Derby, open to the world, which is held at Douglas Bunn's All England Jumping Course at Hickstead in Sussex, and the French Jumping Derby, held in the seaside resort of La Baule.

The Hamburg Jumping Derby used to be renowned as the most gruelling show-jumping competition in the world. Initiated in 1920, it did not produce a single clear round until 1935.

The British Jumping Derby came into being in 1961. Most prominently featured among its sixteen obstacles is the Derby Bank, with its precipitous drop of 10 ft 6 in (3·2 m), which alarmed many riders. But over the years there have been comparatively few falls or faults at the bank, apart from a most unfortunate fatal accident in 1972. The most prevalent penalty area has proved to be the notorious tripartite Devil's Dyke, with its sunken middle element over 8 ft (2·4 m) of water, which has taken the heaviest toll in faults and refusals.

Although three riders—Seamus Hayes, of Ireland, on Goodbye (the winner in the inaugural year and again in 1964), Nelson Pessoa of Brazil on Grand Geste and Harvey Smith for Britain on Mattie Brown—have each won the Jumping Derby twice, the last in two consecutive years, only a dozen clear rounds have been jumped since its beginning in 1961. Three of them have been achieved by Marion Mould on Stroller, the ladies' world champion in 1965 and the winner of the Olympic silver medal in 1968. Other notable winners have been Pat Smythe with Flanagan, David Broome with Mister Softee, Alison Dawes with The Maverick and Anneli Drummond-Hay with Xanthos. Although the United States team has taken part more often than any other visiting force, they have yet to win it. Germany came very close in 1970, when Alwin Schockemohle and Donald Rex finished as runners-up after falling at the oxer in the barrage, but the first German victory was recorded in 1972, when Hendrik Snoek won on Shirroko. This time there were no clear rounds, and Snoek, still a student at Munster University, won after a jump-off with Paddy McMahon, riding Fred Hartill's Pennwood Forgemill, the top horse of the year in Britain, for the home side. Marion Mould and Stroller are the only British combination ever to have won the Hamburg Jumping Derby.

The Derby competition is undoubtedly the event of the future, for its element of danger and the type of setting in which it is held makes it a welcome change from the stereotyped stadium contest which is basically much the same all over the world. The risk involved is such that high prize money is imperative, and stakes today may total as much as £6,000, with £2,000 going to the winner. PMM

Derby (Jumping). The original Derby Bank at Hickstead. Its position and slope have been modified.

Derby

The Epsom Derby, one of the most famous

races in the world, was founded in 1780, but is not the most senior of the five 'CLASSIC RACES', the Doncaster St Leger having been instituted in 1776.

The Oaks, a race for three-year-old fillies, was started in 1779 by the twelfth Earl of Derby, who entertained his friends for Epsom races at his nearby country house, The Oaks. After its success, it was decided to run another three-year-old race for both colts and fillies over 1 mile (1·61 km) the following year. There is a story that a toss of a coin decided whether the race was to be called the Derby Stakes or the Bunbury Stakes, Sir Charles Bunbury being the foremost racing man of the day and a guest at The Oaks. Perhaps the guests insisted on naming the race in honour of their host. As the fifth Earl of Rosebery observed a hundred years later, 'A roystering party at a country house founded two races, and named them gratefully after their host and his house, the Derby and the Oaks. Seldom has a carouse had a more permanent effect.'

The winner of the first Derby was Sir Charles Bunbury's Diomed, who, at the advanced age of twenty when his sphere of usefulness was apparently over, was exported for 50 guineas to America. He survived for a further ten years, founded a dynasty, and from him are descended many famous horses in American racing history.

When the Derby was founded, English racing was still conducted on primitive lines, horses competing on rough, unprepared ground. The sport was ignored by the newspapers, details being available only in the *Racing Calendar*.

The growth of the Derby into eminence was gradual; it hardly attained national fame until fifty years after its foundation and then largely through being boosted in *Bell's Life in London*, a popular sporting newspaper first published in 1822. By 1847 the prestige of the Derby was such that it became the custom, now discontinued, for Parliament to adjourn from Tuesday to Thursday in Epsom week. In the mid-Victorian era, Derby Day was a great national festival. People went to Epsom less to see the race than to have a good time at the gigantic fair on the Downs. Towards the end of Queen Victoria's reign, the festival spirit was dying and the race itself assumed increasing importance.

In 1784 the distance of the Derby was increased to $1\frac{1}{2}$ miles (2·40 km) and has remained so ever since. The present Derby course was first used in 1872. It provides a splendid test for a Thoroughbred. A true-run mile and a half demands both speed and stamina, eliminating both short-runners and plodders who cannot accelerate. The gradients require a horse to gallop both up-

Derby (Racing). *Above left:* Diomed, the winner of the first Epsom Derby, was later exported to the United States where, at the age of 23, he became the progenitor of many racehorses and influential sires.
Top: Persimmon, here winning the Derby in 1896, also won the St Leger, and the Ascot Gold Cup and Eclipse Stakes in 1897.
Above: The 1971 Derby was won by Geoff Lewis on Mill Reef. Here the field is at Tattenham Corner, with Mill Reef and Geoff Lewis (striped cap) in fourth place.

Derby Winners

1780	Diomed	1845	Merry Monarch	1909	Minoru
1781	Young Eclipse	1846	Pyrrhus the First	1910	Lemberg
1782	Assassin	1847	The Cossack	1911	Sunstar
1783	Saltram	1848	Surplice	1912	Tagalie
1784	Serjeant	1849	The Flying Dutchman	1913	Aboyeur
1785	Aimwell	1850	Voltigeur	1914	Dunbar II
1786	Noble	1851	Teddington	1915	Pommern
1787	Sir Peter Teazle	1852	Daniel O'Rourke	1916	Fifinella
1788	Sir Thomas	1853	West Australian	1917	Gay Crusader
1789	Skyscraper	1854	Andover	1918	Gainsborough
1790	Rhadamanthus	1855	Wild Dayrell	1919	Grand Parade
1791	Eager	1856	Ellington	1920	Spion Kop
1792	John Bull	1857	Blink Bonny	1921	Humorist
1793	Waxy	1858	Beadsman	1922	Captain Cuttle
1794	Daedalus	1859	Musjid	1923	Papyrus
1795	Spread Eagle	1860	Thormanby	1924	Sansovino
1796	Didelot	1861	Kettledrum	1925	Manna
1797	Br. c. by Fidget	1862	Caractacus	1926	Coronach
1798	Sir Harry	1863	Macaroni	1927	Call Boy
1799	Archduke	1864	Blair Athol	1928	Felstead
1800	Champion	1865	Gladiateur	1929	Trigo
1801	Eleanor	1866	Lord Lyon	1930	Blenheim
1802	Tyrant	1867	Hermit	1931	Cameronian
1803	W's Ditto	1868	Blue Gown	1932	April the Fifth
1804	Hannibal	1869	Pretender	1933	Hyperion
1805	Cardinal Beaufort	1870	Kingcraft	1934	Windsor Lad
1806	Paris	1871	Favonius	1935	Bahram
1807	Election	1872	Cremorne	1936	Mahmoud
1808	Pan	1873	Doncaster	1937	Mid-day Sun
1809	Pope	1874	George Frederick	1938	Bois Roussel
1810	Whalebone	1875	Galopin	1939	Blue Peter
1811	Phantom	1876	Kisber	1940	Pont l'Eveque
1812	Octavius	1877	Silvio	1941	Owen Tudor
1813	Smolensko	1878	Sefton	1942	Watling Street
1814	Blucher	1879	Sir Bevys	1943	Straight Deal
1815	Whisker	1880	Bend Or	1944	Ocean Swell
1816	Prince Leopold	1881	Iroquois	1945	Dante
1817	Azor	1882	Shotover	1946	Airborne
1818	Sam	1883	St Blaise	1947	Pearl Diver
1819	Tiresias	*1884	St Gatien	1948	My Love
1820	Sailor		Harvester	1949	Nimbus
1821	Gustavus	1885	Melton	1950	Galcador
1822	Moses	1886	Ormonde	1951	Arctic Prince
1823	Emilius	1887	Merry Hampton	1952	Tulyar
1824	Cedric	1888	Ayrshire	1953	Pinza
1825	Middleton	1889	Donovan	1954	Never Say Die
1826	Lapdog	1890	Sainfoin	1955	Phil Drake
1827	Mameluke	1891	Common	1956	Lavandin
1828	Cadland	1892	Sir Hugo	1957	Crepello
1829	Frederick	1893	Isinglass	1958	Hard Ridden
1830	Priam	1894	Ladas	1959	Parthia
1831	Spaniel	1895	Sir Visto	1960	St Paddy
1832	St Giles	1896	Persimmon	1961	Psidium
1833	Dangerous	1897	Galtee More	1962	Larkspur
1834	Plenipotentiary	1898	Jeddah	1963	Relko
1835	Mündig	1899	Flying Fox	1964	Santa Claus
1836	Bay Middleton	1900	Diamond Jubilee	1965	Sea Bird II
1837	Phosphorus	1901	Volodyovski	1966	Charlottown
1838	Amato	1902	Ard Patrick	1967	Royal Palace
1839	Bloomsbury	1903	Rock Sand	1968	Sir Ivor
1840	Little Wonder	1904	St Amant	1969	Blakeney
1841	Coronation	1905	Cicero	1970	Nijinsky
1842	Attila	1906	Spearmint	1971	Mill Reef
1843	Cotherstone	1907	Orby	1972	Roberto
1844	Orlando	1908	Signorinetta	1973	

*Divided after a dead heat

Below: **Destrier.** Dürer's *St George on Horseback* shows a late medieval warhorse.

hill and down, and in particular the steep descent to Tattenham Corner ensures that the race is seldom won by a horse of poor conformation. The crowds, the air of tension, and the lengthy parade in front of the stands combine to form a test of a horse's temperament. See colour plate on page 170. See also Kentucky Derby. RM

Destrier

A great war horse or charger, from Latin, *dextrarius* (the right side), the side on which the squire led his master's horse. See Warfare, Horse in

Difficult Horses

The horse and pony throughout the long

period during which they have been subject to man's dominance have remained in varying degrees difficult in their behaviour and have caused their riders and drivers countless accidents and untold periods of fright and mental upset. Curiously, however, the ass, which is of the horse family, does not suffer these disabilities, or only in the smallest degree.

It is generally accepted that all foals are born free from vice and the many shortcomings to which the horse is prone. The savage horse, i.e. one that will attack human beings without provocation with teeth and fore legs, is an exception. These are extremely dangerous and should be destroyed, as the condition is hereditary. If, then, the newborn foal is free from vice, what causes it to develop into a problem horse? The answer almost certainly lies in its upbringing. In considering this, one vital factor must be borne in mind. How intelligent is the horse? Opinions vary surprisingly, many knowledgeable horsemen rate it rather highly, many others hold it to be low.

It may be confidently asserted that most forms of vice can be cured by a fairly long long period of careful retraining to recreate confidence. The horse has a long and retentive memory, thus time must be given to forget the troubled past. Obviously this is by no means always possible. How then is the horseman to deal with any of the vices which may suddenly and embarrassingly confront him? Happily for him the horse, probably because of its rather simple mind, is easily confused. Thus the horse which refuses to go forward, declines to enter a horsebox or starting stall at a racecourse, rears or runs backwards, will often do what is required after being circled sharply on its hocks once or twice and then urged forward. Some covering over the head to confuse it generally has the same effect. Many horses shy at or refuse to pass a certain object. To cure this, familiarize them with the object.

There are many vices and bad habits of a different kind, however, such as crib-biting, wind-sucking, weaving, bed-eating, biting and rug-stripping. All these may well have been produced by overfeeding and lack of sufficient exercise. The cure is less food and more exercise. When the cause is found, common sense usually suggests the remedy. See also Vices, Mind of the Horse. RSS

Disabled, Riding for the

Ever since Greek athletes put crippled people on horses after the Games, we may suppose that the disabled travelled by horse in some way as horses were the principal means of transport. But today, as we are used to mechanical transport, the idea of using horses, now associated with sport, for disabled persons surprises most people.

After the 1947 poliomyelitis outbreak in Britain when there were many children in hospital for long stays, the idea came more or less simultaneously to Miss S. Saywell at Winford Orthopaedic Hospital in London and to a hospital in Norway that the endless and boring exercises these children had to do would be much more interesting and exciting if performed on a pony's back. This proved to be so, and was so successful that the Advisory Council on Riding for the Disabled was formed in 1964. Its groups of volunteers all over England, Scotland and Wales provide physical help, ponies and their transport, professional help in the form of physiotherapists and doctors, and organize regular rides for disabled children and adults. This work was taken over in 1969 by the Riding for the Disabled Association (a registered charity) with headquarters at the National Equestrian Centre, Kenilworth, Warwickshire. In 1971 there were 150 groups in the British Isles, with regional representation on the Council. Some are connected with riding schools, some with residential schools for the physically or mentally disabled and some are independent. Organizations from five other countries were represented at the Association's annual conference in 1971.

Almost every type of disability can be helped by regular riding under professional guidance. Apart from the obvious emotional and social benefits of regular contact with outsiders (including one-up-manship over the rider's normal brothers and sisters!) the physical benefits vary from a general improvement in health to specific increase in mobility, coordination and balance. An extraordinary widening of interests and ambitions is also achieved. Two examples: a seven-year-old spastic who had never spoken before produced full sentences at his third ride; a bed-bound, and later chair-bound, boy who had never walked learned to manoeuvre himself and pony in space so well that he learned the highway code, passed his driving test in an invalid car and is now a self-supporting journalist.

The ponies and horses used must be carefully selected, although most well-trained animals pick up the idea very quickly; a surprising empathy is established between the disabled and their mounts. Equipment is kept as simple and normal as possible, although various adaptations become necessary from time to time, for example extra-long looped reins for armless children, basket saddles for the legless and paddings for vulnerable areas.

An indoor school is ideal so that these activities can occur regularly despite the weather. Where there is no school any fenced-off area will do. At the start it is usually necessary to have three helpers, one to lead the pony and two to steady the rider. However, very soon riders can manage almost alone, with only a leader alongside in case of trouble. Suitable exercises are performed, first at the halt and later at different paces. Mounted games are a great source of enjoyment; remarkable relaxation and co-ordination are achieved in this way.

There are also established riders who become disabled. Their determination to ride again and their ingenuity can be helped by a local group with experience in methods of mounting and special equipment. GTP

Horsemanship for the handicapped began to be organized in the United States in 1967, originally following British practice but the size of the country with its varied geography and climate made certain innovations necessary. Opportunities for academic credit courses and career training are available. The use of Western saddles and neck reining is very helpful to armless or legless riders. The smooth gait of the PASO horse eases riding for the severely handicapped. MHW

Dished Face (Stag Face)

A concave face, characteristic of the ARAB

Docking

In 1948 it became illegal in Britain to dock or nick a horse's tail, except where a veterinary surgeon deems it necessary to amputate the tail or part of it to combat disease. In the past it was the practice to remove the lower part of the tail of harness horses and some types of riding horses. Before it became illegal to dock a horse (for a time it was allowed to be done under an anaesthetic on certain classes of horses) it was the cruel practice just to cut off the dock and apply a hot docking iron to the end to stop bleeding. It is illegal in most of the United States. DRT

Døle, Dølehest see Gudbrandsdal

Domada see Mounted Games

Don, Donsky

The Russian Don was important to the Tsarist cavalry and is now used as a riding horse and also in harness. It was the foundation of the new BUDYONNY breed; it was also used to improve many native Russian breeds such as the KAZAKH and the KIRGIZ. The head is medium-sized, often light, with a straight or hook-nosed profile. The ears are small and mobile; the brow is wide, eyes large, nostrils delicate. The neck is medium long, often straight; the withers medium long and low. The back is straight and wide, the loins straight and solid, the croup wide, long and slightly lowered. The shoulder blade is usually steeply inclined and not long; this limits the amount of ground the Don covers in a stride. The chest is well-developed, the ribs are long and tight, and the thigh is short. The hindlegs have a tendency to be sickle-hocked, and the fore legs often have fallen-in, 'calf' joints. The hoofs are large, with strong bone. The Don has a calm but energetic character. Average height at withers for stallions is about 15·2½ hands (1·59 m), for mares 15·2¼ hands (1·56 m); bone below the knee for stallions 8 in (20·6 cm), for mares 7½ in (19·3 cm).

The Don has a regular but not very elegant or elastic movement. The shoulder, often straight and steep, and the pelvic corner, often strong and uncovered, tend to limit the forward movement at trot and canter. Moreover, the pastern is frequently very perpendicular, producing a jolting gait, while the poll is frequently short and thus interferes with collection.

In developing the Don and Kazakh breeds, horses of the South Russian steppe, obtained by the Cossacks from nomads and distant droves, were used. KARABAKH, TURKMEN, and PERSIAN HORSES obtained as trophies were the best of the foundation stock. More recently, Russian riding stallions (Orlov and Orlov-Rostopchinsky) were used, and also English Thoroughbreds. At first, the breed was light, hardy and very mobile. Then a more powerful animal was

Don, Donsky. A popular cavalry horse, the Don is also used in harness.

developed, with a better conformation; golden chestnuts became predominant in this period. By 1920, the Don was fully developed as a cavalry horse in studs in Rostov, Volgograd, Astrakhan, Saratovsky, Kazakhstan, and Kirgizia. WOF

Dongola

The Dongola takes its name from the district in Nubia and is still to be found in Alfaia and Gerri. Emperor Haile Selassie of Ethiopia has a stud and breeds Dongola horses for racing. See Africa. DMG

Doping of Racehorses

A horse's performance can be either improved or reduced by the administration of various drugs but such an alteration of form cannot be achieved without endangering the horse and its rider. Doping can be used to perpetrate gigantic betting swindles. If doping went unchecked, performance on the racecourse would cease to be a guide to the selection of the best horses for breeding.

British and U.S. racing rules forbid the administration to a racehorse of any substance (other than a normal nutrient) that could alter its racing performance at the time of racing. Horses are subjected to veterinary inspection before a race. Immediately after racing samples of urine and saliva may be examined in the laboratory for the presence of drugs. Trainers of racehorses shown to have been doped may, if proved to have been at fault, lose their licences to train or they may be fined. Legal action for fraud may be instituted. British racing statistics suggest that about 80 horses might be doped out of 50,000 declared runners per year.

In the past most drugs used for doping were stimulating alkaloids: caffeine, cocaine, strychnine and morphine, or, later, amphetamine, all easily identified by modern analytical methods. In the 1930s there were horrific stories of over-stimulated horses bolting down the course completely out of control. Then came the turn of the 'stoppers' or depressant drugs, as, for instance, when in the early 1960s a number of ante-post favourites were found 'nobbled' in their stables, having been given barbiturates to prevent them running. More recently, dopers have tended to favour tranquillizers and anti-inflammatory drugs, such as butazolidin, as well as hormones.

Drugs may be administered by all kinds of methods: by mouth, in drinking water or feed, or as a drench, ball, powder or electuary, by injection, perhaps even by aerosol spray or rubbing into the skin. A doper must have close access to a horse and to achieve the best effect he must give an exact dose at exactly the right time before the race. The best precaution against such interference is good security, not only at the home stables and on the racecourse but also at stopping places between them.

Routine laboratory testing of horses' body fluids has for long been a useful deterrent to the practice of doping. Today, improved analytical techniques allow the detection of minute residues of drugs days after they have been administered. At one time it was thought safe to stop veterinary therapy 72 hours before a race; now, especially with anti-inflammatory drugs, it is advised that medication should cease at least eight days before a race. JC

Dosanko Horse see Japan

Double Bit see Bits and Bitting, Bridles

Drag Hunting

Drag hunting or hunting an artificial scent made by a linesman trailing something of strong smell to allow hounds to follow at speed, is becoming increasingly popular in many countries. The object is to allow riders to travel at speed across country over a variety of fences laid on by the hunt in agreement with farmers to avoid galloping over young grass or crops. Foxhounds are mainly used for drag hunting as they follow the scent really well. There is, of course, no real quarry and hounds receive a reward at the end of the hunt. JHew

Dragoon see Warfare, Horse in

Draught Horses horses used for drawing a vehicle. The breeds are described under individual headings.

Draw Rein a rein fixed to the girth and passing through the bit rings to the rider's hand.

Dressage

This term, which is the French for training, has by extension been applied to academic equitation, though its original and basic meaning is merely the systematic training of the horse. This is subdivided into three main phases: breaking in, basic training, and the fairly advanced schooling that is popularly associated mostly with 'dressage'.

The first phase produces, in about ten months, a physically fit horse, going forward keenly and in a natural attitude on the bit at the three paces, its calm testifying to trust in its rider.

The second phase produces a gradual engagement of the hind legs through growing flexibility of quarters and a neck proceeding toward the *ramener*, a head carriage obtained at the rider's demand by a flexion at the poll, not to be confused with *self-carriage*, the way the horse naturally carries its head. Maximum length and elasticity of its 'springs' is developed through *lateral suppling* (circles, serpentines, half-turns on the fore hand and quarters) and *longitudinal suppling* (speed-ups, slow-downs, halts, rein backs, transitions between paces) and *the work on two tracks*, all conducive to good balance (see Movements). This phase, including its work outside the school and over fences, is part and parcel of any horse's education; only the stress laid on one or the other activity varies in accordance with its prospective career.

The third phase brings the horse up to its 'speciality'. For example, where the goal is *haute école*, one gradually improves to near perfection the lightness which much more than any specific movement constitutes the hallmark of this art, where the horse's forces are harmonized to allow perfect balance in motion, where constant eagerness to advance never disrupts calm or disturbs straightness, where all this is combined with instant response to the slightest indications, whatever the demand, so that the image arising is that of a horse moving of and on its own. JF

Dressage Tests

Dressage tests are designed to demonstrate and evaluate training results. They are competitive, taking place in an arena (full size 60 × 20 m, modified size admissible in some national competitions 40 × 20 m; see diagram under Movements) in front of a judge or jury giving marks for each movement and for a number of 'general impressions', such as lightness, impulsion, correctness and discretion of aids.

Each national federation elaborates its own tests for home use, the top test directly preparatory to the first of an upper-level series established by the FÉDÉRATION ÉQUESTRE INTERNATIONALE, called *Prix Saint-Georges* (Number Five). Number Six (*Reprise Intermédiaire*) and Number Seven (*Grand Prix* or *Reprise Olympique*) follow. They and the dressage test of the C.C.I., C.C.I.O. and C.C.E.O., also designed by the F.E.I., are the only ones admitted in international competition. See page 169. JF

Driving

Although horses have been used as draught animals for many centuries, driving as a branch of equestrian recreation dates from about the last quarter of the eighteenth century. The art of driving may be divided into three general schools, each developed for a distinct purpose. The first may be called the working-horse school in which the main function of the driver is the guiding of the horses and the control of their pace. Horses performing heavy work usually learn how to make the most effective use of their weight and strength without depending on any assistance from the driver through the reins. Indeed for some tasks the driver may direct the horses by voice alone, or he may use a single rein for guidance as in 'jerk-line' or 'check-rein' driving, in which a team of several horses is guided by one rein attached to the near-side lead horse, who is taught to turn to the right when the rein is jerked and to the left when it is given a steady pull. With horses and ponies in lighter work the driver may have a continuing contact through the reins to govern the pace, but his aim is only to ensure that the task is done without wasted effort in the time allowed without much concern for style. The working-horse school is a broad grouping of all those different styles of driving where utility is the keynote as to harness, vehicles and performance of the horses.

The second school is concerned with driving fast trotters where speed is a first aim. This school of driving was developed in those countries where fairly long distances had to be covered over unpaved roads or tracks that were at times deep in mud or

Dressage. *Top:* Horst Kohler, riding Immanuel, demonstrates a pirouette to the left at the canter. *Above:* Josef Neckermann, on Mariano, performs an extended trot.

soft sand, hard and stony or covered in snow in winter, conditions calling for light but strong vehicles. Such conditions are found in parts of eastern Europe and North America and it is in those places that the driving of fast trotters has been most developed. The style of driving them has been called the 'firm contact' style because the forward positioning of the horse's balance which fast trotting demands often needs support from the driver through the reins, hence the use of snaffle bits. The overdraw bearing rein is usual with the American type of harness, and its function is to promote the correct extension of head and neck to achieve the maximum forward thrust of the horse's weight. This overdraw check, or bearing rein, is attached to its own bridoon bit by straps which come together across the horse's face and pass upwards between the eyes, through a loop on the bridle crown-piece between the horse's ears, from there down the neck to a hook on the pad. The American patterns of racing harness and sulkies have now been adopted in most countries where the sport flourishes. When driving racing trotters it is usual to hold a rein in each hand, and sometimes hand holds, or loops, are used on the reins to give a firmer hold. If the reins are held in one hand, as when driving a roadster, the off rein is passed over the first finger and down through the hand while the near rein is brought round the outside of the little finger and up through the hand. A straight whip with a short 'snapper' but no thong is carried.

With Hungarian harness various snaffle bits are used; the two reins are buckled to a short hand-piece which is so adjusted that it can be held in the full left hand without leaving any slack in the reins. When the handpiece is held at the centre, both reins should be of equal length and the horse will move straight forward. Turns are made by sliding the left hand along the hand-piece to the appropriate side, the right hand taking the reins while this is done. A pair is driven in the same manner and the four reins used for four- or five-in-hand driving are buckled into a single hand-piece in a similar way, the length of the reins being carefully adjusted so the draught is shared by both wheelers and leaders.

The third school, generally known as the English school, admits of greater development as a form of equestrian skill and is the style usually followed by amateurs of driving. Edwin Howlett, a professional coachman of English parentage who lived in Paris in the latter part of the last century, was one of the early pioneers of the English school. Among his pupils was the German, Benno von Achenbach, who became acknowledged as the leading exponent of driving in Germany and who wrote a valuable textbook on the subject. Achenbach was largely responsible for the survival of driving as a sport in Germany after the advent of the car. Howlett's pupils also included several wealthy Americans, one of whom, Fairman Rogers, wrote a classic work on coaching, *The Manual of Coaching* (1900). The English style of driving, as well as the kind of harness used with it, became known in North America as 'heavy harness' to distinguish it from the native 'light harness' style as used with fast trotters, roadsters and fine harness horses. The English school aims at precise control of direction and pace. The horses, by the use of curb bits, move in a more collected manner, and when the aim is movement with considerable presence and style rather than speed it has been called 'park driving'. The high-stepping Hackneys seen in the show ring are an extreme development of the park-driving school.

In the English school the reins both for single and multiple harness are held in the left hand, and the whip, of the bow-topped pattern, in the right hand. With single and pair harness the near, or left, rein passes over the forefinger and the off rein between the second and third fingers, and both reins pass together down the palm of the hand against which they are gripped by the lower fingers. Well-trained horses can be made to make slight changes of direction without assistance from the right hand. For a left-inclined turn the left hand is rotated in a clockwise direction so that the back of the hand comes uppermost and the hand is moved in the direction of the right hip; these movements draw back the near rein and let out the right rein a similar amount. For a right inclined turn the left hand is turned anticlockwise and brought towards the left hip. For shorter turns the right hand is used on the appropriate rein. When driving a pair it is convenient to make turns by shortening the selected rein by drawing it back with the right hand to form a loop over the left forefinger where it is clasped by the thumb. The right hand is then free to use the whip should the outside horse need urging up to its work, and the loop can be allowed to slide out when the turn has been completed. In driving a show-ring stepper it is usual to keep the right hand on the right rein to help the horse make a good exhibition, but both reins still pass into the left hand so that, if the whip is needed, the right hand can be taken off the rein. It is a cardinal rule of driving that the whip should not be used when the whip hand is holding a rein.

Tandem driving, that is driving one horse in front of another, requires considerable skill and well-trained horses. It is usual to drive tandem to a two-wheeled vehicle which need not be extremely high, as fashion once demanded; certain types of four-wheeled carriages are also thought proper to use for tandem work. The reins are held in the left hand in the following order: near lead over the first finger, off lead and near wheel together between the first and second fingers, and the off wheel between the second and third fingers. All the reins pass together down the hand where they are secured by the lower fingers. On level going the leader may not be required to take much share of the load, and never should it be drawing the vehicle unless the wheeler is taking its share. When making short turns the leader should be out of draught. Inclined turns can be made by turning the left hand as described for single harness. The assistance of the right hand is needed for shorter turns, always turning the leader before the wheeler and being ready to counter any tendency for the latter to cut the corner. Loops may be made in the leader's reins for turning as described for pair harness but, especially with a well-schooled pony-tandem, the change of length of rein needed for turning may be too small to allow for looping.

Unlike a rider, the driver of a horse can only communicate his directions through his reins, hence the need for a continuing contact. Careful bitting is, therefore, of the greatest importance in harness work. Most curb bits used for this work provide alternative positions for fastening the reins, each giving more or less leverage on the curb, from the 'plain cheek' with no curb action, to 'bottom bar', the so-called 'duffer's slot', which is the most severe position. As in riding, the basis of good hands is a good seat and its is essential to adopt a good position on the box. The driver should not perch insecurely on the edge of the seat with his body inclined forwards, but firmly upon it, body erect with back slightly hollowed, and feet on the footboard with the legs suitably bent at the knees to give support should the need for strength arise. TR

Driving Competitions

Organized competitions to test the skill of the coachman as well as the fitness and standard of training of the horses, have been held in various forms in different countries for many years. In 1909 a coaching marathon was held at the International Horse Show, Olympia, London, and before then some other horse shows had tandem-driving tests. Similar events were included at some North American horse shows, but it was in Germany that driving competitions were chiefly developed. In 1969 a committee of the FÉDÉRATION ÉQUESTRE INTERNATIONALE was formed to establish rules and tables for the standardization of driving competitions. These rules were designed for teams of four

Driving. *Far left, above:* Mr M. C. Hughes drives Hackney gelding Hurstwood Scotch Mist to a dogcart to win the British Driving Derby at Hickstead, 1970.
Far left, below: Mr John M. Seabrook drives his pair of Oldenburg geldings to a game cart at the Essex Hunt Races, New Jersey.
Above: Mr Sanders Watney drives his tandem at Worminghall, Buckinghamshire.

Driving Competitions. 1971 European Driving Champions, Imre Abonyi and the Hungarian driving team, in Budapest

horses, but are adaptable for competitions for six-horse teams, pairs, tandems and horses in single harness. The F.E.I. rules set out tests under three tables: (A) Presentation and Dressage; (B) Marathon; (C) Obstacle Driving. Organizing committees may arrange Combined Driving competitions under any two or all three tables, but in Continental or World Championships the competition must consist of all three tables. Under Table A marks are awarded for presentation, turnout, condition and matching of horses as well as for the execution of movements at the walk, working trot, collected trot and extended trot, with a halt at a prescribed point and a rein-back movement. In the marathon (Table B) a referee must ride on each vehicle taking part. The course is divided into five sections, each to be completed in a prescribed time if no penalties are to be incurred, and at a specified gait; two sections at the walk, the others at different speeds at the trot. The minimum weight for the vehicle when empty is laid down at 500 kg (1,102 lb) for a four-horse team, and at least four persons must ride in it during the marathon. Table C is held in an arena over a course of 500–800 m (1,620–2,625 ft) in length with not more than 20 obstacles. The time allowed is worked out at a speed of 220 m per minute. Scoring may be calculated in one of two ways. In fault competitions penalty faults are given for knocking down obstacles, etc., and to this total are added penalty faults for exceeding the time allowed. In time competitions penalty seconds are given for faults made on the course and this total is added to the actual time taken to complete the course. In both cases the lowest score decides the winner. Exceeding twice the time allowed means elimination. The F.E.I. Rules apply only to international competitions; local societies may arrange driving competitions under their own rules to suit their particular circumstances. TR

Driving Harness

The basic components of driving harness, the equipment borne by the horse to enable it to draw a burden and to provide its driver with control over it, are the bridle, the collar with traces, the pad or saddle to support the shafts or traces, and the breeching.

Driving bridles usually have *blinkers*, stiffened blinds attached to the cheekpieces to prevent the horse seeing to the side or rear, but bridles without blinkers are also used. Blinkers are made in several traditional patterns, the choice being determined by the type of harness. With coachman-driven carriages and the more formal types

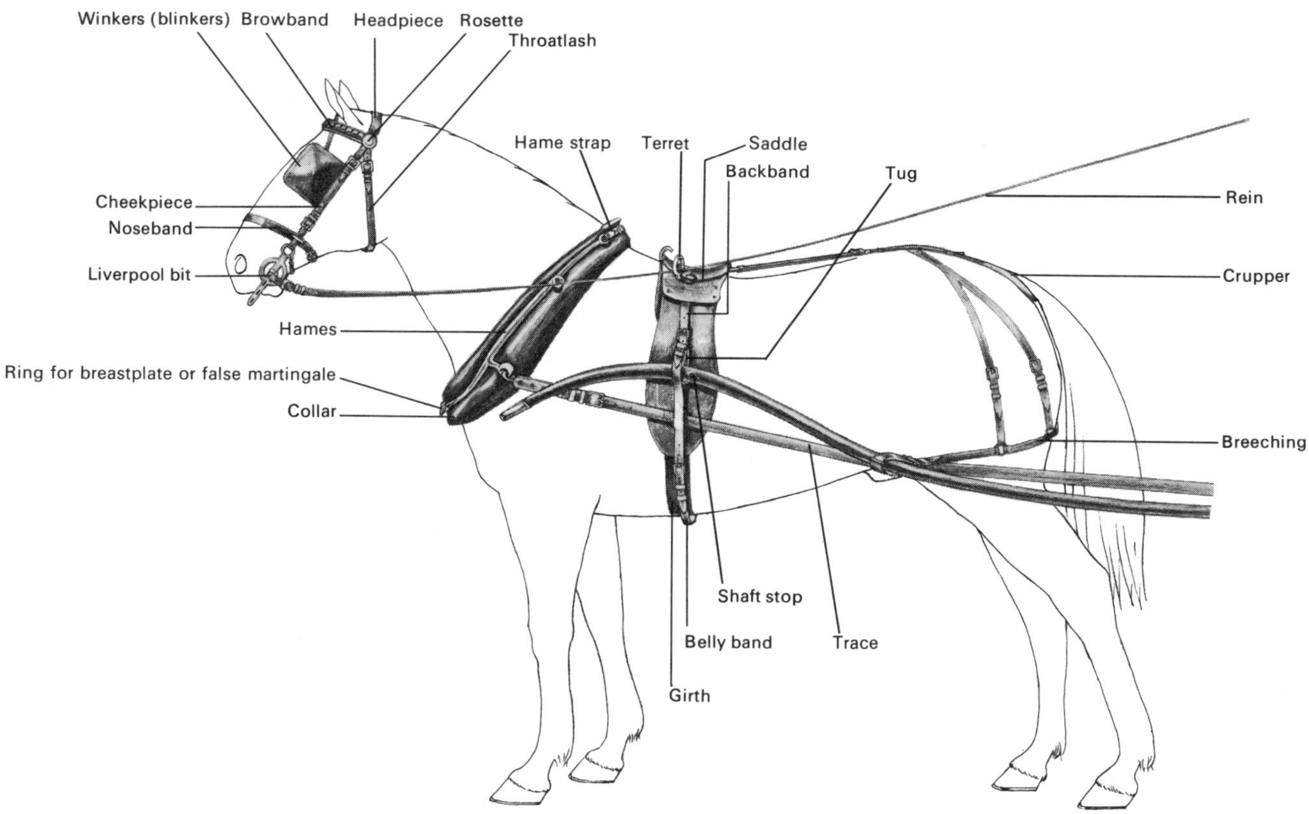

Driving Harness

of harness square or D-shaped blinkers are used; with sporting and lighter types of carriages hatchet-shaped or round blinkers are more appropriate. Bearing reins, used to keep the horse's head in position, are sometimes added. With the English type of harness the latter are either of the plain bridoon or pulley bridoon patterns. With racing harness the bearing rein is usually of the overdraw type (see Driving).

Collars are made of two general types, the neck collar and the breast or Dutch collar. The former is stuffed with rye or wheat straw and shaped to lie closely around the base of the horse's neck following the line of the shoulder. It may be lined with cloth or basil leather. Hames, made of metal or wood and metal, fit tightly in a groove round the outside of the collar, and the trace tugs are attached to them. The hames are joined together at the top, and sometimes also at the bottom, by hame straps, which are vitally important pieces of the harness and must always be of sound, strong leather. Neck collars must be so made that no pressure is brought to bear on the windpipe to restrict the breathing of the horse. They are made in different weights and shapes to suit the type of harness. A breastplate or false martingale connects the lower part of the collar to the pad girth of double harness and its function is to prevent the collar riding up the horse's neck when the carriage is being slowed down or is descending a hill. A breast collar consists of a strong band of a width suited to the work passing horizontally round the horse's breast a few inches above the point of the shoulder, held in place by a carrying strap running across the place where the neck joins the withers. The traces may be attached by buckles or stitched directly on to the breast collar. Breast collars are commonly used for quite heavy work in some European countries, also they are usual with racing harness and many other types of light harness.

The *harness saddle* for single harness is wider and more heavily padded than a double harness pad, which need only support the traces; both kinds have a pair of ring terrets on their upper panels to serve as guides for the reins, also a hook on the top to which the bearing rein can be fastened. It is held in place by the crupper, i.e. a padded leather loop under the horse's tail, which is connected to the saddle by the backstrap. The breeching, if used, passes round the horse's quarters roughly half-way between the dock and the point of the hock. Breeching straps connect it at each side to the shafts with single harness, or to the trace tugs with double harness. Its function is to hold back the vehicle when descending hills or slowing down.

Driving reins must be made of the best quality leather. They are much heavier than riding reins, and about 1 in (2·54 cm) wide. Double harness reins consist of a pair of draught reins which are buckled to the outside of each horse's bit. Buckled on to each draught rein at a point between a half and two-thirds of its length is a coupling rein which will be fastened to the inner side of the other horse's bit. In other words the draught rein on the near-side horse is buckled to the left side of the bit and its coupling rein to the left side of the off-horse's bit. The off-side draught rein and coupling rein are similarly fastened to the right side of the horses' bits.

The collar is usually put on the horse first; if it is a neck collar, it is held upside down so that the widest part can be passed over the horse's eyes. If it is not wide enough to slip on without undue force, then the hames must be removed and the collar opened out by stretching it over one's knee. The hames can then be put back on, the collar turned right way up, and dropped onto its place on the shoulder. The saddle, or pad, follows and this is not girthed up until the crupper has been placed under the horse's tail and the backstrap adjusted for length. One must ensure that no hair has been trapped between the crupper and the horse's dock, also that the backstrap is not overtight. The bridle is put on next and should be fitted so that the blinkers allow plenty of freedom of movement for the eyelids while the cheekpieces remain close to the horse's cheeks, held there by the noseband. The bit should be of a comfortable width and buckled at a height that will not cause it to pinch the corners of the mouth. When a curb chain is used it should always be at the length found to be most suitable for that particular horse. Nosebands on harness bridles are seldom made short enough to do more than hold the cheekpieces in loosely, whereas they can often be of much greater service to the driver if they can be buckled tight enough to keep the horse's mouth closed. The throatlatch should be no more than comfortably tight while not being so loose that the horse may shake his bridle off. If a bearing rein is used, its length should be adjusted according to the driver's judgment before the horse is put to the carriage. The reins are put on last and buckled to the bit. It is usual for the driver to take up the reins from the off-side and it is on this side that they are looped up ready for him.

When putting to in single harness the horse is led into position, the shafts are lowered and their points passed through the shaft tugs. The traces are then fastened to the carriage and their length adjusted so that when they are drawn tight the shaft tugs will lie in the middle of the saddle side-panels. The breeching straps, when used, are fastened last, leaving sufficient freedom to avoid chafing the horse's rump. With a two-wheeled vehicle it is important to arrange the balance before starting so that, with all the passengers in their places, the shafts bear down in the tugs with only a slight weight. Some carriages have a sliding seat which varies the balance, but raising or lowering the tugs on the backband will have an effect upon it also. With four-wheeled carriages the shaft tugs are usually of the French or Tilbury patterns which tighten round the shafts and are used with a tighter bellyband than the open pattern tugs.

Before putting to in double harness the driver should first see that the carriage is ready in a good position with the pole fitted and secured by its pin; also that the pole-pieces or pole-chains have been put on. The horses are led up from the rear of the carriage each on its appointed side so that they may be stopped nearly parallel to the pole and properly in position. The pole-pieces are then put on loosely buckled, many careful drivers having them passed round the collars, a much safer method than merely going through the rings on the kidney links. The traces are next attached to the splinter bar, outside traces first; followed by buckling the coupling reins to the bits. Lastly the pole-pieces are taken up to their proper length and the reins passed over and looped up on the off-side.

Before taking up the reins and mounting his seat the driver must always walk round his horse or horses to make sure that every strap is in its proper place and correctly adjusted, paying particular attention to the bridle and bit. For history of driving harness, see Accoutrements. TR

Dülmen

The Dülmen ponies are kept in a reserve in the Meerfelder Bruch on the estate of the Duke of Cröy in Germany, near to the Dutch frontier. Like the now extinct, semi-wild SENNER ponies, the Dülmen were mentioned as early as 1316. Basically they are native stock, although recently pony stallions have been imported from Poland and Britain. Because of these outcrosses, the ponies are by no means linebred but are rather a mixture of a number of other pony breeds. There are about 100 mares and there is an annual festival when the yearling colts are caught and sold. DMG

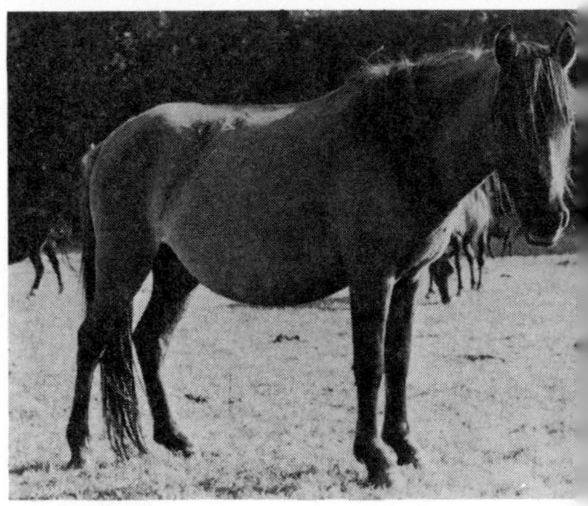

Above: **Dülmen**

Dutch Draught Horse see Netherlands

Dutch Warmblood

The Dutch Warmblood is a halfbred horse, originating from the GRONINGEN and GELDERLAND horse crossed with THOROUGHBRED, HOLSTEIN, TRAKEHNER, ANGLO-NORMAN and other light horse breeds. It is principally a riding horse but a few are bred as coach horses. Height is about 15·2½–16·1 hands (1·60–1·70 m). WS

Top: **Dutch Warmblood**

Above: **East Bulgarian.** Gondola, an East Bulgarian mare, jumping in a pre-Olympic trial at Munich

East Bulgarian Horse

The East Bulgarian horse was developed at the stud of the Vassil Kolarov state agricultural farm (formerly Kabijuk) near Shumen. For more than fifty years horses crossed with Thoroughbreds were bred at the Kabijuk stud (founded 1894), and at the military stud at Bojurishte, near Sofia (founded 1896), gradually developing into the East Bulgarian breed. In 1951 the horses at Bojurishte were transferred to the present state stud, Stefan Karadja in Dobrudja.

The East Bulgarian was created by crossing local ARAB, ANGLO-ARAB and halfbred English mares with THOROUGHBRED and half-bred English stallions, imported from Hungary, Russia, Poland, Germany and other countries. Some Arab stallions were used. The following Thoroughbred stallions played a particularly important role: Laudon, Kozak, Woostershire, Gremy, Neron, Tihany, Edelknabe and Zenger, and the halfbreds Betjar, Fenek, Gallion and Furioso VII-3, used as foundation stock. The East Bulgarian has been purebred in strains for many decades and regularly obtains new blood from Thoroughbred stallions. By selection over many years, improvement of feeding and rearing methods, training and testing performance on racecourses and in harness, the East Bulgarian has become a universal breed, suitable for riding, competitive sports and agricultural work. It is hardy, has a rather long body and active movements. Colours are chestnut, bright chestnut, or black. Average height is about 15·3 hands (16·2 m).

East Bulgarian horses have also performed well in dressage and riding competitions, taking part in almost every International Steeplechase at Pardubice, Czechoslovakia. In 16 years (1955–70) 137 Bulgarian horses have participated, being placed among the first five 91 times: 17 times first, 24 times second, 15 times third, 16 times fourth and 19 times fifth. They have won the most important steeplechase, the Labe (5,000 m or 5,468 yd), for halfbred horses three times; the Kladrub steeplechase (3,600 m or 3,937 yd) five times; the Amateur steeplechase (4,000 m or 4,374 yd) one; the Maritza award (3,800 m or 4,155 yd) once, and the Danube prize (3,200 m or 3,500 yd) twice. The most outstanding win at Pardubice was at the Jubilee Contests in 1970 (the 80th) when the East Bulgarian mare Vezna II won the GRAND PARDUBICE Steeplechase (6,900 m or 7,646 yd) from 22 competitors.

East Bulgarian horses also work well in harness. The stallions Fetish and Frak reached seven metric tons and six metric tons respectively in gradual-loading pulling tests (in which the first load of two tons is pulled for 200 m, and after a break of 3 m, an additional ton is added every 200 m until the horse stops). East Bulgarian horses are now bred in the districts of Shumen, Razgrad, Torgoviste, Varna, Tolbuhin, Burgas, and some parts of Silistra, Russe and Jambol; numbers of them are exported. VP, II.

East Friesian Horse see Germany

East Prussian Horse see Masuren

Egypt

The arrival of the horse in Egypt has been connected by most Egyptologists with the invasions of the Hyksos, for it supposedly entered the Nile Valley about the time of

Egypt. A dancing horse performs in front of the pyramids of Giza.

their conquest. Since about 1580 B.C. the horse has played a vital role in Egyptian culture. The Old Testament is liberally sprinkled with references to Egyptian horses. Solomon sang: 'I compare thee, O my love, to a company of horses in Pharaoh's chariots'. Indeed the early Egyptian steeds showed the type, spirit, grace and subtle power of the pure Arabian breed as it is known today. With the decline of the Egyptian empire and the advent of Islam, the Arabian breed came to the fore again through the Mameluke Sultans. Most famous among them were Kala'un and Sultan Barkuk, A.D. 1382, whose stud eventually numbered some 7,000 horses.

Mohammed Ali the Great (1769–1849), originator of modern Egypt's renaissance, also obtained excellent Arabian horses with the help of one of his sons, Ibrahim Pasha. The most famous and eccentric collector of them all, however, was Abbas Pasha, Viceroy of Egypt (1848–1854). His horses were said to rival those of King Solomon, and it is from Abbas' collection that most of the present day Arabians in Egypt, America and England descend.

The Egyptian Agricultural Organization, near Cairo, maintains a 60-acre farm devoted exclusively to breeding purebred Arabians descending from the finest stock gathered by Egypt's past royal families. Horse racing is popular the year round and many of the Organization's horses compete against privately bred ones. The recent E.A.O.-bred Arabians are experiencing a new wave of popularity in Europe, South Africa, Australia and America and their wins at horse shows in the United States have been spectacular.

The specially trained and gaily caparisoned dancing horses, exclusive to Egypt, are a great attraction at sporting events, festivals and weddings as they dance to the flute-like strains of the rababa. Their cadenced rhythm and steps can be likened to such dressage movements as the *piaffe, levade* and *passage*.

Equestrian sports are practised by local riding clubs. Horse shows featuring jumping competitions are held in Alexandria and Cairo annually. Polo was once popular but now has practically faded from the sporting scene. As in the days of the pharaohs, the Egyptians still hold their Arabian steeds in great esteem and continue to breed some of the finest in the world today. JEF

Einsiedler

The existence of a stud at the Benedictine Abbey of Einsiedeln, in the Swiss canton of Schwyz, is recorded as early as A.D. 1064. Breeding of Einsiedler and Schwyzer horses reached a peak during the sixteenth century; after the French Revolution almost all these horses were taken as loot to France and breeding declined. At the beginning of the twentieth century English HACKNEYS were imported; since 1922 breeding has been based on ANGLO-NORMAN stallions. Today's Einsiedler does not differ from the Swiss Warmblood (see Switzerland). EW

Endurance see T.P.R.

Endurance Riding see Long Distance Riding

English Thoroughbred see Thoroughbred

Entire see Stallion

Eohippus 'dawn horse' see Evolution of the Horse Family

Epistaxis

Bleeding from the nose due to haemorrhage in the upper part of the nose, the guttural pouches or the lungs. It is more often seen in racehorses than other riding types. Attacks are usually towards the end of a race but may be spontaneous and unpredictable. CF

Epona

A pre-Roman Gallic goddess of horses and all concerned with them. See France

Equine Research Station

The Equine Research Station, established at Newmarket in 1946, is one of the Research Centres controlled by the Animal Health Trust, a registered charity relying for its income on voluntary support. It is the only centre in the British Isles which devotes itself exclusively to the study of the problems of the horse in health and disease. It comprises Departments of Haematology, Pathology including Mycology and Parasitology, and a Clinical and Surgical Wing with specialists in orthopaedics and ear nose and throat surgery to assist veterinary surgeons in practice. JHM

Equitation

Equitation, or the art of horsemanship, has been practised in varying forms throughout the centuries (see Horsemanship, History of). Equitation in the mechanized world of today has reverted primarily to a civilian interest and to the majority of equestrian-minded people it implies the systematic training of a horse for a particular sphere of activity. The primary object of schooling is to make the horse obedient to the rider and the secondary object is to prepare it for the special purpose the trainer has in mind. All horses undergo the primary training in varying degrees, for most horses are required to carry man and be obedient to a certain extent. The racehorse is well handled from birth but its breaking and backing is a comparatively hurried affair and results in its never progressing beyond the minimum requirements of equitation. One has only to watch the horses going down to the post to realize they know little more than how to gallop.

A well-schooled horse, a riding horse, hack or hunter, is another matter. The finished article should be a pleasure to ride, obedient to the aids and capable of following hounds safely across country. It has to be trained systematically and according to the principles of equitation.

The predominating factor in the character of the horse is fear and its chief method of defence is flight. It is imperative therefore that the horse learns to look on its trainer as a friend and to have confidence in him. The trainer must learn to make use of the horse's memory, which is prodigious; it never forgets places nor things which have happened to it. It is invaluable for schooling purposes when the training is carried out on the right lines but equally disastrous if the schooling is bad. A trainer must make absolutely clear from the start the difference between right and wrong. He must above all be consistent so that the horse is not confused. Misunderstanding leads to doubt, in a generous horse to its offer of other answers in its desire to please, and finally to confusion and fear. The frightened horse soon learns bad habits and in this way it becomes nappy. The bad horse has yet to be born; it is made by man.

A horse well handled from the time it is a foal will be supremely confident in humans and perfectly amenable when it is time for its education to begin in earnest. Already it will lead quietly in hand and it must learn to go on the lunge. The equipment required is a leather headcollar, a lungeing rein preferably with a swivel end, a cavesson and a lungeing whip (see Tackle, Breaking). The horse must learn to walk, trot and canter at the word of command to either rein. It will have difficulty at first on the right rein as it has always been used to being led from the left or near side but an assistant to lead and guide the horse on the circle will soon settle this problem. The voice is an invaluable aid at this stage and the horse's appreciation of the words of command will be a tremendous asset in its later training. The horse must learn also the use of the whip, never to punish it on the lunge, but as as a directive, pointing at the quarters to encourage it to go forward in its paces or pointing at the shoulder to keep it out on a true circle. Once it has mastered this stage the trainer can begin to accustom the horse to a saddle on the lunge and eventually to a rider and the subsequent and almost unnoticed acceptance of simple rein aids to right and left. The horse soon becomes used to the rider's weight and its education progresses so that it can be mounted without fuss, moves forward when asked, rides quietly on either rein and learns to become more responsive and obedient to the elementary aids. The 'direct' or 'opening' rein aids it will have begun to learn on the lunge, and it soon associates the aid of 'both legs' to obtain forward movement and impulsion by the use of the word of command after applying the aid. In the same way it will learn to stop when the rider simultaneously 'closes his hands' and 'closes his legs' on the girth. General education is immensely important and the horse must learn to go out into the country either alone or with other horses and to cope with the sights and sounds of the world outside in a calm and relaxed manner.

The school work is extended to include changes of direction across the diagonals, circles, counter changes of hand, doublers, serpentines and half voltes (see Movements). These school figures are all valuable exercises and help to balance the horse, to build up its back muscles and to strengthen and supple its loins. In this first stage of training the horse's centre of gravity is forward and the object is to have it 'long and low' in outline. The trainer's goal should be to acquire pure basic paces and a horse that goes freely forward and straight. It should show the correct bend in a corner or on a circle so that its body follows the line of the transitions from one pace to another should be smooth and flowing. The best pace for working the horse at its school figures in this first stage is the trot, simply because the trot is a two-time movement and is therefore the easiest pace at which to maintain rhythm. Continual changes of direction will help to shift the centre of gravity from the inevitable too far forward of the early days to further back. As this happens the horse will be less inclined to go 'on its fore hand' and its hind legs at last begin to work more underneath it or become 'engaged'.

Next the horse learns to go away from the leg ('leg yielding'). This is a prelude to work on two tracks (see Movements). It is also invaluable for general education as it is an obvious advantage when opening and shutting gates and for innumerable other situations arising in day-to-day riding. The horse trots round the school and on the long side the rider applies his outside leg strongly behind the girth while maintaining impulsion with the inside leg on the girth. The horse's hindquarters move on to an inner track and it is straightened out again before it approaches the corner. This is practised, as are all other exercises, equally on either rein. The horse must also learn early in its career to rein back correctly, that is, for a chosen number of steps and in a quiet balanced two-time. The easiest way to explain to the horse what is required of it is to face it up against the high walls of the school or a fence and halt. The rider closes his legs behind the girth and tilts his body very slightly forward. He 'gives' fractionally with his hands so that the horse takes a hesitant step forward and then because of the barrier inevitably will take a step back. The rider does not pull back with his hands, he simply does not go forward. The horse will soon realize what is wanted if it is made much of as soon as it steps back and it is merely a matter of time and patience before it can rein back correctly facing the fence and then in the open. In a similar way the horse can be taught the aids for work on two tracks. It stands facing the fence and about two strides away from it and the rider asks it to move sideways to the left by taking his left hand out to the left and 'balancing' this action with his right hand so that the horse does not simply turn left. The right leg pushes the horse to the left behind the girth and the left leg maintains the impulsion of the movement. The first attempts will be very ragged and hesitant but this method seems to produce first-class results almost as soon as the horse is asked for shoulder-in or half-pass.

Work at the canter needs plenty of attention while the horse is still in the first stage of training. At a three-time pace it is only too easy for the horse to lose its rhythm and lapse into four-time, a grave fault in the dressage arena, and the rider must avoid this pitfall by asking the horse to canter energetically round the school and to describe a few circles before making a transition to the trot. It learns the aids to canter to either rein easily and quietly by being taught from the first to canter on the inside leading leg on a circle or on the approach to a corner. Its natural balance will make it strike off on the correct leg and once again it absorbs the rider's aids to canter almost without realizing it. The aids are the rider's means of communication with the horse, his daily language; as long as he uses them in a clear cut and understood manner, he will have little difficulty and no confusion. Later on in the canter the horse will have no problem in striking off on the required leg from a walk because it is given the aid to canter and it produces it automatically.

There remains only the exercise of increasing and decreasing the pace in walk, trot and canter. The horse is asked to lengthen and stretch in its increase of pace and to resume the normal carriage of an 'ordinary' pace on the decrease. The horse is expected to lengthen its stride and maintain its rhythm and the whole outline of the horse lengthens in the increased paces. In the subsequent lesson in extended paces the stride lengthens, the horse's hind legs become further engaged beneath it creating a tremendous driving force, its back begins to soften and 'swing' and its rhythm takes on the higher degree of cadence.

The whole art of equitation to this stage is a gradual and systematic process. It cannot be hurried nor can any time limit be set upon it. It depends entirely on the individual talents of both horse and rider, and the trainer's ability to discern his horse's state of mind. His whole attention should be con- concentrated on his horse so that the horse never becomes upset nor confused but maintains its own character and spirit and is happy and generous in all its work.

Equitation is not schooling on the ground alone. The horse must learn to jump all manner of obstacles. The trainer starts by placing a pole on the ground so that the horse can walk quietly over it. Then a second pole is placed some three feet away from the other and the horse trots carefully over these with no attempt on its part to jump them as one obstacle. Gradually the number of poles is increased to a maximum of six or eight. If ever the horse becomes excited it returns to just the two poles on the ground. The next stage is to repeat this

Equitation. Dr Rainer Klimke riding Mehmed at the canter

lessons over CAVALLETTI; the horse learns to balance itself and trot carefully down the line of raised poles. It is an invaluable exercise for suppling the back and building up the muscles of the loins. The horse is now ready to tackle small fences; the trainer places three trotting poles on the ground eight feet in front of a small post-and-rails. The work is still done at the trot and any attempt at cantering except on the take-off stride is quietly checked. The horse then progresses to single small obstacles, both straight-up fences and little spreads, and even simple combinations until it trots over all sorts of obstacles with a perfect *'bascule'*. It learns to get height by jumping wider and wider spreads. It is important never to overface a young horse. The youngster of considerable talent will soon be able to tackle a course over three feet with quiet ease and at a canter. It is important never to allow rushing at a fence; the answer is to turn off in a circle from the obstacle if the horse becomes too impetuous or excited. Again the whole criterion of jumping in the early stages is a perfect '*bascule*' and calmness.

Horses destined for specialized work will require more advanced training than that described in the first stages of equitation. The show jumper, the three-day-eventer, and the advanced dressage or Grand Prix horse all require a great deal more work. The show jumper's training will develop further by learning to cope with bigger fences and a greater variety of obstacles; it may become either a *puissance* or a speed horse in the highly competitive and specialized world of show jumping today. The majority of show jumpers in Great Britain have not had the schooling in work on the ground already described for they are chosen as soon as they show signs of a phenomenal leap. After this little time is spent on any schooling other than over fences. On the other hand, the Germans and the Americans set great store by training their horses to a fairly high standard of dressage and their performances, albeit in different ways, demonstrate the advantages of a well-trained animal. The aesthetic advantages are obvious.

The three-day-eventer has to achieve the second stage of work on the ground. It must acquire 'self-carriage' to a certain extent, certainly if it is to lead the field at the end of the first day's dressage test. This is a test which includes collected and extended paces, work on two tracks, simple changes of leg and counter canter. The horse must also be trained over show jumps and across country and learn to adapt its jumping from the fast steeplechase phase and the tricky and awe-inspiring cross-country fences to the precision of the show jumping on the third day. It is the all-rounder of modern equitation and as such requires the most searching training and preparation of all.

Equitation. Miss Sheila Willcox, riding Fair and Square, takes the sleeper stack at Badminton.

The advanced or Grand Prix dressage horse on the other hand is the prima ballerina to the corps de ballet. Many horses and riders given the opportunity and proper instruction can attain the second stage of equitation with work and application. They achieve 'collection' of the horse so that the horse goes truly up to its bridle, is perfectly obedient and has surrendered itself completely to the combined effect of hands and legs. The degree of control is great but is still short of the elusive third stage, the highest degree of equitation. This quality embraces far more than the perfection of collection; it means the suppleness of the body and of the horse's entire being, the ease and generosity of its movements and the outstanding rhythm and cadence. It takes for granted the extreme lightness of the horse due to the perfect harmony of the mouth and action. It is perfection and the final goal of the master of equitation. See also Dressage, Dressage Tests. SWI

Equus caballus the horse see Evolution of the Horse Family

Equus hemionius onager see Onager

Equus przewalskii Przevalski's Horse see Asiatic Wild Horse

Equus przewalskii gmelini see Tarpan

Estonian see Toric

Evolution of the Horse Family

The oldest known fossils definitely placed in the horse family date from about 60 million years ago and were found in southern North America. The family probably originated in that general area from still older members of an otherwise extinct family known as the Phenacodontidae. Those ancestors, among the most primitive of all hoofed mammals, had five toes on each foot, which were reduced to four on the fore foot and three on the hind in the earliest horses. Each toe ended in a diminutive hoof. As the horse family evolved, other minor changes in limb structure and proportions made for more rapid running, a special adaptation of most horses throughout the history of the family. However, in these early horses the toes were followed by a large pad, more like dogs' paws than the feet of modern horses. The teeth became somewhat more crested than in the ancestors, but remained low-crowned and relatively small and simple, adapted for a soft, leafy vegetable diet and quite unlike the teeth of the now living, grazing horses. The bony eye socket was open behind and the comparatively large eyes were near the middle of the head, from front to back, not far back as now. In fact these earliest horses were so different from our present horses that when the skull of one was first found it was not recognized as belonging to the horse family at all and was named *Hyracotherium*, 'the hyrax (or cony) beast', by Richard Owen, the great nineteenth-century English anatomist. That is still the correct technical name, although 'eohippus', meaning 'dawn horse', is also in use as a more correctly descriptive popular name.

In the early Eocene geological epoch, round about 55 million years ago, *Hyracotherium* or eohippus spread widely and became abundant throughout North America and also quickly reached western Europe, at first in direct contact via a land-bridge with North America. That contact was soon lost, and thereafter the descendants of eohippus had quite different histories in the Old World and the New. In Europe and neighbouring regions of Asia the early descendants of eohippus split up into a number of divergent lines of descent, some members of which became so distinct that they are no longer considered members of the horse family, but are known collectively as palaeotheres, a non-committal name meaning simply 'ancient animals'. They all became extinct without issue, the last of them living into the early Oligocene, about 40 million years ago or a little less.

While that ill-fated diversification was going on in Europe, the more directly ancestral horses in North America were changing steadily, but more slowly and less divergently. Changes through the Eocene (about 55–40 million years ago) were sufficient to make students recognize three successive genera, arbitrarily separated in the gradual progression: *Hyracotherium, Orohippus*, and *Epihippus*. The skeletons changed little and the genera are distinguished mainly by rather technical details of tooth structure, notably that the premolars became more complex, more like the molars, and the outer walls (on the cheek side) of the upper premolars and molars became more strongly crested and more V-shaped. These changes increased the efficiency of the cheek (back or posterior) teeth for chopping leafy herbage.

Those changes in the teeth were carried still further in the next two named stages, *Mesohippus* and *Miohippus*, in the Oligocene of North America, approximately 40–25 million years ago. By the end of that epoch the dentition had reached nearly maximum efficiency for browsing on relatively soft plants, but was not at all adapted for grazing on harsh prairie grasses. By now the feet had changed somewhat, also. The fore foot had lost its fourth toe (which was actually the fifth or outer toe of the remote, five-toed, pre-horse ancestors), and so both fore and hind feet became three-toed. The side toes (second and fourth of the remote ancestors) also tended to become slightly more slender so that more weight bore on the middle toe (the original third). In *Mesohippus*, at least, there was nevertheless still a pad on each foot behind the small hoofs, and the feet gave a broad base adapted to bearing on soft ground. That correlated with life in brushy or wooded areas, which tend to have soft soil and food suitable for a browsing dentition. There was another trend in leg structure that later became more marked. In eohippus leg movement was not entirely loose, not nearly as much as in man for example, but still fairly free. By the time of *Miohippus* it was more strictly limited to fore-and-aft motion, and it is still more so in modern horses.

Size was beginning to change, too. In eohippus there was great variation, some forms being as low as about 10 inches or 0·25 m (2·2 hands) at the shoulders and others up to twice that, about 20 inches or 0·50 m (5 hands), which means that the latter were about eight times as heavy as their contemporaneous small relatives. However, through the Eocene there was no definite trend for the average size of North American horses to become larger. (Some European palaeotheres became much larger in the Eocene, but they were heading for extinction.) *Mesohippus* and *Miohippus* did show a distinct, although irregular, tendency toward increase in average size. It has often been stated that constant increase in size characterized the evolution of the horse family, but that is not strictly true. Modern horses are indeed all larger than eohippus, although the difference in size between a large eohippus and a small pony or Sardinian donkey is not great. However, in the broad history of the family there have been branches of descent that hardly changed in size at all for millions of years, and when increase of size did occur it was as likely to be by fits and starts as by steady progression.

The evolution of the horse family did not consist of constant structural change through a single sequence from *Hyracotherium* (or eohippus) to *Equus* (modern members of the horse family). There were three main important contradictions of that simple concept. In the first place, rates of evolutionary change were far from constant. Now one and now another character would sometimes change relatively rapidly and then slowly or not at all for a time.

Evolution of the Horse Family

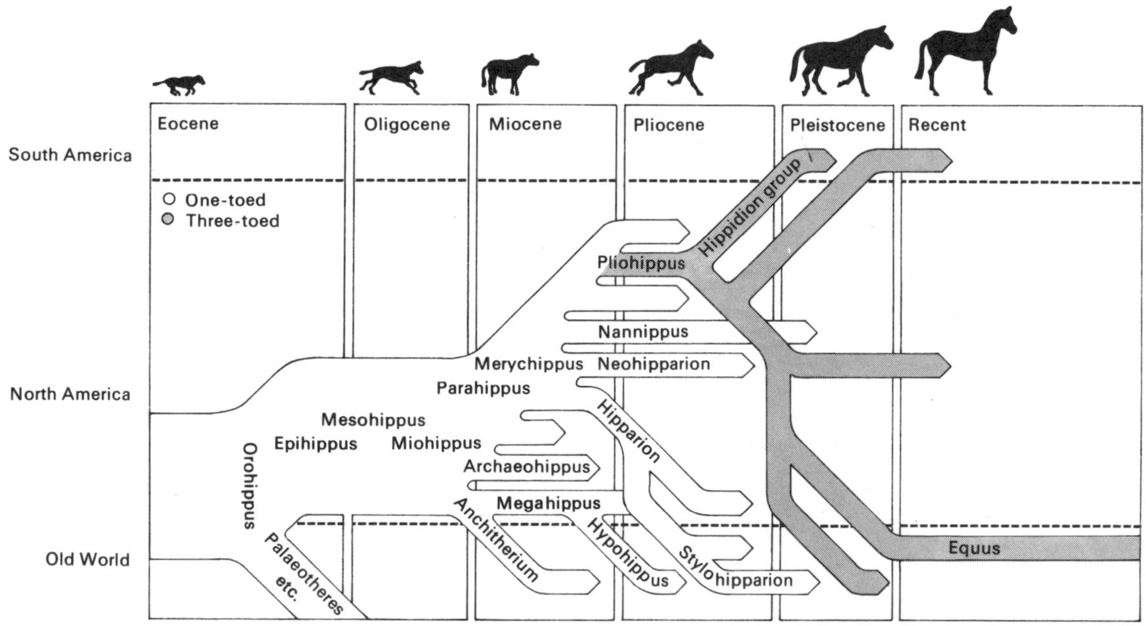

Second, the direction or kind of change was not constant. In most cases structural changes were adaptive in one way or another, but in several lines of descent and notably in that leading to *Equus* the kind of adaptation evolved, and therefore the direction of evolution, changed radically, And third, there was not one or just a few similar lines of descent but eventually a large number of lines, some of them quite different from others and most of them eventually becoming extinct. Those complications in the evolution of the family became particularly important during the Miocene epoch, some 25–10 million years ago. Some horses conservatively continued the same sort of adaptation that had occurred through the preceding Oligocene, glade and forest animals with broad, three-toed feet and low-crowned browsing teeth. Some remained small (*Archaeohippus*) but others increased notably in size and in one of the several different groups (*Megahippus*) became gigantic, even in comparison with modern horses. By the beginning of the Miocene all the descendants of *Hyracotherium* had long been extinct in the Old World, but at least two of these groups of North American browsing horses (first *Anchitherium* and later *Hypohippus*) migrated to Eurasia in the Miocene, now by way of Asia as a direct connection between Europe and North America no longer existed. Both in North America and in Eurasia all the browsing horses eventually became extinct, the last in the early Pliocene, perhaps 7 million years or so ago.

Most important, however, was the appearance of a totally new adaptive type for horses in the Miocene: the evolution of plains-, savanna-, prairie-, or steppe-living, grass-eating (grazing) horses adaptively quite different from the browsers and more like all the surviving members of the family. Changes throughout their anatomy (and surely also in their physiology) were involved, but these were particularly noticeable in the feet and the teeth. After this transition the feet were without pads and the weight was carried almost entirely on the enlarged single hoof of the central toe. When running, this toe was flexed, stretching an elastic ligament and bringing into play also the now quite small lateral toes (originally the second and fourth), still present and each with a tiny hoof. Rebound of the ligament attached to the central hoof eventually led to the typical running gait of modern horses. In the dentition, the grinding teeth (premolars and molars) became increasingly and finally very high-crowned, with elaborate patterns of enamel ridges, and a heavy coating and filling of cement, a tissue absent or slight in browsing horses. Such teeth can stand heavy wear and thus permit the animals to eat harshly abrasive grasses, that is, to graze throughout a lifetime sufficiently long to maintain the breeding population.

That new kind of horse was tremendously

successful and populations split up into numerous different lines of descent. Around the end of the Miocene at least six distinct main groups existed simultaneously on the spreading grassy plains of North America. At about the beginning of the Pliocene one of these (*Hipparion*) crossed into Asia, quickly multiplied across that continent and Europe, and eventually reached Africa —the first members of the horse family ever to occur in the African continent as far as it is known.

Meanwhile back in North America a still more advanced and indeed final model had developed in the horse family: *Equus* in a broad sense, comprising a number of different species. Their most obvious distinction was further reduction of the lateral toes to functionless vestiges so that the animals progressed (and still progress) on the single, ligament-sprung hoof on each foot. Other technical details throughout the anatomy also accompanied this final major step in the evolution of the family. Members of this group spread to South America, which had never had any earlier horses, and became quite diverse there. They also spread rapidly to Asia, across Asia to Europe, and finally down into Africa, and as *Equus* arrived the last of the three-toed horses, *Hipparion*, everywhere became extinct. Finally about 8,000 years ago, *Equus* itself became extinct in North America, so long the centre of evolution of the family, and it and its allies disappeared from the New World when they also died out in South America.

Thus there survived into the modern world only the wild species of Europe, Asia, and Africa, a number of distinct species but all so nearly related that they can be classified as *Equus* in a broad sense: the wild horses, strictly speaking, of Asia and Europe, usually considered two closely related species, from which domesticated horses were derived (*Equus caballus* and *Equus przewalskii*; domesticated forms principally from the former but quite likely from a mixture of both); the Asiatic wild asses, onagers, hemiones, etc. (they have dozens of local names in various languages) (*Equus hemionus*); the true or African wild ass, source of domesticated donkeys (*Equus asinus*); and the three species of zebras in Africa, quaggas, bontequaggas, or Burchell's (*Equus quagga*), the nearly extinct mountain zebra (*E. zebra*), and Grévy's zebra (*E. grévyi*). See also Ass, African Wild, Ass, Asiatic Wild, Onager, Asiatic Wild Horse, Zebra. GGS

Ewe Neck
The crest of the neck is concave instead of convex. CF

Exmoor Pony see Mountain and Moorland Ponies

Extended Paces see Movements

Falabella
This is a miniature horse developed during the last hundred years in the Argentine by the Falabella family on the Recreo de Roca Ranch, outside Buenos Aires. The Shetland pony was the basis of this breed, deliberately developed by down-breeding with crosses of the smallest possible animals; unfortunately no records were kept. In the process the breed lost the toughness of the Shetland and cannot be regarded as a riding pony. Its coat is long and silky, like a Shetland superficially but without that breed's thick, warm undercoat. The height does not exceed 7·2 hands (0·76 m or 30 in) at maturity, so the Falabella can claim to be the world's smallest horse. The breed appears to be stabilized at its present size; specimens are favoured in North America as pets and for use in harness; a few have also been exported to Australia. All colours are found but Appaloosa-marked are the most popular. CEGH

Falconry
Though now practised almost exclusively on foot, falconry was in its inception essentially a mounted sport. Greek authors of the fifth century B.C. mention it as a practice of the SCYTHIANS but it was not introduced into Europe until after the classical age; according to some, not before the lifetime of Charlemagne (742–814). But there is extant the letter of an English (Mercian) king to a German bishop, dated 757, requesting purchase of two falcons, which must argue the firm establishment of the sport by that date. It became more widespread in England, after, and because of, the Viking invasions. In Europe, it usually involved the participation of falconers or austringers on foot also, but even so there was a form of *cadge* (multiple perch for hawks) which was designed to be carried on horseback.

In its mounted form falconry continued in England until the introduction of a really effective shotgun (about 1700) on a wide scale. There are still Hereditary Grand Falconers for England and Scotland. A Wolds Falconers Club, for mounted hawking, was founded in East Yorkshire by Colonel Thornton as late as 1781.

In the Middle Ages it was the summer sport of the nobility *par excellence*. What was demanded of the horse, in falconry, was above all a smooth gait, a 'soft ride', great handiness, and a build that facilitated frequent dismounting and remounting. These the pacing PALFREY offered and the the most frequent employment of the palfrey was in falconry, a sport followed by men and women in about equal numbers. This is one of the reasons why the palfrey is primarily thought of as a ladies' horse. One of the horses provided for Charles II's flight in disguise after the battle of Worcester in 1651 was a trained falconer's mount. AD

Top: **Ewe Neck.** The dotted line indicates the normal line of the neck.

Above: **Falabella.** Carlos, 29 in (0·74 m) high, clearing 3 ft (0·91 m) in the United States

Below: **False Quarter**

Far right: **Feet and Shoeing.**
Top: Dumping. The dotted line indicates the normal outline of the hoof.
Below: The structure of the hoof (right fore foot)
Bottom: Hunter shoes.

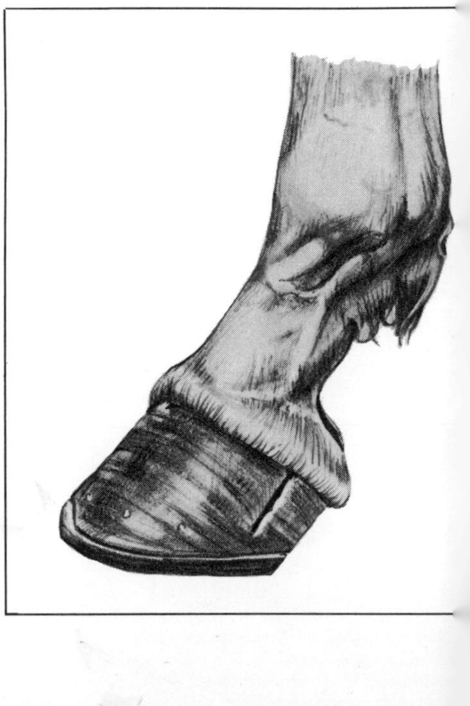

False Quarter
A condition of the hoof where there is a lack of normal horn towards the heel, making it difficult to secure the shoe at that site. It is caused by injury to the coronary band which is responsible for the formation of horn. CF

Fantasia
The fantasia is a traditional way of celebrating festivals in Morocco. Richly decorated horses and riders parade before galloping behind their chief in a furious headlong charge. Nearly 2,000 riders took part in the largest fantasia of this century, to celebrate King Hassan II's birthday in 1969 (see colour plate page 261).

Farriery see Feet and Shoeing

Faxaflói an Icelandic breed resembling the Exmoor. See Iceland

Fédération Équestre Internationale
The F.E.I. was formed in 1921 to act as the official governing body of equestrian sports. Its headquarters are in Brussels. All competing countries are represented and the Bureau or Executive Committee meets regularly and deals with policy complaints and regulations. The F.E.I. is completely authoritative and is strict in the enforcement of its rules. It has a judges' panel and at each international show there has to be an F.E.I. judge and a technical delegate. H.R.H. Prince Philip succeeded H.R.H. Prince Bernhard of the Netherlands as President in 1965. DW

Feeding and Nutrition see Stable Management

Feet and Shoeing
The old adage 'no foot, no horse' is still true. A foot which is neglected or inadequately prepared before being shod can upset the whole balance of the limb and cause stresses and strains on joints, ligaments and tendons. At the same time there are excesses in preparation which can easily ruin a foot such as *opening the heels*, cutting away the bars and thus destroying the continuity and stability of the wall of the foot. Excessive rasping of the outside of the wall, paring the frog and *dumping* (shortening the wall at the toe) are other practices to be condemned. A horse when shod should have its feet attended to on average once a month even if it means replacing the old shoes. If a horse is to be turned out to grass for any length of time it should be fitted with tips or half shoes to prevent the breaking away of the wall at the toe. The fitting of a grass tip also allows the frog to develop and perform its normal function of taking pressure.
Types of shoes: shoes vary according to the type of horse, the work it has to do and the pace at which it is carried out. Hence the aluminium racing plate of the Thoroughbred is vastly different from the heavy bevelled shoe intended to enhance the size of the Shire's foot in the show ring. In the ordinary course of events shoes should be simple in design and as light as is compatible with retaining their shape on the foot and wearing for three to four weeks.
Hunter Shoes: typically the bearing surface is flat and the ground surface is fullered and concaved. The latter prevents suction and in the hind shoes mitigates against OVERREACHING. The front shoe is rounder than the hind and has one toe clip, the heels are bevelled and do not project beyond the bearing surface of the foot. The inner branch is fitted 'close' or slightly under the hoof to minimize the injury caused by BRUSHING. The hind shoe has two lateral toe clips. This enables the shoe to be 'set back' under the toe: another way of avoiding injury from overreaching. The branches of the hind shoe are usually a little longer than those of the front shoe. The outer heel is turned down to form a small calkin and this is balanced by a wedge heel on the inner branch. Nail holes, usually three on the inside and four on the outer, must be correctly stamped. Placed too near the inner margin of the shoe ('coarse nailing'), they may cause the nails to impinge on the sensitive structures (nail bind) or actually prick them (causing 'pricked foot'). Holes stamped too near the outer edge give rise to 'fine nailing'; the nails emerge too soon and too low down and the shoe is insecurely held on the foot.

Shoes for hacks, ponies and most riding horses vary little from those of the hunter apart from size and weight.
Surgical shoeing: variations of the normal shoe are occasionally adopted to assist in the treatment of lameness, e.g. corns, sprained tendons, laminitis, etc. In many instances in the past these measures were aimed at keeping an animal in work and most of them have now been discarded. CF

F.E.I. see Fédération Équestre Internationale

Fell Pony see Mountain and Moorland

Fillis, James
Although he spent the greater part of his life in France, James Fillis, *écuyer* and teacher of equitation, was born in London on 17 December 1834 of English parents. A gifted child, by the time he was eight he was riding difficult horses with success. He had a very fine teacher, François Caron, himself a pupil of BAUCHER, who was undoubtedly largely responsible for his later achievements. Throughout his life Fillis trained horses for *haute école*, many for performances in the Champs-Élysées circus, where he worked from 1873 to 1886. Although small, he had extraordinary strength in his

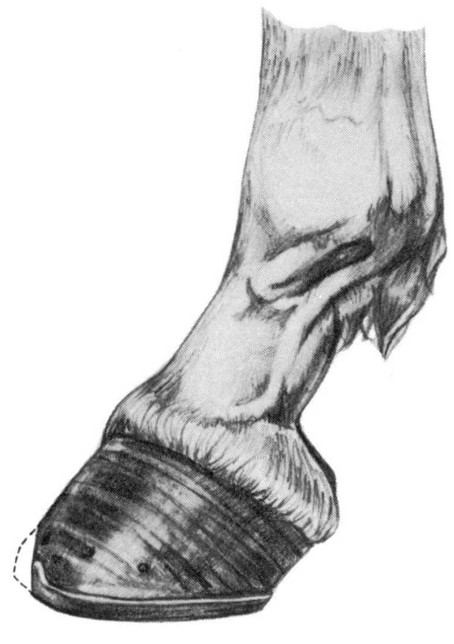

Right fore foot

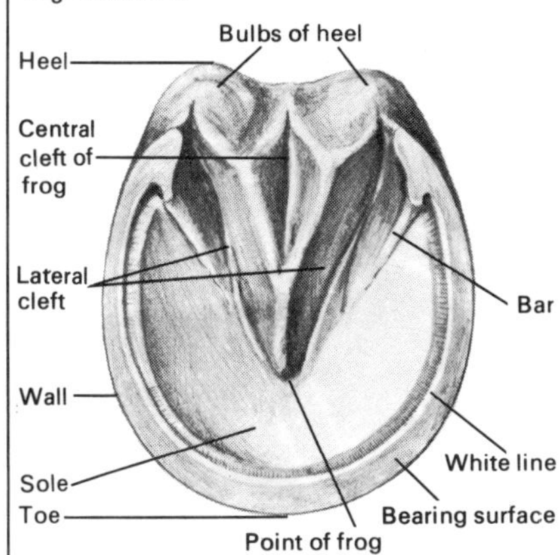

Left fore shoe

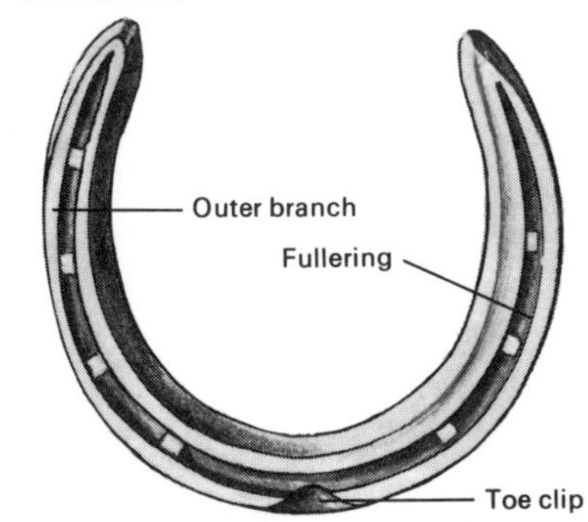

Left hind shoe

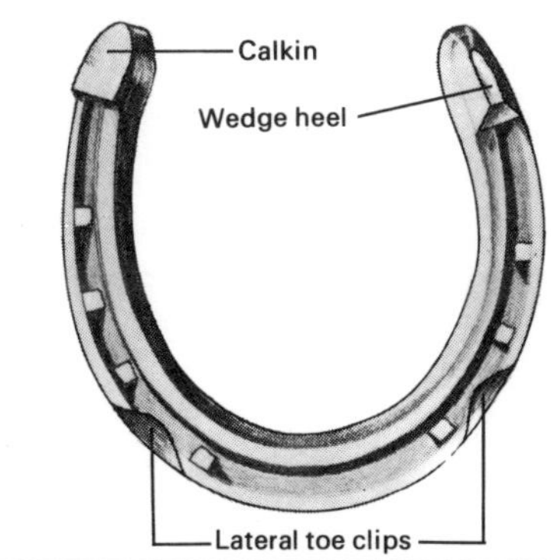

Finland. A Finnish mare

legs and always affirmed that riding was 'legs, not hands'. Though indebted to the classic masters of the *haute école*, he created a new school which is still followed. He was appointed riding master at the School of Cavalry for Officers at St Petersburg in 1898, a post he held until 1910. He died in Paris in 1913.

Author of *Breaking and Riding* and other books, he also gave his name to a snaffle bit: a hanging cheek, double-jointed, ported mouthpiece. DRT

Filly
A young immature female horse over one year old. CF

Filly Foal
A female horse under one year old. CF

Finland
There used to be two breeds of horses in Finland: the Finnish Draught and the Finnish Universal. Increasing use of machinery and higher labour costs have reduced the number of horses needed; there is now only one type of horse bred, a useful all-rounder. Working horses are used in agriculture and forestry, but in two decades the number of horses used for handling timber had gone down from 60,000–80,000 to 30,000. The demand for horses for equestrian sports, however, is increasing and the Finnish horse is bred for trotting races, once a rural sport but now supported by townspeople, and for riding. Light horses of the American, Russian or Orlov breeds also take part in these races since the ban on importing light horses was lifted in 1966. Riding horses number some 500. There has been a decrease in the total horse population since 1950 when 408,800 were registered: in 1968 the figure had decreased to 126,100.

The Finnish horse is believed to be descended from the horses of northern Europe, from both heavy and light ancestors. Its even temper and draught power suggest a heavy horse, but its speed, lively character, stamina and longevity indicate light-horse traits. Generally the colour is chestnut; the old colours of black and brown are no longer common. White markings on the head and white socks are usual. Height of both sexes is 15·1$\frac{1}{2}$–15·2$\frac{1}{2}$ hands (1·56–1·59 m). DMG

First-Cross
When two horses or ponies of different acknowledged pure breeds are mated to one another, the resulting foal is a first-cross. Today it may, for example, mean the foal of any purebred Mountain and Moorland pony crossed with a Thoroughbred or pure Arab; a Cleveland Bay/Thoroughbred cross is common to breed hunters. See Breeding. DRT

Fistulous Withers
An inflammatory swelling on one or both sides of the withers which may result from a badly fitting saddle or from the horse rolling when turned out. In most instances an abscess develops and bursts at one or more points, leaving a series of discharging sinuses leading to necrotic ligament or bones. CF

Fitness and Condition
Condition can be built up by care in feeding, general management and regulated work. It is a gradual development of the skeleton muscles, heart and respiratory organs to withstand fatigue. All superfluous fats and fluid are removed from the body; the volume of muscle and muscle tone, elasticity, response to stimuli, power of contraction and blood supply are increased. The respiratory system is developed so that a far greater amount of blood is oxygenated in a given space of time than in an unfit animal. The heart muscle and walls of smaller arteries (the auxiliary pumps of the circulation) are conditioned to the peak of responsiveness.

In each animal this development will reach a maximum. Unless this is appreciated an animal will 'go over the top' and become 'stale'. At all times work must be geared to the quantity of food (see Stable Management). As each animal varies, not even approximate figures can be given. If for any reason work is cut down concentrated foods must be reduced accordingly, otherwise colic, azoturia or lymphangitis may follow. WSC

Five-Gaited American Saddlebred Horse see Gaited Horses

Fjord Pony
Fjord ponies are mostly 13–14·2 hands

(1·32–1·47 m) high. The colour, in modern times, is a uniform shade of dun, with light mane and tail and a black dorsal stripe running from the forelock to the tip of the tail. This type of pony in general is widely distributed through the Baltic region (the Prussian Schweike and northern Polish varieties of KONIK are typical) and northern Russia. But it has become specialized in Norway through a very strict breeding policy dating from the beginning of this century and earlier which resulted in a pronounced Arabian shape of the head and very substantial bone, producing an all-round utility horse for hill farm work in harness or under the packsaddle and for ridden work. A good proportion of the 50,000 or so horses in Norway belong to this breed.

The characteristic stiff mane is naturally rather coarse but would grow long if left to itself. It has been from early times the custom to hog it carefully, and the traditional method of doing this brings two features into relief. Seen from the front, its profile is a ridge, so that the dark hairs at the centre stand out above the rest; seen from the side the top of the mane is so curved by the use of clippers that a pronounced arch is produced, thus lending even to mares and geldings the silhouette of a stallion. This feature is apparent in medieval farmhouse tapestries and even earlier in the carved runestones of the Viking Age, testifying to the antiquity of the fashion.

Countries which have no native pony breeds, notably Denmark and Germany, have been considerable importers of Fjord ponies in the past, and still import top-grade breeding stock to improve the studs already established outside Norway. AD

Flanders Horse see Belgium

Flat Racing

The development of horseracing in Britain can really be said to date from the seventeenth century, although it is known to have taken place much earlier. Records exist of racing during the Roman occupation, and during the reign of Henry II races took place at Smithfield, then the great London horse market. At Chester there were Shrove Tuesday races on the Roodeye, where Chester races are held today, for a wooden ball embellished with flowers.

It was in the reign of James I that racing first began to be an organized sport. He took a great liking to Newmarket, then an obscure village, and had a royal palace built there. His own enthusiasm was for hunting and hawking but many of the Scottish members of his court were fond of racing, at that period extremely popular north of the border. Recognizing the desirability of im-

Flat Racing. Bay Malton defeats King Herod, Turf and Askam in a 500-guinea sweepstake at Newmarket in 1767.

proving the breed of horse in England, he established public races in various parts of the country. The prize was usually a silver bell; an ancient silver bell is still a trophy at one of the Lanark meetings.

As is the case today, British blood was constantly reinforced by the import of high-class horses from abroad: in 1605 James was given 'a dozen gallant mares, all in foal, four horses and eleven stallions, all coursers of Naples', and the Queen received a dozen valuable horses from her father, the King of Denmark.

Arab stallions were then considered best for siring racehorses and the golden age for the importing of Eastern stallions was from the middle of the seventeenth century to the middle of the eighteenth. The most significant of these imported sires were the DARLEY ARABIAN, the BYERLEY TURK and the GODOLPHIN ARABIAN, who all founded dynasties that exist to this day. All modern THOROUGHBREDS descend from them in the male line though other stallions, whose male line eventually died out, also played a notable part in the evolution of the Thoroughbred.

Charles II loved racing, rode in matches, founded races called the Royal Plates and sometimes adjudicated in the disputes which were becoming more numerous owing to the increase in the volume of betting. The famous Rowley Mile Course at Newmarket, the home of English flat racing, is named after Charles II. 'Old Rowley' was his nickname, derived from his favourite hack which bore that name.

William III founded the Royal Stud at Hampton Court, betted heavily and owned a good horse named Stiff Dick. His trainer was Tregonwell Frampton, who also held the position of 'Keeper of the Running Horses at Newmarket' to Queen Anne, who founded the racecourse at Ascot, to George I and George II. Shrewd, not over burdened with scruples, and detesting women, Frampton possessed an unrivalled knowledge of horses and developed the art of training them for racing. In addition he succeeded in introducing a semblance of orderly rules and methodical organization into a sport then conducted in a lax and haphazard manner. Respect for him, if not affection, increased with the years and at the time of his death he had earned the title of 'Father of the Turf'.

In assessing the type of racing that took place in the seventeenth century, it must be remembered that the horse was all-important in transport, in agriculture and in war. The quality most sought after was 'bottom', a combination of strength, stamina and resolution. Sheer speed was not desired. Races usually consisted of a series of matches between mature horses over distances of 4–12 miles (6·5–20 km) on rough, unprepared ground. 'Give and Take' plates were then common, races with a weight-for-inches allowance based on the height of the horses competing.

The increasing popularity of racing was such that in 1740 Parliament passed an Act restricting it, since it was thought there was too much racing for the good of the country as a whole. To eliminate small country meetings where trickery was rife, the Act decreed that no plate of value less than £50 should be run for. Parliament also fixed the weights to be carried: five-year-olds 10 stone (140 lb or 63·5 kg), six-year-olds 11 stone (154 lb or 69·85 kg), seven-year-olds and upward 12 stone (168 lb or 76·2 kg). Penalties for carrying less were a fine of £200 and forfeiture of the horse. Matches were to be allowed only at Newmarket and Hambleton ('Black Hambleton'), and then only for a minimum stake of £50.

With the growth of racing, a governing body was required to lay down clearly defined rules and to ensure their enforcement. The JOCKEY CLUB came into existence round about 1750 with many rich and influential men among its members. Though it had been founded with no intention of becoming the governing body of the sport, it gradually assumed control, firstly at Newmarket only, but later over racing throughout the country.

The axiom held at the beginning of the eighteenth century that no horse should be raced before the age of five was fading fifty years later. Three-year-old races were introduced at Newmarket in 1756. The first of the five so-called CLASSIC RACES for three-year-olds, the St Leger, was founded in 1776, swiftly followed by the Oaks in 1779 and the Derby in 1780. More and more emphasis was placed on speed. Inevitably there was racing for two-year-olds as well, and the July Stakes at Newmarket, still a major two-year-old event, was founded in 1786. There was even for a time racing for yearlings, and races for yearlings were not offi-

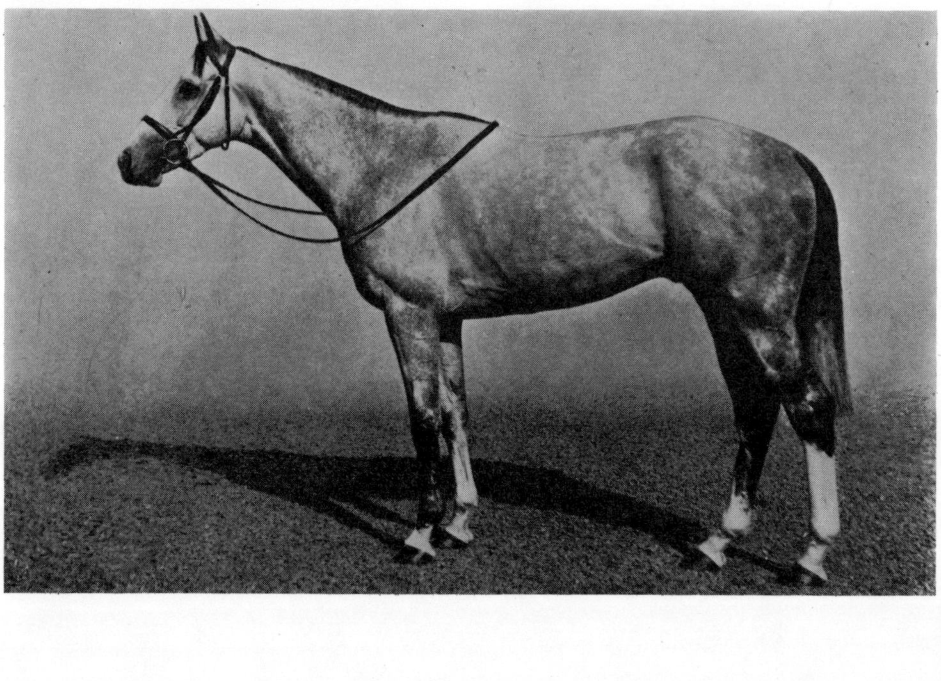

Flat Racing. Mahmoud, winner of the 1936 Epsom Derby

cially banned by the Jockey Club till 1859.

In the nineteenth century the spread of the railway system increased attendances at major race meetings and newspapers began to pay more attention to the sport. For the first time some notice was taken of the comfort of spectators and Lord George Bentinck introduced different-priced enclosures with amenities varying according to price; punctuality; the numbering of each horse on the card; the saddling of horses in a stated place; and the parade in front of the stands. He also improved the standard, then deplorably low, among racing officials, and waged relentless war on the villains who were threatening to drag the sport into utter disrepute.

During the nineteenth century the quality of the Thoroughbred was vastly improved and the selling plater of 1850 was superior to the champion of 1750. Even so, the famous Flying Dutchman in 1849 took 3 min to cover the Derby course, whereas in 1936 Mahmoud took 2 min 33⅘ sec. Gradually the Turf managed to shed most of the rough and raffish element that distressed so many of the primmer Victorian families; the sport gained greatly in prestige through the patronage of the Prince of Wales, later King Edward VII. There were memorable scenes of enthusiasm when he won his first Derby in 1896 with Persimmon.

At the turn of the century anti-racing legislation in America resulted in the so-called American invasion. American jockeys, Tod Sloan in particular, revolutionized English race riding, and English jockeys, to stay in the game, had to pull up their leathers and adopt a more streamlined style of riding. Races ceased to be a dawdle followed by a sprint. Trainers from America introduced beneficial new methods and their plating of horses proved greatly superior. Unfortunately some of these trainers were experts in doping, too, and certain American jockeys were in close touch with the riff-raff of the American Turf.

During two world wars racing, despite some fierce and occasionally unjust opposition, just kept ticking over, thanks largely to the tact and discretion of certain members of the Jockey Club, and in World War II to the efforts of Sir Francis Weatherby, head of the firm of Messrs Weatherby, for so long the Jockey Club's agents.

Since World War II there have been many changes, not least in Britain through the passing of the Betting and Gaming Act 1960, one consequence of which was the legalization of betting shops and the founding of the HORSERACE BETTING LEVY BOARD, designed to collect money from both the bookmakers and the TOTALISATOR, the totalisator having been introduced into British racing between the wars, and to apply that money for the general good of the sport. Innovations have been the photo finish; the patrol camera; sponsored races; starting stalls; twenty-four-hour declarations; racecourse commentaries; televised racing; and routine tests to deter DOPING. Stable and racecourse security has been overhauled and the doping laws revised. The Jockey Club has amalgamated with the National Hunt Committee to control both flat racing and racing over jumps; the administration of the sport has been modernized. In a changed, and still changing, world, racing faces many problems, chiefly financial ones, but its hold on the public persists. RM

Flat Racing. The Paris Grand Prix at Longchamp in 1900

Europe: Thoroughbred racing and breeding were not long confined to Britain. The late eighteenth- and early nineteenth-century sportsmen were great exporters of horses and ideas. Volume IV of the General Stud Book shows the scale of their work, indicating exports of noted stallions to France, Germany, Prussia, Holland, Sweden, Russia, Bohemia, India, South Africa, Sardinia, Australia and America. The initial movement was westward, to the Americas, the natural connection with France being postponed by the Napoleonic Wars.

The French Jockey Club was founded in 1833 and within a few years promoted its own version of the Derby (Prix du Jockey-Club) and the Oaks (Prix de Diane). Racing prospered under the patronage of the nobility, and by dint of judicious imports France was soon able to breed horses as

Flat Racing. *Top:* The Gran Premio at Milan, 1971
Above: The Russian racehorse, Anilin

good as the English. This point was emphasized in 1865, when Gladiateur ('The Avenger of Waterloo') captured the English TRIPLE CROWN. Since then, France has vied with Britain for the title of Europe's premier breeding nation, the pendulum swinging first one way, then the other.

In some respects, French racing leads the world. Vast sums of money are available for provision of prize money to owners and breeders, thanks to the *tiercé*, a PARI-MUTUEL pool which draws huge amounts (over £500,000 on occasions) from punters on a selected race once or twice a week. A percentage of the *tiercé* 'take' also goes to the improvement of public amenities at racecourses, including the sumptuous new grandstand at Longchamp.

The French racing calendar has been imaginatively planned, providing a variety of well-endowed events at all stages of a horse's development. There are ample opportunities for the horse just below the top class to earn good prize money and the very best can race for mammoth sums in the Prix Lupin, Grand Prix de Saint-Cloud and Prix de l'Arc de Triomphe.

The Thoroughbred population of Italy is tiny, compared with those of France or Great Britain. However, Italian studs, particularly the Razza Dormello-Olgiata, have developed the habit of occasionally producing an international champion. Donatello, Nearco and Ribot are examples of Italian-breds who followed brilliant racecourse careers with influential periods at stud. Italy stages her counterparts of the five English CLASSIC RACES with several prestige prizes open to horses of different generations. Imported horses are now permitted to run in many top races and the locally bred horses have generally come off worse.

Germany has produced only a handful of outstanding performers at international level, of which Oleander (foaled 1924) was probably the best. He subsequently became an important influence in worldwide pedigrees. Ticino (1939) and his son Neckar (1948), both winners of the Deutsches Derby, have also made an impression on international breeding. In the early 1970s German-breds have been quite successful in France and they have done nobly in defending their important open events, such as the Grosser Preis von Baden. It seems likely that Germany will eventually supplant Italy as Europe's third breeding power.

Racing takes place in almost all other European countries, but none can boast of a breeding industry which is consistently able to produce horses of a superior calibre. The reasons are varied: climatic conditions, inadequate government support, lack of public interest, dearth of qualified professionals, etc. However, there is a chance of a resurgence in Hungary, still best known for the performances of Kincsem (unbeaten in 54 races) and Kisbér (Epsom Derby winner) in the 1870s. Imperial, a racehorse of international standard, was foaled there in 1960 and he has rapidly established himself as the most successful sire. There is considerable interchange of bloodstock between the central and eastern European nations, but few horses are imported from the West. Imperial could soon wield a tremendous influence in the Communist bloc.

In the U.S.S.R. and other Communist nations, racing and breeding are state-controlled. The horses are government-owned, being bred by and racing for a collection of government studs. After many years in obscurity, the U.S.S.R. began to show her bloodstock in the 1960s. Russian

Melbourne Cup Winners

Year	Winner	Year	Winner
1861	Archer	1918	Night Watch
1862	Archer	1919	Artilleryman
1863	Banker	1920	Poitrel
1864	Lantern	1921	Sister Olive
1865	Toryboy	1922	King Ingoda
1866	The Barb	1923	Bitalli
1867	Tim Whiffler	1924	Backwood
1868	Glencoe	1925	Windbag
1869	Warrior	1926	Spearfelt
1870	Nimblefoot	1927	Trivalve
1871	The Pearl	1928	Statesman
1872	The Quack	1929	Nightmarch
1873	Don Juan	1930	Phar Lap
1874	Haricot	1931	White Nose
1875	Wollomai	1932	Peter Pan
1876	Briseis	1933	Hall Mark
1877	Chester	1934	Peter Pan
1878	Calamia	1935	Marabou
1879	Darriwell	1936	Wotan
1880	Grand Flaneur	1937	The Trump
1881	Zulu	1938	Catalogue
1882	The Assyrian	1939	Rivette
1883	Martini-Henri	1940	Old Rowley
1884	Malua	1941	Skipton
1885	Sheet Anchor	1942	Colonus
1886	Arsenal	1943	Dark Felt
1887	Dunlop	1944	Sirius
1888	Mentor	1945	Rainbird
1889	Bravo	1946	Russia
1890	Carbine	1947	Hiraji
1891	Malvolio	1948	Rimfire
1892	Glenloth	1949	Foxzami
1893	Tarcoola	1950	Comic Court
1894	Patron	1951	Delta
1895	Auraria	1952	Dalray
1896	Newhaven	1953	Wodalla
1897	Gaulus	1954	Rising Fast
1898	The Grafter	1955	Toparoa
1899	Merriwee	1956	Evening Peal
1900	Clean Sweep	1957	Straight Draw
1901	Revenue	1958	Baystone
1902	The Victory	1959	MacDougal
1903	Lord Cardigan	1960	Hi Jinx
1904	Acrasia	1961	Lord Fury
1905	Blue Spec	1962	Even Stevens
1906	Poseidon	1963	Gatun Gatun
1907	Apologue	1964	Polo Prince
1908	Lord Nolan	1965	Light Fingers
1909	Prince Foote	1966	Galilee
1910	Comedy Kg	1967	Red Handed
1911	The Parisian	1968	Rain Lover
1912	Piastre	1969	Rain Lover
1913	Posinatus	1970	Baghdad Note
1914	Kingsburgh	1971	Silver Knight
1915	Patrobus	1972	Piping Lane
1916	Sasanof	1973	
1917	Westcourt		

horses were sent to western Europe and the United States to race, always in the best company. Several were successful, notably Anilin, a brilliant rugged campaigner twice placed in the Washington D.C. International and fifth in the Prix de l'Arc de Triomphe. Anilin now stands at the Voskhod Stud, where he was foaled.

Africa: South Africa is one of the few countries besides Britain that allows bookmakers to operate both on and off racecourses. She relies heavily on purchases from abroad and in the 1970–1 season every one of her leading 20 sires was imported. The accent is on speed, with two-thirds of the prize money allocated to winners of races at a mile or less. The four provinces in the Republic each run a series of classic races, but the most popular events are big handicaps, including the nation's most valuable race, the Rothmans July Handicap, run over 2,200 m ($1\frac{1}{4}$ miles) at Greyville, Natal. The 1960s produced a succession of top-class racehorses in South Africa, like Colorado King and Hawaii, both exported to the United States, where they won prestige events and were retired to stud, proving a fine advertisement for South African stock.

Asia: Malaysia, where racing is graded, imports relatively modest stock from Britain and Australia. The quality of the racing is not high, but the great volume of betting contributes to excellent facilities at the racecourses for horses, trainers, stable staff and public. There are no legal bookmakers or totalisator betting shops, but the Malaysian authorities hit on a new idea to ensure that little revenue is lost. There are only three regular racing centres and when one stages a meeting the other two open their courses, provide a full totalisator staff and relay commentaries on the races. Crowds of over 5,000 regularly attend these 'ghost' meetings.

Hong Kong also operates a graded system of racing, importing extensively from Australia. As in Malaysia, the horses are regarded primarily as gambling media and the quality of the racing is poor.

Japan could be the next great power in racing and breeding, judging by her performance in the 1960s and 1970s. Six Epsom Derby winners and a host of other top-class European horses have been imported for stud duty in the Hokkaido area. Japan's heavy investment in mares, yearlings and foals has been the biggest single factor in the boom in British bloodstock prices in recent years. As Japan has no ideal horse-breeding territory, it appears that she will always be forced to import quite extensively. The popularity of racing is astonishing. Over 100,000 spectators attend the Derby, the Tokyo Yoshun Kyoso, and all tickets have to be bought in advance. On this one race, punters gamble £5,000,000.

Australasia: Australia's importance in the bloodstock world has grown considerably since World War II. The export of Bernborough, Noholme, Pago Pago and Tobin Bronze to the United States and their success there drew attention to the quality of Australian-breds and their reputation has steadily advanced. Australia now enjoys the position of 'middle man' in many profitable bloodstock deals, importing well-bred but often poorly performed horses from Britain at modest prices, establishing them as stallions and selling their offspring at inflated values to the United States. Most Australian tracks are tight ovals with short straights and as the majority of the jockeys like to employ waiting tactics the final two furlongs often prove intensely exciting. Each state runs its own classic events for three-year-olds, but, as in South Africa, the

Flat Racing. *Above:* New Zealand grey Baghdad Note wins the 1970 Melbourne Cup.
Below right: Iroquois, the American winner of the 1881 Epsom Derby

handicaps are more popular. Most famous of all is the two-mile (3·2 km) Melbourne Cup, which brings the nation to a halt for three-and-a-half minutes every year on the first Tuesday in November.

Like the Australians, New Zealand breeders have always been inclined to favour pedigree rather than conformation or performance in their prospective stallions. Their judgment has been proved correct many times, with the production of such as Phar Lap and Daryl's Joy, each the brilliant son of a very low-grade racehorse. Their climate seems particularly suited to the breeding of high-class horses. Their record in the great Australian races, especially staying events like the Melbourne Cup, is outstanding. Many of the best yearlings sold in New Zealand go to Australian stables, winning about 1,000 races there annually. Americans are also becoming very active in the market. The horses that remain have a variety of classic events open to them as three-year-olds on both islands, but more store is set by the long-distance cup events, such as the Wellington, New Zealand and Auckland Cups. These are for three-year-olds and upwards, run at two miles (3·2 km). TM

North America: horseracing in North America began almost as soon as the English colonists could chop out 'race paths' from the wilderness. Originally, because of the pervading forest and the shortage of cleared land, these were only about a quarter-mile long, frequently part of a street or road. The horses competing on them were called QUARTER HORSES.

The first organized racing in North America on the English model took place at a track called New Market, after the English locale, founded in 1664 by the Colonial Governor of New York, Richard Nicolls, on Long Island, only a few miles from the modern Aqueduct and Belmont Park, where today about half of the major North American races are run. Horseracing has become the leading spectator sport on the continent, as measured by attendance at over 100 tracks in 30 states, half a dozen Canadian provinces, two Mexican locales and one Puerto Rican track. All legal wagering is done through the pari-mutuels except in New York City, where legal off-track betting was authorized in 1971 under an independent corporation created by the city. From the mutuel handle a certain percentage, varying from state to state, is deducted, with part going to the state in taxes and the rest to the track for expenses and purses.

In the United States, racing is administered through individual State Racing Commissions (or similar bodies under different names). A 1950 court decision stripped the Jockey Club of all racing authority, although it still issues model racing rules which many states follow. The Jockey Club, founded in 1890 as the Board of Control, also maintains the American Stud Book (although Mexico has a separate one), registers names of horses and provides a clearing centre for racing colours, breeding leases and similar contractual agreements.

Practically all Thoroughbred breeding stock of consequence in North America traces to British bloodlines. The first 'blooded horse' recorded on the continent was Bulle Rock, imported to Virginia from England in 1730. Recently North American breeders have sought good stock throughout the world with particularly successful imports from France, which provided the leading sires Sir Galahad III, Mahmoud and Ambiorix.

North American influence abroad has grown strong recently. Although the American Iroquois won the Epsom Derby as far back as 1881, the more recent achievements in Europe of Never Say Die, Sir Ivor, the Canadian-bred Nijinsky II, Mill Reef, Roberto and Crowned Prince have vastly increased the export market for North American bloodstock.

Since the American Civil War, Kentucky has been the main centre for American Thoroughbred breeding. Although it continues to supply most of the top stock, breeding in other states has grown rapidly recently, particularly in California and Florida.

Major racing is concentrated in New York, Chicago, Miami and Los Angeles, with important minor centres in New Jersey, Maryland, Delaware, Massachusetts, Kentucky and New Mexico. The three-year-old classics (the 'Triple Crown') are the KENTUCKY DERBY (founded 1875), Preakness Stakes (1873) and Belmont Stakes (1867). The major event for three-year-old fillies is the Coaching Club American Oaks (1917). The richest race is the Garden State Stakes (1953) for two-year-olds. The richest handicap is the Hollywood Gold Cup (1938) but it does not carry as much prestige as the weight-for-age Jockey Club Gold Cup (1919). Although most racing is conducted on dirt ('skinned') ovals, recently competition on grass ('sodded') courses has grown more important. The best-known race on grass is the Washington, D.C., International (1952).

Canadian racing and breeding of international consequence is concentrated in Ontario; Woodbine is the major racecourse. The Queen's Plate there, for Canadian-foaled three-year-olds, is North America's oldest continuously run race, founded in 1860. The more modern Canadian International Championship (1938) on grass often attracts runners from the United States. A number of Canadian-bred horses have won championships in the United States, including the 1971 leading sire in North America, Northern Dancer.

Breeding and racing in Mexico and Puerto Rico is not yet of international rank. Both countries have active native-bred racing and breeding programs but are largely still satellites of the sport in the United States. Mexican racing has been concentrated at Mexico City since the 1971 burning of the Caliente track, scheduled to reopen in 1972. El Comandante is the only track in Puerto Rico. FTP

South America: the racing and breeding of Thoroughbreds are of great importance in seven of the ten South American nations, led by Argentina with a production of more than ten thousand foals a year, many of which are exported to the rest of South and Central America and to the United States. In what has proved to be a permanent preference for English bloodlines, the Argentinians, at the beginning of this century, despite strong opposition from the British House of Lords, bought for stud Diamond Jubilee, son of St Simon-Perdita and winner of the English Derby. Horse racing in Argentina has been developing since 1850, when Dr Carlos Pelegrini founded the Jockey Club. In his name an internationally famed classic race is run each year over $1\frac{7}{8}$ miles (3 km) with a $100,000 purse. Other important races include the Jockey Club, $1\frac{1}{4}$ miles (2 km), since 1853; Gran Premio Nacional, $1\frac{9}{16}$ miles (2·5 km), since 1857; and the Polla de Potrillos over 1 mile (1·6 km). Thirty-six racetracks operate in Argentina; San Isidro and Palermo are the most important, the latter being an exact replica of Longchamp in France. Palermo has night racing with the daily attendance exceeding 50,000 and with bets surpassing one million dollars. Peppermint, Old Man, Yatasto, Cara Palida, Botafogo, Rico Monte, and, more recently, Make Money, Forli and Pronto have placed Argentina high both in racing and breeding. Chile not only ranks second in South America in the production of Thoroughbreds but also exports a great number of them to the United States and Venezuela. Chile's main tracks are Hipodromo de Chile, de Santiago and de Valparaiso. One of Chile's greatest moments in racing was when Yumbel won the 1969 Widener Handicap at Hialeah.

In Venezuela racing and breeding are booming, especially since the 1959 inauguration of La Rinconada, the pride of the Venezuelans and of all Latin Americans. Venezuelans have a betting system called the Five and Six, in which great sums of money are bet every Sunday. Their most important races are the Simon Bolivar, run over $1\frac{1}{2}$ miles (2·5 km) with a $70,000 purse, the Fuerzas Armadas and the J. de Julio Stakes.

Uruguay, with the Hipodromo de Maroñas, offers the Clasico Jose Pedro Ramirez and the Gran Premio Municipal. Brazil has the Hipodromo de la Gavea, where the Gran Premio de Brazil is disputed over $1\frac{7}{8}$ miles (3 km). Peru, with the Monterrico, has night racing; and Colombia, with the Hipodromo de Techo, follows in importance.

Central America: Panama is the only country in Central America that has horse racing. The modern Presidente Remon race track offers 166 racing days a year. Breeding is becoming more important with imports from Argentina, Chile and the United States. Even though Panama does not rank high in horse quality compared to its neighbours, it can be proud of its contributions to world turf with top-ranked jockeys like Braulio Baeza, Laffit Pincay, Manuel Ycaza, Jorge Velazquez, Heliodoro Gustines, Jorge Tejeira, Victor Tejada, Angel Santiago, and many others. Panama also has the only jockey school in Latin America, directed by two saddle greats: Bolivar Moreno and Blas Aguirre. RC

Flying Change of Leg see Movements

Fontainebleau see France

Forest Tarpan see Huçul, Tarpan

Fort Riley

Fort Riley, an army post in Kansas, was the location of the United States Cavalry and Light Artillery School from 14 March 1892 to 26 September 1907, the Mounted Service School from 26 September 1907 to 19 September 1919, and the Cavalry School from 19 September 1919 to 1 November 1946; it is now the Army General School. Originally established to pacify 'hostiles', as the Indians were called, the fort's history is closely tied to the U.S. Cavalry's 7th Division, the 'Garry Owens', and their dashing second-in-command, Gen. George A. Custer, killed at the Battle of the Little Big Horn. After its establishment as the Cavalry and Artillery School, subjects taught included Hippology, Tactics, Equitation, Horse Training, Horseshoeing and Topography. As the Mounted Service School, student officers enrolled averaged 892 hours in the saddle on school horses, plus riding their private mounts. The first U.S. Army show-jumping team to compete in a National Horse Show was trained at the fort in 1909 and it remained the principal training base for U.S. Olympic Equestrian teams even after the Cavalry had been completely mechanized; the first civilian Olympic team (1952) was selected there in 1951. HCA

Forward Riding

Forward Riding is a development of CAPRILLI's *Sistema*, preserving the latter's fundamental principles, but it has enlarged upon its theory and its practices. Additions to Caprilli's very brief theory were imperative because much had been learned since his death about the mechanics of the horse's jump and of his gaits. While these alone improved some practices, further changes were necessary to keep the method in step with the changing conditions of equestrian sport. For instance, the various forms of competitive jumping, so popular today, were in embryo when Caprilli was alive. Forward Riding, as an American version of *Il Sistema*, is adjusted to the American equestrian scene, and it differs from the European adaptations of the same, often called Natural Riding. The cornerstone of Forward Riding is the belief that jumping and cross-country riding are most efficient if based on the free travelling gaits used by the horse in nature only when it is calm and moves to get somewhere. Thus this method rarely employs even semi-collection and never any artificialities.

Forward Riding as a complete method consists of three parts: The Forward Seat, Forward Schooling and Forward Control.

The Forward Seat: places the rider over the area of the average centre of gravity of a free-going horse, thus uniting him with a horse moving naturally in *forward balance*, which is particularly predominant at speed. Mechanically, however, this particular Forward Seat differs from the original Italian Seat. The stirrups are two or three holes longer; consequently the forward inclination of the rider's torso is less at ordinary gaits; the rider's forward balance is based on the stirrups and not on pinched knees; when a strong grip is required, pressure with the upper calves plays the predominant role.

Forward Schooling: begins by teaching the horse voice commands. For this purpose the education of a completely 'green' horse starts on a lunge. A horse thus started, if all goes well, can be ridden (at first in the ring) at slow ordinary gaits on loose reins, controlled by voice to start gaits, to change them, and to halt. Almost simultaneously, the horse is taught to approach low fences on loose reins, at first at a trot and later at a canter: CAVALLETTI (on the ground) are used to 'stabilize' the horse's approach at a trot, and very low in-and-outs (at least triple ones) are used for the same purpose at a canter.

The next step is to teach the horse not to object to a *soft contact* between his mouth and the rider's hands. From then on, the horse is taught all the standard leg and hand AIDS. Familiarity with voice commands is a great help in teaching the horse obedience to gentle aids. Thus the term

Forward Riding. This is an entirely free, natural, easy jump. The horse is not disturbed by the rider's position, nor by his hands or legs.

'soft contact' replaces 'on the bit'. Throughout schooling, calmness rather than 'brilliance' is the foremost goal.

Forward Schooling restores (under the weight of the rider) the *natural balance* of the horse, without any special effort of its trainer. Much riding across country, with some mild ring exercises and jumping combinations (mostly low) added to it, will increase the horse's strength and agility to the point where it will easily be able to handle the weight of a Forward Seat rider and will move efficiently on the basis of its restored natural forward balance.

Ring exercises such as changes of gaits and speeds, halts, reining back, turns in place, etc., are practised as in most types of schooling. In comparison with DRESSAGE, however, they are here simplified both for the horse and for the rider. For example, no lining up of legs is required in halting; during the turn on the haunches in place, no attention is paid to whether the hind legs mark all the beats or skip some. Thus Forward Schooling eliminates anything that makes merely a good show rather than good practical horse sense.

Forward Control: in riding is the same as that used in schooling, but it has to be taught to the rider on a schooled horse before he undertakes his own schooling of a colt.

Forward Riding is particularly suitable for riding to hounds, showing hunters over fences, and for junior jumping in horsemanship tests. It is also a godsend to innumerable riders whose ambitions do not go beyond hacking. The fact that Forward Riding has produced a number of top riders and horses does not alter its main function of being a method of riding for the majority. VSL

Reference: V. S. Littauer, *Common Sense Horsemanship*, 2nd ed., New York, 1963; V. S. Littauer, *Schooling Your Horse*, New York, 1956; J. M. Dillon, *School for Young Riders*, New York, 1958; H. D. Chamberlin, *Training Hunters, Jumpers and Hacks*, 2nd ed., New York, 1952.

4-H Horse Project

The largest organized youth horse program in the United States is the 4-H Horse Project, sponsored by the Cooperative Extension Service of the United States Department of Agriculture. The 1971 enrolment was 256,791 compared with 37,531 in 1959, the first year of official statistics. The project strives to develop leadership, citizenship, self-reliance and sportsmanship in addition to teaching equitation and proper management. Activities are varied: horse shows, judging, trail riding (competitive and recreational), and educational experiences such as public displays and knowledge contests. Projects range from breeding, rearing and training young horses to equitation. Young people who do not own horses may participate in this program. Volunteer leaders guide the clubs, which average 20 members aged 9–19. FH

Foxhunting. The Curre Hunt moving across country near Llansoy, Monmouthshire

Foxhounds see Hounds

Foxhunting

Hounds have hunted the fox in Britain since earliest times, but it was only in the eighteenth century that packs began to hunt the fox exclusively, although there is evidence that the fox was frequently the main quarry for a pack of hounds, especially in the north of England. For this reason several northern packs of hounds have claimed to have the longest history. Certainly in Sussex, in the south, there is evidence that at the beginning of the eighteenth century the Charlton Hunt, now extinct, hunted the fox and nothing else. The Brocklesby kennel came into being in 1710. Here hounds were bred exclusively to hunt the fox. At Milton, the Fitzwilliam family had a firmly established kennel. Their pre-1760 stud books have unfortunately been lost in a fire. Halfway through the eighteenth century there were some fifty people breeding foxhounds. These included such names famous in the annals of hunting as the Duke of Beaufort, Lord Middleton and Mr Hugo Meynell.

In the eighteenth and early nineteenth centuries huge tracts of lands were hunted, the Berkeley for instance hunting from Berkeley to Chorley Wood, the Beaufort from Bristol to Banbury, but the sport was entirely the private recreation of big landowners who invited their aristocratic friends to join them. Towards the middle of the nineteenth century the cost of maintaining lavish establishments became too much even for the great landowners of those days, and gradually subscription packs were introduced. This largely altered the character of hunting. Subscribers not only swelled greatly the number of people following hounds, but felt entitled to a say in the organization of the hunt. Above all they wanted sport. With almost limitless grass and the comparatively few fences now part of the English countryside it was not difficult to produce sport of the order demanded by those who reckoned to do very little other than hunt during the winter months. Great names were associated with this era: Mr Osbaldeston, Sir William Lowther, Mr Assheton Smith, Mr Tom Smith, Mr Corbett, the Selby Lowndes, Parson Milne, and many others in addition to the great landowners, many of whom retained their control of the family packs.

That hunting's survival in the nineteenth century was largely due to the subscription packs cannot be denied. It enabled hunting, moreover, to be carried on in a very lavish manner right up to World War I. Thanks to the existence of cavalry regiments, enabling many fine horsemen to hunt army horses, hunting continued between the Wars; but while 'Joint Masters' were virtually unknown before 1914, during the 1920s and 1930s more and more hunts had two or even three masters to share the ever-increasing costs not met by the hunt guarantee.

Hunting has continued to flourish since 1945, largely due to the newly formed 'supporters' clubs which not only help hunts financially, but produce enthusiasts in all walks of life who are able to rebut the various accusations of those opposed to the sport. The 1970s have brought inevitable changes, amalgamations, hunts run by committees, shorter terms of office by masters, and huge increases in costs necessitating smaller staffs. Yet with more than 200 packs in action in Britain, and larger fields, foxhunting has never been more popular. See also Hunting. DW

France

Equitation: equitation and love of horses, on the increase for several years, have very ancient roots in France although perhaps not so deep as in England.

The Romans used a large body of Gallic cavalry. EPONA, the horse goddess adopted by them, was a Gallic deity, and Caesar wrote that only two classes counted in Gaul: the Druids and the knights.

It was in the sixteenth and seventeenth centuries, with a peak in the eighteenth, that France set standards for the world. After the Italian Renaissance with its masters, the instinctive equitation of the past became a rational science taught in academies. In 1680 Louis XIV transferred to Versailles the large and small royal stables and what was to become the Riding School of Versailles. This, under the influence of a number of extremely talented masters, became a true training school of equitation, especially of academic equitation of *haute école*, 'high school' riding. It was soon to become the accepted model for all Europe, and notably for the SPANISH RIDING SCHOOL OF VIENNA, which still adheres to the principles of the most famous French master of the time, LA GUERINIÈRE. Among famous Englishmen who studied equestrianism in France were William Pitt, Canning and the Duke of Wellington.

France. The *reprise des sauteurs* presented by the Cadre Noir

The Napoleonic wars seriously affected the Riding School of Versailles and it disappeared in 1830. From then to the present the Cavalry School at Saumur, and essentially its corps of officer instructors of equitation called the Cadre Noir, have been the most representative of what can still be called the French School. Its great principles can be summed up as the pursuit of calm, impulsion, straightness, lightness, suppleness, and their application to all equitation whether performed outdoors or indoors.

The riding school at Saumur has a long history and the fame of this little town on the Loire as an equestrian centre is well established. At the end of the sixteenth century Saumur was a Protestant stronghold. There was an academy there, comprising a riding school intended for training young Huguenot gentlemen. Ruined by religious wars, the town declined and the academy disappeared. It was not until 1763 that it was reopened, when a carabineer regiment of the Comte de Provence (later Louis XVIII), grandson of the reigning Louis XV, was stationed there. Eight years later, thanks to the exceptional quality of its military and equestrian instruction, Saumur had progressed to become the seat of the French Cavalry School. Closed during the Revolution and the First Empire, it was reopened in 1815; it was then that the famous corps of riding instructors, the Cadre Noir, was formed, taking their name from their uniform of black tunic, white buckskin breeches and, in full dress, black cocked hat, which has remained almost unchanged since then. At first the instructors of the Cadre Noir were civilian riding masters. Towards the middle of the nineteenth century they were all replaced by officers and noncommissioned officers selected from cavalry regiments. Today the Cadre Noir is still composed of military men (either active or retired, not assigned to a particular corps), but the creation in 1968 of a National Institute of Equitation, replaced in 1972 by a National School of Equitation, both civilian, should bring civilian instructors back to their ranks. There is often confusion between Saumur, the cavalry training school, and the Cadre Noir, limited to a dozen officers (*écuyers* and *sous-écuyers*) and an equal number of noncommissioned officers (masters and under-masters). The corps is commanded by a Chief Écuyer, always a high-ranking officer, at least a major, usually a Lt-Colonel or Colonel, never a General. Instructors must be all-round horsemen. They do not specialize exclusively in dressage leading to *haute école* although this takes precedence. They also race, show jump and compete in horse trials, and they must school their own horses. To the public, in France and abroad, the Cadre Noir is known mainly for its presentations of the *reprise des écuyers* (instructors' dressage test) of the high and low school, and *reprise des sauteurs* (jumpers' dressage test) presented by the under-masters commanded by a captain. In the course of the latter the ancient school jumps, *courbette, croupade, cabriole,* are executed. The instructors are mounted mostly on English Thoroughbreds or Anglo-Arabs, the under-masters on French Saddle Horses.

For some time the Republican Guard of Paris has been the only mounted regiment in France and Saumur has become the Training School for Tanks, Armoured Cars and Cavalry (1945). Equitation is, however, still used to develop the traditional qualities of the officer corps and is compulsory at Saumur for young officers. Every year in July they still present the traditional display of lances and equestrian games alongside motorized demonstrations. Needless to say, the Cadre Noir takes part in these displays and is the most popular part of them. Today the Cadre instructs both the military and civilians. It trains equitation instructors to teach in equestrian sections of the military schools of the various arms such as Fontainebleau, Saint Cyr-Coëtquidan, Paris, etc.; the corps also trains civilians of both sexes (many of them instructors themselves) in courses of general instruction as well as high school dressage. In the present structure of the National School of Equitation, the Cadre Noir of Saumur still concentrates on dressage and improvement of the best riders as military or civilian instructors, while training and preparation for competitive equitation (field trials and show jumping) is carried out at the centre at Fontainebleau, a town in wooded, hilly country about 35 miles south of Paris. In the autumn each year the French Championships in Dressage, Show Jumping and Horse Trials take place there.

Apart from racing and stag- and fox-hunting, which are outside the scope of this article, and polo, which is too expensive for most people, equestrian activities are becoming increasingly popular in France, as in many countries over the last few years and are encouraged by the State; a new interministerial Council of Equitation, and a superior committee of equitation created by decree in August 1971, are charged with the general direction of equitation in France. On a more modest scale, public authorities work to make riding more democratic. The increased popularity of riding generally can be attributed to an improving standard of living, more leisure, more interest in physical fitness, reaction against intensive urbanization, and fashion. Private and individual initiative coexists with official organization at all levels, from the modest hirer of a horse by the hour or pony trekker, to the member of a club of international show jumpers. The French Federation of Equestrian Sports is affiliated to the FÉDÉRATION ÉQUESTRE INTERNATIONALE. The Union Nationale Interprofessionnelle du Cheval (U.N.I.C.) keeps in touch with national and private studs and is in charge of publicity and all commercial matters; while the recently formed National Federation of French Saddle Horse Associations groups breeders by breeds. The State Stud Administration, founded in 1663 by Colbert, Louis XIV's Minister, has from time to time been suppressed, but always re-established. It is at

France. Officers at Haras du Pin, Normandy, riding French Saddle Horses

present divided into 21 areas of which the most famous are Le Pin in Normandy, Pompadour in Limousin, and Tarbes in the Pyrenees. The role of the studs is fundamental in promoting the preservation and improvement of French horse breeds. The State Stud Administration is under the control of the Minister for Agriculture. ES

Breeds: as in all countries, the majority of French breeds come from crosses between ancient local breeds and foreign introductions. These crosses, which took place fortuitously at first (through invasions etc.) but which, more recently, were arranged to improve the breeds, were marked everywhere by important additions of both Oriental blood (Arab or Barb), Thoroughbred and blood from those English breeds derived from pure blood such as the NORFOLK TROTTER and HUNTER. Climate, soil and methods of rearing also played an important part in the success or failure of these crosses. There are now only a very reduced number of Arabs in public or private studs; their essential role is to conserve the obligatory 25 per cent of Oriental blood in the Anglo-Arab, which in France has been elevated to the status of a breed.

Apart from the English THOROUGHBRED and the Arab, the State Stud Administration now recognizes three large families of saddle horses: the Anglo-Arab; the French Saddle Horse, mainly derived from the Anglo-Norman; and the Trotter, an Anglo-Norman specially bred for trotting races, which has become a separate breed. See separate articles on Arab, Anglo-Arab, Norman, Anglo-Norman and French Saddle Horse, French Trotter, Camargue, French Ponies, Percheron, Boulonnais, Breton and Breton Heavy Draught, Ardennais, Trait du Nord, Auxois, Comtois and Poitevin. ES

Franches-Montagnes (Freiberger)
see Switzerland

Frederiksborg
see Denmark

French Ponies
see Ponies, French

French Saddle Horse
see Norman, Anglo-Norman and French Saddle Horse

French Trotter

In the nineteenth century there was a demand for trotting horses and for coach horses with a naturally high action. E. Houël, a stud official, realized the necessity of choosing a horse not only for its build and way of moving but also for its racing performance. The first trotting race took place at Cherbourg in 1836. The sport soon became very popular, spread, and was officially recognized and subsidized. In 1864 a society to encourage the French Halfbred Horse was formed. From the stallions Young Rattler, Normand, Lavater and particularly Fuchsia (foaled 1883), ancestors of the present elite, a new breed was established, which also had Russian and American blood. Progress in speed, gaits, and conformation were constant in spite of a tendency to a rather straight shoulder due to the effort of the racing trot.

At present 5,000–6,000 trotting races take place in France each year, the horses harnessed either to a sulky or mounted,a French speciality. Reserved for trotters which have already shown their speed, the highlight is the Prix d'Amèrique at Vincennes, which attracts the best trotters in the world. The Stud Book was opened in 1922 and closed in 1941. The Trotter is native to Normandy (see Norman, Anglo-Norman and French Saddle Horse). ES

French Trotter. *Top:* Tidalium Pelo wins the 1971 Prix d'Amèrique at Vincennes.
Above: A French Trotter stallion at Haras du Pin

Friesian Horse

The Friesian is an old horse, black in colour, without markings (only a very small star is allowed). It stands at about 15·1 hands (1·55 m), has high action and an upright neck. It is principally bred in Friesland in the Netherlands. Friesians, harnessed to an old chaise with the driver and his wife in nineteenth-century costume, are one of the traditional sights of Friesland. See also East Friesian, Oldenburg. WS

Furioso
see Hungary

Gaited Horses

This term is generally employed to distinguish the Five-Gaited American SADDLEBRED Horse from the Three-Gaited variety of the same breed (the 'Walk-Trot' horse). The latter, who is groomed with a roached mane and tail, is trained to walk, trot and canter with a high degree of refinement and animation. The 'Gaited Horse' is usually heavier in build and its mane and tail are long and flowing. Both types carry their tails high, due to a surgical operation that severs the depressor muscles. In addition to the walk, trot and canter, the Five-

Gaited Saddlebred is taught the stepping pace and the rack (see Gaits). The latter gait is seldom performed well by any other breed.

In the larger sense, 'Gaited Horse' may refer to any breed trained to perform an artificial gait, such as the TENNESSEE WALKING HORSE or the HACKNEY PONY. MAS

Gaits

The natural gaits of the horse are the *walk*, a four-beat gait, the *trot*, a two-beat gait in which the left front and right hind feet strike the ground simultaneously, then the right front and left hind, and the *gallop*, a three-beat gait. The *canter* is a restrained gallop executed on the right lead (i.e. the right front foot strikes in advance of the left) when turning to the right or on the left lead (i.e. the left front foot strikes in advance of the right) when turning to the left.

In the United States, in addition to the walk, trot and canter, Five-Gaited SADDLEBREDS are taught the *stepping pace* and the *rack*. The stepping pace is a slow gait, not faster than 10 m.p.h., with a slight break in cadence from the *pace* proper in which the left front and left hind feet strike the ground simultaneously, then the right front and right hind, a highly uncomfortable gait for the rider as it gives him side motion in the saddle. The break in cadence of the stepping pace gives the rider an extremely smooth ride. The *rack*, formerly called the 'single foot', is a smooth, fast gait in which each foot strikes the ground separately. The *amble* is a slower form of pace. See also Movements. CJC

Galiceño

The Galiceño horse, a breed since about the fifteenth century, was produced by the forces of evolution and not by man. It is believed to have come from Galicia, in northwestern Spain, and was among the sixteen horses landed on the mainland of America when Cortes invaded Mexico from Cuba. The Galiceño horse, when mature, measures 12–13·2 hands (1·22–1·37 m) and weighs 625–700 lb (283·5–317·5 kg). Its gentle disposition, high intelligence and versatility make it an excellent competition horse as well as a natural ranch horse. Its natural running walk sets it apart from the pony. HJS

Galloway

This term is still used in the north of England to signify *any* pony, often a Dales pony. Despite great historical confusion and some mistaken derivations, it seems indubitable that the Galloway was originally a riding pony, about 13 hands (1·32 m), dark bay or black in colour, with a great turn of speed and much endurance, bred in the region between Nithsdale and the Mull of Galloway; on these the more dangerous of the Scottish border raiders were mounted in the days before the union of the crowns of England and Scotland in 1603. They had ceased to exist as a breed before the end of the nineteenth century, though individuals of the type still abounded. Photographs are extant of the Isle of Man variety of Galloway. Galloway blood has contributed much to the foundation stock of the Fell Pony (see Mountain and Moorland) and to North Country harness trotters. AD

Below: **Friesian**

Above right: **Galiceño**

Right: **Galloway.** This Manx Galloway, photographed in 1864, was believed to be one of the last bred from the old Isle of Man stock.

Galls

Bruised and often raw areas caused by ill-fitting harness and irregular pressure. Saddle galls occur principally at the base of the withers and either side of the spine.

Above: **Gelderland**

Below right: **Germany.** An East Friesian horse

Collar galls are seen in draught horses working in badly-fitting collars and in conditions conducive to sweating. They respond readily to rest and simple forms of treatment, e.g. bathing with antiseptic solutions. CF

Garranos see Portugal

Garron

Garron (English), derived from Gaelic *gearran* (gelding) means today in English the larger 'mainland' type of Highland pony (see Mountain and Moorland). In Spain the term *Garón* is applied to any of the North Spanish pony types of the Galician/Cantabrian region otherwise known as *jacas* or *asturiones*. The Irish ponies of the sixteenth century were also known as 'garrans' to English authors when they did not call them 'hobbies'. Obviously there cannot be a breed exclusively of geldings but since the principal use of geldings was in pack trains, walking loose-headed after a bell-mare, the term *gearran* came to be applied to a pony suitable for pack work. AD

Gaucho

The gaucho, a South American cowboy of the Argentine and Brazilian plains, usually of mixed South American and Indian blood, is noted, together with the American COWBOY of the West, as an expert 'rough rider'. His horses are often half-broken broncs on which he rounds up immense herds of lean, fast and fierce long-horned cattle. Like the American cow-puncher, or the VAQUERO and the BUTTERO, he carries a lasso (*reata*); as his saddle has no horn, the *reata* is attached to the cinch-ring of the girth. His tack is generally elaborately decorated and his long rowelled spurs sometimes made of old Spanish silver coins. LFB

Gayoe see Batak

Gelderland Horse

The Gelderlander is a Dutch warmblood horse originating from the Dutch FRIESIAN and the German EAST FRIESIAN with ANGLO-NORMAN, HACKNEY and OLDENBURG blood. Until ten years ago it was a farm horse, performing well in harness and in country riding clubs. It is now a riding horse, crossed with THOROUGHBRED and other breeds (see Dutch Warmblood). WS

Gelding a castrated male horse

German Trotter see Germany

Germany

There are no fewer than 18 breeds of horses and ponies in East and West Germany including the Arab at Marbach-Weil Stud (but excluding those pony breeds originating in Britain). They are the TRAKEHNER (East Prussian), HOLSTEIN, WÜRTTEMBERG, OLDENBURG, EAST FRIESIAN, HAFLINGER, PINZGAUER (Noriker), Rottaler, Trotter, ARABIAN, THOROUGHBRED, DÜLMEN, SCHLESWIG, South German and Schwarzwald heavy horse breeds and the HANOVERIAN, Brandenburg and MECKLENBURG. The last three breeds have similar bloodlines. The Hanoverian has, in recent years, been greatly improved with Thoroughbred and Trakehner blood. With the exception of the Dülmen there are no native breeds of ponies in present-day West or East Germany. Warmblood or crossbred breeding has always received first consideration. As their names show, most of the light-horse breeds were given the name of the province where they were selectively bred, according to the needs of local farmers and horse owners. Breeding is strictly controlled by stud directors responsible to the State or the *Länder*. Colts of all breeds have to pass both a veterinary and a physical test under the saddle and in harness, including a one-day event, trotting to a sulky and pulling a load (a weighted sled on runners). Those failing the test are gelded and sold as saddle horses, for agricultural work or as remounts. Mares must have a certificate of health and suitability before they are allowed to be covered by a state-registered stallion. Owners are advised of the best stallions, which stand at allocated stations throughout the spring and summer. Foals are registered on birth and are issued with a foaling certificate which accompanies them throughout their lives. They are later branded with the breed mark. These procedures are universal throughout continental Europe and the U.S.S.R. and are responsible for the excellence of many of the warmblood breeds.

Since World War II Thoroughbred racing in Germany has not reached the peak of pre-war years and it is nothing like as popular as in France, Italy and Britain. This is largely due to lack of press and television coverage. Racecourses are at Cologne, Baden-Baden and Hamburg, where the 'Derby Week' takes place. Trotting races, however, draw larger crowds. Trotting is popular both in Hamburg and Munich, to name two tracks. Show jumping is enorm-

Germany. Purebred Arab mares at Marbach National Stud, West Germany

ously popular and there were some famous riders before World War II and after, including the internationally-known Fritz Tiedemann with the Holstein gelding Meteor and Hans Winkler with Halla, the offspring of a Trotter/Thoroughbred cross. Germany, like Sweden, produces her own international horses for dressage, show jumping and military trials (otherwise known as three-day events or horse trials). These warmbloods bred in Germany have gained gold and silver medals in the Olympic Games held in Japan (1964) and in Mexico (1968). Classes for teams of harness horses are popular in Germany. Holsteins, Hanoverians and Oldenburgs are used in harness teams and all three breeds are represented in international harness events.

There is very little private driving at present, although the Trakehner, Rottaler and Haflinger may be seen in harness in their respective localities: the Trakehner as a refugee in Holstein; the famous chestnut Rottaler from the 'classical country of horse-breeding', the Rottgau in Lower Bavaria; and the equally famous chestnut Haflinger of southern Germany, although it actually originated in Austria. The Haflinger is valued as a pack horse in the mountains, where even hay is brought down from higher slopes on its back. In winter, harnessed to a sleigh, the Haflinger often provides the only means of transport and communication.

The number of heavy horses is rapidly decreasing. There are a few mares and stallions of the Schwarzwälder breed, the South German Heavy Horse (see Noriker) and the Schleswig of northern Germany where they are still used on the land. The 1969 figures for the Federal Republic show only 254,000 horses, a decrease of 3·6 per cent on the previous year. DMG

Gidran see Hungary

Girth

The girth is the attachment of nylon cord, woollen web or leather used to secure the saddle. Leather girths are generally made to one of three patterns which, in Great Britain, are given the names Balding, Atherstone and Three-Fold. The two former, although differing in their construction, are both shaped back from the horse's elbow and tapered at that point to obviate chafing in this often sensitive area. The Three-Fold is, as the name suggests, a length of soft baghide folded in three, the rounded edge being at the front of the girth. This type of girth should have a piece of serge cloth laid inside the fold. The serge when well-greased keeps the leather soft and supple. Web girths, not now in such common use outside racing, are always worn in pairs. The girth currently in most general use in Great Britain is probably that made of nylon cord. It is soft, and so unlikely to chafe, and has the advantage of being easily washed as well as being comparatively cheap. With the possible exception of the nylon variety it is possible to fit elastic ends to all girths. The object of such inserts is to allow expansion when the horse makes a big effort as when jumping or racing. Other materials used in the manufacture of girths are lampwick, a soft tubular fabric in a 3¼ in (8·25 cm) width, and the narrower tubular web frequently seen on show ponies. EHE

Godolphin Arabian

A lop-eared bay of just under 15 hands

(1·52 m), the Godolphin Arabian was purchased in Paris by Mr Edward Coke of Derbyshire in 1729 and after his death in 1733 was acquired by the second Earl of Godolphin, in whose ownership he died at Gog Magog in 1753. The Godolphin Arabian is recorded as having covered about ninety mares; his most notable son was Cade (1733), who in 1747 sired Matchem. In 1850 came the Godolphin Arabian's most noted descendant West Australian, who sired Solon and Australian, from whom came the noted American sires Fairplay and Man-o'War. Solon's grandson Marco by Barcaldine ensured the line in Great Britain through such famous horses as Marcolve, Hurry On and Precipitation into the present-day big winners and famous sires and dams. The only authentic picture of this Jilfan Arab is that by Wootton, now in private ownership, painted when the horse was seven. This very fine painting shows him as a very good example of his day. DRT

Golden Horseshoe Rides see Long-Distance Riding

Goose Rump

An exaggerated slope of the quarters from the croup to the dock. CF

Gotland Pony see Russ (Gotland) Pony

Grading up see Breeding

Grand National

The most famous steeplechase in the world, the Grand National, is run at Aintree, a suburb of Liverpool, over a distance of 4 miles 856 yd (7·22 km). It is therefore the longest race of the season. There are 30 fences to be jumped, and though in recent years these have been rendered less formidable than they were, chiefly by the provision of an inviting slope on the take-off side, they are still far more severe than the jumps to be found on park courses.

The best-known jump is Becher's Brook, which has to be crossed twice and forms the sixth and twenty-second obstacle. It is named after Captain Becher, who rode in the race in its early years and was precipitated into the little brook that crosses the course, emerging to declare that he had no previous conception of how unpleasant water tasted without brandy. The present Becher's Brook fence has a ditch and a drop on the landing side, and horses are very inclined to pitch or knuckle over. Equally formidable are the Canal Turn fence with its sharp turn to the left on landing, Valentine's Brook, which, like Becher's, has a perceptible drop; and the gigantic open ditch called 'the chair fence', which is only to be met on the first circuit.

The course calls for jumping ability, stamina and courage on the part of the horse; for nerve and skill on the part of the rider. The exceptionally long run-in from the final fence makes added demands on the resolution of a tiring horse and on the physical fitness of its jockey.

The Grand National is sometimes called the 'Blue Riband of Steeplechasing' but this is a misnomer as the Grand National is a handicap. The 'Blue Riband' in the United Kingdom is in fact the Cheltenham Gold Cup, in which the competitors meet on level terms. In modern times the top weight in the Grand National is rarely asked to carry more than 12 stone (168 lb or 76·20 kg) and therefore has to concede 28 lb (12·70 kg) to rivals at the bottom of the handicap. In the old days, the top weight was always given 12 st 7 lb (175 lb or 79·38 kg) while the bottom weights carried 3 stone (42 lb or 19·05 kg) less.

The race was first run in 1837 and was designated the Grand Liverpool Steeplechase. The name was changed to the Liverpool and National Steeplechase in 1843, and finally to the Grand National Steeplechase in 1847. The course was very testing in those early days and one big field had to be crossed that was half plough, and the jumps included some post-and-rails. Until late in the

Grand National Winners

1837	The Duke	1881	Woodbrook	1925	Double Chance
1838	Sir Henry	1882	Seaman	1926	Jack Horner
1839	Lottery	1883	Zoedone	1927	Sprig
1840	Jerry	1884	Voluptuary	1928	Tipperary Tim
1841	Charity	1885	Roquefort	1929	Gregalach
1842	Gaylad	1886	Old Joe	1930	Shaun Goilin
1843	Vanguard	1887	Gamecock	1931	Grakle
1844	Discount	1888	Playfair	1932	Forbra
1845	Cureall	1889	Frigate	1933	Kellsboro' Jack
1846	Pioneer	1890	Ilex	1934	Golden Miller
1847	Matthew	1891	Come Away	1935	Reynoldstown
1848	Chandler	1892	Father O'Flynn	1936	Reynoldstown
1849	Peter Simple	1893	Cloister	1937	Royal Mail
1850	Abd el Kader	1894	Why Not	1938	Battleship
1851	Abd el Kader	1895	Wild Man from Borneo	1939	Workman
1852	Miss Mowbray	1896	The Soarer	1940	Bogskar
1853	Peter Simple	1897	Manifesto	1941–45	No Race
1854	Bourton	1898	Drogheda	1946	Lovely Cottage
1855	Wanderer	1899	Manifesto	1947	Caughoo
1856	Freetrader	1900	Ambush II	1948	Sheila's Cottage
1857	Emigrant	1901	Grudon	1949	Russian Hero
1858	Little Charley	1902	Shannon Lass	1950	Freebooter
1859	Half Caste	1903	Drumcree	1951	Nickel Coin
1860	Anatis	1904	Moifaa	1952	Teal
1861	Jealousy	1905	Kirkland	1953	Early Mist
1862	Huntsman	1906	Ascetic's Silver	1954	Royal Tan
1863	Emblem	1907	Eremon	1955	Quare Times
1864	Emblematic	1908	Rubio	1956	E.S.B.
1865	Aclibiade	1909	Lutteur III	1957	Sundew
1866	Salamander	1910	Jenkinstown	1958	Mr What
1867	Cortolvin	1911	Glenside	1959	Oxo
1868	The Lamb	1912	Jerry M.	1960	Merryman II
1869	The Colonel	1913	Covertcoat	1961	Nicolaus Silver
1870	The Colonel	1914	Sunloch	1962	Kilmore
1871	The Lamb	1915	Ally Sloper	1963	Ayala
1872	Casse Tête	1916	Vermouth	1964	Team Spirit
1873	Disturbance	1917	Ballymacad	1965	Jay Trump
1874	Reugny	1918	Poethlyn	1966	Anglo
1875	Pathfinder	1919	Poethlyn	1967	Foinavon
1876	Regal	1920	Troytown	1968	Red Alligator
1877	Austerlitz	1921	Shaun Spadah	1969	Highland Wedding
1878	Shifnal	1922	Music Hall	1970	Gay Trip
1879	Liberator	1923	Sergeant Murphy	1971	Specify
1880	Empress	1924	Master Robert	1972	Well To Do

Grand National. *Above right:* The Grand Liverpool Steeplechase in 1839
Below right: The Grand National in 1968

nineteenth century, the race used to end with a couple of flights of hurdles to be jumped.

There are countless strange and romantic stories of Grand National winners. Voluptuary had carried Lord Rosebery's colours in the Derby only three years earlier and later in life jumped the water every night in a melodrama at the Drury Lane Theatre, London. The French horse Lutteur III won as a five-year-old within just over a year of his first steeplechase. Rubio had pulled the hotel bus at Towcester, Master Robert a plough. Jack Horner had carried the Master of the Blankney for 15 miles (24 km) in a famous run when hounds made a 14-mile

(22·5 km) point and covered 26 miles (42 km) in all. Tipperary Tim, the 100/1 winner of 1928, was tubed, had a parrot mouth, and was on offer for £200 up to the morning of the race.

There has been a wide variety of successful riders, too. Count Kinský was an Austrian diplomat; Lord Manners a Grenadier Guards officer with scant racing experience; Major J. P. Wilson had shot down a Zeppelin in World War I; Mr Bill Dutton was a Cheshire solicitor when he won on Tipperary Tim; Bruce Hobbs a mere boy of seventeen when he triumphed on the little American horse Battleship.

The first American-bred National winner was Rubio (1908). Owned by Major F. Douglas Pennant, who lived to be over a hundred, he was anything but sound and had at one time changed hands for £15. Billy Barton very nearly won for the U.S.A. in 1928 but crumpled up at the final fence. In 1938 there was an American triumph when Mrs M. Scott's little entire horse Battleship, who stood only 15·2, beat the gigantic Royal Danieli. In 1965 there was the splendid success of Jay Trump, ridden by the American amateur, Mr Tommy Smith.

Opinions of course vary as to the finest performance in the race. Golden Miller remains the one horse to have brought off the Gold Cup–Grand National double and he achieved a marvellous performance as a seven-year-old in 1934 when he carried 12 st 2 lb (170 lb or 77.11 kg) and beat an exceptionally strong field in record time. Memorable, too, was the gallant failure of Easter Hero in 1929. Not built to carry big weights and running on soft ground that did not suit him, he was second with 12 st 7 lb (175 lb or 79·38 kg) in a field of 66 after leading from the start and despite spreading a plate badly at a critical stage of the race.
RM

Reference: M. Seth-Smith, P. Willett, R. Mortimer, J. Lawrence, *History of Steeplechasing*, London, 1969; C. Graham and B. Curling, *The Grand National,* London, 1972.

Grand Pardubice

This difficult steeplechase in Czechoslovakia was founded in 1874 by Count Octavian Kinský and since then, except in 1876, 1908, 1914–19, 1938–45 and 1968, has been held annually, usually on the second

Grand Pardubice. *Below:* The Taxis ditch *Bottom:* Plan of the course

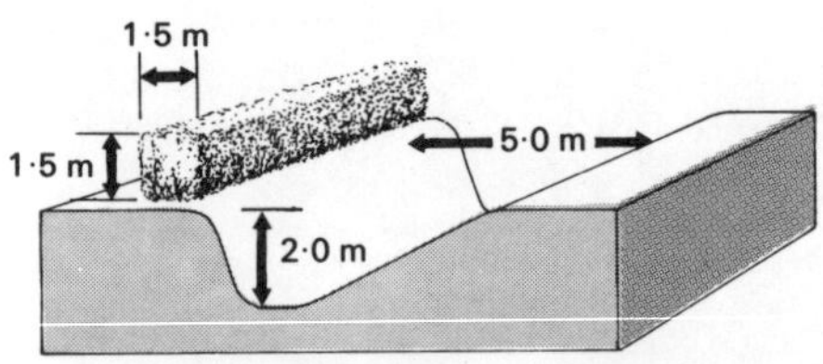

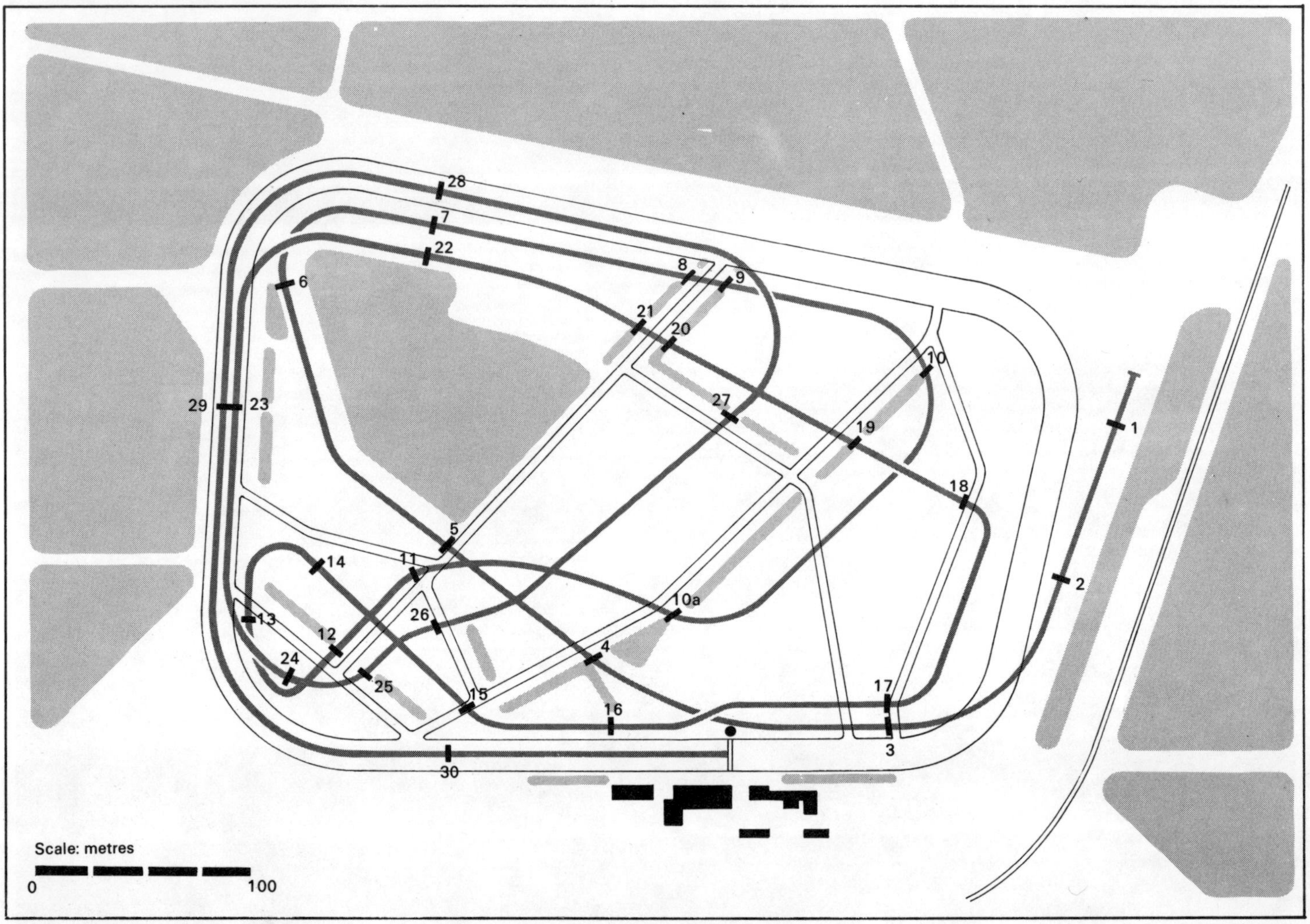

Sunday of October. The course measures 6,900 m (4¼ miles) and has 31 jumps. The most difficult is the Taxis ditch, where many competitors come to grief. The ditch is 5 m (16 ft 5 in) wide × 2 m (6 ft 6 in); in front of it there is a natural fence 1·5 m (5 ft) high and 1·5 m wide. The Grand Pardubice is often compared with the English GRAND NATIONAL. The main difference lies in the course: the Pardubice goes mostly over meadows and fields, which are ploughed deeply the day before to preserve the original character of the race. Every year the race is seen by about 70,000 spectators and another million watch it at home on television. PNe

Great Britain

It is significant that the two legendary leaders of the first English immigrants into Britain in the fifth century A.D. bore the names Hengist and Horsa, both of which mean 'stallion'; *pace* certain nineteenth-century historians who thought Horsa meant 'mare'. It is also significant that the only persons of Celtic ancestry who were of any consequence in the households of early Anglo-Saxon kings were the 'Welsh horsethegns', presumably stud managers. Quite apart from its practical significance almost exclusively as a riding animal to the warrior class of the Migration Age, the horse for the still pagan Anglo-Saxons, as for their allies the Jutes and the Friesians, was of deep religious importance, and was the attribute of more than one god. As a fertility symbol it was associated with Frey, as a symbol of death with Woden, and in a 'secondary' sexual capacity it stood for masculine courage and aggressiveness, as evident in the duels between stallions on free range in the mating season. To the Welsh, the more or less romanized Britons living in the petty successor-states into which the Roman province of Britain had fallen apart, the horse had ceased to have any overt religious significance, since all of them were nominally Christian. But they looked back to a past in which, five centuries earlier, the island had been ruled from Cornwall to Caithness by an aristocracy of chariot drivers. The interlude of Roman rule had done nothing at all to detract from the equation of horsemanship with social rank in Celtic society; all that had happened was a shift of emphasis from the charioteer to the mounted swordsman, bringing with it the demand for a larger horse than the Exmoor-type pony which had sufficed the pre-Roman British princes as a status symbol.

This demand had been filled, under the Roman occupation, by the introduction of remounts from every quarter of Europe and some from Western Asia, for the cavalry regiments which made up (not counting the legions of which there were never more than three) half the complement of the Roman garrison at the beginning, and much more than half by the end. Some of these were very large by the standards of antiquity: 15 hands (1·52 m); all were stallions, and by the end of the fourth century the result of crossing these with 'native' mares who themselves were by no means of uniform type must have produced a diversity which only the comparative isolation of the next three centuries served to reduce. There is little evidence for the introduction of fresh stock during the Anglo-Saxon period, and none for its necessity. Probably the only significant imports were of the black Friesian horses, already present in later Roman times, into the region surrounding the Wash and the Humber in which Friesian traders operated. This horse was the ancestor of the OLD ENGLISH BLACK, which in turn was the ancestor of the SHIRE HORSE.

Great Britain. An Old English Black stallion, ancestor of the Shire Horse

To revert to a much earlier age, Britain as an island had been, in late Pleistocene times, on the outer fringe of the habitat of all Eurasian fauna, including horses. The great majority of British (and Irish) wild equines stranded here after the flooding of the plains which became the North Sea and the English Channel must have belonged to two of the four primeval equine races now believed to have existed before domestication produced, almost from the beginning, an infinite variety of cross-breds. These races were: Type I, a pony roughly resembling the modern Exmoor (see Mountain and Moorland), not above 13 hands (1·42 m), and Type II, a more heavily-built pony represented by the ASIATIC WILD HORSE (Przevalski's), seen only in zoos today. All other types may be regarded as having been introduced by human agency, but it should be borne in mind that such im-

Great Britain. Ponies in the Scottish Highlands

Colour plate: **Dressage.** Liselott Linsenhoff riding Piaff at the C.D.I.O. in Wolfsburg, 1971; they won the individual Olympic gold medal for Dressage in 1972

ports began as soon as transport of horses by sea, even one at a time, became a practical possibility; probably early in the Bronze Age.

After the Roman period, the next era of serious importation began with the incursion of the Vikings from A.D. 800 onwards; they probably brought the ancestors of the SUFFOLK HORSE to East Anglia from Jutland; a certain type of Highland pony closely resembling the FJORD PONY from western Norway, and a certain component in the ancestry of the Dales Pony (see Mountain and Moorland), from Gudbrandsdal in central Norway. They also introduced the custom of gelding, hitherto unknown in Britain. By their conquest of certain stretches of the Irish coastline they gave rise to a situation in which the same Norse king ruled, for instance, in Dublin, the Isle of Man and York, thereby laying the foundations of the one-way Anglo-Irish horse traffic which has gone on ever since. But Irish horses themselves had from very early times carried a high proportion of Spanish blood, and this tended to reinforce the Iberian strain already present in British horse stock, a legacy of Roman times, and destined to be refreshed by more direct traffic with Spain until the seventeenth century (always in the upper price brackets).

The end of the Viking Age coincided with the Norman conquest of England whereby the pattern of English society, civil and military, was forced into the common West European 'feudal' mould, in which France set the tone. In war the tactical unit was built up of knights on armour-carrying chargers, and in peace the economic unit was the manor, identical in theory with the 'knight's fee', which had to produce, beyond the requirements of subsistence for the landlord and the tenants free or unfree, the keep of at least one charger. Only a very small minority of horses bred in England before

63

1066 were suitable to carry an armoured man in battle and chargers (*destriers*) were introduced from the lands from which the host of William the Conqueror had been drawn. This region centred on his own duchy of Normandy, but extended to west and east from Brittany to Flanders; so that the whole range of heavy horses represented today not only by the heavy NORMAN but by the BRETON, the BOULONNAIS, the ARDENNAIS, the PERCHERON, the TRAIT DU NORD and also, again, the FRIESIAN, went to make up the charger of English chivalry. Its diversity of origin is symbolized by the surviving muster-rolls of knights' horses in which every coat-colour imaginable is mentioned. The only common factor appears to have been bulk, weight, mass. The descendants of these stallions by native mares were the only horses in Britain that were not, until the seventeenth century, bred on the waste lands outside the enclosed field. They were fed as young stock from the never quite adequate grain surplus, and were housed in winter even when not working. The more expensive chargers came from Mediterranean sources: the ANDALUSIAN, and the much heavier Lombard from the Po valley. The Andalusian remained, in Britain as in the rest of western Europe, the 'prestige' horse, until at the very end of the seventeenth century it began to be replaced by various Oriental breeds, the distinction between which was imperfectly understood by English breeders, although their amalgamation with selected native mares gave rise to the THOROUGHBRED, called, outside England, the 'English Thoroughbred'. Even so, the Andalusian was only displaced in those roles which demanded speed, never its strong point. The 'running horse' or 'courser' in England before the Stuart age had been of the most diverse origin, and seldom deliberately bred; but from the fourteenth century, perhaps earlier, horses from southern Italy, especially Apulia, which owed a great deal to Arab blood introduced by the Moslem emirs of Sicily, had been brought to England for fast work, of which racing was only an unimportant department compared, say, to dispatch riding by which the rulers of the kingdom received information and issued their commands.

Why the Thoroughbred should have taken shape in England and only in England at a time when every ruler in Europe was trying to produce something similar for military purposes is an unsolved mystery. Perhaps the answer lies in the very frivolity of the English effort and the fact that initiative in this matter was not the sole prerogative of the Crown. The only comparable results at that period were achieved in Poland and Hungary, two countries where the authority of the sovereign as such was as limited as it was in England, and where equally arrogant and self-sufficient aristocrats more comparable with English magnates than with the necessarily more disciplined nobility of Western absolute monarchies were to be found. The fact that England was a leading naval power (when not actually *the* naval power) for so many centuries meant that military requirements have never been foremost in the mind of the English breeder since the end of Elizabeth I's Irish campaigns. Requisitioning only took place at rare intervals and in the direst emergency, and the remount buyer with his niggardly outlay in the open market was not the customer at whom farmers and other breeders aimed. A gentleman's hunter, a gentleman's coach horse, a nobleman's steeplechaser, a lady's hack, rather than an officer's charger, much less a troophorse, dominated the market. It is worth noting that in all the long struggle against Napoleon it was only in the last battle at Waterloo that the British army fielded a whole division of cavalry and that contained allied elements.

By the end of the eighteenth century the pattern of the British horse population as we know it today, was set, except for the shrinkage that has taken place all round (outside racing) since the advent of the internal combustion engine. A considerable sector of the horse-owning population, by then, had a background of service in India where, in the absence of suitable indigenous breeds, a taste for Arab riding and driving horses had been formed, even if the 'Gulf Arabs' used for all purposes in India were of unknown pedigree and all stallions. The HUNTER, the HACKNEY, the quality carriage horse, the COB, were all on the scene, as was the 'new' stamp of agricultural horse: SHIRE, CLYDESDALE, SUFFOLK. These last were all produced by crossing regional types of heavy harness horse, themselves the descendants of redundant armour-carrying chargers, with Flemish carthorses, further height being induced, at a later stage, by a Thoroughbred cross. An enormous expansion of all types of harness horse began with the growth of the railways, gaining momentum from about 1850 onwards. By 1950 it had utterly run its course, and the English equine scene today is filled almost entirely by the 'fun' horse, for riding purposes only. There is (see other articles) a marked over-production of Thoroughbreds, of ponies of all breeds and none, of partbred Arabs, an excessive proportion of entire stallions among purebred Arabs which partly accounts for the partbreds; and an acute shortage of weight-carrying hunters at a time when the number of packs of hounds in existence has never been higher. AD

Great Horse see Destrier

Greece

Although in classical times Greece held an important place among the lands that bred

Colour plate: **Derby.** The Epsom Derby, 1971

horses, and was particularly noted for breeding chariot horses for the Olympic races, that position has sadly deteriorated and there are now few breeds of horses of any importance.

There are now 264,996 horses, 199,492 mules and 410,343 asses. The only pony breed about which information is obtainable is the very small SKYROS pony, bred on the island of that name. It is generally used as a children's pony. Other riding horses are the Lipizzaner and Arabian, and the Thessalian, which is now the only native saddle horse that has any importance at all. DMG

Grisone, Federico

A mid-sixteenth-century Italian nobleman who established a riding school in Naples and wrote the first systematic manual of horsemanship, *Gli ordini di cavalcare* (1550). See Horsemanship, History of. DRT

Groningen

Groningen Horse

A Dutch Warmblood originating from the Dutch native horse (FRIESIAN) with EAST FRIESIAN and OLDENBURG blood. Before 1945 it was a very heavy farm horse with little action. After World War II it virtually disappeared. Some mares are used for light-horse breeding (crossed with THOROUGHBREDS). WS

Grooming

Grooming Kit: dandy brush, body brush, water brush, rubber curry comb, metal curry comb, hoof pick, two sponges (nostrils and eyes; dock), wisp, stable rubber. **Method:** short rack, using a quick release knot. (a) *Grass-kept horses:* if muddy, dry by packing straw under a rug, using a surcingle. When dry, brush off all dried mud with the rubber curry comb. Then remove scurf and dust with the dandy brush. Groom the near side first, then the off. Frequently pat the coat to bring the dust to the surface while brushing. Especially brush between the legs and elbows. Do not use the dandy brush on mane and tail unless they are caked with mud, as it pulls out the hairs. Sponge eyes and nostrils and clean the dock with the second sponge. Pick out feet with hoof pick, working outwards away from the frog. (b) *Stable-kept horses: Quartering* ('knocking over'): removing night stains and dust before exercising. Use the body brush on a clipped horse; dandy brush bristles are too prickly. Sponge eyes, nostrils and dock. In cold weather turn rug back over withers and groom the forehand (near and off sides) and fore legs; replace rug and throw it forward off the hindquarters. Groom hindquarters and hind legs on both sides; replace rug. Brush out mane and tail. Pick out feet. Groom the head and ticklish parts especially gently (e.g. belly and between hind legs). Face hindquarters while grooming them; hold the hind leg while grooming it to prevent kicking. *Strapping:* thorough grooming after exercise while pores of skin are open. Starting at the head, groom all the near side thoroughly; use rubber curry comb and body brush. Clean brush frequently on the metal curry comb, tapping the latter on the ground to remove dust. Repeat on the off side. Then use the wisp on the neck, back and hindquarters, bringing it down smartly with a semicircular movement in the direction of the hair; avoid all sensitive parts. Continue for about 20 minutes each side: this tones skin and muscles, promotes circulation, and gives the coat a beautiful sheen. Then use a slightly damp water brush. Finally polish with the stable rubber. Brush mane and tail with body brush, finishing with a slightly damp water brush. Pick out feet; apply hoof-oil to hoofs. Bandage tail to keep it in shape. See also Clipping, Plaiting, Trimming. GW

Guarapuavano see Brazil

Gudbrandsdal, Dølehest

The Gudbrandsdal takes its name from the great central valley of Norway connecting the Oslo region with the North Sea coast around Kristiansund. Through this ran the only considerable overland trade route of Norway until recent times, and the horses bred in this valley were employed in pack traffic just as the Dales Ponies of Pennine England were, before wheeled traffic became important in either country. Half the present horse stock of Norway is either purebred or partbred Dølehest.

The general appearance of the breed is strongly reminiscent of the English Fell Pony and still more so of the Dales breed (see Mountain and Moorland). This is not fortuitous, since all three must be derived from much the same wild stock in prehis-

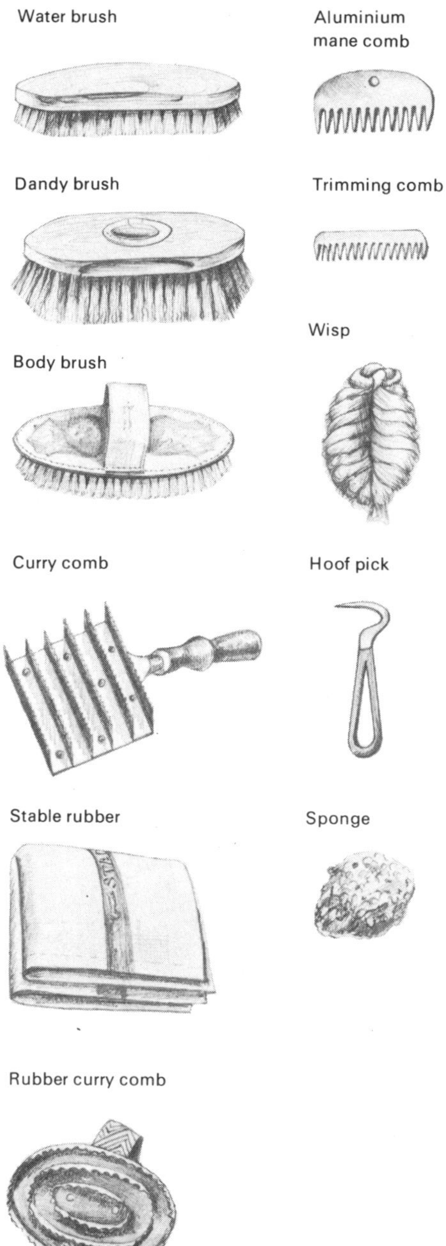

Above: **Grooming.** Grooming kit

toric times, and in the historical era (800–1066) the very considerable immigration from western Norway to the Pennine and Cumbrian regions must necessarily have had its influence on horse breeding in the new homeland. In the period between the late Roman Empire and the onset of the Viking expansion (say 400–800 A.D.) considerable seaborne trade between Britain, Norway and the Rhine delta was carried on by Friesian merchants, who may have exported their own breed of black Friesian horses, also of the same general type, both to Norway and to England. The best gait of all these breeds is a trot, and the Norwegian racing trotter has considerable Døle blood at its taproots.

As in the Dales, the principal colours are black, brown and bay, with black manes and tails. The 'utility' Gudbrandsdal has all the characteristics and build of a draught horse, being capable of great pulling power in relation to its size; this is typical of horses with a background of pack traffic. A lighter riding and fast draught type is nowadays becoming increasingly common, showing the long-range influence of the Thoroughbred stallion Odin, imported in 1834. AD

Guérinière, François Robichon de la

Guérinière, François Robichon de la see La Guérinière, François Robichon de

Gymkhana

'Gymkhana' is apparently a combination of Hindustani *gend-khana* (ball-house or racket court) with *gymnastics*, indicating a public resort for athletics and games. To the horse world it means a place where mounted games are played.

Introduced to Britain by army officers returning from India, where mounted games had been played for centuries, gymkhanas became extremely popular and still are; it was from them that the Pony Club Mounted Games Championship (for the Prince Philip Cup) came into being in 1957. Most riders have taken part in gymkhanas; they teach young riders a great deal if care is taken to ensure that they do not become rough.

The principal games or events in British gymkhanas are: *bending*, where the rider weaves his horse through a line of poles; *musical sacks* or *poles*, like musical chairs, the rider cantering round until the music stops and then dashing to sack or pole; *ball and bucket*, in which the rider carries a ball to the far end of the arena, drops it into a bucket and returns for another; *walk, trot and gallop*, one circuit of the ring at the proper pace with a penalty for breaking it. These are usually run in heats of 4–6 riders and ponies at a time with a final. Small showing and jumping classes are usually also held to give as wide a choice of events as possible.

To succeed a skilful pony is required and a child or adult with a sense of timing and a marked degree of agility. The average child with a pony that is not a 'show' pony can gain a great deal of fun from these events. DRT

Hack

The name of this riding or saddle horse is a shortened form of HACKNEY, now purely a carriage horse but once used for riding. Hacks are variously distinguished as *ordinary* or *road hacks*: country riding horses with easy GAITS and possibly an ability to negotiate low jumps, and in American show rings required to demonstrate an extended trot; *park hacks*: high-class show-ring saddle horses with almost perfect

Above right: **Hack.** Shalbourne Last Waltz, ridden by David Tatlow

conformation, graceful carriage and good manners—in England either THOROUGHBREDS or well-bred horses with low easy trot and canter, in the United States more generally American-bred Saddlers (see Saddlebred) with high head and tail carriage, high knee action and in some cases five gaits. LFB

Hackamore

The hackamore is a rawhide and leather headgear for controlling the horse without

Right: **Hackamore**

a bit in the mouth. The name is derived from the Spanish *jaquima*, and is applied to the rawhide noseband (*bosalillo* or bosal), the headstall and its fastening device (*fiador*), and combination woven hair reins and lead rope (*mecate*) used for breaking and training horses with the old Californian method. The rawhide noseband, to which both *fiador* and *mecate* are fastened with especially intricate knots, allows the horseman to apply pressure to the sensitive nerves on the underside of the lower jaw. After a horse is completely broken to rein with the hackamore it is usually switched to the bridle and bit. See also Western Tack. RS

Hackney. *Below:* Eastertide, driven by John Black
Far right: Outwood Florescent, driven by Mrs Haydon

Hackney

This English breed of high-stepping trotter is descended from the Norfolk trotters. The term was formerly used to describe an active riding horse for roadwork. It was adopted as the breed name when the Hackney Stud Book Society was formed in Norwich in 1883, and spelled afterwards with a capital letter to distinguish it from the old usage. The native trotting horses of East Anglia became renowned for their superiority through the descendants of the original Shales, a half-bred son of the celebrated racehorse Blaze by Flying Childers, foaled about 1755. Shales had two noteworthy sons, Scot Shales and Driver, and it is from a son of the latter, Jenkinson's Fireaway (foaled *c.* 1780), that most modern Hackneys are descended. During the early nineteenth century Norfolk trotting stallions were

used in parts of Lincolnshire and East Yorkshire as well as in their native county, and there are many contemporary records of the trotting prowess of their stock, several having covered 16 miles (26 km) and more on the public roads in one hour, carrying sizeable men. Jary's Bellfounder, foaled in 1816 in Norfolk, was sent to the United States in 1822 where he had a prominent role in the development of the STANDARDBRED trotting breed. Continental breeders also made good use of Norfolk trotters throughout the century, taking both stallions and mares. From 1885 the Society held an annual spring show in London to which eager buyers came from all over the world seeking stallions to improve native stock. Partly through the depletion of East Anglian stock by foreign buyers, the breed show soon came to be dominated by Yorkshire horses, and of the five head sires four were bred in that county. Many wealthy and influential people became interested in breeding Hackneys, notably Sir Walter Gilbey and William Burdett-Coutts, M.P., who saw the need for other classes of light horses besides the Thoroughbred.

During the last quarter of the nineteenth century an increasing number of agricultural and horse shows began to include classes for light harness horses, and showing these horses soon became an expensive luxury which the Hackney breeders were ready to supply. After the coming of the car the export of breeding stock to foreign countries rapidly fell away; the modern Hackney owes its survival after World War I to the continued demand both in Britain and North America for high-stepping show horses. Certain strains soon showed themselves pre-eminently suited to supplying this special demand. By 1940 almost the only stallions left were the descendants of the brown horse Mathias, bred by the Earl of Londesborough in 1895.

The modern Hackney is 14–15·3 hands (1·42–1·62 m) in height and is bay, brown, black or chestnut in colour, usually with some white markings on the legs. The line of the face is straight or convex in profile with eyes and ears expressive of a vigorous and alert personality. The neck is of average length with some crest and generally more muscular than that of the Thoroughbred. The head must be well-hung, allowing ample scope for flexion. The shoulder should be flat and laid well back to give a good range to the action of the fore legs, and the withers, though they are less prominent and a little thicker than those of a Thoroughbred, must not be excessively fleshy. The back should be of average length and strongly coupled, with a good depth of body standing on limbs clean and flat of bone. The feet are most important. They should not be flat and spreading, but fairly upright with a good strength of wall particularly at the heels. The walk is characteristic and should be brisk and elastic, denoting muscular tone and activity. At the trot the front action should be lofty, smooth and progressive with the feet meeting the ground neither on the heels nor the toes, nor yet forcibly slammed down, and the hind legs should be well flexed and propelled forward under the body. TR

Hackney Pony

This can be described as the Hackney horse in miniature, being under 14 hands (1·42 m), with the addition of the distinctive but difficult to define 'pony character'. Although there must have been many small Hackneys before then, the breed dates its origin from the Wilson ponies of the 1880s, a type developed by Christopher Wilson in Westmorland, who followed a selective breeding program based on the small Yorkshire Hackney, Sir George. Other influential stallions have been the Norfolk-bred Confidence, a brown standing 15·2 hands (1.57 m) high, and Sir Horace, a pony bred by Wilson in 1891. Sir Horace became the chief stud pony at Sir Gilbert Greenall's Tissington Stud in Derbyshire and his influence was very marked in Walter Cliff's Melbourne Stud in Yorkshire, the two principal nurseries of the Hackney Pony in its formative years. The Hackney pony is today treated as almost a separate breed from the Hackney horse although both are registered in the same stud book. Volume I of the Hackney Stud Book contains a detailed early history of the breed, the result of many years of painstaking research on the part of the first secretary of the Society, Henry F. Euren. TR

Hadbe see Persian Arab

Haflinger

The Haflinger is probably the most useful and hard-working of the Austrian horse breeds (see Austria). Primarily a horse of the mountains and originally bred in the district of Hafling near Merano, this chestnut horse with flaxen mane and tail can carry or pull loads up and down the steepest mountain slopes. It is thought that the East Goths who retreated after the battle of Vesuvius (A.D. 555) to the Tirolese valleys in the ancient Roman province of Rhaetia left behind them the ancestors of these horses which may have had a considerable amount of Oriental blood. Breeding is in the hands of the farmers. The Government has an option on all foals; the best are raised at Ebbs. There is now a Hafling Society of Great Britain. DMG

Haiti see West Indies

Halfbred Arabian see Partbred Arabian

Half-halt

The horse's balance is changed by a shift of weight from fore hand to quarters, accomplished by one type of hand action that raises the neck, or another that engages the hind legs.

The first method is generally and particularly used in training on the flat when fighting 'weight resistances', where in defence or from bad conformation the horse puts excessive weight on its fore hand. Preceded by leg action engaging the hind legs, this hand action, with fingers closed over the reins, consists of an upward turn of the wrists without loss of contact with the mouth, followed by a return to the original hand position. Since it is the upward movement, not the raised position, that brings about the half-halt, if the desired effect is not forthcoming the movement is immediately repeated. Depending on the stage of

training, it may vary from the sketchiest upward motion to a quite considerable shift. Needless to say, there must be neither jerk nor retraction. Decarpentry compares it with the action of someone at the foot of the stairs lifting a paving stone delicately off one step and placing it as delicately onto the one just above.

Done properly, the half-halt causes no slowdown of the pace; for 'balance', says the classical formula, 'must be obtained without changing the movement and, conversely, movement must proceed without interfering with balance'.

The second method is mostly used in jumping where the horse's stretched neck causes hand action to be transmitted directly to the quarters, increasing their engagement. Since the engagement pulls more weight to the quarters, the fore hand is lightened by as much. See also Dressage. JF

Half-Pass, Half-Turn see Movements

Halt see Movements

Hamdani see Persian Arab

Hames metal or wood and metal arms linking the traces and the collar. See Driving Harness

Hand (measurement) see Height

Handicapped Rider see Disabled, Riding for the

Hanoverian

The Hanoverian breed has been 'modernized' over the last twenty years in the German Federal Republic to meet the demand of riders for a horse to compete in international show-jumping competitions and three-day events (military events).

The Hanoverian was formerly a harness and carriage horse and some even had ungainly heads and straight shoulders. Now these faults have been bred out by infusions of TRAKEHNER (East Prussian) and THOROUGHBRED blood and the Hanoverian has emerged as one of the best saddle horses for sporting events. An auction takes place annually at Verden/Aller, the home of the Hanoverian. At the Landgestüt Celle some 200 stallions receive training. On the last Sunday in September and the first Sunday in October, these stallions give special displays lasting about 2½ hours. Later many of them stand at stations throughout the province of Hanover. They are always accompanied by their own grooms, who start on leaving school and are responsible for feeding, grooming, schooling and training the 2½-year-old colts in their care. At 3½ years old, when the horse has passed the stringent tests required by the State for licensed stallions, horse and groom are sent to the stations and may remain together for most of their lives. They return to Celle, once the capital of the Electors of Hanover, when the stud season is ended. Hanoverian brood mares are owned and kept by farmers and private owners. They may work on the land as occasion demands, although much agricultural work is today done by tractors.

The Hanoverian owed much to royal encouragement. When the Elector Ernest Augustus (1629–1698) took the white horse for his coat-of-arms he showed symbolically his affection for an animal which had long been a part of the tradition of the early German tribes. At Herrenhausen, a royal residence, the famous white or cream Hanoverian coach horses (see Isabellas) were bred at the instigation of the Electress Sophia. In 1714, when George, Elector of Hanover, became George I of England, the opportunity was taken of using Thoroughbreds to improve the Hanoverian breed. The Landgestüt at Celle was founded 'for the benefit of our subjects' in 1735 by George II. The King had a private stud at Neuhaus in the Solling, where Hanoverian horses are still bred, at Memsen near Hoya and at Radbruch in the Lüneburger Heide.

Gabriel Roger Brown, probably of English or Scottish descent, was the first Stud Director at Celle and was actively engaged in improving the breed. This improvement continued in spite of difficult times and the French invasion of the eighteenth century, thus making the Hanoverian one of the oldest breeds in West Germany. DMG

Harewood

Harewood, some eight miles from Leeds, in Yorkshire, was built in 1760 in a wooded park and is the home of the Earls of Harewood. Between 1953 and 1959 the horse trials held there in the autumn became as well known as those at BADMINTON. In 1960 it was not possible to hold the event there; it was subsequently moved to the southeast and replaced by the BURGHLEY Horse Trials in 1961. DRT

Harness see Driving Harness

Harness Racing see Trotting Racing

Harriers

The harrier is a hound, smaller than a foxhound, of similar colouring and looks and should be used exclusively for hunting hare. Today, however, several packs hunt fox though the majority still hunt hare with success. Many harrier packs in Britain were established before the days of foxhunting. See Hunting. JHew

Height

The height of a horse is measured from the ground to the highest point of the withers. In the English-speaking world the height is usually quoted in hands plus inches, a hand being 4 in (10 cm); in other countries it is quoted in metres and centimetres.

A typical measuring stick consists of a graduated upright carrying an adjustable cross bar in which is incorporated a spirit level. Care is required in measuring a horse or pony; it is essential to have the animal standing on a level surface. CF

Hickstead the site of the All-England Jumping Course, established by Douglas Bunn in 1960. See Derby (Jumping)

Highland Pony see Mountain and Moorland Ponies

Highway, Horses on the

It is essential to know and understand the Highway Code as it relates to horses. No horse or pony that is not used to heavy traffic should be taken on busy roads. It is unsafe both for the horse and rider and for other road users. No horse is ever entirely reliable so the rider must constantly be prepared. All ridden horses and ponies should conform with the rule of the road (in Great Britain moving on the left of the road in the same direction as the traffic). Led horses should be between the person in charge (whether mounted or unmounted) and the curb. If the rider is mounted with a led horse they should conform to the rule of the road; if the rider is on foot it is permissible to walk

Harewood Horse Trials Winners

1953	Miss V. I. Machin Goodall on Neptune
1954	Miss P. Molteno on Carmena
1955	Lt-Col F. W. C. Weldon on Kilbarry
1956	Miss S. Willcox on High and Mighty
1957	Mr I. H. Dudgeon on Charleville
1958	Herr O. Pohlmann on Polarfuchs (Germany)
1959	Major H. Schwarzenbach on Burn Trout (Switzerland)

Horses on the Highway

The rider intends to move out or turn to her right.

The rider intends to pull in or turn to her left.

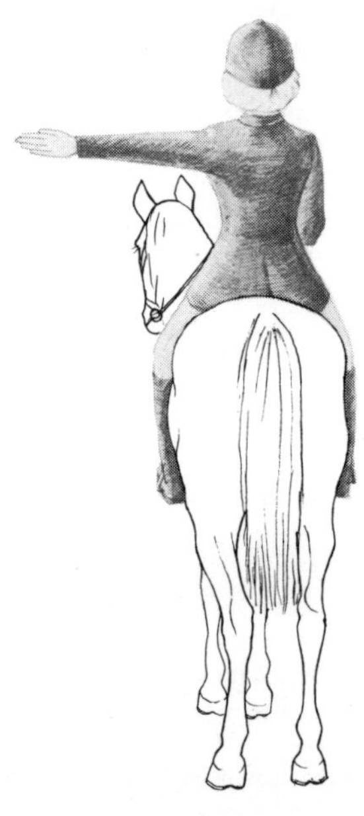

The rider is asking vehicles behind her to stop.

The rider is asking vehicles behind her to slow down or stop.

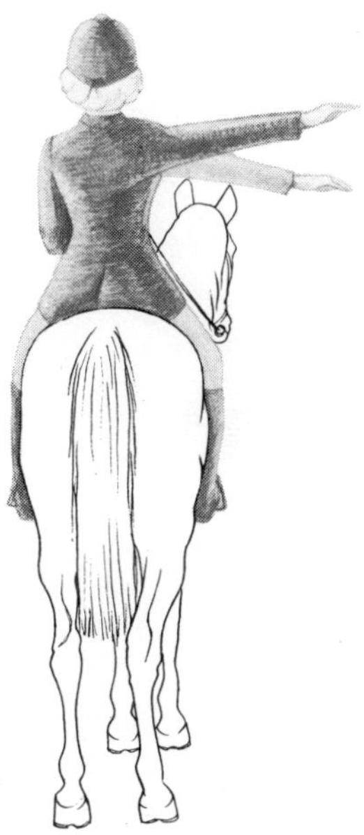

against the traffic if the horse will not lead from the off side. Give the Highway Code hand signals. It helps to warn fast-moving traffic if, as the vehicle approaches, the rider halts the horse close in to the side of the road and stands there. The horse lets the vehicle pass and the driver slows down and pulls well clear. DRT

Hinny see Jennet, Hybrids

Hipparion see Evolution of the Horse Family

Hippological Texts

Hippologica Hethitica: the first hippological book extant (*c.* fourteenth century B.C.) was written by Kikkuli of Mittani, an expert trainer of chariot horses engaged by the Hittite King Chattusili of Chatti. The clay tablets, probably intended as a military textbook, were discovered in Bogazköy during excavations (1906–12). The language is Hittite with both Aryan and Hurrian technical terminology.
Hippologica Accadica: a cultural historical investigation into draught, pack and saddle horses/asses used by the peoples of ancient Mesopotamia, texts translated by Armas Salonen, 1955.
Hippiatric texts from Ugarit: possibly the earliest veterinary textbook, translated by M. B. Gordon, 1942. DMG

Hippology

The study of the genus *Equus* (horses, zebras, asses and onagers) including breeding, breeds, genetics, history and geographical distribution. DMG

H.I.S. see Hunters' Improvement Society

Hispano Arab see Arab in Spain, Spain

Hittites

A people of complex racial origin but Indo-European speech, the Hittites occupied in the second millennium B.C. a key position athwart the southward progress of the domesticated, chariot-yoked horse from the region of its first taming in Transcaspia, in eastern Asia Minor, north Syria, the present Kurdistan and Armenia, towards Syria and Egypt.

By 1600 B.C. at the latest the Hittites had adopted as a weapon of war the chariot with spoked wheels drawn by two horses. One of the greatest chariot-to-chariot engagements in antiquity, at Kadesh in 1286 B.C., was a victory for the Hittites over the forces of the Pharaoh Rameses I. Hittites were the first, and one of the few, peoples of antiquity to have chariot crews of three men, driver, shield-bearer and archer, instead of the customary two. Their chariots therefore had to be larger and their horses stronger proportionately. The earliest book on the training of harness horses, by Kikkuli the Mittanian, was written for the instruction of the Hittite chariot corps, *c.* 1360 B.C. The Hittite empire ceased to be a major power after about 1190 B.C. AD

Hobby

Today's Connemara Pony (see Mountain and Moorland) was in the sixteenth and seventeenth centuries called an 'Irish Hobby' (earlier *hobyn*). Like 'Dobbin', the word is a diminutive of Robert/Robin; it meant a general-purpose riding horse, especially one for use in the towns ('street nag'), docile, with easy paces, handy and well-schooled. It was essentially a pony in size, and rather narrowly-built, so that, like the ass in Eastern cities, it could easily negotiate narrow alleyways. AD

Hobdayed

When a horse has had a throat operation to relieve ROARING or WHISTLING it is said to have been 'Hobdayed', after Sir Frederick Hobday (1870–1939) who pioneered the operation in Britain. CF

Hodh see Africa

Hog Mouth (Undershot)

The lower jaw protrudes. CF

Hokkaido see Japan

Holland see Netherlands

Holstein

The German Holstein was primarily a horse of the marshes surrounding the Elbe and nearby rivers; later it was bred further afield. The old breed, which had Neapolitan and Spanish blood and therefore very high action, was improved with CLEVELAND BAY and YORKSHIRE COACH HORSE stallions, the latter having THOROUGHBRED blood. Burlington Turk 1825 was also used. The Holstein has always been a big, strong horse. One type was the heavy coach/artillery horse; a second developed into a useful heavyweight saddle horse. Horses of the latter type sometimes make good show jumpers; they generally belong to the Tobias branch of the Achill line. Some two hundred years ago the Holstein was used to improve other German warmblood breeds. Both Dillenburg and Celle used it, as did Mecklenburg, Oldenburg and Westphalia. Strong, deep horses capable of working on the land, in harness and under the saddle, were required.

As early as 1300 there is mention of a stud belonging to Uetersen monastery in the Haseldorf marshes. In the Middle Ages, both the kings of Denmark and the dukes of Schleswig-Holstein encouraged the breeding of suitable war and tourney horses. In the sixteenth to eighteenth centuries the market for Holstein horses covered most of Europe. In 1680 the first regulations for breeding were issued and, in the royal stud of the dukes of Holstein at Esserom, the breeding of the famous cream horses (see Hanoverian), descended from the Holstein stallion Mignon, was started. The stud at Traventhal (closed in 1960) was founded in 1876. Although it was not at first used to breed Holstein horses, they soon became important. The school at Elmshorn, Schleswig-Holstein, is now the main centre of activities connected with this breed. See also Germany. DMG

Horse Brasses

From early days, horses and oxen, important sources of power and transport, were protected by amulets which flashed with the animal's movement to distract the 'evil eye'. People in triumph were particularly vulnerable so horses were always decorated on fair or show days and often still are. A big, heavy horse may be decorated with a facepiece on the forehead, a pair of brasses behind the ears, three or four on each side of the shoulders, and five or six (sometimes even ten) hanging from the martingale. There are about three thousand different designs of horse brasses, which are very much a British phenomenon; but the basic and very ancient patterns were the sun circle, or sunflash, the crescent, the heart and the horseshoe.

Most brasses found today were made between 1850 and 1910 when the largest maker of brasses in Britain ceased operations. Though earlier specimens can be found, the general manufacture of brasses appears in trade catalogues around 1860. About 1890 a very popular design was a central boss of coloured glass or bone china set in a brass with a serrated edge.

Queen Victoria's first Jubilee (1887) started a series of commemorative brasses; over 40 were issued for her Diamond Jubilee (1897). Commemorative designs have also been supplied, mainly for collectors, for all subsequent monarchs and for many important people including Gladstone, Disraeli and Sir Winston Churchill. The Royal Society for the Prevention of Cruelty to Animals has issued two designs: a shield for the annual parades of cart- and light horses in Regent's Park, London, and a circular design for other shows. Their small circular one marking the world's first television broadcast of a horse show, by the B.B.C. in 1939, is very rare since only 30 were made.

Edwardian designs embody agricultural pursuits, trades (the barrel for brewers, the churn for dairymen, the anchor for dock teams, the engine for rail transport) and motifs for various counties (the wheatsheaf for Cheshire, the prancing horse for Kent, the boar for Lincolnshire.) Nearly all were set in the conventional sun or crescent.

Horse shoes were naturally common as a symbol of good luck (see Myth and Legend, Horse in). They were usually cast and often show the profile of a horse's head inside. Oddly enough, most horse brasses show the shoe pointing down instead of up, the traditional lucky position. Worshippers of fire

Horse Brasses. Various designs, including the sun circle, the heart and the prancing horse, can be seen on this pair of Clydesdales.

used symbols with the apex pointing up since the property of fire is to ascend, while worshippers of water used a crescent pointing down since water descends. Accordingly crescents or horse shoes pointing up were used in towns or country districts where there was fear of fire, while near the sea the common design pointed down to protect against the dangers of water. A modern collector's piece shows a sea horse surrounded by a horse-shoe pointing down.

Genuine used brasses of 1850–90, increasingly hard to find, can be recognized by the careful handwork performed on the edges and interstices and modelling of the figure parts. Modern reproductions usually have very rough edges with odd pieces of metal left and are finished with a wheel or brush to give a bright surface. Old cast pieces show the perfect smoothness and softness produced only by wear: the loop is worn smooth by running against its strap and the foot is worn thin and smooth by hitting the leather martingale. RAB

Horse Clothing see Clothing, Horse, Accoutrements

Horsemanship, American Indian

The Plains Indians' acquisition of the horse was sudden and almost universal throughout the plains country of North America. By the early part of the eighteenth century every tribe on the Plains was well supplied with horses, either stolen or escaped from the Spanish herds in the Mexican provinces. Knowledge of the Spanish methods of handling horses seems to have been passed on from one tribe to the next, starting at the Rio Grande in what was then northern Mexico, swiftly spreading up the eastern slopes of the Rocky Mountains, and then eastward until horses and the art of riding and handling them covered every tribe on the Plains. Almost miraculously, the Plains Indian, who had no previous knowledge of the horse, transformed himself from a sedentary resident of the river valleys to a fierce nomad, following the buffalo herds for a new existence, and waging unceasing warfare against neighbouring tribes.

The Indian made his own saddles in imitation of those used by the Spaniards. But his bridle remained two simple half-hitches around the lower jaw until the end of his wild free days near the close of the nineteenth century. The two principal types of Indian saddles were the frame saddle, and the simpler pad. Both had stirrups and each had its purpose. The frame saddle was made in a style similar to the Spanish, with a pommel and cantle made of wood or horn, fastened to side bars, the whole covered with wet rawhide sewn in place. When dry, this crude tree had the strength and rigidity of iron. Stirrups, made from bent slabs of wood covered with rawhide, were suspended from the tree, and a single rawhide girth held the saddle firmly on the horse's back. Pads of buffalo hide under the saddle, with the hair side down, protected the horse's back, and tanned hides over the saddle, held in place by a crude surcingle, protected the rider's person. The pad saddle was a leather envelope stuffed with grass or animal hair, to which were attached stirrups and girth. These simple pads were used by young, active warriors, while the frame saddle was preferred by older men and women.

The Plains Indian seldom relied on the wild herds for replenishing his supply of horses, although the warriors caught and broke some wild horses. The most common method of acquiring new animals was to raid the herds of enemy tribes. This was an honourable practice to the Plains Indians, and very much a part of their culture. A few tribes, such as the Nez Percé, practised gelding, but most left their male horses entire. The result of this lack of selectivity had reduced the quality and size of the Indian horses by the end of the nineteenth century.

American Indian Horsemanship. George Catlin, painting in the nineteenth century, depicts the riding skill of the Plains Indians.

The riding skill of the American Plains Indian astonished the American immigrants and the mounted troops of the U.S. Army when they found themselves embroiled in savage war with the warriors of the Plains. Cavalry leaders on every part of the American frontier declared the mounted Plains warriors 'the best light cavalry in the world'.

With their crude riding gear, often on horses stripped of saddles, these wild fighters performed feats of riding almost unbelievable to their white opponents. Dropping over on one side of their mounts, the warriors were able to loose volleys of arrows under their horses' necks at the enemy with only a heel exposed. During more peaceful times the young warriors delighted in showing off before the young maidens by vaulting on and off their horses and standing on the horses' backs, all at top speed.

Most Plains Indians broke their horses by allowing the young boys to play with them as colts so that by the time they were mature they were broken to ride, and gentle. Horses caught from the wild herds were mounted and ridden in water or deep sand so that efforts to throw off their riders were ineffectual.

Until late in the first decades of the twentieth century the Plains Indian continued to count his wealth in the number of horses he owned. RS

Horsemanship, History of

Although a lengthy text on the training of chariot horses had been written in the fourteenth century B.C. by Kikkuli in Hittite Asia Minor (see Hittites) XENOPHON's (fourth century B.C.) much shorter work is the earliest extant one on riding horses. This deals with the choice and care of horses, and has less than twenty pages (out of a total of fifty-three in a modern translation) on riding proper. These consist mainly of commonsense advice and not of a description of well-defined techniques. Some two hundred years before Xenophon, in the Greek colony of Sybaris (in southern Italy) horses were taught to 'dance' to music.

Not enough is known of riding in ancient Rome to visualize a method, but there is evidence that in circuses horses executed the *piaffe* (tripudium).

Medieval manuscripts discuss stable management, bitting and diseases of the horse, merely adding here and there elementary, disconnected suggestions on riding. Roman display practices survived in European travelling circuses, and at least two medieval illuminated manuscripts depict horses, at liberty, performing formalized rearing, kicking, and a leap similar to the *capriole*.

The first book that attempted to present a reasoned method of horsemanship appeared in Italy in 1550. It was written by Federico GRISONE, who, with the inquiring approach of the Renaissance, improved on what he saw around him, which was knights in parades and jousts and the performances of circus horses. His book is considered to mark the beginning of the development of the various forms and related techniques of western European academic riding, which continued to evolve and change up to today. Several Italian books followed Grisone's, and the Neapolitan School attracted young pupils from the rest of Europe. One of these, Salomon LA BROUE, published the first book in French (1593–4); with this, leadership in equitation began to pass from Italy to France, where it was maintained until the twentieth century.

Riding has never been practised in a vacuum; its aims and ideals have changed with the changing social scene. In short, the history of formal riding on the European continent since the sixteenth century may be divided into three main periods: (1) the Aristocratic, up to the end of the eighteenth century, (2) the Military, up to World War I; and (3) the Democratic, the twentieth century. No period was completely uniform; England was always a special case, and eastern Europe even more so.

The Aristocratic Period: this was the period of the development of complicated movements, executed in small *manèges*, at slow, highly-collected gaits. This form of riding, in the baroque taste of the time, suited perfectly the sumptuous life of princes and their courtiers, and served to animate parades and CARROUSELS, and to glorify the ruling class. A dozen or so noblemen, splendidly attired, performing a program which consisted of highly dramatic movements, made an unforgettable display which clearly put them above the rest of the population. Today the echoes of such displays can be seen in the SPANISH RIDING SCHOOL OF VIENNA. Although the seventeenth-century masters could make their horses execute the difficult airs above the ground, there was little science in their pragmatic skill. Even the easy-to-see order of beats at a canter was correctly described only in the 1730s. Ignorance of the horse's mentality provoked cruelty; the horse was considered to have a better brain than he actually had and any resistance on his part was attributed to contrariness rather than to lack of understanding. The severe medieval bits were not only preserved but even elaborated; they were considered the answers to all problems. But, as what was left of the illiterate knight of the Middle Ages was gradually replaced by the cultivated gentleman of the Renaissance, riding techniques moved from the frequent brutality of the sixteenth century to the refinements of the eighteenth. While the nobility practised High School, their teachers such as Antoine de PLUVINEL (1555–1620) and François Robichon de LA GUÉRINIÈRE (1688-1751) belonged to the gentry and dedicated their books to aristocratic patrons. It was different in England, where the nobility spent most of its time not at court but in the country, amusing itself by hunting, racing, and breeding better animals. There *manège* riding never became popular, even though one of its protagonists was a very important person: the Duke of NEWCASTLE (1592–1676).

In the second half of the eighteenth century texts appeared suggesting simplifications of *manège* dressage for the use of mounted troops. The writers, while still belonging to the privileged class, were progressive cavalrymen, such as Henry, Earl of Pembroke (1734–1794) in England and Comte Drummond de Melfort (1721–1788) in France. They were all influenced by the successes (in the Seven Years War) of the relatively modernized cavalry of the King of Prussia, Frederick the Great. In 1789 the French Revolution destroyed the royal riding schools, and with the Napoleonic Wars began the new Military Period.

The Military Period: the Napoleonic wars

consumed a prodigious number of horses. Replacements had to be quickly produced; there was no time for elaborate schooling and military riding consisted mostly in permitting horses to go freely and men to sit as they wished. With such elementary equestrian education the French cavalry 'made the tour of Europe'. Soon all civilians began to copy the victorious army and, for a while, rode on loose reins with legs 'on the dashboard', as many prints testify. After the fall of Napoleon, during the Restoration of the Bourbons, and later, through the Second Empire, the educated riding of France was represented by the mostly peace-time army, which supported the much-diminished royal throne. It was natural for the young royalist officers to feel nostalgic for the days of sumptuous courts and for the pageantry of *manège* riding. The military set the style for civilian riders. In all European countries the nobility was still able to live in a formal manner in castles and palaces. At the same time, the new industrial and the old commercial bourgeoisie was trying hard to imitate its betters. The simplified, but still formal, *manège* riding was in accord with the renewed formality of the life of the upper classes. In surroundings where carriages were drawn by high-stepping horses, infantry was goose-stepping in one way or another, and cavalry paraded at collected gaits, one could hardly expect a self-respecting horseman to let his mount move in a simple natural manner, at least when he was riding in city parks. The English country squire was unaffected by it all, and, joined by some city people, continued to hunt the way his ancestors had, and to race the horses which he bred. Hunting and racing in the nineteenth century were particularly the glories of England, and the English sporting attitude eventually affected continental Europe.

Because competitive jumping (except in steeplechasing) did not play a great role until the twentieth century, all outstanding professional riders of the nineteenth century practised High School. And because dressage competitions did not exist yet, riders showed in circuses, which were the only places (outside the cavalry schools) in which to demonstrate the talents of both horses and riders; these exhibitions enjoyed great prestige among connoisseurs. The influence of one of these riders, François BAUCHER (1796–1873) persists in some High School circles even today and is known as 'Baucherism'. His wide influence was threatened only by that of one other great rider about forty years later, James FILLIS (1834–1913). In pursuit of yet greater fame both these men tried hard to sell their methods to the army. Baucher failed but Fillis eventually succeeded, and later in life was the chief instructor of the Russian Army, which accepted his method, much simplified for the occasion. Some cavalry officers also continued the old attempts to introduce more field schooling and reduce *manège* riding. Comte d'AURE (1799–1863), at one time chief instructor of the French Cavalry School (Saumur) was the best-known leader of this movement. But none of the attempts to adapt *manège* schooling for field riding were crowned with great practical success, as half-measures rarely are. The army's mixture of elementary dressage with more natural cross-country riding produced competition for officers' horses, which was the ancestor of the modern THREE-DAY EVENT.

History of Horsemanship. Equitation in the early eighteenth century

History of Horsemanship. A kind of early Forward Seat was employed by the Polish rider painted by Rembrandt.

The man who had enough imagination to propose a radical change in the method of military riding was an Italian officer, Federico CAPRILLI (1868–1907). He suggested that collection should be completely abolished and horses allowed to move at their natural travelling gaits. There was nothing new in this: it was how most Asian tribesmen, Russian Cossacks, and the eastern European mercenaries employed by western Europe as light cavalry (in the seventeenth and eighteenth centuries) had ridden for centuries. Some of these even used a kind of Forward Seat, as Rembrandt's painting *The Polish Rider* proves. The English foxhunter, although lacking the Forward Seat, also rode on long reins, and a hundred years before Caprilli, an English professional John Adams described (*c.* 1800) a mechanically poor Forward Seat. A variation on the latter was also used by some jockeys a few years before Caprilli. Caprilli, however, did more than merely abolish collection and conceive an efficient Forward Seat, he created a complete method of riding, including a new type of schooling. His method was accepted by the Italian Army in 1904, and many other cavalries sent officers to Italy to learn it. World War I doomed cavalry by proving its inefficiency in machine-age warfare, and, when peace was restored, riding took a different trend.

The Democratic Period: the several revolutions of the current century largely destroyed the aristocracy and the old bourgeoisie, while taxes diminished the wealth of those remaining. At the same time, an ever-growing class of professionals and technicians was earning more than ever before. Many of these people took up riding or gave this opportunity to their children. Never before had so many people ridden for recreation. The more ambitious of these newcomers were naturally attracted by the competitive possibilities in riding. Today the most popular mounted game is jumping in a horse show and, next to this, jumping in various cross-country competitions.

Jumping was barely mentioned in the Aristocratic Period, and it remained in the second place during the Military one until the time of Caprilli. Only in England and Ireland did the enclosing of fields make jumping an important part of foxhunting, practised in an uneducated but effective manner. Caprilli, who emphasized jumping, would have been forgotten with the passing of the cavalry had his teaching not been picked up by sportsmen. Ironically, the success of Caprilli's method in schooling and riding show jumpers permitted the raising of fences and eventually the making of courses so complicated that to allow the horse to perform almost on its own (that is, on Caprilli's principles) became impractical. In riding modern courses, precise control became imperative, and this led to the revival of the army type of dressage in schooling and riding jumpers while preserving the Forward Seat for the jump itself. The success of German International riders who preached collection in jumping influenced many horsemen. Hence today Caprilli is known for the Forward Seat more than for his complete method. Imitating the great is inevitable, and soon collection for riding on the flat was taught indiscriminately by some teachers even to children and 'Sunday riders'. It is only in foxhunting, in showing hunters over fences, and in junior jumping (the last two in the United States) that Caprilli's method, modernized in various ways (see Forward Riding), still holds its own.

The High School of the eighteenth and nineteenth centuries is not practised today by amateurs, whose highest ambition is the Olympic level of dressage, without airs above the ground, cantering to the rear, etc. Although improved modern horses perform technically better than those of the past, the art lacks the importance which social conditions gave it in the Aristocratic Period. VSL

Reference: V. S. Littauer, *Horseman's Progress*, New York, 1962. English ed., entitled *The Development of Modern Riding*, London, 1968; C. Chenevix Trench, *A History of Horsemanship*, London and New York 1970; L. Picard, *Origines de l'École de Cavalerie et de ses Traditions Équestres*, Saumur, 1890.

Horsemanship, Oriental

The horse cultures of the East were derived from the nomadic tribes of Central Asia, whose conquests extended from the China Sea to the Adriatic, from the Arctic to the Indian Ocean. While Western horsemanship was distorted by the requirements of the tournament, Eastern horsemen, 'riding short in the Turkey fashion', developed an easy, relaxed style ideal for covering long distances. Their saddle was high-arched, deep-seated; the stirrup iron broad and flat in the sole, the inner side furnished with a short spike or sharp edge for use as a spur. Bits varied: in Central Asia jointed snaffles were usual; Arabs and Indians generally favoured curb bits of various forms, including spade- and ring-bits which required the lightest of hands. Captain Lewis Nolan, the nineteenth-century British cavalry expert, who was killed at the Battle of Balaclava, had no doubt that Turkish cavalry were as individuals the best horsemen and swordsmen in the world. CCT

Reference: L. E. Nolan, *The Training of Cavalry Remounts,* 1852; V. S. Littauer, *Horseman's Progress*, 1962.

Horseman's Word, Society of the

This association of old-time waggoners, ploughmen and others whose daily work was with heavy horses, extending up the east of Britain from Kent to Orkney, has been in existence since at least the seventeenth century and partly resembles a clandestine trade union, with some ceremonies reminiscent of the seventeenth-century witch covens. The 'Word' is a secret imparted to members on initiation as in Freemasonry. AD

Horserace Betting Levy Board

The purpose of the Horserace Betting Levy Board, set up in 1962, is to accrue money betted on horseraces in the United Kingdom with the TOTALISATOR and bookmakers and redistribute it for the general benefit of racing in increased prize money, new and improved grandstands, security (anti-doping) precautions, horse transportation and publicity for racing. The Board also controls Racecourse Technical Services, Ltd, directly responsible for the starting stalls, course commentaries, camera patrols and photo finish. Its first chairman was Lord Harding (Field Marshal Lord Harding of Petherton), succeeded in 1967 by Lord Wigg, under whom the amount available for redistribution has risen to an estimated £5m for 1973–4. GE

Horserace Totalisator Board see Totalisator

Horseracing see Flat Racing, Steeplechasing, Trotting Racing, etc.

Horse Trials

Horse Trials, or COMBINED TRAINING, produce a horse fit and sound and pronounced ready to go by a veterinary surgeon.

The French phrase in common European use is the *Concours Complet d'Équitation,* an accurate description of the required form of horsemanship. The first horse trials in the form of three-day-events in the Olympic Games occurred in 1912; this type of equitation was already very popular on the Continent, where many cavalry officers used it regularly, but although there was a British team in the 1912 and 1924 OLYMPIC GAMES, horse trials were not popular in Britain until after some success had been shown by British riders in the 1948 Games.

To perform horse trials correctly it became necessary to organize three-day-events, arranged as follows. On the first day the dressage test takes place. The second day is used for the endurance test, generally thought to be the hardest as the horse and rider must travel a distance of over 25 miles (40 km) with many and varied obstacles. It requires the greatest fitness of both. It begins with a road and track test over a distance of about 4 miles (6·4 km) to be taken generally at about 8 miles (13 km) an hour. This is followed immediately by an individual steeplechase of 2½ miles (4 km) over twelve fences. Time is important so fences have to be taken fast as well as accurately. Then follows a hack of 8 miles (13 km) at the same pace, crossing lanes and tracks of many different surfaces. After this the horse must at once enter the cross-country course, about 5 miles (8 km) long, during which at least 30 fences of various designs must be jumped. All parts of the course are under observation by judges and stewards at all times. The third and last day begins with a full veterinary examination for all competing horses. When it has been

Horse Trials. *Below:* Blitzkrieg, owned and ridden by Major J. N. D. Birtwhistle, clears a formidable criss-cross fence at Badminton. *Bottom:* H.R.H. Princess Anne, riding Doublet, competing to win at Burghley in 1971

passed sound, the horse is then ready to enter the last phase, show jumping: a small solid course of no fewer than twelve jumps. Marking is by penalty points for faults: the horse with the lowest number of points is the winner.

To compete in horse trials at international level requires an absolutely first-class horse and rider, and to produce a horse fit enough requires intensive preparation and work by rider, trainer and groom. After much study it has been found that THOROUGHBREDS are usually most suitable for this type of work although there have been successes with crossbred horses. When successful, schooling and fitness for this work produce one of the finest horses in the world.

The European Horse Trials began in 1953 and a British team was entered. The following year a British team won; the individual winner was A. Hill, riding Crispin and representing Great Britain. The interest in Horse Trials has grown in Britain ever since. The two most important events in this country are the BADMINTON Horse Trials held in spring each year and the BURGHLEY Horse Trials in late summer. JHew

Hounds

Hounds are dogs used for hunting by scent. The types used for this purpose are beagles, bassets, bloodhounds, otterhounds, harriers and foxhounds. The last two are usually followed on horseback.

All hounds should be bred for work. The working qualities a hound must have are: (a) a good nose to hunt over the bad scenting ground and to avoid over-running the line of the quarry; (b) a good tongue to let the Huntsman and followers know where the pack is and keep them together; (c) plenty of drive to get over the bad scenting ground. In addition a hound must be active and have a strong constitution.

All hounds hunting in the British Isles are descended from those introduced by the Normans after 1066. Recently efforts have been made to improve performance by crossing the standard hound with rough-coated Welsh Mountain hounds. There are over 200 packs of foxhounds in the British Isles, four packs of staghounds, 80 packs of beagles and a number of harrier and otterhound packs. See Hunting. CGEB

Huçul (Huzul)

The Huçul pony is a native of the Carpathian Mountains, from the Huzulei district which was part of Austria before World War I. It is closely related to the widely distributed European KONIK, which it closely resembles. A considerable amount of Arab blood has been introduced. Huçuls are hardy, willing, untiring pack and draught ponies covering the most difficult terrain. Characteristics are a short neck and marked croup. They are rather over-built with sickle hocks.

The German writer Hackl believes that the Huçul is descended from the TARPAN and should be described as the Forest Tarpan. The breed is also thought to have Przevalski blood. There are said to be three types, now very mixed: the Tarpan-Huçul (North), the Bystrzec-Huçul (West) and the Przevalski-Huçul. Heights range from about 12·1 to 13·1 hands (1·24–1·34 m). The small ones are considered the best. Huçul ponies were bred chiefly in Austria, Rum-

Above left: **Horse Trials.** Lt Mark Phillips and Great Ovation competing in the dressage phase at Burghley in 1971

Below: **Huçul.** A Huçul stallion in Poland

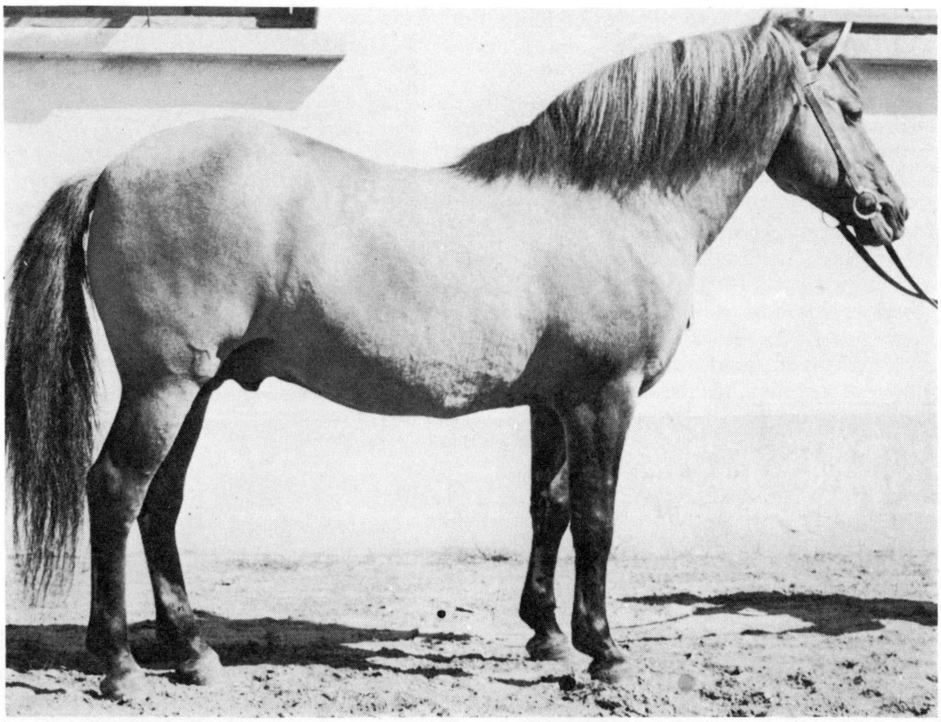

Hungary. Harness racing in Budapest

ania, Czechoslovakia and Poland. There is now a stud in Wiltshire, England. DMG

Hungary

Horse breeding in Hungary was already prosperous when the Magyars settled here at the end of the ninth century, adding expert knowledge as well as their own horses.

In the period of the Turkish occupation the tough Hungarian *parlagi* horse was interbred with Oriental, mainly ARAB, horses, improving its strength and carriage. Interbreeding with the LIPIZZANER (called Lippizan in Hungary) in the eighteenth century increased its size. Then Oriental horses were imported again and also Spanish horses, becoming especially popular in Transylvania. The English THOROUGHBRED was introduced in the second half of the eighteenth century. In Kisbér, after which the 1876 Epsom Derby winner was named, a state-owned stud was founded in 1853 to breed Thoroughbreds and halfbreds. Buccaneer, North Star and Kincsem, the 'wonder-mare', the daughter of Cambuscan and Waternymph, are the most famous of them.

Towards the end of the nineteenth century breeding stations were founded. During their golden age (1867–1914) only English and French horses were of better quality.

Between the two world wars, some good breeds were developed (e.g. the 'lick' Nonius) in order to achieve a suitable agricultural type.

As a result of crossing with English and Arab blood and the effect of Nonius, Furioso, Shagya and Gidran, breeding showed marked progress. For developing the farm horse type mainly Nonius, Gidran and the halfbreds of Kisbér and Mezöhegyes were used. In western Hungary the settlers after the Turkish occupation brought with them coldblooded horses and their breeding was begun at Bábolna in 1897. These coldblooded horses were interbred with Arab and Lipizzaner stallions. After 1920 Belgian Ardennes draught horses became common in western Hungary.

Today Hungary has a stock of 231,000 horses, 80–85 per cent used in agriculture. The most important breeds are the Anglo-Norman Nonius, the Anglo-Arab Gidran, the English halfbreds, English Thoroughbred/Hungarian warmblood crosses, belonging to the Furioso and North Star stock in the Mezöhegyes stud, founded in 1784), the English halfbreds of Kisbér (Maxim, Kozma and other stocks), and the Lipizzaner of Szilvásvárad (Conversano, Incitatio, etc.).

Races were held as early as the sixteenth century. The first 'popular' contests began in 1804 and the first official flat race was held in 1827. The Equestrian Club of Pest was founded in 1842.

The Hungarian Equestrian Association

(1949) oversees 54 regional clubs with 1,351 members and 831 horses and also organizes 'spectaculars' at Nagyvázsony, where various historic events are re-created. Hungarian riding schools and pony trekking attract many tourists every year.

The Arab: the Arab horse was introduced into Hungary together with other Oriental breeds by the Turks (see above). Its supremacy lasted for two hundred years, until the age of the Spanish horse. Brought back again in 1814, its importance continues today. In the Bábolna stud (founded in 1789) Arab breeding was begun in 1816. With the exception of the Lipizzaner all the other breeds were improved by the Arab horse, which became popular for its sound constitution and fecundity. Its blood also improved the NONIUS, the halfbreds of Kisbér and the coldblooded horse of Muraköz. The typical Hungarian horse is basically of Oriental and Arab origin. The Arab increased the size and improved the carriage of the small Hungarian horses and its hardiness qualified it for improving other breeds (e.g. the coldblooded mares of western Hungary).

As increasingly greater importance was attached to smaller horses, the Arab horse came into prominence and now every breeding station has an Arab stallion to improve characterless or poor strains.

Horses living in adverse circumstances cannot be immediately improved by Thoroughbreds, so Arab horses are used. In Bábolna Gazal, Kemir, Kuhaylan, Mersuch, Obayan, Shagya, Saqlawi and Saqlawi-Bagdady are the most important lines. PN

Hunter

The hunter is a riding horse of size, substance, depth and considerable quality, suitable for carrying a rider following hounds in the pursuit of live quarry, usually a fox, sometimes hare or deer. Horses are often described as being 'of hunter type'.

Hunters have been bred in the British Isles for the last two centuries. The sire is nearly always THOROUGHBRED. The dam was originally a draught horse—SHIRE, CLYDESDALE, SUFFOLK PUNCH, CLEVELAND BAY, YORKSHIRE COACH HORSE, or, perhaps ideally, the Irish Draught Horse. Welsh Cobs have also proved to be excellent foundation stock for the breeding of hunters. In more recent times the dam has tended to be a crossbred animal with a high proportion of Thoroughbred blood in her veins, the result of putting the offspring of the original cross back to the Thoroughbred for generation after generation. Breeders have also used occasional infusions of British native pony blood, and the resulting progeny have been hardy and exceptionally surefooted.

In the type of work required and the extent and nature of this work, the hunter has more stringent demands made upon it than almost any other type of horse. The season, which in Britain lasts from November to April, is a long one. A day's hunting starts at 11 a.m. and may well continue until the dusk of a winter evening. Horses are often out of their stable for eight hours at a stretch, and they spend their day galloping and jumping out of and into deep mud. In a wooded country they must be sufficiently temperate to crawl and creep under overhanging branches, often taking off at a fence from a standstill. In a galloping country they must have sufficient courage and ability to tackle big, strange and sometimes trappy fences at speed. Everywhere they must be content to stand about while hounds are drawing without becoming fidgety, they must be bold without being over-impetuous, and they must be content to go first or last at the pace that the rider dictates. Most important, perhaps, they must possess the type of conformation, and above all the type of limbs, that enable them to do the maximum amount of work without falling victim to those manifold unsoundnesses to which the horse of less than classical conformation is subject, e.g. navicular disease, curbs, spavins, sidebones and ringbones.

The primary requirement of a hunter is a good, open foot with a well-developed frog to absorb concussion and one that is made of hard, flinty horn. Medium-length, well-sloped pasterns lead up, in the fore leg, to a large, prominent, convex knee and a strong and muscular fore arm leading into a well-laid, sloping shoulder. It is said that a good shoulder is a luxury and a good hind leg a necessity, but they are each of nearly equal importance in the riding horse.

In the hind leg, which should be straight from the fetlock joint to the hock, the hock is of extreme importance; indeed, it can hardly be overrated, for it is the vital propelling force, the engine as it were, behind every stride taken and every fence jumped. The hocks should be big and bony and completely devoid of fleshiness or puffiness, a sure sign of trouble, either present or imminent. Then come strong, muscular second-thighs leading up to the stifle joint, which has a patella and corresponds to the knee in man.

The horse's body should be deep and wide through the chest, denoting great heart room and therefore stamina. Its shoulder should be laid right back so that the saddle sits well behind it and its back should be short. Strength and muscle behind the saddle are very important—a horse slack over its loins is invariably weak and unthrifty, and its croup should be short and its tail set on high. It must have a good, round rib-cage and barrel or in hard work it will run up as light as a greyhound.

The neck should be neither too long, which implies weakness, nor too short, which implies lack of quality. The head, which gives the surest indication of a horse's quality, character and tempera-

Colour plate: **Horse Trials.** Rosalyn Jones riding Farewell at the 1972 Badminton Horse Trials

DIVERSION HICKSTEAD →

ment, should be fine and lean, tapering down to a small muzzle. The bones should be prominent, the eye bold and kindly, and the front of the face should be straight or slightly convex. If the ears are finely-made and readily pricked so much the better, but there have been some great lop-eared horses and it is said that a bad lop-eared horse has never existed.

The hunter may range from 15 hands to 17 (1·52–1·77 m) or over, but the ideal height, depending on the requirements of each particular hunting country, is 16–16·2 hands (1·65–1·72 m). Weight-carrying capacity is defined by depth through the girth and the amount of bone below the knee. For the latter, 8 inches (20·3 cm) is minimal and 9–9½ inches (22·8–24.0 cm) is good.

Bay is a favourite colour with most people, but browns, greys and chestnuts are popular. Odd-coloured horses such as piebalds and skewbalds are not in demand. For one thing, those who ride them find that they are very conspicuous, not always an advantage in the hunting field. Odd-coloured horses are, moreover, usually underbred.

Since the draught horse population has decreased so greatly in recent years, hunters tend to become more and more Thoroughbred. Some people refuse to hunt anything that is not either in the Book or 'on the front page' but with increasing age many prefer a little less quality and a little less temperament. After two hundred years and more of selective breeding, British and Irish hunters have proved themselves superior to any other riding horse. They are in great demand all over the world, particularly for international competitive sport such as show jumping and three-day horse trials. In Britain, a constant supply of good sound stallions standing at a reasonable fee, is ensured by the PREMIUM STALLION SCHEME. PMM

Hunter Classes

Showing classes for hunters are held at all the major horse and agricultural shows in the British Isles. They include a section for brood mares and young stock (foals, yearlings, two-year-olds and three-year-olds, all shown in hand) as well as for ridden hunters (four-year-olds, lightweights, middleweights, heavyweights, ladies' hunters under side-saddle and small hunters, not exceeding 15·2 hands (1·57 m) in height). Classes for working hunters, which originated in the United States, were introduced to Britain after World War II; they are judged partly on the horse's ability to jump a small course of fairly natural fences.

Hunter classes are probably the most important and valuable ingredient of any horse show, for they provide the prototype and thus establish a type which the breeders strive to perpetuate. It would be no exaggeration to say that the present excellence of British and Irish horses in every type of equestrian sport, particularly in horse trials, is due to the standards set in the hunter classes.

Judges are drawn from a panel published annually by the HUNTERS' IMPROVEMENT SOCIETY and recruited from ex-cavalry officers (now, regrettably, a diminishing source), from the hunting field and the steeplechase course, from breeding studs and from horse dealers. They are required to ride most of the horses that come before them in the ridden classes, and they base their conclusions on the relative assessment of conformation and movement, quality, type, ride and manners. Ability to gallop on, covering the ground with long, low strides, is a primary requisite in a champion hunter, who must defeat the winners of all the other classes to achieve its title.

In the breeding classes the exhibits are required only to walk and trot. The most valuable brood mares are those with sufficient bone, depth and substance to produce a weight-carrying animal when mated to a Thoroughbred horse. The young stock championships are generally won by three-year-olds, whose comparative maturity gives them a great advantage over the yearlings and most two-year-olds.

Although the best type of Thoroughbred is quite capable of winning hunter championships, and indeed, is the typical show

Hunter. Chiming Bells, owned and ridden by Donald Owen

Colour plate: **Show Jumping.** Ted Williams riding Carnaval at Hickstead hunter in the United States, the majority of winning hunters in England are generally three-quarter bred, that is to say by a Thoroughbred stallion out of a mare who is herself by a Thoroughbred, but can be traced back in the female line to a heavier type of animal. Irish Draught mares are the best foundation stock for the hunter, for they are clean-legged, active and lighter in build than any of the British draught horses such as Shires, Clydesdales or Suffolk Punches.

The procedure for judging is for the judge to stand in the centre of the ring while the exhibits walk, trot, canter and gallop around its perimeter. He then asks his steward to call them into the centre of the ring, lined up in order of merit. He walks down the line for a closer inspection of each horse before he rides it. Then it is stripped of its saddle, led out for a further inspection and trotted up and down before him, so that he can see whether its action is true and straight. PMM

The Hunter Division of American horse shows is composed of breeding and model classes (shown in hand and judged on conformation only), conformation classes (shown under saddle, with both performance and conformation scored), and working hunter (winners determined by performance and soundness only). The last group attracts the largest number of entries at many shows, with the class for amateur-owned working hunters recently enjoying a veritable boom. Most horse shows schedule hack classes on the flat as well as jumping classes for both conformation and working hunters, but the jumping classes predominate by far.

The American Horse Shows Association outlines the current regulations in its annual Rule Book. A show may schedule separate classes according to weight, age, or breeding, as well as a Corinthian class (for amateur members of a recognized Hunt), Appointment, Local, Junior and Ladies' classes, Handy Hunters, Pony Hunters, Pair, Teams and Hunt Teams, among others, and Open and Stake classes.

Unlike their British counterparts, American hunter judges never ride the horses. After the competitors have jumped the course, the judge merely verifies the horses' soundness as they are ridden or jogged around the ring. Performance is thus the prime factor in his decisions. MAS

Hunters' Improvement and National Light Horse Breeding Society

This British society was founded in 1885 to improve and promote the breeding of Hunters and other horses used for riding and driving and for general purposes. In addition to its Premium Schemes for stallions and mares, the Society organizes two annual national shows, the Thoroughbred Stallion Show and the National Hunter Show. GWE

Hunter Trials

Hunter trials are modified cross-country events, usually consisting of some 15–20 fences, some of them natural hazards, spread over a course of about a mile long and usually typical of the hunting country in which they are found. There is often a gate to be opened and closed, or a slip rail to be removed and put back, to test the training and the handiness of the horse. There is often a degree of controversy as to the code under which hunter trials should be judged. It is usual for faults to be awarded for every fence knocked down. Refusals can be penalized, but when the trials are timed and judged on the clock refusals are sometimes unfaulted as the additional time incurred will carry its own penalty. Points are sometimes awarded for style, particularly in a tie, but it is sometimes considered that too much reliance is placed on personal opinions, which can vary and may produce an unsatisfactory result.

Since the advent of HORSE TRIALS, hunter trials have declined in popularity in parts of the country which are well served by COMBINED TRAINING, although they are still held in more remote hunting areas and provide a popular day out for Pony Club members. PMM

Hunting

In a variety of forms, hunting continues to provide horsemen and women with the challenge of riding to hounds, despite modern difficulties such as: urbanization, which reduces hunting areas; fuel fumes on roads and chemical fertilizers on land, which destroy scent; modern farming methods, involving the rooting out of hedges and the increase in arable land, which lessens the pleasure of riding across country.

Hunting in which hounds are followed by mounted supporters is principally found in

Hunting. *Below:* The Duke of Beaufort's hounds move off from a meet at Badminton, Gloucestershire, home of the Duke (right).
Above right: The Exmoor Hunt ride across the moors near Honeymead Cross, with Master and Huntsman Mr J. Hosegood on the right.

Great Britain, Ireland, parts of Continental Europe, some British Commonwealth countries, and the United States. British Army officers have long been instrumental in spreading foxhunting abroad during service overseas. The Duke of Wellington took hounds to Spain to hunt during lulls in the Peninsular War (1808–14). The practice persisted into recent postwar years; even Cyprus had a military pack. Withdrawal of British troops from many parts of the world has reduced such packs. For example, in India there were twenty hunts in the 1930s; now only one remains, the Ootacamund, hunting jackal in South India. The disposition of hunts with mounted followers throughout the world is broadly as follows: Great Britain has more than 200 packs of foxhounds, an increase of about 40 since 100 years ago, mainly because hunts tended to split into smaller units immediately after World War II because of difficulties in transporting horses and hounds. The trend is now towards amalgamations, and some closures, but hunt subscribers are more numerous than ever.

The Irish Republic has some 30 packs of foxhounds (see Hunting in Ireland).

Foxhunting dates from the eighteenth century in the United States (see Hunting in North America). Hunts use American hounds, sometimes crossbred with English foxhounds, and some packs include some purebred English hounds.

Canada lists 11 packs of foxhounds, in Ontario and Quebec; some supplement their sport with drag lines (following a line of scent laid artificially by man). Two also hunt hare. In Australia there is foxhunting by the Melbourne Hunt and the Pine Lodge in Western Australia. Three packs in Tasmania hunt kangaroo, wallaby and deer, and follow drag lines.

For the mounted follower in Britain and Ireland, HARRIER packs are the most frequent alternative to foxhunting. These have decreased in this century in Britain, but still number 28; there are 30 harrier packs in Ireland. New Zealand, where there are no foxes, has 17 packs of harriers, and some drag hunting. Horses frequently jump New Zealand barbed wire fences with aplomb while following hounds, not a popular practice in Britain. South Africa has two packs of hounds hunting jackal, or following drag lines; there is drag hunting in Kenya, with deer as an alternative quarry. A pack in Mexico hunts deer, hare and fox.

There is limited foxhunting in Italy, near Rome, and in Portugal, near Lisbon. In Germany game laws forbid hunting wild animals with hounds, but some drag hunting is run by German packs and by a pack of British military hounds. There is some drag hunting in Denmark, Holland and Belgium. The current spread of rabies among wild life on the Continent, carried principally by the fox, makes foxhunting impossible in most countries. Rabies has already reached northern France; if it should cross the Channel and become endemic in British wild life, all forms of hunting throughout the United Kingdom would be gravely threatened. Significantly, drag hunting is pursued by only seven packs in Britain and is not regarded as an adequate alternative to foxhunting, but purely a substitute providing fast runs across country in areas where foxhunting is unsuitable or for those with no time to follow foxhounds.

Several private packs in Britain, at present no more than four, use bloodhounds to hunt 'clean boot' (the line of scent left by a man). Followers of the hounds are mounted.

All forms of hunting, especially foxhunting, have become increasingly expensive in recent years. Hunts vary enormously in scope and size; in Britain their subscriptions vary from a few guineas to more than £100 per person each season. See also Foxhunting, Hounds, Staghunting. MC

Reference: *Baily's Hunting Directory*, London (annual).

Hunting Horn, Music of the

The music of the hunting horn, like the art of venery, is of ancient origin. Horns were originally made of the horns of animals, generally oxen, embellished with silver-work or engravings. Later they were made of copper and/or silver. Horn music was originally intended to inform the field or members of the hunt. This was and is especially necessary when hounds are hunting quarry in heavily wooded areas or forests, when hounds can easily be lost to mounted followers. The different calls are set to music and, although many are no longer heard today, some Masters and Huntsmen do still inform the field of hounds' activities.

Reference: L. C. R. Cameron, *The Hunting Horn,* London, n.d.

Hunting in Ireland

No country in the world is so ideally suited to hunting as Ireland, that is, hunting in the accepted European sense by the pursuit, without guns, of fox, hare, stag and otter. The climate, the nature of the country and the attitude of the landowning community are the major factors in its extraordinary popularity.

The origins of hunting are lost in the legends of the Irish and bound up with two separate breeds of hounds, the Irish wolfhound and the black and tan Kerry beagle. The former is now purely a show animal; but the Kerry beagles and their descendants have provided some of the gamest hunting hounds in the world. The Ryan family of Knocklong, Co. Limerick, have bred the black and tan hounds and hunted them as the Scarteen Hounds as an unbroken family pack for over two hundred years. Aside from the few packs that breed hounds exclusively from the old black and tan lines, such as the Scarteen, the majority of the Irish packs are a mixture of Irish and British bloodlines. Outcrossing with fashionable stallion hounds from leading British packs, and indeed, drafting bitches, has kept the breed strong. In West Waterford Captain Morgan has successfully introduced Fell hounds.

For a relatively small island a very wide variety of hunting country is encountered. In the west of Ireland the Galway Blazers hunt a big country of fearsome stone walls. Generally good firm going on limestone land, with few banks or hedges, it is a fast country suited to a fast Thoroughbred type that takes its fences going on. In Munster the big double banks of Limerick and Tipperary need a clever, locally-bred horse, the short-backed handy sort that can cope with unexpected emergencies at the back of a huge bank. In the Wexford country the fields are small and fenced with tall, narrow, stone-faced banks that need a locally-bred specialist if they are to be jumped with safety. In the Kildare and Meath country the huge enclosures of the big farms are often divided by 'Meath ditches' resembling small canals. Here again the big long-striding horse of scope is the best.

Urbanization of the countryside close to major cities is eroding some hunting country but this is not yet as obvious a problem as it has become in Britain. And in line with a steady increase in national affluence more and more people are turning to hunting as a recreation, particularly in the city areas. Of course horses are very easy to hire in Ireland, where half- and three-quarter-bred hunters are bred on many small farms.

There are only two staghound packs: the Ward Union near Dublin and the County Down Hunt near Belfast. Curiously, neither pack kills its quarry. In both cases stags are kept in a deerpark and set free on hunting days. Some become very tame after a while and have to be replaced. The late Sir Alfred Munnings painted a remarkable portrait of the Ward Union going home after a day's hunting with the stag trotting on the road with the hounds.

Music of the Hunting Horn. Some of the many calls are shown here, including 'When Drawing On' (Straking from Covert to Covert) and 'Breaking Covert'. The hunting horn became an art instrument in the seventeenth century. There are many impressions of the sport in French and German baroque and later music; Haydn used calls in his symphony no. 31 ('Hornsignal') and Mozart in his Horn Concertos.

At the moment about 30 packs of foxhounds and 30 packs of harriers hunt regularly. The number varies slightly each year. Recently beagling has gained in popularity among students; during December 1971 the first meet of basset hounds was held. But generally speaking the strength of hunting lies with the foxhounds and harriers, with the beagles an accepted and valued method of introducing young people. TP

Hunting in North America

Mounted hunting of the red fox, indigenous to most areas of North America, started at least two hundred years ago. The first President of the United States, George Washington (1732–99), was among those who hunted regularly in colonial times.

The best foxhunting country is found, for the most part, in Virginia, Maryland and Pennsylvania, but there are many suitable areas in other parts of the country and interest has spread widely across the United States and into Canada.

The Masters of Foxhounds Association of America (112 Water Street, Boston, Mass.) was organized in 1907, generally based on the British Masters of Foxhounds Association. In 1972 it listed 136 hunts, 125 in the United States and 11 in Canada. Hunting continues to be most popular in Virginia, Maryland and Pennsylvania, but there are organized hunts in at least 30 states, with especially significant activity in Kansas, New York, Illinois, Massachusetts, North and South Carolina and Tennessee. All these hunts except two are active. Seventeen report drag hunting only; 16 have both fox and drag.

The red fox found in the United States is not significantly different from the red fox of the British Isles. However, it seems to be less successful in adapting itself to survival in settled areas, so that nowhere in North America are foxes as plentiful as in the best hunting areas in Britain. Accordingly, there is less pressure from farmers for the control of foxes, and, except for an occasional kill, most Masters prefer to have the fox go to ground and be preserved for another day. Earths are rarely stopped and terriers almost never used.

There are important differences in terrain between North America and Britain. In most areas the country is more heavily wooded and more rugged. A covert is generally a strong woodland of considerable extent, intersected by irregular crooked rides. Getting a fox to break from covert is substantially more difficult.

Most hunting is over ground which is firm or even hard, so horses travel on top of rather than in the ground. It has often been said that a horse can carry at least one stone (14 lb or 6·35 kg) more under American than under British conditions. Many hunters admirably suited to American hunting would be considered lacking in substance or even weedy in Great Britain. Such horses do go extremely well on American terrain, as British visitors often find to their surprise. Again, because of different conditions, many good horsemen regularly fly their fences at a speed which would be considered stupidly reckless in Britain, especially over solid timber, a common type of fence in many areas.

Most of the horses used as hunters are Thoroughbred or part-Thoroughbred. In some areas, the rocky, hilly terrain requires a heavier and sturdier type with little or no Thoroughbred blood. Almost any type may be seen, particularly as a child's pony. Quarter Horses and Appaloosas, often crossed with Thoroughbreds, are increasingly popular.

In the north, most hunts close down as soon as frozen ground and snow begin to make hunting difficult or impossible. However, many Masters carry on under conditions that would be considered unacceptable in England or Ireland; many good runs are

Hunting in Ireland. The Galway Blazers

reported on snow-covered ground. Further south, hunting continues into early spring with only occasional interruptions for frost.

In some Western states, where there are few foxes, the coyote is hunted, giving a fast run over open country where the obstacles are apt to be dry watercourses. Holes of prairie animals are often a serious hazard but western-bred horses can be surprisingly skilful in detecting them.

In more conventional hunting countries a wide variety of obstacles is found. Timber jumps may be posts-and-rails, snakes or board fences. Stone walls are sometimes faced with a solidly-supported telegraph pole on top. The chicken coop is a common fence, often used as a panel over wire. The Hitchcock, or Aiken, is a splendid artificial fence: it is a rail fence with brush piled on each side to a height of 3 ft (1 m) or more, and extending 4–5 ft (1·2–1·5 m) each side of the fence; this invites both horse and rider to jump cleanly and boldly. WSF

Hunting, Language of

The voice in hunting is no less important than the horn. A good Huntsman has a good voice and uses it to encourage or help his hounds. Over the centuries hunting has developed its own vocabulary, of which the following glossary of terms is typical:

All on: when the pack is complete at the end of a run.
Babble: when a hound speaks but is not on the line.
Blank: when a covert has no fox in it.
Blood: a fast-disappearing practice of daubing a young person with blood at his first kill.
Break Covert: when a fox goes away.
Brush: a fox's tail.
Bye-day: an extra unofficial day's hunting.
Cap: the subscription paid to the Hunt Secretary at the start of a day's hunting.
Cast: when the Huntsman helps hounds to look for the lost scent.
Chop: to kill a fox in covert before it has been hunted.
Couple: two hounds; a pack is always counted in couples.
Course: when hounds chase a fox in view.
Draft: the hounds not needed in a pack and sold or given away.
Enter: training young hounds to hunt the fox.
Foil: when scent fails because it has been ridden on.
Heel: when hounds hunt the line in the wrong direction—where the fox has come from instead of where it is going.
Hold-up: when a covert is surrounded as in cubhunting.
Holloa: the call that is made when a fox is seen.
Huic: a hunting call when a fox is seen.
Lark: to jump fences unnecessarily when hounds are not running.
Lift: when a Huntsman takes hounds from the scent to where a fox has been seen.
Line: the trail of a fox.
Mark: when hounds bay at a hole when the fox has taken refuge.
Nose: the ability of hounds to hunt a scent well.
Over-ride: to get too close to hounds.
Pad: the fox's or hound's foot.
Pink: often used to describe the colour of the red coat.
Point: the furthest distance in a hunt.
Stub-bred: foxes born above ground.
Tail hounds: those at the back.
Tally-ho: a hunting cry derived from the French.
Trencher-fed: hounds brought up and kept at separate homes not in kennels.
Walk: to bring up puppies away from the kennels for 4–5 months from 8 weeks old.
Whelps: unweaned puppies. DW

Hurdle Racing

Hurdle racing is one of two integral parts —STEEPLECHASING is the other—which make up racing over jumps. The obstacles are smaller and quite different from steeplechase fences and most horses start their jumping careers as hurdlers. In Britain hurdles are required to be not less than 3 ft 6 in (1·07 m) in height between the bottom bar (virtually on the ground) and the top bar. There are usually three bars with birch and/or gorse interwoven and the hurdles are set in the ground at an angle of about 45 degrees.

The first recorded hurdle race was held at Durdham Down, near Bristol, on 2 April 1821 but steeplechase followers were not enthusiastic, considering hurdling no more than glorified flat racing with a few small jumps. The rules lay down a minimum of only four hurdles per mile as opposed to six fences in steeplechasing and thus hurdle races are on average run at a faster speed.

However, hurdle races gradually became a regular feature of jump racing and in

Hurdle Racing. The Singleton Novices Hurdle Race, Fontwell Park, a typical English hurdle race for horses that are not yet in the top flight.

Language of Hunting. Lt-Col F. Mitchell, joint-Master and Huntsman of the Hambledon Hunt, takes hounds to a 'holloa' near Hambledon.

Britain are now an accepted part of the winter calendar, with many valuable prizes to be won. The most important is the Champion Hurdle, run at Cheltenham's March Festival, sponsored for the first time in 1972 by Lloyds Bank. Other major events are the Schweppes Gold Trophy, the Welsh and Scottish Champion Hurdles, the Imperial Cup and the 'Fighting Fifth' Hurdle. There are also important races confined to four-year-olds (horses can start hurdling in the autumn of their three-year-old days), chiefly the Victor Ludorum and the Daily Express Triumph.

France is the only other country in which jump racing now has very much importance and only in the British Isles is it as popular as flat racing. French hurdles are less rigid and can be jumped through rather than over. The principal French jumping races, including the Grande Course de Haies and the Grande Course de Haies de 4 Ans, are held at the Paris track of Auteuil. GE

Hurlingham

After polo matches between the 9th Lancers and the 10th Hussars at Hounslow in 1870–1 a polo club was formed at Lillie Bridge, now Earls Court, London. Since the ground was only 200 yd (183 m) long there was soon demand for a bigger one. In 1873 the members of The Hurlingham Club (formed in 1868) bought Hurlingham House and grounds and the celebrated No. 1 Hurlingham Polo Ground was finished in 1874 and the opening match played on 6 June in the presence of the Prince and Princess of Wales. The Hurlingham Club Committee drew up official Rules of Polo from 1 May 1875 and continued to control its developments for the next thirty years. Then a separate Polo Committee was formed which now has its own secretary and office and is called The Hurlingham Polo Association.

From the beginning Empire polo associations and clubs wished to play under Hurlingham Rules and soon had representatives on the Council. Though some countries have by now left the Commonwealth, all have remained as members of the H.P.A. with their own representatives: the All Ireland Polo Association and others of India, Pakistan, South Africa, Rhodesia, New Zealand, Australia, Kenya, Nigeria, Malaysia, Malta, Cyprus, Hong Kong, Jamaica and Ghana. The Clubs of Tangiers, Düsseldorf and Hamburg also play under rules without representation. JRCG

Hussar see Warfare, Horse in

Huzul see Huçul

Hybrids

All the species of the genus *Equus* (horse, ass, zebra and onager) are fertile and can interbreed. Indeed, there are many instances quoted of hybrids, apart from the recognized cross, jackass × mare which produces the mule; and the horse × she-ass which produces the hinny. Both offspring depend for size on that of the female parent. Both the mule and the hinny are considered to be sterile although insufficient research has been done in this field to confirm this. The most useful hybrid cross is that of the large Poitou mule of France, which has been exported in large numbers for draught purposes (see Poitevin). DMG

Reference: W. B. Tegetmeier and C. L. Sutherland, *Horses, Asses, Zebras, Mules and Mule Breeding*, London, 1895.

Iceland. These hardy Iceland ponies are descended from horses brought over by Norse settlers.

Iceland

The most northerly country, except for Siberia, to have an 'indigenous' breed of horses. During the period when Greenland was inhabited by Europeans (*c.* 1000–1500) there were horses in Greenland, but these, like the Norse settlers, came from Iceland.

The Iceland pony is descended almost exclusively from the horses brought over by the settlers, *c.* A.D. 860–935. These settlers came from Norway and from Norse colonies in Scotland and its offshore islands, Ireland and Man, and their foundation stock of horses (or ponies) was drawn from all these regions. The various strains have blended to a considerable extent but experts can still recognize four separate types, one of which, the Faxaflói breed of the southwest (where the rainfall is highest) bears a marked resemblance to the Exmoor. Average height is 13 hands (1·32 m) but there are very few examples below 12 hands (1·22 m) or above 14 hands (1·42 m). All possible coat colours are seen, including piebald and skewbald. Preferred colours are in the range dun/chestnut, and include ISABELLA, PALOMINO, and the liver chestnut with flaxen mane called, in English, mulberry. Even today there are about as many ponies as there are people in Iceland; but not all are bred for work. The climate is such that beef cattle will not winter out, though the summer keep on the fells is good. Therefore horsemeat has always been a staple of Icelandic diet, and today separate breeding herds are kept for meat and work horses. In the absence of roads, and practically of wheels, the use is entirely for riding or pack. As in medieval Europe generally, the best quality saddle horses are those which pace and rack (see Gaits). AD

Ili see China

India and Pakistan

To try to trace the distinctive breeds of Indian horses and ponies, it must be remembered that in the many internal wars the cavalry, including the cavalry of the British armies, were mounted on countrybred horses, i.e. those foaled in India. Possibly the best horses in Wellington's successful campaigns in the south were the extensively bred Deccanis in central to south India. These were also used by his enemies.

The Mahratta cavalry seem to have had a large supply of the best horses of the period: the Marwari (an outstanding breed of the Rajputs) and the Kathiawari breeds. The Punjab also produced a large supply of horses of which the mares showed both quality and more substance than most breeds, though the stallions were apparently not outstanding. The Pindaree, gangs of mounted marauders who raided Hindustan, were mounted on the horses of the north.

As the British advanced to the north the breeding of countrybreds began to decline as wars between Indian states ceased. Still the demand for them from the British serving in India remained; they bought them from dealers.

Some foreign breeds were imported by traders: TURKOMANS, Persian ponies, ponies from Waziristan and small Kabulis from Afghanistan. Kabulis crossed with ARABS could produce fair-sized remounts. Imports of Arabs began and were soon used for crossbreeding.

There has been no deterioration in the breeds of small riding or pack ponies in northern hill states. No man walks in the mountainous areas of Chitral, Hunza, Nagar, Gilgit or Kashmir; he rides on various breeds or crosses of hill ponies, practically all under 14 hands (1·42 m), down to 13 hands (1·32 m) and under. In most small towns and villages polo is regularly played, frequently on the main village street and with eight or nine a side. 'Always' is the answer if asked how long they have been playing.

Prof. E. Warts in *The Horse of the British Empire* (1907) considered the Mongolian horse to be nearer to the original horse than any other breed. The Tartars bred them and, by turning them out in herds in bitter winter on the steppes to feed on what they could find, they produced the hardiest type with great endurance.

Genghis Khan's great army was mounted on Tartar ponies; it is written that along his line of communications just north of the Karakoram and Pamirs he had depots of fresh supplies of these ponies to replace casualties. Some of these hardy stallions must have left their mark among the breeds along India's northern states and individual well-known true pony breeds developed, especially in Bhutan, Yarkand and Spiti. The Mongolian Tartar Pony has a rough coat and legs of iron, muscles of steel and the hardy constitution that results from a tough upbringing. Capt. Hayes wrote that he saw no distinctive difference in the breeds mentioned above, but by the nineteenth century they were producing some ponies of fine quality. BURMA PONIES, chiefly bred in the Shan Hills where they were used as packhorses, continued in use among the British till they left the country. The Manipur ponies are another strong little breed, very likely introduced by the Tartars who invaded in about A.D. 700, settled and must have brought polo with them. With their Mongolian ponies they continued to breed polo ponies of 13 hands (1·32 m) or less. British soldiers stayed for a time in Manipur after a minor war there and, with the tea planters of Assam, played polo with the local players. A visit of a Manipuri polo team to Calcutta resulted in the formation of the Calcutta Polo Club (1860) and polo spread rapidly all over India, particularly in the British and Indian armies, and in the Indian princely states.

From its start it was agreed that ponies not over 13·3 hands (1·40 m) should be used. This rule lasted till 1899 and gave an impetus to the smaller breeds. The height limit was later raised to 14·1 hands (1·44 m), then 14·2 hands (1·47 m) in 1907. The use of countrybred ponies for polo was affected by the ever-increasing numbers of Arabs imported to Bombay. The best ones had originally been brought by rajahs for riding, but there was a lower class of Arab that could still pass the 13·3-hand test and about half the average team were Arabs, half countrybred. When the height limit was raised to 14·2 hands the Arabs began to be replaced by the better-bred Australian WALERS or New Zealand ponies. When the height limit was abolished after World War I the Arab gradually dropped out of first-class polo.

Walers imported as army remounts also affected the countrybreds. By the nineteenth century all British cavalry, Royal Horse Artillery and Field Artillery regiments were mounted by the Remount Department on Walers, and, of the 39 Indian Cavalry regiments, three were mounted by the Remount Department. The remainder, up to World War I, bought their own horses, Walers from Bombay or Calcutta gradually predominating, though in some cases a

India and Pakistan. *Above top:* A Baluchi stallion. This is a deep-chested, strong horse famous for its capacity to carry weight and comfortable ride. Bred in the Marri, Bugti and Barkhan districts of Baluchistan, it may be chestnut, grey or bay.
Above centre: A Kathi or Kathiawari stallion. This horse has a naturally fine gait and smooth action. In the purebred Kathi the tips of the ears touch each other above the centre of the poll.
Above: A Spiti mare
Right: A Bhutia mare

smaller proportion of countrybred Marwaris or Kathiawaris were used, and also breeds from outside India: Waziris from Waziristan, Kabulis from Afghanistan and Baluchis from Baluchistan.

After World War I the Remount Department mounted the Indian Cavalry with Walers. With these and a few countrybreds, the Indians evolved a system of crossing selected mares, mostly from the Punjab, with Arab stallions, the resulting fillies covered by English THOROUGHBREDS. After partition in 1947, Pakistan successfully followed on with Thoroughbred stallions and now has a good supply of horses of 15–15·2 hands (1·52–1·57 m) suitable for good polo or for riding.

Today neither India nor Pakistan permits imports of foreign breeds although in India one horsed cavalry regiment is still mounted on imported Walers. Except at Delhi, where the cavalry play polo regularly, less polo is now played in India. In Pakistan too polo to Hurlingham rules is largely played by the cavalry. Wide use of the car has probably reduced the number of countrybred horses, though the ponies of the northern districts remain in demand and use. Racing for countrybred horses, developed in the nineteenth century from older relay races, is still flourishing in India and Pakistan. Great improvement in pace and quality has developed through imports of Thoroughbred stallions for breeding, maintained after the departure of the British Army by the governments and private owners. Pakistan now has its own stud book. See also Nepal. JG

Reference: Capt. M. H. Hayes, *The Points of the Horse,* London, 1893, 7th revised ed. 1969; Sir H. F. de Trafford (ed), *The Horses of the British Empire,* London, 1907.

Indians, American see Horsemanship, American Indian

Indonesia

Horses play an important part in the life and economy of Indonesia. There are some very small primitive types on the islands. Others have been improved with the introduction of Arab blood. These include the good-looking ponies on the State stud farm near Padang Mengabas and the Sandalwood pony, named after one of the chief exports of the islands of Sumba and Sumbawa. Selected mares are sent to imported Arab stallions standing at Menangkabau, Central Sumatra, where the BATAK pony is also native. This stud was under Dutch control in the days of the Netherlands East Indies, and the Dutch were reponsible for improving the ponies bred throughout the many islands. The best of the Sandalwood ponies are raced over a distance of $2\frac{1}{2}$–3 miles (4,000–5,000 m). Neither saddles nor bits are used but plaited leather bridles with hard nosepieces similar to those used some 4,000 years ago in Central Asia. These ponies have distinct Arab characteristics including the head, hard legs and joints, deep girth allowing for plenty of heart space, and fine coat. They are of all colours. Some ponies on other islands are small and primitive and appear to be a mixture between the TARPAN and the ASIATIC WILD HORSE, as indeed they may well be, for although they were originally imported their actual provenance appears lost in antiquity. DMG

Industry, Horse in

Industry in the modern sense of the word was only made possible by a system of transport that could bring raw materials to the workplace, and convey the finished goods away, in sufficient quantities to permit operations on a 'factory' scale. The foundations of such a system were laid, in Britain, in the immediate pre-railway age, in the form of the canal network, the barges being towed by horses. Mining and metallurgy, before steam-power, were also inseparable from the use of horses. (At the beginning of February 1972 the last five ponies working in Yorkshire pits, at Wheldale Colliery, Castleford, were retired.) Quite apart from pit ponies, unknown before the nineteenth century because there were then only vertical shafts and no horizontal 'drifts'

Horse in Industry. *Far right:* A British canal horse

along which horses could walk into the mine, and no 'cages' in which horses could be lowered down the shaft, horses worked near the pithead throughout the history of mining, for instance, turning the windlass of the hoist. This was only one of a large range of heavy machinery worked by horses (or asses, or mules); the prototypes of these machines were probably the oil and wine presses of the Mediterranean region. In regions where water power was scarce, and windmills unknown or impracticable, there were horse mills, often powered by lame or blind animals. Grist mills and machinery for chopping and pulping roots for cattlefeed were a feature of progressive Scottish agriculture in the nineteenth century; these were operated by horses, and the round structures housing them can be seen today, not only in the eastern Lowlands but also in areas such as Exmoor where farms were managed by Scottish agents of English landlords. There was never such a breed or type as an 'industrial' horse: it was almost always a demoted pack or draught horse. AD

Insurance

Horses and ponies generally can be covered by insurance against death from accident, sickness or disease. Death from accident normally includes fire, lightning or any form of accident while the animal is in transit. Premiums depend chiefly on the age of an animal and the use for which it is kept. Often the lowest rates apply to two-year-olds up to 12-year-olds. The lowest rates of premium may apply if a horse or pony is used for hacking, driving, gymkhanas or polo. An additional premium is generally charged for show jumping; hunting is more expensive. Steeplechasing is one of the worst risks from an insurer's point of view. If a horse does not race very often, sometimes additional insurance is taken out specifically for each race.

Before insurance can be arranged, it may be necessary to obtain a certificate from a veterinary surgeon to the effect that the animal is in good health. Sometimes nothing more may be required than a declaration of health from the owner. This will say that, to the best of his knowledge and belief, the animal is in good condition with nothing existing which would be detrimental to good health and satisfactory breeding. If the risk of foaling, including pregnancy and parturition, is to be insured, some insurers require an additional premium.

When a policy to cover death is in force, it automatically covers any operation undertaken to try to save the animal's life. If, however, any other form of operation is decided upon, generally there will be no cover under a policy unless the insurers have agreed to it in writing. An additional premium is often required to extend a policy in this way.

There is normally no cover for intentional slaughter. On occasions, however, insurers will agree to the destruction of an insured animal. They may appoint their own veterinary surgeon and require from him a certificate that destruction is necessary so as to terminate incurable suffering. If it is not possible to contact the insurers in advance, it is essential to obtain a certificate from a qualified veterinary surgeon stating that immediate destruction was imperative for humane reasons and that it would have been morally wrong on this account to wait for the insurers to appoint their own veterinary surgeon. Nevertheless, insurers may well reserve the right to have a postmortem examination carried out by their own veterinary surgeon.

In some cases, it is possible to insure a proportion of the value of a horse or pony if it should suffer an accident and be quite incapable of performing the work expected of it. This insurance is relatively expensive and there can be no claim under it for the death of the insured animal. Only relatively few insurers will extend a conventional policy in this way. Loss due to theft and/or straying is often not covered but can usually be added quite cheaply. Any policy covering the death of a horse or pony stipulates that the owner must provide care and attention. Usually a policy states that a veterinary surgeon must be called in without delay in the event of any illness, lameness, accident or injury. Insurers usually insist that they must be notified of any illness or accident. They may appoint their own veterinary surgeon to look after their interests. Although it is a condition that an owner must call in a veterinary surgeon, a policy covering the risk of death does not include his fees. However, arrangements can often be made for them to be covered; the insurance usually applies in excess of a relatively low figure in respect of each incident.

In view of the liability for damages which can be incurred by keeping a horse or pony, it is important to make sure that there is an adequate indemnity for liability under an existing policy, or to make special arrangements.

A variety of other insurances are available to meet specific needs. 'No foal no fee' insurance will cover fees and expenses if a mare proves barren or fails to produce a live foal. This insurance is expensive and usually insurers will give cover only where they have proved the breeding records of the mare for the previous five years. Stallion infertility insurance can be arranged. If there should be total infertility of a stallion during the first season at stud, with no mares in foal, the insurers will pay the full value of the stallion. Cover may also be available for the loss which will be incurred if a stallion should prove to be wholly and permanently infertile, or incapable of serving mares as a result of an accidental external injury or sickness or disease. JG

The insurance protection available in the United States, and the terms and conditions upon which insurance is issued, are substantially the same in the United States and in the United Kingdom.

While no statistics are readily available, it appears that insurance against death is carried for the most part only with respect to animals of considerable value and by very few owners of 'pleasure' horses. Horse owners in the United States are more concerned with protection against liability for damages. An example of this is the requirement imposed by the United States Pony Clubs, Inc. that each club, as a condition of membership, must carry approved liability insurance to protect the officers and other persons involved in club activities against liability arising in connection with such activities. The U.S.P.C. also strongly urges, though it does not require, accident insurance to protect the members of the club in the event of accident or injury resulting from participation in Pony Club activities. Most riding establishments carry liability insurance, and such insurance on a day-to-day basis is commonly provided for specific sporting events.

Many horse shows and similar sporting events whose receipts will be materially reduced by rain take out rain insurance, which provides for the payment of a stated sum if the rainfall exceeds an agreed minimum amount.

Apart from insurance related specifically to the ownership and use of horses, many persons carry broad liability and accident protection, which includes coverage for horse-related liability or accidents. Such liability policies frequently are written to cover all animals owned by the insured. The insured should examine carefully the terms of his policy to determine the extent of the coverage. In the event of a horse-related accident, many insurance companies terminate at once further coverage of such accidents as a condition to the continuation of the policy. WSF

International Horse Show, London

see Royal International Horse Show

Interval Training

Interval training, a system of conditioning horses to get the best performances of speed or endurance, is based on the observed fact that animal physique adapts itself, if given time, to feasible demands made upon it. An effort that would seriously injure a horse when not fit is easily within its capacity when it is fit. A limiting factor in the effort that an unconditioned physique can sustain is the ability of the circulatory and respiratory systems to remove the accumulation of lactic and carbonic acids that results from the combustion of glucose to produce heat and energy. When an excess of these acids accumulates in the muscle fibres, the muscles lose their elasticity and tire.

Interval Training improves respiration, circulation, and removal of waste products, by exposing the physique progressively to the stress of limited effort, alternated with rest. This effort creates a demand for oxygen which, without risk of injury, stimulates the lungs and heart to supply it. Athletically efficient muscle can be developed by short gallops at speeds just below the maximum of which the horse is safely capable, regularly repeated, with intervals of walking between—the number of gallops being progressively increased. Each gallop should be started after a period of walking while the blood is still slightly short of oxygen before the horse has fully recovered from the previous gallop—to stimulate the lungs and heart to supply the shortfall of oxygen.

The horse at rest normally has a pulse of 32–40. Warmed up at the canter it might have a pulse of up to 65; after a short sharp gallop a pulse of 100, or more. If it falls from 100 to 65 in two minutes, the interval of walking before its next gallop should be 75 per cent of two minutes, so that the horse starts its next gallop before its pulse comes down to 65 while its blood is still slightly short of oxygen. During the first months, the trainer gradually increases the speed of each series of gallops until the horse reaches the speed required for the trial in view. Concurrently, he improves the horse's stamina by galloping it over a constant distance (around 700 yd or 640 m) a fixed number of times (not more than five on any one day) with a constant interval of walking (1½ min) between each gallop, and perhaps twice a week. In the following weeks the trainer prepares the horse to stay the whole distance required, and at this increased speed, by progressively increasing the number of gallops on any one day (from five to even nine)—still over 700 yards or more and with a fixed interval of walking between gallops. To develop mainly speed the trainer uses a few short gallops at increasing speeds; to develop stamina, he relies on an increasing number of slightly longer gallops at slower speeds. GNJ

Reference: G. N. Jackson, *Effective Horsemanship,* London, 1967.

Iomud

The Russian Iomud was originally bred as a riding horse, but has been adapted to more varied work. Healthy and adaptable, and well-suited to mountain roads, it has been used as a cavalry horse, field horse, and racehorse over long distances. Stallions, noted for their strength and endurance, are

Iomud

widely used in breeding. Iomuds have covered 1,600 m (1 mile) in 1 min 52 sec, 45 km (28 miles) in 1 hr 39 min, 4,300 km (2,672 miles) in 84 days over difficult terrain, 360 km (224 miles) in 3 days, 800 km (497 miles) in 7 days.

Showing Arab characteristics, the Iomud has a thin, medium-sized head with a straight or concave profile, small lively ears, large wide-set eyes, wide and delicate nostrils. The neck is long and straight, withers high, back straight, loins wide and sound. The croup is straight or moderately lowered, and very occasionally sloping. The shoulder is long and sloping, the chest quite deep. Legs are thin with well-pronounced tendons; hoofs are medium-sized, with strong bone. The coat is fine and soft, with sparse mane and tail. The overall constitution is slender and muscular. Grey is the most usual colour, followed by bay and chestnut.

Average height at withers for stallions is 15·1 hands (1·52 m), for mares 14·3½ hands (1·50 m); bone below the knee for stallions 7½ in (19·0 cm), for mares 7¼ in (18·3 cm).

The Iomud has a fast walk, a short trot and canter. When racing, it stretches its head and neck down and forward and has a light, balanced gallop. Its home is Central Asia, in the Turkmen country, south of the foothills of Kopet-Daga and the valley of Atreka, and north of Tashauzsky. See also U.S.S.R. WOF

Iran see Persia

Ireland

The Irish horse, so firmly established in the racing and the hunting fields, owes its basic quality of bone formation to the native terrain containing large deposits of lime salts and phosphates.

The first major introduction of imported equine blood to the indigenous pony of the country came with the Celtic invasion of about 500 B.C. One of the distinctive qualities of these ponies of the Celts was their great adaptability, and their adjustment to almost every kind of climate and living conditions has caused the variations of conformation and character of the different breeds. Thus, while the ponies retained by their masters in their progress westwards remained unchanged until they reached the western seaboard of Ireland and could go no further, those shed on the way acquired fresh characteristics and became crossed over the centuries with other imported animals.

The combined Celtic and indigenous ponies that found sanctuary in the mountainous region of the far west were preserved in their purity for hundreds of years, until the wreck of the Spanish Armada and the foundering of many vessels on the rocky coast with the subsequent escape of the ANDALUSIAN horses aboard eventually diluted them. In 1900 their descendants were discovered by Professor Ewart of Edinburgh and his recommendations as to future selective breeding are responsible for the well-known Connemara pony of today (see also Mountain and Moorland).

Of other developments, the one that has most influenced modern breeding is the Irish Draught Horse. This was an all-purpose animal, used by the country people for ploughing, transport and riding, and bred to no specific pattern. However, across the years a certain uniformity has become established and certain crossings, notably the CLYDESDALE, have become apparent, although it has remained conspicuously clean-legged. The Irish Draught mare, crossed now with the THOROUGHBRED, produces the kind of horse that is sought by sportsmen all over the world.

At home in Ireland there is no lack of sporting fixtures where the quality of the native equine product can be judged to the best advantage. Few would question, for instance, the statement that the best hunting in the world is to be found there, over an unrivalled variety of terrain and fences.

The point-to-point is a natural derivative of the hunt, arranged by the Hunt Committee. The earliest record of the sport in Ireland is held by the O'Brien family of Dromoland who possess a document describing a cross-country race in County Cork between a Mr O'Callaghan and a Mr Blake, who raced from Buttevant to St Leger, using the steeple of St Leger church as a landmark (see Steeplechasing).

In flat racing, too, Ireland ranks among the leaders and since Hard Ridden won the Epsom DERBY in 1958 it has become a major racing country. Within a decade Ballymoss, Ragusa and Santa Claus were champions of their year in England and in 1964–7 Irish trainers saddled the winners of seven of the twenty English classic races.

Polo is played in Phoenix Park, Dublin, and has had many enthusiasts since the first game was played in Ireland in 1872.

Flapper meetings, or unlicensed race meetings, are held throughout the country during the summer, as are horse shows. The Dublin Horse Show is internationally famous and in recent years the Westport one, held in the grounds of Lord Sligo's house, has become a major event. For Connemaras the highlight of the year is the Clifden Show in August.

The less professional rider has also plenty of opportunity for enjoyment as pony trekking is becoming increasingly popular in Ireland, the most prominent centres being in Counties Wicklow and Kerry, the Killaloe area and Rostrevor at the foothills of the Mourne Mountains. See also Hunting, Show Jumping, Flat Racing, Point-to-Point. SK

Irish Draught Horse see Hunter, Ireland

Ireland. An Irish draught stallion in Kerry

Irish Martingale see Martingales

Isabellas ('Royal Hanoverian Creams')

Named after the Spanish Queen Isabella (1451–1504), this breed of small cream coach horse with *café-au-lait* manes and tails from the Royal Celle Stud of Hanover was used in British royal processions from the reign of George I to that of George V, when they were replaced by WINDSOR GREYS. They have no connection with PALOMINOS. LFB

Italian Heavy Draught Horse see Italy

Italian Military Riding School see Passo Corese

Italy

It appears that in antiquity Italy had no native horses or ponies. All the equine stock, however long ago, was brought into the peninsula from Spain, Persia, and probably from Noricum, where there was already an ancient breed of mountain horse known as the Abellinum to the Romans and represented today by the HAFLINGER and the AVELIGNESE, the mountain horse of Avellino.

For the past two thousand years, Italian horse breeding has held an important position, especially in the Middle Ages and the seventeenth century, when it reached a peak. The breeds originated from Spanish, Barb and Arabian horses; the most important, the Neapolitan, was bred near Naples and Sorrento, where the Italian School of Horsemanship was founded. The Neapolitan was regarded as the finest horse possible to express the art of riding. It had high action and extremely strong hocks; although the shape of the head and profile is not considered a good point today, then it was much admired. There were other characteristics which would not have pleased a modern judge of horses. The Neapolitan influenced the breeding of both the KLADRUBER and the LIPIZZANER.

The classical regions where the horse was mostly used and still is are Sicily, Sardinia, Tuscany and the Po valley. Nowadays the highest concentrations per square kilometre are found around Milan, Turin and Naples. In the province of Maremma, there are several studs, some breeding on semi-feral lines with crosses to English horses. Italy imported over 300 Norfolk Roadsters between 1867 and 1881. In Sicily and Sardinia some good animals are bred. These are lighter mountain horses with crosses of ARAB and BARB blood, used for work and also for riding. Italy also produces some of the best THOROUGHBREDS the world has known; the original stock was of course imported from Great Britain. The stud of the late Federico Tesio was famous. Other studs breed first-class Trotters, largely based on Russian stock imported in the late eighteenth century and subsequently also from the United States. Trotting races are as popular as flat racing. Other breeds are the warmblood Calabrese, the Salerno and the heavy, very dark liver chestnut Italian Heavy Draught Horse. In 1969, when the census was taken, there was a horse population of 310,000 in Italy. DMG

J

Jaf see Persian Horse, Plateau Persian

Jalfan (Jilfan) a strain of ARAB. See also Persian Arab

Jamaica see West Indies

Japan

Horses have played an important part in Japanese history from early times. Equitation and archery were mentioned as the most important *bujutsu* (military arts) for *samurai* (warriors) to master among the many other arts including those of fencing, judo, wrestling, using the spear, etc. However, horses used to be much smaller than those of present-day Japan. Twelfth-century novels described the average height of the horse as 1·40–1·45 m (13·3–14·1 hands); horses of 1·50 m (14·3 hands) were few in number and those over 1·55 m (15·1 hands) were considered exceptional. Equitation too in the early days was quite different from that of today as emphasis was placed on fighting on horseback. Two Japanese generals famous for cavalry warfare were Yoshitsune Minamoto (twelfth century) and Nobnaga Oda (sixteenth century), each of whom commanded his compact cavalry himself, attacked his enemy from the rear and won.

Since the seventeenth century, when Japan became one nation and internal wars ceased, cavalry has been used more for ceremonial occasions than for fighting. At the end of the nineteenth century European equitation was introduced. *Yabusame,* classical Japanese equitation, has survived only as a Shinto ceremony in which fully-armed *samurai* gallop, shooting arrows at a target.

From the end of the nineteenth century, Japanese horses have been gradually improved by imports from abroad. There are still a few pure Japanese horses such as the Dosanko of Hokkaido, the Kiso horse of the central part of the main island and the wild horse of southern Kyushu; they are all really ponies in size. At the beginning of the twentieth century, horseracing in the European style began in Japan, also the breeding of Thoroughbreds. From the end of the nineteenth century to 1945, equitation in Japan

Japan. *Top left:* A Tsushima stallion
Centre left: A Hokkaido stallion
Bottom left: A Kiso horse

was virtually that of the Imperial Army. Yoshifuru Akiyama, a Japanese army officer trained in France, built up the cavalry and surprised the world by defeating the Cossack cavalry, then considered the most powerful in the world, during the Russo-Japanese war (1904–5). From that victory Japanese equitation advanced: for example, Captain Nishi won the Show-Jumping gold medal at the 1932 Olympic Games.

After 1945 the Japanese Army was abolished and the number of horses in Japan dropped sharply to a third or a quarter of the prewar 1,500,000. Equitation declined sharply too, but it has gradually recovered and is now supported mainly by civilian riding clubs of various kinds and college and university clubs. There are still only some 2,000 horses formally registered with the Japanese Equestrian Federation. At present C.H.Is are not held in Japan. C.H.Ns or their equivalent are held several times a year. However, riding has recently been booming and it is hoped that there will be rapid advancement based on popular support before long. HA

Jaripeo see Mounted Games, Mexico

Jennet (Hinny, Bardot) the offspring of a horse sire and a female ass. Compare Mule, see Hybrids

Jilfan a strain of ARAB. See also Persian Arab

Jockey Club

No precise information exists as to how, when and why the British Jockey Club was founded; the first intimation of its existence came in 1752. The word 'jockey' then meant an owner as much as a rider, as many owners of the period rode their own horses in races. The word 'club', too, was used in a wider sense and then merely denoted any group of friends that met at regular intervals to discuss matters of common interest.

There are no grounds for believing that the Jockey Club was founded with the intention of becoming the governing body in English racing. The original intention was probably no more than to promote good fellowship among racing and horse-breeding gentlemen of the north and south. However, as the early members of the Club included some of the richest and most influential men in the country, it swiftly began to acquire authority and prestige.

The Club first used to meet at the Star and Garter in Pall Mall and also at other London premises including The Corner, Hyde Park, where Mr Tattersall provided a room and a cook. Eventually the Club's London headquarters were established with their agents, Messrs Weatherby, in Old Bond Street. Naturally the Club also wished a place in which to foregather at Newmarket and in 1752 a plot of land was obtained. On that plot a building known as the Coffee Room was erected; the room of that name in the present Jockey Club building stands on its site.

It was not until 1835 that an official list of Jockey Club members was published but the Club began to exercise authority long before that: every competitive sport needs clearly defined rules and a governing body to ensure that those rules are maintained; the Jockey Club was ideally constituted to be that body. The most important member of the Jockey Club in its early days was Sir Charles Bunbury, the 'perpetual president' and 'first dictator' of the English Turf. It was he who handled the notorious scandal of a horse called Escape, owned by the Prince of Wales (later Georve IV) and allegedly dishonestly ridden by the Prince's jockey, Sam Chifney.

In 1827 the Duke of Portland, by action for trespass against Mr S. Hawkins at Cambridge Assizes, established the right of the Jockey Club to warn an individual off Newmarket Heath, evidence being produced by the Jockey Club that it had been invested with the proprietorship of these grounds as tenant of the Duke since 1753. The two outstanding personalities of the Club in the nineteenth century were Lord George Bentinck and Admiral Henry John Rous. Bentinck, aristocratic, aloof, often arrogant and sometimes open to criticism in the way he conducted his own racing affairs, brought order, discipline, punctuality and a higher standard of integrity into racing. Rous, shrewd, vigorous, straightforward and at times impulsive, revised and modernized the rules, greatly improved the Club's financial position and established a new standard of competence in handicapping. He forms the link between the haphazard racing of the old days and the highly organized sport of today.

The Jockey Club is perhaps something of of an anachronism today, being self-perpetuating and composed for the most part of members drawn from a narrow section of society. It has at times been accused of ultra-conservatism, of a disinclination to accept modern attitudes, and of outdated methods in the application of disciplinary measures. By and large, though, the Jockey Club has served racing well and in recent years it has made strenuous efforts to improve its relationship with the public and the press, and to modernize the organization of the sport. In General Sir Randle Feilden it has a Senior Steward worthy to rank with Admiral Rous. The danger to its future existence lies less in public resentment of its composition or conduct, than in the difficulty experienced nowadays in finding men of first-rate ability who have the means and the leisure to devote their time to unpaid service in the cause of the Turf. For the United States Jockey Club, see Flat Racing. RM

Jomud see Iomud

Jousting see Chivalry

Jumping see Show Jumping, Horse Trials, etc

Jumps

Cross-country: obstacles used in cross-country competitions — HUNTER TRIALS and HORSE TRIALS (THREE-DAY and ONE-DAY EVENTS) — should represent as far as possible fences met in various hunting countries: posts-and-rails, hedges, stiles, open ditches, oxers, double oxers, and open water (either to be jumped over or into). As a cross-country course contains anything from 20 jumps (novice one-day event) to over 30 (three-day event), as much variety as possible should be provided, by using walls, gates, banks, bullfinches, hay racks, water troughs, lamb creeps, hen coops, straw bales, timber wagons, pit props (upright), log piles (table fences), logs or fallen trees, garden seats, churn stands (table fences), parallel bars, triple bars, piano steps, ditches, trakeners, tiger traps, drop fences, and combinations of the above. Most of them speak for themselves, but some need explaining. A *trakener* is a post-and-rails set in the bottom of a dry ditch, the top bar being higher than the level of the lips of the ditch. A *tiger trap* is a spread jump consisting of a series of poles sloping up to a centre pole and sloping down on the other side; the effect is similar to that of a double oxer, only it looks different. The *piano step* is a series of two or three hops, either using the natural ground or cutting steps in a slope, and, if necessary, revetting them; it can be taken up or down. A regular obstacle in three-day events is the *coffin*, receiving its somewhat grim name when it was first introduced at the Badminton Three-Day Event of 1949. It is a combination of two post-and-rail fences in front of and behind a slope into an open ditch or stream and up again. For some reason horses dislike this obstacle.

The ingenuity of the course builder welds the types of fence and materials available into sundry combinations, often requiring a choice of action on the part of the rider. Two hedges or rails coming to a V in the corner of a field, for example, can either be taken at the corner as one big but chancy jump or safely in two bites but losing time. Or a bank and post-and-rails can be combined with a big drop on the far side, as in the 'Normandy Bank' at Badminton in 1970. Dimensions of cross-country obstacles are strictly controlled by the F.E.I. for international competitions, and by national federations. The maximum height everywhere is 3 ft 11 in (1·20 m). The maximum spread for water jumps where there is no height element is 12 ft (4 m); and for normal spread fences (oxers, parallel bars, etc.) 6 ft 6 in (1·80 m) at the highest point, 8 ft (2·80 m) at the base. Minimum dimensions in one-day events (novice) are 3 ft 6 in, 9 ft, 4 ft and 7 ft (1, 2·75, 1·22 and 2·1 m) respectively.

Show jumping: originally regarded as a projection of the hunting field into the arena, show jumping has now developed into a separate sport with its own technique, and the fences, although derived from hunting obstacles, rails, walls, stiles, oxers and so on, are now completely stylized. They are either upright or spread. Uprights include post-and-rails, gate, wall, and their many variations. Spread jumps are of four basic types: parallel, staircase, pyramid and water. Most of the components of these fences, except the water jump, are uprights in some combination or other. The parallel has two upright posts-and-rails, the same height for a true parallel bars, the first lower than the second for a more usual, and easier, jump. The staircase is three posts-and-rails in graduated heights: the triple bar. The pyramid is basically a double oxer: a high centre upright fence with lower elements, which can be rails, brush or wall, on either side. The pyramid can also be a single unit, like a chicken coop or an African pig pen. The decorated, painted, flower-bedecked fences seen in international show rings are sophisticated versions of the basic types. Jumps must be made to look solid, and be solid, but all elements, poles, bricks, etc. must be able to fall down when hit reasonably hard. The cross poles are usually hollow, except natural (rustic) poles; and the woods used are mainly larch, Douglas fir, and, for 'rustics', silver birch. The cups to support the poles are metal, deep enough to allow the pole to lie snugly, not liable to fall at the lightest touch but requiring a good rap. The width of a fence should be 12–15 ft (3·50–4.50 m). Most fences are given a *ground line*, that is a pole on or not far off

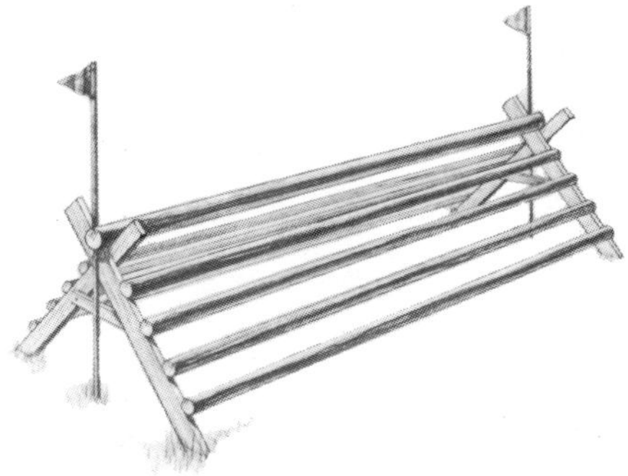

A tiger trap

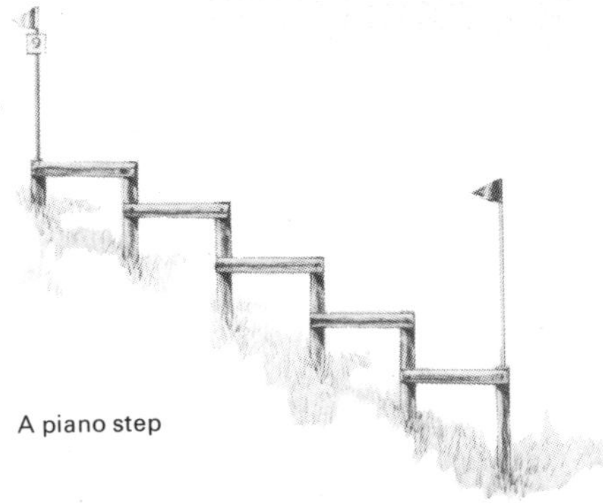

A piano step

A bullfinch

Jumps. *Above:* Three typical cross-country jumps
Below: Bridget Parker (Great Britain), riding Cornish Gold, comes through the open water in the cross-country section of the 1972 Olympic Three-Day Event.

the ground to guide the horse in the take-off. For normal competitions the starting height of the jumps is 4 ft 3 in (1·30 m), and the spread 4 ft (1·22 m) (5 ft or 1·52 m for a triple bar). In championships and international competitions jumps usually start at 4 ft 6 in–5 ft 3 in (1·37–1·60 m), rising higher for jumps-off. Water jumps are 13–15 ft (4–4·50 m). For a *puissance* type of competition the fences start at about 5 ft (1·52 m) and finish in the final round at 6–7 ft (1·83–2·13 m). The 'Irish' bank is occasionally found on permanent show grounds, such as Balls Bridge, Dublin or Hickstead, Sussex. It is not popular with many show jumpers on the ground that faults can only be incurred for a refusal or a fall. The 'Derby' bank, first introduced at the Hamburg Show Jumping 'DERBY', is in essence a 10 ft 'slide', followed immediately by a post-and-rails. See also Course Building. CEGH

Reference: Lord Hugh Russell, *Notes on Cross-country Course Design and Fence Construction,* London, 1964.
Lt-Col C. E. G. Hope, *The Horse Trials Story,* London, 1969.
Col Sir Michael Ansell, *Show Jumping Obstacles and Courses,* London, 1951.
Col. J. Talbot-Ponsonby, *Harmony in Horsemanship*, London, 1964.

Junior International Equestrian Events

Junior Events are primarily training grounds for riders for adult international competitions. The Junior European Championships held annually in any European country at the discretion of the FÉDÉRATION ÉQUESTRE INTERNATIONALE are, like their adult counterparts, split into two separate forms of competition: COMBINED TRAINING, or THREE-DAY EVENTING, administered in the United Kingdom by the Combined Training Committee of the BRITISH HORSE SOCIETY, and SHOW JUMPING administered by the BRITISH SHOW JUMPING ASSOCIATION. Other nations have comparable organizations. Their rules for domestic competitions vary but for international events they all subscribe to the rules of the F.E.I.

For both forms of competition a series of international trials is held annually throughout the United Kingdom. There are no restrictions on the grading of horses and ponies brought before the selectors but riders must be in their 14th–18th year in the year of the Championships, a regulation binding upon all competing nations. It is emphasized by the B.H.S. and the B.S.J.A. that the size and difficulty of courses are such that younger riders and ponies are unlikely to meet the standard required for team selection.

Except for the host nation, which in Combined Training is permitted more than two individuals, each nation is allowed to take up to six horses and riders from which a team of four is selected with the marks of the best three counting for team placings. The remaining two combinations from each nation compete as individuals. The individual European Championship can be won by any individual combination of horse and rider whether a team member or not, so for every competitor there exists a chance of glory. DR

Jutland

The heavy horse of Denmark, first mentioned specifically in the twelfth century, existed at least from the Viking period, which began about A.D. 800. Like the

Jutland. *Below:* Horses of Jutland type, ridden by Danish warriors invading England in the eleventh century
Bottom: Jutland stallion Bjarne

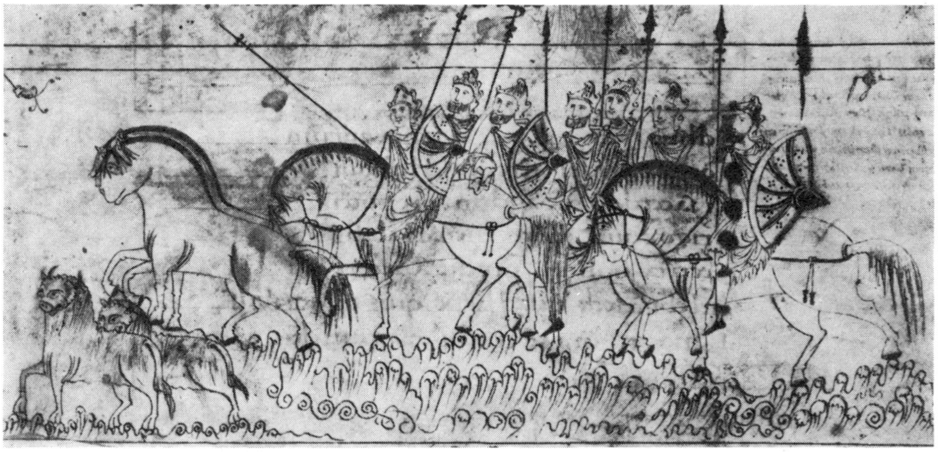

BOULONNAIS and other heavy breeds of the English Channel and North Sea coastal region, the Jutland horse is very deep in the body with a pronounced dip at the saddle. Measurement from elbow to withers greatly exceeds that from hoof to elbow, as length from breast to rump exceeds height at the withers. Prevailing colours are sorrel, chestnut, and roan. Foundation stock of the SUFFOLK PUNCH visibly owes something to the Jutland horse, imported during the Danish invasions. Anglo-Saxon pictures of invaders driving away prisoners show the former mounted on horses of Jutland type. In 1955 the stud-book showed 405 studs of mares, totalling 14,416, and there were then 2,563 stallions. In the middle of the nineteenth century YORKSHIRE COACH HORSE blood was introduced but proved unsuitable (predictably, since the prime use was for work on the land); since then the influence of such sires as Oppenheim, who stood from 1862 to 1869, has been quite bred out. See also Denmark. AD

K

Kabardin

This Russian mountain breed does not show much speed in races but has extremely high fertility and longevity, and the mares give excellent milk. Kabardins are used for riding and as pack horses. Noted for their surefootedness, they can traverse steep mountain tracks at dizzying heights and ford stormy mountain streams under saddle. There are three distinct types: the Eastern light horse, the basic type, and the thick type. All three have a rather long back and characteristic large, straight ears, with tapered tips pointed inwards. They are often sickle-hocked. Hoofs are regularly formed with powerful bone. Bay is the most common colour, but dark brown, black and grey occur occasionally.

Average height at withers for stallions is 15·0½ hands (1·53 m), for mares 14·2½ hands (1·49 m); bone below the knee for stallions 7½ in (19·35 cm), for mares 7¼ in (18·4 cm).

Opinion differs regarding the Kabardin's origin. What is certain is that it somehow resulted from crossing horses of the southern group (PERSIAN, KARABAKH, ARAB) with Nogaisty and eastern steppe horses. The breed developed in the Caucasus. See U.S.S.R. WOF

Karabair

The Karabair is an ancient breed from the Central Asian mountains, a small riding horse, substantial, with good bone, and usually of a coarse, thick-set build. Well adapted to work in a hot, dry climate, it is useful under saddle and in harness. It has been successfully used to improve the KAZAKH and KIRGIZ strains, and is now bred primarily in Uzbekistan. It is a fast, beautiful Eastern-type horse. There are three distinct types: the riding and harness horse, massive and quiet; the riding horse, thick-set, with a powerful constitution but proportions more suitable to riding; the harness horse, with a longer and very strong back. In all three types, the head is medium-sized, with a straight profile and rather 'breedy' appearance. Ears are medium or long, wide apart, mobile; eyes are large, prominent and lively. The neck is massive and short, the withers medium high. The back is short and straight, with good loins; the chest is wide, the croup powerful and wide. Legs have good bone and strong tendons. The hind legs often have close-set hocks and a tendency to sickle hocks. Hoofs are not large, but upright and strong. The coat is delicate and the contours of the blood-vessels are well-developed and clearly visible. The mane and tail are sparse. Grey is the predominant colour, followed by bay and chestnut. Average height at withers for stallions is 15 hands (1·52 m), for mares 14·2 hands (1·47 m); bone below the knee for stallions is 7¾ in (19·7 cm), for mares 7 in (18·2 cm). Free and light movement is characteristic.

Uzbeks brought the Karabair from Central Asia, and the breed was already well known in the eighteenth century. Arab influence was very important in the nineteenth century, though there were also crosses with Mongol, Kirgiz and Turkmen horses. See also U.S.S.R. WOF

Karabakh

This ancient Russian breed, probably the same as the Iranian KARADAGH, was well-known as early as the fourth century A.D. It has greatly influenced the DON, KABARDIN and other southern breeds, and is found in the mountains of Karabakh in Azerbaidzhan. A horse of great presence and substance, it is feared to be dying out at present, but Karabakhs have been successfully imported into England, notably by H.M. the Queen. It is usually 14·1–14·3 hands (1·45–1·50 m) high. The head is small, light, and fine, with large prominent eyes and a prominent forehead. The torso is relatively massive and the legs clean and strong. The coat is fine and tender, and the general appearance elegant. The movement is calm and pleasant and the temperament energetic. Chestnut, bay, grey and dun are the prevailing colours. See also U.S.S.R. WOF

Above left: **Kabardin**

Below left: **Karabair**

Below: **Karabakh**

Bottom: **Kazakh**

Karadagh

The Karadagh is from the province of Azerbaijan in the northwest of Iran, across the border from the Russian Azerbaidzhan and is probably the same animal as the KARABAKH. Once bred in great numbers, it is now represented by a very few specimens. Ranging in height from 14·2–15·2 (1·47–1·57 m), with a fine head, large eye, moderately arched neck, strong quarters, short back and long legs, it excels at mountain and carriage work. Colours are bay, chestnut and dun with a pronounced metallic sheen to the coat. LF

Karst see Austria

Kasansky, Kazansky see Viatka

Kathiawari Pony see India and Pakistan

Kazakh

The Russian Kazakh horse resembles the Mongolian (see China) and occurs in two types: one is massive and called the Dzhabye, the other lighter and called Adayevsky. The Adayevsky type is used for riding in Central Asia. In long-distance races, the Kazakh has covered 53 km (33 miles) in 1 hr 58 min and 106 km (66 miles) in 4 hr 30 min. It is a good cavalry horse, especially when crossed with the DON, BUDYONNY, AKHAL TEKE, or others of this type. The mares give good milk which is used for kumiss. Average height at withers for the eastern Kazakh is 12·3 hands (1·30 m), for the western Kazakh 13·2 hands (1·36 m), for the Adayevsky 13·2½ hands (1·39 m); bone below the knee for the eastern Kazakh is 6½ in (16·7 cm), for the western Kazakh 6¾ in (17·4 cm), for the Adayevsky 7 in (17·7 cm). See also U.S.S.R., Cossacks. WOF

Kehailan, Kehilan variants of Kuhaylan, a strain of ARAB

Kentucky Derby

The Kentucky Derby, the most famous Thoroughbred race in the United States, for three-year-olds carrying 126 lb (57 kg) over 1¼ miles (2·0 km), has been run in the spring at Churchill Downs in Louisville, Kentucky, since 1875. Ever since its inauguration (originally over a distance of 1½ miles or 2·4 km, reduced in 1896), 'The Derby' has attracted leading American three-year-olds and some from overseas as well, not only because of its prestige, but also because it is the first of the events that lead to the coveted Triple Crown (see Classic Races).

The fastest time to date, as well as the track record for the distance, was set by Northern Dancer, the Canadian champion, on 2 May 1964, in 2:0. The runner-up for speed honours in the Derby is Decidedly, with a winning time in 1962 of 2:00 2/5. See also Flat Racing. MAS

Kerry see Mountain and Moorland

Khersan see Persian Arab

Khis-Koubou see Mounted Games

Kiang see Ass, Asiatic Wild

Kirgiz see China, New Kirgiz, Horse Breeding under U.S.S.R.

Kiso Horse see Japan

Kladrub Horse see Czechoslovakia

Klepper a word similar to 'nag', indicating not a breed but a type of light draught horse used in Estonia. See Toric. DMG

Knabstrup

This Danish breed of spotted horses dating from the Napoleonic Wars is said no longer to exist as such, having become very much mixed to preserve the spotted colouring. A few have been imported into Britain where they are used generally for circus work. DMG

Reference: Graf Lehndorff, *Ein Leben mit Pferden,* 1956.

Knight see Chivalry, Warfare, Accoutrements

Kohdban see Arab under U.S.S.R.

Koheilan, Kohaili variants of Kuhaylan, a strain of ARAB

Kokburi see Mounted Games

Konik

The Konik (small horse) is a native of Poland. In the pure form it closely resembles the TARPAN, the wild horse of the steppe, from which it is descended. Although there is a tendency to sickle hocks, the Konik has good conformation, is good-tempered and willing. The PANJE pony is very similar. Both these types of pony are found throughout the countries of north-eastern Europe. DMG

Korush see Persian Arab

Kuhaylan (Kuhailan, Kuheilan, Koheilan, Kehilan, Kochlani, Kohaili, Kehailan, etc.) a strain of ARAB. See also Czechoslovakia, Persian Arab, U.S.S.R.

Kulan (Dzigetai) see Ass, Asiatic Wild

Kurdistan Plateau Persian Jaf strain see Persian Horse, Plateau Persian

Kentucky Derby Winners

Year	Winner	Year	Winner	Year	Winner
1875	Aristides	1908	Stone Street	1941	Whirlaway
1876	Vagrant	1909	Wintergreen	1942	Shut Out
1877	Baden Baden	1910	Donau	1943	Count Fleet
1878	Day Star	1911	Meridian	1944	Pensive
1879	Lord Murphy	1912	Worth	1945	Hoop Jr
1880	Fonso	1913	Donerail	1946	Assault
1881	Hindoo	1914	Old Rosebud	1947	Jet Pilot
1882	Apollo	1915	Regret	1948	Citation
1883	Leonatus	1916	George Smith	1949	Ponder
1884	Buchanan	1917	Omar Khayyam (England)	1950	Middleground
1885	Joe Cotton	1918	Exterminator	1951	Count Turf
1886	Ben Ali	1919	Sir Barton	1952	Hill Gail
1887	Montrose	1920	Paul Jones	1953	Dark Star
1888	Macbeth	1921	Behave Yourself	1954	Determine
1889	Spokane	1922	Morvich	1955	Swaps
1890	Riley	1923	Zev	1956	Needles
1891	Kingman	1924	Black Gold	1957	Iron Liege
1892	Azra	1925	Flying Ebony	1958	Tim Tam
1893	Lookout	1926	Bubbling Over	1959	Tomy Lee (England)
1894	Chant	1927	Whiskery	1960	Venetian Way
1895	Halma	1928	Reigh Count	1961	Carry Back
1896	Ben Brush	1929	Clyde Van Dusen	1962	Decidedly
1897	Typhoon II	1930	Gallant Fox	1963	Châteaugay
1898	Plaudit	1931	Twenty Grand	1964	Northern Dancer
1899	Manuel	1932	Burgoo King	1965	Lucky Debonair
1900	Lieut Gibson	1933	Brokers Tip	1966	Kauai King
1901	His Eminence	1934	Cavalcade	1967	Proud Clarion
1902	Alan-a-Dale	1935	Omaha	1968	Forward Pass
1903	Judge Himes	1936	Bold Venture	1969	Majestic Prince
1904	Elwood	1937	War Admiral	1970	Dust Commander
1905	Agile	1938	Lawrin	1971	Canonero II
1906	Sir Huon	1939	Johnstown	1972	Riva Ridge
1907	Pink Star	1940	Gallahadion	1973	

Above: **Kentucky Derby.** The first turn in the 1971 Kentucky Derby, won by Canonero II

Above left: **Knabstrub.** Stallion Mala

Below: **Konik**

Below, centre: **Kulan.** This Asiatic wild ass of North China, Mongolia and southern Siberia has a dorsal stripe but no shoulder or leg stripes.

Bottom: **Kustanair**

Kustanair

The Russian Kustanair is a general-purpose horse, suitable for riding and draught work. Stallions are widely used for crossbreeding. A massive, short-legged horse with splendid bone, the Kustanair produces an excellent, harmonious animal when crossed with the English THOROUGHBRED or the DON or KAZAKH. The head is medium-sized, the neck long, not very high-set, sometimes with a prominent Adam's apple. The withers are high, the line of the back very good, the croup often short and drooping, the chest deep and wide. Legs have good bone and pronounced tendons, and the hoofs are not large but very strong. There are three distinct types: the steppe horse, riding horse, and basic type. The steppe horse is massive, with evidence of the influence of Kazakh and Don blood, and is a very adaptable, fertile horse (the mares giving much milk), but not as fast as horses of the riding type. The riding type is more like the Thoroughbred, more difficult to feed and keep in condition, less useful for range life, but when properly fed is well adapted to riding. The basic type is a compromise between the other two types. Bay is the most common colour, and then chestnut. Average height at withers for stallions is 15·2 hands (1·57 m), for mares 15·0$\frac{1}{2}$ hands (1·53 m); bone below the knee for stallions 8 in (20·3 cm), for mares 7$\frac{3}{4}$ in (19·4 cm).

The walk, trot, and canter are true and cover much ground. One stallion of the breed covered 50 km (31 miles) in 1 hr 35 min; another covered 100 km (62 miles) in 4 hr 1 min. In races, the records set by the breed are 1,200 m ($\frac{3}{4}$ mile) in 1 min 16·4 sec, and 7,000 m (4$\frac{1}{3}$ miles) in 8 min 51 sec.

The Kustanair is bred in the Kustanaisk, Akmolinsk and Kokchetavsk regions of Kazakhstan. Northwest Kazakhstan has long been noted for its herds of massive horses. The harsh, bitter climate, with snowy winters and hot, dry summers influenced the development of small (13 hands or 1·32 m) but unusually hardy horses. Until the 1880s, no attempts were made to improve the breed; thereafter it began to be used for cavalry, which stimulated more care in stud organization. In 1886 the first official studs were formed; foals were corn fed and stabled in winter, and turned out in droves on the steppes in summer. As a result, the height increased to 14·0$\frac{1}{2}$ hands (1·43 m) by the turn of the century. Further improvements were sought, and from 1920 the Kustanair was crossed with other breeds including English Thoroughbreds. See also U.S.S.R. WOF

Kuznetsky see Horse Breeding under U.S.S.R.

La Broue, Salomon, de

This noted seventeenth-century French horseman and author was a Gascon and a pupil of the celebrated Italian *maestro*, Pignatelli. The exact dates of his birth and death have not been established. Although less famous than PLUVINEL, he preceded him in advocating kindness and persuasion in the schooling of horses in lieu of the harsh methods of coercion then in vogue. He became *Grand Écuyer* to the Duc d'Éperon in 1593, but it was not until his old age that he began to write books on equitation, the best known being *Traités d'Équitation* and *Cavalarice François*, the latter published in three volumes in 1602 and running into several editions. LFB

La Guérinière, François Robichon de

This famous French horseman (1688–1751) was equerry to King Louis XIV at the Tuileries, where he was instructor in the classical seat in which the rider's body is held upright, the small of the back well braced, seat well down in the saddle with fairly long leathers, the lower leg slightly behind the vertical. On the training of the

Below, far right: **La Guérinière.** François Robichon de la Guérinière, Écuyer du Roi, in 1769

horse he wrote that the object of dressage was, in systematic work, to make the horse calm, light and obedient, so that it might be pleasant in its movements and comfortable for the rider. This, La Guérinière taught, was as true for the horse for the chase and for the military charger as for the school horse. He and his immediate successors practised *manège* or school riding as an art and spectacle for its own sake, and held that the same principles of riding and schooling applied to outdoor sport as well. However, as hunting in France at that time involved practically no jumping, he gives almost no advice on this subject. The development of jumping was to follow in later years as better horses were bred for racing and hunting.

Nonetheless, La Guérinière was probably the greatest of the eighteenth-century masters, and had more influence on the development of school riding and training than any other single person. He was the first to develop the shoulder-in as it is known today, the first to use the counter-canter, and the first to teach his horses to do the flying change of leg.

Under his influence the great French School of Versailles (see France) reached its apogee; and his teachings, published in his book *École de Cavalerie* (1733), were adopted as the basis of instruction at the SPANISH RIDING SCHOOL OF VIENNA and continue to this day to be the main source of that school's doctrine. See Horsemanship, History of. LFB

Lameness. *Below:* The left fore leg (medial aspect)
Bottom: The left stifle joint (anterior view)

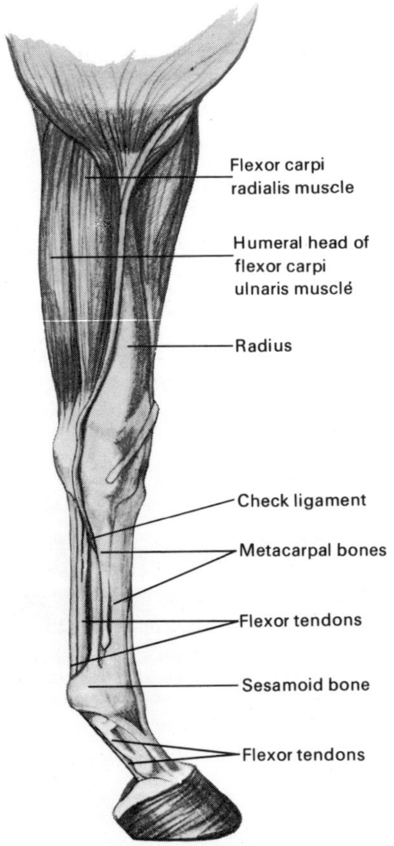

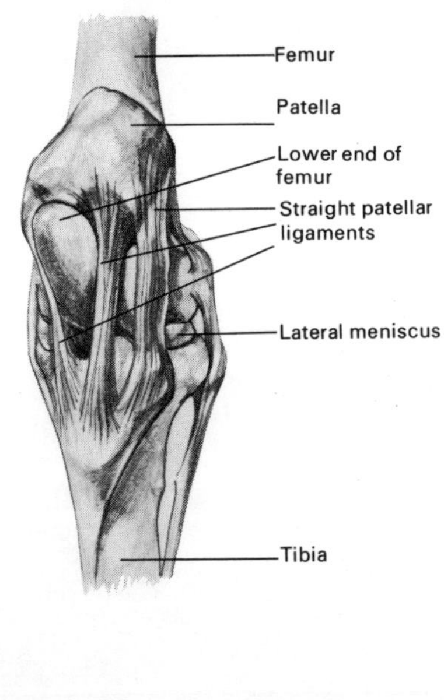

Lameness

In most instances lameness is a manifestation of pain due to disease or injury. It can be so acute, as in cases of fracture, that the animal is reluctant to move. Or it may be so slight as almost to defy detection. In determining the lame leg the horse should be trotted in a snaffle at a 'jog trot' on a hard road, preferably with a slight incline. Free movement of the head must be permitted. Front-leg lameness is diagnosed by observing a nodding action of the animal's head as it is trotted towards one. The head falls as the sound foot comes to the ground and rises with the lame one. In hind-leg lameness the horse is trotted away from the observer, and attention is focused on the disparity of movement of the quarters. The quarter tends to sink on the sound side at each step and rise when the lame foot comes to the ground. In general terms front-leg lameness is often associated with the foot region and in the hind leg with the hock. In all cases of lameness, fore or hind, examination of the foot is essential. CF

Laminitis (Founder)

An inflammation of the sensitive laminae of the pedal bone with exudation and separation of the bone from the hoof wall. The toe of the pedal bone quite often tilts downwards and penetrates the sole of the foot. This may affect front or hind feet or all four at the same time. It is extremely painful in the acute form, common in overfed and underworked ponies and extremely serious when a sequel to womb infection after foaling. CF

Landais Pony see Ponies, French

Latvian Harness Horse

This is a general-purpose harness horse used in farm work, city transport, and sport, under saddle. Rather thick-set, with a well-developed long torso and good bone, the Latvian harness horse has a powerful but harmonious frame, often quite well-fleshed, with well-developed muscles and a deep, wide chest. The head is sturdy, with a straight profile and large eyes. The withers are well-defined, the shoulder bone long and sloping, and the profile of the back is good, though some mares have a tendency to develop a soft back. Tendons are well developed, hoofs strong, but hind legs are sometimes sickle-hocked. Bay, dark brown, black and chestnut are the predominant colours. There are three distinct types: the basic type, the harness type, and a lighter type. The basic type is well proportioned, with good bone and a powerful but hardy conformation; about 85 per cent of the breed are of this type. The harness horse is taller and better fleshed. The lighter horse has softer bone, and resembles a trotter. Average height at the withers for stallions is 15·3½ hands (1·64 m), for mares 15·2½ hands (1·58 m); bone below the knee for stallions 9 in (22·9 cm), for mares 8½ in (21·4 cm).

Movement in general is ample and wide, with a productive walk. The lighter type gallops and jumps well. Latvian harness horses have walked 2 km (1¼ miles) in 13 min 40·7 sec under burdens of 150 kg (331 lb), and trotted 2 km in 4 min 58·6 sec carrying 50 kg (110 lb).

The breed was established in 1952. Before that, Latvian horses of the forest and northern types were well known from the seventeenth century and were often crossed with heavy horses and with Arabs. Horses imported from Germany, Sweden and Lithuania were also crossed with Latvian horses, widely used for transport before the advent of railways. During the second half of the nineteenth century, the breed was improved by the use of Estonian, ARAB, ARDENNES, TRAKEHNER, and THOROUGHBRED blood; five OLDENBURG stallions were also particularly influential. Latvian Harness stallions are used in the north for riding and harness sport and in the south for draught work. See also U.S.S.R. WOF

Law, Horse and the

Numerous aspects of the law in the United Kingdom affect horses; only the barest summary of English law can be given here. **Riding Establishments:** the law has been altered principally by the RIDING ESTABLISHMENTS ACT of 1970. Riding establishments must be licensed by their local authority. Only establishments which can satisfy the authority that they can comply with the strict conditions now required by the 1964 and 1970 Acts will be granted a licence, which however may be a renewable provisional one for three months in the first instance.

Horses' accommodation and forage, bedding, stable equipment and saddlery must be suitable; there must be sufficient grass at all times available for horses maintained

Latvian Harness Horse

at grass; the horses must be adequately supplied with food, drink and bedding; they must be adequately groomed, exercised and rested. There must be adequate precautions against fire and appropriate provision must be made for the protection and extricating of horses in such an emergency. The name, address and telephone number of the licence holder or other responsible person, must be kept posted up in a prominent position on the outside of the premises, together with instructions as to action to be taken in the event of fire.

It is also necessary to satisfy the authority that horses to be used for instruction are fit for such purposes; that the feet of the horses will be kept properly trimmed and that their shoes will be properly fitted and in good condition; that veterinary first aid equipment and medicines will be provided and maintained on the premises; that a horse found on inspection of the premises to be in need of veterinary attention must not be returned to work until the licence owner has obtained and lodged a fitness certificate.

Horses aged three years or under and mares heavy with foal or who have foaled within the previous three years may not be hired out or used for instruction.

Rides must be supervised by a responsible person not less than 16 years of age, unless the licence holder is satisfied that the rider is competent to ride without supervision.

A licence will only be granted to a suitable and qualified person over the age of 18 years of either sex, though it may be granted to the Secretary or President of a Company, or other body, provided that the conditions of suitability and qualifications are satisfied. The business, however, must not be left at any time in charge of a person under 16 years of age.

The licence holder is required to be insured himself against liability for injury occasioned to a rider, and to insure his riders against liability for injuries occasioned by them to third persons. This insurance is distinct from the further compulsory insurances required to be taken out by *employers* against bodily injury or disease suffered by their employees in the course of their work, and against injury or damage suffered by them as the result of the use of defective equipment.

A riding establishment may be inspected from time to time and a licence may be revoked if the inspector's report indicates that it is not being satisfactorily conducted.

Planning Consent: Town Planning consent will generally be required for use of land as a riding establishment.

Negligence: a riding establishment may be liable for negligences both to the public and to their riders. Rides *must* now be under the supervision of, and must be accompanied by, a responsible person. Care must be taken in the selection of the horses alotted to each rider, whose competence must be judged strictly with the utmost caution.

Employment: contracts of employment, and indeed the whole relationship between employer and employee, are now governed by the new Industrial Relationships Act 1971.

Partnerships: many riding establishments are run as partnerships; a number of problems can arise as to the rights of the respective partners, competition by ex-partners and the taxation of the partnership.

Leasing of Buildings: where the premises on which the establishment is carried on are leased, the application of the Landlord and Tenant Acts, now amended by the Law of Property Act 1969, with regard to the rights of the landlord and tenant in relation to such matters as security of tenure, the rent and other terms of the new lease, compensation for the refusal of a new lease on the ground of the landlord requiring the premises for demolition or alterations or for his own purposes, is likely to arise.

The position of tenants who are partners or companies is the subject of special provisions in the Acts. Even gallops may be the subject of a 'business tenancy'.

Taxation: horses used for the purposes of a *riding establishment* may, in the writer's view, be regarded as 'Plant' for which allowances for depreciation might be claimed. This is a question, however, which may be debated. Horses owned for private purposes, or as a hobby, or for sport, are capital assets. Profits on their sale, however, do not attract any liability to Capital Gains Tax. Horses which are the subject of a trading activity, such as horses at stud, or forming part of the trading stock of their owners, stand on a different footing: if they are transferred out of stock, to racing, for instance, they will be treated in the trading accounts as having been disposed of at their market value.

Sporting Events: competitors at sporting meetings such as point-to-points, gymkhanas, race meetings and the like in general will not be held responsible in law for accidents to spectators. The latter are to be regarded as accepting the risks inherent in events of this kind. Organizers of such events, however, are not in so happy a position. They must show that they have taken all reasonable precautions for the protection of the public, by erecting rope or other proper barriers and the like, and by exercising some sort of control over spectators who wander across the proper boundaries and thus expose themselves and the riders and horses, too, to the risk of injury. Special care should be taken to block all escape exits, particularly where the events are held in fields.

Trade Descriptions Act, 1968: trade descriptions may apply to horses. The misdescription of even the age of a horse has been held to be an offence under the Act.

With regard to horses and all animals in general, the Act makes it an offence to apply a false description as to sex, breed, cross, fertility or soundness, and in the case of semen, the identity and characteristics of the animal from which it was taken.

Negligence of Riders: riders may be liable for negligence, not only towards other riders but also to members of the public. Galloping past a horse which is proceeding even at a walking pace, is liable to make it bolt. Such action would be crass negligence. So also would be the leading of a horse while on the highway without the interposition of the leader between the horse and the traffic. The British Horse Society has published a set of general rules on this subject with which every rider should acquaint himself.

Straying Horses: the Common Law rule was that the owner or keeper of a horse would not be liable for any harm or damage caused by an animal straying on to a highway, not even if he was negligent in allowing it to escape. This rule, however, has now been abolished by the Animals Act 1971 which makes important alterations to the law in relation to liability for injury and damage caused by horses. The straying of a horse *onto the highway* as distinct from a third person's land, will now be an actionable breach of duty, rendering the owner or the keeper liable for any damage caused thereby. The question as to whether or not there has been such a breach will depend on a consideration of several factors. Liability for damage to land or to any property on it, caused by a horse straying from another person's land, is imposed on the person who, at the time, has *possession* of it. TJS

Each of the fifty separates states of the United States establishes, either by statute or judicial decision, the law applicable within the state to matters relating to animals. Although in many respects the applicable law is more or less the same throughout most of the United States, differences do exist which reflect the customs, manner of life and historical background of the various sections of this large country. An example is the relative freedom from liability for straying animals in the West and Southwest where grazing on an open range is the normal way of raising stock, also in many western states the registration of brands and the branding of stock including horses to evidence ownership and written evidence of ownership is required if the horse is transported by van or trailer. The following general comments are applicable in most sections of the country.

No state has so far enacted any statute comparable to the British Riding Establishments Act of 1970, although the advisability of enacting such a law has been discussed in some of the eastern states. Apparently no state has as yet imposed licensing requirements either with respect to the conduct of a riding establishment or the giving of instruction in riding.

In most urban areas, zoning restrictions prohibit or at least require approval for the setting up of any riding establishment, or even the stabling of horses in residential areas.

The general laws of negligence apply to the maintenance, care and use of horses. The liability of the owner for damage caused by a straying animal is in most states based on negligence, but what constitutes negligence is regarded quite differently in different sections of the United States. In most areas, laws which are enforced with widely varying degrees of severity may be asserted where animals are abused or neglected.

Liability of competitors and of organizers of sporting events is much the same in the United States as in England, except that the standards of due care vary considerably. For example, due care in conducting a rodeo in the West or Southwest would probably be measured by less strict standards than would be considered reasonable in conducting a horse show, a race meeting or a combined training event in the eastern states. See also Insurance, Highway. WSF

Levade see Airs, Classical

Liberty Horses see Circus, Horses in the

Libyan

The Libyan is the horse of North Africa although, like the ARAB, there are many types and local 'breeds'. It seems probable that the Libyan or Barb, formerly the native horse of Barbary, has its origin in the Numidian horse but was crossed with Oriental horses during the various Arab invasions of North Africa, of which the first took place in A.D. 700 when 75,000 horsemen are said to have appeared. Count Wrangel, a noted nineteenth-century horseman and writer, considered the ancestor of the Numidian to be the prehistoric African horse. Apart from Arab invasions, there was constant traffic through Egypt with Syria, so that the Barb is related to breeds found there. The 'purest' are in Morocco and have a characteristic concave head, pronounced fore hand with sloping croup, stamina and speed over short distances. The Barb also contributed to the ancestry of the THOROUGHBRED. See Africa. DMG

Limousin see France

Lipizzaner

During the 700 years of Moorish occupation of Spain, horse breeding was developed to a very high standard. The Moors introduced ARAB and BARB stallions and bred them with ANDALUSIAN mares to produce a proud and elegant horse with graceful movements and great stamina, much appreciated at the royal courts of Europe and eventually bred

Right: **Libyan.** This Moroccan Barb has a concave head, rounded chest, flat shoulder and sloping croup.
Below right: A Moroccan Arab

Bottom right: **Lipizzaner.** Horses of the Lipizzaner breed grazing in Hungary

in countries other than Spain. Emperor Maximilian II of Austria began to breed Spanish horses in Kladrub (Czechoslovakia) in 1562 for the Imperial court in Vienna and his brother Archduke Charles did the same in 1580 in Lipizza near Trieste. The foals born in Lipizza were named Lipizzaners. In 1918 the part of the Imperial stud farm allotted to the republic of Austria was transferred to the government stud farm of Piber in the province of Styria, but the name of the breed remained Lipizzaner.

There are six lines of Lipizzaner stallions and 18 families of mares. The stallions' lines are: Pluto, Maestoso, Favory, Conversano, Neapolitano and Siglavy. The stallions have double names, the first being that of their sire's line (for instance, Neapolitano) the second that of their mother (for instance, Santuzza). Characteristics of the Lipizzaner are harmonious conformation, elastic paces with a high knee action, intelligence, docility and sweetness of character. Its body is well muscled with a strong neck, slender legs and small feet. The back is somewhat long and the withers little marked. The head is fine with large dark eyes, small ears and wide nostrils. The coat is sleek and mane and tail silky and abundant. Originally of all colours, grey now prevails. There are very rarely bays. The foals are born dark brown or grey and turn white between their third and seventh year. The average life expectancy is 24–26 years. The Lipizzaner is a small horse, 14·2–15·2 hands (1·47–1·57 m).

The SPANISH RIDING SCHOOL OF VIENNA trains stallions from Piber only and those that have proved themselves at the School return to Piber as sires. AP

Literature, Horse in

The horse has been an inspiration in all forms of art, not least in literature. In English literature, its treatment depends very much on the status of the horse at the time of writing. There are many romantic descriptions in medieval chivalrous tales. But Chaucer in his *Canterbury Tales*, for instance, describes horses in practical terms: a horse can be 'lean as a rake' or a 'stot'; even an 'ambler' is scarcely complimentary. In Chaucer's time the horse was purely functional, a beast of burden and taken for granted. By Shakespeare's time, however, the beautiful Arab had been imported into Britain, and all over Continental Europe the nobility were establishing magnificent riding centres where talented riding masters taught *haute école*. The horse had become socially important. Thus Shakespeare in his first major work, *Venus and Adonis,* describes the stallion:

> Sometimes he trots, as if he told the steps,
> With gentle majesty and modest pride;
> Anon he rears upright, curvets and leaps,
> As who should say, 'Lo, thus my strength
> is tried . . .'

Round hoof'd, short-jointed, fetlocks
shag and long,
Broad breast, full eye, small head, and
nostril wide,
High crest, short ears, straight legs and
passing strong,
Thin mane, thick tail, broad buttock,
tender hide...
Venus and Adonis, 11.277–280, 295–298

In different vein, however, Shakespeare describes the horses of the exhausted English army:

...and their poor jades
Lob down their heads, dropping the hides
and hips,
The gum down-roping from their pale-dead
eyes,
And in their pale dull mouths the gimmel
bit
Lies foul with chew'd grass, still and
motionless...
King Henry V, IV, ii, 46

But Shakespeare was a psychologist, too, as is shown in the little scene between Richard II and the groom when the latter clumsily describes how Bolingbroke rode Richard's favourite horse at his coronation. Richard would like to hear that the horse refused to go for his new, usurping master but, no, he went 'so proudly as if he disdained the ground'. This is the last straw for Richard:

That jade hath eat bread from my royal
hand;
This hand hath made him proud with
clapping him.
Would he not stumble? would he not fall
down,
Since pride must have a fall, and break
the neck
Of that proud man that did usurp his
back?
King Richard II, V, v, 85–9

Literature. This illustration from a fifteenth-century manuscript about the life of Richard II shows the victorious Bolingbroke being welcomed by Londoners.

How many children have not felt just this bitterness when a beloved pony has passed to someone else and gone equally well, even better perhaps, for the new owner?

The eighteenth century for the most part paid scant attention to the horse. It was a peaceful age and the horse was very much taken for granted. It was nothing to be particularly excited about since it was the only means of transport and stood in every stable. In the following century, however, the pressures were on: the Industrial Revolution arrived. The horse was no longer a means of leisurely transport, it was a beast of burden. There was a hard, practical, unromantic streak in writing about horses. Even the great Robert Smith Surtees whose Jorrocks stories endeared him to horsemen seldom describes a horse with any sense of affection or admiration. His horses are 'rakes', 'unwilling', 'you ugly beast'.

Dickens is little better. His knowledge of the horse, unlike that of Surtees, was limited to the fact that it was a necessity of life. 'Orses and dorgs is some men's fancy' but not Uriah Heep's (*David Copperfield*). The description of Mr Pickwick's drive to Dingley Dell with Mr Snodgrass and Mr Tupman in *Pickwick Papers* is anything but flattering to the horse, which displayed various peculiarities 'highly interesting to a bystander, but by no means equally amusing to anyone seated behind him'. Nevertheless Dickens showed all the perception of a great writer in the second chapter of *A Tale of Two Cities* where he describes the Dover Mail labouring up the hill in the fog and bitter cold.

There are, of course, many delightful Victorian passages about horses: the description of the runaway in Blackmore's *Lorna Doone* and George Borrow's magnificent cob in *Lavengro*. Particularly interesting is Charles Kingsley's chapter in *Hereward the Wake* about the dealer trying to sell 'the ugliest as well as the swiftest of mares', for Kingsley obviously had a remarkable eye for a horse. Even Lewis Carroll was anything but ignorant of riding. His description of the White Knight in *Through the Looking-Glass* is not only hilariously funny but extremely penetrating.

In the twentieth century the horse is a luxury and so, as in Shakespeare's time, writing about it is flattering and even inspiring but not, for the most part, especially distinguished from a literary point of view. This is, of course, because the twentieth-century poet or painter generally has little contact with horses. Nevertheless in the last fifty years there has been quite a pleasing output of equestrian literature. John Masefield, the Poet Laureate, gave a magnificent description of the favourite in *Right Royal* (1926). In his own genre Will Ogilvie, the New Zealander, is without equal. His enjoyable poems, 'The Clydesdales' for example, have given pleasure to thousands.

Today there is an almost limitless output but few books are destined for the immortality of Anna Sewell's *Black Beauty*, written nearly a hundred years ago. Its perennial popularity should not blind the reader to its excellence. It is well written, has great feeling, is surprisingly full of practical knowledge (it is the only work of an invalid) and certainly played an important part in influencing people to treat their horses more humanely. DW

Lithuanian Heavy Horse

This calm but energetic Russian breed is used for city transport and farm work. It is noted for its hard constitution and free paces. There are two types, the basic and the lighter. The former has a massive stature, a long, deep and wide torso, and a wide, bifurcated drooping croup. The musculature is good and the legs are short but with rather round bone and some feather. The temperament of the basic Lithuanian heavy horse is so calm that it is sometimes lazy. The lighter type, however, shows the exterior influence of the Zhmudky horse (*Equus samogitarius*); it is taller than the basic type but has a smaller circumference of chest and bone. Medium high, with a light head and wide forehead, this type has a comparatively short torso, a round rib-cage and a long croup which is not very bifurcated or rounded. The legs are hard and strong, with small fetlocks; the mane is long and thick. This type is easy to feed and has good paces. Both types occasionally result in excessively massive horses closer to the Belgian and German heavy horses. In approximately 8·3 per cent of the breed, over-spreading occurs in the fore legs; in 7·6 per cent bandy-legs; in 32 per cent sickle hocks. Stallions of five years and older weigh 610–820 kg (1,345–1,808 lb), averaging 706·2 kg (1,556 lb), mares 530–815 kg (1,168–1,797 lb), averaging 646 kg (1,424 lb). Average height at withers for stallions is 15·2$\frac{1}{2}$ hands (1·58 m), for mares 15·0$\frac{1}{2}$ hands (1·54 m); bone below the knee for stallions 9$\frac{1}{2}$ in (24·4 cm), for mares 8$\frac{3}{4}$ in (22·3 cm). Chestnut is the predominant colour. They may also be bay, roan, black or grey. The walk is fast and covers ground well; the trot is good and free. Lithuanian heavy horses have covered 2,000 m (1$\frac{1}{4}$ miles) in 5 min 24 sec and have carried 300 kg (661 lb) 1,281·2 m (1,402 yd).

Lithuania has long been famous for its tiny but strong and hardy Zhmudky horses, first mentioned by Lissitsiasa in 1554.

Lithuanian Heavy Horse. Stallion Valetas

During the second half of the nineteenth century, studs were organized, breeding from ARAB, ARDENNES, BRABANT, SHIRE, and English THOROUGHBRED stallions. After World War I, Swedish horses, particularly Swedish Ardennes, were widely used. See also U.S.S.R. WOF

Livery Companies see City Livery Companies

Lofoten Pony see Mountain and Moorland Ponies

Loire Horse see Percheron (French)

Lokai

The Russian Lokai is a typical saddle and packhorse, widely used for transport and

Lokai. This Russian breed is widely used in the mountains of Tadzhikstan, in this case for hawking.

work in the mountainous parts of Tadzhikstan, where it is bred in the central and southwestern districts and the western and eastern river valleys. The head varies between fine and coarse; it is similar to that of the Mongolian horse, and sometimes has Arab contours. The profile is straight or hook-nosed; the short head is wide at the forehead. The neck is straight, medium long, sometimes with a protruding Adam's apple. The withers are not high, the back short and straight, the loins wide, short and sound. The croup is usually drooping and sloped. The chest is well developed, the ribs tight and long. Legs have good bone and good joints. Common faults are a short thigh, spreading of the fore legs, closeness of the hocks, and sickle-hocks. The pasterns are sloping, the hoofs medium erect and sound. Mane and tail are sparse. Bay is the most common colour, followed by grey, chestnut, and rarely black or dun. Average height at withers for stallions is 14·1½ hands (1·46 m), for mares 14 hands (1·42 m); bone below the knee for stallions 7½ in (19·0 cm), for mares 7 in (17·9 cm).

Lokai horses move freely at the gallop and walk, but the trot is not well developed as it is not often used in mountainous country. In flat races, the Lokai is generally slower than the KARABAIR: 2-year-olds have covered 1,500 m (1 mile) in 1 min 52 sec, and 3-year-olds have covered 2,400 m (1½ miles) in 2 min 59 sec. Carrying a rider of 65–75 kg (143·3 lb or 10 stone 3 lb–165·34 lb or 11 stone 8 lb), the Lokai can cover 60–80 km (37–50 miles) a day in the mountains, maintaining a speed of 6–7 km (3¾–4¼ miles) an hour over steep rises and drops and on narrow cliff-side tracks.

Like the Karabair, the Lokai can be traced back to the Uzbeks; the Lokai tribe of Uzbeks developed the Lokai horse in the sixteenth century when they came from the northern shore of the Aral Sea. These horses were small, but they were improved by crossbreeding with Argamats and later with IOMUD, Karabair and ARAB stock. The Lokai was used for the game of kop-kopi (see U.S.S.R.), which required stamina, courage and strength. Nowadays, the breed is usually kept pure by inbreeding, but a small proportion of the mares are crossed with TERSKY, Arab, and THOROUGHBRED stallions. See also U.S.S.R. WOF

Long-Distance Riding

Great Britain: the inception of long-distance riding in Great Britain was due to the initiative of the *Sunday Telegraph* newspaper which organized the first Golden Horseshoe Long-Distance Ride over 50 miles of Exmoor country in September 1965. At that time there was little experience in Britain of techniques of training and of competing in such events. Some competitors drew on the reports of overseas competitions such as the U.S. Tevis Cup Ride; many based their plans on their experiences in activities such as foxhunting and usually underestimated the difficulties.

This first ride demonstrated that with intelligent training and suitable horses this activity was well within the scope of the average horseman; many competitors turned in good average times approaching 10 mph over 50 miles of difficult terrain. In the following years there was a rapid development of interest and enthusiasm for this new type of competition. Inevitably problems arose through excessive demands by inexperienced competitors on unfit and unsuitable horses. The adage that there is nothing a horse can do that a Thoroughbred horse cannot do better became patently obvious. The lightly-framed athletic type of Thoroughbred or Arab became the obvious choice of mount to the exclusion of the heavyweight or cob type. In particular, Arabs and partbred Arabs have figured prominently in the lists of award winners.

For the protection and wellbeing of both horse and rider the BRITISH HORSE SOCIETY enforces strict standards of veterinary control at all stages of these competitions; great emphasis is laid on the satisfactory condition and fitness of the horse after completing a long-distance ride. This has eliminated excessive demands on the horse and the risk of the ride being treated purely as a race against time. In recent years a competition has evolved requiring a ride of 50 miles on the first day and then, subject to passing the fitness checks, a ride of 25 miles on the next morning. In order to win a Gold Award an average speed of 9 mph is required on both days together with full veterinary marks. The primary objective is to train and condition a horse to be capable of competing in this contest, which usually takes place in September. Training of both horse and rider occupies several months during the summer, building up to a peak of 3–4 hours riding a day as the climax approaches.

It is now necessary for competitors taking part in the Golden Horseshoe Ride to qualify over a one-day course of approximately 45 miles. This helps both horse and rider to become fit and ready for the main event and takes place during the spring or summer. The Golden Horseshoe Ride itself has evolved an atmosphere and camaraderie of its own. Competitors from all parts of the country join together in three days of mutual interest and shared competition. This competition also creates fellowship between horse and rider. The long period of training and the many hours spent with the horse as sole companion tend to produce a much closer understanding between horse and rider. The meticulous and successful attention to every detail of exercise, feeding and shoeing, work and rest can in itself be a rewarding experience. LC

United States: endurance riding in the United States started in 1919 when the U.S. Cavalry set up tests to compare the quality of Arabian with Thoroughbred horses for use as remounts. Each horse and rider had to cover 300 miles, averaging 60 miles a day for five days and carrying weights from 200 to 245 lb (90·72–111·13 kg). Everybody connected with these rides learned much about the conditioning, feeding, riding and care of horses on forced marches.

The annual Vermont One-Hundred Mile Three-Day Competitive Trail Ride was started to perpetuate the knowledge thus gained. In the western United States the N.A.T.R.C. (North American Trail Ride Conference) set up a series of rides based on the Vermont event but with shorter distances of 20–30 miles for one or two days to be covered in 6½ to 7 hours' riding time, plus a lunch break. Basically, these rides provide recreation and promote interest in the care of the horse rather than test endurance. The awards for first to sixth place are given for horsemanship, which is fundamentally the riding of the horse on the trail, and care after the ride. A rule peculiar to N.A.T.R.C. demands that all horses be tied, generally in a large arena, from 10 p.m. until the 8 a.m. veterinary check and cannot be moved or even touched during the night. This is to circumvent the use of exercise or massage to overcome stiffness and swelling.

Riders finishing early are eliminated and there is a time penalty of one point a minute over the maximum time with elimination after 30 minutes. Horses are judged on condition, soundness, manners and way of going. Hidden judges watch from the trail to observe these points. Condition is based upon the recovery of the pulse and respiration after a climb, on the horse's willingness to eat (checked by the judges during the evening) and by signs of dehydration and the quality of the sweat. Horses are penalized for sore backs, heat bumps, stiffness, filling in the legs, and nicks and cuts generally attributed to tiredness or poor gaits.

In the eastern United States there are six major 'One Hundred Miles In Three Days' rides that cover 40, 40 and 20 miles a day. The 40 miles are ridden in 6½ to 7 hours and the 20 miles in 2¾ to 3¼ hours. Most competitive trail rides are divided into several divisions: lightweight, middleweight and heavyweight, also junior and novice, the last covering a maximum of 20 miles. Other awards are given for breeds and breed types.

Endurance rides differ from competitive trail rides in that they generally cover 50 to 100 miles in one day with a maximum time limit but no minimum. There is an award for the first horse to cross the finish line and for the horse in best condition among the first ten to finish. All others who finish within the allowed time receive a completion award which is usually a belt buckle or a pin. Unlike the competitive trail rider, an endurance rider can dismount and lead his horse, and the winning riders invariably lead and run down the steeper grades and many also tail up hill.

The 'One Hundred Mile, One Horse, One Rider, One Day Endurance' rides started in 1955 when Wendell Robie, with four other riders, set out to prove that the modern horse is as tough as the mounts that carried the mail on the old Pony Express Route. They rode from Tahoe City, Nevada, to Auburn, California, following the same steep and hazardous trail over the Sierra Nevada Mountains that the Wells Fargo Express riders used. This event has been repeated each subsequent year and is now known as the Western States Trail Ride (often referred to as the Tevis Cup Ride). It is considered the toughest ride in the country with a total aggregate descent of 15,250 feet (4,680 m) and a climb of 9,500 feet (2,900 m) leading through snow and cold winds at Squaw Pass and then into 100-degree heat in El Dorado Canyon. Approximately 40 per cent of the contestants are eliminated each year and the percentage of women who finish regularly exceeds that of men. All but two of the winning horses (one Mustang, one Thoroughbred cross) have been Arabians.

There are three one-hour required stops with veterinary examinations and a 30-minute veterinary check at the 55-mile point, which is after a long difficult climb. At the one-hour stops the horses are check-

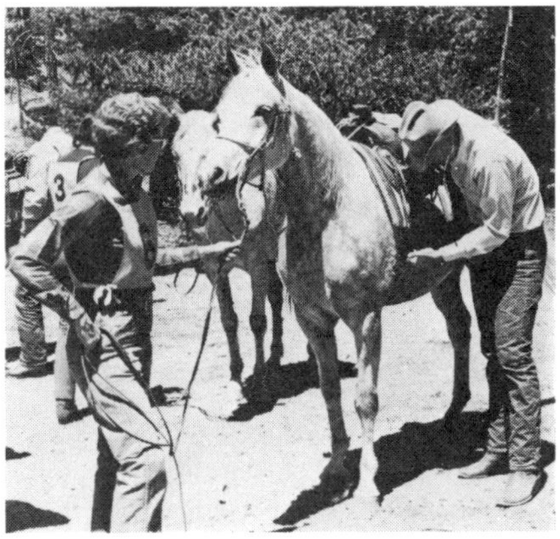

Long-Distance Riding. *Above:* A horse is examined at a veterinary checkpoint on a Western endurance ride.
Below: British horses and riders soon after the start of the first Golden Horseshoe ride across Exmoor, September 1965

ed by vets immediately upon arrival for pulse and respiration and again after 30 minutes. If the horses have not recovered to a pulse rate of 70 or less, they are not allowed to continue. Temperature recordings were discontinued three years ago because of the time involved. The Tevis Ride now limits entries to approximately 175 riders. The record winning time in 1968 was 11 hr 18 min. The Haggin Cup (best condition award) is given to one of the first ten horses. All riders who finish within the 24-hour time limit are awarded the famous silver and gold buckle.

The popularity of endurance riding has increased tremendously since 1968. There are over thirty 50- and 100-mile endurance rides in the United States now, with from 50 to 200 competitors in each one. LTJ

Reference: Wentworth and Linda Tellington, *Endurance and Competitive Trail Riding Manual,* California, 1966.
Albert W. Harris, *The Blood of the Arab,* Englewood, Colorado, 1941.

Long Reining

Long reining is a form of unmounted training by driving the horse on two extra long reins. The objects are to break in and mouth a young horse or pony, or to re-school a spoiled one. The advantages are to work the horse without weight on him and to school the horse before he is ever mounted.

Schooling horses from the ground is a very old form of training. The masters of the sixteenth-century Neapolitan school are known to have used a form of long reins. There are several different methods, the best known the British and the Viennese. There are also Danish and French methods. In the British method, the reins go from the bridle or cavesson through the stirrup irons and along by the horse's hocks. In the method used by the SPANISH RIDING SCHOOL OF VIENNA the horse wears no surcingle; two extra long bridle reins are held by the trainer, who walks at the horse's quarters. This is to show off fully trained horses, whereas other methods are used to train unschooled horses. The Danish method, akin to the Neapolitan one, is probably the most refined for schooling the young horse. Here the reins go through terrets on a roller or driving pad, the terrets placed high up near the withers; the reins do not go round the quarters, but come directly back to the trainer's hands, thus giving a very sensitive feel through the reins with the horse's mouth. All dressage movements can be taught through this method. In the French method a collar is used as well as a surcingle, in order to keep the horse's neck well raised. See also Tackle, Breaking. SS

Ludus Troiae see Mounted Games

Lundy Island

There is no long-standing tradition of breeding horses on Lundy, an island in the Bristol Channel, but like all islands, it offers certain advantages to the horse breeder. The only fences needed are those round the standing crops. The grazing in general is good, enriched by the manure of seabirds, and the climate equable. The mares may wander at will but the danger does not exist, as it would on mainland common grazings, of their being covered by a scrub colt from the next parish. For the same reason a chosen stallion introduced to the island will very soon stamp his type on all the progeny. Inbreeding is the only danger but with a good foundation sire this is not altogether undesirable. The type bred at present is a dun-coloured pony of medium size, about 13 hands (1·32 m). AD

Lunge, Riding on the

The practice of riding on the lunge is used as an exercise to train the rider and particularly to correct and strengthen his position in the saddle, improve his balance and develop a seat independent of both reins and stirrup irons.

The novice or complete beginner is often introduced to riding by this method. The advantages of beginning the instruction on the lunge are considerable. As long as the horse is well-schooled in the exercise and quiet and entirely obedient to the trainer's voice, the latter can concentrate on placing his pupil in the correct position without the pupil having to think about controlling his horse in any way. The fact that the horse is connected directly to the trainer by means of the lunge rein and is under his control encourages the pupil's confidence and consequent relaxation.

Since the object is to improve the rider's seat and balance, the latter being furthered by the horse working on the circle rather than on a straight line, the rider sits without reins and without stirrups to encourage him to ride and maintain his balance without their assistance. To help the pupil to maintain his balance, he is instructed to hold the front arch of his saddle with his *outside hand*, i.e. right on the circle left and *vice versa.* If the inside hand were employed it would tend to cause the trunk to be inclined too far inwards. Working without stirrups helps the rider to stretch downwards with the thigh, improving the security and effectiveness of the seat by bringing the seat bones deeper into the saddle. The hand resting on the front arch may be used to pull the rider towards the pommel, placing his seat centrally in the saddle, should a tendency to slip towards the rear become evident. The first lessons are at the walk; with the addition of stirrup irons, the rising trot can be taught. Once the rider is secure at both walk and trot without irons, cantering can be commenced; it is also possible to introduce instruction on the simple leg aids.

Work on the lunge is essential in the training of the beginner; it is also very useful for the more advanced rider. All riders may develop individual faults in posture and these are most easily corrected on the lunge under the guidance of an experienced instructor. EHE

Lungeing

Lunge work varies in form with the purpose and stage of training. Early on, when the only purpose is to win the inexperienced horse's trust, teach it to obey the voice – precious aid in subsequent lessons under the saddle – and develop its muscles without encumbering it with the rider's weight, the line is fastened to the front ring of a simple cavesson and the work takes place on a large circle, to both reins. It includes walk, trot, halt; rarely, and only by the time the trainer may be sure it will not disrupt the calm, the canter. The trainer also lunges in this way when schooling over fences and when exercising a horse temporarily unfit to ride.

When the time comes to teach the horse to accept and keep contact with the bit, side reins and snaffle are introduced. The reins must be even and long enough to sustain the neck as naturally as possible, since they are supposed to teach the horse to balance itself while on the bit, neck stretched forward and arched slightly downward.

Ultimately, a special lunge-line arrangement lets the trainer act directly on the mouth and neck when working toward a *horse in hand*, a term signifying a horse relaxing at the jaw in correct head carriage and readiness to obey.

The circle worked should never be too small, the cavesson and other gear should always be properly adjusted and the paces maintained unbroken while the lunge line is kept taut by the horse. JF

Lunge Rein see Tackle, Breaking

Lusitano see Portugal

Madison Square Garden see National Horse Show, New York

Maine Horse see Percheron

Manège an enclosure used for teaching equitation or schooling horses. See Movements

Mangalarga

The Mangalarga (see Brazil) is descended from ALTÉR and ANDALUSIAN stallions crossed with local mares, also descended from horses of Spanish origin. The breed is about a hundred years old. The horses are of elegant appearance and are used in competitions in the south of Brazil. DMG

Mangalarga. In Chile this horse is known as the Caballo Chileño.

Manipur Ponies see India and Pakistan

Mare an adult female horse. CF

Maremmana, Maremma

The Maremmana is the best-known indigenous Italian breed, deriving its name from the lowlands north of Rome where it is bred. This thickset, sturdy, general utility animal is used by the mounted police and more especially by the BUTTERI or mounted herdsmen (cowboys) of the Roman *campagna*. It was, never, as is frequently erroneously stated, trained to jump by either Italian civilians or the now non-existent Italian Cavalry (mechanized after World War II in 1945), probably being confused with the smaller, more active SARDINIAN horses which are on rare occasions seen in the smaller Italian show rings. Today in the hunting field or international events Italians are invariably mounted on Thoroughbred or halfbred Irish and English horses. LFB

Martingales

Martingales include all those devices used to assist or correct the positioning of the horse's head. The two simplest forms are the *standing* and *running*. The former is basically a strap fastened at one end to the girth, then passing through the fore legs to be attached to a plain cavesson noseband at the other. Its purpose is to prevent the horse carrying or throwing its head so high that it becomes out of control. Modern equitational practice tends to regard its use as a substitute for poor training and riding and to hold that it restricts the scope of the horse when jumping large fences, particularly spread ones. The running martingale, having the same object, differs by operating directly on the mouth instead of on the nose: the main strap is divided into two branches at the base of the neck, each ending in a ring through which the rein passes. Adjusted so that the rings are in line with the withers it is relatively harmless but if shortened so that the rein makes an angle between bit and hand it can provide a severe lever action on the mouth. An improved form of running martingale is made with a *pulley* at the point of division, the 'branches' being a cord fitted with rings at either end. Since the cord slides in the pulley as the horse bends its head in the direction of a turn no contrary and restricting pressure is applied to the outside of the mouth as may occur with the ordinary running martingale. Where running martingales are used with a double bridle or a Pelham it is thought logical that it should be attached to the lower (curb) rein to accord with the head lowering action of the latter. A further variation on the running martingale is the old-fashioned Cheshire, in which the branches are fitted with clips instead of rings and fastened directly onto the bit rings. Its use is now largely confined to the more forcible methods of horse breaking or schooling and it is generally held to be inhumane.

More sophisticated versions of the martingale are two schooling devices of French origin known as the *chambon* and the *de Gogue*, both intended to lower the head. Each operates by forming a triangle between the base of the neck, the poll and the mouth and seeks to induce a low head carriage with the nose as the foremost point of the progression. Such an attitude results in the horse moving with tensed and rounded back and encourages the engagement of the hind legs under the body. The *chambon* and its near but less complicated relative the *Continental*, operating against nose and poll, are both used for dismounted training on the lunge, and the de Gogue, the logical extension of the Chambon, can also be used in a variety of arrangements from the saddle, and can be operated by the rider's hand to give an infinite degree of control over the position of the head.

The simplest form of martingale is the *Irish Martingale*, in fact, no martingale at all since it has no effect on the positioning of the head. It comprises a 4-in (10-cm) strip of leather joining two rings through which the rein passes. It assists the directional placing of the rein to a degree but its principal object is to prevent the reins being pulled entirely over the horse's head in the event of a fall. EHE

Marwari see India and Pakistan

Maryland Hunt Cup

One of the oldest, most prestigious and challenging steeplechase events in the United States, the Maryland Hunt Cup has been run annually since 1896 at Glyndon, Maryland, some ten miles from Baltimore, over a permanent course built in natural hunting country.

Often compared to the Aintree GRAND NATIONAL, it is actually quite different, since the fences are solid timber, up to 5 ft 6 in (1·6 m) in height. The only race of its meeting, the Hunt Cup is run through natural hunting country. There is no official betting, no admission charge, no grandstand, and until 1972 there was no purse, a silver trophy being awarded to the winner. Only amateur riders are eligible. It is an important social as well as sporting event. There are far fewer entries than in the Grand National, resulting in a slower pace and little danger of interference. Though it is usually considered a jumping race rather than a running race, with speed secondary to jumping ability, it is worth noting that Jay Trump won both races and Billy Barton, the Maryland winner of 1926, ran second in the 1928 Grand National. MAS

Masuren

Masuria is a land of lakes and forests lying in the heart of East Prussia, formerly a province of Germany, now occupied by Poland. The Masuren horse is bred by Polish stud directors on the same lines as the TRAKEHNER (East Prussian) horse, with extreme care and attention to bloodlines, for the Poles are both great horsemen and horse breeders. There are a number of State studs, formerly in private hands, now breeding Masuren horses. The most important is Liski (Liskien) a former German remount depot near Bartenstein. There are three herds of brood mares containing about 50 mares each, divided by colour, as was done in Trak-

Maryland Hunt Cup Winners

1894	Johnny Miller	1933	Captain Kettle
1895	Sixty	1934	Captain Kettle
1896	Kingsbury	1935	Hotspur 2nd
1897	Little Giant	1936	Inshore
1898	The Squire	1937	Welbourne Jake
1899	Reveller	1938	Blockade
1900	Tom Clark	1939	Blockade
1901	Garry Owen	1940	Blockade
1902	Garry Owen	1941	Coq Bruyère
1903	Princeton	1942	Winton
1904	Landslide	1943–5	No Race
1905	Princeton	1946	Winton
1906	Princeton	1947	Winton
1907	Garry Owen	1948	Peterski
1908	Judge Parker	1949	Pine Pep
1909	Sacandaga	1950	Pine Pep
1910	Sacandaga	1951	Jester's Moon
1911	Pebbles	1952	Pine Pep
1912	Conbe	1953	Third Army
1913	Zarda	1954	Marchized
1914	Rutland	1955	Land's Corner
1915	Talisman	1956	Lancrel
1916	Bourgeois	1957	Ned's Flying
1917	Brosseau	1958	Ned's Flying
1918	Marcellinus	1959	Fluctuate
1919	Chuckatuck	1960	Fluctuate
1920	Oracle II	1961	Simple Samson
1921	Mazarin	1962	Mountain Dew
1922	Oracle II	1963	Jay Trump
1923	Red Bud	1964	Jay Trump
1924	Daybreak	1965	Mountain Dew
1925	Burgoright	1966	Jay Trump
1926	Billy Barton	1967	Mountain Dew
1927	Bon Master	1968	Haffaday
1928	Bon Master	1969	Landing Party
1929	Alligator	1970	Morning Mac
1930	Brose Hover	1971	Landing Party
1931	Soissons	1972	Early Earner
1932	Trouble Maker	1973	

Maryland Hunt Cup. Horses take a solid timber fence in the 1969 steeplechase.

Masuren. Horses at a state stud in Masuria

ehnen: chestnut, bay/brown, and mixed. Masuren stallions stand at stud throughout Poland. They make excellent saddle horses and are used in a variety of competitive events. Some are sold to Switzerland for army remounts. See also Poland. DMG

Meadow Brook
This former centre of American polo is located at Westbury, Long Island, N.Y. The Meadow Brook Club, founded in 1881, was originally organized as a hunt club, which it has always remained. But its world renown derived from its role in polo, particularly as the home of the finest high-goal international polo teams ever mustered in the United States and the scene of the greatest matches ever played there, during the golden age of American polo in the late 1920s and early 1930s. It was at Meadow Brook that the Open, Senior, 20-Goal, and International matches were held, often before tens of thousands of spectators.

Since that brilliant era, polo in the United States has increased in quantity but not in quality. Indoor 'arena polo' has developed while outdoor polo has declined; the headquarters of the Polo Association have moved west to Oak Brook, Illinois. MAS

Mecklenburg
The Mecklenburg horse, with bloodlines similar to those of the HANOVERIAN, can be traced back to the fourteenth century. It was one of the first German breeds to be improved through the introduction of THOROUGHBRED blood at the end of the eighteenth century. Hanover obtained its first Thoroughbred to improve the Hanoverian from Mecklenburg and there has been a constant exchange of breeding material. About 70 per cent of the brood mares and stallions were lost in 1945 as a result of World War II. In 1946 a new start was made in Schwerin, with the object of breeding horses similar to the Hanoverian, and 10,000 mares were registered. In 1956 the number was given as 14,000, of which two-thirds had the same bloodlines as the Hanoverian. Mares are generally owned by small farmers; the German Democratic Republic owns and keeps the stallions in State studs. See also Germany. DMG

Megiddo
A royal mews, built by King Solomon, with stabling for about 450 horses and coach houses for 150 chariots, has been excavated at Megiddo in Israel, which was on the caravan route from Syria to Egypt. 'And Solomon gathered together chariots and horsemen: and he had a thousand and four hundred chariots, and twelve thousand horsemen, whom he bestowed in the cities for chariots, and with the king at Jerusalem.' (I Kings, x, 26). DMG

Melbourne Cup see Flat Racing

Mérens Pony see Ponies, French

Mesopotamia
The first civilized, literate, record-keeping men to use horses were the inhabitants of Mesopotamia. The horse was not indigenous to their country, but the onager (wild ass) was; during the third millennium B.C. they drove and, from the evidence of a single cylinder seal, occasionally rode the domesticated onager.

About 2000 B.C., however, there descended from the north into the plains the HITTITES, an aggressive people speaking an Aryan language and armed with the two-horsed chariot. The driver, his feet braced against the footboard, controlled his yoked pair with half-moon or jointed bronze snaffles, the cheekpieces sometimes fitted with spikes to increase their nutcracker effect. The warrior fought either from the chariot or, using it merely for rapid movement, on foot. In fact the chariot combined the roles of the tank and infantry carrier of today. The fact that this particular horse culture was fairly sophisticated is proved by a fragmentary Hittite manual, written in the fourteenth century B.C., on the care and training of chariot horses.

The first definite reference to horseriding dates from about 1800 B.C. The King of Mari, a tributary of Babylon, advised his son, 'My lord should not ride upon a horse. Let my lord ride upon a chariot or even on a mule, and let him respect his royal status.' Probably the horse of that day, perfectly adequate for drawing a light chariot, was too small and too slow to carry an armoured man into, and out of, battle; the smooth-paced, quick-stepping mule was a more dignified and comfortable ride for a person of consequence. But Syria and Mesopotamia provide perfect conditions for horse breeding: the sparse grazing of the limestone desert gives horses hardiness and good bone, while civilized nations could, from the fertile river valleys and oases, provide a surplus of barley for grain feeding. So, although during the long rivalry of the Babylonian and Assyrian empires charioteers, not cavalry, were the *corps d'élite* on both sides, selective breeding in these conditions was producing a horse fit to carry kings and warriors.

It is not known precisely when cavalry became a useful arm. Certainly it was so by the reign of the Assyrian King Assurbanipal (885–860 B.C.) It may be due to his use of this new arm that he established a definite superiority over the rival power and captured the city of Babylon. Curiously enough the cavalry of Assurbanipal (and an Egyptian depicted in the Horenhab tomb five hundred years earlier) sit right back on the horses' croups, clinging apprehensively with heel and calf. Each archer is on a leading-rein, held by a comrade, so that his hands are free to shoot. These, clearly, are poor horsemen, and we may assume that this is how Babylonians rode. Donkeys are ridden thus in the East to this day, so it seems that early Egyptian and Mesopotamian horsemen simply used the seat they had found most comfortable on onager or ass. It was left to the Assyrians to discover how horses should be ridden. See also Babylonia, Assyria. CCT

Reference: J. K. Anderson, *Ancient Greek Horsemanship,* Berkeley, California, 1961; F. E. Zeuner, *The History of Domesticated Animals,* London, 1963.

Mesteño see Mexico

Métis Trotter

The Métis Trotter is a cross of the best bloodlines between the American STANDARDBRED and the Russian ORLOV TROTTER. It has been bred in the U.S.S.R. only within the last twenty years. The grey horse Veterok is an excellent example of the breed, which is not yet fixed. DMG

Mexico

Of the over four million horses in Mexico at present, the great majority are medium-sized saddle and work horses widely used on farms and in small country towns. What can be said to be a characteristic Mexican breed is the ranch horse of the cattleman and its more refined counterpart, the country gentleman's *charro* mount, half or quarterbred, properly broken and trained for ranch riding and for ceremonial occasions. It is this latter variety that has brought Mexican horsemanship to international attention.

The general foundation stock was the early sixteenth century Arab-Moorish horse, crossed with Andalusian and Navarrese strains, brought to the New World by the Spaniards, by way of the Caribbean Islands. This was no selected stock, but drawn from all-round common work or war horses, later upgraded by stallions sent over from the royal studs in Spain. As early as 1529, the possession and use of horse ownership brands were prescribed by regulation in the Americas. In New Spain, this stock multiplied in great numbers, producing variations such as the Cow pony, the Indian pony, the Bronco and the Mesteño. For lack of a specific breed, differentiation rests principally on colouring.

Specimens range from 13 hands (1·32 m) or less for the average farm or work horse, through the *charro* type not exceeding 15 hands (1·52 m) and weighing up to 900 lb (410 kg), to the regulation army horse, 14·2–16·2 hands (1·47–1·72 m) high.

The process of breaking in and reining a *charro* stock horse is attended to in Mexico more methodically and scrupulously than in many other parts. A *charro* mount must be trained to serve the rider well in the most important performances of the cattle range, either in open field or in a corral: in roping the front legs, *manganear*; the hind legs, *pialar*; mounting unbroken stock, *jinetear*; tailing, *colear*, etc. Each individual round is known as *suerte*, and a combination of all is a *jaripeo*. These peculiarly Mexican skills have brought about a whole range of customs, expressions, dress, accessories and ceremonials that lend a great deal of colour to local culture and folklore.

The breeding of good *charro* stock is at a low ebb at present, as a trained mount costs about £560 and can be as high as £1,600, restricting it to the luxury class. Nevertheless, there exists a nationwide Federation of some 340 *charro* groups with approxi-

Mexico. The *charreada* or *jaripeo* is an exhibition of horsemanship and test of skill. Here the rider has roped a wild mare.

mately 10,000 members who practise the *charreria* as a vocation and sport, in addition to the professional working cattlemen. JH

Reference: *La Charreria,* Museo Nacional de Artes Populares, Mexico, 1954; *Charreria*, Artes de Mexico, Coleccion, 1967; *Manual de Equitacion Militar,* Estado Mayor, Mexico, 1954; Inspecteur Lefour: *Le Cheval, Races, Utilisation, Equitation,* Paris, 1886; Jo Mora, *Californios*, New York, 1949.

Mezensky see Horse Breeding under U.S.S.R.

Mierzyn

This working horse bred by farmers in Poland is today found only in isolated forest areas and crossed with other breeds. Standing 14·1–14·3 hands (1·44–1·49 m), it is strong and hardy and an economical feeder. The type is thought to have originated from the wild forest horse and is much larger than the KONIK. DMG

Military Events see Combined Training, Horse Trials

Mimoseano see Brazil

Mind of the Horse

The horse's mental abilities tend to be judged in comparison with man's and to be categorized like his in such terms as intelligence, memory, temperament, etc. Modern animal psychologists, however, prefer to concentrate on the measurement and description of behaviour together with the situations (including the stimuli) associated with it, and to classify the acts according to the need each one fulfils. In wild animals these needs are concerned only with the preservation of the self or species. In domestic animals, in addition, certain acts are encouraged or taught which help to satisfy the needs of man. Thus horses are trained to race and jump to satisfy man's competitive propensities, to pull carts to satisfy his physical requirements, to do circus tricks or parade to satisfy his aesthetic tastes. It is in the process of training and using horses for these purposes that man makes his closest contact with the horse's mind.

The behaviour of all animals is found to depend on both the presence of innate or inherited patterns of sensory-muscular co-ordination, and on the conditions within the environment when these are elicited or practised. Since both nature and nurture are involved in every aspect of behaviour, it is no longer found very profitable to discuss one without the other.

Motor Activity: the horse's repertoire of motor skills is fairly limited, but those it does possess have been highly specialized through selective breeding to the tasks required of it. Apart from the activities involved in running and jumping (which are of physical more than of psychological interest), it has a repertoire of acts involved in feeding, elimination, reproduction and social signalling. Some of these acts die out with maturation, like suckling and 'snapping' (an action with the lips and teeth used to signal submission to an older horse and inhibit its aggression), which are seen only in youngsters; others (such as copulation) appear only with maturity.

Although every animal tends to show some idiosyncracies in the way it performs an act, some acts have altered basically little over the centuries. For example, according to Frank Ödberg (1969), the modern domestic horse paws the ground when excited in much the same way as does the Przevalski horse, although the ancestors of both these species died out many centuries ago (see Evolution). However, even the innate acts can be refined with practice and may develop at different rates in different equine breeds. For instance, according to Peter Rossdale (1967), the modern Thoroughbred foal takes an average of 57 min to stand for the first time after birth, and 111 min to suckle, whereas Stephanie Tyler (1969) noted that New Forest ponies stand after 41 min and suckle after 52 min.

Perceptual Behaviour: it is now widely recognized that visual perception in all animals is influenced by practice. Although all horses show initial fear of stepping into water or into space, and also show fear of half-hidden objects on the ground (which presumably bear shapes similar to those of the predators of their ancestors), and although, according to Grzimek (1949), they also show recognition of any horse-shaped silhouette, they very quickly learn to distinguish harmless from harmful stimuli, and to recognize the contours of their surroundings. Unlike many animals, particularly man, this rapid visual learning seems to continue into maturity, but whether it is influenced by the 'richness' of the environment in which the foal is raised is not known. Most people who breed and raise horses feel that a mature horse is better equipped if it is subjected to a variety of experiences when young than if it is not, but there have been no very systematic studies of the subject.

The part played by other senses, especially smell and hearing, has been very little studied, but smell may be particularly important in territorial and social recognition. For instance, all horses like to smell the ground when entering strange territory and they show a particular interest in piles of dung. Moreover, foals separated from their mothers will gallop up to any horse they see in the distance, failing to recognize their own mothers from among others till near enough to smell them.

Alarm calls are mostly made by sound (perhaps because sound can be more easily attended to than sight when the animal has its head down grazing), and horse trainers often find it easier to teach a horse to associate new actions with auditory signals than with those in any other sensory modality.

Emotional Activity: although it is now known that in a wide variety of animal species anxiety in the mother during both pregnancy and lactation tends to increase the nervousness of the offspring, no attempts have been made to study or control this in horses. In the majority of Thoroughbred studs, mares are subjected to long, arduous and sometimes undoubtedly frightening journeys before and shortly after foaling, which may be one of the factors leading to the reputed excitability of this strain.

Social Behaviour: any group of horses living together develops a hierarchical structure or 'peck order' in which each animal assumes a position of relative dominance. This order is maintained by a series of sounds and gestures by means of which dominance is signified and acknowledged, so that actual violence is kept to a minimum. The extent to which a horse's natural dominance or submissiveness in its own society is carried over into its relationships with man is unknown, but it seems quite possible that, in common with a number of other species, its submissiveness to man is dependent on the extent to which it regards him as a superior member of its own hierarchy, and that many of the resistances shown during training are 'testing out the limits' at which obedience will be enforced.

Learning: learning may take place after a single experience (such as learning that a hypodermic needle hurts) or only as a result of repeated practice (such as learning to change legs at a canter in response to the rider's aids). It may take place by association (as in the second example) or by insight (a sudden realization of the solution to a problem), but more often it involves a mixture of both these processes. The speed and stability with which learning takes place varies very much between individual

animals. Learning usually involves the shaping or modifying of behaviour through the acquisition and refinement of specific motor skills in connection with perceptual generalization and discrimination.
Generalization: the extent to which a lesson which has been learned in one situation is carried over to others varies with individual animals; but compared with some other species, particularly dogs and monkeys, generalization seems to be very limited in horses. Any new element in a situation appears to alter it, so that sights and sounds to which a horse has grown accustomed while unmounted may appear novel to it when it is ridden past them for the first time. This may be one of the reasons why horses are often considered unintelligent.
Discrimination: perhaps to compensate for their poor powers of generalization, horses have very good powers of discrimination if they are given the opportunity and encouragement to develop them. This is especially so in the visual field. (Their powers in other sensory modalities are virtually unknown.) One of Bertram Mills' circus horses could pick out its trainer's signal to lie down even when the latter was moving about among the audience outside the ring; and the famous 'calculating' horse, Clever Hans, could pick up the minute movements of its trainer's head which indicated to it the moment it should stop pawing, even though the trainer was unaware that he was making movements at all.
Habit Formation: most horses have some way of signifying displeasure by an evasion strategy. This is very often a repetition of the first reaction adopted by the animal when frightened and its repetition can become a serious training hazard, for once a pattern of behaviour has been established in a horse, it tends to show remarkable persistence, i.e. it quickly becomes a habit. Although behaviour patterns learned in early life may be inhibited by those learned later on, there is always a tendency for the earlier ones to reappear in moments of stress. For this reason, great care is taken by professional trainers not to let their animals develop unwanted habits (VICES), and to make sure that at all stages of training and maturation only those acts are performed which it is desirable to perpetuate.
Mood: although the consistency of behaviour among horses has just been stressed, the reactivity and excitability of an animal can vary greatly from time to time. Diet plays an important part in causing this variation. A high protein diet lowers the threshold at which flight reactions are triggered off, thereby putting an animal on its toes or making it 'fresh'. Social dominance may also be raised by good feeding, making a corn-fed animal more likely than a grass-fed one to defy its trainer's commands and develop undesired habits.

It has also been observed, especially by those working with handicapped riders, that some horses appear to alter their mood with different riders. Animals which tend to be aggressive, overactive and volatile with an experienced rider may be very gentle and docile with an inexperienced one (see Disabled, Riding for the). MOW

Reference: Moyra Williams, *Horse Psychology,* London, 1956; *Adventures Unbridled,* London, 1961; *A Breed of Horses,* Oxford, 1971.

Minho see Portugal

Mongolia

In the narrower sense the People's Republic of Outer Mongolia; in the wider sense, also the Chinese province of Inner Mongolia and adjacent regions of the U.S.S.R., the population of which is wholly or partly of Mongolian race and language. The northwest corner of Outer Mongolia, especially the Takin Shar Nuru (Yellow Horse Mountain) range is the last refuge of the only surviving subspecies of wild horse, Przevalski's Horse (see Asiatic Wild Horse). The government of the People's Republic has passed stringent laws prohibiting its hunting, and is doing what little can be done to preserve it. Outer Mongolia has the largest number of horses per head of human population in the world. The national drink, kumiss, is a mildly alcoholic liquid produced by foment-

Mongolia. *Below:* A Mongolian pony mare in Inner Mongolia
Bottom: Chinese drawing of a Mongolian mounted archer (fifteenth- or sixteenth-century)

ing mares' milk, and there are co-operative equine dairy farms where kumiss is produced commercially and kept in cold storage after fermentation. Yoghurt, now widely consumed in the West and made from cows' milk, is also probably a Mongol invention, originally made from mares' milk.

Most of the highly energetic mounted team games (see Mounted Games) played over a wide area of Central Asia appear to have originated in Mongolia. Horse racing is practised there, but the riders are almost exclusively children. Girls are often winners of important events, but there are no races for girls only or boys only.

If there is any one place in the world that can be regarded as the (pre-) historic 'cradle of horsemanship' it is Mongolia; certainly as regards the practice of riding, and perhaps also in regard to horse breeding. Horses of many breeds are now kept and bred in Mongolia, but the characteristic local stamp of pony, which has very low withers and a relatively large head, is the race that goes farthest back into antiquity. There has been much dispute as to whether this pony is simply the domesticated form of the Taki (*Equus przewalskii*) since it is well known that domestication itself produces after some generations physical, even anatomical, features not present in the wild ancestor. The balance of zoological opinion is that the Mongol herdsman's pony is a mixture of one or more domestic strains that may well have been under human management before the Taki developed some of its special features under the very heavy environmental pressure that turned it from a grassland into a desert animal. Even so, one or more of the original wild strains that went to make up the Mongol pony was also the ancestor of the Taki and the direct influence of the Taki on the tame herds made itself felt from time to time down to the present day, by wild stallions abducting tame mares from pastures and horselines. These mares may be recaptured, in foal to the Taki sire or with his foal at foot, or else 'wild' horses (in fact the halfbred descendants of such abducted mares) are captured and broken. The converse process has exercised little influence on the now rapidly dwindling wild herds; although domestic stallions run away into the desert, sometimes in pursuit of 'horsing' Taki mares, they stand no chance whatever of reproducing themselves, since before they can get near a mare the Taki stallion or even colt will reduce them to mincemeat. Physical conformation apart, what chiefly distinguishes the truly wild from the feral ('run-wild') or domestic horse is the deadly fighting ability of the male from about two years onwards. Therefore whatever 'tame' blood has infiltrated the Taki herds is through runaway mares. Such mares are the first to succumb to all the dangers and hardships of the wild existence—the attacks of wild beasts, hunger, thirst, exhaustion—as are their halfbred progeny, though to a lesser degree. See also China. AD

Morgan Horse

This American light breed, standing 14–15 hands (1·42–1·52 m) high traces back to one foundation sire, Figure, better known as Justin Morgan after his second owner, who took him for a bad debt at the age of (probably) two in 1795. He was foaled at Springfield, Massachusetts, and taken to Randolph, Vermont, where he passed the rest of his life, dying, like Napoleon, in 1821. Morgans are ideal general-purpose saddle horses, but in draught also have enormous pulling power for their size and are capable of high speeds as roadsters. Extensive and intensive research has been able to prove nothing about the breeding of the foundation sire, but taking into account the general appearance of the breed and the background of Morgan family friends and neighbours with names like Evans and Rice there can be little doubt that Figure was essentially a Welsh Cob with a touch of either Thoroughbred or Arabian blood. Headquarters of the breed is the University of Vermont Morgan Horse Farm, Weybridge, Vermont. AD

Morocco see Africa, Fantasia, Libyan

Morven Park International Equestrian Institute

This American riding school in Leesburg, Virginia, is co-sponsored by the U.S. Combined Training Assn and Springfield (Mass.) College for training professional riding instructors. Founded in 1967, the institute is headed by Major John Lynch. It stands in a part of Morven Park, an estate made over to the Commonwealth of Virginia by its former governor, Westmoreland Davis.

The ten-month course at the institute counts in the requirements for baccalaureate degree in physical education at Springfield College. HCA

Motion Pictures, Horse in

Probably no other national cinema has made such varied and extensive use of the horse in films as has the American. The circumstances of American Western history, particularly the cowboy and the wild horse, have offered a dramatic setting for much of American film production, and a unique training for horses as cinema actors.

As far back as the middle 1920s one of the more famous film horses, Rex, starred in a series of movies and serials under the sobriquet, *Rex, King of the Wild Horses*. Even before the advent of sound in films, the Western cowboy actor, William S. Hart, shared billing with his pinto horse, Fritz, who was trained to play significant parts in the heroic adventures of his rider. And since dramatic action is the core of Western film themes, horses were frequently used in startling stunt performances such as falling at a gallop and leaping off cliffs. Thus, throughout the years a casting system has arranged film horses into three classes: starring horses playing lead roles or significant parts; horses used by leading actors, often selected for their handsome bearing; and stunt horses. A fourth type, both non-descript and non-specialized, are the cast horses. These are used for atmosphere purposes, mounting the extras who fill town scenes or act as a posse, and for pulling coaches and wagons. A cast horse's main attribute is a docile nature.

The starring horses, and those that once shared billing with their cowboy stars (a style that has passed into movie history and is exemplified by Roy Rogers and Trigger, Gene Autry and Champion, Ken Maynard and Tarzan, etc.), are selected for their beauty, intelligence and adaptability. Adaptability is foremost. Unless a horse adjusts adequately to cameras and lighting equipment, the dozens of personnel scurrying about, sound trucks and the usual tension which pervades a set, it may not be sufficiently reliable to take cues quickly and quietly. Just as with human actors, beauty may not count if the temperament is too flamboyant. The American SADDLEBRED, the peacock of American horses, is highly desired by film horse trainers since this breed combines beauty, intelligence and an evenness of temperament suitable to film work. In addition, it has substantial size. But the Saddlebred does not reign exclusively in the Hollywood roster of star film horses. One of the finest of all performers was a THOROUGHBRED named Misty. This stallion performed in countless films for almost twenty years and learned, as does any long-time campaigner, that once he was in front of the camera, a performance was expected. Colour types, especially the palomino and snow-white horses, are also popular.

Training horses to take part in films is given by a small group of specialist trainers. Although each has his particular technique, virtually all trainers start training by whip breaking. The horse is taught to come to the trainer when signalled, to stop immediately when cued (this is important since stopping behind or ahead of a designated spot will place the horse out of camera focus), to stand still, turn right and left, back up, lie down, limp, pretend pain (by nuzzling a sore leg, for example) and rear. This set of dramatics is a standard film repertoire. Trigger, probably the most famous of all movie horses, performed these actions in addition to a considerable number of tricks. Fury was another horse of equal talent.

Sometimes a horse displays a particular ability and is used to double for a star horse which does not give as convincing a performance. Misty had a natural propensity for the fighting stallion routine. He would rear and lunge, lay back his ears and bare his teeth. When the cue was stopped he reverted to his quiet self.

Horse in Motion Pictures. Probably the best-known of movie horses was Trigger. He was certainly the most extensively trained.

All the basic actions are performed on cue from the trainer who uses body movements, arm and hand signals, or a whip to signal the horses. For example, the trainer tells the horse to come to him by turning his back. If the trainer is standing behind the camera, the horse comes toward the camera. If the trainer stands to one side of the camera the horse passes in front of the camera lens. To stop the horse at the precise moment the trainer turns and faces the horse, usually placing a hand or whip in front of his chest. Whichever style of cueing is employed, silent cues are necessary as filming is often under live sound.

Some horse actions on the screen rely more on the special effects staff of a studio than training. Probably scenes of two stallions fighting cause the most apprehension to audiences who feel cruelty is involved in allowing the animals to fight. But the fierceness of the fight is optically created, although to an extent the combat is real. Two stallions left together are bound to start fighting. But a tape, coloured to match the horse's coat colour, is wrapped lightly around its muzzle, and hoofs are shod in sponge rubber to lessen blows from kicks. The camera contributes by a process called *undercranking*. The fight scene is filmed at a slow speed. When the scene is projected on the screen at normal speed the action appears fast and furious. In reality the fight is stopped whenever one of the combatants becomes too serious.

Stunt horses are as meticulously trained. The American Humane Association is present on all sets using animals (to assure the public that animals are treated humanely) and stunt horses, in spite of rather rough-appearing scenes, are specially trained to fall and jump off cliffs. All falls at a gallop are performed on churned-over earth which covers mattresses or foam rubber to cushion the fall. Besides, stuntmen work freelance and their horses represent a considerable investment. If a horse should hurt itself, it might thereafter refuse to fall.

About three major stables supply the bulk of trained and cast horses to the American film industry. In addition, these suppliers rent saddlery and wagons to match any historical period from Genghis Khan's warriors to a matched pair of harnessed bays for a plantation scene in a Civil War movie. AA

Mountain and Moorland Ponies

This phrase, supplanting 'British Native Ponies', is not really comprehensive enough; it should run 'Mountain and Moorland, Forest, Fen, Heath and Bog'. These breeds are essentially those which have been successfully bred on land called 'marginal' for agricultural purposes. Apart from the genetic inheritance of the original stock, it is the nature of this land and the manner of keeping the herds on it that have moulded the breed in every instance. It should be borne in mind also that this technique of horse breeding on the outer edge of cultivation and beyond was universal in Britain and Europe in general throughout the Middle Ages and for some centuries thereafter in some regions: the sole exception was the DESTRIER, or great warhorse, which was the creation of the weatherproof stable and the carefully enclosed paddock or 'horse-close'.

British native ponies were once a representative sample of West European stock, imported as part of the process of human migration up to but not including the Norman invasion of 1066 (see also Ponies). Some of these types have disappeared from other European countries; some remain to offer striking comparisons, as that of the Exmoor with the old-fashioned stamp of Gotland RUSS, the Fell pony with the traditional type of West Friesian and so on. The British (and Irish) native breeds are now rigidly codified as only nine in number but this is due to the fact that a systematic registration in stud books for the whole of the British Isles did not begin until just before World War I. By that time many local types had ceased to exist in such numbers as to constitute breeds. It is estimated that at the beginning of the nineteenth century there were as many as twenty local races so distinct that they would be recognized as breeds today, had all survived.

It is possible to group the nine surviving breeds in three divisions, of which the northern one contains the largest types: Highland, Dales and Fell. Out beyond the Pentland Firth is the joker in the pack, the Shetland, a very small joker indeed, typical purebred specimens standing 9½ hands (0·96 m), four inches lower than the maximum height for inclusion in the Shetland Stud Book. These ponies are probably a dwarf variety, split off from the main body of ponies of Exmoor type before domestication, since recognizable 'Shetlands' are to be seen in Old Stone Age cave paintings near the Biscayan coasts of France and Spain. As one of the earliest waves of human immigration into Britain came from this region, coasting along the Atlantic shore of France and up to the Irish Sea, it is very likely the Shetland represents the first equines to be brought to Britain by human

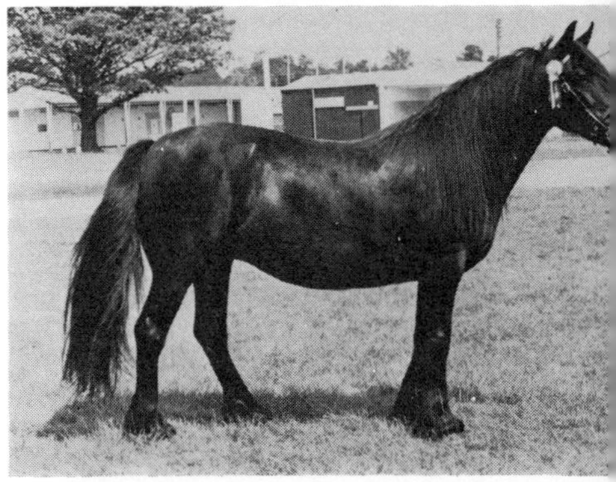

Mountain and Moorland Ponies. *Top:* A Fell pony stallion
Above: A Shetland pony stallion
Below: Highland ponies

agency. Perhaps this very small breed was specially selected by the immigrants, being the only breed that could be shipped over in their boats. Use of horses in the Shetland islands themselves was limited. Virtually roadless, with no point very far from the sea, the islands could for most purposes be best served by boat. But not for all: in a treeless land, the bringing of turf for fuel down to the coastal settlements from the moors was an essential chore; so was the carrying up of seaweed from the shore to the small enclosed fields for manure, and also the carrying of burned seaweed (kelp), the product of the islands' primitive chemical industry. All this work was done with panniers on a wooden pack saddle. The nearest relation to the Shetland was the extinct Lofoten Pony of Norway. This was small and black and also adapted to island life.

Geographically next come Highland Ponies, all registered in one book; most breeders agree, however, in recognizing two different types: the small, fine-limbed Western Isles variety and the taller and stouter Mainland GARRON. Indeed the ponies of some islands such as Barra were quite as small as Shetland Ponies down to the last century and unquestionably the large Garron is the creation of the last hundred years. It would perhaps never have attained its present size but for the influence of the Department of Agriculture for Scotland, which was at one time strongly influenced by the demands of forestry and the necessity for sheer weight to be laid into the collar and not attainable in an animal, however stoutly built, below 14 hands (1·42 m). The present height limit is 14·2 hands (1·47 m). The predominant colour is dun, so prevalent that various shades of dun, such as sandy, blue, yellow, etc. have to be specified for stud-book identification. About 66 per cent of all registered ponies are of this colour. Next most frequent is grey. Bay is unusual, chestnut not uncommon, black not unknown. There are no broken colours, and even roan is rare.

There has throughout historical times been a constant flow of livestock from the western Highlands and Islands into Galloway and the western Lowlands, thence into northwestern England; ponies have been no exception, channelled mostly through the markets of Dumbarton and Carlisle. The link between the Highland Pony and the hill-bred ponies of northern England was the Galloway, now extinct as a breed but of a type still remembered by older people today. It took its name from the region on the north shore of the Solway Firth, stood about 13 hands (1·32 m), was mostly dark bay, dark brown or black in colour with hard 'blue' hoofs, and was a fast and tireless trotter in harness or under the saddle. The Galloway exerted a strong breeding influence on the Highland Ponies of the west, especially on the 13-hand (1·32 m) *gocan* ('skylark') stamp from Mull, famous for its trotting powers.

The Galloway also had a powerful effect on the Fell Ponies of the Border and Cumbrian regions, reaching right down the Pennine range almost to the Peak District. The North Country as a whole, and the adjacent parts of Lowland Scotland, had for many centuries a way of life and an economy that demanded only two types of horse, in both of which height beyond a certain point was a disadvantage. Generally, stock-rearing was more important than arable farming; mining from Roman times onwards was important, though the mineral won changed from age to age; and wool, either raw, as yarn or as cloth, steadily increased in importance right up to the Industrial Revolution of the late 1700s. Up to a late date, though main roads, including Roman ones, leading to Scotland traversed the region, minor roads were really tracks seldom more than a yard wide, often consisting only of 18-inch-wide flags. All the inhabitants, urban and rural, except the very poor and the numerically small upper class, needed a riding horse that would travel all day at a 'soft' pace (see Pacing) herding sheep and cattle on the fells, hunting, travelling, and taking part in the constantly-smouldering Border feuds and skirmishes, of a build that would facilitate frequent mounting and dismounting: also a stout packhorse. It is a great error to write down the packhorse as an equine reject. Work in the pack train (ten horses to move one ton) demanded great strength of back and loins, hard feet, day-long endurance, a mile-devouring stride, surefootedness. Too great height was inconvenient for loading and unloading. Travelling for any distance, herding on horseback, cattle-droving, hunting, and most of all Border raiding meant crossing stretches of upland; smelting, sheep-shearing, walking and dyeing wool, took place down in the Dales. This is the true distinction, in function, between Dales and Fell ponies; it is a question of altitude rather than whether they are from east or west of the Pennines. Dales Ponies became, when the state of the roads and the standard of wagon-building eventually permitted this, harness ponies, for the same reason that everywhere the best packhorse strains became the best draught strains. But the Fell Pony remains primarily a saddle type, with a fast untiring trot without high action. Its resemblance to the black FRIESIAN, making due allowance for the change from a marshy environment to a mountainous one that took place perhaps seventeen hundred years ago, is not a coincidence. The presence of Friesian communities in the north of England from late Roman times to the eve of the Viking invasions is well attested historically. They were mercenary soldiers, merchants and

Mountain and Moorland Ponies. A Dales pony stallion

Mountain and Moorland Ponies.
Below: New Forest ponies
Bottom left: A Dartmoor pony stallion
Bottom right: Exmoor ponies
Above far right: Connemara ponies
Below far right: A Welsh Mountain pony stallion

agricultural settlers and needed a good riding horse. The maximum height for acceptance in the Fell Stud Book today is 14 hands (1·42 m). Colour is overwhelmingly black with a few browns and bays, still fewer greys. No white feet are allowed. Nor is the resemblance in name and appearance between the Dales Pony and the Norwegian DØLEHEST a matter of chance; this is a legacy of Norse settlement (so also is the similarity between a certain type of Highland Pony and the Norwegian FJORD PONY). Dales Ponies can be up to 14·2 hands (1·47 m), more massively built than the Fell, with the same range of colouring but less absolute preponderance of black. White markings within reason are acceptable.

An identifiable 'southern' group comprises New Forest, Exmoor and Dartmoor Ponies, smaller than the northern breeds because South Country heathland in general affords poorer keep than the northern hills. The old type of Dartmoor and the old type of New Forest more closely resembled the Exmoor than either does today. The slightly 'Welsh Mountain' look of the modern show-class Dartmoor is admittedly the result of the devastating effect of two world wars on the Moor; fresh blood has had to be brought in from Wales. Up to the last century the Dartmoor was larger than the Exmoor. Now the maximum height for Dartmoors is 12 hands (1·22 m), for Exmoor mares 12·2 hands (1·27 m), and Exmoor stallions 12·3 hands (1·29 m). The New Forest, unlike other 'classic' pony-breeding areas, has always been much open to outside influence. Main roads traverse the Forest and there are, and have long been, two major ports on its outskirts. Uniformity of type has been maintained, despite the ability of New Forest commoners to acquire mares from any source and every type, simply by the abrasive action of New Forest climate and herbage which in the end allows only one type to survive, a weatherproof and thrifty one. New Forest Ponies can be any colour; only piebald and skewbald are barred from the stud book. Dartmoor Ponies are predominantly dark-coloured, some grey. Exmoor Ponies, purebred, can only be brown, brown-dun, or bay with no white marks, not even a star.

The third, 'western' group, the Welsh and Connemara, have little in common. Formerly other breeds of Irish pony were recognizable, for example the Kerry (see Ireland), even though they never had a stud book. The Connemara Stud Book was begun in 1924, registering ponies between 12·2 hands (1·27 m) and 14·2 hands (1·47 m) in height, but a stature around 13·2 hands (1·37 m) is preferred and the best types seldom exceed this. There is much Spanish blood in the Connemara, especially that of the North (Asturian, Galician and Biscayan *jacas,* and *asturiones* have all contributed) and this is very evident in their conformation. So too is the influence of the taller ANDALUSIAN, which is a horse not a pony. There is some ARAB blood, some recent, some going back to the eighteenth century.

Welsh ponies and cobs are registered in one stud book with four sections. The Cob at one extreme is also the product of an Andalusian cross deliberately introduced in the twelfth century; no better upgrading cross could have been sought since the Andalusian was the undisputed super-horse of western Europe from Roman times until the 'invention' of the THOROUGHBRED. Registerable stature is from 14 hands (1·42 m) to 15·1 hands (1·54 m). It is a ride-and-drive type. At the other extreme the Welsh Mountain Pony, descendant of the original British stock onto which the Andalusian was grafted to produce the Welsh Cob, has received some Arab and some Thoroughbred blood, without increasing its stature above the permitted 12 hands (12·2 m). Between these come the Welsh Riding Pony (Section B) and the Welsh Pony, Cob Type (Section C), both up to 13·2 hands (1·37 m), the latter being more stoutly built. They may be regarded as intermediate in type, the former between

the Welsh Mountain and the Thoroughbred pony, the latter between the Welsh Mountain and the Welsh Cob. See also Riding Ponies. AD

Mountain Ass (*Equus hemionius onager*) see Onager

Mounted Games

Equestrian games, many of them ancient in origin, still exist in modified form today. Not a few of them are derived from the everyday work of the participants, such as the buck-jumping (see Bucking) indulged in as a recreation by the cowboys of North America and Australia and the South American gauchos. Many of the latter also play POLO, perhaps the oldest goal game in the world world, which spread from Persia many centuries ago.

Abats le Sultan is a Russian game played by riders wearing feather-covered fencing masks and bearing keenly-honed swords. In the free-for-all which ensues, the object of the exercise is to cut off the feathers from the opponents' masks.

Buzkashi (or *Kokburi*) is a game played in Afghanistan and originating from the nomadic tribes which roamed the steppes. It is a wild and tough game. A slaughtered sheep or goat is jammed between the knee and saddle of a player who gallops off while the others chase him and try to snatch it away. It can also be played by two teams, one attacking, the other defending the carcass. It was sometimes combined with

khis-koubou, the bridal chase of the nomads, with the bridegroom chasing after his beloved to kiss or caress her. Several men might pursue the same girl. Armed with a leather knout, she defended herself with spirit and often sent her pursuers and would-be wooers reeling back with livid weals once she had reached the goal, usually a pole on the steppe, a fertility symbol, and rounded on her swains.

Above: **Mounted Games.** Kokburi, a game that originated among nomadic tribes in Afghanistan, is still popular in the U.S.S.R.

Below: **Mounted Police.** A Basuto mounted policeman
Right: The 'Star' forms part of the musical ride performed by the world-famous Royal Canadian Mounted Police.

Da-kyu or *spoon polo* is a Japanese variation of polo, once popular in China as well. Each team has several balls, each weighing about an ounce, and the bamboo mallet has a net tied to its end. On a small polo field the goal is a hole, 4 ft 4 in (40 cm) in diameter, in a wooden wall. In Tibet players had to hold their hands high in the air, and whoever touched a rein incurred elimination—sometimes the entire field.

In the Argentine the *domada* is the sport of the proud and courageous gauchos. It consists of riding wild, completely unbroken horses of the pampas for as long as heart, nerve and sinew can stand the strain.

In Turkey, since time immemorial, there have been javelin games and races for horsemen, known as the *dzerid*. Similar contests are pursued with great enthusiasm in Ethiopia.

In Chile and other South American countries one of the most popular mounted sports is *jaripeo*. It consists of working in pairs, to grab a calf by the tail and throw him at the gallop. Every cattleman has attempted this trick while herding a recalcitrant calf, but the competitive element is introduced by the speed factor; the fastest man against the clock wins.

Ludus Troiae is a javelin game played on 12 May, the day which commemorates the foundation of the temple of Mars on the Capitoline hill, and it is played again on 1 August, the anniversary of the foundation of the temple of Mars Ultor. The game is played with cypress javelins of about 5 ft (1·52 m) long, the type used by cavalry in antiquity. The game is believed to have no association with the city of Troy. Indeed, it may be Etruscan in origin, deriving from a Latin word for playground which stems from the Etruscan *truare*, to move vigorously. The game as it exists today could be a Turkish adaptation of Greco-Roman equestrian games (cf. *dzerid* above), or a game with a military background, or even a hunting game from the heart of Central Asia. Riders attempt to hit one another, the teams facing one another, with light, blunt javelins. The first to throw is pursued by the others, and expert players contrive to pick up fallen spears from the ground at the gallop when their own supply of two or three is exhausted. The winner must score three hits, which can take two hours, and he must also win a race, in which all protagonists are involved, from the contest field to the city.

Pato-Lorraine is played in France and related closely to the Argentine game of *pato*. It is akin to netball on horseback, played with a large ball with leather handles, and hit with a curved stick which can lift the ball from the ground into a goal which is hung in the air. *Pato* is similar to *kokburi*, but the 'ball' consists of an oven-ready fowl, sewn into a leather bag with sturdy handles. The winner (he who snatches the bird) is allowed to roast it, but must entertain his opponents to the meal.

Push Ball, played on horseback with enormous 'medicine balls' in Russia as a somewhat ponderous type of soccer, is also played in Holland and made its appearance at the Horse of the Year Show at Wembley, London, a few years ago, played by Pony Club members.

Tent Pegging, familiar in Britain thanks to various mounted regiments and the military and civil mounted police, originated in India. A line of tent pegs is lifted, for a strike or a carry, with the lance carried by a rider on a galloping horse. See also Horse Sports under U.S.S.R. PMM

Mounted Police

Sections in many police forces still ride horses. Duties include ceremonial escort, public relations, traffic and crowd control, patrolling city parks and remote countryside. The famous Canadian 'Mounties', now mechanized, retain horses and men to perform their spectacular Musical Ride;

Dutch sections patrol North Sea beaches, throwing life-lines or swimming with their horses to aid bathers in distress; the Metropolitan Police of London used to provide a horse for H.M. the Queen at the Trooping the Colour.

Incorporated in 1839, the Mounted Branch of the London Metropolitan Police stems from 'two Persuit horses with Proper Persuers' of 1758 which developed into a regular Bow Street patrol in 1805. Australia's old-time Trooper Police were first drafted in 1825; New York's squadrons, now the largest mounted force, started with 15 horses in 1871; the Jamaican Police acquired horses in 1961.

Teheran's Mounted Police ride fiery Persian stallions; the Bahrain horses come from the Royal Stables; Lesotho has the only fully mounted Police Force, and they ride sturdy, native ponies; the Camel Corps, part of the Desert Patrol, utilize fast camels to police the Jordanian borders. Police horses are usually quality HUNTER or THOROUGHBRED-type geldings, of about 15·3 hands (1·62 m), often colour-matched like the Australian sections.

The men first train 'on the beat', then graduate to experienced horses carefully chosen to suit each rider's temperament. Police horses are highly schooled and receive special 'nuisance training', accustoming them to the noise and emotional stress of crowds, to firearms, bands, and every type of traffic. JCa

Movements

Movements are figures and paces executed in dressage tests and/or training:

Volte: a circle, 6 m in diameter, the smallest a horse (estimated length 10 ft or 3 m) can describe on two tracks, as it does in a *pirouette*, with one hind leg serving as a pivot at the centre of the circle. As in all work on circles or bends, the greatest difficulty is to bend the horse's entire spine evenly from head to dock to conform to the curve being travelled. When it is so bent,

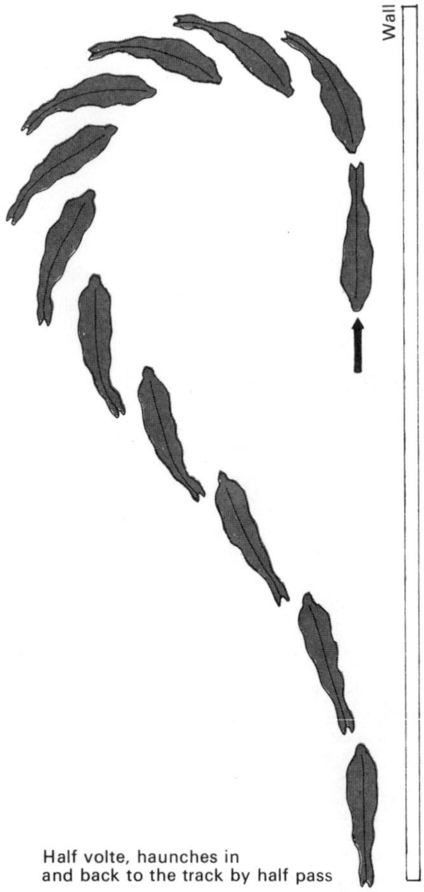

Half volte, haunches in and back to the track by half pass

Reversed half volte, haunches out
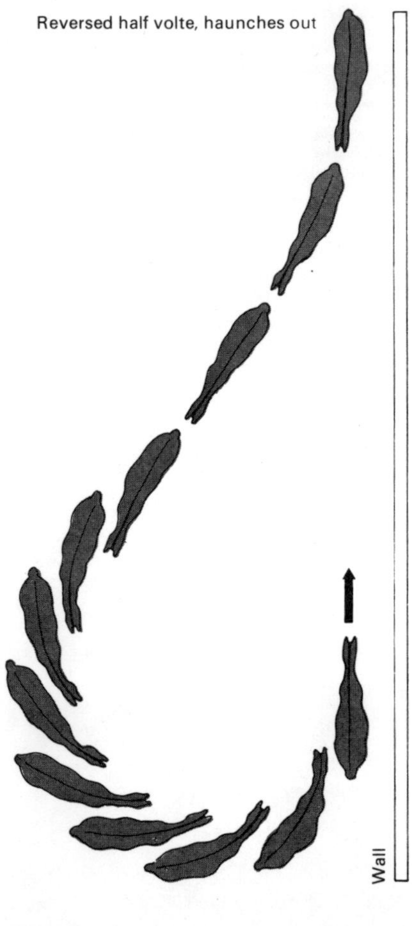

the tracks of the hind legs follow those of the fore legs, as is always required in classical equitation.
Corners: in classical equitation, corners are turned in the form of a *quarter-volte*.
Half-turn on the fore hand: the horse pivots around one fore leg, the other (outer) fore leg describes a small circle round the inner fore leg, while the hind legs describe outer concentric circles round the inner fore leg. Generally performed at the walk, it is also feasible at the *piaffe*. At either pace, the pivot leg should never fail to mark time in the rhythm of the pace, any immobility being a serious fault. At the walk, the hind leg on the inner side should cross well in front of the outer hind leg, a crossing obtained by flexing the principal hind-leg joints: coxofemoral, stifle and hock. This exercise, used to develop engagement of the hind legs, is also called *half-pirouette in reverse*, becoming a full *pirouette in reverse* when the turn is completed and the horse ends up facing in the original direction.
Half-Turn on the Haunches or Half Pirouette: one hind leg serves as a pivot; the horse turns round it, the other (outer) hind leg describing a small circle round the inner hind leg, while the fore legs describe larger, concentric circles round the inner hind leg. It may be carried out at the walk, *piaffe* and canter. Again, the pivot leg should remain mobile in the rhythm of the pace of the movement and the outside fore leg should cross in front of the inner fore leg in a rounded gesture. This movement loosens the shoulders, lightens the fore hand and gets the balance of the horse back onto its quarters. When a full circle is performed, it is called the *pirouette*.
Halt: in a dressage test this signifies total immobility of the horse, and specifically of its head, in perfect straightness; its legs form the four corners of a rectangle, its mouth never loses contact with the bit, ready to relax only at the rider's demand, spontaneous slackening, twitching or tensing being a serious fault.
Rein Back: a pace of two time by alternate touching down of the diagonal bipeds. For correct performance, the feet of each biped must rise and fall simultaneously, the strides being of equal scope, in no way affecting the over-all position; the horse remains straight, keeping contact with the bit and starting forward again on its own as soon as the rein-back aids are relaxed.
Passage: an air originating in the trot, but of slower cadence, the movement of the legs gaining in height what it loses in length, marking a brief pause in the air, cannons vertical, any lateral swing of the haunches being a serious fault.
Piaffe: a *passage* executed on the spot, but with less elevation. For both airs, greater importance is attached to cadence and regularity of pace than to degree of elevation.

Collected Paces: higher but shorter steps than those of ordinary paces. Shortening the pace at will is done largely by correctly raising the neck, with head position nearly vertical, in conjunction with the engagement of the hind legs.
Extended Paces: ampler, flatter, steps, but not faster than ordinary; these are obtained by lengthening the entire topline of the horse and most particularly the neck.
Counter-Canter: this is performed by the horse when cantering on circles or curves on the outside lead, and is conducive to lateral straightening and improvement of balance. Because in tests its sole purpose is to test the horse's balance, any constraint exercised by the aids robs this movement of its value and should receive a low mark.
Flying Change of Leg: a new strike-off, without change of pace, on the lead

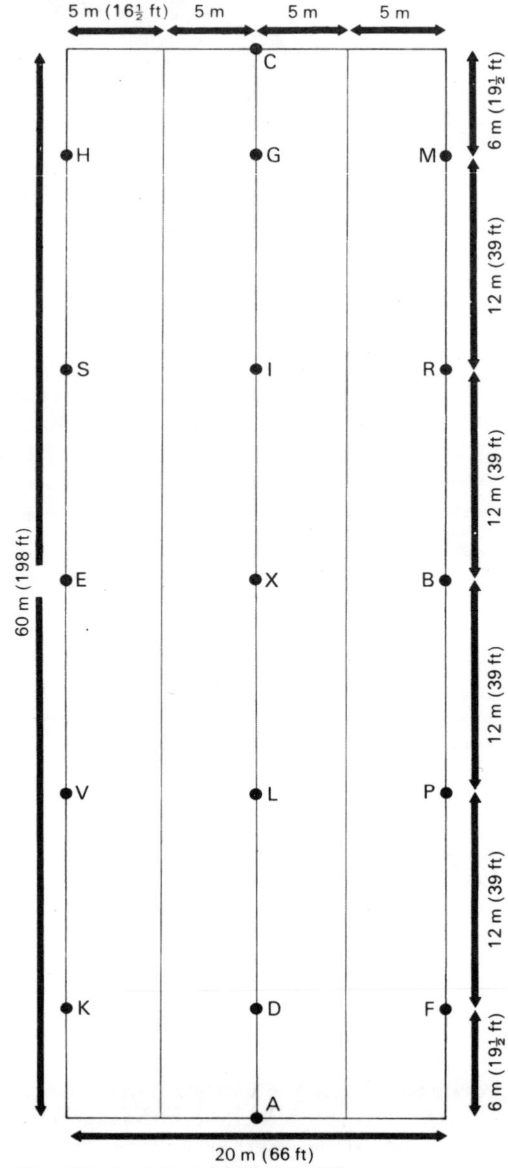

Plan of the large dressage arena, used for International Competitions including the Grand Prix (the small arena, 132 × 66 ft, 40 × 20 m, is used for the British Pony Club, Novice and other Tests of Elementary Standards)

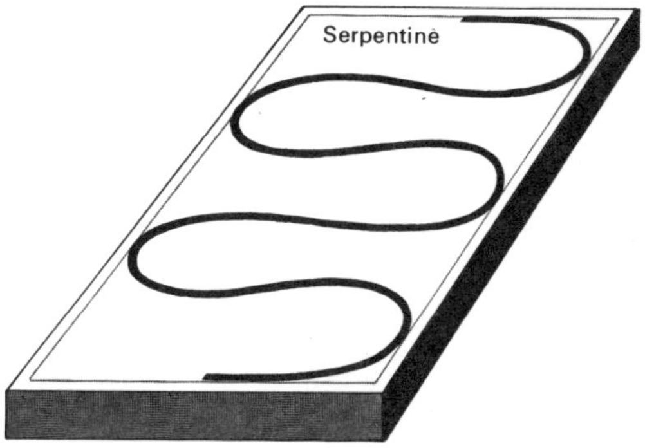

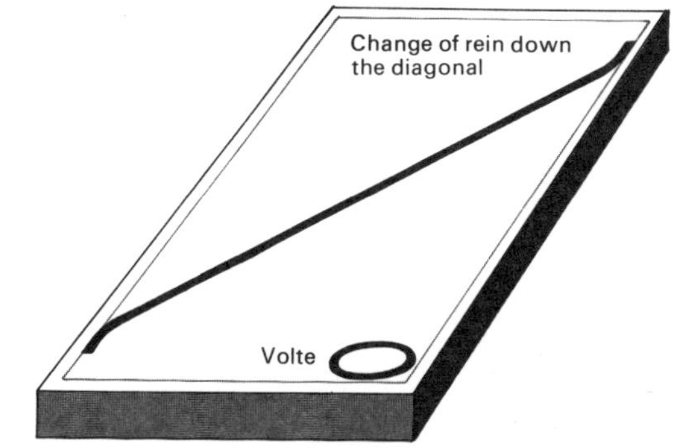

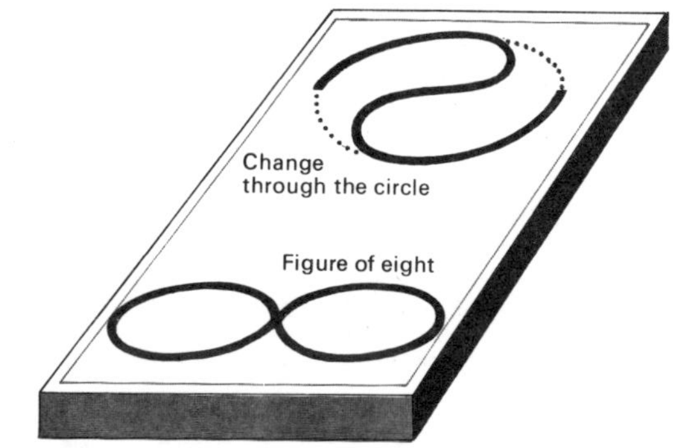

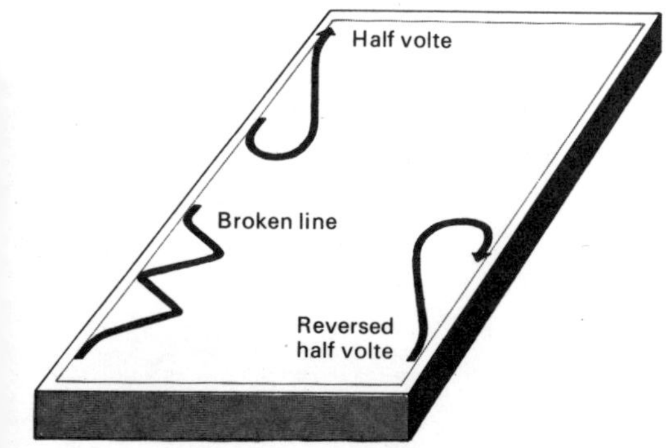

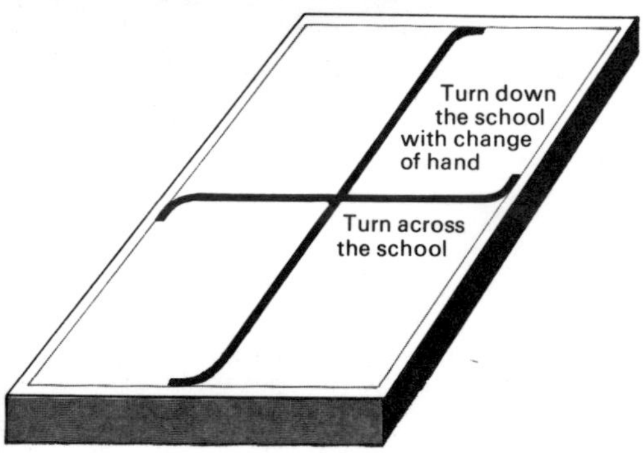

opposite to the one the horse has been cantering on. To be correct, the change of fore and hind lead should be made simultaneously. Flying changes are performed singly or in a series, at every fourth, third, second, and eventually, every stride.

Work on Two Tracks: takes its name from the fact that the hind legs travel on a track parallel to, but distinct from, that of the fore legs. There are two principal movements: *shoulder-in*, bending the horse evenly while moving sideways and forward in the direction of his convex side; *half-pass*, keeping the horse straight with a slight *placer* (lateral turn of the head at the poll) making it look in the direction it is travelling. When performed with fore legs on the outer and hind legs on the inner track, it is called *head to the wall*, or *travers*; done the other way round, it is called *tail to the wall* or *renvers*. It may also be performed from the long side of the arena towards the centre line or *vice versa*; or along the entire diagonal. A *volte* can also be ridden on two tracks; the movement is called *haunches-in* when the croup is closer to the centre than the shoulders. This movement leads, as it is tightened, to the *pirouette*. In the reversed position, with shoulders closer to the centre than the haunches, it is called *haunches-out*, leading, as it is tightened, to the *pirouette in reverse*.

Other school movements are: *turn down the school, turn across the school, change of rein on the diagonal, half-volte, reversed half-volte, figure eight, broken line, change through the circle and serpentine.* JF

Mule

Offspring of mare by jackass (see Jennet, Hybrids). Among early laws of the HITTITES is an ordinance fixing the price of a mule at 60 shekels while that of a chariot horse was only 20 shekels. The greater value lay in its versatility. The mule could plough, be ridden, carry a pack, go in harness. Israelite kings rode mules and the heir apparent was designated by being ceremonially mounted on the king's mule. Heavy draught horses, saddle horses, pacers, trotters, can all be 'simulated' by mules out of mares of appropriate type put to a comparatively small range of jackass types, of which the POITEVIN heavy draught and the Maltese saddle ass are the best examples. AD

Muraköz see Hungary

Murgese

The present Murgese horse bred in the Murge district of Italy is in no way related to the old breed which died out. The modern breed is a light draught/saddle horse and when correctly bred sometimes a riding horse of distinction. DMG

Mustang

The term 'mustang' applies to the 'wild'

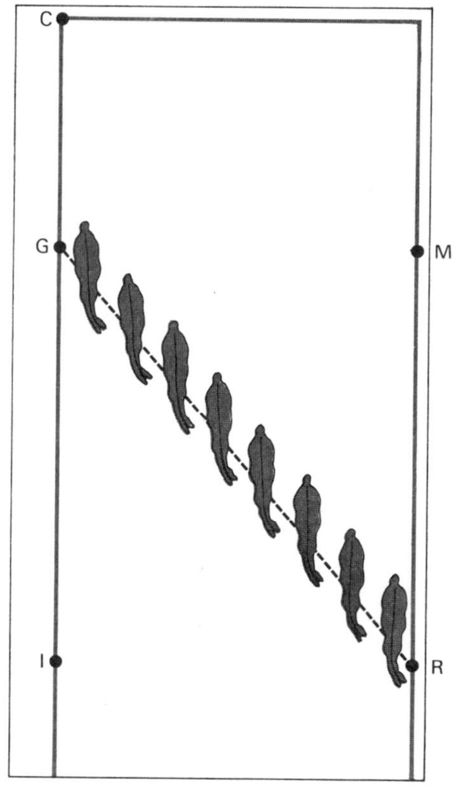

Above: Diagonal. **Below:** Tail to the wall.

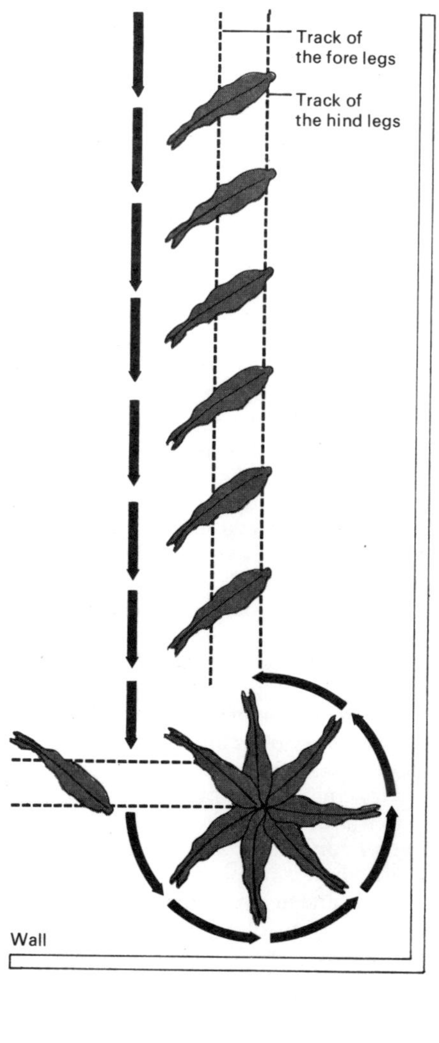

horses of the American West; it derives from the Spanish *mesteña* (group or herd of horses).

When the Spanish first landed on the American continent there were no native horses. As herds of both cattle and horses were introduced into Mexico, after conquest of the Aztecs and the other Indian peoples, numbers of the Spanish horses escaped and became the nucleus of the great herds of wild horses that soon spread all over the plains country of North America. Both Indians and white settlers chased and caught great numbers of these wild horses, using many different methods besides running them down and catching them with thrown loops. During the latter half of the nineteenth century thousands were rounded up by men on relays of fast horses and driven into corrals to be broken to the saddle or harness, then sold to a demanding market. As late as the 1950s, mustangs, or in this late period more correctly called feral horses, were caught and sold to meat packers for dog food. During the past decade the United States government has passed laws protecting the wild horse, and has established areas for them to range. RS

Myth and Legend, Horse in

Of all folklore and legend connected with horses some of the most fascinating concern the Centaurs, the mythical race, half human, half horse, who lived on the mountains of Thessaly and slopes of Arcady. Some were friendly to the Greeks, like Chiron, who was tutor to Jason, the hero of the Argonauts. Others were wild and violent like the ones conquered by Herakles and the Lapithae. They were the offspring of Ixion, King of the Lapithae, and Nephele, a cloud substituted for the goddess Hera, and they drew the chariot of Dionysus. The Babylonian sign for the constellation Sagittarius was a Centaur as early as the eleventh century B.C.

When Jason cut off the head of the Gorgon there appeared Pegasus, the winged horse. This famous myth typifies the fact that the horse in early times was considered to have an almost godlike quality. Even St George is supposed to have changed the pagan god for the noble horse at the Well of St George at Abergele in Wales. It is not difficult to understand the reason for this near worship of the horse. Learning to control such a remarkable beast was probably the most exciting development in man's history next to the invention of the wheel. The horse, of course, was not as big then as it is today. But it was still powerful and fast. There is a legend that the first use of the horse by man was as a weapon of war: a herd of wild horses could be driven against the enemy like a tank. Its exploits were built into legends and myths in many cultures. In Muslim tradition the horse is given great importance (see Arab).

The Pegasus legend is comparatively straightforward: the offspring of Medusa, the Gorgon, and Poseidon, the sea-god, Pegasus was caught by Bellerophon with a golden bridle and ridden by him to kill the Chimera. From one of his hoofprints on Mount Helicon sprang the river of the Muses known as Hippocrene. There are many versions of such tales.

Various ideas connected with the colours of horses are also very ancient although they have little substance in fact: the true black, with no brown, not even on its muzzle, is supposedly badtempered; the pale chestnut lacks courage; the white horse in particular has almost divine qualities. Its use as a fertility symbol and emblem of power survives in many forms of heraldic art. Although only the Celtic goddess Epona and the horse of Diomedes in Thracian mythology seem to have been considered actually divine, horses were closely connected with gods and goddesses and heroes in many mythologies throughout the Near East and Europe from early times. The Norse god Odin had a semi-magical eightfooted steed called Sleipnir. The names of the Anglo-Saxon Hengist and Horsa (see Great Britain) imply their mythological

Horse in Myth and Legend. *Top:* An eighteenth-century representation of a centaur *Above:* The winged horse, Pegasus, drinking *Right:* Napoleon's horse, Marengo

origin. The English taboo against eating horseflesh may derive from the Church's proscription of an Anglo-Saxon horse cult. The magical properties of the horseshoe, however, seem to be related both to its crescent-moon shape and to its being made of iron, a powerful metal repellent to evil spirits. Its use as a good luck charm survives in many forms including HORSE BRASSES.

More interesting are the legends associated with certain horses which, even if their exploits are hard to believe, are known to have lived and to have been ridden and owned by real people. An obvious example is Bucephalus, the horse of Alexander the Great (356–323 B.C.), a magnificent black animal reputedly quite unridable until mastered by Alexander. After a dramatic career he carried his master though 'pierced with many spears' to safety and then died by the Hydaspes (now the Jhelum) river in northern India. Alexander founded the city of Bucephala by the Hydaspes in his honour.

This 'impossible to ride until . . .' is often found. Here is the inevitable conceit of the horseman who has tamed the great animal. Were this not so it is likely that we should never have heard of Marengo, Napoleon's famous horse, or Copenhagen, owned by the Duke of Wellington; indeed there might have been no charge of the Light Brigade (led by the Earl of Cardigan on his magnificent chestnut at Balaclava). In spite of the praises sung by the author of the *Book of Job,* what horse would face the fire and noise of battle unless it allowed itself, despite its superior strength and speed, to be subjected by man?

From early times, the artist, of course, has been as much inspired by the horse as the storyteller. It was depicted in cave drawings (see Prehistoric Art, Horse in). It dominates the famous sculptures of Ancient Greece such as the Parthenon frieze (see Art, Horse in). In the Iron Age (the date is disputed) the great White Horse at Uffington in Berkshire was carved out of the chalk on the downs. Other horses cut in the chalk downs of southern England are of much later date.

Such a wealth of material gathers round the horse in legend that only one or two of the more famous can be mentioned here. A highly romanticized but attractive story is that of Dick Turpin's Black Bess. One of the best tales, *The Smuggler's Leap*, in which the hero is a supernatural dun horse, is to be found in Barham's *Ingoldsby Legends*. Another well worth reading is that of *Malek Adel* by Ivan Turgenev: about Pantalei Eremeich's search for the horse that he had sold, his fear that what he found was not after all his horse, and the terrifying proof. Better known, perhaps, is the Mongolian Legend of Tarpan by Jose Antonio Benton about the Torguls, a tribe descended from a stallion. On the day of the birth of Torgut, son of the lovely Irgit and magnificent Tarpan (which means stallion), mares, foals and stallions come from North, South, East and West. After a fierce fight with wolves in which the stallions rout twenty thousand of them, Tarpan, immortalized, trots proudly away with the young prince on his back. See also Literature, Horse in. DW

Nanfan (Tibetan Pony) see China, Nepal

Narimsky see Horse Breeding under U.S.S.R.

Narragansett Pacer

A now extinct American light-horse colonial breed noted for its swift and easy pacing gait. Developed on the shores of Narragansett Bay in Rhode Island, these horses were probably a cross between imported English 'ambling horses' and Indian ponies or Spanish JENNETS. In any case, they were small in size, generally sorrel in colour, and endowed with an easy, swift, natural pacing gait. Hardy as well as smooth-moving and surefooted, they were ideal mounts over the rocky, rough tracks of the early colonies.

Although Puritan laws forbade horse-racing in most New England states, pacing races were popular in Baptist Rhode Island, where Narragansett Pacers, it was claimed, could pace a mile in a little over two minutes. During the American Revolution, they were used as cavalry horses by the Continental Army. By the middle of the nineteenth century the Narragansett had practically disappeared as a separate breed. It now survives only as one of the progenitors of the American SADDLEBRED, the TENNESSEE WALKING HORSE and the American STANDARDBRED. MAS

National Equestrian Centre

The N.E.C., comprising the administrative offices of the BRITISH HORSE SOCIETY and the BRITISH SHOW JUMPING ASSOCIATION who are jointly responsible for its management, was founded at Stoneleigh, Warwickshire, England in 1967 with Dorian Williams as its first Honorary Director and Chairman of the Management Committee. It has 300 Founder Members who shared with the Government the cost of establishing the Centre; many firms and individuals contributed towards its equipment.

The Centre is on the site of the Royal Show Ground at Kenilworth and easily accessible from all over Great Britain. In addition to a wide variety of courses at all levels regular competitive events take place there, many of which are televised. About 5,000 people pass through the Centre each year. The indoor riding school is probably the finest in Britain. There are also an outdoor *manège* and a cross-country course. DW

National Federations

Each country affiliated to the FÉDÉRATION ÉQUESTRE INTERNATIONALE has a Federation responsible for administering the international affairs of that country. The official Federation for Britain was the BRITISH HORSE SOCIETY until 1972, thereafter the BRITISH EQUESTRIAN FEDERATION. The Federation for the United States is the AMERICAN HORSE SHOWS ASSOCIATION, for Canada the Canadian Horse Shows Association. DW

National Horse Show, New York

The American National Horse Show, held each November in Madison Square Garden in New York City, features international team jumping and competitions for hunters, national jumpers, fine harness horses, saddlebreds, and classes in equitation. The show began in 1883 and the second Madison Square Garden was built in order to house it. It is now held in the fourth Madison Square Garden.

Cornelius Fellowes was the president of the show from 1883 to 1909. Alfred G. Vanderbilt, the next president, started the international jumping classes in 1909, when the U.S. competed against Britain. The highest fence was 4 ft (1·22 m) and Britain won two of the classes, led by Major John Beresford. A Grand Prix class, the Canadian Challenge Cup, was held in 1910. The course was four fences, 4 ft 3 in (1·29 m), jumped twice, and was won by Britain's Lt C. F. (Taffy) Walwyn on The Nut, with team mate Lt Geoffrey Brooke second. France, Holland, Canada and the host nation also competed. It was not until 1925 that the show was international again. The top class for officers was the Remount Service Cup, which had a $1,000 stake, now called the International Stake. After a succession of brilliant years in the 1930s, in 1941 only the U.S.A., Cuba and Mexico competed. The show was not held during World War II but was resumed in 1946, with the U.S.A. competing against Peru and Mexico. Of 46 classes of the Grand Prix type held through 1970, 13 were won by the host nation, six each by Britain and Mexico, five by Germany, and four each by the Irish Republic and Canada. France won twice, and Belgium, Poland, Chile, Peru,

New York National Horse Show. Rodney Jenkins and Main Spring competing in an Open Jumper class

Argentina and Holland won once each.

A team event was first held in 1911, following the style of that time in which three officers from the same nation rode one after the other. Holland won the first competition from Canada, Britain and the host team. One of the most thrilling competitions was in 1936 when Britain, the Irish Republic, Chile and the United States all had 0 faults after the first round. (Britain won in the second jump-off.) In 1946 Mexico won, and repeated this success in 1947, 1948, 1949, 1951 and 1952, led by Capt. Humberto Mariles. In 1950 Mariles did not ride because of an injury. There was no U.S. team in 1948 and 1949, but in 1950 the new civilian U.S.E.T., of Arthur McCashin, Miss Norma Matthews, and the late Mrs Carol Durand, won. The U.S.E.T. won again in 1957 after Mexico, still led by Mariles, had won in 1954, 1955 and 1956. Germany won in 1958, and Canada's civilians won in 1959. In 1962, the U.S.E.T. began a string of victories that lasted until 1970, when Germany won. Bill Steinkraus, Frank Chapot, Mary Mairs Chapot and Kathy Kusner formed the U.S.E.T. team most of those years. Of the 47 team classes the United States has won 16, Mexico 10, Germany 4, France, Poland, Canada and the Irish Republic 3 each, Holland 2, and Argentina, Britain and Sweden 1 each. Because of limited stabling in the latest Garden, the National has had to limit entries, eliminating hunter ponies and demanding a specified number of wins in recognized shows of all entries. HCA

National Hunt Races see Steeplechasing

National Pony Society

The N.P.S. was formed in England in 1893 'to promote the breeding of ponies for polo, riding and military purposes' and also 'to encourage the native breeds'. The aim was to use small Thoroughbred sires and good polo-playing mares to produce a recognizable polo pony type within the prevailing height limit which would breed true. A Polo Pony Stud Book was set up and the foundation polo pony sire was generally recognized as being Sir Humphrey de Trafford's Thoroughbred Rosewater. Because of the difficulty in preserving the height limit then in force of 14 hands (1·42 m), MOUNTAIN AND MOORLAND ponies were introduced into the Polo Pony Stud Book, Volume V, 1898–9. It was suggested by Lord Arthur Cecil in the introduction to that volume that the small but tough native breeds might make suitable sires. Progress in the polo world overtook this idea, but it was to bear fruit in the future for a different purpose. Inclusion of the native stallions was by inspection, and District Committees were formed to draw up a schedule of points for the guidance of inspectors, which were the forerunners of the present-day Mountain and Moorland breed societies. In 1921 the Board of Agriculture set up committees to advise on the improvement of Mountain and Moorland ponies. Their principal recommendation was for 'the encouragement of pony associations in each district, which would administer the grants through a local committee, under the guidance of the Board of Agriculture and Fisheries'. Among their responsibilities were: the registration of suitable sires and mares in recognized stud books, the award of premiums to Mountain and Moorland stallions to roam at large and to pony-bred stallions to travel; the award of premiums to young mares until they produced a foal. Separate stud books were then opened for the various breeds, some of them being maintained by the National Pony Society and included in the Stud Book in sections separate from the polo ponies, some, as in the case of the Welsh and, later, the New Forest, being maintained locally.

After World War I the emphasis of the objectives gradually shifted away from the polo pony to the development of children's riding ponies, children now having the monopoly of ponies up to 14·2 hands (1·47 m), which had formerly been ridden at polo by adults (see Riding Ponies). The Polo Pony Stud Book was still maintained but its connection with the actual game of polo became more and more tenuous.

After World War II the Board of Agriculture grant to Mountain and Moorland ponies was transferred to the Totalisator Charities Trust under the Racecourse Betting Control Board, taken over in 1962 by the HORSERACE BETTING LEVY BOARD. The grant is paid in bulk to the National Pony Society, which then distributes it to the nine recognized Mountain and Moorland breed societies, retaining a portion for the running of the annual show. In 1950 the

National Pony Society. Welsh ponies, like other British native breeds, have benefited from the activities of the National Pony Society.

Society's responsibilities for the showing of children's riding ponies were taken over by the British Show Pony Society. Today, besides administering the grant and maintaining the Stud Books and Registers, the National Pony Society runs the annual National Pony Show, a Study Management Diploma Training Scheme, pony sales and an advisory organization for the export of ponies. CEGH

Nations' Cup

The Nations' Cup is an international team jumping competition, held at a Concours de Saut International Officiel (C.S.I.O.). It is open to teams of three or four riders and decided over two rounds, with only the best three scores counting in each round. A team with only three riders is therefore at an obvious disadvantage since it cannot discard its two worst scores. It is through Nations' Cups that points are earned for the PRESIDENT'S CUP. GM

Natural Riding a European adaptation of CAPRILLI'S *Sistema*. See Forward Riding

Navicular Disease

A disease confined to the front feet of all riding horses involving the navicular bone (a small, boat-shaped bone) and the deep flexor tendon which glides over its posterior surface. The lesion consists essentially of ulceration of the bone and fraying of the tendon fibres. Adhesions often occur between the bone and the tendon. The disease is insidious in onset; one of the first symptoms is a shortened stride, a 'pottering' action. At rest the foot on the lame side is intermittently held slightly in front of the other, 'pointing'. CF

Neapolitan see Italy

N.E.C. see National Equestrian Centre

Nepal

Among the ponies of Nepal three main types are distinguished: Tarai, Bhotia and Tibetan. The Tarai is the slenderest though not quite the smallest. With a withers height of 11–12 hands (1·12–1·22 m) and a weight of 330–440 lb (150–200 kg) it is a true pituitary dwarf. In size and general conformation it nearly resembles the weedy ponies of the plains of northern India, from which it is doubtless derived. It is quite distinct from the sturdier breeds and varieties of the hill and mountain regions of Nepal, which are partly or wholly derived from Tibetan stock and related to the Mongolian.

The Bhotia hill and mountain ponies are classed into three varieties: Tattu, Chyanta and Tanghan. The Tattu, with a height of 11–12 hands (1·12–1·22 m) and a weight of 440–550 lb (200–250 kg), is the smallest Bhotia type. It is used mainly for baggage work in the mountains. The Chyanta, which stands 12–13 hands (1·22–1·32 m) and weighs 550–660 lb (250–300 kg), is a saddle horse for high mountain travel; it is a good climber with a short stepping walk. The Tanghan is the largest Bhotia type, 13–14 hands (1·32–1·42 m) in height and 660–770 lb (300–350 kg) in weight. It is used mainly as a riding horse; its normal pace is an ordinary walk, but it is also capable of a slow or short trot.

The Tibetan is found in the trans-Himalayan areas of Nepal, which form an extension of the Tibetan tableland. Since the early 1950s, when the government of China established their suzerainty over Tibet, Tibetan ponies have also been seen about the camps of recent Tibetan immigrants in the mountain and hill regions of Nepal. They are ill adapted to the summer heat of the Nepalese hill region and central valleys, and mares in foal or with foals at foot must be taken into the mountains for the summer. The Tibetan is much more compact than the average Bhotia pony. On steep trails it moves sure-footedly at a steady plod; on level ground it is a fast walker in spite of its short, tripping steps. Nearly all Tibetan ponies have a white coat with unpigmented skin. HE

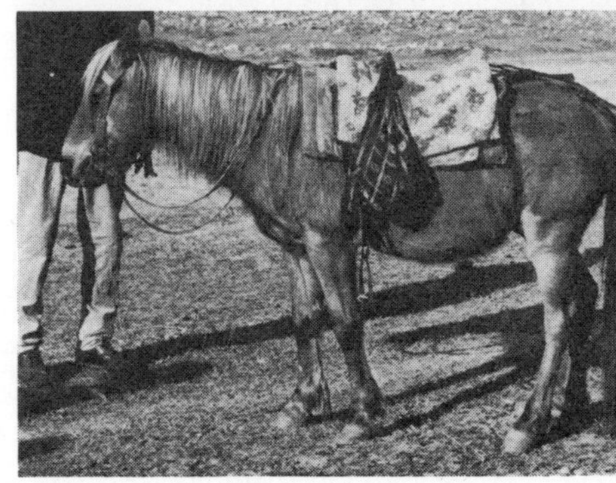

Nepal. *Top:* A Tibetan pony gelding
Above: A Bhotia (Tattu) pony

Nesman see Persian Arab

Netherlands

The Dutch have never been natural horsemen and have tended to be dealers more than breeders, but they have bred good horses. These have had an important influence on breeds in other countries including Great Britain, the United States (trotter), the U.S.S.R. (Orlov trotter) and South Africa (farm horses). The fast horses they have bred have been trotters not racehorses, for the Dutch largely prefer driving to riding. Today in the Netherlands trotting races, held at a number of tracks, are more popular than flat races which are run only at one racecourse, in The Hague. Trotter breeding flourishes: Dutch trotters are of international calibre with many horses that have reached a speed of 1,600 m in 1·20 min.

Thoroughbred breeding is not yet of great importance, but more and more British and German Thoroughbred stallions are imported, not only for breeding racehorses but also light horses for riding. Up to ten years ago DUTCH WARMBLOODS were draught horses, used for farm work. They were of old native (FRIESIAN) origin crossed with (German) EAST FRIESIAN and OLDENBURG stallions or (in the province of Gelderland) with ANGLO-NORMANS and sometimes HACKNEY blood. They were shown in harness, singly and in pairs. Two types were bred: the GRONINGER, a very heavy draught horse like the Oldenburg, and the GELDERLANDER, a horse with higher action and upright head.

With increasing mechanization of agriculture after World War II the breeding of

Duke of Newcastle. 'Monseigneur le Marquis' (the Duke) stands in the centre of this illustration from his *General System of Horsemanship*, instructing Captain Mazin in various movements.

Groningers and Gelderlanders has declined. The Groninger has now almost disappeared; the Gelderlander is used by young farmers for riding. Hundreds of farmers and their families belong to riding clubs. Before the war they had to ride the horses they used on the farm; now they ride what they like. Imported 'halfbred' horses (Trakehner, Holstein, Westphalian) are popular. Post-war changes in breeding in Holland mean that three categories are bred today: (a) riding horses; (b) harness horses; (c) dual-purpose horses. The last group is likely to disappear eventually. Harness horses are in a minority but a flourishing one since show and recreational driving are increasing.

Riding is very popular today. At a rough estimate there are more than 100,000 riders in the Netherlands, including those at riding schools, in riding and pony clubs, and private owners of horses or ponies. In the last ten years riding schools have been built all over the country. Hundreds of pony clubs have been started with members riding Shetland, New Forest, Welsh, Dartmoor or Connemara ponies. Icelandic Ponies are imported for adult pony trekking. FJORD and HAFLINGER horses, formerly imported for agricultural work, are now being bred in the Netherlands for riding and are finding a place in clubs and schools, and in recreational activities. There are also a few good Hackneys, the best blood being imported from England.

The only old truly Dutch breed is the FRIESIAN, found principally in the province of Friesland. Now that there is less demand for farm horses, its future may be as a 'holiday' horse, for it has a very quiet and gentle nature. The Dutch draught horse is of Belgian origin. Although mainly replaced by the tractor, these heavy horses are still bred by a considerable number of people. Every two years a large show for the best of this breed is held at 's-Hertogenbosch.

Competitions in dressage, show jumping and driving are held all over the Netherlands. Classes for horses and ponies in hand are organized by the breed societies, which also run competitions for children on ponies of their breed. WS

Newcastle, William Cavendish, Duke of

Tutor to Charles II when Prince of Wales, the Duke of Newcastle (1592–1676) fought in the English Civil War, after which in exile he wrote *Méthode et Invention Nouvelle de dresser les Chevaux*, printed at Antwerp in 1658. After the brutal coercion advocated by Renaissance writers on horse training his method represented a return to the patient gentleness and psychological subtlety of XENOPHON. Of riding he wrote: 'What exercise is there more noble, more healthy and more esteemed at court than this?' For the purpose of High School riding he esteemed most the Barb, after that the Andalusian breed. Of bits he said. 'Put as little iron in your horse's mouth as you possibly can'. He was the best riding master and the worst cavalry leader of the entire seventeenth century. AD

New Forest Pony see Mountain and Moorland Ponies

New Kirgiz

This is a Russian mountain horse, used for riding, harness, transport and sport; the mare's milk is very good for making kumiss. In races, the New Kirgiz has covered 1,000 m (0·62 mile) in 1 min 15 sec, 1,400 m (0·87 mile) in 2 min 54·3 sec, and 4,800 m (3 miles) in 6 min 16·6 sec. Over longer distances, New Kirgiz horses have travelled 500 km (310 miles) in 54 hr, carrying 100-kg ($220\frac{1}{2}$-lb) loads. Bay, grey, and chestnut are the predominant colours. A massive, muscular torso, quite long, is set on short, powerful legs. The joints are well developed, the hoofs medium-sized with strong bone. The New Kirgiz is usually docile. Average height at the withers for stallions is 15·0$\frac{1}{2}$ hands (1·53 m), for mares 14·2 hands (1·47 m); bone below the knee for stallions is $7\frac{3}{4}$ in (20·0 cm), for mares $7\frac{1}{4}$ in (18·7 cm).

The New Kirgiz has a good gallop and a free walk and trot. It is very hardy, has great stamina and is also good-looking. It moves surefootedly and quickly under saddle or carrying loads over snow-covered mountain trails.

The breed was developed in the Kirgiz republic and the bordering parts of Kazakhstan. The basic stock was the Kirgiz, crossed with the DON and the THOROUGHBRED. The Kirgiz is a very ancient breed, used in studs as far back as the fifteenth century in Altai.

Before the arrival of the Mongol and Turkic tribes, horses of the southern type inhabited Kirgiz territory. The Mongols changed the Kirgiz studs, sent some horses south, and interbred others with Mongol horses. The resulting crossbreds were sturdy but small (13·1 hands or 1·34 m). In a scientific program to develop them into suitable riding and harness horses (1930–1940), Kirgiz mares were crossed with Thoroughbred stallions as well as with AKHAL TEKE, KARABAIR, and IOMUD stallions. Since the second generation of these Anglo-Kirgiz crosses were not as good as the first, it was decided to cross the Anglo-Kirgiz with Don, Anglo-Don, and Kirgiz-Don stallions. The resulting crossbreds surpassed both the Don-Kirgiz and Anglo-Kirgiz in stamina and adaptability. From this group the desired types were selected and interbred, producing hardy, adaptable, fertile horses, easy to keep in condition on a varied diet. The stallions of this group were then put to Don-Kirgiz and Anglo-Kirgiz mares, resulting in a breed approximately 50 per cent Don, 25 per cent English Thoroughbred, and 25 per cent Kirgiz. WOF

New Kirgiz. *Top:* A horse of the Kirgiz type *Above:* A New Kirgiz stallion

Newmarket

Newmarket, Suffolk, has been the principal centre of horseracing in Britain since the reign of Charles II (1660–1685), who had a palace there, and is the headquarters of the JOCKEY CLUB.

The most important races at Newmarket are the Two Thousand Guineas and One Thousand Guineas, in the spring, and the Cesarewitch, the Cambridgeshire, the Champion Stakes and Middle Park Stakes in the autumn. About 2,000 horses are trained in some 35 stables in the town.

Among the historic buildings are the Palace House stables, where Charles II's horses were kept 300 years ago. Bruce Hobbs trains in them today. The National Stud has been at Newmarket since 1967 and there are more than 40 other studs in the area. RO

New York National Horse Show

see National Horse Show, New York

New Zealand

The early European settlers imported horses into New Zealand primarily as a means of locomotion, then to break in the virgin land, for this country has no indigenous placental mammals. The first recorded entry was of three horses landed on 3 December 1814 by the missionary Rev. Samuel Marsden, others following rapidly with importations of livestock from Australia.

Thoroughbreds: the first was the stallion Figaro from Mr T. Icely's Cooming Stud in Australia in the early 1840s, the second of any note the great mare Flora McIvor in 1853. The first to come directly from England, the fine stallion Traducer (by The Libel), arrived in 1862 and when in 1878 the equally famous Musket arrived the New Zealand Thoroughbred industry might be said to have been firmly established. Musket sired the remarkable Carbine and Trenton, both later sold to England, and Sir Modred, exported to the United States where he headed the winning sire's list in 1894.

The country proved ideal for rearing young stock, which rapidly found a ready market overseas; this, together with the consistent emphasis by breeders on middle distance and staying blood, has made the New Zealand Thoroughbred known the world over for bone, stamina and size. In 1927 National Yearling Sales were established which have grown from a turnover at the first sales of $NZ50,000 to one of over $NZ1,500,000; of the 343 yearlings sold there in 1971, 66 per cent went to overseas buyers for a total of $NZ1,204,800. The first Turf Register was produced in 1876 and Volume 1 of the Stud Book in 1900, though records go back to the late 1850s. There are at present 280 stallions standing, and 7,200 mares registered.

Among the great racehorses bred in New Zealand are Moifaa (which went to England in 1904 to win the Aintree GRAND NATIONAL); Carbine; Desert Gold (f. 1912 by All Black); Gloaming (f. 1916 by The Welkin); Phar Lap (f. 1926 by Night Raid); Tullock (f. 1954 by Khorassan); Il Tempo (f. 1964 by Time and Again).

Trotting and Pacing: this is considered the fastest-growing spectator sport in the country, especially since night-racing was introduced in 1958. About 2,000 horses compete each season at the 133 meetings run by the 47 non-proprietary clubs, total attendance in the 1970–1 season exceeding 1,000,000 while betting amounted to almost $NZ44·5 million, more than $NZ25 million coming from legalized off-course investments.

All Standardbreds here trace back to imports from the United States, the first of note being the stallions Berlin and Blackwood Abdallah and mares Blue Grass Belle, Fannie Belle, Jeannie Tracey, Messenger Maid, Queen Emma and Woodburn Maid, in 1882. The sport was formally established in 1896 with the formation of the N.Z. Trotting Association, which in 1950 became the N.Z.T. Conference. Records and Stud Book have been kept since the earlier authority.

During the 1960s and early 1970s a multi-million-dollar business has been developed and more than 200 horses are exported annually to Australia and the United States, most of those to the latter country being proven race performers whose staying power and courage have brought them remarkable success. World fame was brought to the industry when Cardigan Bay (by Hal Tryax from Colwyn Bay) was sold to the States for $NZ100,000 for his racing career and there became the first pacer ever to win more than $NZ1,000,000 in stakes. More than 3,400 mares were put to 193 stallions in the last breeding season.

Organized Horse Sports: colonized comparatively late and extremely difficult in terrain, New Zealand was dependent upon the horse for work and transport until well into the twentieth century, so naturally all forms of horse sports developed along with racing. Agricultural shows were held from early days and each contained classes for hacks, hunters, draught horses, ponies, stock horses and for jumping.

The jumping competitions were of the 'round the ring' type, judged on style, until the N.Z. Horse Society was formed in 1950 and show jumping under international rules was introduced. New Zealand sent its first equestrian competitor to the OLYMPIC GAMES in 1960, at Rome. This was a lone and courageous effort by Adrian White riding Telebrae and, considering their lack of experience, horse and rider acquitted themselves well. This was followed by a full team to the Tokyo Games in 1964, where again New Zealand horses and riders showed they had great potential. Show jumping, horse trials and dressage are now firmly established and the N.Z.H.S. has a current membership of 3,100.

The New Zealand Pony Clubs Association (formed 1946) has a membership of 10,454, with annual championships and competitions at the biennial Inter-Pacific Rallies (established 1959).

Hunting began in the 1880s; the first club, the Pakuranga, was actually formed in 1873. The N.Z. Hunts Association (established in 1900 with nine member clubs) now has 26 hunts affiliated, subscribers numbering 6,738. Harriers are used, the quarry introduced being hare, though two hunts are solely drag and two others partly so.

The N.Z. Polo Association (1891) has 225 players registered from 22 clubs, the major competition being the Savile Cup, contested annually since 1890.

Rodeo has a keen following, with a membership of over 1,000. Competition is based on international rules and the country has produced two world champions: Warwick Stegall of Gisborne won the Ampol World Championship Bareback Ride in Australia in 1958 and Evan Rayner of Wanganui the Saddle Bronc title there in 1967. Thirty-two clubs form the N.Z. Association of Rodeo.

Other organized forms of riding include pony safaris, trekking, 100-mile endurance riding, and various types of riding schools and equestrian centres.

Breed Societies: necessarily, the heavy draught horse played a major role in New Zealand's early establishment, not only in the country's essential economy but in proving, along with the Thoroughbred, that here was a nursery for young stock second to none in the world. CLYDESDALES proved the most suitable breed, and imports such as Berlin Congress and the famous mare Loch Leven in 1871, followed by the sire Junior Chief and the mare Maid o' Threave, with countless others of Scotland's choicest blood, soon gave New Zealand young stock world ranking. Indeed between 1878 and 1929 the largest and finest stud in the Southern Hemisphere was recognized as being that of Sir Douglas McLean in Hawkes Bay. Though vastly reduced since its heyday in the 1930s, the Clydesdale Society is still active, the Stud Book is still meticulously maintained, the horses are still bred, still worked in parts of the country, and still exported.

One of the first ARAB stallions to come in was Arab Child in the 1880s; there have been many since. The first Registry was started in 1954 and later incorporated as the Arabian Horse Registry of New Zealand and includes Anglo-Arabs and Partbreds. There are currently 51 purebred Arab stallions listed and as many mares.

The Pony Breeders' Society was formed, and published its first Stud Book, in 1957. Purebreds are mainly Welsh Mountain, with Welsh, Shetland and one New Forest. The ponies registered are evolved from crosses with these, the Arabians, and Thoroughbreds.

The first QUARTER HORSES, the stallions Di Bar Flit and Mike Stead, were brought to New Zealand in 1969 by the American businessman and landowner W. B. Mendenhall. The N.Z. Quarterhorse Association was formed in 1970, and in 1971 the N.Z. Quarter Mile Racing Association was incorporated. There are now two studs comprising five imported stallions and a dozen mares imported with foals. DH, TH

New Zealand. Show jumping at the Lake Hayes Show near Queenstown, Otago

Top: **Nonius.** Stallion 50

Centre: **Norman, Anglo-Norman** and **French Saddle Horse.** An Anglo-Norman stallion
Above: A French Saddle Horse stallion at Haras du Pin

New Zealand Rug see Clothing, Horse

Nicking
(1) The operation of cutting the small tendons under the tail of a horse, so that when they heal they are slightly longer than they were before. This enables the tail to be set much higher by means of a special crupper, with the object of giving a higher and more showy tail-carriage. This is an operation confined to the United States, mainly carried out on gaited horses (see Saddlebred).
(2) The practice, mainly in Thoroughbred breeding, of mating two bloodlines which seem to have an affinity for each other and produce exceptional results, the result being called a 'nick'. For example Bend Or 'nicked' with mares by Macaroni to produce, among others, the TRIPLE CROWN winner Ormonde (out of Sister Agnes), and Ornament, the dam of Sceptre. Another significant 'nick' was that of Phalaris with Chaucer mares. CEGH
Reference: Sir Charles Leicester, Bt, *Bloodstock Breeding,* London, 1957.

Nisaean Horse see Persian Horse

Nivernais Horse see Percheron

Nivernais-Charollais see Norman, Anglo-Norman and French Saddle Horse

Nonius
This Anglo-Norman strain originated in the Hungarian stud at Mezöhegyes. At present it is bred in Yugoslavia, Rumania and Czechoslovakia. The branch was founded by the stallion Nonius, taken as a prize of war as a five-year-old colt by Austrian cavalrymen when they occupied the stud at Rossières in France. According to French records, Nonius was sired in 1810 at a stud in Calvados (Normandy) by the English halfbred stallion Orion from a Norman mare. Records decribe Nonius as a fair bay, 16·1½ hands (1·71 m) high, with a heavy head, small eyes and long ears, a short neck, long back, a narrow pelvis and a low-set tail, suggesting a not very handsome horse. He was therefore not much used at first. Until it was discovered that he sired very good and reliable stock of the right type, the Mezöhegyes stud used him indiscriminately on Spanish, Lipizzaner and Kladrub mares as well as on Arab, Norman and English halfbred mares. He was very prolific and sired 79 stallions and 137 mares. The Nonius strain is now very popular with farmers in Czechoslovakia, Hungary and Yugoslavia. The horses do not mature until six years of age, are usually black or brown in colour, with a very good temperament, well-disposed for harness, but rarely used for riding. In Czechoslovakia they are bred at the Topolčianky stud in Slovakia. See also Arab in Czechoslovakia. PNe

Norfolk Roadster, Norfolk Trotter
A strong, fast-trotting horse which had great influence on the development of the HACKNEY and STANDARDBRED trotting breeds.

Noriker see Pinzgauer Noriker

Norman, Anglo-Norman and French Saddle Horse
The Norman Horse, benefiting from an exceptionally good climate and soil, has always held an important place in French breeding. As early as the seventeenth century, there were imports of mostly Scandinavian and German stallions, sometimes BARBS and ARABS. This policy of improving stock was followed in the eighteenth and nineteenth centuries by imports of English THOROUGHBREDS, NORFOLK TROTTERS and HUNTERS. From all these crossings with the native breed came the Anglo-Norman halfbred, which in turn became the principal stock for the halfbred of the central part of France, *demi-sang du centre* (Nivernais-Charollais) and the halfbred of the west, *demi-sang de l'ouest* (Maine, Vendéen-Charentais), both of which were specially bred for the saddle earlier than the Anglo-Norman. According to demand and at different periods, the Norman halfbred was in turn bred as a coach horse, racing trotter, charger or saddle horse. Since 1965 the Anglo-Norman has been the main foundation of the French Saddle Horse (*selle français*), which is a halfbred born and reared in France and produced by different crossings (Anglo-Norman, Trotter, Thoroughbred, Anglo-Arab, Arab) but bred essentially for riding. It is bred mostly in Normandy but also in Anjou, Charollais (southern Burgundy), Ain (border of Switzerland), Vendée and Charente (Atlantic coastal regions). The Trotter and the French Saddle Horse, now separate breeds, have their own stud books, but that of the latter is the continuation of the former Anglo-Norman stud book.

The Anglo-Norman is a larger horse with a bay or chestnut coat. It can be higher than 16·1 hands (1·70 m). It has a ram-shaped head, rather long ears, a long and strong neck, ample chest and powerful shoulders. Its very muscular hindquarters make it a fine jumper. It is a powerful and courageous riding horse with a good temperament. ES

Northern Draught Horse (French) see Trait du Nord

North Star see Hungary

North Swedish Horse
This breed is descended from a small native horse which stood between 14·2 hands (1·47 m) and 15 hands (1·52 m) and was crossed with various other breeds. There was thus no distinct type until 1890 when

a breed society was formed and a more uniform type of horse began to be produced by using stallions of the closely related Norwegian GUDBRANDSDAL breed. In 1900 the breed became known as the North Swedish Horse, and in 1924 the breed society became a national one with its own registry and stud book.

The North Swedish Horse is a middle-sized cold-blooded horse averaging between 15·1 hands (1·55 m) and 15·3 hands (1·62 m), the stallions being somewhat larger than the mares. It has an especially good temperament and has very good and energetic movements, like those of a riding horse. It is also very easy to look after, not requiring sophisticated handling or attention, which makes it an excellent horse on the farms and in the forests. It is a magnificent trotter and is much used in the north for the popular trotting competitions. The Swedish army used it formerly for pulling guns and other heavy loads, and even as a cavalry remount. PL

Norway

This was the first European country for which there are records (contemporary with the English King Alfred) of the horse-drawn plough, and through its dissemination in the period of Viking expansion it exercised an enormous long-range economic influence (see Agriculture, Horse in). The practice arose because on steep slopes horses are more efficient than oxen in the plough, even if more expensive to keep. But so using horses entailed the invention or adoption from (Asiatic?) sources of a type of harness also suitable for use with carts or wagons, not a mere adaptation of the ox-yoke, under which the horse cannot work with maximum effect. Thus the beginning of the slow technological revolution which made the fast horse-drawn carriage possible can be traced, in the West at least, to Norway.

The rural economy of Norway relied heavily on seasonal occupation of mountain pastures (*sœter*) by dairy cattle and goats; to get the products down to the main farm, as liquid milk, or butter or cheese, strong and surefooted packhorses were essential, using tracks too narrow and steep for any kind of wheeled vehicle. On the flat, if narrow bottoms of the valleys, wagons were, however, in use. Thus from an early date a dual-purpose pack-and-harness animal was favoured, corresponding in many respects to the Fell and Dales Ponies of northern England (see Mountain and Moorland Ponies).

From the Bronze Age onwards the horse, either ridden or driven, was a symbol of prestige in Norway, although for many purposes its function could as well be carried out by boat: it is significant that wedding customs among the wealthier Norwegian peasant proprietors included a procession of *either* decorated boats *or* of riders on decorated horses for the bridal cortège.

Thus in a country without a native aristocracy in the feudal sense the horse for all its practical utility remained also a status symbol. In the mid-nineteenth century fashion displayed itself in the rural communities by the quality and elaborate ornamentation of the sidesaddles on which the wives of Gudbrandsdal farmers rode to church. The Scottish traveller Samuel Laing observed on his Norwegian tour of 1834–6: 'There is no part of Europe less adapted for cavalry movements than this part of Norway, . . . yet cavalry is the passion of the country'. Laing wrote at the dawn of the Railway Age. Yet even at its zenith, Norway, because of the mountainous terrain and heavily indented coastlines, had a very small railway network by western European standards and, until the advent of the car, travel was by ferry-boat or horse-drawn sleigh in winter and horse-drawn gig (*stolkjœrre*) in summer. As a matter of utility therefore a fast-trotting harness horse was an inevitable product of the country, and as an entertainment today trotting in harness is the form of horseracing that flourishes most in Norway.

The utility of the Norwegian native breeds as pack animals in mountain country led, inevitably, to wholesale requisitioning by the Germans as soon as their occupation began in 1940; as the war dragged on with ever deeper commitment of the Wehrmacht in areas (Italy, the Balkans, Russia) where motorized transport could not be used aside from certain main road axes, horse breeding was compulsorily expanded in the interests of the occupying power. By 1945 the horse population of Norway stood at a surprisingly high figure, partly accounted for by the scarcity of fuel for civilian vehicles, and reliance on the horse for domestic purposes was higher than in peacetime.

Since then it has declined, as everywhere in Europe, the more so as the economy of *sœter*-style dairy farming becomes less and less viable under modern marketing conditions and obtaining hired labour to man the upland shielings becomes more difficult. But despite the increasing number of small tractors for use in mountain country there will always be a hard core of upland which can only be travelled over or worked by means of the horse; this, together with the possibilities of tourist traffic in the inland parts of the country and the increasing popularity of the horse for the leisure activities of town-dwellers, combines with the Norwegian farmers' traditional high regard for the horse, emotional as well as practical, to ensure that the Norwegian stock of horses of all breeds will not fall far below the present level in the foreseeable future. AD

Below: **North Swedish Horse**

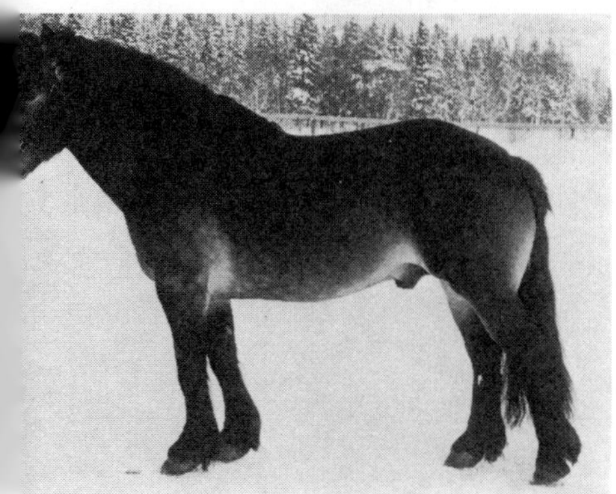

Nosebands

Nosebands of the plain cavesson type came

into general use in England in the latter half of the nineteenth century and can be regarded as largely decorative. They serve one useful purpose as an anchorage for a standing martingale but otherwise add nothing to the rider's control of the horse, although a partial closure of the mouth may be effected if the noseband is buckled tightly. Of more practical value is the *drop noseband* originating in the Continental military schools. This is fastened under the bit with the nosepiece some three inches above the nostril and effectively prevents evasion of the bit action by the opening of the mouth. Furthermore, it adds to and alters to a degree the action of the snaffle bit. Pressure on the rein induces a retraction of the lower jaw through the bit and consequently, since the jaws are encompassed by the noseband, pressure is exerted on the sensitive portion of the nose itself and may possibly cause a slight momentary restriction on the breathing. The result is that the horse drops its nose in response, thus placing its mouth in relation to the hand in a position that gives the greatest measure of control to the rider. Clearly it is an effective method of checking an over-exuberant animal and it also allows the rider to obtain a certain flexion in the lower jaw before introducing the horse to the double bridle.

The principal remaining nosebands are the *Figure 8*, now indistinguishable from the *Grakle*, so named after the winner of the Grand National, and the *Puckle* or *Kineton* noseband, Puckle being the name of the inventor and Kineton being the village in which he lived. The Grakle, fastening by crossed straps both above and below the bit, is thought to prevent a horse evading the bit by crossing its jaws. The point of pressure at the juncture of the crossing straps is higher on the nose than in the conventional drop noseband and the action upon the head position is therefore less definite. The Kineton is a device to be confined to the inveterate puller and its action on the nose is a strong one. It comprises two metal loops adjusted inside the bit rings and in contact with the rear of the mouthpiece on each side; these loops are joined by an adjustable nose strap, into which a strip of metal is frequently inserted. Pressure on the reins produces a direct and corresponding pressure on the nose causing a momentary restriction of the breathing which ceases when the horse drops its nose and comes back to hand. EHE

N.P.S. see National Pony Society

Nubian Ass see Ass, Wild African

Numnah

A protective pad cut to the same shape and slightly larger than the saddle and placed between it and the horse's back. It is usually made of sheepskin or artificial sheepskin; foam (rubber or plastic) on its own or covered in linen or man-made material, leather or felt may also be used. It is held on by straps that pass over or fix onto the girth straps under the saddle flap. The term is derived from an Urdu word of Persian origin meaning 'carpet, rug'. See Clothing, Horse. DRT

O

Oaks, The see Classic Races

Obvinka, Obwinki see Viatka

Oldenburg

The Oldenburg breed of northwestern Germany goes back to the FRIESIAN horse, which had both Andalusian and Oriental bloodlines; even before the Thirty Years War (1618–48) there were records of Friesian-Oldenburg horses of big, strong conformation and high action with plenty of scope. Some of the Spanish lines inherited the markedly Roman nose. Needing a strong horse for agriculture, Oldenburg farmers later organized themselves into a society to improve the breed. In about 1897, THOROUGHBRED stallions were imported from England, as well as CLEVELAND BAYS and the potent Normann 710, a NORMAN stallion descended from the imported and very active NORFOLK ROADSTER horse. HANOVERIAN and the old SENNER blood was also used. Breeding was judicious and served to strengthen the Oldenburg. Hardly any further outside blood was used once the type was establish-

Far right: **Olympic Games.** A fourth-century B.C. chariot rounds the turning post in the hippodrome.

Below: **Oldenburg**

ed. Breeders aim for a strong, capable horse which is fertile, long-lived and a good doer, with strong joints and hoofs, a marked shoulder, deep body, good muscles, powerful quarters and vigorous action. In 1950 Condor was imported from Normandy to improve and consolidate. See also Germany. DMG

Old English Black Horse ancestor of the SHIRE. See Great Britain

Olympia see Royal International Horse Show

Olympic Games

Classic Times: the Olympic Games of ancient Greece were held every four years in honour of Zeus, although their origin is thought to have been the contest between Pelops of Phrygia and Oenomoos, King of Elis. The hero Herakles is credited as the originator of competitive games and founder of Olympic rules and regulations.

Chariot races were introduced in the Hippodrome in 680 B.C. The Hippodrome, 770 m (2,526 ft) long and 100 m (328 ft) wide, had to be traversed at least ten times in both directions. At first quadrigas (four horses abreast to a chariot) were used; later it is said that mules were driven but after 408 B.C. pair-horse chariots were favoured. There were also competitions in which the riders had to leap from their horses and run beside them, as well as races between riders wearing cuirasses.

The Olympic Games, as the name suggests, were held at Olympia in Elis, on the plain between the rivers Alpheios and Kladeos, guaranteeing peace after a sacred agreement between King Iphitos of Elis and Lycurgus of Sparta. At the beginning it appears that the neighbouring Pisatans presided over the Games but early in the sixth century B.C. Olympia won control. The buildings were erected over a period of time.

The fifth-century B.C. historian Herodotus wrote that Solon explained to the Scythian Anacharsis that only a few could win prizes but every individual representing his country could enjoy the laurels, not of ivy or olive, but of mortal bliss. Philip II of Macedonia, being told of victory by his generals, the birth of his son (later Alexander the Great) and the success of one of his horses in the Olympic Games, found the last piece of news the most pleasing and issued a coin to celebrate the event.

Under the Romans, the quadrigas raced under colours and political factions followed their chosen teams enthusiastically. Olympia was destroyed during the great Asiatic invasions, the river Kladeos flooded the plain, covering the ruins and eventually the meaning of Olympia disappeared. DMG

Reference: Dr R. Keller, 'Die Olympische Reiterspiele von Anbeginn unter Kulturhistorische Aspekt', *Sankt Georg Almanach*, Düsseldorf, 1956; D. Machin Goodall, *The Horseman's Year,* London, 1965.

Modern Times: there were no equestrian events at the first modern Olympic games in Athens, Greece, in 1896, nor was riding included in the programs of the 1900, 1904 and 1908 games. The equestrian sport became an Olympic event in the 1912 Games in Stockholm, Sweden, thanks to the untiring efforts of Count Clarence von Rosen, Master of the Horse to the King of Sweden.

The program for this first Olympic Equestrian Games consisted of an individual dressage with maximum six riders per nation; a three-day event with teams of four riders, of which three counted toward the team championship; an individual jumping with six riders and a team jumping with four riders per nation, of which three counted. Except for the addition of a team championship in dressage (from 1928) and that only three or four riders (instead of six) are allowed in the individual classes, the 1972 version of the equestrian program at the Olympics is virtually the same as the one created over sixty years before. Although some alterations have been attempted over the years, the wisdom of the Swedes of 1912 has prevailed.

Ten nations sent their representatives to the first Olympic Games. Only two, however, came with full teams: Sweden and Germany; other countries such as France, Great Britain, Belgium and the United States entered the same four riders and horses in several if not in all of the four competitions. The 1912 Games were dominated by Sweden and, to a lesser degree, by Germany. The former won four of the five gold medals, and Germany got three silver and one bronze. One gold, one silver and one bronze medal were won by France.

The success of Stockholm secured a definite place in the Olympic program for equestrian sport. World War I, however, preven-

Olympic Games
Winners of Equestrian Events

Games	Event	Winners
1896 Athens	*No Equestrian Events*	
1900 Paris	*No Equestrian Events*	
1904 St Louis	*No Equestrian Events*	
1908 London	*No Equestrian Events*	
1912 Stockholm	*Three-Day Event*	Team: Sweden Individual: Lt A. Nordlander, Lady Artist (Sweden)
	Show Jumping	Team: Sweden Individual: Capt J. Cariou, Mignon (France)
	Grand Prix de Dressage	Team: No Competition Individual: Count C. Bonde, Emperor (Sweden)
1916 Berlin	*Not Held*	
1920 Antwerp	*Three-Day Event*	Team: Sweden Individual: Count H. Mörner, Germania (Sweden)
	Show Jumping	Team: Sweden Individual: Lt T. Lequio, Trebecco (Italy)
	Grand Prix de Dressage	Team: No Competition Individual: Capt J. Lundblad, Uno (Sweden)

Olympic Games. *Right:* William Steinkraus (U.S.A.) riding Snowbound in the 1968 Show-Jumping Grand Prix to win the individual gold medal
Far right: Jim Day (Canada) riding Canadian Club at the 1968 Games in which Canada won the team gold medal for show jumping

1924 Paris	
Three-Day Event	Team: Holland Individual: Lt A. v. d. V. van Zijp Silver Piece (Holland)
Show Jumping	Team: Sweden Individual: Lt A. Gemuseus, Lucette (Switzerland)
Grand Prix de Dressage	Team: No Competition Individual: General E. Linder, Piccolomini (Sweden)
1928 Amsterdam	
Three-Day Event	Team: Holland Individual: Lt Ch. Pahud de Mortanges, Marcroix (Holland)
Show Jumping	Team: Spain Individual: Capt F. Ventura, Eliot (Czechoslovakia)
Grand Prix de Dressage	Team: Germany Individual: Baron C. F. von Langen, Draufgänger (Germany)
1932 Los Angeles	
Three-Day Event	Team: U.S.A. Individual: Lt Ch. Pahud de Mortanges, Marcroix (Holland)
Show Jumping	Team: Not Awarded Individual: Baron T. Nishi, Uranus (Japan)
Grand Prix de Dressage	Team: France Individual: Comdt F. Lesage, Taine (France)
1936 Berlin	
Three-Day Event	Team: Germany Individual: Capt L. Stubbendorf, Nurmi (Germany)
Show Jumping	Team: Germany Individual: Lt K. Hasse, Tora (Germany)
Grand Prix de Dressage	Team: Germany Individual: Lt H. Pollay, Kronos (Germany)
1940 Tokyo, Helsinki	
Not Held	
1944 London	
Not Held	
1948 London	
Three-Day Event	Team: U.S.A. Individual: Capt B. Chevallier, Aiglonne (France)
Show Jumping	Team: Mexico Individual: Col H. Mariles Arete (Mexico)
Grand Prix de Dressage	Team: France Individual: Capt H. Moser, Hummer (Switzerland)

ted the celebration of the sixth Olympic Games, scheduled for 1916 in Berlin, and it was only in 1920 at the seventh Olympic Games in Antwerp, Belgium, that the second equestrian games were held. Antwerp was a satisfactory, although in organization not entirely successful, beginning soon after a long and devastating war. Eight nations sent riders. Sweden was the winner again, getting four gold, two silver and two bronze medals. Italy, participating for the first time, did well in jumping and to a lesser degree in the three-day event.

The equestrian events of the eighth Olympic Games, held in Paris, France, in 1924, had excellent participation from 17 nations, many of them, especially eastern European nations, competing for the first time. Nevertheless, Sweden again was the winner, getting two gold and two silver medals. The surprises were the riders of two small nations: the Dutch won the three-day event, while the Swiss won individual gold and team silver in the jumping, held for the first time as one event. The three-day event found its present formula: dressage on the first day; endurance ride in two phases with steeplechase in between and followed by a cross-country ride on the second day; jumping on the third day. Only the relative importance of the various parts has changed over the years.

Germany, whose non-invitation by France to the 1924 Olympics had created quite a furore, was back in 1928 at the ninth Olympic Games, held in Amsterdam, Holland. They were successful, especially in dressage, where they not only won both gold medals, but also had the satisfaction that eight of the twelve top placed horses were German-bred. The Dutch, on their home ground, repeated their 1924 three-day victory with a near-total triumph, when their three riders placed first, second and fourth. Only three teams out of 14 finished the event, a direct result of the reduction of riders allowed per team from four to three.

The easiness of the 1928 jumping course caused the maximum height of the fences to be raised from 1·40 m (4 ft 7¼ in) to 1·60 m (5 ft 3 in) for the 1932 Olympic Games. It was a necessary decision, but because the 1932 Games were held outside Europe for the first time, had a very unfortunate result. Only three full teams competed for the team medals in Los Angeles, none brought all three riders over the course and consequently no team medals were awarded. None of the top jumping powers at that time was represented in Los Angeles. In the three-day event, the only European teams came from Holland and Sweden, and in dressage, the European representation consisted of Sweden and France. The Americans, winning one gold, two silver and two bronze medals, got the biggest share of prizes. Berlin (1936) was different. Equestrian sport, still entirely dominated by the mounted services, had reached its peak with most countries having permanent jumping, dressage, even three-day stables, which competed against each other all year long in Europe and America at a well-organized circuit of international shows. For the eleventh Olympic Games, Nazi Germany provided near-perfect organization and unmatched enthusiasm from the population. This preparation was richly rewarded when Germany won all six equestrian gold medals. Altogether, 127 riders with 133 horses from 21 countries competed. The

Grand Prix de Dressage was the last encounter of the three nations who had dominated dressage all these years. Germany won, France was second and Sweden third. In the three-day event, the rule that only three riders were allowed resulted in the elimination of all favoured nations except Germany. The course for the jumping event was, relative to the standards of that time, extremely difficult and, although built by a German, nearly caused the downfall of the much favoured German team, which won its sixth gold medal only after the third rider of the leading team had failed.

The 1940 Olympic Games, originally scheduled for Tokyo, then switched to Helsinki, were finally cancelled, as were the 1944 Games, awarded to London. In 1948, after World War II, the fourteenth Olympic Games were held in London. With Germany and the eastern European nations absent, the 21-nation record of Berlin could not be matched. Still, 17 nations sent 103 riders with 108 horses. There was no clear-cut over-all winner, although the United States, with its last army team, won the most medals. A Swiss won the dressage, but since he was the only representative of his country, the team gold medal went to Sweden, until one of their riders was disqualified. The gold medal then went to France. The three-day event, like the dressage, was considerably easier than in the 1936 Games. The main consequence was that this Olympic three-day event in Aldershot was the initial spark that got the British interested in eventing; an interest which has led to their current world dominance.

The 1952 Olympic Games were awarded to Helsinki, Finland, which staged them in a very dignified manner as, probably, the last small-scale Olympics. Twenty-five nations, a new record, sent 134 riders. Germany was back in the Olympic arena, as was the Soviet Union, the latter after an absence of 40 years. Sweden won four gold medals. For the first time in Olympic history non-commissioned officers and women were allowed to compete, the women in dressage only. In this event, four non-commissioned officers and two women were placed among the top ten.

The equestrian events of the 1956 Olympic Games were held in Stockholm, Sweden, because the quarantine rules in Australia, to whom the sixteenth Olympic Games were awarded, made it impossible to send horses there. The result of this separation was the most perfect horse Olympics ever; but it was feared that the Olympic touch would be missing if this separation were repeated. West Germany, winning medals in all three events, individually and on a team level and the host nation, Sweden, were the big winners.

The 1960 Olympic Games in Rome brought new records in participation: 73 riders in the three-day event, 60 in the individual

jumping. There was no team competition in dressage, the result of unfortunate nationalism by the 1956 judges which prompted the International Olympic Committee to consider the abolition of all equestrian team events. There were also, as in 1912–1920 and from 1968 on again, two jumping competitions: one for individual, the other for team honours. The Soviet Union was the not entirely unexpected, but still surprising winner in the dressage, and Australia dominated the three-day event. In the jumping events, Italy was placed first and second in the individual jumping held on the Piazza di Siena, but lost the team gold to Germany.

Four years later, the equestrians met for the second time outside Europe: in Tokyo, Japan. Despite the long distances for many teams participation was, in contrast to Los Angeles 32 years before, truly Olympic. In dressage Germany overtook the Russians again, but the coveted individual gold medal went to a Swiss. After 1952, when women were allowed in dressage and 1956 when the first woman participated in jumping, the Olympic three-day event finally became open to the female sex too. In jumping the Italians repeated their success in the individual event and Germany, against all predictions, won the team gold medal.

In 1968, Mexico was host for the nineteenth Games, the twelfth to include riding. In the three-day event heavy rain played a part. The surprise of the dressage event was the strong showing of the East Germans, while in the three-day event, the British proved their superiority in finishing second, fourth and fifth, although individual gold went to France. The jumping produced an old favourite from the United States Eques-

1952 Helsinki	
Three-Day Event	Team: Sweden Individual: Capt H. von Blixen-Finecke, Jubal (Sweden)
Show Jumping	Team: Great Britain Individual: P. J. d'Oriola, Ali Baba (France)
Grand Prix de Dressage	Team: Sweden Individual: Maj H. St Cyr, Master Rufus (Sweden)
1956 Melbourne (equestrian events in Stockholm)	
Three-Day Event	Team: Great Britain Individual: Sgt P. Kastenman, Iluster (Sweden)
Show Jumping	Team: Germany Individual: H. G. Winkler, Halla (Germany)
Grand Prix de Dressage	Team: Sweden Individual: Maj H. St Cyr, Juli (Sweden)
1960 Rome	
Three-Day Event	Team: Australia Individual: L. Morgan, Salad Days (Australia)
Show Jumping	Team: Germany Individual: Capt R. d'Inzeo, Posillipo (Italy)
Grand Prix de Dressage	Team: No Competition Individual: S. Filatov, Absent (U.S.S.R.)

Olympic Games. *Right:* G. Mancinelli (Italy) riding Ambassador in the 1972 Show-Jumping Grand Prix to win the individual gold medal *Below:* Richard Meade (Great Britain) riding Laurieston in the show-jumping section of the 1972 Three-Day Event. Great Britain won the team gold medal, Meade the individual gold medal.

1964 Tokyo	
Three-Day Event	Team: Italy Individual: M. Checcoli, Surbean (Italy)
Show Jumping	Team: Germany Individual: P. J. d'Oriola, Lutteur (France)
Grand Prix de Dressage	Team: Germany Individual: Sgt H. Chammartin, Wörmann (Switzerland)
1968 Mexico City	
Three-Day Event	Team: Great Britain Individual: Adj J.-J. Guyon, Pitou (France)
Show Jumping	Team: Canada Individual: W. Steinkraus, Snowbound (U.S.A.)
Grand Prix de Dressage	Team: West Germany Individual: I. Kisimov, Ikhor (U.S.S.R.)
1972 Munich	
Three-Day Event	Team: Great Britain Individual: R. Meade, Laurieston (Great Britain)
Show Jumping	Team: West Germany Individual: G. Mancinelli, Ambassador (Italy)
Grand Prix de Dressage	Team: U.S.S.R. Individual: L. Linsenhoff, Piaff (W. Germany)

trian team as winner, and Canada was an unexpected winner of the team jumping.

At the 1972 Games in Munich, the British again won the three-day event, West Germany the individual dressage and the show jumping, although the individual gold medal went to Italy, and the U.S.S.R. won the team dressage. MEA

Onager

Name applied in antiquity to all ASIATIC WILD ASSES but in modern zoological terminology only to the Indo-Persian *(Hemionus onager indicus)*, Syrian *(Hemionus onager hemippus)* and Mesopotamian *(Hemionus onager)* races. The last-named is probably the one tamed in antiquity to draught by the Sumerians, but never since then, and never tamed to ride. The ancient siege engine called *onager* reflected the belief that in flight they deliberately threw stones backwards with their hoofs; they do not, but inevitably kick them backwards whe[n] travelling over rocky ground. Their ears a[re] shorter than those of true (African) asses, longer than those of horses. They have no stripes on spine, shoulder or legs. The hea[d] is 'lumpier' than in the horse. Height up t[o] 13 hands (1·32 m). Prevailing colour is yel-low, sometimes brownish dun. AD

Onager. This detail from the Standard of Ur shows a Sumerian chariot drawn by a pair of yoked onagers.

One-Day Event

A modified version of the three-day event (see Horse Trials). The first held in Great Britain (1950) was found to be popular an[d] full programs were drawn up to give a sta[n]dard for the country which was approved and promoted by the BRITISH HORSE SOCIE[TY].

The one-day event is very useful to trai[n a] horse in its early days for much harder an[d] more advanced work in three-day events. [It] takes three seasons to bring a horse to its best. The one-day event is usually divided into Preliminary, Intermediate and Open sections so that any horse and rider of a re[a]sonable standard may compete. Entering [a] young horse in the Preliminary section is [a] great help to the novice; horse and rider a[re] seen by experienced judges and may gain much useful advice for the future.

The one-day event usually consists of dressage, cross-country work and show jumping. The dressage section is always held first. Its classification varies from ve[ry] simple elementary dressage to Olympic o[r] Badminton standard. After the dressage, horse and rider prepare for the cross-coun[try] section. The final part of the three-day event does not occur in a one-day event.

It is often necessary to make local varia[tions] in the jumps and cross-country goin[g] to suit the country covered, rather than simply copy courses elsewhere (see Cours[e] Building). The course may be varied by judges to allow horses in different classes [to] use it according to their ability; the final scores on various occasions will help a rider judge his horse's progress.

As in a three-day event the organizatio[n] is in the hands of a committee, and officia[l] judges and stewards are present, as well a[s a] veterinary surgeon who will attend to an[y] lameness or ailment in the horse. It is oft[en] necessary, in the one-day event, for the rider to bring his horse and box it straigh[t] home after the event; so horses are check[ed] before being allowed to compete. JHEW

Oriental Horsemanship

see Horsemanship, Oriental

Oriental Horses

see Arab

Orlov Trotter

This horse, formerly called the RUSSIAN TROTTER, is a powerful, thick-set harness horse with a strong constitution. It is per-haps the most widely known and used of a[ll] Russian horses, and has exerted a powerf[ul] influence on Russian breeding, particula[rly]

Orlov Trotters. Average height at withers for stallions is 15·2½ hands (1·60 m), for mares 15·2¼ hands (1·58 m); bone below the knee for stallions 8½ in (20·2 cm), for mares 7¾ in (19·8 cm). The trot is very good, though sometimes the fore legs are raised too high.

on the Bitiug, Kuznets, VORONEZH HARNESS HORSE, and Russian trotter, as well as on the village farm horse. The Orlov is widely used for sport and is a good cavalry horse. There are many types, but certain characteristics are largely shared. The head is usually heavily proportioned but breedy, often with a convex forehead. The ears are erect, eyes large and wide-set, the neck long and straight but often swan-like. Withers are medium high, the back rather long, loins medium long, croup slightly lowered. The chest is quite wide but not too deep, making the trotter look rather high on the leg. The legs have good bone and large hoofs. The mane, tail and forelock are luxuriant, and most Orlov trotters have heavy feathers. Grey is the most common colour, followed by black, bay and rarely chestnut.

The Khrenov stud, birthplace of the Orlov trotter, was founded in 1775. There Count Orlov crossed his Arab stallion Smetanka with a Danish mare. Since then, Danish and Dutch mares as well as Eastern stallions, MECKLENBURG horses, NORFOLK TROTTERS and ARABS have been used in the development of the Orlov. The breed's record holder, the stallion Ulov, covered 1,600 m (1 mile) in 2·02 min. In spite of the prevalent belief that no pure Orlovs exist, there are more than 30,000 purebreds in the Soviet Union at present. WOF

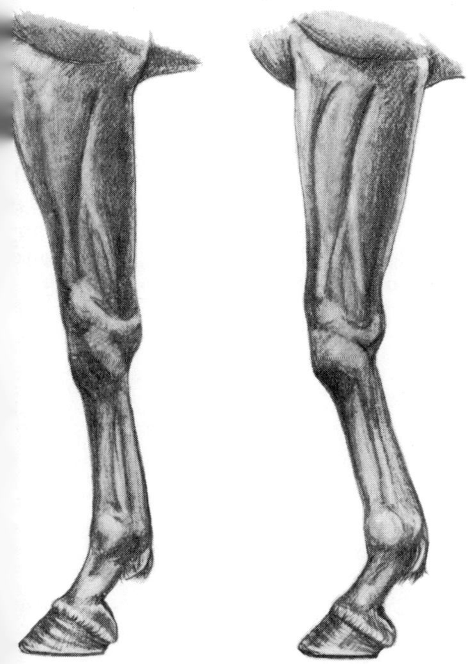

Above: **Over at the Knee.** *Left:* Normal fore leg *Right:* Fore leg over at the knee

Over at the Knee

In profile the anterior line of the leg is more convex at the knee than normal. CF

Overo see Colours and Markings

Overreach

Injury to the back of the fore leg caused by the toe of the shoe of the hind foot on the same side. The anterior lower edge of the shoe is responsible for injuries to the back tendons and back of the fetlock joint and the posterior lower edge is similarly responsible for lesions at the bulbs of the heel. CF

Overshot see Parrot Mouth

Pacing

In those parts of the English-speaking world where the gait is no longer in use, modern terminology is rather loose but in the United States it is defined (see Gaits). It is a racing gait in the United States and may also be seen at north of England harness meetings, confusingly called 'trotting races'. Ponies racing in sulkies often wear 'hobbles' at knee height which are used to train the colt to move its legs laterally. Probably all MOUNTAIN AND MOORLAND PONIES have the inherent ability to amble or pace, which was a speciality of the PALFREY, hence the seventeenth-century proverb: 'Trot sire, trot dam, how shall the foal amble?' and this tendency has only been bred out during the last 200 years. See also Trotting Racing, United States. AD

Pahlavan see Anglo-Persian and Pahlavan

Pakistan see India and Pakistan

Palfrey

The palfrey, called from about 1600 onwards a 'pad', was a light saddle horse that did not trot. It either paced or racked (see Gaits). Until 1539 the best English palfreys were bred on the estates of abbeys such as Fountains and Jervaulx in Yorkshire. Irish ones were better. Best of all were those from Galicia in Spain. Knights when not actually wearing armour and carrying shields (i.e. not in contact with the enemy) rode palfreys on the march; otherwise palfreys were used for hunting, especially for falconry, and for travelling. They were not specifically a lady's ride until the introduction of the side-saddle in the fourteenth century; this offered so insecure a seat that only the smooth gait of the palfrey permitted its use. Palfreys in England virtually became extinct about 1700, due to the spread of coach travel. AD

Palio

A type of horserace run in Siena twice a year, on 2 July and 15 August, in honour of the Virgin, in which countrybred nags ridden bareback by jockeys representing the various *contrade* (boroughs) of Siena race around the paved central *piazza* of the city. It originated in the twelfth century, as a survival of the chivalric games played throughout medieval Italy; glorious with pageantry and followed fanatically, it is unique. It takes its name from the prize of a silk banner or *palio*, a word derived from the Latin *pallium*. LFB

Palomino

Palomino indicates not a breed but a horse of golden colour, with no smudge or dorsal stripe and possessing a flaxen or silver tail and mane. White is not allowed except on the face; blue or chalk eyes are unacceptable. A few Palomino ponies exist but only those over 14·2 hands (1·47 m) are acceptable for registration. Palominos are especially prized in the United States where in shows they are distinguished as Parade (of Thoroughbred Arab or Saddlebred origin) or Stock (Standardbred, Morgan or Quarterbred). The American Palomino breeders' associations hope eventually to create a Palomino that breeds true to type and can be defined as a breed. Claims are made that the Palomino dates back to Homeric times and was favoured by the Yemen kings. These statements refer more probably to the ISABELLAS or HANOVERIAN CREAMS. See also Colours and Markings. LFB

Pan American Games

The Pan American Games, a competition on the Olympic model but limited to nations in The Pan American Union (North, South and Central America), was created during a conference of delegates in London who decided that the rules and regulations of the International Olympic Committee would apply to the competition. After being scheduled for 1942 and then 1946, the Pan American Games were first held 25 February–8 March 1951 in Buenos Aires, Argentina, and every four years thereafter in the year preceding the Olympic Games. Because of the great distances involved and various diseases, not every 'major' nation has entered every year. The United States, for example, did not compete in 1951 nor 1971.

The first Pan American Games included polo (won by Argentina in three straight games). Since then the events have consisted of a three-day event, dressage competition, and show jumping (NATIONS' CUP). HCA

Panje

This is a type, not a breed, of all-purpose pony, a cross of many breeds from Arab to Belgian, standing under 14 hands (1·42 m), sometimes of faulty conformation but always extremely hardy and resistant to hunger and thirst. The Panje is a very useful type found in central and eastern Europe. DMG

Paperchase

In a paperchase, a trail of paper is followed by mounted riders. Two persons ride ahead to leave the trail and after a suitable interval the field follow in pursuit, finishing at a predetermined place. Damp sawdust may be used in place of paper and must be cleared after the chase is completed. JHew

Pardubice, Grand see Grand Pardubice

Pari-Mutuel

The pari-mutuel, the French equivalent of the British TOTE (Totalisator), is organized by the government and all legal horserace betting in France is conducted through it. It operates a win and place pool on the same basis as the Tote as well as a type of forecast. Its real money-spinner, however, is the *Tiercé*, on which the prosperity of French racing depends: the backer nominates the first three for the biggest race each weekend, with the prospect of a huge win if outsiders fill the first three places. All tickets are sold off-course. Because of the big dividends, the *Tiercé*, like British football pools, attracts people whose knowledge of racing is limited. On course the pari-mutuel is not renowned for its speed; visitors on a busy day often find it impossible to bet and watch the race as well. GE

In North America, all on-track betting is conducted through the pari-mutuels, with efficient mechanization and electronic handling of wagers. On major classic days at the larger tracks over $6,000,000 may pass through the betting machines.

In addition to win, place and show (first, second and third) betting, the Daily Double, in which the backer tries to select the winners of two straight races, usually the first two on the day's card, is the most popular.

Some tracks also offer the Exacta or Perfecta (the nomination of the first and second in their precise order in the same race), the Quinella (Spanish, *Quiniela*) (first and second but not necessarily in the correct order), the Superfecta (Perfectas on two succeeding races), 'Big Q.' (Quinellas on two succeeding races) and the relatively new Trifecta (similar to the French *Tiercé*). FTP

Parrot Mouth (Overshot)

The upper jaw protrudes over the lower. CF

Partbred Arabian

Partbred Arabian horses in the British Isles must possess a minimum of 12½ per cent Arabian blood in their pedigrees, the other ingredient being from any breed other than Thoroughbred. From 1 January 1974, however, the Arab Horse Society has ruled that requirements for registration of Partbreds will be raised to a minimum of 25 per cent Arab blood.

Definitions vary widely in continental Europe. In the United States the Partbred is known as the Halfbred Arabian; the sire or dam must be pure Arabian, thus giving a

Pan American Games Winners

Year	*Event*	*Team*	*Individual*
1951 Argentina	Polo	Argentina	—
	Three-Day Event	Argentina	Capt. Julic C. Sagasta (Argentina
	Dressage	Chile	Capt. Jose Larrain (Chile)
	Show Jumping	Chile	Capt. Alberto Larraguibe (Chile)
1955 Mexico	Three-Day Event	Mexico	Walter Staley Jr (U.S.)
	Dressage	not held	Capt. Hec Clavel (Chile)
	Show Jumping	Mexico	Lt Roberto Viñals (Mexico)
1959 United States	Three-Day Event	Canada	Michael Page (U.S
	Dressage	Chile	Patricia Galvin (U.S.)
	Show Jumping	United States	not awarded
1963 Brazil	Three-Day Event	United States	Michael Page (U.S
	Dressage	not held	Patricia Galvin (U.S.)
	Show Jumping	United States	Mary Mai (U.S.)
1967 Canada	Three-Day Event	United States	Michael Plumb (U.S.)
	Dressage	Chile	Kyra Downton (U.S.)
	Show Jumping	Brazil	Jim Day (Canada)
1971 Colombia	Three-Day Event	Canada	Manuel Mendevi (Mexico)
	Dressage	Canada	Christilot Hanson (Canada)
	Show Jumping	Canada	Elisa P. c las Heras (Mexico)

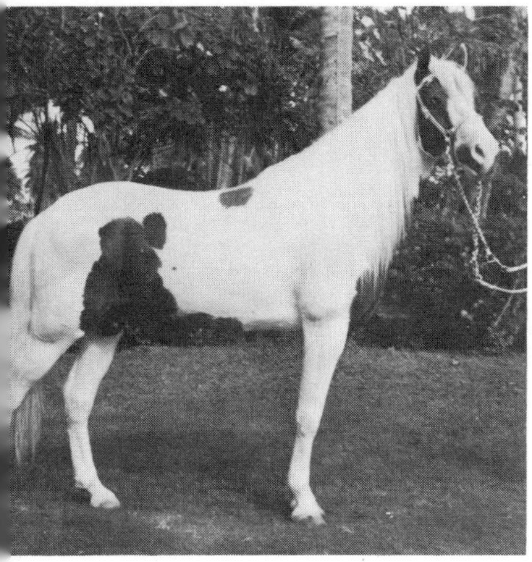

Paso Fino Horse. El Conquistador, photographed in Puerto Rico

minimum of 50 per cent Arabian blood. Australia also demands this percentage with the sire or dam being either pure Arabian or a registered Anglo-Arabian, carrying at least 50 per cent of Arabian blood, or of registered Partbred Arabian parents. SAW

Paso Fino Horse
The Paso Fino is a naturally-gaited riding horse developed in the Caribbean and South America. It is known primarily for its inherent lateral four-beat gait which is very comfortable for the rider. This gait is traceable to the Spanish JENNETS chosen as mounts for the early expeditions to the Western Hemisphere and was refined principally in Puerto Rico, Colombia and Peru. These separate strains are now being blended in the United States where the breed is known as the American Paso Fino. Standing between 14 and 15 hands (1·42–1·52 m) and of every equine colour, Paso Finos combine the ordinarily incompatible characteristics of sturdiness and elegance. RMacW

Passage see Movements, Airs, Classical

Passo Corese
At Passo Corese, a small town in the Tiber valley twenty miles north of Rome, the last of Italy's four ancient cavalry schools survives as the *Scuola Militare di Equitazione* (Military Riding School). Its present-day strength of 80 officers and 200 horses provides entrants for most international riding events in which Italy competes. Officer-pupils, sent to Passo Corese from various branches of the Italian armed forces, are trained exclusively in horsemanship and never return to ordinary military duties.

Horses are bred at the School and there is an annual intake of three-year-olds from the military stud at Persano, south of Naples, and from Sardinia and Ireland. Animals selected for competition work undergo four years of schooling.

The establishment's covered schools, obstacle and cross-country circuits, racecourse and replica of the Piazza di Siena (the international arena in Rome) are spread over 20 square miles of heath and woodland. 'Open days' are frequently held. The Hall of the Lances (officers' mess) contains a display of old cavalry regimental trophies dating from 1683. LG

Patella (Upward Fixation)
A 'locking' of the stifle joint due to the internal straight ligament of the patella becoming 'hooked up' on the medial condyle of the femur, resulting in extension of the limb backwards. It is common in Shetland ponies. CF

Pato, Pato-Lorraine see Mounted Games

Pazyryk
Burials of rich herd-owners with remarkably well-preserved horses dating from the Scythian period have been found in the Altai mountains in western Mongolia near Pazyryk. The richest *kurgans* or burial mounds were opened and robbed during the Middle Ages. Florov (1793–1830) was the first archaeologist to discover them; he sent contents of value to the Hermitage Museum, Leningrad. In 1856 W. Radlov found more burials in the southern Altai, Adrianov discovered more *kurgans* in the high Altai and in 1924 an 'Altai Expedition' was launched under S. I. Rudenko, one of Russia's greatest explorers and archaeologists, and M. P. Grjaznov. The Pazyryk group, probably seventh century B.C. to first century A.D., was opened in 1939. Bronze horse bits indicate communication with eastern Europe. Pazyryk *kurgan I* horses showed ten different ear marks (by snipping). As some of the horses marked differently were similar in conformation while others were of varying sizes, it is accepted that the ear marks indicated (tribal) ownership. Pazyryk *kurgan II*, in the east Altai, was opened in 1947–8 by Rudenko, who found seven dark-coloured horses, heads to the east, buried in ice although they may have thawed and been refrozen several times. All horses were harnessed, four had handsomely-carved wooden bit-bars, some had decorative bridles and headpieces. Two horses wore masks of leather and felt and saddles of leather with felt saddlecloths, and pommels decorated with gold leaf. They had been

Passo Corese. A group of officer-pupils jump one of the cross-country obstacles at the military riding school.

killed by pole-axing. Professor Vitt (described by Hançar) found four different types of horses, ranging from 13 to 14·3 hands (1·32–1·50 m). The largest were apparently imported from Turan, were of the TURKMEN type and were all stallions, varying in colour from dark chestnut to light gold chestnut with black manes and tails. DMG

Reference: K. Jettmar, *Die frühen Steppenvölker,* Baden-Baden, 1964; F. Hançar, *Das Pferd in prähistorischer und früher historischer Zeit*, Vienna, 1955; D. Machin Goodall, *History of Horse Breeding*, London, 1973.

Pechora, Pechorsky

An extremely hardy and active draught breed, native to the valleys of the river Pechora in the northern U.S.S.R. See U.S.S.R. DMG

Percheron

The Percheron, native to the rich hills of Perche (south of western Normandy and west of the Parisian basin), has from an early date been exported to England and many other countries. In France, other breeds are derived from it: the draught horses of Auge (near Lisieux and Caen in Normandy); Maine (north of the Loire round Le Mans); Berry (immediately south of the Loire valley); Nivernais (from the Nièvre, northwestern Burgundy); and the Loire. Each of these breeds has its own stud book for the pure Percheron must be born in its original breeding zone, which covers parts of four *départements*. In spite of different infusions of foreign blood, Oriental influence can be traced as early as the Middle Ages. Some describe the Percheron as an enlarged Arab. One of the most important sires, Jean le Blanc, was the son of a purebred Arab. The Percheron has a grey or sometimes black coat; it is energetic, strong, docile and hardy, with a straight head, expressive eyes, open nostrils, wide chest, short loins, high and thick tail. There are two varieties, the small, which is disappearing, and large (16–17 hands or 1·70–1·77 m), weighing about a ton, which used to be much in demand by American importers and has continued to be popular in France and abroad. ES

The English Percheron: is clean-legged (devoid of feather) with strong hard feet, popular as a farm horse and for draught work. It is strong and powerful, has good bone and should be well put together with an impression of balance. Its height is not less than 16·3 hands (1·75 m) for stallions and 16·1 hands (1·70 m) for mares. It is quiet and docile, easy to handle and break. It is frequently used for crossing with THOROUGHBREDS in order to breed hunters up to weight. This cross is responsible for many grey heavyweight hunters, for the Percheron is always grey or black, with the minimum amount of white. It also possesses a fine coat and skin. DRT

Periodic Ophthalmia (Moon Blindness)

A serious disease of the eye, the early symptoms of which are not inconsistent with those of a blow. Recovery from a first attack is not unusual but subsequent attacks, a feature of the disease, almost invariably produce changes, including cataract, that may lead to blindness. CF

Persian Arab

The Arab strains raised predominantly in the province of Khuzistan in southern Iran are said to have been developed from Persian plateau stock many hundreds of years ago. There is no doubt that some mixing with blood from the Arab countries to the west has occurred, but the Persian Arab has been jealously guarded for centuries for its purity and absence of foreign (non-Persian) blood. The principal strains are: Khersan, Hamdani, Kuheilan (Kuhaylan), Sharak, Nesman, Hadbe, Korush, Jalfan (Jilfan) and Vasne.

Because the tiny indigenous horse of Iran (before the invasion of Indo-European warrior horsemen, *c.* 2000 B.C.) was a prominent, although not strategically important, feature of the early equestrian picture, the Persians have long laid claim to owning the forefathers of the Arab horse. Whether or not the Arabs gained their original stock from the spoils of the conquered Assyrians or from Iran in the seventh century A.D., a strong case can be made for the antiquity, purity and originality of the Persian Arab strains. The Persian Arab was bred from the original mixture of Indo-European import and tiny native horse, but a return to the basic qualities of the native horse gradually occurred in the hot, dry climate of Khuzistan, particularly in the last 1,000 years when Mongol devastation and destruction of the vast irrigation systems rendered the area a dusty waste with scant forage for horses. Those raised in these areas soon altered their appearance, reverting more to the size and shape of the native horse of Media, the principal differences being a longer ear, higher stature and leaner appearance.

The Persian Arab is 14–14·3 hands (1·42–1·49 m) high, with a fine, dry head, small muzzle, large eyes, arched neck, short back and high-set tail. The body is tight and well muscled due to a diet of camel's milk and dates as a foal and scant forage high in protein thereafter. The bone is fine and strong and the hoofs are small with tucked up frogs as natural protection against stones and rocks. Colours are grey, bay and chestnut with occasional blacks. The principal breeders are the Arab tribes of Khuzistan although Sardar Mohtashem Bakhtiar for long kept a large stable of the various strains

Pazyryk. Part of the Altai barrow treasure now in the Hermitage Museum, Leningrad, this four-wheeled wagon was reconstructed from parts found in the frozen barrows. The wagon, drawn by four horses, had carried the chief's body to his burial and was interred with the chief and the horses.

which, upon his death, were divided among his sons. Imported Arabs are registered separately. See also Arab. LF

Persian Horse

Although recent findings confirm the presence of an indigenous (wild) horse in prehistoric Iran there is, at present, little evidence of domestication before the arrival of the sturdy steppe horse introduced by the Indo-Europeans *c.* 2000 B.C. Terra-cotta relief plaques, standards and statuettes from third millennium B.C. Mesopotamia, however, illustrate the practical use to which the onager and a small horse, which the Mesopotamians claim came from the Zagros mountains of western Iran, were put. Why the Persians from the plateau area of Iran seem to have restricted their use of the native equines (onager and horse) to the cooking pot is not yet certain, but with the introduction of the steppe horse from the north some time after 2000 B.C. horse breeding started in earnest in the fertile watered valleys of the Zagros mountains.

As far as is known, large, saddle-sized horses like those ridden today were first bred by the Medes in the cool grassy country of western Iran near Hamadan (Carleton S. Coon, *History of Man,* London, 1954, 1967). This horse, known to the Greeks as the Nisaean, was the result of a peculiar set of circumstances: a blend of the small fine native horse and the sturdy steppe horse selectively bred over a period of 1500 years on some of the best pasture land in the Middle East. The result was a tall, for the time (14·2 hands or 1·47 m), strong horse with great muscle development in the neck, shoulders and croup eminently suited for the cataphracts of the successful Achamaenian armies and extolled by contemporary writers as the best of all known horses, a veritable Thoroughbred of the past.

The heavy Nisaean horse remained popular as a cavalry mount throughout the Parthian and Sassanian periods until the Arab conquest of Persia in the seventh century A.D. A distinct change in the conformation of the Persian horse occurred around this time and the trend moved away from the sturdy, massively built horse, of which the Nisaean was the prototype, to the light, elegant horse of the central plateau portrayed in countless miniatures of polo and hunting scenes. Describing this horse in 1686, Sir John Chardin writes (*Travels in Persia, 1686,* London, 1927): 'The horses of Persia are the finest of all the East. They are taller than the English saddle-horses are, straight before, a little head and legs that are wonderfully thin and fine, exactly proportioned, mighty gentle, good travellers and very light and sprightly. They carry their noses to the wind when they run a course, and gallop with their heads lifted high in the air and this they are bred and taught . . . The king has very large studs in all of the Kingdom. In Media and in the Province of Persia (Fars) chiefly near Persepolis, where the most beautiful horses of the Kingdom are bred.'

Strangely enough, with all the magnificence of the PLATEAU PERSIAN horse, Sir John Chardin observes that the Arab was preferred. He does not seem to feel quite the same way but says: 'I have told you that they (the Persian horses) are the finest in the East: but they are not for that reason the best, nor the most sought after. Those in Arabia surpass them far, and are mightily esteemed in Persia for their lightness. They are in their make like perfect jades and being lean and withered, they make a wretched figure.'

Of the TURKOMAN, whose slim beauty can be seen galloping on Teheran's racetracks in the spring and fall, he says: 'The Persians have several Tartarian horses too, that are lower than those of Persia and more burly and ugly, but will bear more fatigue, are more lively and nimble for the race.' It would seem that the Turkoman bore more resemblance to the Mongol pony at this stage than to the elegant creature it is now.

Iran's unique geographical position, situated at the crossroads of the earliest human migrations and encompassing a wide range of topographical and climatic features, has been instrumental in the development of a wide range of native breeds. Khuzistan in the south, where a statuette of a ridden horse dated to 2200 B.C. was found, is now famous for the various strains of Arabs it raises (see Persian Arab). Nestled in the cool valleys of the middle Zagros mountains the area of Kurdistan is famous for a strain known as the Jaf, descendants of the strong, elegant horses once the pride of the Achamaenian Empire. The central Persian plateau still produces the horses that Sir John Chardin enthusiastically described and the Turkomans to the north on their steppes stretching endlessly into Russia cherish their felt-blanketed steeds. Last of all, the CASPIAN, believed to be a remnant of Iran's prehistoric wild horse, has found a last refuge on the forested slopes of the Caspian littoral.

The recently formed Royal Horse Society, of which H.I.H. Crown Prince Reza is the patron, recognizes the following breeds in Iran today: Plateau Persian (encompassing all of the various Persian strains such as Shirazi, Quashquai, Darashouri, Basseri, Jaf and also including the 'Arab' strains which have traditionally been raised in Iran; see Persian Arab), Turkoman, Tchenaran, Caspian, Karadagh, Anglo-Persian and Pahlavan. Imported Arabs are registered separately. LF

Peru

During the turbulent history of the Republic of Peru the horse has played a lesser role than might be expected, probably due to the

Peru. A Paso Horse (stepping horse)

unfavourable topography of the country, whose present boundaries, including much unexplored jungle territory, were established only in 1929. Horses were introduced to Peru by Pizarro, who made a rapid conquest of the native Indian population in 1652. The intermingling of their Spanish and Arab blood with that of horses from neighbouring South American countries and, more recently, imported strains from Europe and North America, have produced a number of native Peruvian breeds, including the Peruvian Criollo (a small, close-coupled, sturdy pony of Argentine origin), the Costeno, Morochuco and Serrano ponies (small, surefooted mountain ponies) and the Peruvian stepping horse.

The latter, also called the 'Peruvian Paso Horse', is the triumph of Peruvian horse breeding. Developed some 300 years ago, it is believed to possess approximately three-quarters Barb and one-quarter Andalusian blood. The *paso* is a unique lateral gait that can be maintained even over rugged terrain for an astonishing length of time without tiring horse or rider. It is a natural gait, somewhat like the rack, the pace, the running walk and the singlefoot, but identical with none of them. It can produce a top speed of 15 m.p.h. and an easy average of 11 m.p.h. No other breed performs a true *paso*, with its characteristic paddle-like movement of the fore legs, while the hind legs move forward in a straight line often overstepping the track of the fore feet, with the hind quarters held low and the back straight and rigid. Although they vary greatly in size (13–15·2 hands or 1·32–1·57 m) and include almost every equine colour, all Paso Horses have very long hind legs, long pasterns, strong bone and hoofs, enormous lungs and hearts for their size, and unusual flexibility of the joints. This Peruvian strain has contributed to the American PASO FINO.

Equestrian activities in Peru are similar to those in other nations, particularly in nations where the military has retained its prestige and importance. The Peruvian Federation of Equestrian Sports is affiliated to the FÉDÉRATION ÉQUESTRE INTERNATIONALE and Peruvian teams compete in international competitions (see Show Jumping). There are a number of Peruvian riding clubs, the most important being the Club Ecuestre Huachipa in the capital, Lima. Although restricted to an elite, interest in riding sports is keen. Polo is popular, played all year round. Hunting too, is practised, but without foxes. Horse racing is extremely popular. There are four racetracks and more than fifteen Thoroughbred breeding and training establishments. The principal racetrack is the American-designed Hipodromo de Monterrico in Lima, one of the most modern in the world, with a sand surface and both night and day racing four times a week throughout the year. Peruvian Thoroughbred breeders have produced racehorses that have made a name for themselves throughout South America. MAS

Pesade see Airs, Classical

Piaffe see Movements, Airs, Classical

Piebald see Colours and Markings

Pig-sticking

This very hazardous, intensely exciting and exhilarating mounted sport was practised in Bengal early in the nineteenth century by British sportsmen as a substitute for bear-spearing when bears became scarce. At first the spear was thrown at the hog and competitors tied coloured ribbons to their spears to identify them. Soon it was found to be better sport to hold on to the spear which could then be used in defence. Favourite localities were the Kadir or riverine flat country of the Ganges and Jumna rivers at Meerut and Muttra. This was usually hard as a rock and full of pitfalls hidden from view by high grass and *jhow* or tamarisk. The quarry was the Asiatic wild boar (*Sus scrofa*) of four years or more armed with razor-sharp lower tushes. Its average height was 33 in (84 cm) at withers, average weight 250 lb (113 kg). When hunted it would gallop as fast as a horse for a while and then suddenly turn and charge its pursuer. The best height for horses was 15·2 hands (1·57 m) though originally 14·2 hands (1·47 m) or less. Locally-bred horses or imported WALERS were favoured. The sportsman in Meerut and Muttra was armed with an underhand spear, about 7 ft long. In Bengal and Upper India a short (5 ft) jabbing spear was used, as the thickness of the jungle impeded the long spear.

The Kadir Cup was founded in 1869 and run at Meerut until 1939 with rare breaks due to war. Individual competition was for 'first spear' i.e. first blood. The pig was not necessarily killed. The best exponent ever was Captain (now Brigadier) J. Scott-Cockburn (4th Hussars) on his countrybred Carclew. He won the cup in 1924, '25 and '27 and still rides to hounds. The Hog-hunter's Cup Steeplechase took place over four miles of the same country for the Kadir Cup. In 1922 the Prince of Wales (Duke of Windsor) won. In the Muttra Cup, a team event, the pig had to be killed and produced.

The golden rules were: ride with loose rein; deep hunting seat; gallop at a charging boar; always take the boar on the off-side. RT

Reference: Lord Baden-Powell, *Pig-sticking or Hog-hunting*, London, 1924; Gen. Sir A. E. Wardrop, *Modern Pig-sticking*, London, 1914.

Pinerolo

This famous Italian cavalry school, situated near Turin, was founded on 15 November 1823 by King Carlo Felice of Sardinia.

Originally called The Royal Military School of Equitation, its name was later changed to Royal Cavalry School. It was temporarily disbanded on 24 March 1848 when war against Austria was declared, but the benefits from its teaching were so noticeable during the conflict that it was immediately re-established by royal decree at the close of hostilities; one branch was moved to Modena.

As in the early nineteenth century France and Austria were the acknowledged leaders in equestrian matters it was natural that the then commanding officer at Pinerolo, Col Lanzvecchia di Burri, chose as instructor for the school a graduate of the SPANISH RIDING SCHOOL OF VIENNA, Cesare Paderni, an advocate of dressage and high-school. Pinerolo owes its greatest fame, however, to the young lieutenant, Federico CAPRILLI, who proved that Viennese methods were useless for getting cavalry across country, and eventually succeeded Paderni as instructor. LFB

Pinkafelder
A medium-weight Belgian draught horse used in Hungary to improve draught breeds. DMG

Pinto
Pinto (Spanish, 'spotted') indicates not a breed but a colour pattern (see Colours and Markings). In coaching days pintos were popular everywhere as leaders for road coaches and sporting tandems. LFB

Pinzgauer Noriker
The Pinzgau horse (from the Pinzgau district of Austria) is the same as the Noriker, the correct term being the Pinzgauer Noriker breed. The chief colours are brown and chestnut but spotted colouring frequently appears, particularly in Lungau and Murtal. It used to be typical of the breed two hundred years ago, probably due to eighteenth-century ANDALUSIAN crosses, since spots and odd colours are a dominant factor. Specialized breeding began in 1903 when the Pinzgauer Stud Book opened with 450 stallions and over 1,000 brood mares. The type is a mountain heavy horse with a long back and very short pasterns. It is extremely hardy and surefooted.

The Noriker is said to be increasing in numbers, particularly in southern Germany (where it is called the South German Heavy Horse), in Czechoslovakia, Hungary, Yugoslavia and Italy. DMG

Pit Ponies see Industry, Horse in

Plaiting (Braiding)
The number of mane plaits varies according to the length of the horse's neck. In *English (Hunting) style* the conventional number of plaits is seven; a long neck may have eight, a short one may have six. In *Continental style* and in the United States there are a number of small plaits right down the neck, as many as sixteen. Remove plaits and comb out the mane as soon as possible after a show or hunting. Never leave them in overnight as this tends to make the hair brittle and split. Always sew plaits, using thread to match the colour of the horse. Never use rubber bands. In bygone days the mane was always plaited for hunting but left unplaited for cubhunting. It should be plaited for showing and show jumping. The forelock should be plaited; also the tail for showing classes. GW

Pinzgauer Noriker. Spotted horses in Salzburg, Austria

Plateau Persian
This includes all of the various Persian strains such as Shirazi, Quashquai, Darashouri, Basseri, Bakhtiari, Jaf and also the 'Arab' strains traditionally raised in Iran. These horses have a common background dating to before the foundation of the Achamaenian Empire in the sixth century B.C. Regional variations have occurred through selective breeding, specific geographical and climatic conditions and differences in degree of crossing with horses of invaders from the west or north during the 3,000 years of their history.

The average height of the Plateau Persian is 15 hands (1·52 m) although variations to 15·2 hands (1·57 m) and 14 hands (1·42 m) are not unusual. The head is elegant, with a pronounced bulge over the interparietal bones; it has large eyes, flaring nostrils, arched neck, wide chest, sloping shoulder, short back, strong hind quarters, high-set tail, slim bone and very tough hoofs with receding frogs for protection against rocks. These horses make strong, surefooted mountain horses and at the same time their gaits are long and free-moving. They are also much esteemed for use as jumpers in Teheran shows. Colours are grey, bay and chestnut with very little white marking. Blacks are occasionally found. Bred principally by the tribes of the provinces of Fars, Isfahan and Kurdistan, these horse live under typical tribal conditions and may migrate as much as 620 miles (1,000 km) in a year over rough mountain passes, swollen streams and hot dusty plains. They are extremely tough as, for generations, none but the hardiest can have survived their first journey as foals. For the (Arab) strains included in the Plateau Persian see Persian Arab. LF

Above: **Pleven**

Below: **Pluvinel.** M. de Pluvinel demonstrates the use of his pillars to the 16-year-old Louis XIII (right)

Pleven Horse

The Pleven was developed on the Georgi Dimitrov State Agricultural Farm (formerly Klementina) near Pleven, Bulgaria, from Anglo-Arabs bred there since 1898. Several Anglo-Arab stallions were imported from Russia and crossed with local, improved, Arab and other mares. The stallion Sivori, acquired from the Strelets stud, was the ancestor of a strain continuing today. For the first two or three decades several Arab stallions from the Kabijuk and studs in Hungary also had considerable influence. Anglo-Arab breeding took a more precise direction after stallions of the Gidran strain were imported from Hungary, a process covering three decades (1911–38). Since then the Pleven has been purebred in strains. It also obtains some blood from Thoroughbreds. The Pleven is of a robust, well-balanced constitution. Its beautiful conformation resembles that of the Arab. Its colour is bright chestnut. It stands about 15·2½ hands (1·61 m).

The Pleven is used for riding, competitive sports and in agriculture. It is an excellent jumper and is therefore greatly favoured in competitions. Several horses have done well at international events, among them Avion, Pagon, Essetra and Evropeetz.

The Pleven is now bred on a large scale in northern Bulgaria, in the districts of Pleven, Tarnovo, Lovetch and in part of Vratza; it is also bred in southern Bulgaria, in some parts of the Plovdiv and Pazardjik districts. VP, II

Pluvinel de la Baume, Antoine de

Famous founder of the French classical school of riding and a disciple of the Italian Master, Pignatelli, Antoine de Pluvinel de la Baume (1555–1620) became Master of the Horse to King Henry III, Henry IV, and Louis XIII. For Louis XIII he wrote *Instruction du Roi en l'art de monter à Cheval* (1625), notes in the form of a dialogue between himself (the author) and the King, his pupil. Pluvinel's methods of training were entirely artificial, the horse being trained to perform such High School AIRS as *courbette* and *capriole* by a sign of the hand or long whip. He was the first to introduce the use of 'pillars' to which a horse was tied while being schooled at a standstill. See Horsemanship, History of, Accoutrements. LFB

Points of the Horse see Conformation

Point-to-Point

It is not possible to fix the date of the first point-to-point, a form of steeplechasing for certified hunters, with any certainty. Its origins are bound up in the origins of steeplechasing; there is documentary evidence of a point-to-point held in Worcestershire on 2 March 1836, although before 1884 point-to-points were 'unrecognized meetings' and any horses running at them were

perpetually disqualified from racing in Britain under National Hunt Rules. In 1885, a point-to-point was held at Towcester, Northamptonshire, without permission having been obtained from the National Hunt Stewards; owners complained that this had rendered them liable to disqualification and the Clerk of the Course was fined 25 sovereigns.

Early point-to-points, like early steeplechases, were run literally from one point to another, over 'natural' countryside. The rules (when they existed) were rough and ready and there were no marking flags.

Today hunting may be said to be subsidized by point-to-point racing and consequently the public has to be given value for money. Although no charges are made for admission, substantial sums accrue from carpark fees and the sale of racecards; there are additional benefits in the shape of the annual grants made by the HORSERACE BETTING LEVY BOARD and direct donations from bookmakers.

The first mention of prize money seems to have been in 1899, when, after a conference between the Masters of Foxhounds Association and the National Hunt Committee, a ceiling of £20 was imposed. Hunts were empowered to hold any number of races (today there is a limit), over not less than three miles, and facilities for staging point-to-points were extended to regiments and clubs. Various other regulations were introduced over the next few years but it was not until 1913, when the M.F.H. Point-to-Point Committee was formed, that point-to-point racing got its own charter. After a growing difference of opinion between the M.F.H. Point-to-Point Committee and the National Hunt Committee, in 1934 point-to-point racing came under the direct control of the National Hunt Committee, who were, however, prepared to be guided by suggestions made by the newly-formed Joint Advisory Committee, which later replaced the old M.F.H. Point-to-Point Committee. The new set-up finally received the seal of approval from the doyen of the point-to-point fraternity, Arthur W. Coaten, who claimed in his editorial to the *Point-to-Point Calendar* 1937–38 that 'in 1937 it could be said that a situation of perfect accord between the two responsible bodies had come to pass'. 'Perfect accord' is probably an exaggeration, but certainly the system worked fairly well, and the appointment of official course inspectors made for almost immediate improvement in the construction of courses and the building of the fences, resulting, in the long run, in better facilities for the public and a higher standard of racing. By 1950, D. W. C. Brock was able to write in his book, *Point-to-Point Racing,* that most horses seen out hunting or at point-to-points were at least seven-eighths thoroughbred.

It was therefore getting much more difficult for the ordinary man on his ordinary hunter to win any kind of race, and the top point-to-pointers were not all that far behind the top steeplechasers. Many of them, in fact, graduated with distinction to National Hunt racing; horses which have won the GRAND NATIONAL in the postwar years include the following point-to-pointers: Russian Hero (1949), Teal (1952), Oxo (1959), Merryman II (1960) and Highland Wedding (1969); four point-to-pointers have won the Cheltenham Gold Cup over the same period: Four Ten (1954), Limber Hill (1956), Linwell (1957) and Woodland Venture (1967). The list would be even longer if horses point-to-pointed in Ireland were to be included.

Point-to-Point. Heythrop Hunt Point-to-Point, Stow-on-the-Wold, Gloucestershire

The distinction of riding the greatest number of point-to-point winners outside Ireland belongs to Major Guy Cunard, who remained an amateur throughout his riding career. Born in Yorkshire on 2 September 1911, he had his first ride in a race when he was still a schoolboy at Eton. When Major Cunard was compelled to give up race riding as a result of a fall at the Derwent Point-to-Point in March 1968 he had ridden 251 point-to-point winners and 61 under N.H. Rules. He subsequently became a professional trainer.

The only amateur known to have exceeded Major Cunard's total is the veteran Willie Rooney, who rode over 350 winners in Ireland and was still riding in 1971.

Point-to-point racing since World War II has been regenerated by some exciting new ventures, beginning perhaps with the creation in Yorkshire of a point-to-point 'Grand National' when the distance of the Grimthorpe Cup at the Middleton and Middleton East was increased to $4\frac{1}{2}$ miles (7·24 km) in 1954. The point-to-point equivalent of the Cheltenham Gold Cup is the Lady Dudley Cup at the Worcestershire, first competed for in 1898. The re-forming, by Lance Newton, of the Melton Hunt Club in 1956 has

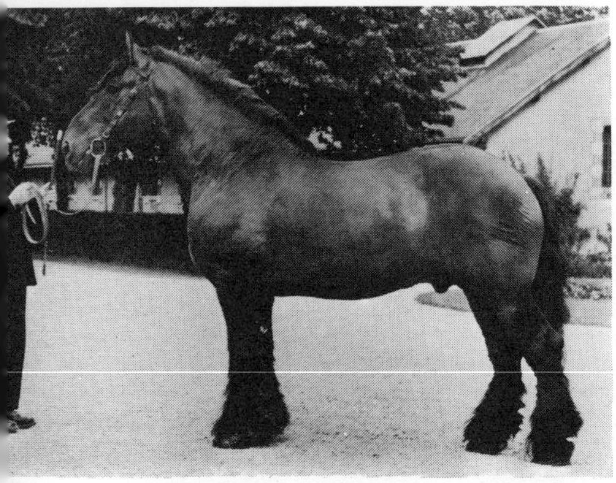

Poitevin. *Top:* A Poitevin ass
Above: A Poitevin horse

Colour plate: **Fantasia.** Traditionally dressed tribesmen taking part in a Moroccan fantasia

Overleaf: Polo. Tournament between the Argentinian teams of Colonel Suarez (red and blue shirts) and La Alicia (red and white shirts). *Inset:* A seventeenth-century game on the Maidan at Isfahan, where remains of the ancient stone goal posts can still be seen

resulted in a memorable fixture on the permanent course at Garthorpe, Leicestershire; the events include an established championship for novice horses, and the national lady riders' championship, sponsored by Goya, introduced in 1972, which in time will no doubt find its way on to a professional racecourse.

An extra dimension was added to point-to-point racing when John Player & Sons launched their Gold Leaf Trophy championship in 1968, with qualifying races at some 40 point-to-points and a final on a professional racecourse; local rivalries are now sharpened by various regional championships, of which the pioneers were the French champagne firm of Laurent Perrier in 1969.

The postwar years have also seen numerous alterations in the rules. In 1957 girls employed professionally with horses were permitted to ride in point-to-points, a concession which does not apply to men, who are ineligible to ride in point-to-points if they have ever held a professional jockey's licence or, within the period of the previous three years, been professionally employed with horses.

In 1961 the ceiling for prize money went up to £40 for the winner of an open event and to £30 for the winner of any other race.

In 1962 a rule forbidding girls under the age of 18 to ride in point-to-points was introduced. In 1967 the ladies were once more permitted to ride against the gentlemen, though only in members' races; and in 1968 the minimum height of the fences was raised from 4 ft (1·22 m) to 4 ft 3 in (1·52 m).

Perhaps the most controversial piece of legislation will prove to be the recommendation made by the Committee of Enquiry into Point-to-Point Racing, set up under the chairmanship of Lord Leverhulme in 1971, that no horse which, from 1 July of the previous year, has run under the Rules of Racing or been with a licensed trainer, shall be eligible to run in point-to-points. The position before 1972 was that, so long as they were not winners, prospective point-to-pointers could run under Rules up to 1 November, and be with a licensed trainer up to 1 January of the current hunting season.

The Jockey Club Regulations for Point-to-Point Steeple Chases are published annually by Messrs Weatherby; copies may be obtained from the Racing Calendar Office, Sanders Road, Wellingborough, Northants, NN8 4BX, England. MW

Poitevin

This breed from the Poitou (central western region round Poitiers, south of the Loire), despite motorization, still has an essential role in furnishing heavy draught mares of which the best are crossed with jackasses to produce mules. Used for draught or with a pack-saddle, many were exported because they were useful for work in difficult terrain. The Poitevin is a large horse, of undistinguished appearance, with gaunt lines and feet decorated with long hair. Sober and strong, it is descended from various French breeds of heavy draught horses and from Dutch horses imported centuries ago to drain the marshes. Its stud book contains one section for horse breeding and another for mule breeding. ES

Poland

In spite of, or perhaps because of, their varied history, the Poles have been excellent horsemen and horse breeders for many centuries. For many decades, before World War II, the privately owned Arabian studs were famous throughout Europe. At first Eastern horses were brought to Poland as booty, later members of the nobility organized direct importations from the Near East. Prince H. Sanguszko was the first to send an envoy (1803) to acquire horses for his stud at Slawuta; Count Potocki, a descendant of Prince Sanguszko, founded the famous Antoniny stud and also bred odd-coloured horses with considerable success. Count Dzieduszycki's Jarezowce stud housed the legendary grey Bagdad. Today the great Arabian studs of Guminska, Pelkinie, Sawran, Jarezowce and Bialocerkiev are no more. But those of Michalow and Janow Podlaski, which lie on the river Bug, near Brest, keep alive the great tradition and breed some of the best Arab horses in Europe. Lady Wentworth bought her famous Skowronek from Janow Podlaski, which was removed to Germany during the war and later was almost destroyed by Soviet troops. Now rebuilt, this stud has some beautiful mares and Saqlawi (Siglavy) and Kuhaylan stallions. Pure Arabs and Anglo-Arabs are trained and raced at Warsaw racecourse, since the furtherance of the hardy Arab horse still amounts to a national duty. Arabians are trained at 2½ years old for a Derby course of 3,000 m (1·86 miles).

There are a number of other breeds of horses and ponies native to Poland, including the regenerated wild TARPAN herds at Popielno, the native KONIK, the PANJE pony of the peasants, the HUCUL of the Carpathians, the strong and active carriage and light harness horses of Posen, the Skólsk Vanner type which may be seen in the district round Brest, and the Ermland or Stuhm horse from the western district of East Prussia, which is similar in type if a little heavier. Heavy BELGIAN, GUDBRANDSDAL and ARDENNES horses are also bred.

Other breeds, developed as a direct result of the war and the acquisition of former German territories, are the MASUREN, whose breeding adheres strictly to East Prussian and TRAKEHNER bloodlines. The chief stud is at Liski, the former remount depôt Liskien, whose lands border the Soviet-occupied northern half of the former province of

Colour plate. Above: **American Stagecoach.** A Wells Fargo coach in California

Below: **Rodeo.** Chuckwagon racing, a colourful event which came to the rodeo via the Wild West show

Below: **Poland.** A Wielkopolski or Masuren horse

Right: **Polo.** Hindu women playing polo in the sixteenth century A.D.

East Prussia. At the end of hostilities many homeless and ownerless horses, whose breeding was known only by the elk-antler brand mark, were sent by the Poles to reorganized studs and formed the nucleus of the new Masuren breed. In addition, 18 mares of Trakehner or East Prussian origin were acquired from the Russians, from the distant Don steppes where they had been taken as booty and left to fend for themselves through several winters. These mares were exchanged for six stallions and were taken to Liski but because of their run-down condition were unable to breed to East Prussian or Thoroughbred stallions—although subsequently a Tarpan stallion was successful. The resultant cross is interesting. There are said to be 800 East Prussian or Masuren mares and 900 Posen mares at the State Studs and it is not uncommon to find 150–200 stallions standing at the stallion depôts at Starograd, Kwidzyn (Liebenthal) and Gniezno. The number of horses in Poland is reckoned to be about three million.

The Raçot and Iwno studs also contain some Thoroughbred horses but breeding is not entirely successful and the type has deteriorated. Whether this has something to do with the continental climate as opposed to the wetter maritime climate which is more suited to the Thoroughbred horse, or whether breeding stock is inferior to the specialized product originating in Britain, or whether breeding policies are to blame, is hard to say. Poland's political situation for the past forty years has had its effect on horse breeding although the State studs are now exporting horses, especially to Switzerland.

Breeding is entirely under the control of the Polish Ministry of Agriculture through the Directors and Inspectors of the State studs, who control the studs for brood mares, the stallion depôts and stallion training schools. Farmers still retain a few mares on their present holdings and these are bred. The foals accompany their dams to work on the fields, a truly delightful sight. DMG

Reference: D. Machin Goodall, *Die Pferde mit der Elchschaufel*, Berlin, 1966, translated as *Flight of the East Prussian Horses*, Newton Abbott, 1972; *Horses of the World*, London, 1965.

Poll Evil

A painful inflammatory swelling at the poll, precipitated in most cases by injury and accompanied by necrosis and suppuration of the underlying tissues. CF

Polo

A stick and ball game on horseback for teams of four players.

Early History: the earliest references to the game appear in connection with Alexander the Great and Darius, King of Persia, the country which has strong claim to the honour of originating polo – although it seems to have been played in some form or other all over the East, especially in China and Mongolia. The game reached Japan, too, where a form of it called *da-kyu* (see Mounted Games) was adopted, as in so many countries, as part of equestrian and military training. It was a kind of mounted netball, played with up to 12 balls which had to be got into a central goal. Persian paintings of the sixteenth century show it as an elegant, aristocratic game played by kings and their courtiers, and also by women, it being definitely considered a co-educational sport there from earliest times. A seventeenth-century English observer (George Mainwaring, *The Journey into Persia*, 1613) describes something rather like the present game, but with 6 players a side. Remains of ancient stone goal posts (8 ft apart as today) still stand here and there, notably on the

Maidan at Isfahan (see plate p. 262) and at Kishtwar in the Himalayas.

Polo reached India with the Moslem invaders from the northwest, and from China in the northeast, but with the decline of the Moghul empire it virtually disappeared, lingering on only in the hill states of the Himalayas and Assam, such as Gilgit and Manipur. A rough version of the game survives in Gilgit; the teams line up at one end of the main street, the ball is hit to the other end, and a mad chase ensues, the winner of which has to dismount and hit the ball back up the street before being overwhelmed by the charging *melée*. In Persia the game was called *chaugan* (mallet), but its present name derives from the Tibetan *pulu* (root), from which the ball was, and still is, made.

Modern times: the game made no impact on the West until English planters discovered it in Assam in the 1850s. It was played on the local MANIPURI ponies and was called *kangjai*. Silchar, capital of the district of Cachar, has the honour of being the birthplace of modern polo, and the Silchar Club, founded in 1859, is the oldest polo club in the world. The founder members were Captain Robert Stewart, Deputy Commissioner, Lieutenant Joe Sherer, Assistant D.C., James Davidson (Soubong),

Polo. A British officer playing polo with the Wazir and Nawabs of Baltistan at Skardo, North Kashmir in 1889

Julius Sandemand (Chutla Bhil), James Abernethy and Arthur Brownlow (Hailakandi), Ernest Echardt (Silkuri), W. Walker (Bograghat) and J. P. Stewart (Larsingah). They drew up rules which were the foundation of the present ones. Nine players made the original team, later reduced to 7, and finally, as the ponies became bigger and faster, to 4. The original Manipuri ponies on which the Englishmen played were barely 12 hands (1·22 m) high, the height limit being fixed in 1876 at 13·2 hands (1·37 m) in India, 14 hands (1·42 m) in England. In 1895 the limit was raised to 14·2 hands (1·47 m), and finally abolished in 1919. The optimum height has settled now to about 15·1 hands (1·55 m).

In 1869 some officers of the 9th Lancers, 10th Hussars, 1st Life Guards and Royal Horse Guards played polo on Hounslow Heath, near London, which people called 'Hockey on horseback'. It was an instant success, the HURLINGHAM Club became the headquarters of English polo, and in 1875 the Hurlingham Club Polo Committee issued the first English Rules. The Indian Polo Association was formed about the same time and maintained its own rules until World War II. The first Inter-Regimental Tournament was played in 1878, and in 1893 the NATIONAL PONY SOCIETY was founded to promote the breeding of POLO PONIES.

The game quickly spread to the rest of the world, especially to the British Empire (now the Commonwealth) and to the United States and Argentina. International polo started in 1886 with the series of matches between Britain and the United States for the WESTCHESTER CUP. Between the wars brilliant Indian State teams came periodically from India, where the bulk of the polo played was regimental, and from Australia, but the lead remained with the United States, only beginning to be challenged by Argentina. Since 1945 that country has been supreme, unbeaten in the Cup of the Americas, the only international contest in existence now. Argentina has about 3,000 active players, compared with 1,000 in the U.S.A. and 500 in Britain.

In England after World War II, Hurlingham, Ranelagh and Roehampton ceased to be the headquarters of polo and the game nearly died, but a revival took place in 1950 thanks to the energy and munificence of Lord Cowdray supported by a group of prewar players, and to the patronage of H.R.H. the Duke of Edinburgh. The Hurlingham Polo Association was reconstituted to incorporate overseas associations and local clubs, and English polo is now in a very healthy condition, but not of a standard to challenge the Argentinians or the Americans on level terms.

Equipment: apart from the ponies (see Polo Ponies) the essential requirements for a game of polo are the ground, goal posts, ball, polo sticks or mallets, and the rider's own wear. The total length of the ground must not exceed 300 yd and the goals must not be less than 250 yd apart and 8 yd wide. Without side boards the width is 200 yd, with boards 160 yd; the boards must not exceed 11 in in height. The goal posts are at least 10 ft high, of light, easily breakable material. The ball, made of willow or bamboo root, has a diameter of not more than $3\frac{1}{4}$ in and weighs $4\frac{1}{4}-4\frac{1}{2}$ oz. The *polo stick* (called *mallet* in the United States) is a cane of varying degrees of whippiness, 48 in to 54 in long, according to the individual needs of the players, having a hand-grip at one end, the other end being inserted into a transverse head, which provides the hitting surface. This head is either cylindrical or cigar-shaped; square and other shapes are rarely seen in modern polo. The head is $8\frac{1}{2}$ – $9\frac{1}{2}$ in long, $1\frac{5}{8}$ – $1\frac{13}{16}$ in in diameter, and weighs 6 – $7\frac{1}{2}$ oz. It is made of sycamore, ash or bamboo, the latter sometimes covered with vellum. The angle of the head to the cane enables it to meet the ball parallel to the ground for a normal stroke. The inner end of the stick head is called the heel, the outer end the toe. In uncovered heads the heel and toe can be tapered on the lower side to facilitate far out and close shots respectively. The ball is hit with the centre of the long side of the head, which, in order to get a loft on the ball without sacrificing strength, is usually made elliptical. The cane is usually Malacca or Moonah, or a combination of the two, the Moonah cane, the lower part, being spliced into the upper part of Malacca, the object always being to have the greatest whippiness at the lower end. A whippy cane can obtain length of drive with the minimum of effort but is less manœuvrable in close work; a stiffer cane can be more accurate, but requires great strength and accuracy of timing. At the top of the cane is the grip, the best type being the O.H.K. or Rugby, which broadens on the inside, facilitating the prolongation of the line of the wrist and arm by the stick. Another type, the Parada, widens a few inches from the top, giving a kind of pistol grip, which adds to the strength of the hold. The grip is held by the fingers and thumb rather than by the whole palm. There is always a sling attached to the grip for security. The handle can be bound with leather, rubber, cotton wick, or (in hot climates) towelling.

Polo sticks are liable to break in the stress of a game, so a stock of six to twelve should be kept; when not in use they should be hung up by their slings, not by their heads. If the head is oiled (but not ash or bamboo) keep the oil away from the binding or the entry of the stick into the head. Bamboo heads can be painted to keep out damp. Rubber rings on the canes, a few inches above the head, will protect them from mis-hits.

Personal equipment: spurs are usually worn, blunt or without rowels; the rules expressly forbid sharp spurs. Protective headgear is obligatory: helmet (*topi*) type or reinforced polo cap with a peak, with chin strap. Boots by custom must be brown (to prevent blacking rubbing off on to opponents' white breeches), and, by rule, must have no outside buckles or projections. Under the breeches it is as well to wear long thin stockings or tights to prevent chafing, there being considerable movement in the saddle during a game. The polo whip should be about 40 in long and flexible. Hitting the pony with the stick is totally forbidden. A polo saddle should be light with moderately forward-cut flaps so as to provide a secure grip with the knees. For the pony boots or bandages, preferably boots with low-cut inner flaps, are compulsory, and coronet boots are advisable; tail bandages are used during play to keep long tails from interfering with the polo stick.

Playing the game: the most desirable qualities for a polo player are: courage; coolness; aptitude for ball games (such as rackets, squash rackets, tennis), with which goes a good natural eye; horsemanship; team spirit. Taking the last first, polo is essentially a team game in which all the members cooperate in plans and manœuvres to get the ball into the enemy's goal. The individualist, however brilliant, who tries to do it all himself, is harmful to the game both for players and spectators. Horsemanship, surprisingly, is not an essential quality; basic horsemanship, good balance and ability to stick on are the necessary attributes. Not all the top players of the world have been outstanding horsemen. A good natural eye for a moving ball is a *sine qua non*. The need for courage and cool judgment in a game played at a speed of 20 to 30 m.p.h. goes without saying.

Training: the first thing an aspiring polo player must learn, before he ever gets into a game, is to hit the ball accurately and correctly at all angles, forwards and backwards. The strokes are: *off-side forward, off-side backhand, off-side under the pony's neck, near-side forward* (in effect a backhand shot as at tennis or rackets), *near-side 'backhand'* (in effect a forward shot to the rear), *near-side under the pony's neck*, also *off-side* and *near-side back shots under the pony's tail*. Other effective shots are the *push*, an off-side stroke for which the rider bends low, using the full length of arm and stick to anticipate a normal strike by an

Polo. *Below left:* A good polo player is not necessarily a first-class horseman, but he must be good at ball games. This player is about to make an off-side backhand stroke.
Below: The rider nearest the camera prepares to make an off-side forward shot while the rider next to him aims a near-side 'backhand' (really a forward shot to the rear).

oncoming player, and *lateral*, underneath the pony's body and between his legs, for which very accurate timing is necessary, effective when in front of the goal.

Mastery of these strokes is only obtained by constant practice, preferably at first on a dummy horse in a *polo pit*. The horse is placed at the centre of a circular, square or oblong pit, 20–30 yd diameter, with gently sloping sides. The top perimeter should be surrounded by a netting or canvas screen, divided into 10-ft-wide numbered sections. The dummy horse should be solid, firmly based, and equipped with saddle and reins and a neckstrap. As for all striking games a secure base is needed at the moment of impact, which in polo is provided by the support of the stirrup irons and the grip of the knees and calf. For a forward shot the ball must be taken when it is in front of the withers, and for rear shots when it is roughly level with the quarters. For cross shots the ball should be taken as far in front of the fore legs or behind the hind legs as possible; for lateral strokes the ball is taken well to the side and about level with the rider in the saddle. First lessons in the pit consist of swinging practice without a ball. With the finger grip, for a forward stroke the thumb is bent round the handle below the first finger; for the backhand shift the thumb lies along the rear side of the handle. The rider should lean forward and down, bracing himself with his knees and stirrups, aiming to get as close as possible to the ball. The ball is struck with a swinging motion of the stick and arm, the former being an extension of the latter; everything depends on the exact timing of the swing so that the head strikes the ball at the instant of maximum momentum, helped by a final flick of the wrist. After the strike the swing is carried on round until the stick returns to its normal position, the carry, i.e. held vertically with hand and forearm horizontal.

When practising with a ball, every shot should be aimed at one or other of the numbered sections, starting of course with the ones straight ahead. The ball returning down the slope provides practice in hitting a moving ball. Once the swing and accuracy have been established in the pit, the beginner can progress to mounted work and to slow chukkars in practice games. Polo clubs in all countries usually provide these facilities for their members, and also, in some clubs, ponies for hire at reasonable fees.

Match play: the game is played in periods (*chakkar*, Urdu for 'circuit') of 7½ min each: 4,6,7 or 8 according to the nature of the competition, the normal ones now being 4 and 6. The normal interval between chukkars is 3 min, with a 5-min break at half-time. Except for the last chukkar (when the sides are not level) play continues after the signal for the end of the period until the ball goes out of play or into a neutral position on the ground. So the last chukkar is usually a short one, since the total time allotted for play must not be exceeded. If the sides are level at the end of the last chukkar play goes on until a goal is scored or the ball goes out of play. In the latter case an extra chukkar is played with widened goals until a goal is scored. Every time a goal is scored the teams change ends. A *team* consists of 4 players: Forwards (Nos 1 and 2); Half-back (No 3); Back (No 4). Each player must carry his number conspicuously on the back of his polo jersey. No 3 is the pivot of the side, the one who initiates attacks, or covers No 4 in defence; needless to say he has to be very well mounted, and be a long and accurate hitter in all directions. Nos 1 and 2 follow up the attacking moves initiated by their No 3, and also mark their opposing Nos 4 and 3 in defence. Both, No 2 especially, must be accurate forward hitters. No 4 defends his side's half of the territory, but should be ready to support and interchange with No 3.

Handicaps: most games are played on a handicap basis, all players being assessed at their worth in goals or minus-goals, with a range of minus 2 to 10, which is based on the assumption (now seldom true) that matches will be of 8 chukkars. In handicap tournaments the total individual handicaps are added up, one subtracted from the other, the balance being the number of goals start given to the lower handicapped team by the higher. In a 4-chukkar match the amount is halved, because calculated on an 8-chukkar basis, and proportionately adjusted for longer matches.

Polo. The dimensions of a boarded polo ground. If no boards are used the size of the ground is 300 × 200 yd. Flags should then be used to show the 30-, 40- and 60-yd marks but they must be placed behind the side lines.

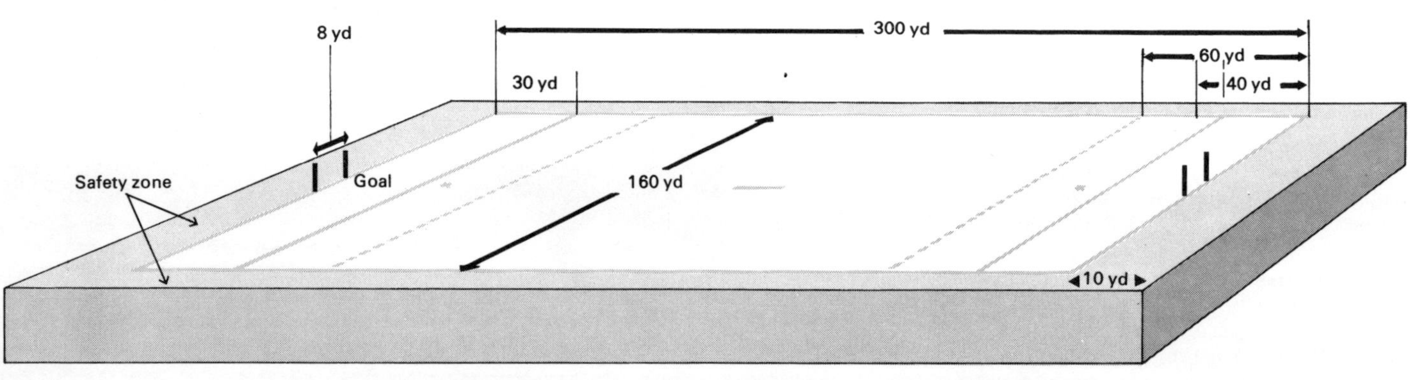

Top: **Polo Crosse**

Above: **Polo Pony.** A champion Argentinian Polo Pony mare

Rules: the rules of polo are mainly devised to ensure safety in a very fast-moving game, so they mostly aim at clarifying the right of possession of the ball (right of way), prescribing penalties for infringing that right and causing danger, e.g. by crossing the line of the ball in front of a player who is either the last to hit it or has acquired a 'right of way', except at such a distance away as to preclude all risk of a collision. A player on the line of the ball and taking it on his off-side has the right of way over all other players; the same applies to two players riding each other off and following the line of the ball; but one player may not ride another off across the right of way. Players meeting each other on the line of the ball must do so off-side to off-side. Other infringements are: riding into a player at a dangerous angle, zigzagging in front of a player at full gallop, pulling across a pony's legs, intimidation, sandwiching a player between two opponents, hooking an opponent's stick from the far side. Penalties vary according to the nature and gravity of the offence. A deliberate foul to save a goal is penalized by the award of a penalty goal. Dangerous fouling carries 30-yard or 40-yard free hits at an open, undefended goal. Lesser penalties are a 60-yard hit, also awarded when a ball goes behind off a defending player or pony (corner), free hit from where the foul occurred or from the centre. The game is stopped if a pony falls, or is lame, if player or rider is injured, if there is a potentially dangerous accident to the pony's gear, or if a player loses his headgear and if the ball goes out of play. CEGH

References: Marco, *An Introduction to Polo*, London, 1931; John Board, *Polo*, London, 1956; W. B. Devereux, Jr, *Position and Team Play in Polo*, New York, 1914; Newell Bent, *American Polo*, New York, 1929; William Cameron Forbes, *As to Polo*, Manila, 1919; Lt-Col E. D. Miller, *Modern Polo*, London 1896, 6th rev. ed., London, 1930; Lt-Gen Sir Beauvoir de Lisle, *Polo in India*, Bombay, 1924.

Polo Crosse

Polo crosse, derived from polo and lacrosse, began before World War II as an indoor game, sponsored by the National School of Equitation, Kingston Vale, London. In 1939 an Australian of Ingleburn, N.S.W., introduced it as an outdoor game to his own country, where it was played by the Ingleburn Horse and Pony Club. Before long it swept Australia. In Australia the standard field is 160 yd long by 60 yd wide. Goal posts 14 ft high, 8 ft apart, stand at each end with a semicircle of 11 yards diameter drawn in front of them, beyond which goals must be thrown in. Thirty yards from each end is a penalty line over which no ball may be carried; it must be grounded and picked up again which calls for good timing and wrist work. A soft ball is used, carried in a net on a stick similar to a polo stick; the net is the size of a squash racket and not unlike a lacrosse stick. Ponies do not exceed 15 hands (1·52 m). The teams are made up of six players, three taking the field for each side at a time, playing alternate chukkars of eight minutes each. Reintroduced into England in 1947, polo crosse became very popular before polo came back into its own. DRT

Polo Pony

Horses of about 15·1 hands (1·55 m), which in polo are still called ponies, with seven-eighths or more of English Thoroughbred blood, seem to be generally accepted as most suitable for modern polo.

They are usually found by selecting from large numbers of horses bred primarily for other purposes – such as handling cattle or racing – those few that show outstanding natural aptitude for polo. They are then trained to allow the player to hit the ball all round him, to gallop straight on the line of the ball, to face an onrush of other ponies, to jump from a standstill into a gallop, to stop and turn handily, and to ride into the other ponies as and when required. Concurrently with this they are played, slowly at first, and they generally improve as they gain experience of the game.

Today the majority of ponies playing polo come from the Argentine, where the number and skill of Argentine players, the scale of horse breeding, and the indigenous skills in horsemanship cheaply available, enable Argentine exporters to sell in quantity high-class ponies more cheaply than breeders in most other countries can produce them. See colour plate, page 263. GNJ

Ponies

The official definition of a pony is a male or female horse not over 14·2 hands (1·47 m) (see Height). Although both ponies and horses belong to the one species *Equus caballus*, all races of which will interbreed to produce fertile offspring—even the union of a Clydesdale with a Shetland is possible and has been produced—it is not now believed that ponies are simply small horses. There are elements of conformation as well of scale that divide the one from the other, and these differences are observable not only in the living animal today but in fossil remains.

The most recent theory of the origins of the domestic horse distinguishes four separate types already in existence in the wild before domestication took place in Eurasia. Two of these are classified as horses and two as ponies. Their habitats overlapped widely in every instance, even before domestication, so that it is only possible to say that *most* of the wild equids in a given area belonged to this or that type; it is also probable that in border regions there will have been individuals, perhaps whole herds, of half-bred wild horses showing some characteristics of more than one type defined below. As the terminology has changed several times, to the confusion of the student, since this subject was first seriously studied in the early 1800s, the present most respected authorities, Speed in Scotland, Skorkowski in Poland and Ebhardt in Germany, have agreed to stop coining fancy names like Diluvial Horse, Forest Horse, Plateau Pony etc., and adopt a simple numerical scheme as follows:

Pony Type I: in northwest Europe and its offshore islands, insofar as the latter were joined to the Continent after the Ice Age. Unspecialized, broad forehead, wide nostrils, small ears, broad croup, brush on base of tail, straight or S-shaped facial profile, height at withers 12·2 hands (1·27 m). Like the Pleistocene fossil ponies of Mendip; approximately the Exmoor (see Mountain and Moorland Ponies) of today.

Pony Type II: more massive, heavier and coarser head, longer ears, split up behind, more sloping croup, erect mane with little or no forelock, height to 14·2 hands (1·47 m), light-coloured when living in the open, mostly closely resembling the Przevalski horse of today (see Asiatic Wild Horse). The most northerly, but yet the most widely distributed of the wild varieties: the majority of European horses of the Old Stone Age appear to have been of this type, the result of migrations from Siberia. In forests and swamps an extremely massive variety of this type with low withers and much bone developed; it was darker in colour.

Horse Type III: as an element in the make-up of ponies in historical times this type entered least frequently, therefore it is not illustrated here. It had a long back, somewhat slab-sided, a long head, very long ears, narrow forehead, convex facial profile, sloping croup. No brush on base of tail. Sparse hanging mane and forelock. Habitat Central Asia. Height to 15 hands (1·52 m).

Horse Type IV: fine-boned, short in the back. Short narrow head with wide muzzle, broad brow, concave facial profile, small inward-curving ears, tufted at tips, narrow quarters with high-set tail. Height to 12 hands (1·22 m). No brush on base of tail. Habitat western Asia. Nearest living representative is the CASPIAN PONY of northwest Persia.

No living breed of horses exhibits, exactly, all the points of any one of these primeval races, but occasional individuals of almost any breed will unpredictably do so, once in several thousand births. This is because about four thousand years of crossing between all four types, mostly haphazard or dictated by necessity, have taken place. Even the occasional Thoroughbred turns out like Horse Type III. The extinct TARPAN of eastern Europe and the Ukraine seems to have been a relatively simple mixture of

Pony Type I

Pony Type II

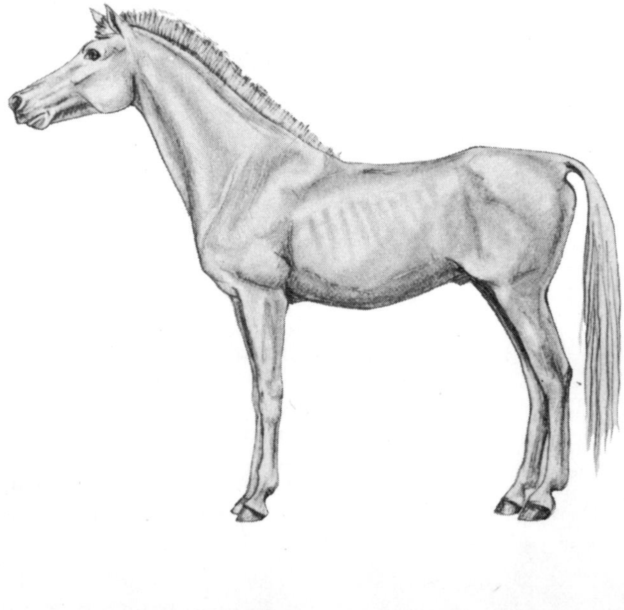

Horse Type IV

Pony I and Horse IV and its blood today runs in the Polish KONIK, the Carpathian HUÇUL, the BOSNIAN PONY, the Prussian Schweike, and other local races of eastern Europe from the Balkans to the Baltic; as one goes further north, so the visible proportion of the blood of Pony Type II becomes more obvious, mostly manifesting itself in low withers and a short thick neck.

Domestication probably took place in the following order: Type II, for riding and pack work, probably by reindeer herdsmen who some while previously had adopted the unique habit of riding their reindeer, as the Uryanchai and Yakut nomads of Siberia do today. Type IV, followed by Type III, initially only in harness (chariots) by people already practising a crop-rearing economy involving the use of draught oxen. Lastly Type I, in imitation of the charioteers who worked mostly with Type IV and its derivative the Tarpan, and whose influence spread slowly northwestwards across Europe. Type I was also used early in its domestic career as a pack horse, because the ass and mule, not found wild in Europe but brought to western Asia as pack animals in late prehistoric times, were not available in Europe north of the Alps until about the beginning of the Christian era. Thus in terms of size nearly all the horses driven or ridden in ancient times, at least down to about 600 B.C., were ponies.

By this standard, the capacity of the four primeval races to grow larger varies very greatly. Thus Pony I had also a diminutive prehistoric variant, seen on the walls of the painted caves of France and Spain, where it is often shown piebald, that became the modern Shetland (see Mountain and Moorland Ponies). But without the admixture of other blood, and even under the most favourable conditions of feeding, Type I would not grow much above 13·2 hands (1·37 m). The most frequent admixture of blood to Type I, due to geographic proximity, was of course Type II, resulting in increased weight and stature and decreased speed and handiness. The capacity of Type III, when not crossed to increase in size, is limited only by the amount of food it can get and the amount of shelter from cold and damp available. In the forests it had shelter from cold, dry ground, and abundant but not very nutritious browsing. In the marshes it had much better keep, but it was never dry and got only moderate protection from the cold. The ponies of northern Europe (for instance Scandinavia) are the result of a cross of Types I and II, living out all the year round, usually spending the summer on the hills and the winter on the low ground. The tall heavy agricultural (formerly war-) horses of northern Europe are the result of a cross of Types II and III, artificially fed and housed in winter. Light horses of 'oriental' type, other than Arab, up to 16 hands (1·65 m) high, are basically crosses of Types III and IV in varying proportions, artificially fed in the dry season and protected from the worst heat of summer. The capacity of Type IV, uncrossed, to grow larger over the generations where there is adequate food is almost as great as that of Type II. Hot damp is almost as stunting as cold damp. Thus the ponies of southeast Asia (for instance Java), which are a combination of Types III and IV, are both low in stature and narrow. Mountainous country does not lead so much to a low height as to short legs in proportion to depth of body. Ponies about 13 hands (1·32 m) high but relatively high on the leg are the product of flat open country.

The distribution of pony types in Europe is confused because they have been eliminated from the central mass by the economic demands of man and the fact that the mule is available in the South. Thus they are present in Spain, Portugal, Sardinia (but not the Italian mainland), western France, where they have been much mixed with BARB blood (the Barb is basically not a pony), the British Isles, Iceland, Scandinavia, the Baltic, Poland, the Carpathians. Then comes a gap corresponding to the Danube Valley in the widest sense, then the Balkans and Greece, including the interesting island breed of SKYROS in the Aegean. Within this margin is a 'dead centre'. Formerly ponies were abundant in the Alpine regions; now the only Alpine ponies are HAFLINGERS, which owe their colour to a highly prepotent Arab sire of Napoleonic times and their conformation to the large agricultural PINZGAUER NORIKER horse of the Danube region. The 'lost' Alpine ponies appear to have been predominantly of 'northern' (Type II) stamp and they extended northwards through the Black Forest as far as the Vosges until about 1600. Type I ponies survive in some Atlantic districts of France between the Gironde and the Pyrenees, where they merge imperceptibly into the ponies of Spanish Navarre. These Landais ponies (see Ponies, French) are now greatly reduced in numbers but have gained in esteem; within living memory drives have been organized against them, as vermin to be killed rather than to be caught and broken. There is no doubt that the light-horse breeds of Gascony and Limousin are built up on a foundation of this pony blood, mixed with that of the Barbs which even two hundred years ago were common in that region; '. . . if you send to Languedoc or Provence in France, Barbs can be bought there for forty or fifty pistoles a horse' (Fielding and Walker, 1778). The white horses of the CAMARGUE are regarded by some as *the* aboriginal pony race of France but it is more than probable that they are of virtually unmixed Barbary blood, introduced during the Saracen invasions of that region that took place during the ninth century. AD

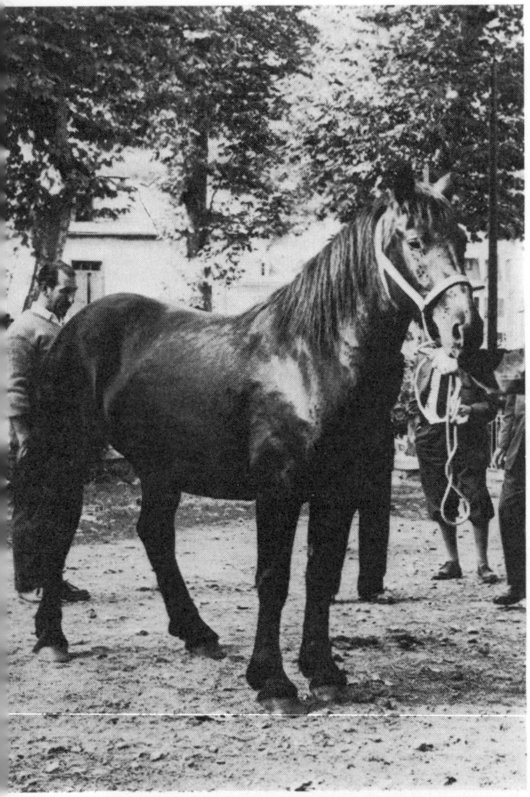

Ponies, British Native see Mountain and Moorland Ponies

Ponies, French

Recent fashion, the demand for ponies for children and consequent imports of ponies, mostly British, should stimulate breeding in France. Most native ponies are found in the Basque and Pyrenean regions. The Poney Landais lives in a semi-wild state in the wooded areas of the Landes, the biggest forest in Europe. It is grey, with a small, expressive head, light and straight neck, long mane and tail, thin but solid limbs and sloping croup. It stands about 11·3½ hands (1·20 m) high. A larger, because better nourished, relation is found in the plains of Chalosse near the Adour river. The Barthais, another closely related pony, lives in the marshes of this river. Both are often crossed with Tarbais. They are chestnut or black and are worth protecting.

The Mérens, described by Caesar, probably of oriental origin, is an ancient breed like the CAMARGUE. Found semi-wild in the mountains and high valleys of the Ariège river, they are used as packponies or for light draught work. They are black, sturdy, compact and surefooted, with hairy coats, about 13·3 hands (1·40 m) high. They have had their own stud book since 1948.

French Ponies. *Top:* A Mérens stallion *Above:* Pottok ponies

The little Basque Pottok is completely wild, living among sheep. It is very rarely used.

The Corsican Pony, dark grey or black and of Arab origin, height 12·3½ hands (1·30 m), has been modified by its wild life in the high mountains of Corsica. It is lightly built and of rather primitive shape but sober and sturdy. The breed is unfortunately disappearing. ES

Pony Breeding see Breeding, Pony, Riding Ponies

Pony Club

In 1927 a number of people advocated the forming of a junior branch of the Institute of the Horse (now the BRITISH HORSE SOCIETY). In 1928 three branches were formed, attached to Hunts, as these were considered to be in suitable geographical areas. Prime movers at this time were Major Harry Faudel-Phillips, Colonel Guy Cubitt, Chairman for 20 years, Mrs Corbett and Colonel V. D. S. Williams.

Within three years there were over 100 branches and the movement quickly spread overseas. Today the Pony Club is stronger and more active than ever, with more than 300 branches in Britain and over 600 branches overseas. In Britain alone there are over 30,000 members. Most of Britain's leading riders have been members, many admitting they owe much of their success to their early Pony Club days.

It is likely that membership would be even larger if Pony Club rallies were not restricted, as they are, mainly to boarding-school holidays, though more and more branches are catering for day-school children by providing Pony Club activities every weekend. In most country districts enormous distances have to be covered and most Pony Clubs depend entirely on voluntary assistance. This makes it difficult to organize rural clubs on any but a school holiday basis. The highlight of the year in most Pony Clubs is a camp held during the summer holidays when 50–200 children congregate for a week in one area and can benefit daily from instruction in addition to the fun of a community holiday. DW

The United States Pony Club, Inc. had its inception at informal meetings in New York in 1953 and was formally incorporated early in 1954. Although not officially associated with The Pony Club of Great Britain, the U.S.P.C. adopted in most respects its program, standards and training methods. The initial assistance from Great Britain has ripened into a friendly and continuing cooperation between the two organizations.

The U.S.P.C. works closely with other U.S. horse organizations, including the Masters of Foxhounds Association of America, the American Horse Shows Association and the U.S. Combined Training Association, but is not affiliated with or a part of any other organization. Its officers are elected by, and control of its activities is entrusted to a Board of Governors (at present thirty in number), who in turn are elected by over 2,000 'Sustaining Members', whose annual dues are a major source of funds to finance its operations. The Pony Club children are members of local pony clubs affiliated to the U.S.P.C. In 1972 there were about 250 member clubs throughout the United States, with about 9,000 members. The numbers continue to grow steadily.

Pony Club activities include regional rallies in each of the 21 regions, a national rally, international exchange visits to other countries, inter-club exchanges within the United States, and a continuing program of instruction at the member clubs, including camping and games. The U.S.P.C. emphasizes equally horsemanship and horsemastership. These are reflected in the examinations which pony club members must pass to attain the highly coveted rating as a 'B' rider, or the even more exalted status as an 'A' rider. To compete successfully at a regional or national rally, a competitor must combine ability as a rider with both 'book knowledge' and practical competence in stable management. WSF

Pony Express

William Russell, the last surviving Pony Express rider, died at Stockton, California, in 1934. So vivid is the American legend of the Pony Express that few people realize that it existed for less than two years. It first ran in April 1860 from St Joseph, Missouri, through Kansas, Nebraska, Colorado, Wyoming, Utah and Nevada to Sacramento, California. The last run was made in October 1861. The fastest was by Bob Haslam, who carried the mail 120 miles from Smith's Creek to Fort Churchill, Nevada, in 8 hours 10 minutes in March 1861.

It was neither a Federal nor a State service, but a contract undertaken by the transport firm of Russell, Majors and Wadell, who were also engaged in goods and passenger haulage by road and employed 5,000 men. Although there were only about two dozen riders at any given time, the service was uneconomic because the ancillary services required to support the actual riders took up too many man-hours of the labour force as a whole. Four hundred horses were used, including spares, to cover the 1,966 miles of route in ten days. It was literally a pony express as few of the animals were over 14 hands (1·42 m) high; none was materially above this height. But they were greatly superior in quality and price to the general run of Western cow pony. They had to be because sometimes at the very end of their stage they had to outdistance hostile Indians mounted on fresh ponies. This risk also affected the weight carried. Saddle, bridle and mailbag together only weighed 13 lb (5·90 kg), whereas the common Western saddle of that day weighed more than that by itself. Twenty pounds (9 kg) of mail (say 300 ordinary letters) were carried. Since most of the men were smallish and lightly built, their all-up weight unarmed would be about 12 stone (168 lb or 76·20 kg). But since the Pony Express era coincided with that of one of the most dangerous Indian risings, each man carried a carbine as well as two revolvers, with ammunition. Parts of the Pony Express route coincided exactly with that of the Wells Fargo Overland Stage. The service cost $100,000 to equip initially, and $80,000 a month to run. The company finished operations $20,000 in the red, but this was a case where success and service to the public could not fairly be measured in financial terms. AD

Below: **Pony Express.** A messenger on his way from the Missouri River to California in 1861

Bottom: **Pony of the Americas.** The first registered Pony of the Americas, originally owned by Leslie L. Boomhower

Pony of the Americas

The Pony of the Americas is an officially recognized American pony breed with its own stud book and registry. Created by Mr Leslie Boomhower of Mason City, Iowa, who produced the first stallion by crossing a Shetland pony with an APPALOOSA mare, the Pony of the Americas has Appaloosa markings: round or elliptical spots on the coat with emphasis over the hindquarters, white circling round the eyes, often striped hoofs, and mud-coloured shading round the mouth and nostrils. The neck is slightly arched and clear cut, the face often 'dished' as in the ARAB, eyes large; the body is round, full-ribbed and well-muscled. The walk is straight with long, easy stride, the trot prompt, balanced and free. A mature pony must stand 11·2–13·2 hands (1·16–1·37 m) high and must have visible Appaloosa colouring. In December 1971 there were 12,598 registered ponies of this breed. GBL

Pony Trekking

Trek is a loan-word from Afrikaans, and originally meant a journey, march or migration. Its speed used to be measured by that of the ox-wagons or Cape carts. Trekking today in the British Isles is of course quite different. In fact, the name is misleading, for it is undertaken from a centre, either residential or non-residential, from which riders go out daily from approximately 10 a.m. to 4 p.m. to ride along previously reconnoitred routes, attended by the proprietor and/or one of his staff, and returning each evening to the base centre. A different route is taken each day from Monday to Friday. A halt is made at midday for a rest and picnic lunch. Trekking is undertaken almost entirely at walking pace. Short intervals of trotting may be permitted should the terrain be suitable and provided those taking part are sufficiently experienced, which actually is often not the case. For one of the attractions of trekking is that it is possible for people with little or no experience to take part.

If the trekkers ride out and either camp out overnight or put up at an hotel or inn, then ride on again the next day, and so on for varying periods of from three to five days, this is called *post trekking*. It is provided by only two or three centres, because of the difficulty of organization in country full of barbed wire and other boundaries, of T.T. accredited herds, coupled with the lack of stabling and the reluctance of farmers to graze the ponies overnight. It is in any case only suitable for experienced riders.

Pony Trekking. Riders set off for a day in the hills of Inverness-shire.

In most trekking centres little or no instruction is given and there is no supervision after trekking hours. It is therefore unsuitable for children aged 12 years or under. In fact even young teenagers are usually much happier at a riding holiday centre with others of their own age group, but for older teenagers and adults it is an extremely popular, health-giving and enjoyable recreation. It is advisable to patronize only 'approved' centres.

Trekking takes place where the terrain lends itself to this, in Britain on Dartmoor and Exmoor, in the New Forest, the fells and dales of Westmorland, Cumberland, Yorkshire and Northumberland, all over Wales (notably in Breconshire), in Perthshire (notably the Trossachs), Inverness-shire, Ayrshire, Angus, Aberdeenshire, the border countries of Roxburghshire and Dumfriesshire, and in the Lammermuir, Ochill and Eildon Hills. The ponies used are mostly indigenous (see Mountain and Moorland Ponies).

A few lessons at a good riding school beforehand are advisable since they give more njoyment to the rider and less discomfort to the pony, by exercising muscles not previously used, which otherwise tend to get very stiff for the first day or two. People with no previous riding experience are accepted, but due notice should be given so that proprietors can provide suitable mounts and at least elementary instruction.

It should be noted that in substandard centres the ponies are deliberately kept in low condition to render them spiritless enough for novices to ride them. Trekkers should refuse to ride animals that are obviously in poor or weak condition or badly shod, or use badly maintained and therefore dangerous equipment.

'Ponies of Britain' does not itself run trekking centres but inspects such centres and awards its Certificate of Approval to those attaining a good standard. It should be remembered, however, that standards fluctuate and the society cannot be responsible for any sudden deterioration. A full descriptive list of over 150 approved trekking and riding holiday centres is available from 'Ponies of Britain', Brookside Farm, Ascot, Berks. on receipt of 25p. GS

Portugal

In the twelfth century A.D. Portugal became a kingdom (see Spain), freed itself of Moorish influence and, with the marriage of Alfonso III (1248–79) of Portugal to the daughter of Alfonso X of Leon and Castile (Spain), obtained its present European boundaries. It is from this period that the breeding of horses in the two countries diverged slightly, although basically the ANDALUSIAN and the ALTÉR are from the same stock. To the north, in the provinces of Garrano do Minho and Traz des Montes, Portugal has its own breed of native ponies, the Minho or Garranos, which stands between 10 hands (1·02 m) and 12 hands (1·22 m). They are used by the army and local people as packponies.

The Sorraia pony has inhabited the plains between the rivers Sor and Raia (in both Portugal and Spain) from ancient times. It stands between 12 hands (1·22 m) and 13 hands (1·32 m) and was possibly one of the first breeds of horses to be domesticated, probably during Neolithic times. This pony is almost always dun or grey in colour, often with zebra marks on the legs and a dorsal stripe. Some specimens have a distinctly concave face, while others seem to have a profile similar to that of the TARPAN. The Sorraia is extremely hardy and was used by cowboys. The d'Andrade family keeps a purebred herd of Sorraia ponies in their natural state.

The Lusitano, once used by the army, is another old breed which has the same background as the Spanish Andalusian. These horses are used for light farmwork and also for the bull ring. In Portugal bullfighting (see Rejoneador) is a far more artistic sport than in Spain, requiring great expertise in horsemanship. The Altér-Real is still bred at the National Stud, Vila de Portel in Alentejo province. This breed also has connections with the Andalusian, since 300 mares were used by the House of Braganza in 1747 to lay the foundations of a court stud. Later, after political disturbances when the breed had been almost ruined by outcrosses of foreign and ARABIAN horses, it was re-established by introducing Andalusian stallions from the Zapata Stud in Spain. In 1910, when Portugal became a republic, almost all the documents and data relating to breeding were destroyed, but in 1932 the Ministry of of Economy took over its management and reduced the number of brood mares, keeping only the best together with two first-class stallions. Today the Altér horse is an all-round warmblood horse of exceptional quality. It is a beautiful saddle horse and

Top: **Portugal.** A Lusitano horse

Centre: **Horse in Prehistoric Art.** A pregnant mare struck by arrows at Lascaux suggests magic for success in hunting.
Below: A string of ponies, one a skewbald, also at Lascaux

can be schooled for *haute école*, for which it was originally bred.

Anglo-Arabs, Arabs, Thoroughbreds and Irish horses have been imported into Portugal. Even so, horse breeding is not as important to the economy of the country as the breeding of asses and mules, which are used all over the Iberian Peninsula.

The Portuguese Ministry of the Army maintains a well-developed Military School of Equitation at Mafra, near Lisbon. DMG
Reference: D. Machin Goodall, *A History of Horse Breeding*, London, 1973; *Horses of the World*, London, 1965.

Posen see Poland

Post Trekking see Pony Trekking

Pottering (Pottery) Action
A term describing a short stride with a tendency to throw the weight on the heels, typical of NAVICULAR DISEASE. WSC

Pottok see Ponies, French

Poznan (Posen) see Poland

Prehistoric Art, Horse in

Rock drawings and engravings of the prehistoric horse date from approximately 30,000–10,000 B.C., covering the Aurignacian, the Solutrean and the Magdalenian culture periods, and take an important and graphic place in these ancient animal representations, especially remarkable in the Magdalenian period.

Cave pictures appear in various parts of the world. It was predominantly, however, in the small western European area, on the southern edge of the glacial belt in the limestone region of the Pyrenees, where the fauna was dominated by mammoth, giant antelope, woolly rhinoceros and a race of wild horses, that Palaeolithic man, animals and artists found the most suitable habitat. Over 70 grottoes with paintings and engravings are known to exist in France and 33 in Spain. The cult of secret religious beliefs and hunting magic inevitably dominated artistic inspiration, for postglacial man was primarily a hunter and food gatherer: horsemeat provided a vital element of diet. Pregnant mares, therefore, are frequently portrayed to invoke fertility and also pictures of horses killed or struck by arrows to suggest conditions for success in hunting. The irregularity of the rock wall is often employed to emphasize the design, the same sites being used repetitively, several drawings being superimposed over earlier works. Figures of horses appear frequently in the art of the Magdalenian period in the Montespan cave in the Garonne and on the floor of the Bedheilac cave in Ariège; both show tough little horses with big strong heads and erect manes, resembling Przevalski's wild horse (see Asiatic Wild Horse). These prehistoric artists obviously possessed a keen eye and confident hand, especially noticeable in equine figures in the Lebastide cave in the Hautes-Pyrenées and in the cavern of Niaux near Tarascon.

Palaeolithic pictures began as simple outlines but increased pictorial sophistication came with the application of colour. Pigments derived from oxide, white marl, ochres and charcoal with some medium, possibly fat, were used, sometimes applied by a feather. Later a type of coloured crayon was also employed, several being found neatly sharpened in the caverns at Altamira, discovered in 1879 and richly endowed with animal pictures. Two especially striking drawings here are of horses, one galloping, depicted in thick deft lines comparable in style to a study by Picasso or Cézanne.

Most remarkable in all Palaeolithic art are the painted pictures of Lascaux in the Dordogne. Considered to have been executed in the late Aurignacian or early Magdalenian period, and discovered in 1940, the caves had been hermetically sealed naturally and the colouring had retained all its original brilliance. In the main hall several horses are depicted in black outline, with black manes and bodies of yellow-brown. A frieze 11 ft 6 in (3·5 m) long of five pregnant ponies, one a skewbald, is painted with vivid realism in brown and black, the colour within the contours having been applied by a small bone blowpipe. An in-foal wild mare in yellow and black struck by arrows repeats the hunting theme. In some representations of these horses surprising elegance and accuracy prevails, for artists ranked as magicians to enchant the primitive gods and on the realism of their pictures depended the ultimate success of their invocations. Unfortunately a fungus infection began seriously to damage the Lascaux paintings and the caves had to be closed to the public.

The later Palaeolithic artists worked in an individual style though still using rock formations to enhance their compositions, as in the little spotted horses in the huge caverns of Peche Merle. Here appears an almost unique feature in the suggestion of a dished facial profile reminiscent of the modern Welsh Mountain Pony. The figures of the horses are bordered by outspread hands demanding fertility and plenty. Within this same period many engravings on bone, tiny and meticulous, use the horse as subject. Four heads from Isturitz in the Basses-Pyrenées vary from only $\frac{1}{5}$–$\frac{1}{2}$ in (5–12 mm) in length. In Vienne the artist successfully copes with the problems of perspective in a bone engraving showing two herds of wild horses.

The Palaeolithic artistic heritage lived on for millennia into the dawn of history. In Levantine Spain, in rock paintings of approximately 2500 B.C., artists began depicting in silhouette actual sporting scenes in monochrome, usually red. At Los Canforos de Penarubia there are paintings of human figures leading a horse and foals with halters, showing that domestication of genus *Equus* had begun. SAW

Prehistoric Horses see Evolution of the Horse Family

Prehistoric Remains see Prehistoric Art, Megiddo, Pazyryk, Qualat Jermo

Premium Stallion Scheme

The Premium Stallion scheme as operated by the HUNTERS' IMPROVEMENT AND NATIONAL LIGHT HORSE BREEDING SOCIETY (H.I.S.) throughout Great Britain is unique. Most other countries have national studs, state-controlled and financed, where stallions of various types are available to small breeders at low fees. In Great Britain the National Stud has only high-class Thoroughbred stallions which stand at extremely high fees, far outside the reach of small breeders and in any case not catering for owners of non-Thoroughbred mares.

The H.I.S., backed by the HORSERACE BETTING LEVY BOARD, makes available to small breeders approximately 65 good strong Thoroughbred stallions allocated as evenly as possible throughout the country; in many areas they still travel to call at farms and cover any mare which farmers may want to breed from.

The Premium Stallion scheme began in 1894, mainly due to the fact that very large sums of money were being spent on importing horses from abroad. The scheme was first financed by the War Office as they were very concerned about the shortage of horses for the Army. Twenty-nine premiums of £150 each were awarded to suitable stallions in 1894, but now the H.I.S. awards some 65 premiums, each of £445, every year. The stallions are selected at the Thoroughbred Stallion Show at Newmarket in March, and usually about 85 stallions compete for the awards. In addition to the basic premium of £445, the top 14 stallions receive additional prize money ranging in value from £270 to £80. These additional prizes are known as super premiums.

When a stallion is awarded a premium he is under contract to the H.I.S. from March until the end of July; he has to be made available as the Society directs in the district to which he is allocated. He then either travels or stands at stud where mares can come to him. Members of the H.I.S. are entitled to have their mares covered at a fee of £12·60; non-members pay £23·10. The premium paid to the stallion owner is therefore intended to subsidize the fee which mare owners are charged. Breeders who send their mares to premium stallions are assured of the services of a thoroughly sound animal as all the stallions have to undergo a most rigorous veterinary examination before they can be considered for an award. They must be certified free from cataract, roaring, whistling, ringbone, sidebone, bone spavin, defective genital organs, navicular disease, shivering and stringhalt. They must also acquire a certificate stating that they have not been hobdayed or tubed and that they are not parrot-mouthed.

The 65 premium stallions cover nearly 4,000 mares each year; as a result some 2,500 foals are produced annually, many of which achieve international fame. Three GRAND NATIONAL winners in the past ten years have been sired by premium stallions: Merryman II, Highland Wedding and Specify; among show jumpers are the immortal Foxhunter and Sunsalve, both of which won medals for their riders at the OLYMPIC GAMES. Perhaps most important of all, the majority of the stock sired by premium horses is used for hunting and general riding purposes. The achievements of the premium stallion scheme are reflected in the fact that the general standard of riding horses in Great Britain is higher than anywhere else in the world. GWE

President's Cup

Instituted in 1965, during H.R.H. Prince Philip's first year as President of the FÉDÉRATION ÉQUESTRE INTERNATIONALE, the President's Cup is based on the results of NATIONS' CUPS and is therefore a World Championship for teams. To encourage NATIONAL FEDERATIONS to give a chance to their up-and-coming riders, the rules stipulate that each country must be represented by no fewer than six riders in Nations' Cups during the year. Only the best six scores for each country can be counted. Points are awarded in all Nations' Cups competitions according to the number of teams taking part. When there are five or fewer teams, the winning country gains five points; when there are six teams the top score is six points; for seven or more it is seven points. In each case the second team receives one point less than the winner, the third team two points less, and so on. Every team that starts is automatically awarded one point towards the President's Cup. GM

President's Cup Winners	*points*	*wins*
1965 Great Britain	37	6
1966 U.S.A.	27	3
1967 Great Britain	37	6
1968 U.S.A.	34	6
1969 German Federal Rep.	39	6
1970 Great Britain	27·5	4
1971 German Federal Rep.	37	6
1972 Great Britain	33	4

Priobsky see Horse Breeding under U.S.S.R.

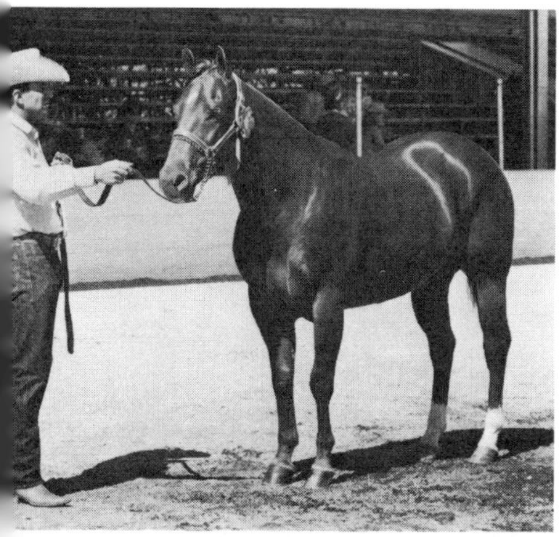

Quarter Horse. *Top:* Joe Hild Man, an American Quarter Horse gelding
Above: Mentirosa, an Australian Quarter Horse

Przevalski's Horse see Asiatic Wild Horse, Evolution of the Horse Family

Puerto Rico

There are three general types of horses in Puerto Rico. The PASO FINO, the native breed, mostly used for pleasure and by country people on their farms, is a descendant of the ANDALUSIAN brought during Spanish colonization. THOROUGHBREDS were introduced into the island for racing and are, economically, the most important breed. Constant improvement of bloodlines is accomplished by the introduction of English, United States and Argentine stock. There are 152 racing days annually, eight races per day on San Juan's racetrack. A new track has been licensed for the southern part of the island (see Flat Racing). Show classes for Western hunters and jumpers were started about seven years ago. These horses, usually Thoroughbreds, are generally brought from the United States. The great majority of competitive riders are juniors and a Junior International Show is held in San Juan every year. JH

Pulse (Heartbeat) see T.P.R.

Push Ball see Mounted Games

Quadrille

Developed from military methods of schooling horse and rider to greater agility and suppleness, horse ballets and quadrilles on horseback became favoured amusements at the royal courts from the sixteenth to the eighteenth century. Today the classical quadrille is presented by the Cadre Noir (see France) with twelve riders and by the SPANISH RIDING SCHOOL OF VIENNA (four riders before 1942, twelve riders until 1945, eight riders now). At gymkhanas and horse shows a quadrille is ridden as a display confirming the degree of accomplishment of horse and rider.

A classical quadrille is performed by four riders, or a number divisible by four, who execute simultaneously various exercises and figures timed to music. *Haute école* movements at the different paces and of varying degrees of difficulty are composed into a dance, the evolutions of horses and riders often reflecting as in a mirror. The precise performance requires of horses and riders an equally high standard of training and uniformity of appearance. AP

Quagga see Zebra

Qualat Jermo (Kerkuk)

This site of an early Mesopotamian farming community, on a tributary of the river Tigris, is the earliest find of a developing breeding centre of more than one domestic species. Remains of *Equus onager Pall.* (*c.* 5000–4500 B.C.) indicate that the onager was domestically bred here, together with horned cattle and pigs. DMG

Quarter Horse

The American Quarter Horse was the first breed developed in the Americas, originating during the colonial era in the Carolinas and Virginia, where match racing was the leading outdoor sport, with races run on village streets and along country lanes among the plantations. These horses were seldom raced beyond 440 yd (400 m), hence the colloquial name 'quarter miler'.

The breed's foundation came from the Arabs, Barbs and Turks brought to North America by Spanish explorers and traders. Selected stallions were crossed with mares brought from England in 1611, producing compact, heavily-muscled horses which were faster over short distances than any other breed.

The uses of the Quarter Horse were manifold. As the white man moved west he took the Quarter Horse with him to help conquer and settle the continent. The breed survived time and change because it excelled in qualities which were of major importance to people in diverse occupations and geographical areas. It was early adopted by ranchers and cowboys as the greatest round-up and trail-driving horse they had seen, for it possesses inherent 'cow-sense'.

The American Quarter Horse Association was established in 1941 in Fort Worth, Texas. Today, Association headquarters are in Amarillo, Texas, where more than 200 employees handle registrations, transfer of ownership, and other pertinent information for the world's largest equine registry. With more than 800,000 American Quarter Horses registered in the United States and 42 other countries, the breed is by number the most popular in the world. BW

Quashquai see Persian Horse, Plateau Persian

Quidding

The falling from the mouth during feeding of partially masticated food, indicating that close apposition of the cheek teeth is painful. In most cases irregularities in wear of the teeth, e.g. sharp edges, are the cause. CF

Quittor

A chronic suppurating lesion at the coronet towards the heel consisting of one or more channels leading to a focus of necrotic lateral cartilage within the hoof. CF

Rejoneador. Bullfighting in Portugal

Racecourse Betting Control Board see Horserace Betting Levy Board, Tote

Racing see Flat Racing, Hurdling, Point-to-Point, Steeplechasing, Trotting, etc.

Rack see Gaits

Records

The official F.E.I. record for high jump is 8 ft $1\frac{1}{4}$ in (2·47 m), cleared by Huasó, ridden by the Chilean Capt. Alberto Larraguibel Morales at Vina del Mar, Santiago, Chile on 5 February, 1949, improving on both the American and the European records (see chart). The official long jump record over water is 27 ft $2\frac{3}{4}$ in (8·30 m), by Amado Mió, ridden by Lt-Col Lopez del Hierro (Spain) at Barcelona, Spain on 1 July, 1951.
MEA

Red Indians see Horsemanship, American Indian

Registration

Every horse racing under the rules of the British JOCKEY CLUB must have its name registered with the Club's secretaries, Weatherby and Sons, before it can race. The name can only be changed in exceptional circumstances. The list of registered names is published by Weatherby's annually.

Similarly, any horse qualified to be entered in the General Stud Book, which is the property of Weatherby's, must also go through a process of registration. The owner of every Thoroughbred stallion holds covering certificates issued by Weatherby's. When a mare is covered, the stallion's owner completes a certificate of covering with details of the mare's name etc., which is given to the owner of the mare.

The certificate is attached to the Stud Book return form which is sent to Weatherby's the following year together with a foal identification certificate when there is progeny. GWe

Rein Back see Movements

Rein Effects see Aids

Rejoneador

The *rejoneador* is a mounted bullfighter who rides highly-trained horses to 'course' and kill a fighting bull. This aristocratic mounted bullfighter of the Spanish-speaking countries displays highly-skilled horsemanship ranging from the precise performance of *haute école* to a weaving, dodging gallop just ahead of the wide-branched horns of a charging bull.

The *rejoneador* rides four or five horses during the course of his twenty-minute performance in the bullring. One of these mounts will be schooled to the highest degree in the airs of *haute école*, and will be ridden by the *rejoneador* during the opening parade into the arena. Then the horseback bullfighter rides ahead of the men on foot, his spectacular stallion performing a slow, proud and lofty *passage*. After the parade has crossed the ring, he will entertain the crowd by putting his ANDALUSIAN through one impeccably-performed high-school movement after another: the Spanish walk and Spanish

Speed Records

Distance	Time	mph	Name of Horse	Course	Date
$\frac{1}{4}$ mile	20·8 s	43·26	Big Racket (U.S.A.)	Lomas de Sotelo, Mexico	5 February 1945
$\frac{1}{2}$ mile	44·8 s	41·29	Tamran's Jet (U.S.A.)	Sunland, New Mexico	22 March 1968
$\frac{5}{8}$ mile	53·6 s	41·98	Indigenous (Gt Britain)	Epsom	2 June 1960
$\frac{3}{4}$ mile	1 m 07·4 s	40·06	Zip Pocket (U.S.A.)	Phoenix, Arizona	6 December 1966
	1 m 07·4 s	40·06	Vale of Tears (U.S.A.)	Ab Sar Ben, Omaha, Nebraska	7 June 1969
1 mile	1 m 32·2 s	39·04	Dr Fager (U.S.A.)	Arlington, Illinois	24 August 1968
$1\frac{1}{2}$ miles	2 m 26·0 s	36·98	Meneleck (Gt Britain)	Haydock Park, Lancashire	1 July 1961
2 miles	3 m 15·0 s	36·93	Polazel (Gt Britain)	Salisbury, Wiltshire	8 July 1924
3 miles	5 m 15·0 s	34·29	Farragut (Mexico)	Agua Caliente	9 March 1941

Development of North American High Jump Record (recognized by the A.H.S.A.)

Ft/in	Metres	Horse	Rider	Place	Date
7 $10\frac{1}{2}$	2·40	Heatherbloom	Dick Donnelly	Richmond, Va.	1902
8 $0\frac{1}{2}$	2·45	Confidence	Jack Hamilton	Ottawa, Canada	14 Sept 1912
8 $0\frac{13}{16}$	2·46	Great Heart	Fred Vesey	Chicago, Ill.	8 June 1923

Development of European High Jump Record (recognized by the F.E.I.)

Ft/in	Metres	Horse	Rider	Place	Date
7 $1\frac{3}{16}$	2·23	Conspirateur	Capt Crousse	San Sebastian, Spain	1904
7 $2\frac{3}{4}$	2·35	Conspirateur	Capt Crousse	Paris, France	1906
7 $3\frac{1}{8}$	2·36	Montjoie III	René Ricard	Vittel, France	17 Aug 1912
7 $3\frac{1}{8}$	2·36	Biskra	F. de Juge	Vittel, France	17 Aug 1912
7 $3\frac{5}{32}$	2·38	Vol-au-Vent	Lt de Castries	Paris, France	10 April 1933
8 0	2·44	Osoppo	Capt Gutierrez	Rome, Italy	27 Oct 1938

trot, half and full passes at the trot and canter, the *passage* and *piaffe*, perhaps one of the great, soaring 'airs above the ground' leaps.

The *rejoneador's* other horses are educated to a very high standard in 'Andalusian dressage', the end product of which is a cross between a high-school horse and highly-trained cow pony. As well as being able to whirl on their haunches, start, stop and weave in fluid, almost instant transitions, these horses can perform half and full passes, the Spanish walk and often the Spanish trot and *passage* as well.

The *rejoneador* rides into the ring on one of these horses to await the entry of the bull. The first horse he uses will usually carry a lot of Thoroughbred blood to give it the dose of speed needed to outrun the fast-starting, quick-sprinting fighting bull when it rushes fresh and full of force into the ring. The *rejoneador* will be armed with a *rejon*, a short steel blade attached to the end of a stick. As the *toro* charges, the man adroitly curves the horse around its uphooking horns and plants the blade in the bull's withers.

After placing two more *rejones*, the mounted bullfighter will change his horse for the planting of the three pairs of shorter *banderillas*. By this time, the bull will be slower and will have started to go on the defensive. The horseman will have to get much closer to it before it will charge, and so he rides a muscular mount that starts fast, stops quickly and can spin on the spot.

Finally, after changing mounts at least once more, the *rejoneador* will kill the bull with the long, thin blade of the *rejon de muerte*. ND

Remedial Riding see Disabled, Riding for the

Resinback see Circus, Horses in the

Respiration see T.P.R.

Rhenish, Rhineland

These terms used to mean a very heavy cold blood horse of Belgian or Brabant ancestry. Although specimens may still be seen in Germany, it no longer ranks as a breed and does not officially exist. Modern methods of mechanization and industrialization of agriculture have made the heavy horse redundant. In its place, however, the Rhenish Stud Book caters for registered warmblood horses, small horses and ponies; there was a considerable increase of entries and members in 1970 over previous years. Many of the new members do not own or breed horses. Breeds which now come under the Rhenish umbrella are Shetland, Welsh, Fjord, 'riding ponies', Iceland, Haflinger, Arabian and warmbloods with Thoroughbred, Trakehner and Hanoverian/Westphalian blood; they are sired by stallions bred or registered within the area of the Hanover/Westphalia Stud Book directorate (see Germany).

It is currently hoped that suitable stallions may be found among the halfbreds to establish a new 'Rhenish' breed of warmbloods. The quality of the mares is improving and it is hoped to produce a recognizable saddle- or riding-horse breed. For the first time at the Deutsche Landwirtschaftliche Gemeinschaft (German Agricultural Association) exhibition in Cologne in 1970 a group of three mares was shown; they gained two first prizes and a second. Their action and conformation were impressive although they were said to be lacking in bone. The future for the warmblood in the Rhineland is considered to be expanding. DMG

Rhodesia see Southern Africa

Rhum see Mountain and Moorland Ponies

Riding Clubs

In the United Kingdom and Northern Ireland the Riding Clubs Committee of the BRITISH HORSE SOCIETY administers the Society's affiliation scheme for riding clubs, which in 1971 numbered 366, including 36 university, 56 service and 5 overseas clubs in Germany, Cyprus and Rhodesia. Total individual membership is about 22,800. The scheme aims to encourage riding as a sport and recreation, to improve and maintain the standard of riding and horsemanship, to keep bridle paths open and improve and maintain facilities for riding. Activities include riding instruction in all forms, competitive events including contests against other clubs (e.g. gymkhanas, jumping, dressage, horse trials, quizzes and brains trusts), lectures and demonstrations, rides, visits to shows, hunt stables, and social events. Clubs must have a minimum of 12 adult members before applying for affiliation. A junior section can be formed if there is no local Pony Club. Affiliated clubs may take the Riding Club Tests, designed to test practical horsemanship; approximately 1,000 certificates are awarded annually.

National competitions are held for all standards of riding including National Dressage, Horse Trials, Prix Caprilli and Show Jumping Championships. The Golden Horse Ride is run in conjunction with the Arab Horse Society. MBe

Rhenish, Rhineland. A Rhenish Belgian draught horse

Riding Establishments Acts

The Riding Establishments Act of the United Kingdom became law in 1964 after much pressure from societies and individuals dedicated to animal welfare. It had become necessary because of the tremendous increase in public demand to ride and to be instructed, unfortunately against a background of appalling ignorance. Many first-class establishments and trekking centres were providing the right kind of animals, supervision and instruction. There was, however, an ever-increasing number of ignorant persons who quickly took advantage of the demand.

The 1964 Act clearly laid down general requirements for an establishment which made a charge for hiring out horses and ponies: the experience of the proprietor, type of stabling, condition of animals, provision of feed and grazing, sanitation, fire precautions, the supervision of rides and the qualifications of instructors. It provided for the licensing authority to issue a licence at a statutory charge to cover one year, the issue of such a licence to be subject to an inspection by a veterinary surgeon appointed by the authority. It was soon obvious that in many cases lip service only was paid to the provisions of the Act. Some Local Authorities showed little interest, inspectors were lackadaisical or even ignorant of equine requirements. More and more unsuitable proprietors had come into the field.

Backed entirely by charitable funds a survey was carried out in 1968–9 in the south of England. More than a quarter of licensed establishments were found to be below an acceptable standard. Accordingly an amending Act was passed in 1970, which tightened up many clauses and provided for the issue of a provisional licence for three months only, in doubtful cases stipulating that necessary improvements should be carried out before a normal licence could be considered. Since the survey, now extended over most of Britain, still shows a quarter of establishments to be substandard, it is clear that much still has to be done to make these Acts effective and the public must play their part. GHC

Riding for the Disabled see Disabled, Riding for the

Riding Ponies

Most riding ponies and many horses in Great Britain are based on the nine British native breeds (see Breeding, Pony). Throughout the centuries these ponies were an integral part of British national life, carrying their owners and all kinds of merchandise. Fell and Dales ponies bred in the north of England transported lead from the mines to the seaports along tracks used today by trekkers. All the larger breeds were used extensively in agriculture.

Because breeders naturally breed to meet demand there have been many and various infiltrations of foreign blood over the years. When roads were built and wheel traffic invented the ponies drew all manner of vehicles and, crossed with other larger animals such as THOROUGHBREDS, NORFOLK ROADSTERS, Welsh Cobs (see Mountain and Moorland Ponies) or HACKNEYS, produced larger, fast-trotting horses. Trotting races became popular and prodigious feats of pace and stamina were achieved. A succession of Eastern traders introduced ARAB blood whose influence may be seen to this day, especially in the Welsh breed.

Mechanization gradually but increasingly removed horse-drawn traffic from the roads and by World War I the main outlet for the smaller breeds of ponies were as children's mounts. After the war there was little demand and little was known by the general public about the native breeds. When horse shows became more and more popular, and the demand for children's show and jumping ponies and small horses increased, breeders began crossing their native mares with small Thoroughbreds and Arabs to obtain larger animals with better performance. This, however, was checked by World War II when horses were bought up by the War Office and the ponies which were not broken to harness because of the fuel shortage went in thousands to slaughterhouses. Again dedicated breeders saved the native ponies by wisely retaining some foundation stock.

Since World War II there has been an explosion in riding and, to a lesser extent, in driving. The demand for children's ponies of all kinds has increased at a fantastic rate.

The popularity of PONY TREKKING, a relatively recent recreation, has saved the larger native breeds from extinction. Highland, Dales, Fell, the larger New Forest, and Welsh ponies of cob type are ideal for this.

Crossbred ponies, i.e. mixture of Native, Thoroughbred and/or Arab blood in varying proportions, dominate the riding pony classes, show-jumping and Pony Club events, hunter trials and cross-country events. These British ponies are unparalleled and there is an increasing demand for them overseas. Supply, however, has by now outdistanced demand and only the best should be bred from.

Since the passing of the Ponies Act 1969, there is a minimum value under which ponies may not be exported (see Pony Breeding). This was introduced to stop the trade in 'scrub' ponies to Continental markets and abattoirs, and to protect overseas buyers from misrepresentation and overpricing.

Besides the show and show-jumping market, there is an enormous outlet for good utility ponies, for which classes are increasingly being held. These ponies play an essential part in the Pony Club, in riding establishments and in private homes. See also Mountain and Moorland Ponies. GS

Riding Schools

The emergence of riding as a major form of recreation for an ever-increasing number of people has resulted in greater need for high standards of tuition, animal welfare and coaching facilities at the base, the riding school.

In Great Britain the BRITISH HORSE SOCIETY, the 'Ponies of Britain' and the Association of British Riding Schools attempt to maintain and improve existing standards of horsemanship and facilities provided by affiliated schools. There are more than 2,000 riding schools in Britain; about a quarter have been approved, graded or licensed to the standards set by these authorities. Statutory control of animal welfare and instructor qualification already exists under the RIDING ESTABLISHMENTS ACTS but these do not provide prospective clients with satisfactory guidelines to the quality of instruction they can expect. It is with the latter that the B.H.S., P.O.B. and A.B.R.S. concern themselves, laying down minimum requirements covering the whole spectrum of riding-school operations from beginner coaching to the perfection of skills in the advanced rider, and ensuring that animals are cared for, equipment is satisfactory and facilities are adequate.

The A.B.R.S., formed in 1954, is mainly a body of riding-school proprietors. It deals with the general problems that arise in school management while maintaining a high standard of instruction and facilities. It is not their policy to grade schools on the basis of categories of client. The size of the school is generally irrelevant; as long as it can match the basic requirements it is eligible for approval. Once that approval has been granted the school should provide clients with a praiseworthy service. The Association lists 250 schools that have passed their inspection of tuition, facilities, equipment (including saddles and necessary riding gear), animal accommodation and welfare standards. Of prime importance is the condition of the animals; the presence of adequate grazing facilities at all schools is demanded by the Association. The school must also have at its disposal a covered school, an outside *manège* or some enclosed space for instruction. The standard of instruction is assessed on the basis of lessons given at elementary, intermediate and advanced grades.

Elementary: the quality of instruction at this level is of vital importance; young riders need confidence from the start. The instruction needs to be comprehensive and tolerant. The basic rudiments of riding should be taught.

Intermediate: the early work on riding technique is continued and polished. At this level riders are introduced to dressage and cross-country activity. Again the Association demands sound instruction that will make progress fluent and natural.

Advanced: the talented rider begins competition work and possibly development into top-class riding. The instruction will ensure the rider's progress into all kinds of equestrian activity.

The B.H.S. grades instruction and facilities in four grades, ranging from Grade One, which covers elementary facilities, to Grade Four, which requires the school to provide, among other things, a cross-country course, a show-jumping course and a covered school or outdoor *manège*. This system matches instruction to facilities and ensures satisfactory teaching and supervision at each stage. Each school seeking Society approval is visited by an inspector who makes a thorough tour, noting riding facilities and provision made for care of the animals. He also studies a ride. From his report the Society decides whether or not to approve the school and, if approval is granted, to which grade the school may operate. This enables each school to use its facilities to the full without attempting to provide more than it can cope with. The Society has approved more than 250 schools to various grades.

'Ponies of Britain' has an approval scheme covering trekking centres (see Pony Trekking).

A groom's diploma can be obtained from the B.H.S. or A.B.R.S. The rider can gain an Assistant Instructor's Certificate, an Instructor's Certificate, or can, although few do so, apply for a B.H.S. Fellowship.

The rise in the number of riding schools in Britain reflects the enormous popularity of the sport. Prospective clients should be aware of the pitfalls in choosing unapproved schools. Approved schools have to provide good facilities and sound instruction. Instruction, however, is not all the riding school has to offer. Most schools involve themselves in competitions and gymkhanas, provide facilities for keeping members' horses or ponies and hacking. Many schools co-operate with other schools and pony clubs for some events. Riding has also for some time been recognized as an important form of therapy for disabled people and special centres have been established in most parts of the country (see Disabled, Riding for the). SG

Rig

A male horse with one or both testicles retained in the abdomen. CF

Ringbone

An inflammatory outgrowth of bone connected with the pastern or phalanges. *High ringbone* involves the lower end of the first phalanges and the upper end of the second phalanges. *Low ringbone* or pyramidal disease mainly concerns the pedal bone. Both forms cause lameness and in time may result in fusion of the pastern or pedal joints. *Coronary ringbone* is confined to the second phalanx and lameness is usually temporary. CF

Roaring

An abnormal sound on inspiration during

forced exercise, due to paralysis on the left side of the larynx. It is seen more commonly in heavyweight hunters and the bigger breeds of horse, and seldom or never in ponies. The disease is believed to be hereditary but systemic disorders, e.g. STRANGLES, appear to be predisposing factors. CF

Robichon de la Guérinière, François see La Guérinière, François Robichon de

Rodeo

Rodeo (Spanish, 'cattle-ring') began in the early days on the American frontier when the trail crews who drove cattle hundreds of miles to the railheads for shipment to the markets of the East held informal contests of skill in roping, breaking horses, etc. to relieve the boredom of waiting for days or weeks for their cattle to be loaded. Private contests naturally progressed to public exhibitions; on 4 July 1886 the first rodeo with a paying audience was held in Prescott, Arizona, and many Western rodeos are still held on Independence Day.

Around 1900 rodeo began to merge with the Wild West show, a combination of circus and carnival devoted to Western lore. There were staged Indian massacres, exhibitions of trick roping, fancy shooting and riding, and eventually rodeo. Competition and cost soon brought the Wild West show to an end but rodeo survived and grew in popularity, particularly in the West of the United States and in Canada. Its brief marriage with the Wild West show resulted in the addition of bull riding, steer wrestling, wagon races, etc. which, although related to the professional tasks of the working cowboy, had no counterpart on the range as did bronc riding and calf and steer roping.

Today rodeo is a multi-million dollar business. In hundreds of Western communities it is the only live entertainment. Over 3,000 rodeos are held annually, most of the larger or better-known ones sanctioned by one of two professional leagues, the Rodeo Cowboys Association (about 550 rodeos a year including the Cheyenne Frontier Days, the Pendleton Round-Up and the Calgary Stampede) and the International Rodeo Association (about 300 rodeos a year). There are also hundreds of semi-professional and amateur rodeos. Most of the colleges of the West and many high schools have regular rodeo teams.

Eight regular events in professional rodeo are used to determine the national championships: bareback bronc riding, steer wrestling, saddle bronc riding, steer roping, calf roping, bull riding, team roping and barrel racing. Bareback, saddle bronc and bull riding are judged events. The contestant must stay on his animal for 8–10 seconds, depending on the event, in order to have a qualifying ride. The roping events and barrel racing are timed contests with the fastest contestant winning.

In *bareback bronc riding*, the cowboy must secure himself to the horse with one hand only on a handle on a rigging going around the animal approximately where a saddle girth would fit. The bronc wears no halter or bridle of any kind. In *steer wrestling*, a rider must overtake the steer, jump off his horse onto the head of the animal and twist it to the ground so that all four feet are in the same direction. In *saddle bronc riding* the horse has a modified saddle and a halter to which is attached one rein which the cowboy must hold in one hand only. In *steer roping* the contestant ropes the steer round the head and rides past it, looping his rope round its hind legs so that it falls. In *calf roping* the cowboy must rope the calf, dismount and tie any three legs together. In *bull riding*, the most dangerous of the riding events, the cowboy must secure himself to the bull's back by using a loose rope wrapped around the bull's middle and held in place with one hand. *Team roping* involves two contestants roping each end of a running steer. In *barrel racing*, the only women's event in rodeo, the contestant must ride a cloverleaf pattern around three barrels. See also Australia. CL

Roman-nosed

Viewed from the side the face is somewhat convex, a desirable feature. CF

Rosinback (Resinback) see Circus, Horses in the

Rottaler see Germany

Rouncy see Cob

Royal International Horse Show

The Royal International Horse Show, granted its prefix after World War II, started at Olympia, London, in 1907, and was held there, with the exception of the war years,

Royal International Horse Show. Carol Hofmann (U.S.A.) riding Salem at Wembley

until 1939. It went outdoors after the end of World War II, being resuscitated at White City Stadium as the National Horse Show in 1946, and finally resumed its international status the following year. When the new Western Avenue motorway encroached on the approach roads to the White City in 1967 the show was moved to Wembley Stadium, but after complaints by footballers about damage that horses were said to have caused to the turf during a wet week in July, the show moved indoors again to the Empire Pool, Wembley, in 1970. A year later the show was held in two parts, the first at the All England Jumping Course at Hickstead, Sussex, to enable the Prince of Wales' (Nations') Cup to be held over an outdoor course.

The Royal International caters for all categories of ridden show horses, in addition to staging hackney driving and other harness classes such as coaching and private turnouts. Top-class international jumping takes place daily and includes such classics as the King George V Gold Cup and the Queen Elizabeth II Cup. PMM

Russ (Gotland) Pony

This pony has existed on the Swedish island of Gotland in the Baltic Sea since the Stone Age. It used to live in a semi-wild state all over the island, and there is still a herd in the forest at Löjsta. Today they are also bred on the Swedish mainland, generally living out the year round. The breed is fairly pure with a sprinkling of Arab and English pony blood.

The Russ stands 11–13 hands (1·12–1·32 m) and is usually bay or black, although all colours occur. A black line along the back is common and a star and blaze occur, but rarely socks or stockings. It has a rather heavy head, dry, strong legs, good hoofs, good shoulders, usually a rather long back and a sloping croup. It generally has a good temperament although it can be rather stubborn, and shows great endurance. It has good movements at walk and trot, but a poor gallop. It is an outstanding trotter and a good jumper. Formerly used for light farm work and road transport, today it is mainly a children's pony for jumping and trotting competitions. See also Sweden. PL

Russian Heavy Draught Horse

This is a clean, short-legged draught horse, smaller than the SOVIET HEAVY DRAUGHT HORSE (not over 15 hands or 1·52 m) but very strong and active. It is bred by crossing local mares with small Belgian stallions. Colours are bay, chestnut or roan. DMG

Russian Steppe Horse see Kustanair

Russian Trotter

This breed was known as the Orlov-American crossbred until 1949. There are three distinct types: thick, medium, and sporting. The thick type has the proportions of a harness horse: a strong constitution, well-developed chest cage, massive body, short legs, long torso, good bone and generally hard limbs. Compared with the ORLOV TROTTER, the Russian Trotter has a more delicate constitution but a more robust musculature, stronger tendons and ligaments, and a better line of the back and loins. The head is light, with a straight profile; the neck is straight and long. The withers are high, the back straight, the loins solid. The legs are of fine bone, with a short cannon bone; the hoofs are medium large and strong. Faults which tend to occur in this breed are a shortening of the torso, sickle or close hocks, sloping or hanging croup; these and other flaws in the legs occur more often in the Russian trotter than in the Orlov. Black and bay predominate, with rarer greys, chestnuts and dark-brown horses.

Average height for stallions is 15·2½ hands (1·61 m), for mares 15·2 hands (1·57 m); bone below the knee for stallions 8 in (20·2 cm), for mares 7¾ in (19·5 cm).

The trot is productive, low, and covers much ground; there is a tendency to pace or rack. Russian Trotters have covered 1,600 m

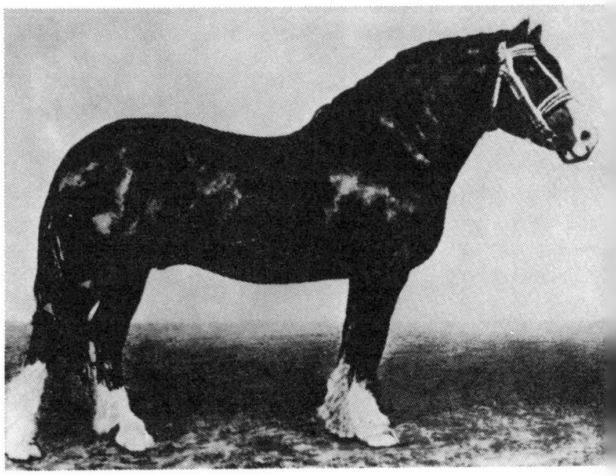

Top: **Russ (Gotland) Ponies**

Above left: **Russian Trotter**

Above right: **Russian Heavy Draught Horse**

S

Sable Island. These ponies run wild among the dunes of an island sandbank off Nova Scotia.

(1 mile) 2–2½ sec. faster than the Orlov, the breed record being 59·6 sec.

The Russian Trotter was officially established in 1949. In the 1890s American Trotters were crossed with Orlovs for use at the Moscow racetrack; 156 stallions and 220 mares were brought from the United States, but this import ceased at the beginning of World War I. In 1926 scientific breeding began, and in 1961 two more American stallions were imported. See U.S.S.R. WOF

Sable Island

The Sable Island ponies, on an island sandbank in the Atlantic off the coast of Nova Scotia, are said to descend from New England stock brought to the island early in the eighteenth century. The several small herds of ponies, with one stallion to about 6–8 mares, feed on the dune or scrub grasses. They are used by the lighthouse keepers in harness and under saddle. The ponies are lightly built and of all colours, although chestnut seems to predominate. Their height is about 14 hands (1·42 m). DMG

Saddlebred

The American Saddlebred Horse is a distinct breed tracing its ancestry to the imported English THOROUGHBRED stallion Hedgeford, brought to Fayette County, Kentucky, in 1832. He was the sire of the stallion Denmark, considered one of the foundation sires of the breed. Another important foundation sire was Harrison Chief, who traced to the imported Thoroughbred stallion Messenger on his paternal side and to the Thoroughbred Bulk Elk on the dam side. From these two horses came the Denmark and Chief strains, now thoroughly intermingled. The Denmark strain was noted primarily for length of neck and beauty of conformation; the Chief for greater ruggedness and endurance, now represented by the STANDARDBRED used almost exclusively for harness racing at the trot or pace. The maternal side of the Saddlebred pedigree traces to the MORGAN breed, founded in Vermont.

The Canadian Pacer, also figuring in the maternal side of the Saddlebred, came to Canada from France, descended from horses brought to France from England, where they were able to carry the weight of a knight in armour and at the same time give him a comfortable ride due to their ambling gait. Their predisposition to amble accounts for the Saddlebred's susceptibility to training to do the five gaits: walk, trot, canter, stepping pace and rack (see Gaits).

The American Saddlebred originated in Kentucky at a time when there were no roads, simply footpaths through the heavily wooded hilly country. It was a family horse which pulled the plough and carried the family to church, often having more than one rider. It later pulled the family carriage over the newly-made roads. Today it is ideally suited for family use in trail riding and foxhunting and is the most popular breed at horse shows.

The American Saddle Horse Breeders' Association was incorporated in 1891 to record and preserve the pedigrees of every horse of this breed in the world. Its office at 929 South Forest Street, Louisville, Kentucky 40203, has the five-generation pedigree of about 140,000 horses. It registers approximately 4,000 per year. CJC

Saddles

Saddles vary in shape according to the purpose for which they are intended. Western riding apart (see Western Tack), these purposes can be defined as jumping, hunting, dressage or show-ring riding and racing. All, however, have a common foundation, the *tree*, although this varies in shape according to the particular type of saddle. In every case the objective in designing a saddle is to help the rider to place his weight as nearly as possible in line with the centre of balance of the horse; a point which moves according to the posture and speed. In extension, as when galloping, the centre of balance moves forward, whereas in collection, as in many dressage movements, the centre shifts slightly to the rear, since the greater portion of the weight is carried over the quarters.

The tree itself, upon which the saddle is built, is made of wood reinforced with metal, particularly across the front arch, and it

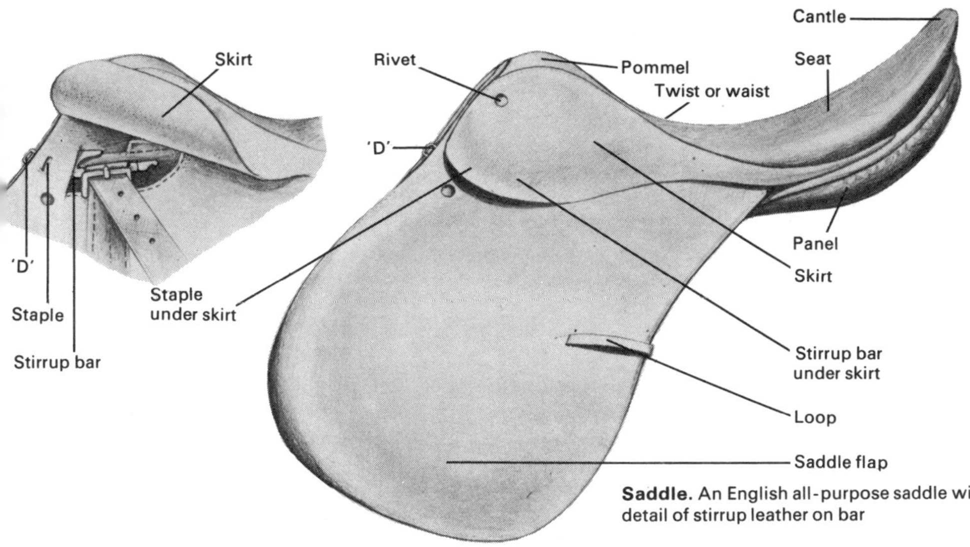

Saddle. An English all-purpose saddle with detail of stirrup leather on bar

incorporates the *stirrup bars*. Onto this framework is built the *seat* (in English saddles always of pigskin), the *flaps* and the *panel*, which is the 'cushion' between the tree and the horse's back and is made with a central channel to ensure that the weight is carried on either side of the spine and cannot therefore inhibit the movement of the back or cause it to become galled. The shape of the panel and the setting of the flap must inevitably follow the shape of the tree.

In the *jumping saddle*, where it is necessary to position the rider's weight to the front to correspond with the horse's moving centre of balance, the bars are placed further forward by inclining the lower ends of the front arch (the *points* to which the bars are attached) towards the front. The flap then follows this line and so does the panel, which, in order to give greater security to a rider sitting, or perching, with a shortened stirrup, is extended to provide a roll to support the knee and the portion of thigh immediately above it. To give additional security to the rider and to assist him further in maintaining his position in the centre of the saddle, the tree, and consequently the seat, is given a characteristic dip. In the majority of modern saddles the tree will be of the 'spring' type. A spring tree is one in which two pieces of tempered steel are laid lengthwise along the underside of the tree from front arch to cantle. The effect of the steel strips is to give a greater resilience to the seat, enabling the rider to be in closer contact with his horse and causing the driving thrust of his seat bones to be more easily transmitted. This spring seat, offering infinitely more comfort to the rider, is also employed in the modern *hunting* or *cross-country saddle*, often called an 'all-purpose' or 'general-purpose' saddle. Otherwise this saddle follows the line of the jumping saddle but with a less forward inclination of flap and panel to permit riding with a longer stirrup leather.

Dressage, an activity demanding a considerably lengthened stirrup, calls for a much straighter-cut saddle, although again the seat will be dipped and support will be provided for the lower thigh by a roll being incorporated on the forward edge of the panel. Rarely, however, is a dressage saddle made with a spring tree.

The *show saddle*, possibly the prototype of the modern dressage saddle, carries the straight-cut flap to its extreme but without offering the security of a dipped seat. Its object is to present an unbroken back line to the judges and to flatter the appearance of the horse's shoulder in front of the saddle. To assist the illusion, the saddle fits more closely to the back than might be normally considered permissible and to do so employs a skeleton type of panel, often made of felt instead of being stuffed with wool as in most of the other types, which terminates about halfway down the flap and is not extended to give any knee or thigh support. The majority of modern saddles have their panels, whether stuffed or of felt, covered in light, flexible leather. Older patterns were frequently covered in wool serge, either left as such or given a top covering of linen.

Racing saddles, many of which are within the 1–2 lb (0·45–0·91 kg) weight range, must be made of the lightest materials and in the majority of cases conventional bars will be omitted, the leathers passing over the side bars of the tree. The seat is relatively unimportant in racing as the jockey makes no use of it and even though the extra-light flaps will be cut very well forward they offer little in the way of support, the rider remaining in contact with his mount by means of the leathers and stirrup irons. Since no proper panel is possible, because of the weight factor, racing saddles, always placed as far to the front as possible, have to employ a pad under the front arch to prevent them from galling the withers.

A saddle is said to be 'mounted' when it is fitted with girth, leathers and iron. See also Accoutrements, Western Tack. EHE

Saddleseat Equitation. Cathy Noble riding Ridgefield Genius Again, a three-gaited Saddlebred

Saddle Seat Equitation

Because of the distinctive high head carriage, extreme leg action and long neck of the American Saddle Horse (see Saddlebred), coupled with the fact that it has two acquired gaits in addition to the three natural gaits, Saddle Seat equitation is probably more individual than any other form of riding. Equitation, as judged in the show ring, is confined to the natural gaits: walk, trot and canter.

The rider's hands are held approximately at waist height to maintain the horse's front elevation. The seat is firmly down in the saddle, which is longer than the Forward Seat saddle and the heels drop almost directly below the rider's centre of gravity. This position is obtained by pointing the knees somewhat forward of the stirrup leathers and drawing the shins rearward until the heels are in position. Firm pressure on the stirrup bars will force the heels below level and should be maintained at all times in order to stabilize the seat and enforce the discipline of leg control on the horse. Length of stirrup is determined by adjusting the leathers so that the hanging stirrup bars touch the rider's ankle bones. Knee grip is a result of the upward and outward slope of the balls of the feet on the stirrup bars, which tends to force the knees into the saddle and give constant easy pressure at the knees, rather than clutching, which results from gripping with the thigh muscles.

Since the high action of the American Saddlebred gives considerable hindquarter propulsion, posting should originate from the thrust of the horse, a blending of movement between horse and rider rather than a movement which precedes the trot to avoid being bounced by the saddle.

The rider's torso is erect, head and chest lifted, with a slight forward tilt from the hip joint. This tilt ensures the position of the lower legs and prevents out-thrust feet and a backwards body position (possibly the worst fault that any rider may commit) and which immediately brings to mind the old misnomer 'backward seat', used to denote the Saddle Seat in the past.

The position of the rider's hand on the reins is of paramount importance since a sensitive, consistent restraint coupled with strong, steady leg pressure from mid-calf to crotch, will engage the horse's hindquarters strongly, resulting in the desired balance and action so characteristic of the Saddlebred. Reins are held above or slightly forward of the pommel with equal pressure on the snaffle and curb. Double-bitted bridles are always used as the lifting action of the snaffle combined with the tucking influence of the curb results in the high-arched neck and head position.

Presence and brilliance exemplify the Saddle Horse; therefore, the rider's task is multiple. He must employ the diverse aids of hands, body and voice to extract the most animation from his mount, while keeping it under complete control. Obviously, there must be much practice and great co-operation between horse and rider to achieve what may appear to be opposing natural tendencies. The fact that the American Saddle Horse has been bred for many years to develop a natural exhilaration and extreme motion makes a seemingly difficult task relatively easy. The universal term 'good hands' in reality translates into 'good brains'. The mastery of riding saddle horses is the combination of perfect balance and co-ordination which frees the rider's mind to approach his equitation with the quality of his mount's performance uppermost in his thoughts.

The walk and canter are ridden with the basic position. Most important is the maintenance of animation, which means ever-present collection. A show walk may be slightly prancing. The canter is slow and high, never flat or dispirited.

The two trainer-taught gaits are the slow gait and the rack. These are speed and action versions of the walk pattern in which the rider does not post since the gaits are four-beat with no bouncing of the horse's back as in the two-beat trot. In the five-gaited classes, the trot and rack are very fast. The slow gait is more restrained, high and showy. At no time should there be any mixture of the lateral pace in the acquired gaits. Only the horse is judged in five-gaited competition. Three-gaited classes may be open (where only the horse is judged) or equitation, where the rider is judged. HKC

St Leger see Classic Races

Salerno see Italy

Sandalwood Pony see Indonesia

Sandcrack

A fissure or crack in the wall of the hoof from the coronet downwards, beginning at the toe or the quarter. If the crack is deep enough to expose and pinch the sensitive laminae it causes lameness. CF

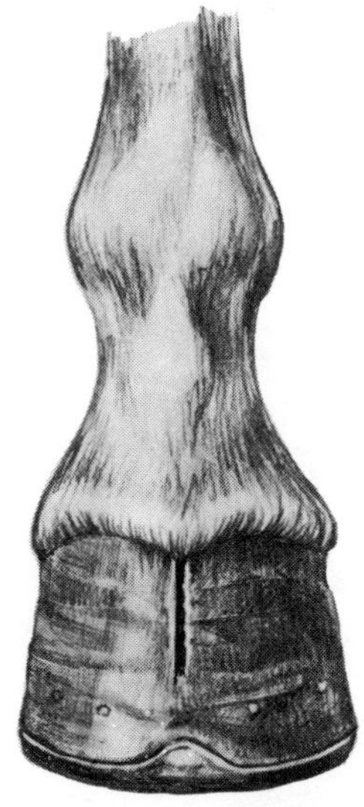

Sandcrack

Santini, Major Piero

Piero Santini (1881–1960), Major in the Light Horse Cavalry of Lucca, introduced the FORWARD SEAT which revolutionized modern riding to the English-speaking world.

A friend and pupil of the great Captain Federico CAPRILLI and completely bilingual, he became as well-known as Caprilli in both Great Britain and America by means of his lectures and books: *Riding Reflections* (1932), *The Forward Impulse* (1936) and *The Riding Instructor* (1952). His translations of the very few notes Caprilli ever wrote down first appeared serially in *The Light Horse* in 1951 and were published in book form posthumously as *The Caprilli Papers* in 1969. LFB

Saqlawi (Seglavi, Saglavi, Sacaloui, Siglavy, etc.) a strain of ARAB

Sardinian Horse

The Sardinian horse, indigenous to the island of Sardinia, is usually bay or brown and, like the cattle and even the people, probably for climatic reasons, fairly small, rarely more than 15–15·2 hands (1·52–1·57 m). It is extremely hardy, sturdy and surefooted and, with schooling, often good at jumping. Before the mechanization of the Italian Cavalry at PINEROLO and TOR DI QUINTO it was often used, either purebred or mixed with foreign stock, as a troop horse and by Italian officers riding in international teams. Today its use is confined to the *Carabinieri* or private riding schools. LFB

Saumur see France, Equitation in

Right: **Schleswig**

Below: **Seedy Toe.** The hoof seen from below
Bottom: Vertical section of hoof

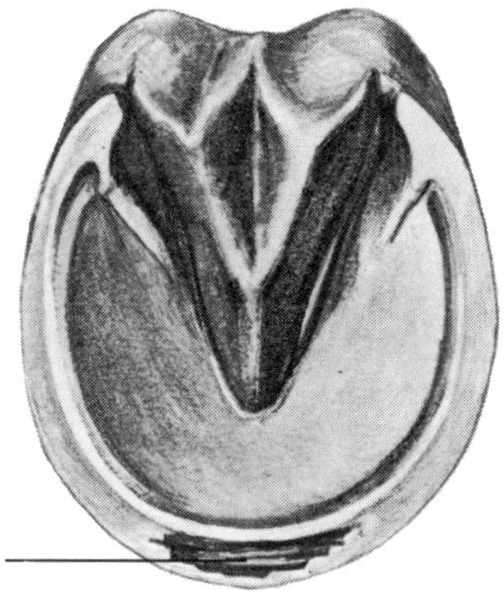

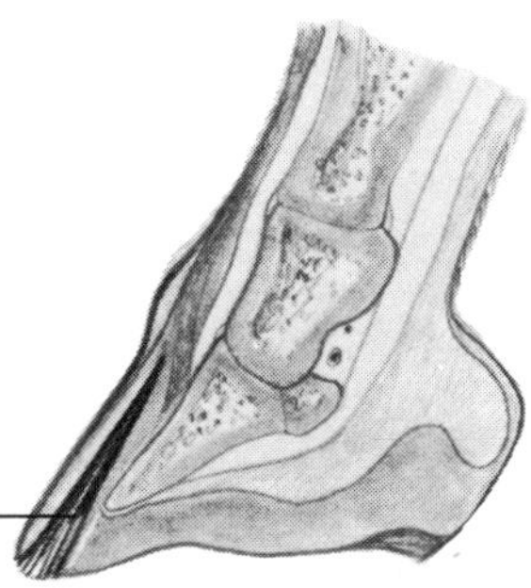

Schleswig
The foundation ancestor of the Schleswig medium heavy horse is the JUTLAND horse from Denmark. These active, short-backed horses were principally used for draught work and light haulage. In 1888, regulations for breeding were laid down; in 1891 the Stud Book was opened by the Verbanddes Schleswiger Pferdezuchtverein. As Jutland stallions were constantly used, the blood-lines are the same but since 1938 no Danish stallions have been employed. The extremely potent chestnut SUFFOLK PUNCH stallion Oppenheim LXII (see Jutland), helped to found the Schleswig. Through his son Munkedal 445 and inbred descendants Prins af Jylland 1000 and Høvding 1055, he became virtually the founder sire of the Schleswig breed. There is sharp discrimination against any horse not conforming to the desired characteristics of the breed which is now 95 per cent chestnut in colour. DMG

Schooling see Dressage, Equitation, Aids

School Movements see Movements

Schwarzwald Heavy Horse see Germany

Schwyzer see Einsiedler

Scythians
A collective term used by the Greeks for the mounted nomads of South Russia, speaking an Indo-European language, whose raids on horseback reached Egypt in 611 B.C. They moved into what is now Hungary and the Carpathians in the sixth century, and raided as far west as the upper Seine valley at the end of the century. A riding, not a chariot-driving people, they used on migration lightly-built four-wheeled wagons with tilts on a wickerwork superstructure, like gypsy caravans. Through their own highly dramatic pictorial art and that of the Greeks who came into contact with them on the Black Sea coast we know all that we are likely to know about the appearance of horses and saddlery in antiquity; they had a custom of burying rich men with several horses and saddlery besides weapons and jewelry which provides information about the anatomy of the Iron Age riding horse (see Pazyryk). The snaffle bit and bridle with Y-shaped cheek-pieces most widely used in Europe during the first millennium were of Scythian type.

Most of the horse stock of classical Greece was ultimately of Scythian origin, bred from stock that reached Greece through a long chain of dealers across the Danube and the Balkans: Dacians, Thracians and others. Although they kept other livestock, the Scythians lived very largely on the horse, drinking mares' milk, eating foals' flesh and in certain circumstances drinking blood drawn from living horses. The superiority of the Scythian-bred horse lay chiefly in the fact that unlike the Mediterranean peoples the Scythians regularly practised castration and were not plagued with scrub stallions. As a political power the Scythians ceased to count after about 330 B.C. when they were conquered by the Sarmatians, a related group of horse-nomads from further east. AD

Seedy Toe
An affection of the wall of the foot at the toe, extending from the ground surface towards the coronet. It is characterized by cavitation between the outer and innermost layers of horn, occupied by crumbly degenerated horn and other debris. CF

Seglavi variant of Saqlawi, a strain of ARAB

Senner
Now extinct, the Senner pony ran wild or semi-wild in the Senne (central Germany). The Senner Stud, at Lopshorn in the Teutoburger forest, first mentioned in 1160, produced extremely hardy animals. The Senner was 14–14·3 hands (1·42–1·49 m) high; it was obviously of cob type. In the eighteenth century it was hunted as game. In 1876 sixteen Senner mares were taken into the BEBERBECK Stud, then under Prussian direction, and horses of extreme hardiness were bred. See also Dülmen. DMG

Sertanejo see Brazil

Shagya
This is the purest halfbred strain of Oriental horse, started at Bábolna (Hungary) by the Arab stallion Shagya, of the Kehil/Siglavi (Saqlawi) strain born in 1830 in Syria and bought for the Austro-Hungarian stud by Major Herbert in 1836 from the Bedouin of the Bani Sahaer tribe for 1,800 gulden. He was a cream-coloured horse 15·2½ hands (1·59 m) high who stood at the Bábolna stud until 1842. Of his sons the most outstanding was Shagya IV from Siglavi I. Afterwards he sired the Mezöhegyes stud horse Shagya X, born from 307 Samhan II in about 1855. His three sons Shagya VI, VII, and VIII returned to Bábolna where Shagya VIII out of 25 Aga was the most successful, and founded the

whole Bábolna breed of Shagyas. Some of his descendants were brought over to the Czechoslovak stud at Topolčianky; others went to Radovec stud farm where another strain of Shagya was established.

Shagya X was a most important stallion who as a four-year-old colt was chosen, for his breed characteristics and brilliant paces, as the main stallion for the Hradovec stud. He was an outstanding sire who left a number of his stock at Radovec. Forty-five of his daughters were retained as brood mares. After World War I he was transferred in 1921 to the biggest Czech stud at Kladruby-on-Elbe.

The Shagya strain has spread all over Europe. Shagyas are currently bred in Czechoslovakia, Austria, Hungary, Rumania, Yugoslavia, Poland and Germany as well as in the United States. In Hungary, Shagya XXXII served 16 stock mares at the age of 28 at the rate of 75 per cent. They have excellent characteristics; are hardy, tireless under saddle and as draught horses; they are good movers. Their efficiency as cavalry horses was proved in the Austro-Hungarian and later Hungarian, Czechoslovak and Polish armies.

The best stallion of the Shagya strain currently standing in Czechoslovakia is Shagya XV, owned by the Albertovec stud, whose stock make excellent competition horses. See also Czechoslovakia, Hungary.
PNe

Shan Pony see Burma Pony

Sharak see Persian Arab

Shetland Pony see Mountain and Moorland Ponies

Shirazi see Persian Horse, Plateau Persian

Shire Horse

Traditionally evolved from the medieval 'Great Horse of England' which carried knights in armour into battle, the Shire is both in height and weight the greatest purebred horse in the world. Many stand over 17 hands (1·77 m). These mighty horses can pull 5 tons (5·08 metric tons) and are invaluable for farm work. They are so docile that they can be worked as three-year-olds. Bays and browns are colours permitted by the Shire Horse Society; also, although in fewer numbers, blacks and greys. White is found on fetlocks and to below the knee.
RSS

Shire Horse. A pair of purebred Shires with ploughman Robert Dash

Shoe Boil see Capped Elbow

Shoeing, Shoes see Feet and Shoeing

Show Jumping

Britain: show-jumping competitions, originally called 'leaping contests', were first introduced into the programs of agricultural shows around the 1870s. At that time rules were non-existent and judges were therefore free to decide whether the main criterion should be style or jumping ability. There was a suspicion, apparently quite well founded, that some competitions were decided before they had even started. This naturally led to a good deal of dissatisfaction but, though Olympic show-jumping rules had been drawn up before the Games of 1912, it was not until after World War I that a hard-and-fast set of rules applied to all Britain's big national shows.

The first International Horse Show, since given a 'Royal' prefix, took place at Olympia in London on 7–13 June 1907. Competitions for 'high jumps' and 'wide jumps' were included in the program. Considering the value of the pound at that time, the prize money was exceptionally generous since it included top awards of no less than £120.

Though civilian riders, like Tommy Glencross and Fred Foster, were making a big name for themselves at home, international show jumping was largely confined to army officers. Indeed there were no civilian riders in the Olympic show-jumping competition until after the 1948 Games in London. Both civilians and military men were, however, involved in the meeting at Olympia which was to lead to the founding of the BRITISH SHOW JUMPING ASSOCIATION in the early 1920s. The need for standardization of the rules had, by this time, become imperative for, while the FÉDÉRATION ÉQUESTRE INTERNATIONALE (founded 1921) had responsibility for all international rules, the big national classes were out of their jurisdiction.

Between the World Wars two British army officers, who had a far-reaching influence on the future of British show jumping, appeared on the scene: Mike Ansell and Jack Talbot-Ponsonby, both members of the British team that triumphed at the International Horse Show in New York in 1936. The former, now Col Sir Michael Ansell, became the inspired leader and administrator of postwar British show jumping; the latter was a renowned course designer until his death in 1970.

Mike Ansell had been badly wounded during World War II and as a result eventually lost his sight; he had also spent some

Show Jumping. *Top:* Colonel Harry Llewellyn and Foxhunter
Centre: Marion Mould and Stroller
Above: Captain Billy Ringrose on Loch an Easpaig

years in a prisoner-of-war camp before being repatriated in 1944. His plans for British show jumping, germinating during his time in captivity, took their first major step towards fruition when he became Chairman of the British Show Jumping Association in December 1944, a few months after his return to England. His aims were clear and precise: to build up a powerful British team and to make show jumping in Britain a popular spectator sport. Although the foundation of the B.S.J.A. had resulted in the much-needed standardization of rules, there was still vast room for improvement in other directions. Before time limits were introduced, competitions could be agonizingly slow, and the courses over which they were contested were completely unimaginative. Normally there were three fences down each side of the ring, with one (usually a triple bar) in the centre; combination fences and 'related distances' were then unheard of in national classes. Judging was made more difficult by the use of thin strips of wood ('slats') placed on the top poles of obstacles; the rider was penalized if his horse knocked one down. Quite often a slat would be swept off by the horse's tail, or even by a high wind, and the judges' decision, though 'final', was therefore often contested. The use of slats imposed the necessity of jumping clean which led to various abuses, such as rapping, but although they were both inconvenient and unnecessary, they continued to be used in Britain until the late 1940s.

It was not until 1954 that judges of national classes were spared the problems of determining whether a fence had been knocked down by the horse's fore or hind legs. International rules had long since abandoned the distinction but, under national rules, British horses continued to incur four faults for knocking down a fence with their fore legs and two for dislodging it with their hind.

Other major considerations at the time involved the use of more interesting courses and the introduction of a time limit, later to be followed by jump-offs 'against the clock'. Inevitably, these changes sparked off some heated controversies; riders were virtually made to change their whole approach to the sport and in many cases they even had to find new mounts since the more pedestrian type of animal lacked the speed which was necessary in order to win a timed jump-off. The better class of horse also proved far better suited to the more sophisticated courses slowly being introduced.

During the 1950s there was still a predominance of vertical fences in British show rings and, for this reason, British horses tended to run into difficulties when they encountered big spreads, especially combinations of spreads, in continental Europe. But fortunately a few British riders, with considerable international experience behind them, had acquired a certain expertise in jumping big Continental courses. Thanks to their efforts, Britain won an Olympic team gold medal at Helsinki in 1952 and thus provided postwar show jumping with one of its biggest boosts. The successful trio were Colonel Harry Llewellyn on Foxhunter, Wilf White on Nizefela and Douglas Stewart on Aherlow. Their splendid achievement helped to bring more competitors, spectators and sponsors into the sport; the fact that this was Britain's only gold medal at Helsinki meant that show jumping was right under the publicity spotlight.

For the next six or seven years still only a small handful of British riders were able to hold their own against the Italians and the Germans in international competitions, but they were of the highest quality. Apart from Llewellyn, whose Foxhunter must be considered as one of the all-time greats, and Wilf White, who had achieved the best British score in Helsinki, the leading riders of the day included Pat Smythe (with Flanagan and Prince Hal) and Peter Robeson (with Craven A).

It was not until the end of the 1950s that new British names began to appear on the lists of international honours. Among them was that of David Broome, who made his debut in the British team in 1959 and won an individual bronze medal at the Olympic Games in Rome the following year. He has since won another individual Olympic bronze, plus three European Championships and one World Championship, which gives him the best international record of any British rider. Marion (Coakes) Mould, who became a worthy successor to Pat Smythe as the top British woman of the 1960s, won two more prestige awards for Britain, the individual Olympic silver medal and the Women's World Championship, both on her inimitable pony Stroller. Other riders like Harvey Smith, Alison (Westwood) Dawes and Anneli Drummond-Hay (Wucherpfennig) helped to strengthen Britain's hand and, by the start of the 1970s, Graham Fletcher and Ann Moore had moved into the same category.

Since the establishment of the All-England Jumping Course at Douglas Bunn's home in Hickstead in 1960, the sport has achieved the standing at which Sir Michael Ansell was aiming some 20 years earlier. Increased television coverage, many generous new sponsors and an impressive list of international successes have all helped to arouse public interest; in Britain show jumping has moved into the top league of popular spectator sports. GM

Ireland: Ireland was one of the first countries, if not *the* first, to stage show-jumping competitions. The earliest records show that contests for 'wide' and 'high' leaps were included in the Royal Dublin Society's show of 1865. Since that time, Irish horses have proved their talent for the sport

Show Jumping. *Top:* Captain Raimondo d'Inzeo and Merano
Above: Hans Günter Winkler (West Germany) and Torphy competing in the Nation's Cup at the 1972 Olympic Games, in which West Germany won the team gold medal

though, more often than not, their triumphs have been achieved with riders of other nationalities. Italian success, for instance, must be largely attributed to the many good horses purchased in Ireland.

Between the two World Wars, when army officers dominated international show jumping, Ireland had a powerful team in Jed O'Dwyer, Jack Lewis, Dan Corry and Fred Aherne. Both O'Dwyer (on Limerick Lace) and Lewis (on Tramore Bay) won the King George V Gold Cup at Britain's International Horse Show. Part of the credit must go to their trainer, Paul Rodzianko, who was a director of the Cavalry School in Dublin in the early 1930s. Some 20 years earlier, Rodzianko had been a member of the Russian team that won the King Edward VII Cup at London's International for three years running, from 1912 to 1914.

Since the end of World War II, Ireland has produced a few great partnerships, but has rarely succeeded in fielding a top-class team though she has been close to it on a few occasions. Probably the best postwar Irish team was the one which comprised Billy Ringrose on Loch an Easpaig, Ned Campion on Liathdruim, Seamus Hayes on Goodbye and Tommy Wade on Dundrum, who came together at the 1967 Dublin Horse Show and defeated a high-class British team to win the Aga Khan Trophy for the Nation's Cup.

In 1968 the Dublin Horse Show's jumping competitions attracted generous sponsorship and their prizes are now among the most valuable in the world. Ireland's permanent showground at Ballsbridge, where the Royal Dublin Society took up residence in 1881, provides an ideal setting for high-class international show-jumping contests. Since 1968 the Irish show has attracted a large international field, including virtually all the top show-jumping nations. GM

Europe: there are jumping shows nearly all year round in Europe today, and hardly any closed season. The season of unofficial international indoor shows, held in halls in places such as Brussels, Amsterdam and Vienna, take over from the outdoor shows without a break and continue in Germany after Christmas until early spring.

But it is the outdoor itinerary of official international shows (i.e. those permitted by the Fédération Équestre Internationale, to hold their own country's Nations' Cup) which carries the greater prestige. It follows a regular pattern, normally starting indoors in Nice, France, and followed by the great outdoor opening in Rome at the beginning of May, continuing in Spain at Madrid or Barcelona (in alternate years), Lucerne (in even years) and then to AACHEN in Germany in early July.

Then comes the ROYAL INTERNATIONAL HORSE SHOW, divided between Hickstead and London with a rest-day intervening, and on to Dublin in early August. The end of the month brings Ostend and then Rotterdam. Every year the outdoor season is concluded at Lisbon in October. But, biennially, there is another meeting to come, the Swiss official international show in Geneva, held indoors.

All these are regular ports of call for the top teams in Europe; the midsummer shows are also a happy hunting ground for the United States team, and the Canadians and the Mexicans also sent teams to travel Europe in 1970. There are also other official international shows which, due to their geographical location, are less often included by the leading teams in their campaigns: Copenhagen, Olsztyn, Budapest and Leipzig. The unofficial shows in Italy, Germany, Belgium, Holland and France constitute an additional circuit in themselves, and if flesh and blood, both human and equine, could stand the pace it would be possible, with modern methods of transport, for teams and individuals to be in a state of almost perpetual motion, competing at some show almost every day of the week.

The highlight of every show is the Nations' Cup, for teams of four riders with the scores of the best three counting, usually held on the second last day of the meeting. The PRESIDENT'S CUP has been closely contested by Britain and Germany, though the United States have won it twice.

The Grand Prix is the second most prestigious event, and here Britain and Germany are often challenged by the Italians, and particularly by the two famous d'Inzeo brothers, Captain Raimondo and Colonel Piero. It is fitting, moreover, that Italy should have two such distinguished sons, for it was an Italian cavalry officer, Captain Federico CAPRILLI, who conceived the idea of the Forward Seat which did so much to revolutionize jumping style.

The German horses, with their round action and short stride, are ideally suited to show jumping and their disciplined riders are adept at getting the best out of them. The French, who have had to discard their brilliant little Anglo-Arabs to cope with modern courses, have not yet found the ideal homebred replacement except for Thoroughbreds, and they have few outstanding horses at present. They have, however, some outstanding riders, some of whom are able to do remarkably well on mediocre horses, though they must wish that the law confining them to French-bred stock (because French breeding is subsidized by the government) might be abandoned. The Italians, with no such restraints, obtain some of their best horses from Ireland. The Irish have to ride what is left after the foreign dealers have departed.

The enthusiasm for show jumping in Germany is only excelled by that in England, where so many riders are involved in the sport that Britain can field at least five full international teams at one and the same time. Since Britain won the Olympic gold medals in 1952 she has been a force to reckon with in international competitions, though the last decade was the one in which she really made her presence felt.

Riding competitions enjoy wide popularity in the U.S.S.R., where more than 50,000 people ride in the riding schools, or on the collective farms' equestrian sections. There are also 30 championship shows during the year and a further 200 local meetings.

The Russian team made a surprise visit to Aachen in 1958, their first emergence from behind the Iron Curtain, apart from Olympic competitions; a year later they won the Nations' Cup in Paris from Germany and the United States. They have never shown this form since.

Hungary and Poland also field both junior and senior international jumping teams, mounted on state-owned horses, and they are sometimes capable of turning in good performances. In the main, however, they are not consistent. In Scandinavia the sport is carried on at a very amateur level, though in Sweden there are several good riders quite capable of holding their own against the best of the Continental riders, and of defeating them on occasion. Both Spain and Portugal field strong jumping teams, although neither country is the force that it was in the 1950s. This is undoubtedly due, in both countries, to the reduction of cavalry regiments which in former years provided the majority of both horses and riders for the international teams.

Britain and Germany are the leading nations in Europe, followed by France and Italy. Switzerland has several very competent riders, as also have Holland and Belgium, but the greatest depth is to be found first in Britain, then in Germany and then France. Horse sports in Italy are confined to a small but very enthusiastic band. PMM

South Africa: Several of the best South African riders have done a season in Europe during recent years, and have proved to be as good as any of the British except the truly great. The Rand show in Johannesburg also makes a point of inviting course builders from abroad, and they have recently been inviting the world's top riders to compete there, being mounted from a pool of horses. PMM

Australia and New Zealand: Show jumping is a thriving sport in Australia, where over five hundred shows are held during the year. It is featured extensively at the major agricultural meetings such as Victoria and Melbourne, and prize money is big enough to ensure that there is a quite substantial professional element which travels from show to show to make a living from their sport. But the prohibition of the free movement of horses into Australia, where there are no equine virus diseases other than strangles, which is easily controlled, means that international experience can only be gained by the costly expedient of sending teams abroad.

In New Zealand, whose Horse Society was formed as recently as 1950, show jumping is also a thriving sport. It differs from its counterpart in Australia, however, by virtue of the fact that the prize money is very low indeed. Thus the professional rider would have very lean pickings, and the sporting New Zealand show-jumping riders are amateur to the bone. As in Australia and South Africa, the distances are enormous and international competition is virtually non-existent. PMM

North America: the origins of show jumping in the United States are obscure. They go back at least to the second quarter of the nineteenth century although early shows consisted primarily of breeding or bloodstock classes shown in hand. There were no performance classes then but it can be assumed that by the 1860s the jumper made his appearance on the scene, following the English precedent.

In the beginning the jumping classes were merely classes for the best jumpers among the hunters; it was only in the last quarter program of American horse shows came into use. The main jumping class of each show was the high jump; others were a broad jump, a 'touch-and-out', a 'knock-down-and-out', a 'scurry' class and the 'stake'. Most of the famous horse names of early show-jumping history are directly related to the high-jumping classes they competed in and the great heights they cleared. The most famous name of them all is Heatherbloom, a clean-bred Hunter, who in 1902 jumped 8 ft 3 in (2·5146 m) high. This took place on the owner's farm, in front of many witnesses who testified to its accuracy, and also of a 8 ft 2 in effort the same year. Heatherbloom's highest jump in an official and recognized show was 7 ft 10½ in (2·40 m) in Richmond, Va, also in 1902 (see Records).

The standard six-class horse-show program remained basically unchanged up to the late 1940s when civilians became involved in international jumping. (Up to 1949 the U.S. Army team represented the United States in international competitions.) These civilians, organized in the newly formed UNITED STATES EQUESTRIAN TEAM, put pressure on the AMERICAN HORSE SHOWS ASSOCIATION to apply F.E.I. rules in their shows. Two shows claim to be the oldest horse show in the United States: Litchfield, Conn., and Upperville, Va. The former is in its 132nd year, but was not held some years during World War I. The latter was held for the first time in 1853 and seems to be the American horse show with the longest uninterrupted run. In 1883 the NATIONAL HORSE SHOW in New York, then as now the most important Horse Show on the American continent, was held for the first time. In 1909, the N.H.S. became international, when a group of five British officers competed against five officers from the U.S. cavalry school in FORT RILEY, Kansas. In 1925 the TORONTO ROYAL AGRICULTURAL WINTER FAIR HORSE SHOW in Canada, became international too and by the end of the 1920s Boston had become the third leg of the 'Fall Circuit'. After some years Boston was replaced by Washington. After World War II, New York, Toronto and Harrisburg, Pa, formed the Fall Circuit until at the end of the 1950s Washington again joined the group to make it a four-show circuit.

In the nineteenth century, when the first horse shows were held in the United States, civilian riding was predominant. Military riding, the backbone of the equestrian sport in most European countries, began only after 1904, when the U.S. Cavalry school was established in Fort Riley, Kansas. Soon afterwards, the first U.S. Army team, led by Capt Guy V. Henry, later a General and President of the F.E.I., paid its first visit to the N.H.S. in New York.

The first U.S. Army team went to Europe in 1911, to compete at the International Horse Show in Olympia, with little success. In 1912, four U.S. Cavalry officers competed at the first equestrian OLYMPIC GAMES in Stockholm, winning the team bronze medal in the Military Event. Since then, the Americans have competed in each Olympic Games and have crossed the ocean to compete at European Horse Shows over a dozen times. In the 1920s, American officers played only a minor role in international show jumping, but change came when a permanent show-jumping stable was founded in Fort Riley and when the preparations for the 1932 Olympic Games in Los Angeles began. While the medals won by the Americans in Los Angeles do not weigh too much since most of the European powers in Olympic riding were absent, their preparation paid off in their results in the following years at the Fall Circuit shows and on two trips to Europe. Harry Chamberlin, Sloan Doak, William Bradford, Earl F. Thomson, Carl Raguse and Franklin Wing were the outstanding American riders of these years.

After World War II, a special order by General Eisenhower reactivated some former Fort Riley officers for the 1948 Olympic Games in London. They did very well there, but the end of American officers riding in uniform was near. In 1949, the Army team was abolished and the United States Equestrian Team was founded in 1950. The first U.S.E.T. Nations' Cup team, consisting of Arthur McCashin, a very successful civilian rider in the 1930s, and two women, Mrs Carol Durand and Miss Norma Matthews, made a successful debut at the 1950 Fall Circuit, winning two of the three Nation's Cups they entered. The next years, the going was rougher, although a team bronze medal at the 1952 Olympics was a pleasant surprise. The big jump into the small group of top jumping nations was achieved in 1958 on a highly successful trip to Europe. This came three years after Bert de Nemethy had become coach of the U.S.E.T. Nation's Cup squad and was achieved by Bill Steinkraus, Frank Chapot, Hugh Wiley and George Morris, for three years the most successful permanent Nation's Cup squad in the world, although they lost the coveted gold medal in the 1960 Olympics to Germany.

The 1960s brought the emergence of a new crop of young riders who were able to replace Morris and Wiley who retired from the team. Most of these young riders had competed in equitation classes and were placed high in the respective Medal Hunter Seat and Maclay finals, equivalents to American junior championships. Among U.S.E.T. members who won the Hunter Seat medal class finals of the A.H.S.A. or the Maclay finals (or both) were Bill Steinkraus (1940-41), Frank Chapot (1947), Ronnie Mutch (1950), George Morris (1952), Michael Page (1956), Michael Plumb (1957), Mary Mairs-Chapot (1960), Crystine Jones (1965), and Conrad Homfeld (1967). The development of younger riders, which resulted in enlarging the basis of U.S.E.T. activity, was facilitated when in 1960 the U.S.E.T. were able to rent the Hamilton Farm in Gladstone, N.J. The activity of the U.S.E.T. is, however, only a small fraction of show jumping in the United States. Open jumper classes still dominate on a local level: professionals ride against owner-riders, young amateurs and occasionally the members of the U.S.E.T. Many of the horses famous the world over as mounts of the U.S.E.T. Nation's Cup squad, such as Riviera Wonder, Untouchable, Jacks or Better, had already a considerable reputation as open jumpers before they were lent to the U.S.E.T. Ben O'Meara, who tragically died in 1966, and Rodney Jenkins were outstanding professionals, not only as riders, but also as developers of horses. See also U.S. Equestrian Team. MEA

South America: international horse shows are held infrequently because of geographical problems. Even in neighbouring countries, great distances often including jungles or mountains have to be overcome; often the only means of transporting horses is by air which is very expensive. This restricts almost all South American countries to mostly national shows with four or five C.S.Is a year for the whole continent.

National show jumping differs in the various South American countries; some have 400–500 riders, others have about 30. The quality and number of horses vary too: Argentina breeds and exports horses to Europe, North and South America; in Bolivia horses must be imported and acclimatized to altitudes of say 4,300 m or 11,200 ft (La Paz). These obvious differences mean that one country may have horse shows every weekend all the year round while others hold shows on a monthly basis.

Show Jumping. *Top:* Frank Chapot (U.S.A.) riding Anakonda
Above: Nelson Pessoa (Brazil) riding Gran Geste

Sickle Hocks. *Below left:* Normal hind leg
Below right: Hind leg with sickle hock

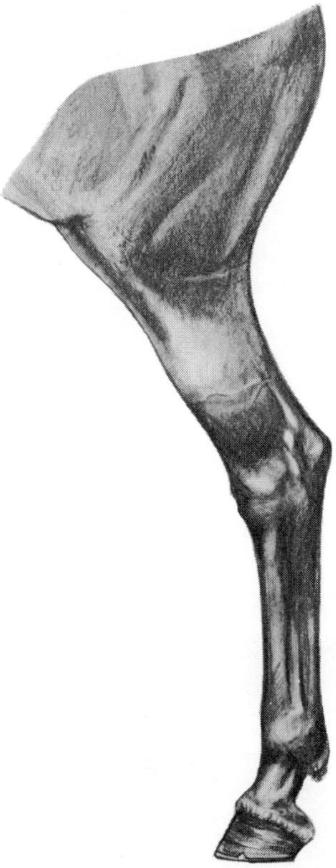

Right: **Sidesaddle.** Queen Isabella of Bourbon wore a most elaborate riding habit for her portrait by Velásquez.

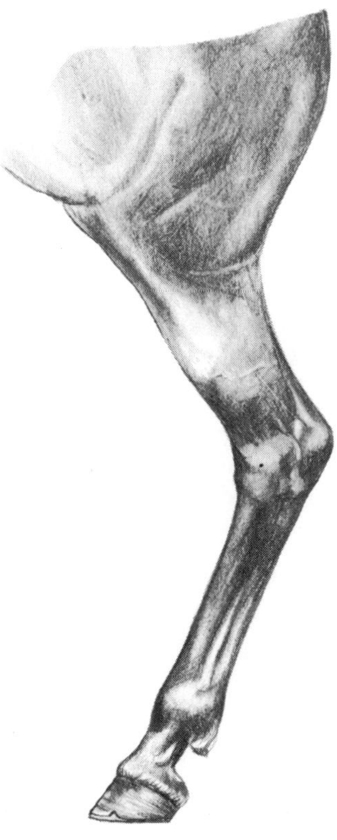

The difficulty of transport has given rise to a special type of show often held in South America: riders arrive with only their boots and saddle—in some cases not even that—and compete in shows where the organizing committee lends horses assigned to the riders by lot. Luck, always a factor in show jumping, takes on an even more important role but this is often the only way the show can be held.

By this means all the South American countries are able to participate in the South American Grand Prix and at the same time renew old friendships. However, the collaboration of the generous owners who lend their horses is essential to the success of the show which gives the public an opportunity to see some of the best riders in the world compete, since riders from Europe often come without their horses. Another characteristic of South American show jumping is that there are almost no cash prizes, although sometimes prizes of minimal value are given.

All countries except Paraguay and the Guianas are affiliated to the F.E.I.; Argentina became a member in 1928, followed by Chile and Brazil (1935), Colombia and Venezuela (1947), Peru (1952), Ecuador (1958), Bolivia (1959) and Uruguay (1960).

Outstanding figures are Alberto Larraguibel (Chile), holder of the high-jump record (2·47 m) since 1949, Carlos Delia (Argentina), finalist in the 1956 and 1960 World Championships and Nelson Pessoa (Brazil), who competes in Europe and is internationally known. There are many other riders, both men and women, known in Europe and who each year contribute to South America's international prestige. POM

Sickle Hocks

Seen in profile the hocks are too concave. CF

Sidebones

Ossification of the lateral cartilages of the pedal bone. This is mainly a disease of draught horses and is more likely to involve the front feet. It seldom causes lameness. CF

Side-Reins see Tackle, Breaking

Sidesaddle

Sidesaddle riding was first introduced to Great Britain by Anne of Bohemia in 1382 at the time of her marriage to King Richard II. Travel for women in those days was usually by cart or carriage and sidesaddle riding was the start of more independent travel. The sidesaddle looks most like the pack

Skyros Pony

saddle, and should not be confused with pillion riding, when the lady, sitting sideways on the rump of the horse, rides behind a gentleman, a style in prominence for centuries and still widely used in Spain.

The sidesaddle has a flat seat with two pommels, usually on the left side, the first shaped like a half moon curved upwards for the right leg to hook over, and the second below it, curved downward to stop the left knee from flying up. There is a stirrup for the left foot. The sidesaddle gives a remarkably fine seat and it is possible that a lády could not control a large heavy horse otherwise.

When jumping sidesaddle, the rider must be sure to get well forward on take-off and to keep the right toe up to maintain maximum firmness over the pommel while keeping the left knee close to the saddle and well down onto the stirrup. She must allow her hands to follow the direction of the horse's mouth in a relaxed manner.

The habit worn by sidesaddle riders used to be a most elegant flowing skirt, waisted jacket with a hat and neck dress to suit the time of day. Later the skirt became much shorter and is now called an apron. In the early nineteenth century many ladies rode to hounds and joined all kinds of sport and some became well-known riders. In those days the saddle had a slightly dipped seat with a slight pommel on the right side of the right leg; this has now disappeared in the modern saddle, which has a nearly straight seat. The pommels were also movable and could be fitted on the other side of the saddle; some hunting ladies had a spare stirrup fitted on the right so that when tired they could ride astride. This was the start of ladies riding astride but was considered most unladylike and was not finally accepted until the late nineteenth century. With the rise in popularity of riding astride for girls, sidesaddle riding has virtually disappeared. JLC

Siglavy variant of Saqlawi, a strain of ARAB

Sit-Fast

A painful lesion in the saddle region somewhat similar to a human 'corn'. It is caused by pressure. If it is complicated by suppuration one should suspect the presence of a maturing warble grub. CF

Skewbald see Colours and Markings

Skyros

The ancestry of the breed of small ponies on the Greek island of Skyros is uncertain but they seem to be of primitive origin. Their small size of about 37 in (0·94 m) is probably due to insufficient food. They are used to carry water and to thresh corn. DMG

Sokolsky see Poland

Somali Ass see Ass, Wild African

Sore Shins

Inflammation of the periosteum of the cannon bones, mainly in the fore legs, marked by a swelling on the front of the bone, localized pain and lameness. It occurs mainly in two-year-old Thoroughbreds and is consonant with immaturity of bone and concussion due to racing on hard ground. CF

Sorraia see Portugal

Southern Africa

South Africa is enjoying the riding revolution that is a modern phenomenon of the western world. Breeding, training racing and riding horses, teaching riders and the organization of horse sports have become a considerable industry that caters for a voracious and increasing demand. The result is a standard in many horse sports that would surprise equestrians in Britain and continental Europe if it were not for a total ban on the importation of horses from Africa due to the fear of African horse sickness. Improved vaccine from Onderstepoort, the outstanding veterinary college and research centre near Pretoria, is mastering the problem. When guarantees of safety are established, horses from the subcontinent will soon travel freely again.

Racing: this is confined almost entirely to the flat and is centred in Durban, Pietermaritzburg, Cape Town, Port Elizabeth, Johannesburg and Salisbury (Rhodesia). The produce of many famous and long-established studs is sold at the annual Yearling Sales under the auspices of the Thoroughbred Breeders' Association. The highest price paid for a yearling (Great Scot by Noble Chieftain/Jaquetta) was R48,000 in 1969. In 1971, 471 lots were sold for an average price of R3,578 and in 1972 nearly 900 lots will be coming up for the Yearling Sales in Johannesburg. The most valuable race is the Rothmans July Handicap run at Greyville, Durban, for R54,000 — an event that creates extraordinary excitement. See also Flat Racing.

Breeds: apart from the Thoroughbred there are some 20 breeds of horse in South Africa, the most popular being the American Saddle Horse (see Saddlebred), the ARAB and the WELSH PONY. The American Saddle Horse is particularly favoured in the farming community. As well as some first-class home-bred Saddle Horses, several of America's great horses, including High Point Supreme and Fancy Fortune's Cookie, have been imported into South Africa, where they are shown in three- and five-gaited classes as well as in fine harness. The Arab has a loyal and expert band of enthusiastic supporters. A purebred Arab mare, Jamani Coreena by Grandchester (U.K.)/Coreeze (U.K.), was Reserve Champion in the Show Horse of the

Top: **Southern Africa.** One of South Africa's most up-to-date riding establishments, the Bryanston Equitation Centre at Diepsloot

Centre: **Soviet Heavy Draught Horse**

Above: **Spain.** The Altér, depicted by Jan van Straet (called Stradanus) in the sixteenth century

Year Competition at Johannesburg's great International Indoor Horse Show in 1971. The Welsh Pony has played a giant's share in establishing South Africa as the home of some of the loveliest and most versatile riding ponies in the world. An important part in this has been played by Miss Ida Illingworth's superlative Section 'B' stallion Valiant by Cribban Victor. See also Africa.

Show Jumping: of all the many riding sports in South Africa, show jumping has the most followers; the standard achieved is among the very best in the world. Before the horse sickness ban the names of Bob Grayston, David Stubbs, Gonda Butters and Ernie Hayward had been familiar in Britain and continental Europe. In 1966 Mickey Louw had a triumphantly successful season in Britain on Mr Len Carter's Trigger Hill. Among hundreds of jumping shows the most famous are the Rand Easter Show, the International Indoor Horse Show, the Rothmans Show Jumping Derby in Johannesburg, the 'Royal' in Pietermaritzburg and, in Rhodesia, the two C.H.I.s of Salisbury and Bulawayo. Southern Africa's only C.H.I.O. is at Lourenço Marques in Mozambique.

Polo: British, Argentinian and Peruvian polo teams have visited South Africa to play the greatest of all games. Some 100,000 spectators watched the Peruvian tour in 1971, closely fought before the visitors won the International Series 2-1. The young Rhodesian player, Patrick Kemple, spent two seasons in Britain in the 1960s during which his handicap went from three to six. Rhodesia has a hard-hitting team that can give South Africa a run for their money and both countries can field twenty-four goal teams.

Horse trials, dressage (South Africa boasts its own team of Lipizzaner stallions), tent-pegging and gymkhana, the Pony Club and driving are all enjoyed in a climate and environment that suits outdoor sport. Pony trekking is also a popular recreation. CC

South German Heavy Horse

South German Heavy Horse the same as PINZGAUER (NORIKER) see Germany

Soviet Heavy Draught Horse

This is a large, almost clean-legged horse, bred up from the Belgian heavy horse (see Belgium). Like its ancestor, the Soviet Heavy Horse is generally chestnut, bay or roan. It is active with a good gait. The stallion Ranet covered 2,000 m (1·24 miles) at the trot in 5 min. 7·2 sec. DMG

Spain

The two countries of the Iberian peninsula are historically bound together, so the native breeds of ponies and horses have much in common. For seven hundred years the peninsula was overrun by successive hordes of Alani, Suevi, Visigoths, Saracens and Arabs, bringing in horses of Eastern origin, ARABS and BARBS. These Oriental breeds and possibly NORIKER horses too, laid the foundations for the ANDALUSIAN breed so famous in antiquity and medieval times. The heavy Neapolitan with its markedly concave profile and high action was used almost indiscriminately in Spain in the fifteenth century by royal edict and thus a heavier 'school' horse was produced. Within a few decades horses of Spanish breeding were being used in many European court studs for they were regarded as the most beautiful horses in the world. However, the Carthusian monastery of Jerez de la Frontera, founded by Don Alvaro Obertus de Valeto in 1476 with a gift of 10,000 acres of land, together with the Carthusian monasteries in Seville and Cazello, refused to use the heavier imported stallions, employing instead selected Barb and Arab stallions, and persisted in breeding the true pure Andalusian or CARTHUSIAN as it came to be called, which must have had its antecedents in an Oriental breed. This breed is therefore nearly 500 years old. The Zapata stud, which originally bred black and chestnut horses until grey stallions were used about fifty years ago, is not so old but the bloodlines have been just as carefully guarded.

One of the best of the modern breeds is the Spanish or Hispano Arab. These fine quality horses are bred in Estremadura and Andalusia and are used for all sporting events and competitions. There are today about 282,000 horses in Spain against 533,000 mules and 368,000 asses. All three species show a decline over previous years. The horse breeds are Spanish (Andalusian/Carthusian), Arab, Spanish Arab, Anglo-Arab and Barb. Some THOROUGHBREDS have been imported. See also Portugal. DMG

Spanish Riding School of Vienna

The Spanish Riding School of Vienna is the oldest riding academy in the world where the classical equestrian art has been practised in its purest form up to the present day. There are no documents to shed light on the beginnings of this institution. The date often mentioned for its foundation, 1735, is just as vague and incorrect as 1572, but in

1572, on the premises of the imperial palace, a covered arena which replaced the outdoor *manège* was built or being repaired, and in 1735, in the reign of Emperor Charles VI, the Spanish Riding School moved into the beautiful riding hall built by Fischer von Erlach which still provides the setting for the daily work and weekly performances of the LIPIZZANERS. There is a satisfactory explanation of the name 'Spanish Riding School'. At the time of its foundation, in the fifteenth or sixteenth centuries, Spanish horses, descended from ARAB and BARB stallions and ANDALUSIAN mares, were much favoured at the royal courts of Europe for their dainty movements and proud carriage. In 1580 Archduke Charles founded the imperial stud farm of Lipizza where these Spanish horses were bred for the use of the court. The foals born in Lipizza were named Lipizzaners and since then have been the only horses trained at the Spanish Riding School.

The institute was a property of the court. The resplendent white hall with its slender columns and suspended stucco ceiling, with the portrait of Charles VI as the only spot of colour, was the scene of gallant pageantry, balls and horse ballets. Beethoven conducted several concerts there and in 1848 the first session here of the newly elected parliament marked a new epoch of Austria's history. Young noblemen were instructed in the classical art of riding and the performances of the powerful stallions were highlights in court life. Whereas the French Revolution and Napoleon's wars set an end to the riding schools at most other courts the Spanish Riding School even survived the breakdown of the Austro-Hungarian Empire in 1918 and was continued as a cultural institution by the Republic of Austria, which opened the training sessions and Sunday performances to the general public. It seems miraculous that it survived the chaos of World War II and the flight from the bombed city of Vienna to Upper Austria. Thanks to the American General Patton, there was no loss whatsoever. During a performance on 7 May 1945, only a few days after the final surrender, he took the old School under his personal protection and upon the special plea of Col Podhajsky, Commander of the School, ordered the Lipizzaner stud farm to be returned to Austria from Czechoslovakia where it had been transferred in 1942 by the German authorities. With these horses from the stud farm (over 200) the continuation of the School was assured.

Spanish Riding School of Vienna. A quadrille in the magnificent hall built by Fischer von Erlach

For over 400 years this time-honoured institute has been governed by tradition. The training strictly follows the classical rules, preserving the natural paces of the horse and developing them to highest perfection. In the course of 3–4 years the stallion is taught all the paces and figures of the *haute école* called 'airs on the ground', which are demanded at the OLYMPIC GAMES dressage test. Talented horses are then taught the 'airs above the ground' (see Airs, Classical). All school jumps are developed from natural leaps and were part of the general training of horses and riders in the seventeenth and eighteenth centuries.

Only stallions are used at the School. They wear black bridles with gold buckles and English saddles for daily work, and gold bridles and traditional white buckskin school saddles for performances.

It takes 4–6 years to teach a young rider to ride a fully trained horse and may take another 2–4 years before he is able to train his own horse to this standard. Traditionally there is one head rider and several riders, assistant riders and apprentices. Only Austrian citizens are accepted. The riders wear the traditional uniform: a dark brown tail coat with a high collar, white buckskin breeches and high black boots. The cocked hat is black with a gold braid indicating the rider's rank. The gala uniform of red coat with gold braid and epaulettes and a cocked hat worn lengthwise was used for special occasions during the time of the monarchy and was revived for Walt Disney's film, *Flight of the White Stallions*. When entering the hall during the training sessions or performances the riders doff their hats in reverence and gratitude to Charles VI under whose patronage the splendid riding hall was built.

Maintaining the tradition was instrumental in bringing the Spanish Riding School through all the difficult times in history; tradition begins to peel off with as little as a glove dropped carelessly, as Colonel Podhajsky explained to Queen Elizabeth when Her Majesty rode his stallion Pluto Theodorosta in London in 1953. AP

Spavin

A bony enlargement on the lower inner aspect of the hock joint, resulting from a localized periostitis. CF

Speedy Cut (Interfering)

Injury on the inside of the leg in the region of the knee or upper cannon, caused by the shoe of the opposite foot during fast work. CF

Spiti Ponies see India and Pakistan

Splints

Inflammatory bony outgrowths involving the small metacarpal or metatarsal bones or 'splint' bones. It can cause lameness but seldom after six years of age. CF

Spoon Polo see Mounted Games, Polo

Spotted Horse see Appaloosa

Sprained Tendons

Sprains usually affect the flexor or back tendons of horses subjected to fast exercise – racehorses and hunters. The degree of sprain, swelling and pain depends on the number of tendon fibres which rupture. Sprain of the suspensory ligament is usually included in this category of injury. CF

Stable Management

The following instructions are general. Routine may vary slightly according to the season. Early morning stables may be later in winter. In summer, further exercise or schooling may be given in the early evening during the longer days. Odd jobs may be done during the afternoon: e.g. tidying the muck-heap, cleaning rugs etc., tidying the tack-room, checking tack for signs of wear and tear, cleaning grooming kit, and so on.

Morning Stables: examine the horse for any injuries during the night. Change night to day rug, clean bucket, refill, and water the horse. Tie it up and give first haynet. Muck out: leave box floor bare except for a thin layer of straw to prevent slipping. Give first short feed. Tidy stable and yard. Short-rack, pick out feet; quarter (see Grooming). Replace rug (or cotton sheet in summer); release horse. About an hour later, tack up and exercise (1½–2 hours), or school (about 45 minutes); after schooling go for a short hack. On return give first short feed, e.g. oats.

Midday: groom thoroughly and strap after exercise (see Grooming). Pick up droppings; put down bedding so that the horse can lie down if it wishes. Refill water bucket. Give second short feed. Refill haynet. Tidy stable and yard. Let horse rest for two hours (e.g. 12–2 p.m.).

Afternoon: brush over; tack up if horse is having further exercise or schooling. On returning, groom. Tidy box, pick up droppings, renew any soiled bedding. Top up haynet and water bucket. Clean tack (see Cleaning Tack).

Evening Stables: brush over; put on night rug. Pick up droppings: set box fair for the night by putting down bedding with fresh straw banked round sides of box. Clean and refill bucket. Give last short feed. Refill haynet; this should be the largest, enough to last the night. Inspect horse before going to bed. If necessary, straighten rug and top up water bucket.

Watering: always water about 30 mins before feeding — never after. Do not give cold water to a hot or sweating horse. Water is best left in the box so that the horse can drink when it wants. Never water directly before exercise.

Feeding: as a horse has a small stomach, feed little and often: four short feeds are better than three, and three are better than two. The largest short feed should be given in the evening when the horse is resting and so best able to digest it.

Composition and quantity of a short feed are directly related to the amount and kind of exercise and work it is having, and to its temperament. Experience and observation are the best guides. A horse needs a balanced diet of protein and carbohydrates, a correct balance of calcium and phosphorus and other essential minerals and vitamins. The short feeds should provide all these. Hay is a natural food (like grass) and provides necessary bulk and roughage, to aid digestion. The smallest haynet should be the first, and the largest the last at night.

Keep the manger and all food and water utensils scrupulously clean. See that all

food is fresh. Remove any uneaten, stale food from the manger. Chaff mixed with a short feed prevents a greedy horse from bolting its food. Feed at least an hour before exercise. Never give a heavy meal to a tired horse as its digestion is not functioning properly. Give it a warm bran mash, followed by a little hay.
Types of Food: oats, broad bran, horse nuts, maize, boiled barley, dried sugar beet (soaked overnight), dried beans and peas (very heating), molasses, boiled linseed, root vegetables, greens (valuable in the winter when grass is not available).
Hay: meadow, mixture, clover, alfalfa, sanfoin. Old hay is best; never give hay under six months old. It should be well saved and free from dust. Never give mildewed or mowburnt hay. Slightly damp the hay if it is dusty, or if a horse is broken-winded.

Daily amounts will vary with the size of the horse and the amount of work it is doing. Stabled horses on hard feed need a rest from it once a week and a laxative food in its place. Do not give oats to children's ponies unless they are doing very hard work; oats make them too excitable and unsafe to ride. A horse that is not working should have a maintenance diet of hay only. Overfeeding and underworking will cause 'filled' legs and digestive troubles (e.g. COLIC).
General Management: while the horse is out of its box, disinfect stable floors once a week and leave bare to dry. Keep drains clear and disinfected. Walls of boxes should be limewashed and kept clean. Avoid direct draughts: a window with the top opening in a V-shaped hopper is best as it prevents draughts from blowing directly down onto a horse's back. Have plenty of fresh air and light. Stables should face south or west (in the northern hemisphere). Keep the upper half of box doors open, unless the weather is exceptionally severe, so that the horse can look out. Provide warmth by rugging up and using woollen (rest) bandages. Have an isolation box well away from the main stables. See also Bedding, Stabling, Clothing, Horse. GW

Stabling

Three factors are of paramount importance when considering stabling for horses. However they are constructed, stables must be safe, secure, and above all sanitary – easy to keep clean and sweet-smelling and well-ventilated.

In the old days, *stalls*, partitioned spaces 6 ft–6 ft 6 in (1·82–1·97 m) wide and 11–13 ft (3·35–3·96 m) long, were in general use. They enabled a far greater number of horses to be housed in a given space than the more commodious *box-stall* or *loose-box*. Stalls are usually approached by way of a passage running behind them which should measure approximately 8 ft (2·43 m) and not less than 5 ft (1·52 m). The disadvantage of stalls is that the horse or pony has to be tied up day and night and has little freedom to move about. To secure a horse in a stall it is necessary for it to wear a headcollar or stall to which a head rope is fixed. The far end of this rope passes through the manger ring and thence through a 'log' – a ball of hard wood suspended on the end of the rope to keep it taut so that the horse has the freedom to lie down without a slack rope in which it may catch a leg. Stalls should have strong, solid partitions, with or without bars along the top, to prevent fighting between horses next to one another, but some rely on the 'bale' system, a plank or heavy pole slung on chains from the roof. The former is safer and more acceptable to most horse owners.

Box-stalls or loose-boxes are built in many shapes and sizes. They can be housed in long barns or stables like stalls but with a partition across the back and a door leading into the passageway, or they can open directly into a yard; in either case the doors must open outwards, and be secured by two bolts — a heavy-duty top bolt and a kick bolt at the bottom — though some of the big high-class stables have sliding doors on the inner boxes. If the yard is sheltered from the prevailing winds, boxes leading directly into the yard are to be preferred for they have access to a greater amount of fresh air that is not being shared with other horses. A really good, well cared for, range of internal boxes is satisfactory, providing there are several horses in the stables to keep each other company. Loneliness is a serious health hazard for horses, for not only do they fret, but also start such undesirable habits as chewing and weaving, windsucking and crib-biting (see Vices). The best boxes are those that look into the yard and have a wide overhanging roof for protection.

Boxes vary in size: the bigger the horse the bigger box it needs. Most standard-size boxes bought ready made for erection on the owner's site are 10 × 12 ft (3·04 × 3·65 m). This, in the writer's opinion, is far too small for a horse, though big enough for a large pony. For a hunter or riding horse 12 × 14 ft (3·65 × 4·26 m) is required; a square box is good: 10 × 10 ft (3·04 × 3·04 m) for ponies; 12 × 12 ft (3·65 × 3·65 m) for horses and small hunters up to 16 hands (1·65 m); 14 × 14 ft (4·26 × 4·26 m) for 16–16·3 hands (1·65–1·75 m) and 15 × 15 ft (4.57 m) for larger horses, stallions, brood mares and foals of hunter type. A square box is safest because a horse will measure the width and then roll or lie down. If the box is narrower than where measured the horse may get stuck against a wall (see Cast).

The doorway into any stable or box should be at least 4 ft (1·21 m) wide, measured from inside the door frame and not from outside: 3 ft 9 in (1·13 m) as in most standard boxes is too narrow. The bottom half (stable doors should be split in half) should measure 4 ft

Stabling. *Above:* A modern loose-box
Left: Stalls, more commonly used in the past than today

3 in (1·28 m) from the ground or else bars or a grid will be required to prevent the horse jumping out.

Stables can be made of stone, brick or wood and other materials. They should be warm, draught-free and easy to keep clean, have good drainage and no projecting objects on which the horse can injure itself.

Mangers are best fixed in the corner at an easy height for the horse to feed from. The new plastic mangers are satisfactory, provided they are boxed in and screwed down to the frame. Otherwise, horses can lift them out with their teeth and tread on them.

Three tie rings are necessary, preferably bolted right through a beam: one by the manger to enable a horse to be racked up for feeding, another to take a haynet and a third to rack the horse up to for grooming.

Every stable should be well provided with windows. In a loose-box the window is best next to the door to prevent cross draughts.

All boxes other than those built of stone or brick should be lined, at least to 4 ft (1·21 m), 6 ft (1·82 m) or right up being better. Heavy duty plywood ⅝ in (16 mm) thick is excellent, and is generally kick-proof. Floors can be of bricks, marl (clay) or concrete and should be laid on a damp-proof surface, for rising damp should be avoided in all stables.

Water can be provided by automatic water bowls or buckets; they should hold at least 4 gallons (4·75 US gal or 18·18 litres) and be placed in the corner of the box so that they are not easily knocked over, handles against the wall and jammed down tight. Hay can be fed in either racks or nets, the former situated so as to prevent hayseeds falling in the horse's eyes.

The roof should be well insulated and preferably pitched, with head clearance of 8 ft (2·43 m) at the eaves for a horse. Tack rooms and feed houses can be built on to the boxes. Field shelters with the same characteristics as the boxes described above are useful in both winter and summer. DRT

Stage, The Horse on the

The history of the horse on the stage is as long as the history of the theatre itself. Greek spectators of the fifth century B.C. must have seen them in the theatre of Dionysus, as when Agamemnon, riding in a chariot with his captive Cassandra beside him, made his triumphal return to Argos in Aeschylus' play. Horses certainly took part in the highly realistic productions of medieval mystery plays; their appearances in theatres of the Renaissance through the eighteenth century have been documented; and today they still figure regularly in outdoor dramas and in spectacular productions of opera, such as those given at the Metropolitan Opera in New York and the Baths of Caracalla in Rome.

It was in the first half of the nineteenth century, however, that the histrionic abilities of these elegant animals were most fully appreciated. Among the many bizarre forms of entertainment that flourished in the theatre during this period, none was more marvellous or elaborately staged than those dramas involving animals. Dogs, horses, stags, bears, and even elephants were the star attractions of these plays. Their activities were invariably directed toward serving or rescuing their human masters, and these activities were thought of not only as expressions of fidelity, but as manifestations of conscious, human qualities possessed by the animals themselves. The horse, on account of its beauty, appropriateness, and the widely held belief in its 'sagacity', was the most frequently seen of these performers, giving rise to what came to be known as *hippodrama*, drama in which horses were considered as actors, with business, often leading actions, of their own to perform.

Deriving from burlesque equestrian interludes given in eighteenth-century riding schools and circuses, by 1807 hippodrama was firmly established as a distinct species of entertainment in England and France, with the United States and other European countries soon to follow. For the most part these plays were performed on the scenic stages of permanent circus buildings, of which Astley's in London and the Cirque Olympique in Paris were the most famous. They could be given on any stage large and strong enough to support them, and from 1811 Covent Garden regularly produced its share of hippodramas, with the rebuilt Drury Lane Theatre shortly following suit. These productions were of mammoth proportions. Hundreds of supernumeraries were engaged to appear in them; vast settings of mountain heights, pathways, bridges, and castles were created by the leading scene designers of the day; and the number of horses appearing in individual scenes (at least in one instance) is reported to have been as many as ninety.

Over the next fifty years hundreds of such dramas were written and produced. In addition to plays in which horses figured as star actors, they were prominently displayed in pantomimes such as *Tam O'Shanter*, in which Meg made her famous dash for the brig (leaving her tail behind); equestrianized versions of Shakespeare's plays and Scott's novels; military spectacles based on historical, often current events; and stirring melodramas which generally concluded with mounted warriors assaulting the villain's castle and, after defeating their opponent's cavalry, setting the castle on fire. Although the horses were usually confined to a handful of scenes in these spectacles, there can be little doubt that audiences took at least as much interest in the four-footed actors as they did in the two-footed. It was not Richard's, but White Surrey's death that spectators flocked to see at Astley's in the 1850s; and when Black Bess, after carrying Dick Turpin safely over the turnpike gate, staggered onstage, fell down, and lifted her head to give her master one last kiss before dying, a new peak in dramatic poignancy had been reached. Sometimes, too, there were real-life fatalities in the course of these representations. Many horses and actors were killed or maimed during performances of *Mazeppa*, for in this play the horse, with Mazeppa lashed to its back, had to dash up a series of ramps extending to the very top of the stage. In reading over the accounts of these disasters, one is impressed

Below: **The Horse on the Stage.** James Holloway in an equestrian version of *Richard III*, performed at Astley's Amphitheatre in London, 1856

Bottom: **Staghunting and Buckhunting.** This mosaic scene from Carthage shows that staghunting dates to at least 500 A.D.

by the curious fact that more pity was often expended on the horses than on their riders.

Even more remarkable were those hippodramas in which the horses, left at liberty and without any human appearing to direct their movements, were given the responsibility of advancing and resolving the actions themselves. In one such play, *Martial et Angélique*, the horse of a murdered nobleman eventually recognized and captured the two culprits who had slain his master, thereby saving the young lover who had been accused of the crime. In *The White Maiden of California* the Arabian palfrey Lily swam ashore from a sinking ship and saved the drowning heroine as well. In *The Woodman's Horse* the steed Beauty climbed a ladder to a loft and removed a dagger holding shut a door, behind which the villain had confined the virtuous characters of the play. And in *Le Cheval du Diable* a phenomenal horse named Zisco, whom Théophile Gautier eulogized as 'a Talma with four feet, a Frédéric Lemaître with flowing mane and tail', searched out and trampled a villain, performed a solo dance, drove off a pack of polar bears, and rescued a screaming infant from a flaming tower by crossing and recrossing a fearful bridge of chains. The horses in these productions not infrequently elicited more praise and applause than did the humans appearing with them, with some critics, perhaps maliciously, going so far as to credit them with superior address and intelligence.

After 1860 the popularity of hippodrama rapidly declined, although two plays, *Mazeppa* and its French counterpart *Les Pirates de la Savane*, continued to experience numerous revivals since they had become vehicles for the display of the feminine charms exhibited by Adah Isaacs Menken and her myriad successors. Melodramas such as *Ben Hur*, whose climactic moments arrived with Virtue triumphing over Vice during the running of a horse race, also helped keep the tradition alive into the twentieth century; and at present, thanks to television and the cinema (see Motion Pictures), the horse continues to play a prominent role in dramatic entertainment. AHS

Reference: A. H. Saxon, *Enter Foot and Horse: A History of Hippodrama in England and France,* New Haven, 1968.

Stagecoach see Coaching, American Stagecoach, Australian Stagecoach

Staghunting and Buckhunting

Prehistoric in origin, staghunting has been recorded as a pastime of royalty and nobles throughout history. The Norman Conquest brought rules and science to deerhunting in Britain. Traces remain today, e.g. *Ty a hillaut,* the old Norman–French warning that a deer was roused, later corrupted to 'Tally Ho'. Staghunting remained the premier sport of the Norman, Plantagenet and Tudor dynasties, but the clearance of the deer's habitat, the great forests, led to a reduction in staghunting, accelerated in the eighteenth century by the improvement of agriculture. Staghunts either disbanded, or in some cases converted to foxhunting. The Duke of Beaufort's Hunt made the change in about 1762.

During the reign of George III (1760–1820) the hunting of carted deer began in Britain. The technique is for hounds to follow the line of a deer released for the purpose, and eventually recaptured completely unharmed. It usually provides long, fast runs for mounted followers. In England this form of staghunting persisted mainly in the southeast, but the hunts have been reduced in recent years, the last to disband being the Norwich Staghounds in 1964. The Ward Union in the Irish Republic, and the County Down in Northern Ireland continue to hunt carted stag.

Hunting wild red deer or fallow buck with hounds is now confined to France and England. There are some 20 packs in France which accept visitors, and others of a more private nature. Elaborate liveries for hunt staff, and the use of the French hunting horn worn over the shoulder, lend colour and music to the sport. In England the red deer is hunted with hounds on or near Exmoor, by three packs: the Devon and Somerset, the Quantock, and the Tiverton. Stags are hunted in late summer, autumn and spring, and hinds in mid-winter. Located in a district previously by a 'harbourer', the stag is first found by a few couple of hounds called 'tufters'; then the rest of the pack is laid on the line and the hunt ensues. If the stag stands to bay, usually in water, it is dispatched at close range by gun. The hunts justifiably claim that as well as providing superb sport in beautiful surroundings, they perform a valuable function in the essential selective culling of the red deer by the most efficient and humane method, since only with hounds can one get within close enough range to guarantee killing, rather than merely injuring, a deer. The New Forest Buckhounds use a somewhat similar technique in hunting the smaller fallow deer, but only males, mature bucks of five years

Standardbred. Albatross, Horse of the Year in 1971

and above. The last true staghounds in England were sold abroad in 1825; ever since packs have hunted successfully using foxhounds. French hunts often include English foxhound crossbreeding, but still retain some old French bloodlines.

Since the English foxhound's ancestors inevitably hunted deer, the modern foxhound can be 'entered' to the pursuit of deer without difficulty. Deer have a stronger scent than foxes, and the line of a stag can usually be 'owned' by a pack with less difficulty, but a mature stag is fast and wily. Hounds need great stamina and persistence in keeping on the line of their original quarry. For the horseman, following staghounds or buckhounds presents a special challenge, since the points achieved are often long, and although there is seldom anything to jump, riding on Exmoor or the New Forest at speed requires judgment. MC

Stallion (Entire)

A mature male horse used for stud purposes.

Standardbred

The American Standardbred developed mostly in New England, where harness racing has been a popular activity since colonial times. It became an official breed in 1880, when the American Trotting Register adopted a set of rules establishing a one-mile speed standard (2 min 30 sec for trotters and 2 min 25 sec for pacers) as an admission requirement, hence the name 'Standardbred'. Breeding restrictions were later added, so that the modern Standardbred is limited to the descendants of certain registered sires.

Although the Standardbred is believed to bear strains of the Norfolk Trotter, Narragansett and Canadian Pacer, Cleveland Bay, Hackney, Arabian, Barb, and Morgan, it is richest in Thoroughbred blood. The official founder sire, Messenger, was a grey Thoroughbred stallion imported into Philadelphia from England at the age of eight around 1788; his lineage traced back to the Darley Arabian through his sire and to both the Godolphin Arabian and the Byerley Turk through his dam. Messenger had been a mediocre flat racer, but he passed on speed to his offspring. However, it was one of his great-grandsons, Hambletonian 10 (often called Rysdyk's Hambletonian, after his owner), foaled in 1840, who endowed the breed with outstanding trotting and pacing ability through no less than 1,335 offspring sired between 1851 and 1875, and he is the undisputed forefather of most modern Standardbred racers.

The Standardbred varies in conformation, since speed has always been of greater importance than beauty. It is generally longer-bodied and shorter-legged than the Thoroughbred, less refined in appearance, and also somewhat smaller, measuring 14–16 hands (1·42–1·65 m) and weighing 900–1,200 lb (408–545 kg). It may be of any of the usual equine colours, but is most often bay. The typical Standardbred has powerful haunches, with the hind legs placed behind rather than under the croup, in order to produce the piston-like action necessary for trotting and pacing speed.

Because of the boom in harness racing in America since World War II, Standardbred breeding has become big business. The major stud farms, such as Hanover Shoe Farms and Meadow Lands in Pennsylvania, Castleton Farms in Kentucky and also in Florida, Nevele Acres in New York, Stoner Creek Farm in Kentucky and others in many states including Ohio, Indiana and as far west as California, where Leland Stanford was one of the pioneers of Standardbred breeding, can be favourably compared to any Thoroughbred establishment. Moreover, a Standardbred racing champion is as valuable as a Thoroughbred racehorse, and syndicate ownership is common. Standardbred racing and breeding are governed by the United States Trotting Association (750 Michigan Avenue, Columbus, Ohio).

The American Standardbred has contributed its blood to trotting breeds in other countries, especially in Italy, Sweden, Germany, New Zealand, Australia, and in the Orient. Russia, however, protects the purity of its own famed Orlov trotting breed; and although the French national breeding centre, the Haras du Pin, imported two top Standardbred stallions, Sam Williams and The Great McKinney, in the 1930s, American outcrosses are no longer permitted in France.

Selective breeding combined with improved training methods and racing conditions have lowered the speed records of Standardbred trotters and pacers throughout the years. Harness-racing records today are broken with disconcerting frequency. The first official trotter of a mile in under two minutes was Louis Dillon (1 min 58½ sec) in 1903, and the first two-minute pacer was Star Pointer, who paced a mile in 1 min 59¼ sec in 1897. The present record holders are the trotter Nevele Pride, who bettered Greyhound's 31-year-old mile record of 1 min 55¼ sec by trotting a mile at Indianapolis in 1969 in 1 min 54⅘ sec, and the pacer Bret Hanover, who covered a mile at Vernon Downs in 1966 in 1 min 54 sec. MAS

Steeplechasing. Racing through a village in the early nineteenth century

Standing Martingale see Martingales

Steeplechasing

Steeplechasing is often called 'the winter sport', a misnomer, as it frequently carries on until June and the summer break is brief: the new season sometimes opens at the end of July. It probably owes its existence to the enclosing of agricultural land in eighteenth-century Britain. Before then, hunting men really only had to cope with brooks and ditches. With the growth of enclosures, assuming they wished to see hounds run, they had to cross hedges, stakes-and-binders, stone walls, banks and posts-and-rails. At the same time the speed of horses was tending to increase and faster hounds were being bred as well. These changes in jumping power and greater speed encouraged hunting men to indulge in friendly arguments over the merits of each other's horses, and so matches between the horses in question were arranged to take place over a line of natural country. The first recorded match was in Ireland in 1752: two gentlemen named O'Callaghan and Blake rode across country from Buttevant Church to St Leger Church. In those days church steeples were usually the most prominent landmarks, so these cross-country matches were frequently from one church to another and were commonly called steeplechases.

For many years steeplechases were run over natural country but at Bedford in 1810 came the first recorded race over made-up fences. The fences in question were 4 ft 6 in (1·37 m) high with a strong bar fixed across the top. The object of these fences was to scare off horses that were not in fact genuine hunters; unfortunately they frightened away the genuine hunters, too, with the result that the enormous crowd that had thronged into Bedford to see the fun had to be content with a field of two. From that date, though, interest in steeplechasing began to grow. Most of the races were over natural country and the country chosen was usually a formidable test for horse and rider. At this period all the riders were amateurs. In 1837 the GRAND NATIONAL Steeplechase was established at Liverpool and owners began to employ professional jockeys. The most famous of these early professionals was Jem Mason, who won the 1839 Grand National on Lottery.

Once the Grand National had been founded, the sport began to develop on modern lines. Racing over a natural country became a thing of the past, and stone walls, posts-and-rails, banks and unfenced brooks were abolished in favour of made-up fences constructed of birch. Arrangements for spectators began to be similar to those at flat-racing meetings, though these were in most cases still somewhat primitive. Many of the main flat-race courses began to stage jumping meetings as well, and hurdle races became an integral part of almost every jumping program. Cheltenham was coming to be regarded as the home of steeplechasing just as Newmarket is regarded as the headquarters of the flat.

There was undeniably a period during the middle of the nineteenth century when steeplechasing passed through the doldrums, primarily because it tended to be a lawless sport, lacking an authoritative governing body. In addition, steeplechasing was anathema to many dedicated fox-hunters, whose views were publicized in forceful fashion by the writer Charles Apperley, better known under his *nom de plume* of Nimrod. However, a turning point, restoring a fast-deteriorating situation, was reached in 1866 with the foundation of the National Hunt Committee, which controlled the sport as the Jockey Club controlled flat racing until the Committee's amalgamation with the Jockey Club at the end of 1968. It is only fair, however, to add that for a good many years the measure of control, particularly at the many minor meetings all over the country, tended to be undesirably lax.

The four-mile National Hunt Steeplechase for maidens at starting (it is now for maidens at entry), ridden by amateurs, was founded in 1860 with the original objective of encouraging farmers to breed good quality horses for hunting and racing. For many years it was a movable feast to provide the right incentive in various parts of the country and the race took place on 22 different courses, among them Cottenham, Warwick, Sandown and Newmarket, before it found a permanent home at Cheltenham in 1911. For a good many years it was the *pièce de résistance* of the great three-day National Hunt Meeting at Cheltenham in March and was one of the most valuable races of the season. Until quite recently it was run over a special course in which no fence was jumped twice, but now it is run on the racecourse proper throughout, attracts far less interest than it did, and is completely overshadowed by such events at the meeting as the Gold Cup and the Champion Hurdle.

The Gold Cup was instituted in 1924, the Champion Hurdle three years later. Originally they were both run on the opening day of the meeting and were worth less than £700 to the winner. In 1972 they were worth to the respective winners £15,255 and £15,648. There used to be four selling races in the program at this important meeting. In 1930 the eighteen winners there earned a total of £8,076, the National Hunt Chase being the only event worth more than £1,000 to the winner; by 1965 the total earned by the winners had risen to £41,159.

Following the 'American Invasion' at the turn of the century when anti-racing legislation in the United States drove many American owners, trainers and jockeys to Europe, the style and method of riding on the flat was revolutionized. This had its repercussions in the jumping world and jockeys shortened their leathers considerably, while races tended to be run at a noticeably faster pace. More attention was paid to the construction of fences, which gradually became less formidably upright and were given a neater, less shaggy appearance. Courses were better maintained. As late as 1881 there were two long stretches of plough on the Grand National course, the first extending from the second fence to Becher's Brook, the second soon after leaving the fence known as Valentine's. It included a field of mangolds, some of which had been pulled to provide a lane through which the competitors could pass. After heavy rain horses were sometimes reduced to a trot.

Between the world wars steeplechasing was still very much the poor relation of the flat and jumping enthusiasts were not infrequently described by the paladins of flat-racing as 'the needy and greedy'. Prize money was exiguous and there were only six races during the entire season worth as much as £1,000 to the winner. There were few rich owners. Patrons of the sport tended to be genuine horse-lovers, or else gamblers who were mainly interesting in betting.

Gradually the position improved, not least on account of the wealthy American owners who started to patronize the sport, such as J. H. Whitney and Mr and Mrs F. Ambrose Clark, chiefly in the hope of winning the Grand National. In addition there were English owners who raced on a big scale like J. V. Rank; Lord Bicester, who was not in the least concerned with betting; and the eccentric Miss Dorothy Paget, who undoubtedly was. Fields began to get bigger and betting tended to take a wider range than it had usually done in the past. The number of clearly 'non-operational' runners decreased; discipline was further improved by the higher standard demanded from local stewards and by the introduction in 1937 of stewards' secretaries.

The pattern of National Hunt racing then tended to be far duller than today. Nearly every meeting started off with a selling hurdle and a selling steeplechase. Because of a total lack of other races of comparable stature, the Grand National dominated the entire season and it was the Grand National horses that provided most of the interest. Sport was very stodgy up till Christmas, most of the programs being made up of uninspiring bread-and-butter events. Only after the publication of the Grand National weights did proceedings really begin to warm up. March was the big month with the National Hunt Meeting at Cheltenham, the Grand Military Meeting at Sandown, and the Liverpool Spring Meeting following each other in swift succession.

During this epoch the Grand National reached the zenith of its popularity and on Grand National day 300,000 people would be packed into Aintree. The sport as a whole was boosted by two brilliant horses that captured the public imagination, Easter Hero and Golden Miller. There were far more minor meetings then that provided opportunities for trainers and riders in a small way of business. Despite the many acts of cheerful villainy that were perpetrated, these meetings were fun and many senior racegoers look back with nostalgic affection on little courses that died during World War II such as Pershore, Hawthorn Hill, Torquay, Bungay, Tarporley, Colwall Park, Wenlock, Bridgnorth and Hethersett.

Possibly since World War II jumping has lost something of the old sporting atmosphere, while changed economics and the disappearance of the horse from the Army have sadly reduced the number of amateur riders. There are fewer big stables that concentrate solely on jumping largely because it is not easy for a jumping trainer to make a lucrative living. On the other hand there is a vast army of permit holders of varying degrees of competence.

On the credit side, the standard among professional jockeys has never been higher. Prize money has greatly increased, thanks largely to the generosity of sponsors. If the Grand National has declined in prestige, the Cheltenham Gold Cup has increased in that respect and there are other good races to enliven the season such as the Hennessy Cup, the Mackeson Cup, the Whitbread Cup, the Schweppes Gold Trophy, the Totalisator Champion Novices Chase and the W. D. and H. O. Wills Premier Chase. Television has not only encouraged sponsorship but has given the sport a far bigger public than ever before. RM

British Army officers were primarily responsible for the spread of steeplechasing in Europe, where it had taken a hold in many countries by 1840; it was also introduced to Canada, where it found instant popularity. The Canadians believed that no race meeting was complete without its jump race and, not surprisingly, that spirit soon spread south to the United States.

The first hurdle race in the United States took place at Hoboken, N.J., in 1844; the appropriate winner was a Canadian gelding called Hops, who had been the best hurdler in his native country. Hops proved to be the only proficient jumper in the field of four, but the race, run in three heats, provided plenty of amusement for a large crowd. There were several falls and objections before Hops, having contrived to lose the first heat, clinched the race by taking the second heat by a furlong and the third by a quarter of a mile.

The first steeplechase in the United States did not take place until 1865, when four hurdle racers attempted 27 more formidable jumps in a 3-mile course at Paterson, N.J. This was a farce. The winner fell and was remounted; the second fell, incapacitating his rider, so another climbed up and rode him home; and the third swerved off the course, a circumstance ascribed to the fact that his jockey, having taken Dutch courage before the ordeal, was drunk. However, steeplechasing grew and prospered. The National Steeplechase Association was formed in 1895, a year after the introduction of the MARYLAND HUNT CUP, which was to become the most famous amateur steeplechase in the world, and 1899 brought the birth of the American Grand National.

The turn of the century also found steeplechasing on a sound footing in many other parts of the world. France instituted its most famous event over jumps, the Grand Steeplechase de Paris, in 1901, and a successful New Zealand 'chaser called Moifaa came to Aintree to land the Grand National of 1904. The same event fell to an American horse in 1908 and a French horse in 1909. Australia, too, was beginning to produce useful jumpers and stage good races over obstacles.

But everywhere jumping was the poor relation of flat racing and over the years it has declined everywhere except in the British Isles. Despite the emergence of a number of spectacular jumpers in the United States, public interest dwindled until in 1971 the New York Racing Association abandoned all racing over obstacles except for a few events at Saratoga. Now only Delaware and New Jersey have major tracks staging jumping.

Paradoxically, the otherwise non-racing state of South Carolina instituted in 1970 an international invitation race, the Colonial Cup. The first two runnings have been only modest successes; despite the pleasant surroundings there can be little future for a fixture in an area where both gambling and the purchase of spirits are outlawed.

In Australia and New Zealand, the few big meetings are well supported, but minor events have little following. The same is true in Scandinavia and in most continental European countries where a tote monopoly obtains. Racecourses have to stage events on which the public will bet; the public tends to invest less on races over obstacles so racecourses stage less jumping and steeplechasing declines. See also Grand Pardubice. TM

Steeplechasing. The Taxis ditch in the Grand Pardubice (Czechoslovakia). On the left is Mrs Eva Palyzová, who has ridden six times in the Grand Pardubice and has come second twice. In this race, men and women jockeys compete, a tradition unknown in Western steeplechasing.

Steer Roping, Steer Wrestling see Rodeo

Strelets (Strelitz)

Steppe Horse see Kustanair

Stirrup
see Accoutrements, China

Strangles
An acute infectious disease of the horse marked by fever, nasal discharge and abscesses in the lymph glands in the intermandibular space. Abscesses may develop in other glands about the head. The disease is said to predispose to ROARING and BROKEN WIND. CF

Strelets (Strelitz)
At the beginning of the nineteenth century, many stallions and mares of Eastern origin were used at the Russian Strelets stud in order to develop a cavalry horse of strong Arabian characteristics. Later, English Thoroughbreds were used, as well as Arab stallions. The Anglo-Arab breed known as Strelets, 15·1½ hands high (1·56 m), was used to improve the native riding breeds. The increase in the measurements of the Arab in the Strelets breed was achieved in the simplest possible manner, by the introduction of English Thoroughbred blood. The Strelets had longer ears than the Arab with an Arab-like or, occasionally, a deer-like neck. Other characteristics of the breed were a wide forehead, powerful rib-cage, long straight croup, long loins, and the tail held in the Arab manner. The general constitution was hardy, and the legs lighter in bone than those of the English Thoroughbred; the hoofs were small with bone of close texture. Grey was the prevalent colour. The Strelets stud and the Tersky stud, near Piatigorsk, were the centres of the breed. The stock of the Strelets stud at the time of its dissolution consisted of 8 per cent Persian and Turetsky, 7 per cent Turkmen, 20 per cent Orlov, 7 per cent English Thoroughbred, 6 per cent Datsky, 43 per cent Arab, and 6 per cent miscellaneous stock. The breed is now extinct. WOF

Suffolk Horse (Suffolk Punch)
A draught horse, originally from the English county of Suffolk, as its name implies. According to William Camden's *Britannia* (1586) the breed dates back to 1506. It is a shortlegged, barrel-bodied horse, always breeds true to chestnut (one of seven shades), is 16–17 hands (1·65–1·77 m) high, is the only British native draught horse to have clean legs, is strong and gentle and economical to keep. Fifty years ago Suffolk horses were a common sight in many counties in England but with increased mechanization their numbers have been reduced. In the last fifty years nearly 200 pedigree mares and 50 stallions have been exported to the United States, South America and more recently to Pakistan for breeding mules for mountain artillery work. In 1938 alone 60 mares and 10 stallions went to the United States. It is a curious fact that every existing Suffolk Horse traces its descent in the direct male line in one unbroken chain to a horse foaled in 1760; today's Suffolk Horse has changed little since then. WJW

Sulky a light two-wheeled cart, having a seat for the driver only, used for trotters and pacers. See Driving, Trotting Racing

Sumba, Sumbawa see Indonesia

Swan-Necked (Cock-Throttled)
The neck is like that of a fowl: long, narrow in the throat region and concave at its base. CF

Sweden
The three native horse and pony breeds in Sweden are the small, stocky RUSS pony from the island of Gotland; the larger NORTH SWEDISH horse, which resembles a Fell pony, and is used mainly in the forests; and the internationally famous riding horse breed, the SWEDISH HALFBRED.

Trotting is a great national sport in Sweden; there are trotting courses all over the country, and more interest is taken in this than in Thoroughbred racing. The horses used are of two types: in the north a light type of the North Swedish horse is used, and further south the horses are mostly imported American or Russian trotters, or animals bred from imported stock.

The three main flat-race courses are at Malmö, Stockholm and Gothenburg, and a few steeplechases are run also. There are many fine Thoroughbred studs, where expensive English and French imported stallions are standing at stud, but the resulting stock are inclined to lack bone and substance and speed, compared to their English cousins, possibly due to the long, cold winters and the short grazing period.

Heavy farm work used to be done by Ardennes cart-horses, many of which were bred in the country, but mechanization on the farms has led to a sharp reduction in their numbers. The remaining ones are mostly used for dragging timber in the forests, and a few still work on the smaller farms and crofts.

Swedish children used to ride mainly Gotland Russ ponies, but these have largely been replaced by enormous numbers of imported British ponies, and their resulting Swedish-born offspring. There has been a tremendous increase in the riding population of Sweden during the last 20 years, and the numbers of children taking to riding increases every year. Great numbers of New Forest, Welsh, Shetland and Connemara ponies have been imported from Great Britain, Ireland and Holland, and there are also Norwegian Fjord and Icelandic ponies in the country. Breeding from all these is enthusiastically carried out, and all the breeds have their own societies, which come under the auspices of the Swedish Pony Society. During the last ten years many fine Arabs have been imported from England and Poland and some top-class stock is being bred here.

The Swedish Army Riding School was started at Strömsholm in 1868 and carried on until 1968, when it was felt to be no longer needed by a mechanized army. Now it is a civilian riding school run by the Swedish Riding Sports Organization, and it holds long and short courses which are filled to capacity not only by Swedish riders, but also by riders from abroad.

When Strömsholm was an Army Riding School it provided a complete training in horsemanship and horse mastership, turning out a continuous stream of superb riders and instructors. These riders competed with great success in the Olympic Games: in 1912 in Stockholm Sweden won both of the gold medals in the Three-Day Event, also the gold, silver and bronze medals in the Grand Prix de Dressage, and the gold medal in team jumping, most of the riders being mounted on Swedish Halfbreds (see below). The 1920 Olympic Games at Antwerp were another triumph for Sweden: Swedish riders won three gold, two silver and two bronze medals.

Since then Swedish riders have won many more Olympic medals and Swiss riders, too, and latterly German, have had great success in International Dressage competitions when mounted on Swedish-bred horses, which seem to have the perfect temperament and action for dressage. The brilliant Piaff, for instance, was formerly a Flyinge stallion. The Swiss formerly bought large numbers of Swedish horses yearly for use as remounts for the Army, and their great dressage riders Chammartin and Fischer were usually mounted on them. PL

Swedish Halfbred Horse

The Swedish Halfbred Horse was originally bred to provide remounts for the Army. About 300 years ago stallions were imported from the Orient, Spain and Friesland; these were crossed with the small rough local horses to produce bigger, livelier horses suitable for the Army. Later imports included Trakehners, Holsteiners and Thoroughbreds; stallion depôts were founded at Strömsholm and Flyinge. All stallions used for breeding in Sweden are subject to rigid examinations and tests under the control of the Ministry of Agriculture, and those that do not pass are not allowed to be used. The stallion depôt at Strömsholm is now closed down, but stallions are sent from Flyinge to their stations all over Sweden. The offspring of these and other privately-owned stallions have been exported in large numbers to Switzerland and even to England and the United States. Swedish Halfbreds are first-class riding and driving horses. Their sensible temperament and tremendous action makes them eminently suitable for dressage: their records in various Olympic Games are second to none, and they are also extremely good jumpers. PL

Switzerland

The origin of competitive riding in Switzerland is closely linked to the cavalry and the artillery, who can generally be said to have begun the sport as well as being its main supporters for many years. The first Swiss international successes were scored by officers on their military horses. It was only after World War II that riding gradually became a civilian sport. Today Switzerland is one of the last countries in the world to maintain cavalry. The artillery's supply echelons also depend heavily on horses and mules in mountain areas. The responsibility of the *Eidgenössische Militär Pferde-Anstalt,* the federal military horse institution in Berne, consists mainly of breaking in to saddle and draught young remounts imported from Ireland, Sweden, France, Germany and Poland, to furnish military horses for future cavalrymen. Men working at the E.M.P.F.A. are government employees. Collaterally the E.M.P.F.A. maintains a small competitive riding stable which has scored many successes, mainly in dressage, during the last few years, e.g. Henri Chammartin, who won the Olympic gold medal on Woermann in 1964 at Tokyo, and Gustav Fischer, awarded the silver medal on Wald in 1960 at Rome. The E.M.P.F.A. drivers are also very good; at the C.H.I.O. at AACHEN they regularly rank among the first.

The future of the cavalry is uncertain and its disbandment in the near future very probable. Civilian riding, on the other hand, has developed very favourably during recent decades under the patronage of the cavalry, with its officers and the E.M.P.F.A. riders (*Bereiter*) setting an example. In future this development should continue with individuals joining associations in order to form large riding centres, engage international experts as teachers, etc. If this materializes a change-over to civilian riding should pose no great problem.

Competitive riding consists of show jumping and dressage; there are also horse trials. In 1970, 24 such events took place. Unfortunately full three-day events are relatively rare in Switzerland as they are not very popular with spectators and it is practically impossible for the organizer to secure a profit or even cover his expenses. Since organizing such events demands much preparation, it is fortunate that devoted individuals and clubs are willing to assist in organizing them. In 1970, 1,427 jumping competitions took place. Of these 393 were solely for troopers and non-commissioned officers, who may start in the easy examinations reserved for them without a qualifying licence. Cavalry officers may also enter

Swedish Halfbred. These horses are popular for dressage. Here Ninna Stoor rides Casanova.

many competitions without a qualifying examination, provided they ride army horses. Civilian riders, however, must first pass an examination consisting of riding skills and theoretical knowledge before they can enter. In 1970 there were 2,884 active licence-holders. Jumping events, depending on size and importance, are either regional or national.

National events are divided into the following categories: L: 10–12 obstacles, 110–115 cm (3 ft 7 in–3 ft 9¼ in) high, 250–300 cm (8 ft 2½ in–9 ft 10 in) wide; M: 12–14 obstacles, 130 cm (4 ft 3 in) high, 350 cm (11 ft 6 in) wide; S: 12–14 obstacles, 150 cm (4 ft 11 in) high, 450 cm (14 ft 9 in) wide. The National Jumping Championship is held every year in the autumn and is open to both sexes. The C.S.I.O. (see Concours) is held alternately in Geneva or Lucerne, the C.S.I. at St Gallen and Davos.

In 1970 dressage riders took part in 84 events, regional and national. Licence examinations are also compulsory for dressage.

Only horses entered in the sports register may be admitted to these examinations; approximately 1,000 horses are entered annually. The majority are imported; only a small percentage are bred in Switzerland. Stock shows do not exist. Driving has recently come back though the number of competitions is still limited.

The central association is the *Schweizerischer Verband für Pferdesport* (Swiss Association for Horse Sports); it has subsections for races. The *Verband Schweizerischer Concours Reiter* (Association of Swiss Concours Riders) has been subdivided into sections for dressage, jumping and three-day events since 1971.

Between the two world wars, races were mainly events for officers, so racing, too, largely owes its origins to the military. This has drastically changed since World War II, however; today amateurs hold the strongest position. Compared with other countries, more amateurs than professional jockeys compete. In 1970, 133 races were held, including those at Divonne-les-bains (in France, but only two miles from the Swiss border). Of these, 30 were over hurdles, 29 flat, 63 driven trotting races; 11 were restricted to troopers and non-commissioned officers. The internationally best-known racecourse in Switzerland is probably St Moritz; during the winter the snow on the frozen lake is carefully levelled into a racecourse. Races also take place every winter on the frozen lake at Arosa. Some of the racecourses (in Switzerland they are all turf) are not permanent. The most important permanent racecourse is at Aarau, where the Grand Prix of Switzerland, a steeplechase over 4,200 m (2½ miles) is held. At Dielsdorf near Zürich a counterpart of this racecourse will soon be built.

Horse breeding in Switzerland is limited to farm horses and warmbloods. The Freiberger bay or chestnut draught horses (French: Franches-Montagnes) came originally from the Jura; they are sturdy and easy to handle. Infusions of Arab blood to improve the stock have added greys. Due to agricultural mechanization the demand for Freibergers is diminishing though they are still important as packhorses in the army; Freiberger mares crossed with asses produce mules. The aim in warmblood breeding was and to some extent still is the multipurpose horse, now increasingly tending towards an efficient horse with a buoyant stride, jumping ability and persistency. For breeding ANGLO-NORMANS and HOLSTEINS are mainly used. EW

Switzerland. Racing on the frozen lake at St Moritz

Tackle, Breaking

The term breaking tackle covers those items of equipment used in the early stages of training before the horse has been accustomed to carrying either saddle or rider. In many instances, however, the equipment will continue to be used after the 'backing' stage.

The objectives in the first phases of breaking ('making') a young horse are to prepare it mentally and physically against the time when it is asked to accept the weight of the rider. The basic element towards this end is the lungeing equipment consisting of cavesson, lunge rein and lunge whip. Later, when the horse is ready to accept a bit and further balancing exercises are practised, a roller, side-reins, bit and possibly long reins will be required.

Modern cavessons consist of a head strap to which is attached a padded noseband fitted with a hinged metal plate having three rings, to any of which, according to circumstances, the lunge rein may be attached. Usually, it is the centre ring, in the nose, which is employed. The head strap is also supplied with a jowl, or throat, strap to prevent the cavesson being pulled across the horse's eye. The lunge rein is made of tubular web up to 35 ft (10·60 m) in length and fastens to the cavesson ring either by a buckle or snap hook set on a swivel to allow the necessary movement of the rein. The most effective form of lunge whip is that made of fibreglass, which is light and easily managed. The whip stock is approximately 5 ft (1·50 m) long and is completed by a thong and lash about 1 ft (0·30 m) longer than the stock. The purpose of the whip is as an extension of the trainer's arm to urge the horse forward. It is not an instrument of chastisement.

Following the first stages of lungeing the horse will be fitted with a bit, either suspended by small straps from the cavesson, or attached to a bridle over which the cavesson is placed. The usual form of breaking bit has a straight metal mouthpiece in the centre of which are fitted 'keys', designed to encourage the horse to salivate and mouth its bit. To accustom the horse to the restraint imposed by the bit side-reins, either of plain leather or of the elasticated type, are attached from the bit to the Ds on the breaking roller.

The latter may be made of leather, web or hemp and differs from the stable roller by being fitted with a number of D-rings set at varying heights down each side. The position of the head and neck can then be controlled by fastening the side-reins to the appropriate D-rings.

For young horses whose development at the withers will be lower than that at the croup it may be necessary to employ a crupper, encompassing the dock and attached to the rear of the roller, to prevent the latter from sliding forward.

Long reins are used to place the horse 'on the bit' and to teach the directional aids of the hand. They are the same in appearance as the lunge rein but need not be fitted with swivels. In the English method of LONG-REINING the reins are fastened to the bit and pass back, through the rings on the roller, into the trainer's hands. He may then drive the horse forward while positioning himself directly behind the quarters, or he may circle the horse around him with the outside rein passing round the horse some 12 in (0·30 m) above the hock. EHE

Taki see Mongolia

Tarbais (Demi-Sang du Midi)

see Anglo-Arab in France

Tarpan

The Tarpan, *Equus przewalskii gmelini Antonius*, is a wild horse widely distributed throughout southern European Russia and eastern Europe including Germany until the eighteenth century. There were two types, the steppe Tarpan and the forest Tarpan. Early explorers confused the issue by calling Przevalski's Horse (see Asiatic Wild Horse) the Tarpan, which it is not.

Breaking Tackle

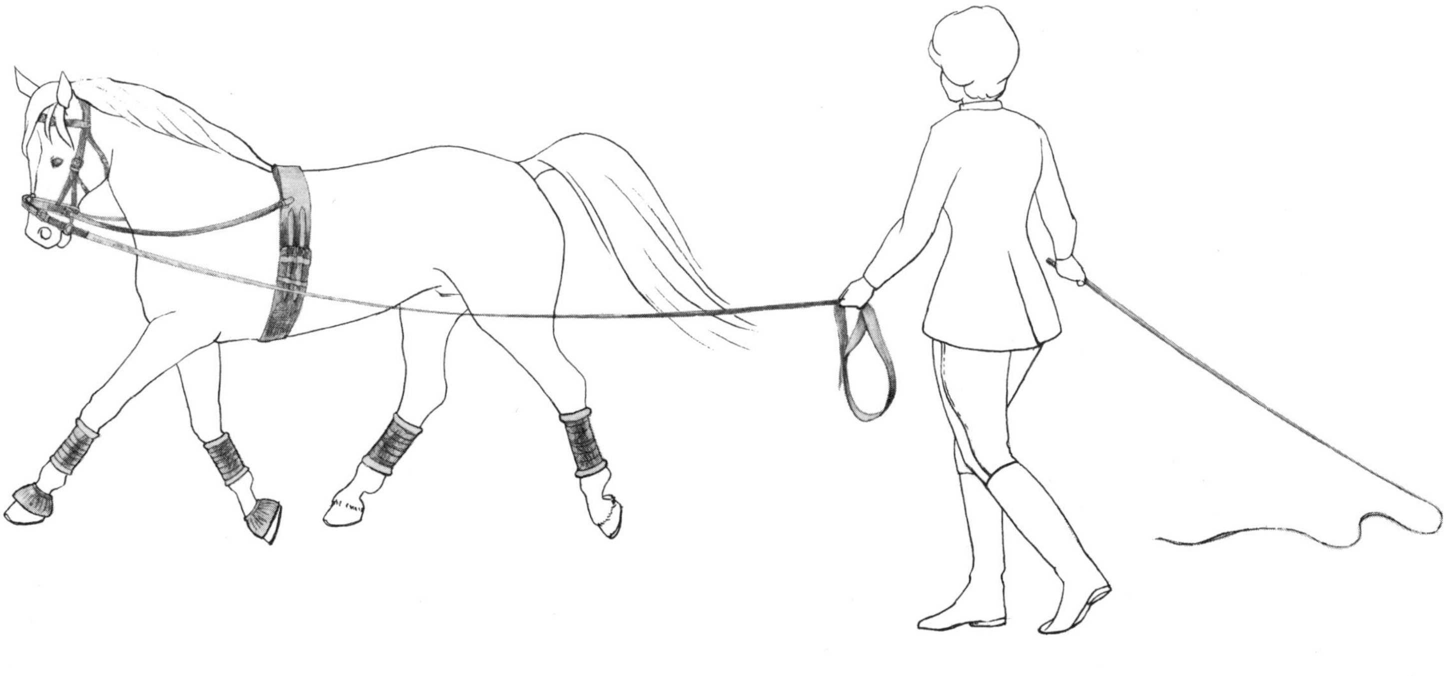

Although the wild Tarpan was domesticated by the peasants, its flesh was regarded as a delicacy and it was hunted almost to extinction. Count Zamojski, one of the great eighteenth-century Polish landowners, founded a reserve; the Bialystock forest later became another. Some of the Bialystock Tarpans came from the Zamojski herd and some from eastern European peasants *c.* 1870 when the last known wild Tarpan died in Munich Zoo.

Today there are two flourishing wild herds in the forest of Popiellen (Polish Popiellno) and a domestic herd at the research station on the edge of the Sperding Lake in East Prussia (Masuria). Research has shown that the Tarpan never aborts, never catches cold or coughs, and if injured the wounds heal without attention. They are extraordinarily hardy. Although many interesting facts about the structure of the hair, hoofs, etc. of the Popiellno domesticated Tarpan have been discovered which could help horse breeders, the West has shown little interest.

The colour generally ranges between mouse-dun and brown-dun with dorsal stripe. There are zebra marks on the legs and sometimes stripes across the body. The coat has a wiry texture like that of the deer. Some Tarpan become lighter, almost white, in winter. Because of the dun hereditary factor, the descendants of the Tarpan (KONIK, PANJE PONY, HUÇUL, LOFOTEN PONY etc.) may be all colours except grey. The domesticated Tarpan at Popiellno are used for light agricultural work. DMG

Tennessee Walking Horse. Stallion Midnight Sun, World's Grand Champion 1945–46

Tartar Pony see Mongolia

Tchenaran
A breed developed in the eastern part of Iran, chiefly in the province of Khorassan. This breed is formed by crossing a PLATEAU PERSIAN stallion with a TURKOMAN mare. The result is a tall horse (over 15 hands or 1·52 m) with breedy, elegant head, moderately arched neck, good withers and shoulders and strong quarters. The first records of breeding for the Tchenaran are from the time of Nader Shah in the eighteenth century and this breed was until very recently popular as a most able cavalry horse and favourite of officers. The Tchenaran is a breed in the sense that the ANGLO-ARAB is a breed, requiring that each time a Plateau Persian and a Turkoman be crossed. Crossing a Turkoman stallion on a Plateau Persian mare does not achieve the same fine results as the opposite cross. LF

Team Roping see Rodeo

Teeth see Ageing

Temperature see T.P.R.

Tendons, Sprains of see Sprains

Tennessee Walking Horse
This American breed of riding horse is of mixed origin, including STANDARDBRED, American SADDLEBRED, MORGAN, THOROUGHBRED, Canadian and NARRAGANSETT PACER blood, developed as a comfortable means of transportation by early Tennessee plantation owners who spent long hours in the saddle surveying their crops. They have been called Tennessee Walkers, Tennessee Plantation Horses, just plain 'Walkers' or, more familiarly, 'Turn-Row' horses, because of their handiness in turning in plantation rows without injuring young plants. Their most distinctive feature is an almost inbred four-beat gait called the 'running walk', in which the front foot strikes the ground just before the opposite diagonal hind foot. The hind foot oversteps the track of the front foot by 6–15 inches, and a speed of 6–9 miles per hour can be maintained. At top speed, the smooth gliding motion is accompanied by a nodding head, swinging ears, and clicking teeth. Walking Horse foals have performed this gait in pasture with their dams, but it has never been successfully taught to any other breed.

Larger-boned than the American Saddlebred, Tennessee Walkers are generally short-backed, deep-chested, and close-coupled, with a low head carriage and a serene disposition. Measuring 15–16 hands (1·52–1·65 m) (with Walking Ponies 14·2 hands or 1·47 m and under), and weighing 1,000–1,250 lb (450–567 kg), they are exceptionally long-lived, often attaining the age of 25 or 30. Originally they were rather plain-headed, with their beauty largely due to their striking gaits and colours. The sorrel, chestnut and yellow varieties often have flaxen or white mane and tails, and others bear extensive white markings. Previously breeding was mostly in the South but the founding in 1935 of the Tennessee Walking Horse Breeders' Association of America (Lewisburg, Tennessee) did much to spread the popularity of the breed, as a show horse rather than as a working farm horse. However, its population is still largely concentrated in the Southern, Middle Western and Western states. MAS

Tent Pegging see Mounted Games

Terrets Two rings attached to the upper panels of the harness saddle or pad through which the driving reins pass. See Driving Harness

Tersky
The Russian Tersky is a good, compact riding horse used in light agricultural work, military patrols, under saddle and in harness; it is particularly well adapted for sport. All the qualities of the Eastern breeds are well expressed, with beautiful movement combined with the hardiness of the horses of the native breeds, and it has been

widely used to improve other breeds in Azerbaidzhan, Armenia, Kazakhstan, and Tadzhikstan. It is very like the ARAB, with certain THOROUGHBRED, DON, and BUDYONNY qualities. There are three closely-related types: the characteristic type, the light/Eastern type, and the thickset. The first has a medium-sized head, usually with a straight profile, large eyes, and long, erect ears. The neck is long and set on fairly high. The withers are well-defined, the back medium long, the loins wide and solid, the croup wide and somewhat lowered, the tail set on high and held in the Arab manner. The shoulder is slanting, the ribs long and round, the bone below the knee fine and flat. Hoofs are of fine texture. Average height for stallions of the characteristic type is 15·0½ hands (1·53 m), for mares 14·3½ hands (1·51 m); bone below the knee for stallions 7¾ in (19·5 cm), for mares 7¼ in (18·7 cm). The light/Eastern type is closer to the Arab, with a very fine head, dished profile and convex forehead, large, wide-set eyes, and flaring nostrils. The neck is more delicate in this type than in the characteristic type, and the light/Eastern type is also more susceptible to tenderness of the back. The body is shorter and the legs even finer than those of the first type; the skin is delicate, the hair thin and silky. Average height for light stallions is 15 hands (1·52 m), for mares 14·3 hands (1·50 m); bone below the knee for stallions 7½ in (18·8 cm), for mares 7 in (18·3 cm). The third, thickset type is powerful, with a longer torso; it is less elegant, but has more bone. Average height for thickset stallions is 15·1 hands (1·55 m), for mares 14·3½ hands (1·51 m); bone below the knee for stallions is 7⅞ in (20 cm), for mares 7½ in (19 cm). Average height for the breed as a whole for stallions is 15·0¾ hands (1·54 m), for mares 14·3 hands (1·50 m); bone below the knee for stallions 7¾ in (19·5 cm), for mares 7¼ in (18·6 cm).

The movement is free, elastic, graceful, and light. The walk is fast and covers much ground; the trot is low, light, and 'floating'; the canter is very energetic and active.

The Tersky was first developed in the northern Caucasus, particularly in the Stavropolsky stud. It is one of the youngest Russian breeds, finally produced at the Tersky stud in 1925 when it was decided to breed a horse with the qualities of the Arab, a good steeplechaser that would keep condition well, with the hardiness and ability to do well in range conditions. The Tersky has the natural intelligence, gentle character, and sturdiness of the Arab; it is suitable for long-distance work and has covered 1,000 m (0·62 mile) in 1 min 9 sec, 3,000 m (1·86 mile) in 3 min 29 sec. The new breed was officially announced in 1948, having been developed from the STRELETS, ARAB, KABARDIN, and DON breeds, with some Hungarian horses of the GIDRAN type. WOF

Tetanus (Lockjaw)

A disease caused by an organism, *Clostridium tetani*, contracted through a wound, particularly if it is infected by pus-producing organisms. This distressing disease of the nervous system is characterized by the progressive development of muscular rigidity. In the advanced case the horse stands rigid with head and neck outstretched and tail extended. The limbs become fixed and abducted. Due to spasm of the muscles of mastication the jaws become locked and eating and drinking become impossible. An early and significant symptom is the protrusion of the third eyelid over the eye. Preventative measures consist of strict attention to all wounds, particularly those about the feet, and the administration of antitoxin. CF

Tetanus (Lockjaw). The afflicted horse stands rigid, with head and neck outstretched and tail extended. The protrusion of the third eyelid over the eye is characteristic.

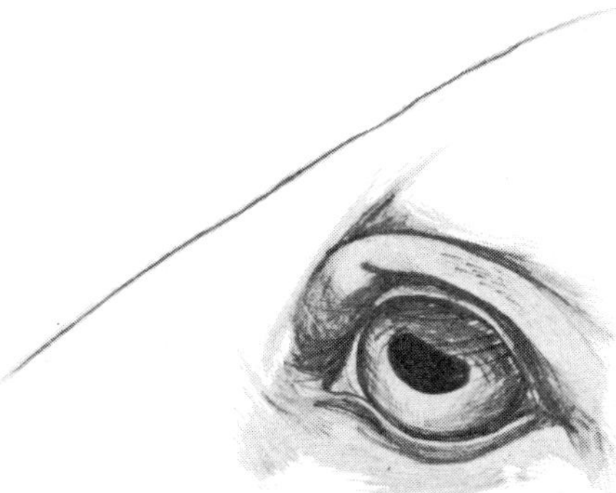

Normal eye

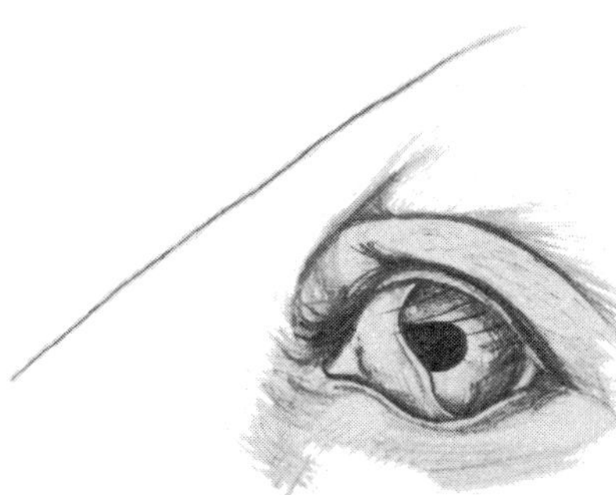

The eye in tetanus with protruding third eyelid

Theatre, Horse in

see Stage, Horse on the

Thessalian

see Greece

Thoropin

see Thoroughpin

Thoroughbred

Horseracing as a sport in Britain has a history dating back to Roman times at least. It probably originated in much earlier times. The Thoroughbred, the breed of horse now employed not only in Great Britain but also in about fifty other countries for racing purposes, has a history of no more than three hundred years. This breed, though of mixed origins, breeds true to type, is not susceptible to improvement by crosses with other breeds, and is noted for its speed, beauty and adaptability to a wide variety of climatic conditions. The modern British Thoroughbred is really the property of two countries, Great Britain and Ireland, whose breeding industries are closely linked and share a common stud book, the General Stud Book.

The animals used for racing in the early days of the sport were mainly GALLOWAYS, fast ponies bred in Scotland and the north of England, and HOBBIES, similar ponies bred in Ireland. Galloways formed the native British racing stock, and races confined to them were run as late as the end of the eighteenth century, though the term was then used to describe all racehorses measuring under 13 hands (1·32 m) rather than a distinct breed. By the first half of the seventeenth century the native stock had been heavily diluted by successive importations, principally from Italy and Spain, and as a result the stock from which the racehorses of early Stuart times were drawn was extremely heterogeneous. Breeding to type and for specific racing purposes had become virtually impossible.

The evolution of a distinct breed of racehorses received a fresh impetus after the Stuart Restoration of 1660, when there was a rapid expansion of racing under the leadership of King Charles II. Charles met the requirements of his racing stable by contracting with his 'Master of the Royal Stud', James D'Arcy, for the annual supply of 'twelve extraordinary good colts' from his stud at Sedbury in Bedale. It is not by chance that the Bedale region of Yorkshire became the cradle of the Thoroughbred.

The fundamental problem confronting D'Arcy and other breeders of Restoration times was how to create a fund of stock capable of breeding to type. Naturally they turned to the most genetically pure breed in the world, the ARABIAN, developed with meticulous care for many equine generations in the Middle East. During the hundred years after 1660 some 200 horses of Middle Eastern origin, of which about three-quarters were stallions and the rest were mares, were imported. Approximately half these horses were Arabians, and the rest were drawn from closely related breeds like Turks and Barbs from North Africa.

Evidence that the imported horses were intended to increase genetic homogeneity and not to increase speed is found in the fact that few ran in English races, although many were of racing age when they arrived in Great Britain. None of the three horses from whom all modern Thoroughbreds trace their descent in the direct male line is known to have raced, though one of them, the BYERLEY TURK, was said to have enabled his owner Colonel Byerley to escape capture at the Battle of the Boyne (1690) by outpacing his pursuers. The other two founding fathers of the Thoroughbred were the GODOLPHIN ARABIAN and the DARLEY ARABIAN. The Godolphin Arabian is believed to have been foaled at the Arabian stud of the Bey of Tunis in 1724. The Darley Arabian was the purest of the pure, as he was certified as being 'of the most esteemed race among the Arabs both by sire and dam, and the name of the race is called Manicha'. He was imported from Aleppo in 1704.

Although the Byerley Turk, the Godolphin Arabian and the Darley Arabian are the most famous of the imported Eastern stallions, they were not necessarily the most potent factors in the formation of the breed. An analysis of the pedigree of Bahram, the Triple Crown winner of 1935, showed that it contained many more crosses of the unnamed Arabian (sire of Old Bald Peg) and of D'Arcy's chestnut Arabian than of the founding fathers.

The origins of the foundation mares are obscured by the contemporary practice of calling mares 'Arabians', 'Turks', or 'Barbs' simply because they were by stallions of those breeds. Many of them may have sprung from pre-Restoration mixed British stock. The difficulties of identification are aggravated by the fact that the first volume of the General Stud Book was not published until 1791, when the pedigrees of some of the foundation mares could not be properly authenticated.

The first great racehorse was Flying Childers (1715). He was described as 'the fleetest horse that ever ran at Newmarket, or as generally believed, was ever bred in the world'. He was never beaten. If the General Stud Book version of his pedigree is accepted as correct, he traced to imported stock exclusively within six generations.

Flying Childers as a stallion had a considerable influence on the evolution of the breed, but it was his brother Bartlett's Childers, unable ever to race because he broke blood vessels, who founded an enduring male line. Flying and Bartlett's Childers were by the Darley Arabian. Bartlett's Childers was the great-grandsire of Eclipse (1764), the second great racehorse. A horse of tremendous vitality, character and commanding presence, Eclipse was never beaten in his 18 races, seven of which were walkovers. Eclipse transmitted his brilliant qualities to many of his progeny and, in combination with his contemporaries, Herod and Herod's son Highflyer, was the mainspring of the transition from the primitive to the modern Thoroughbred. When Herod (1758) and Eclipse were racing, racehorses were mostly mature animals carrying big weights over long distances, and many races were run in heats. By the time their grandchildren were racing, precocity, short distances and pure speed were in vogue; in the second decade of the nineteenth century two-year-old races were established and frequent features of racing programs, and the three-year-old Classic Races (the 2,000 Guineas, the 1,000 Guineas, the Derby, the Oaks and the St Leger) were the accepted criteria of excellence.

Thoroughbred. *Top:* St Simon, leading sire of the late nineteenth century, was never defeated. *Above:* Also unbeaten was Flying Childers, the first great racehorse (right).

In 1797 the 593 horses that ran on British courses included only 48 two-year-olds, or 8 per cent of the total, and 262 five-year-olds and upwards, or 44 per cent of the total. In 1860, 608, or 35 per cent of the 1,717 horses that ran, were two-year-olds and only 286, or 16 per cent, were five-year-olds and upwards. The 1860 proportions have remained practically constant down to the present day.

Thus a lasting balance of speed and precocity had been struck by the middle of the nineteenth century. Likewise selection for racing ability in favourable environmental conditions of feeding and climate had produced dramatic evolutionary changes in the Thoroughbred. At the same period Admiral Rous, the famous 'Dictator of the Turf', expressed the opinion that the worst horses of his own day were superior to the best horses of 1750. There is no reason to believe that Rous exaggerated. The Thoroughbreds of Rous's time averaged 16 hands (1·65 m) in height, about 6 in (15·24 cm) more than the racehorses of the early eighteenth century, and had achieved corresponding increases in length of stride and speed.

Improvement of the Thoroughbred has been much slower since Rous's day, though the influence of great racehorses and stallions like Stockwell and St Simon certainly had a beneficial effect on the breed in the second half of the nineteenth century. Some critics have asserted that the peak of Thoroughbred performance was reached early in the twentieth century and since then the utmost endeavours of breeders have been required to prevent retrogression. This theory implies that The Tetrarch, the invincibly fast horse foaled in 1911, was the model of Thoroughbred perfection. If further improvement has been achieved, it has been slow and attributable mainly to the crossing of bloodlines developed in widely separated areas, notably Europe and the United States, and the stimulus of growing international competition on the racecourse. The former exclusiveness of the General Stud Book has been modified in a realistic spirit in order to take account of this internationalization of the breed.

The greatest threats to the quality of the Thoroughbred in Great Britain and Ireland in the second half of the twentieth century were rapid expansion of the Thoroughbred population and an excessively high rate of export of the best breeding stock. Live Thoroughbred births in the two countries rose from 3,857 in 1945 to 6,361 in 1970, an increase of 67 per cent in a quarter of a century. This rate, though exceeded in some other Thoroughbred-producing countries, could be achieved only by the use of many inferior specimens of the breed for stud purposes.

Nevertheless there was no sign of the demand for British and Irish stock abating; this demand was sustained not only by the primary employment of Thoroughbreds for flat racing, but also by the widespread secondary uses of Thoroughbreds in steeplechasing, hunting, show-jumping, equine events and for the improvement of other breeds. See also Great Britain.

The Thoroughbred is a British creation, but horseracing based on the British model and Thoroughbred breeding have been adopted with enthusiasm in many other countries. The sport is practised in at least fifty countries, of which about ten have breeding industries capable of producing horses of international racing class. Some of these, notably that of the United States, have outgrown those of the homelands of the Thoroughbred, Great Britain and Ireland.

Many countries began to found breeding industries in the first half of the nineteenth century. Foreign breeders acknowledged the futility of trying to develop breeds of their own from native stock, and based their operations exclusively on stock imported from England. Stud-book difficulties arose later only in territories, distant from the homelands of the Thoroughbred, which had been colonized by the British. The colonies in North America, Australia and New Zealand all used some horses untraceable to General Stud Book stock in the early days, though most of those horses probably sprang from the same stock and merely lacked properly authenticated pedigrees. More stringent regulations to control entry to the G.S.B. were introduced as American horses of unauthenticated origin flooded into Europe during the first decade of the twentieth century, and stud-book exclusiveness, summed up by the so-called Jersey Act of

Thoroughbred. *Above:* Flat racing at Florida Downs, Tampa, Florida
Below: Donatello II, bred by Federico Tesio in Italy

1913, aroused bitter controversy until it was modified by the repeal of the Act in 1949. The conditions for entry were finally rationalized in Volume XXXVI of 1969 so as to combine a realistic approach to the problems of a breed transcending national frontiers with adequate safeguards for its purity.

The common ancestry of all Thoroughbreds does not preclude regional and national variations of type and aptitude which have been shaped by factors like soil and climate and, above all, by patterns of racing which differ from country to country. These patterns influence selection and have caused subtle but perceptible shifts in the balance of precocity and later maturity, speed and stamina.

Russia, Germany, Argentine, Brazil, South Africa, Australia, New Zealand and Hungary have all produced horses of world class from time to time, and expansion of the breeding industry in Japan proceeded at a rate unequalled elsewhere during the 1960s. However, apart from the homelands, North America, France and Italy have made the greatest contributions to Thoroughbred progress, and the distinctive features of the Thoroughbreds of those countries require some elucidation.

United States and Canada: the English colonies in North America were the first overseas territories to which horseracing on the English model was transplanted, and there was regular racing there before the end of the seventeenth century. The American Civil War (1861–65) formed a watershed in the evolution of the American Thoroughbred. Before it, races were mostly tests of endurance for mature horses; after it, there was a rapid transition to short races on oval dirt tracks about a mile in circumference, and speed and precocity were cultivated even more intensively than in Great Britain. The KENTUCKY DERBY, the premier American Classic race, is run over $1\frac{1}{4}$ miles (2·01 km) compared with the $1\frac{1}{2}$ miles (2·41 km) of the Epsom Derby, and rich rewards for two-year-old prowess are accompanied by a dearth of races for older horses at distances longer than a mile.

The modern American racing and breeding industry is far the largest in the world, and American breeders have invested heavily in the best stock wherever it has been available. Since the outbreak of World War II the importation of top-class stallions like Princequillo, Mahmoud, Blenheim, Nasrullah and Ribot, and of mares of similar class, has been combined with selection based on pure speed and the rigorous application of the racecourse test to raise Thobred standards in the United States and adjacent Canada to unprecedented heights.

As to quantity, production of Thoroughbred foals in the United States was more than 23,000 in 1968; the quality of American bloodstock is attested by the fact that between 1968 and 1972 four (Sir Ivor, Nijinsky, Mill Reef and Roberto) of the five Epsom Derby winners were bred on the North American continent.

France: France was the first country to produce Thoroughbreds capable of challenging British Thoroughbreds successfully on their own ground. The French filly Fille de l'Air became the first foreign-bred winner of a British Classic race when she won the Oaks in 1864, and the next year the French colt Gladiateur won the British Triple Crown of the Two Thousand Guineas, the Derby and the St Leger. Since then superiority at the Classic level has oscillated between Great Britain and Ireland on the one hand and France on the other. There was a period of French supremacy after World War II when French-bred horses won 15 British Classic Races in 11 years. In the 1960s there was a gradual swing towards parity, but the equilibrium is always unstable.

France has in Normandy a region which, with its temperate climate and lush pastures, is ideal for Thoroughbred production. The French Thoroughbred tends to develop more slowly, possess less precocious speed and more stamina than the Thoroughbreds of Great Britain and North America. For many years the Grand Prix de Paris, for three-year-olds over 1 mile 7 furlongs (3000 m) at first and latterly over 1 mile $7\frac{1}{2}$ furlongs (3100 m), was the supreme test of the Thoroughbred in France, and it still occupies an essential place in the French pattern along with the French Derby (Prix du Jockey Club) and the Prix de l'Arc de Triomphe (for three-year-olds and upwards), both over $1\frac{1}{2}$ miles (2400 m).

The French pattern makes meagre provision for two-year-olds in the first half of the season and for sprinters at ages above two, but gives the strongest incentives to prowess over middle distances of $1\frac{1}{4}$–2 miles (2000–3200 m) at three years of age and upwards. Although the French breeding industry has only about half the annual production of the joint industries of Great Britain and Ireland, it has achieved disproportionate success at the Classic level for more than a century.

Italy: the development of an internationally competitive Thoroughbred industry in Italy was due largely to the efforts of one man, Federico Tesio, who built up his stud on the shores of Lake Maggiore in the first half of the twentieth century. Using as his raw materials mares purchased cheaply in England, Tesio proved himself a genius in the selection and mating of Thoroughbreds. Although the Italian industry in his day was producing only a few hundred foals annually, Tesio bred world-class horses like Nearco, Donatello II and Ribot, whose influence as stallions spread around the world. In 1966 Tesio's successors at Dormello were able to claim that nearly two-thirds of the

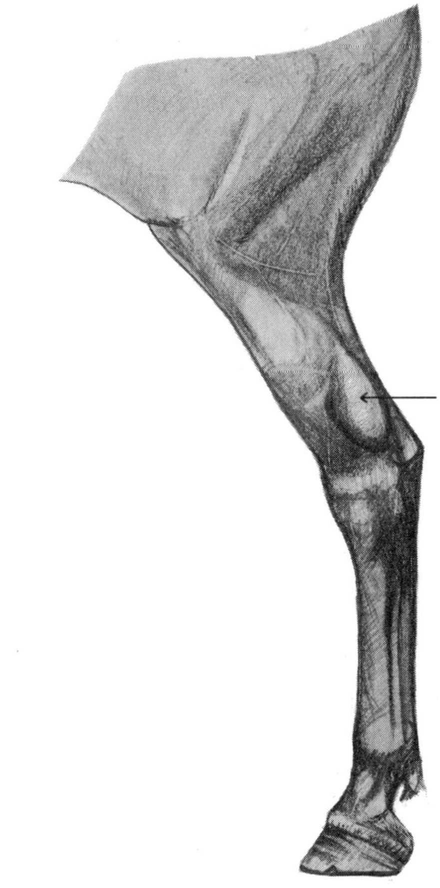

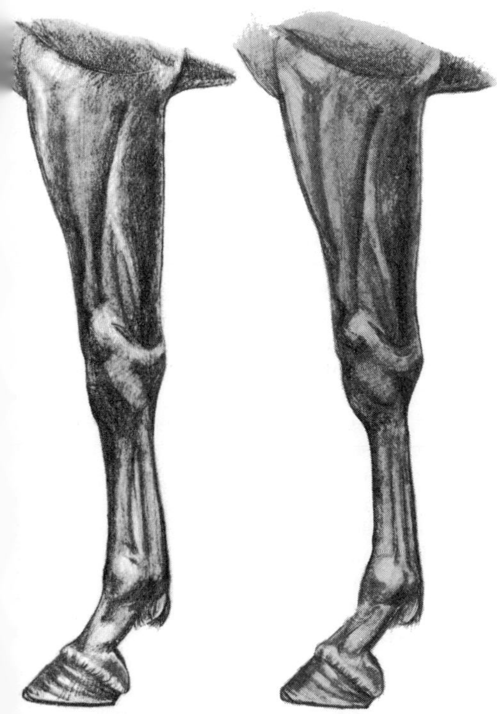

Top: **Thoroughpin**

Above: **Tied in at the Knee.** *Left:* Normal fore leg. *Right:* Fore leg tied in at the knee

Right: **Timor**

important winners in Great Britain and Ireland and more than a third of the important winners in North America that year carried Dormello blood. See also Flat Racing. PW

Thoroughpin, Articular
A chronic distension of the capsule of the true hock joint presented at its postero-lateral aspect. It usually co-exists with BOG SPAVIN. CF

Thoroughpin, Tendinous
A chronic distension of the sheath which surrounds the perforans tendon as it passes through the tarsal arch. It is recognized by a fluctuating swelling on either side of the tendon just above the point of the hock. CF

Three-Day Event see Combined Training, Horse Trials

Three-Gaited American Saddlebred Horse see Gaited Horses, Saddlebred

Thrombosis
Thrombosis of the iliac arteries is well known in the horse and produces a peculiar train of symptoms during fast work. A diminution of the blood supply to the muscles produces a progressive weakness and collapse of the hind legs. The horse sinks to the ground but after a time it recovers and is able to walk or trot. CF

Tibetan Kiang see Ass, Wild Asiatic

Tibetan Pony see Nepal, China

Tied in at the Knee
An evident constriction of the tissues below and at the back of the knee. CF

Timor
There seems to be a parallelism in diminution between the Indonesian anoa, the world's smallest buffalo, an inhabitant of the Celebes mountains, and the small, almost dwarf, pony of Timor: both are only just over 3 ft (about 1 m) in height. The small tough ponies are used in bitless bridles by

native 'cowboys' to round up cattle. The rider's feet often touch the ground. See also Indonesia. DMG

Tobiano see Colours and Markings

Tongue Swallowing
Tongue swallowing ('gurgling' or 'choking up') is a syndrome fairly frequently encountered in the racehorse while racing. All three terms may be consistent with some partial pharyngeal or laryngeal obstruction, causing the horse to fail towards the end of a race. For some years it has been thought to be connected with an abnormally long or flaccid soft palate. CF

Tor di Quinto
The Tor di Quinto, situated just outside Rome, is often erroneously believed to be an autonomous Italian cavalry school but is actually an adjunct of, and has always been dependent on, PINEROLO. Founded by a civilian, Marchese Luciano Roccagiovine, M.F.H. of the Roman Foxhounds, it was instituted as a training-ground to which officers of the parent school went for their final examinations. These took place annually every spring, attended by the King, military staff and foreign dignitaries. The course, designed to teach men to cross a country with speed and precision, consisted of gates precariously placed, broad banks, great walls and the famous *schivalone* (slide)—a perpendicular drop of 18 ft (5·5 m). Like Pinerolo, Tor di Quinto was open to foreign officers. Between 1900 and World War II, 70 officers representing 33 nations took advantage of this, among them five Englishmen and six Americans.

Both Tor di Quinto and Pinerolo were motorized in 1945, the stables of both being turned into equestrian museums. LFB

Toric (Torisky)
The Toric is a Russian farm work horse with great endurance and weight-carrying ability, calm character and good adaptability. It is also used in sport and for cavalry work. There are two types, the light and the heavy. Both share certain qualities. The torso is long with relatively short legs. The chest cage is long and tight, the croup large and longer than it is wide, sometimes bifurcated. The head is medium large, with a wide forehead, medium-sized, erect ears, large lively eyes and wide nostrils. The neck is medium long and muscular; the withers are wide but not high. The back is straight, short, and with strong loins. The legs are hard, with robust joints and flat bone. Hoofs are medium large, and of fine texture. Careful selection has virtually eliminated flaws of the legs. Chestnut is the prevailing colour. Average height for heavy stallions is $15{\cdot}0\frac{3}{4}$ hands (1·54 m), heavy mares $15{\cdot}0\frac{1}{2}$ hands (1·53 m), light stallions $15{\cdot}0\frac{3}{4}$ hands (1·54 m), light mares $15{\cdot}0\frac{1}{2}$ hands (1·53 m); bone below

the knee for heavy stallions 8$\frac{3}{4}$ in (22·4 cm), heavy mares 8$\frac{1}{2}$ in (21·5 cm), light stallions 8 in (20·6 cm), light mares 7$\frac{3}{4}$ in (20·0 cm).

Systematic selection of horses with regular movement has resulted in a breed with a good, even walk and trot, a free gallop, and the ability to jump well.

The Toric was developed at the Tori stud in Estonia from the local KLEPPER, which was a small (13·01–14·01 hands or 1·36–1·46 m) but very sturdy horse with fast movement and good endurance. In the nineteenth century, ARAB, ARDENNES, English THOROUGHBRED and other breeds were used to make the Klepper larger and stronger. In 1888 the ORLOV TROTTER Iantar' was brought from Russia and widely used in Estonia; more Orlov stallions were brought later. The Polish stallion Khetman, a horse with short legs, deep chest, long torso, long and powerful shoulders, and a long, slanting croup produced a very strong influence. In 1908–12 East Prussian stallions were introduced, as well as HANOVERIAN and EAST FRIESIAN horses. The aboriginal Estonian was then reintroduced, but too much inbreeding from the stock of Khetman led to certain faults, primarily sickle hocks and insufficient musculature of the thigh and croup. WOF

Toric (Torisky)

Toronto Royal Winter Fair

The host of one of the finest horse shows on the North American continent, the Royal Winter Fair entered its fiftieth year in 1972. Although it is primarily an agricultural show, the main attraction for many people is certainly the horse show: it has gained the reputation of 'the show place of champions', and, although there are perhaps fewer exhibitors than in a European show of similar stature, the competitors in each division are of high quality.

For the International Jumping Events the 7,000-seat coliseum is filled to capacity every evening. Teams from Belgium, France, Czechoslovakia, Germany, Great Britain, Ireland, Holland, Hungary, Sweden, Chile, Cuba, Argentina, Peru, Mexico, Brazil, Australia and the United States have been represented in these competitions.

Rigid eligibility requirements and limited stabling facilities have kept the number of divisions and classes therein to a minimum: Jumper and Hunter (both working and conformation) have the largest number of entries. Other divisions include harness classes, draught horses and breed classes. There are also dressage tests.

The Royal Winter Fair has enjoyed royal patronage ever since its inception; the official visit of a representative of the reigning monarch is always a highlight of the horse show. Tradition plays a major role: full evening dress is customary for the occupants of the box seats. ML

Tote, The

This alternative to betting with bookmakers was originally known in Britain as the Racecourse Betting Control Board, and now as the Horserace Totalisator Board. It was brought into being by Act of Parliament in 1928, but did not start until the following year. The Tote was designed to make money available for the benefit of racing. It is thus not intended to make profits for itself and any credit balance, after all costs have been deducted, is ploughed back into racing. It pays successful backers a dividend worked out on the basis of dividing the total pool betted (after a deduction for costs etc.) among the number of winning tickets. Unlike when betting with a bookmaker, a backer does not know how much he has won until a dividend is announced. By 1938 the Tote's turnover had reached £9m and after World War II continued more or less permanently upwards to £37m in 1965. In 1966 it started its jackpot, a pool which requires backers to name the first six winners in a day's racing with the prospect of a huge dividend. This proved an instant success but since then its fortunes and finances have slumped. GE

Tournaments see Chivalry

T.P.R.

T.P.R. is an abbreviation for the temperature, pulse and respiration of the horse and is generally associated with endurance riding or competitive trail riding (see Long-Distance Riding).

At an endurance ride or competitive trail ride the pulse and respiration of each horse are taken while at rest, to be compared during the ride with the pulse and respiration while under stress conditions, such as the top of a long climb and after long distances. The recovery rate is usually considered most important.

The average 'at rest' pulse is 32–40 heart beats per minute and the average respiration is 6–12 breaths per minute. After a fast 40-mile ride it is not considered unusual to have a pulse and respiration over 100, but the pulse must return to 70 beats per minute or less within 30 minutes or the horse will be disqualified from the competition.

The temperature is no longer taken on most rides because the number of horses involved in endurance riding makes the time factor prohibitive. The average 'at rest' temperature of the horse is 99·6°–100·6°F. (37·5°–38·1°C.) and it is not uncommon for hotblooded horses to have a temperature of 105°F. (40·6°C.) while under stress, particularly in hot weather.

T.P.R.s are also used by many experienced horsemen to check the day-to-day condition and health of their horses, since a rise in pulse and/or respiration is an early and easily observed indication of possible illness. LTJ

Trail Riding see Long-Distance Riding

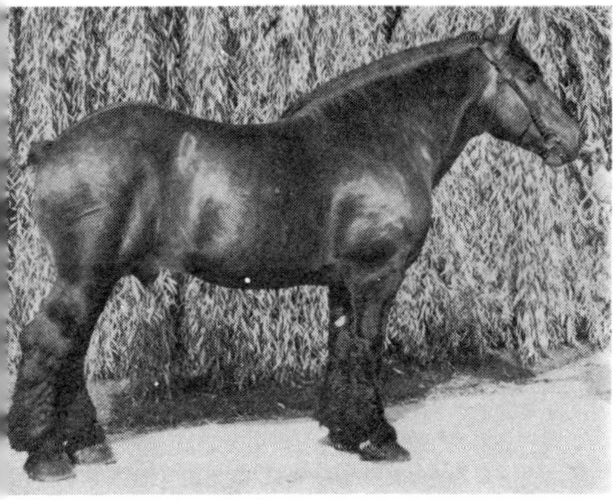

Trait du Nord. A champion stallion

Trait du Nord

Derived from the ARDENNAIS, the French Northern Draught Horse was developed in the nineteenth century. It shares with the Ardennais a breeding zone between the Boulonnais (north) and Ardennais (south) and similar characteristics in physique (compactness of frame and muscles) and spirit (gentleness and docility). Infusions of Belgian and Dutch blood and a rich alluvial soil have given it a larger size (16 hands or 1·65 m) and weight (1 ton). The stud book was opened in 1919 and remains open to permit the reconstitution of the breed which was decimated during World War II. Its coat is bay, roan, strawberry roan or chestnut. ES

Trakehner

The Trakehner (East Prussian) horse belongs to one of the oldest established warmblood breeds in Germany. The Trakehnen stud in East Prussia, now under Soviet rule, was founded by Frederick William I, father of Frederick the Great, in 1732, to provide horses and revenue for the royal stables. The breed is partly based on the native *Schweiken*, a hardy, active little horse, used in agriculture in East Prussia since the knights of the Teutonic Order colonized the province in the thirteenth century. Later on, both Oriental and THOROUGHBRED stallions were imported. Bagdadly, Turkman Atty and Nejed (discovered pulling a cab in London) influenced the breed, as did Persimmon's son Perfectionist, born in England in 1899. Though only three years at stud, he left 131 foals, of which 32 became stallions and 37 brood mares. Three or four of his sons produced 156 stallions and 293 brood mares, all of which were entered in the Stud Book. Trakehnen was to this warmblood breed what Newmarket is today to the Thoroughbred. The stud covered 34,000 acres and 20 premium stallions and 400 brood mares grazed its pastures. The herds of mares were divided according to colours: chestnut; bay/brown; mixed; and black, which were the heaviest. In 1939, there were 25,000 registered brood mares in the hands of some 15,000 breeders, for every estate, farm and smallholding bred horses in this 'paradise for horses' (see Masuren).

Five times during the course of its history the stud was evacuated: in 1812 before Napoleon's armies, in 1914 for the fourth and in 1945 for the last time. Only a small bunch of Trakehner stallions driven by an old groom and two boys reached the West at the end of the war-torn winter of 1945. Seven hundred mares, mostly in-foal, struggled through the ice and snow pulling wagons loaded with refugees, and crossed the Elbe into western Germany. From this small nucleus, the Trakehner survived, was built up and is now exported to North and South America and elsewhere. Trakehner horses are known today as saddle horses of elegance, courage and stamina. Their gentle, reliable temperament makes them particularly suitable for dressage and for show jumping. The stallions are used by a number of European and New World horse breeders to improve their native breeds, Sweden being particularly successful with the famous Swedish warmblood (see Swedish Halfbred). There are many studs in the German Federal Republic including the private stud at Schmoel, and the Trakehner Society's stud at Rantzau in Schleswig-Holstein (see colour plate, page 22). DMG

Reference: D. Machin Goodall, *Die Pferde mit der Elchschaufel,* Berlin, 1966, translated as *Flight of the East Prussian Horses,* Newton Abbot, 1972; *Horses of the World,* London, 1965.

Transportation

Horses have been transported for centuries by ship, but on land travelled mostly on their own four feet until in 1836 Lord George Bentinck devised a vehicle drawn by six carriage horses to take his Thoroughbred Elis from Goodwood to win the St Leger at Doncaster, a journey which took five days instead of the usual two weeks. Since then horses have travelled by increasingly sophisticated means: by road in large air-conditioned horseboxes, by rail in comfortable streamlined wagons specially designed for fast journeys, and by sea in specially constructed but uncomfortable wooden boxes, usually lashed to the deck where they are subject to the full force of wind and weather.

Horses now travel by air, often daily, all over the world. They may be going to race meetings, international shows, bloodstock sales, polo tournaments, or visiting a stallion. They may be worth anything from a few pounds to many millions but all of them are treated in exactly the same way, flying in specially-built enclosed boxes at the same speed as a human passenger.

When horses were first carried by air, they walked up a short ramp into, say, a B170 Bristol normally used for carrying cars or freight; stalls were fixed in pairs down the body of the aircraft. Though the aircraft were noisy by today's standards the horses were unconcerned by the shaking and rattling and travelled without trouble. The low-slung Ambassador or Elizabethan type of aircraft taking eight horses was superseded by the DC4 and DC7 taking 10 or 12 horses. These were higher and the horses had to walk up a long ramp, often rather shaky and uninviting. Occasionally in places where there are no ramps or lifts the horses have to walk down the passenger steps!

A Boeing 707 or Douglas DC8 aircraft can carry 20–30 horses, travelling in strongly-built triple stalls. The front is enclosed but allows the horse to reach a haynet and gives the groom access to the horse in order to calm it during take-off and landing or turbulence. The pilots usually try to make allowance for their cargo, taking off from the runway at a less steep angle than they would for a passenger flight.

The modern loading operation is fascinating to watch. The interior floor of the aircraft is 'palletized' (on rollers). The triple stalls, which are padded for safety and have peat-moss bedding, are pushed along a line of 'dolleys' (trolleys) to a loading ramp where the horse enters the stall. Then the stalls with their horses are rolled onto a scissor lift, which raises them to the level of the aircraft, and are pushed along the body of the aircraft to the required position where they are locked in place by clips. By using this method it is possible to load 27 horses in 45 minutes. Unfortunately, however, veterinary requirements and general customs handling in some countries may make the unloading take longer than the journey. MB

Trappers, Trappings see Accoutrements

Trekking see Pony Trekking

Trick Riding see Vaulting, Circus

Trimming

Trimming is best left to the expert as a badly trimmed mane and tail can look very unsightly.

Mane: start thinning at the head and work downward. Pull the underneath hairs. This is a slow job as single hairs only should be pulled. Twisting the hair round the finger is apt to make it sore; a mane comb can be used. Pull out the hairs to an even length, following the slope of the neck.

Tail: a long, bushy tail makes a small pony look overweighted. Brush the tail out thoroughly and then damp, using a water brush. Pull out the underneath hairs evenly on both sides, working from the top of the dock downwards as far as the end of the tail bone. Pull out only a few hairs at a time at each grooming, to avoid making the tail sore. Never cut the hair with scissors as this makes it grow bristly. Put on a tail bandage at night or after grooming to keep the tail in shape. It should be bandaged from the top of the dock to the end of the tail bone. Do not leave the bandage on for more than about three hours. Never wet it because it will shrink, stop the circulation and cause pain; it can also cause white hairs. A tail can either be *banged* (cut level) at the end, or left as a *swish tail,* which goes to a point. It should gradually narrow to the end of the tail bone and then bush out to the end.

Heels: if a horse has rather thick legs, trimming the hairs (feathers) at the fetlocks helps to make them look thinner. Fell ponies and other British native breeds which have feathers at the fetlocks should not have them removed; nor should Arabs. GW

Triple Crown

The British 'Triple Crown' signifies the three CLASSIC RACES in which colts are entitled to run: the Two Thousand Guineas, the Derby and the St Leger. Although the Crown is purely imaginary and brings no tangible reward to the winner apart from the large prizes awarded for victory in each of the three races, its prestige is immense, for a three-year-old colt capable of beating the best of his age in three races over progressively increasing distances on totally different courses during a period of five months represents the ideal at which the breeder of Thoroughbreds is constantly aiming.

Twelve horses have won the Triple Crown in the proper sense of the term. They are West Australian (1853), Gladiateur (1865), Lord Lyon (1866), Ormonde (1886), Common (1891), Isinglass (1893), Galtee More (1897), Flying Fox (1899), Diamond Jubilee (1900), Rock Sand (1903), Bahram (1935) and Nijinsky (1970). The title of Triple Crown winner is also usually conferred on Pommern (1915), Gay Crusader (1917) and Gainsborough (1918) although they gained their victories in substitute races run at Newmarket during World War I. For the American 'Triple Crown' see Flat Racing. PW

Trotting Racing (Harness Racing)

Trotting racing is an equestrian sport in which horses drawing light gigs or sulkies compete at the trot. Distinction is made between the true trotter, which is diagonally-gaited, and the pacer, which is laterally-gaited (see Gaits). In addition to the light harness needed to draw the sulky, many trotters wear also a head-check, and leg-harness or hobbles, designed to discourage the horse from breaking into a gallop. Special races are sometimes held for ridden horses, trotting 'under saddle', and for these also, restrictive harness such as check and hobbles is usual.

By the middle of the eighteenth century most of the European countries, and the United States, had turned their attention to the production of trotting horses as a specialized breed. In all these attempts the English Thoroughbred played a significant part. In Russia, Count Orlov was at this time producing the famous ORLOV TROTTERS, and these also were later reinforced with English Thoroughbred blood.

In Britain the Norfolk Trotter emerged as the product of local mares and selected stallions descended from the Darley Arabian. One of the resultant foals was Bellfounder, who in turn sired Messenger, the most famous and influential of all trotting sires. After an historic period at stud in this country, he was exported to the United States about 1790, and became the ancestor whose bloodline recurs in virtually every present-day American trotter. English Thoroughbreds, and their progeny Norfolk

Trotting Racing. Ethan Allen and a running mate, in double harness, and Dexter competing in a match for $2000, run over the Fashion Course, Long Island, in 1867; lithograph by Currier and Ives; Yale University Art Gallery, The Mabel Brady Garvan Collection.

Trotters, were also in great demand for crossing purposes in France, the Netherlands, and other European countries.

Towards the end of the following century, the National Association of Trotting Horse Breeders of America laid down a standard of requirements for this type of horse. The standard was based broadly upon the stallion Hambletonian, a lineal descendant of Messenger. The breed became known as the STANDARDBRED. In America, particularly in the South, the breeding, training, and racing of these horses is a major enterprise (see U.S.A.). Despite the prominent part played by English bloodstock in the production of trotting horses both on the Continent and in the New World, the sport did not attain in Britain the national popularity accorded to it elsewhere. Until about 1965, interest in trotting racing as a sport was limited almost exclusively to the six northernmost counties of England and the Scottish Lowlands. Apart from one permanent track at Belle Vue, Manchester, all race meetings were held on grass tracks, the governing body being the Eden Valley Trotting Association, based on Appleby, in Westmorland.

During recent years there have, however, been encouraging signs that trotting is about to take its proper place in Britain. Permanent tracks have been laid down at Prestatyn in North Wales, as well as in the Glasgow, Stirling, and Edinburgh districts of Scotland. Towards the end of the 1971 season a further permanent track opened at Kendal, in Westmorland. The sport has benefited much by the formation recently of the National Harness Racing Club, to which the Eden Valley Trotting Association is affiliated. JKH

Turkey

Few peoples depended more on their horses than the early Turks who roamed the vast horizons of Asia. However, since Turkey has resounded to the hoofbeats of horses bred by the Mittani Hittites, Mongols, Egyptians, Turks, Persians, Greeks, Arabs, etc., the confusion as to what constitutes the 'Turkish horse' is understandable.

The early TURKOMAN horse was identified with the Mongolian horse of Upper Asia (straight or roman nose, ewe neck, rather coarse and common). The AKHAL TEKE, one of the ancient Turkoman breeds, was handsome and much esteemed. However, there appears to be no true Turkish breed.

After A.D. 552 the Turks held sway over all the central Asiatic tribes for about a century. Then the Seljuk Turks conquered Persia and Asia Minor. The Ottoman Turks appeared during the late 1200s, at which time the 'Terrible Turks' became renowned for every equestrian skill. Some Turkoman tribes eventually bred high-caste Arabians. European travellers in the sixteenth, seventeenth and eighteenth centuries mentioned that Turkoman horses were larger than pure Arabians, and had a longer stride. They were generally longer and narrower, bony, horses with long necks and had ugly heads and bad temperaments.

The Turkish horse of Ottoman times, considered to be a mixture of Persian, Arab, Barb and other Oriental breeds, stood 15–16 hands (1·52–1·65 m) high, and was somewhat similar to the modern Thoroughbred. The Ottoman author, Evliya Calebi, described it as very beautiful in appearance, with a short body, long limbs, strong bones, and well-jointed pasterns. Long necks and well-set small heads, short ears and 'apple eyes' were favoured, as were long, flowing manes and tails. Black was a desirable colour and horses spotted with white were also popular.

Many horses taken as spoils of war were not actually Turks. Many captured during battles, or while passing through Turkey via oriental trade routes, acquired their names from the country where they were seized. Most of them were in fact high-quality Arabs. The BYERLEY TURK is credited with bringing the name Turk into prominence, though he was said to be a pure Arab. Zilcaadi, an Arabian from Asiatic Turkey, sired the dam of Gold Dust, the founder of the Gold Dust family of MORGAN trotters. Numerous Turks were very influential in foundation THOROUGHBRED breeding. However, no common Turkoman or halfbred could have been sufficiently prepotent to produce the Thoroughbred horse.

By the sixteenth century the Turkish army was reportedly the largest in the world, and the best mounted. The Empire was divided into various districts, each one being responsible for breeding certain kinds of horses and a required number. Eleven groups were bred, among them warhorses, racehorses, messenger horses, draught horses, ceremonial horses and hunting horses.

Since almost the entire Arabic-speaking world was under Ottoman influence from 1517 to 1915, the Turks acquired superb Arabian horses. But the Empire eventually crumbled, and the breeding programs with it. When the Young Turks established the Republic of Turkey the new Ministry of

U

Agriculture worked in earnest to rehabilitate Turkey's equine population. New programs were formulated for importing and breeding purebred Arabian horses as well as English Thoroughbreds, imported from Europe. To upgrade the local native stock and produce *yarimkans* (halfbreds), the Hungarian NONIUS was also introduced. A general stud book was established for purebreds and seven modern studs were reconstructed or newly erected for horse-breeding purposes.
Today as in the past 'native' Turkish horses are found across the land, products of crosses between Arabians and various other horses. The most valuable horses are Arabian, and of late the English Thoroughbred has also come to the fore on the racing scene. Arabian and Thoroughbred racing flourishes at the major tracks of Istanbul, Ankara and Izmir. JEF
Reference: Judith E. Forbis, *Hoofbeats Along the Tigris*, London, 1971; 'The Arabian Horse in Egypt from Antiquity to Present Day', *Pony*, London, 1968; 'Pearls of Great Price', *Arabian Horse World*, 1971.

Turkoman (Turkmen)

Of the Turkoman, raised on the Turkoman Steppes in northern Iran adjacent to the U.S.S.R., two races are recognized: the AKHAL TEKE and the Yomud (IOMUD). The Akhal Teke, bred primarily across the border in the U.S.S.R., is taller than the Iomud, with longer ears, absence of mane, thin tail, smaller hoof and finer skin. It is said to be a more elegant animal with smaller head, bigger eye and usually of a golden colour. The Iomud, on the other hand, is a slightly smaller (14·3–15·2 hands or 1·50–1·57 m) and coarser animal bred primarily for the long-distance raids that used to be a prominent feature of Turkoman life. Thus, while the Akhal Teke is faster over the short distances of today's race tracks, the Iomud has incredible stamina which will carry it one hundred kilometres to the hapless village to be plundered and one hundred kilometres back, no doubt pursued for as long as possible by irate villagers. The Kirghiz Turkomans who breed the Iomud claim that records for their horses go back 400 years to horses left behind by raiding Mongols. There is evidence, however, that a horse of similar type was bred by the SCYTHIANS in the first cencentury A.D., as indicated by the two classes of horses found in the PAZYRYK burial mounds in the Altai mountains, and it is known that the Baghdad Caliphs' guards were mounted exclusively on Turkomans from the eighth to the tenth centuries A.D.

Turkomans are kept in a fit, tight condition by wearing from four to seven felt blankets the year around and by being fed rations low in bulk and high in protein. Conditioning for racing is done by mixing butter and eggs with barley and feeding *quatlame*, bread dough fried in butter. Colours are grey, bay, chestnut and dun. See also Turkey and page 17. LF

Turn-Row Horse see Tennessee Walking Horse

Tushinsky see Horse Breeding under U.S.S.R.

Tuvinsky see Horse Breeding under U.S.S.R.

Two Tracks see Movements

U.S.A.

The horse has played a vital and immensely varied role in the United States of America. As a warrior, it helped to conquer the New World, then to win independence from the British in 1776; it fought valiantly in the Civil War that divided the young nation less than a century later. As a means of transport, it helped the pioneers to explore and colonize the continent from the Atlantic to the Pacific Oceans; under saddle or pulling a wide range of vehicles, it carried Americans to their destinations through city streets, over country roads, mountain trails, and the untracked desert leading to the Far West. It delivered mail (see Pony Express) as well as provisions of every kind. As a farm and ranch worker, it helped to develop some of the richest farmlands in the world and to raise some of the finest cattle. As a civil servant, it aided urban police forces as well as prairie sheriffs and the U.S. Cavalry to maintain law and order. Sometimes the same horses that had been pulling out tree stumps or rounding up cattle would spend their off-duty hours providing sport and pleasure. At the same time, horses were bred and trained exclusively for sporting purposes: foxhunting, harness, steeplechase, trotting and flat racing, as well as for pleasure riding.

Throughout the years, almost all of these functions have been gradually taken over by more efficient, more powerful machinery. Although horses are still indispensable for working cattle on ranches in some parts of the country (in the face of competition from jeeps and aircraft), they are now confined almost entirely to sporting activities. Although the horse population of the United States dwindled from an estimated 25 million in the nineteenth century to an estimated six million in 1965, horses fortunately gained in quality while losing in quantity. Today the horse population is rising again, the American Horse Council estimating the 1972 figure at over seven million. Selectively-bred horses are not only the star performers in the very big business of flat and harness racing, and the dream of an increasing number of young Americans, but also have become a modern status symbol.

Although forerunners of the horse evolved on the American continent (see Evolution of the Horse Family), they died out; the ancestors of present-day horses returned at the beginning of the sixteenth century with the Spanish *conquistadores*. The American Indians, at first afraid, soon came to appreciate the strange and versatile animal ridden by the Spaniards. The Indians became adept as trainers and riders (see Horsemanship, American Indian) but they were poor breeders, using the best stallions as war-horses, and letting the others roam free to lead a semi-wild life. The Indian Pony or MUSTANG, based on Spanish and Barb strains, grew smaller in size, but happily retained its inheritance of intelligence and stamina.

British officers and aristocrats settling in the eastern part of the American continent at the beginning of the seventeenth century, were often accompanied by English Thoroughbreds or fine coach horses, while the practical-minded Puritan and Dutch settlers brought with them mostly heavier draught horses. As special local needs arose, new breeds were gradually developed from these original imported strains. Many of them still exist today, if only as show horses. For example, in Virginia, where tobacco became an important industry and where the field work was performed by slaves imported from Africa, a comfortable, smooth-gaited SADDLE HORSE was created by selective breeding in order to permit the plantation owners to survey their crops and workers. In Tennessee there evolved an even smoother-gaited breed, the TENNESSEE WALKING HORSE. In Vermont, an extraordinary little horse called Justin Morgan was the sole founder of a breed which bears his name (see Morgan). Among the handy, surefooted, clever little horses in the West, the fleetest and most agile became the founders of the American QUARTER HORSE. Within the past generation, Western horses have been subdivided into numerous separate breeds or types, many of them bearing distinctive colours and markings, such as the APPALOOSA, PINTO and PALOMINO. But the forefather of them all was the ordinary Western horse, whose blood was gradually refined by Thoroughbred and half-thoroughbred crosses, thanks to the remount program of the U.S. Cavalry, which placed some of its best stallions at the disposal of ranchers and farmers who could not otherwise have afforded such a luxury. Some of the other American breeds or equine families to gain fame for their particular abilities were the NARRAGANSETT PACER; the trotting families of the Black Hawks, Mambrinos and the Clays and the superior line founded by Hambletonian; the American HACKNEY HORSE, and its miniature version, the HACKNEY PONY; the Colorado Ranger, Kentucky Saddler, and the Missouri Fox-Trotting Horse, which have become practically extinct after helping to create such breeds as the American SADDLEBRED HORSE and the STANDARDBRED.

Many of the informal competitions on ranches, on country roads and at county fairs developed into major sports. Among these, the most important in the United States in financial revenue and spectator appeal is racing (see Flat Racing). Thoroughbred breeding has become big business too. There are over eleven hundred Thoroughbred stud farms throughout the country, mostly concentrated in the states of Kentucky, Virginia, Maryland, New Jersey, Ohio, Illinois, Florida and California, although horse breeding takes place in every state. As the price of top racing stallions has soared, syndicated ownership has become increasingly common. For example, the staggering price of $5,400,000 paid for Nijinsky at the end of his European racing career was furnished by a syndicate composed of the customary 32 shares, thus greatly limiting the risk as well as the capital investment of his new owners.

Throughout the years, Thoroughbred racing in the United States has produced a number of horses which have become veritable national heroes. The twelve elected to the Hall of Fame since the beginning of the twentieth century are Sysonby (foaled in 1902), Colin (1905), Exterminator (1915), Man O'War (1917), Equipoise (1928), Count Fleet (1940), Citation (1945), Tom Fool (1949), Native Dancer (1950), Nashua (1952), Swaps (1952), and Kelso (1957).

In the West and Southwest, Quarter Horse racing is a major spectator sport.

Thoroughbreds also dominate steeplechasing in the United States, a sport governed by the National Steeplechase and Hunt Association. In fact, a steeplechaser competing on a major track must be a registered Thoroughbred. These races are usually run around an oval course in the infield of the flat racetrack, and may be either hurdle races, with obstacles about 4 ft 6 in (1·37 m) high, or brush races, with obstacles between 4 ft 6 in and 5 ft (1·37–1·52 m), including ditches and water jumps. The most famous big-track American steeplechase events include the Belmont Grand National, the Temple Gwathemy, the Brook Steeplechase, and the Saratoga Steeplechase Handicap, which are almost always ridden by professional jockeys. Amateurs participate, however, in other steeplechase events, most prevalent in the Eastern and Southeastern states, such as point-to-points and hunt race meetings, which generally include a few hurdle races, a timber or brush race, and two or three flat races. Sometimes there is a 'pink coat' race reserved for amateur riders in hunting attire, with a weight allowance as high as 180 lb. The Radnor and Rosetree

U.S.A. Native Dancer (left) first ran and won at Jamaica in April 1952. He won all except one of his 22 races.

Hunt Clubs sponsor famous and fashionable hunt race meetings. The steeplechase Triple Crown events are the Grand National Point-to-Point, My Lady's Manor Point-to-Point, and the MARYLAND HUNT CUP.

Less patrician than Thoroughbred racing, harness racing in the United States, which has existed since the seventeenth century but became really popular only in the 1870s when a trotting association was formed, is no longer the country fair event it used to be. Its development since World War II has been phenomenal. While hundreds of county and state fairs feature harness racing, the major events now take place on a nation-wide circuit of tracks complete with night racing, pari-mutuel betting, mobile starting gates, and meticulously maintained special track surfaces, such as those at Saratoga and Goshen in New York (also the home of the Trotting Hall of Fame), the Meadows in Pennsylvania, Springfield and Du Quoin in Illinois, the Indianapolis Fairgrounds in Indiana, the Delaware Raceway, Lexington Raceway in Kentucky, and Roosevelt and Yonkers in the suburbs of New York City. The governing body of the sport and custodian of the Trotting Register is The United States Trotting Association.

Harness racing in the United States differs from the sport in Europe in several respects. There are no mounted trotting events, all of the horses being hitched to a lightweight sulky. Nor are the horses customarily handicapped by distance at the major tracks where a mobile starting gate is used. Except for fair events and a few historic races, most trotting and pacing events are 'dashes' over distances ranging from six furlongs to one mile, rather than in several mile heats. Finally, pacing is far more popular and prevalent than trotting, perhaps because the lateral pacing gait is more spectacular as well as slightly faster, or because pacers wearing hobbles (or 'hopples'), as most of them do in competition, cannot break gait. Nevertheless, some of the most important harness-racing events on the calendar are for trotters, including the Triple Crown consisting of The Yonkers Futurity in New York, the Hambletonian at Du Quoin, and the Kentucky Futurity at Lexington. Another famed trotting event is the Roosevelt International, in which the entries are restricted to a select group of invited champions from all over the world, with the winner considered to be the World's Champion Trotter. Furthermore, some of the most famous harness horses in America have been trotters rather than pacers, such as the incomparable Hambletonian, the ancestor of the vast majority of modern American harness racers, having sired no less than 1,335 foals.

Still, it is pacing that dominates harness racing programs in the United States, where the major events comprising the Pacing Triple Crown are the Little Brown Jug Trial at Delaware, Ohio (named after a nineteenth-century world champion pacer); the William H. Cane Futurity at Yonkers; and the Messenger Stake (named after the official founder sire of the Standardbred breed, a grey Thoroughbred ex-racehorse imported to Philadelphia from England in 1788) at Roosevelt Raceway. Among the great American pacers of the past, only four have captured the Triple Crown: Adios Butler in 1959, Bret Hanover in 1965, Romeo Hanover in 1969, and Most Happy Fella in 1970.

The postwar boom in harness racing led to the development of a number of large Standardbred breeding establishments, such as Castleton Farm in Florida and Kentucky, and Hanover Shoe Farm in Pennsylvania. But at the same time there are countless small stables, especially in the Middle West, where harness racing is frequently a family affair. Many individuals are at the same time breeder, owner, trainer and driver, devoting their lives to harness racing, moving from one meeting to another all year long.

Horse shows are also an around-the-calendar equestrian activity in the United States, where the first recorded horse show took place in 1883. Now almost 700 shows are officially recognized by the American Horse Shows Association and over 50 affiliated associations organize specialized horse shows of their own. The American Quarter Horse Association, for example, approves over a thousand shows each year, and cutting contests are governed by the National Cutting Horse Association. In addition, there are countless local horse shows sponsored by riding academies, schools, hunt clubs, and pony clubs. The American Horse Shows Association publishes an annual Rule Book, which sets the standard for horse show rules in the United States.

A recognized show is classified as A, B, or C, depending on the amount of prize money and on the number of variety of classes offered. A show may be classed as A for one division, such as hunter and jumper, and B or C for some other division, such as saddle horses. Many shows make a speciality of one of the twenty-odd A.H.S.A. divisions, and some include halter and breeding classes, shown in hand. But almost all of them present an equitation division for an ever-increasing number of participants, with girl riders outnumbering and often outriding the boys. A point system determines the champion hunter and jumper, while other championship awards are generally decided in a championship performance class. In the equitation division, there is also a point system, with riders who have qualified during the year being entitled to compete for the most coveted national horsemanship awards at the National Horse Show in New York City at the end of October: the Maclay Trophy (for hunter seat), the Good Hands Trophy (for saddle seat),

U.S.A. Night harness racing at 'the big red mile' in Lexington, Kentucky

A.H.S.A. Medals for these divisions as well as for stock saddle seat (Western riding), and the United States Equestrian Team Medal, awarded to the winner of a two-phase test over jumps and on the flat. Many talented junior riders (under 18 years of age) have been discovered in the equitation division as well as in nationwide U.S.E.T. trials and selected for advanced training at the U.S.E.T. headquarters in Gladstone, New Jersey. A fortunate few have been named to the United States Olympic Equestrian Team. The United States was handicapped in the past by the fact that its jumping rules did not conform to those of other nations. But since the early 1950s, and despite the opposition of professional horsemen at first, these rules have gradually been adapted to the international F.E.I. show-jumping regulations.

As in the case of many other countries, American representation in international equestrian events was reserved for cavalry officers until the 1940s, when most cavalries were entirely mechanized. At FORT RILEY, Kansas, the U.S. Cavalry headquarters, the stables and riding hall were transformed into depots for tanks and jeeps. The last appearance of an American military Prix des Nations team was during the 1948 Olympic Games in London, after which it was officially disbanded. A group of horse-lovers and retired cavalry officers were the moving force behind the foundation of the UNITED STATES EQUESTRIAN TEAM, INC.

The international and Olympic three-day event and dressage teams have encountered greater difficulties and somewhat less success, due to the limited practice of these activities in the United States, and especially to the shortage of qualified instructors. Nevertheless, American three-day riders have never failed to make an honourable showing, and the Gold Medal for dressage in the Pan-American Games of 1959 and 1963 was won by the Princess de la Tour d'Auvergne (née Patricia Galvin), representing the United States.

The most typically American sport of all is undoubtedly the RODEO. Most rodeos are organized by professional 'rodeo producers', who provide the scorers, the mounted officials, the 'pick-up men' and 'rodeo clowns' (a fearless lot of individuals whose task is to distract the bulls' attention from a fallen competitor), as well as the necessary equipment such as chutes, bulls, and bucking broncs.

The United States entered the polo scene in 1876, when the well-known gentleman sportsman, James Gordon Bennett, introduced the game to riding friends in Long Island, after having learned to play in Paris. Thanks to the support and skill of a group of sports-minded American millionaires, the United States international teams enjoyed a period of glory during the 1920s and 1930s. Then came the income tax, followed by World War II, and American polo suffered a severe decline. The United States Polo Association has sponsored various programs to repopularize the game, and the centre of high-goal polo has moved westward to Oak Brook, Illinois, with Midland, Texas, Meadow Brook, Long Island, and Westchester, New York among the other leading polo centres. New variations of polo have been invented in an attempt to place the game within the means of a greater number of participants. Indoor polo, played on a smaller surface (100 by 50 yd), with only three men to a team and a larger, inflated leather ball, has gained in popularity. The Pony Club program also promotes polo with a simplified set of rules borrowed from the British Pony Club. But at the moment, it seems unlikely that polo in the United States will ever regain the appeal it enjoyed during its heyday in the 1930s.

Foxhunting is another activity that has been unfavourably affected by economic and fiscal factors. Private packs of foxhounds have virtually ceased to exist, although foxhunting is still an important sport in certain states (see Hunting in the United States).

Affiliated with many Hunt Clubs are branches of the United States Pony Clubs, Inc. (see Pony Club). Many Pony Club members, after reaching the maximum age of 17, continue in the program as volunteer instructors, or go on to advanced work with the United States Combined Training Association, which offers advanced training in dressage, cross-country riding and stadium jumping. Over 50 combined training events are held throughout the year in various parts of the country. There are also one-day events, and a simplified version called Jenny Camp Trials, named in honour of a champion American Olympic three-day

U.S.A. Bareback bronc riding in Montana

mare. The number of participants in these competitions is not very impressive for a nation of over two hundred million citizens. But like dressage, which is practised on an even smaller scale, combined training is handicapped less by lack of interest than by the lack of qualified instructors.

There is no shortage of alternate equestrian activities in the United States. Amateur rodeo clubs, cutting contests, and parade clubs abound in the West, and the popular Western diversion of trail riding has spread all over the country. In addition to pleasure trail rides, there is a competitive version, among which some of the most famous events are the Three-Day Hundred-Mile Trail Ride of the Green Mountain Horse Association in Vermont; the Tevis Cup, a hundred mile one-day ride from Tahoe City to Auburn, California; and the Virginia Trail Riders' One Hundred Mile Ride (see Long-Distance Riding).

Finally, almost all of the horse breed associations in the United States, where there are more separate breed registries than in any other country, organize specialty shows and performance competitions. MAS

U.S. Equestrian Team

The organization that trains American riders for international competition is a non-profit, voluntary organization founded after the mechanization of the U.S. Cavalry, which, before 1949, furnished and subsidized the equestrian teams that represented the nation. Except for the dressage horses, which are owned outright by their riders, the team horses are lent or donated outright by interested supporters. The U.S.E.T. is financed through contributions from individual members or organizations, primarily the former.

The office and training grounds are at Gladstone, N.J., in a 55-year-old building at Hamilton Farms, the estate of the James Cox Brady family. The 48 stalls on two levels originally housed the Brady hackneys and hunters. A nearby carriage house is used as a dormitory for grooms and riders. The U.S.E.T. has built its own indoor riding hall.

Bertalan de Nemethy, a former Hungarian Army international rider, became coach of the NATIONS' CUP team in 1955 to provide an insight into the training techniques used in Europe to prepare for competitions conducted under F.E.I. rules, which were rarely used in the United States at that time. De Nemethy insisted that the team should get more competition over international courses in Europe, a practice held to ever since although not supported by some American horsemen who argue that the U.S.E.T. should be represented at the major United States shows during the time the team is overseas.

The three-day event team had been coached by several individuals for short periods before each Olympic or Pan-American Games, but in 1963 Stefan von Visy was named as coach, replaced by Major Joseph Lynch in 1968 and Jack Le Goff in 1970. The eventers have always been at a disadvantage because very few competitions are held each year in the United States and the sport has no really broad base of riders, horses or supporters. Since 1969 U.S.E.T. coaches have received about 160 applications each year from aspiring riders. They hold screening trials around the country and invite the top riders to come to Gladstone 'at their own expense' for further training. From that group about three or four show-jumping and eventing riders are chosen to remain with the team's competitive squads. Candidates for the screening trials must be 16 years or older, U.S. citizens, and possess a valid amateur licence from the A.H.S.A.

The U.S.E.T.'s regular donations are rarely spent on horses. When a horse is recommended by one of the coaches, the team officials try to borrow it, or find a patron who will buy the horse and donate it to the team. HCA

U.S.E.T. Neal Shapiro riding Sloopy in the 1972 Olympic Show-Jumping Grand Prix. He won the individual bronze medal; the United States team lost the team gold medal to West Germany by a quarter point.

U.S.S.R.

Horse Breeding: the horse was domesticated in southeast Russia by 3000 B.C. and highly developed in the southeast Russian Steppes by 1000 B.C. In eastern Skifov, horses were bred for farming, riding, meat, milk, and horsehide in the seventh to third centuries B.C. Kieven Rus in the eleventh and twelfth centuries A.D. developed a lighter horse of the riding type as well as a 'heroic' horse designed to carry heavy armour. In the eighteenth century, the military horse was developed in Russia, and the famous DON breed arose. By the second half of the eighteenth century, the new Russian breeds of ORLOV, Rostopchinsky, and STRELETS were established. Horses were raised on government studs, and English Thoroughbreds were imported for use on the racecourses.

At the turn of this century, there were approximately 20 million horses in Russia. Breeding suffered a severe setback during World War I and the subsequent Civil War, when most breeding animals were destroyed. Half of the Don horses were destroyed during the war, and almost all of the Strelets and Orlov stock. In 1916, the territory included within present Soviet boundaries contained 38·2 million horses; in 1918, the Soviet government began to organize government studs, which were finally established in 1923. Opinion differs sharply on the fate of horses in the period between the two wars; non-Soviet sources maintain that there were still 36·1 million horses in Soviet territory in 1928 but that these numbers were almost halved during the period of collectivization, so that there were only 21·0 million in 1941.

According to the Soviets, however, scientific breeding in government studs caused the equine population of Russia to increase fivefold in 1934–9. All agree, however, that World War II destroyed an extremely high number of Russian horses; the Soviets maintain that 7 million horses were lost during this war, that in 1953 there were 27 per cent fewer horses than in 1940; this agrees with non-Soviet estimates that there were only 10·7 million horses in Russia in 1946. Subsequent figures are again in dispute; the Soviets maintain that their scientific breeding methods have increased the quantity as well as the quality of the herds; others suggest that the equestrian population has continued to decline since World War II as field work has become increasingly mechanized. The Soviets estimate their present equine population at 7·5 million.

Since the Revolution, scientific breeding methods have been used at government studs, and the uniformity of control has enabled the Soviets to produce exact results and detailed statistical records. The breeds of Don and KABARDIN were improved, as was the Orlov, and new breeds were developed, such as the BUDYONNY. Certain Russian breeds, famous in the nineteenth century, became obsolete but provided the stock for new breeds; thus the Bitiug resulted in the VORONEZH work-harness horse, the Strelets in the TERSKY and other related breeds, the Klepper in the TORIC, the Kirgiz in the NEW KIRGIZ, and the Orlov-American trotter in the RUSSIAN TROTTER. The trotters were particularly singled out for attention in the new breeding programs, and were bred for new height and strength. Complex experiments with new strains of blood and new combinations of these strains were also carried out successfully in the development of such breeds as the KUSTANAIR, BASHKIRSKY, and Budyonny. The Don was used as the basis of several new breeds and new strains, and Arab blood was introduced and reintroduced into many breeds, particularly into the IOMUD, KARABAIR, Kabardin, and Tersky. English Thoroughbreds also played an important role in the improvement of such breeds as the Toric, Tersky, New Kirgiz, Budyonny, Don, Kustanair, Strelets, and even in the LATVIAN HARNESS HORSE and the LITHUANIAN HEAVY HORSE. The new VLADIMIR breed was established in 1946; the Budyonny and Tersky in 1948; the new Toric in 1950; the new Kustanair in 1951, and the new Latvian in 1952. Other breeds of lesser importance include the Mezensky, Pechorsky (Pechora), Priobsky, Narimsky, Yakut, Kuznetsky, and Tuvinsky, which were developed in the Ukraine, Latvia, Estonia, the Urals, Middle Volga Region, Siberia, the far East, and Karelo-Finn; these are primarily harness breeds, like the better-known Orlov, Russian trotter, Russian heavy harness horse, and Toric. Supreme among Russian riding breeds are the Don, Budyonny, Bashkirsky, Zabaikal, and Altai, as well as the Arab-influenced breeds and the native breeds of the Transcaucasus, middle Asia, Kazakhstan, Kirgiziia, Moldavia, the Crimea and the lower Volga region; these riding breeds include the Tersky, Kustanair, Kabardin, Karabair, Lokai, Kazakh, Adayevsky, Kirgiz, and Tushinsky.

As evidence of the improvement in the quality of horses in Russia, the Soviets cite the following new records: in 1953, 175 horses of the Russian Trotter type beat the pre-Revolutionary record of 2 min 10 sec for 1,600 m (1 mile); Zhest, a Russian Trotter stallion, covered the same distance in 1 min 59¾ sec in 1953. At present the bay stallion Kreply Zarok (1962) is the leading trotter, having covered 1,600 m in 2 min 3·2 sec; he is now at stud. Great strides have also been made in breeding efficiency, particularly through the wide use of artificial insemination. In 1951, one stallion fertilized 907 mares by artificial insemination; often more than 200 mares can be fertilized by a single stallion, yielding more than 100 foals by him in a year.

The racehorse was also further developed in Soviet studs, and new records were set. In 1951, the stallion Pecheneg, a four-year-old, covered 1,600 m in 2 min 9¾ sec in the Moscow hippodrome. Soviet racehorses trace their bloodlines back to Tagore, Brimstone, Dark Ronald, Gainsborough, St Simon, Teddy (from Eclipse), Blandford, Phalaris and Sunstar. They have raced mainly in eastern Europe until recently; since 1953 they have travelled abroad and Soviet horses have been entered for the Laurel Park Cup in the United States since 1958. Zabeg (bay, 1957, descended from Sunstar) was third in the Laurel Park Cup in 1960, and Anilin (bay, 1961, by Element descended from St Simon, out of Analoghichny) ran third in this race in 1964, second in it and in the Washington D.C.

U.S.S.R. A Yakut horse, used primarily for pack and harness

International in 1966, and finished fifth in a very strong field in the 1965 Prix de l'Arc de Triomphe at Longchamp; he won the Robert Pferdemenges Prize at Cologne by covering 1,800 m ($1\frac{1}{12}$ mile) in 1 min 56·9 sec, and during his five-year career won 21 out of his 27 races, with prizes totalling 169,260 roubles.

There are now 93 studs in the U.S.S.R., 10 specializing in saddle horses, 42 in Orlov and Russian Trotters.

Arab: the Arab has undoubtedly provided the most important influence of any breed in Russia. Arab tribes have lived adjacent to or actually within the confines of the Russian empire from the earliest times; Arab stock was thus in a sense 'native' to Russia for many centuries. Moreover, the Russians have always fancied the sturdy but showy qualities of the Arab stallion as a riding horse; in the nineteenth century, Arab blood was purposely introduced into many native breeds, and again in the Soviet period when 'scientific' breeding was undertaken, Arab blood was at a premium. Several of the 'native' breeds show strong Arab influence with the concave profile, intelligence, docile temperament, flaring nostrils, and proud tail carriage characteristic of the breed; this is particularly obvious in the Iomud, Karabair, Kabardin, and Tersky. The Strelets stud produced a fine breed of Anglo-Arabs in the nineteenth century, and even such breeds as the Lokai, Orlov, Toric, Latvian harness horse and Lithuanian heavy harness horse, which do not have obviously Arab features, have important Arab blood. The purebred Arab is valued in the U.S.S.R. today for its walk and canter, though its trot is considered 'unsatisfactory'; it is used over long-distance races and is bred principally at the Tersky stud. Russian records for the Arab are 1,000 m (0·62 miles) in 1 min 06 sec; 3,000 m (1·86 miles) in 3 min 36·4 sec; and 644 km (400 miles) in 4 days 21 hours, averaging 132 km (82 miles) per day.

Average height at withers for stallions is about 14·3½ hands (1·50 m), for mares about 14·2¾ hands (1·49 m); bone below the knee for stallions is 7½ in (18·9 cm), for mares 7¼ in (18·4 cm).

There are three main strains from which the Arab was developed in Russia: the Khodban, Koheilan (Kuhaylan), and Siglavy (Saqlawi). The Khodban is fairly large (1·56 m or 15·1½ hands), with many characteristics of a racehorse; the Koheilan is smaller (to about 1·52 m or 15 hands) but with a deep chest, solid and compact. The Siglavy is also small, but powerful and elegant. Bay and grey predominate, with a rare black or dark brown. WOF

Horse Sports: the Russians have long been noted for their daring horsemanship and horse sports are still extremely popular in the Soviet Union. In addition to dressage and jumping, the Russians enjoy *dzhigitovka* (acrobatics on horseback, such as riding backwards or underneath the horse, a traditional feature of the Russian circus), tent-pegging, steeplechasing, and flat racing. An annual All-Soviet meeting for the All-Union Race Cup (Kubok SSSR), is held; this is a race over obstacles of the 'field' type over 3¾ miles (6,000 m). National games are very important in Georgia, Kazakhstan, Uzbekistan, Kirgiziia, and Turkmenistan. In Georgia, they take part in *dogi* (a kind of sprinting), and other events called *morula* (10 km or 6·2 mile races), *issindi* (fighting with javelins on horseback), *tskhen-burti* (a kind of tennis on horseback) and *kabakhi* (archery at full gallop). In Kazakhstan, they play *baiga* (a long-distance competition), *kunan-baiga* (testing horses of three years and under in various national games), *zhigig-zharis* (competition in saddling-up), and *zhorga-zharis* (races at the pace or rack). In Tadzhikstan, *kop-kopi*, a strenuous and fierce game, is a national pastime. Every year there is an All-Soviet national games competition.

Russian sports records, as of 1952, include: jumping a height of 2·22 m (7 ft 3½ in); jumping a length of 8·20 m (26 ft 11 in); racing over hurdles, 2 km in 2 min 7·9 sec; 3 km in 3 min 17·9 sec; steeplechasing over 4,000 m (2½ miles) in 4 min 47·5 sec; over 6,000 m (3¾ miles) in 7 min 47·5 sec. In long-distance and heavy-burden races: 50 km (31 miles) in 1 hr 21 min 0·02 sec; 100 km (62 miles) in 4 hr 0·06 min; and covering 311·6 km (193½ miles) within one day.

Recently the Russians have excelled at dressage. Sergei Filatov won the gold medal for the Prix de Dressage at the 1960 Olympics in Rome, riding the Akhal-Teke stallion Absent. Elena Petushkova, on Pepel, won the European Championship at AACHEN in 1970. The Russian team won the three-day event at Burghley in 1962 and came very close to winning the Olympic three-day event in Mexico in 1968. In all of these events, the Russian teams usually ride stallions.

English influence and even Anglophilia is still apparent in Russian equestrian sport. The groom of Vronsky's horse in Tolstoi's *Anna Karenina*, like the grooms of many well-to-do young Russians in real life in the nineteenth century, was an Englishman,

U.S.S.R. *Top:* Troika racing at the Moscow Hippodrome
Above: Tskhen-burti, a national game in the Republic of Georgia

and the English influence remained in the use of such terms as 'steeplechase', 'finish', and 'martingale', which to this day are used in their English form in Russian. James FILLIS was chief instructor in the Officers' Cavalry School in St Petersburg from 1898 to 1910, and even now the Russian style of dressage is closer to the English than to the German: less collected, with a longer rein and freer forward movement.

More than 50,000 people now ride for sport in Russia, at sports clubs throughout the country. Horseracing has remained extremely popular in post-Revolutionary Russia, and Russian racehorses compete successfully abroad as well (see Horse Breeding above). In 1970, 606 Thoroughbred saddle horses competed at 18 Soviet racecourses for prizes amounting to as much as 48,013 roubles a stake. The Red Army cavalry has maintained a Concours Hippique, over fences and ditches, and the Army-Air Force-Navy-Voluntary Society (D.O.S.A.A.F.) is very active in equestrian activities. Civilian sporting societies abound, and it is even possible for individual citizens to maintain horses for sporting purposes. WOF

Vaquero

This Spanish-Mexican term for cowboy or herder is applied to the men who worked the great Spanish cattle herds in the southwestern Spanish provinces. Pronounced 'bah-káir-oh', this name was eventually anglicized to BUCKAROO in the Northwest.

The vaquero, in both Mexico and California, clung to the Spanish dress, equipment, and methods of working both cattle and horses. His saddle was derived from the heavy saddles of the *conquistadores*, and the bit in his horse's mouth continued to be the spade or halfbreed still common along the western slopes of the Sierra Nevada mountains. His traditional saddle rope was the plaited rawhide *reata*, and he took several wraps around his saddle horn with the end of the *reata* when he caught a cow or horse with his rope, giving or taking slack to prevent the breaking of the reata under the strain. This method is still known as the *dally* method of roping, in contrast to tying hard and fast to the saddle horn as is almost universally done in Texas and the Southwest. See Western Riding, Western Tack. RS

Vasne see Persian Arab

Vaulting

Vaulting, gymnastics on the back of the moving horse, began with the Romans as part of their basic riding instruction. In medieval Europe it was also used in training knights in the art of horsemanship. Gradually the exercises became stylized and were practised in the gymnasium instead of on the live horse. This type of vaulting, using the leather or side 'horse', is still a part of international competitive gymnastics. Another outgrowth of the original vaulting on a living horse found its way into the circus, where it is still a popular attraction. Modern cavalries also used vaulting on the moving horse as a foundation for riding; in fact, a vaulting competition among cavalry teams was introduced into the Olympic Games held in Antwerp in 1920.

Today, vaulting as a sport is practised mainly by children's groups and has its strongest support in Germany, where most riding schools have vaulting classes for children. An annual national competition is held among the vaulting clubs of the country, and as a result of the sport's popularity, there are now formal rules and regulations covering competitions. Interest is steadily growing in other parts of the world.

Modern vaulting is performed on the back of a cantering horse which is controlled on a lunge line by the instructor. The horse is equipped with a leather vaulting surcingle having two handles or grips, usually rigid, a ring on the top to which a strap is attached for use by beginners to assist in standing up and loops on each side in which a vaulter can insert his foot in order to perform the Cossack hang exercise. The horse is usually lunged in a snaffle bridle with side reins to keep its neck straight and steady.

There are six basic exercises which are compulsory in competition and which form the basis for countless free-style exercises. These are the riding seat, the kneel and flag, the mill, the flank, the free stand, and the scissors. A competition team is composed of eight members, each of whom must perform all compulsory exercises, for which he is given a score of zero to ten on his form, grace and precision. Then the team is given five to seven minutes in which to present a free-style program with combination exercises performed by two or three vaulters together, as well as difficult individual exercises.

Besides being a competitive sport, vaulting offers many advantages and useful applications in the training of riders. It develops courage, rhythm, balance, grace and a feeling for the movement of the horse. Riding instructors have, for instance, had excellent results with very timid children by taking them out of the riding classes and having them vault for a while. With the constant vaulting on and off and getting used to having the horse move on at the canter, the children gain confidence which carries over when they go back to their riding classes again. EFS

Vendéen-Charentais see Norman, Anglo-Norman and French Saddle Horse

Vaulting. A free-stand exercise by a pair from Kiel, West Germany

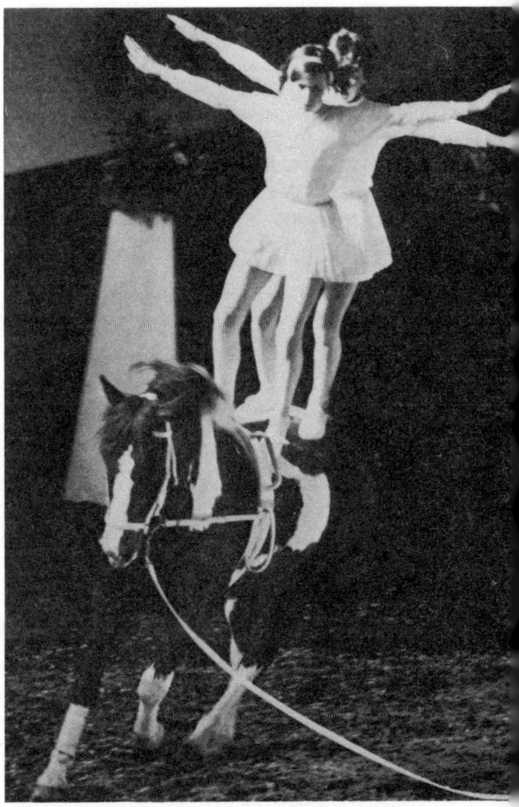

Venezuela

Horses, horsemen, and equestrian skills began to appear in the New World from the sixteenth century onward. The horses brought over from Europe doubtless underwent a degenerative process of adaptation, decreasing in height and bulk in many areas of the New World, particularly in the tropics. However, to compensate, they increased in hardiness and resistance in order to live and work under adverse conditions of climate and feeding.

The main contributions made by horses to the development of the American continent were: (1) their fundamental importance during the period of the Spanish conquest; (2) their value in the penetration of frontier lands and cattle colonization; and (3) their services in the fields of communication and transport. Horses were also a prime factor of military importance in the wars of independence. Today Caracas is the largest centre of equestrian sports in Venezuela, although there are many enthusiasts in other cities. The racetrack of La Rinconada in Caracas attracts, apart from a large number of imported Thoroughbreds, a sizable group of domestic horses, born and bred in the numerous stables found throughout the country.

Riding is divided into that practised with the *criollo* horse, a beautiful, small and strong horse descended from the first imported horses, and competitive international-scale riding, consisting of jumping, cross country and dressage, mainly on horses derived from more recently imported Thoroughbreds. The first type of riding is typically Venezuelan and shows to best advantage the skill and true merit of the popular Venezuelan rider. Long rides are undertaken with the *criollo* horse as well as the *coleo*, in which bulls are thrown to the ground after having been caught by the tail. *Criollo* horses have a comfortable gait which allows the rider to spend many hours on horseback with no trace of fatigue. FIDL

Vermont One-Hundred-Mile Three-Day Competitive Trail Ride

see Long-Distance Riding

Viatka, Viatsky

The Viatka is a light Russian harness horse of the northern forest type, suitable for light farm work, transport, and use in troikas. The head is fairly long, with the wide forehead typical of the northern forest type. The profile is slightly concave at the forehead; the ears are quite large, the neck fairly long and muscular, with a sharp curve in the upper crest. The withers are relatively high and wide, the back straight, the loins wide and strong, the croup round and slightly inclined. The chest is wide and deep, tightly ribbed. The fore legs are set on wide apart, the hind legs often narrowly set on and inclined to be sickle hocked; the legs are hard with well-developed tendons and medium-sized hoofs, with strong bone. Dun is the most common colour, then roan and mousy grey. Many Viatkas have a black band on the back and zebra stripes under the shoulders. The temperament is lively and energetic. Average height for stallions is 13·3½ hands (1·41 m), for mares 13·2 hands (1·37 m); bone below the knee for stallions is 7¼ in (18·7 cm), for mares 7 in (17.5 cm). The walk is hasty and short, the trot small but covering ground.

The Viatka is bred in the Udmurt republic and the Kirov district. It originated in the Viatsky territory, where it was used in troikas. Peter the Great ordered Estonian horses to be brought to improve horses bred on the river Viatka, but no details of this are known. WOF

Vices

Vices in horses cover a group of habits developed from boredom, e.g. WEAVING, WINDSUCKING and CRIB BITING. There is a tendency for all vices to be copied by other horses. All vices are technical unsoundnesses and must be mentioned on any certificate of soundness or guarantee. WSC

Villanos

This very strong, big breed, native to Castile, Spain, was brought to Lipizza in the seventeenth century to become one of the founders of the LIPIZZANER. DMG

Virgin Islands

see West Indies

Vladimir

This heavy, active well-made harness and draught horse, standing about 16 hands (1·65 m), is bred in the districts of Vladimir, Ivanov, Taunhov, Kostrona and Moscow as well as in the Tatar Republic of the U.S.S.R. Crosses of ARDENNES, SUFFOLK PUNCHES, CLEVELAND BAYS and PERCHERONS were used; at the beginning of this century SHIRE blood was introduced. The name Vladimir was given in 1946 when the breed was considered to be fixed. DMG

Volte

see Movements

Voltige

alternative (French) for VAULTING

Voronezh Harness Horse

This Russian breed was developed from the BITIUG. It is a massive and well-boned trotter, with the temperament of a heavy load-puller, very hardy and able to do well on almost any keep. A Voronezh stallion has carried 800 kg (1,764 lb) for 2 km (1¼ miles) in 4 min 40 sec, and a mare has carried 4,364 kg (9,260 lb).

An even back, well-filled loins, and long torso with a well-developed, long croup are characteristic. The fore legs are set on straight; the hoofs are large and rather flat, but with strong bone, and there are extra-

Top: Viatka, Viatsky

Above: Vladimir

ordinary feathers. Occasional faults are badly developed joints, close hocks, and sickle hocks. The average height for stallions is 15·2½ hands (1·59 m), for mares 15 hands (1·52 m); bone below the knee for stallions 8½ in (21·6 cm), for mares 8¼ in (20·9 cm).

The Voronezh has a spacious walk and ample trot. It is noted for its good, calm character but is energetic in all movements.

This breed, now primarily produced at a collective farm in Voronezh, was well-known in the eighteenth and nineteenth centuries as the Bitiug carthorse, bred on the banks of the river Bitiug with its rich pastures. The Khrenovsky stud was particularly influential in its development. The Bitiug can be traced back to the time of Peter the Great, when Dutch stallions were sent to Voronezh, but undoubtedly the greatest influence was from the stud of Count A. G. Orlov. Western breeds were crossed with the Bitiug so much that by 1882 there were almost no pure Bitiugs left. In the 1930s the breed was reorganized and thickset Orlov trotters were put to various local mares, resulting in the Voronezh harness horse. WOF

Vyatka, Vyatsky see Viatka, Viatsky

Waler see Australia

Walk-Trot Horse see Gaited Horses

Warfare, Horse in

This is one of the oldest uses of the horse: not so old as its use in hunting, but arguably arising, in a sense, out of it. The horse at war is first seen in two quite different contexts: in Central Asia, ridden by the bowmen of the steppes, and in Western Asia driven in pairs to a chariot. Both these employments, at the hands of aggressive peoples who were themselves perhaps acting under the compulsion to find fresh grazing ground and more abundant sources of water (the first horsemasters appear to have been primarily pastoralists before they took up with the horse) led to expansion into countries where the domestic horse had not hitherto been seen, and well outside the bounds of latitude (in the Old World, between about 45 and 60 degrees North) between which alone the wild horse occurred.

The chariot-driven phase of this expansion took place shortly before 2000 B.C. but the very presence of horses at all, harnessed under the yoke of people such as the Sumerians, who had previously used the wild ass for this purpose and whose first name for the horse was 'Ass from the Northern Hills' must mean that the Caucasus/Iranian region had already been penetrated by riding nomads from Central Asia, whose incursions were not always peaceful; no other source of horses was available for Mesopotamian peoples, or Anatolians like the Hittites.

Massed squadrons of chariots could be used in the armies of early military empires such as those of Egypt, Babylon, and Assyria, which operated mostly in a flat terrain; in all of these the bow was as commonly used from the chariot as the spear. At the time of the siege of Troy, around 1200 B.C., fighting was still either on foot or from the chariot, but in the more broken ground of Greece and among the Etruscans of northern Italy, where evidence of the earliest chariots in Mediterranean Europe is abundant, opportunities for formations of chariots to deploy were limited and led inevitably to the warrior mounting a single horse, from which he used the same weapons in the same way as he had done from the chariot. Likewise, north of the Alps, the Celts and other European peoples found that hunting from the chariot, much practised in the Near East, was quite impracticable in woods and mountains where narrow defiles abounded. Thus the practice of riding was carried over to the battlefield by Celtic warriors whose chief occupation in peace was hunting. Though chariots were still brought out against the first Roman invaders under Julius Caesar by the Celtic Britons, and against the legions of Agricola in Caledonia a hundred and fifty years later, in both cases they were used interspersed with cavalry, and their impotence against the disciplined Roman array of all arms acting in conjunction only hastened a process of obsolescence which had already begun. The Irish alone, in their isolation, continued to use the war chariot down to about A.D. 400.

The horse in war is not only a means of giving speed to the individual soldier; it serves, ridden or driven, as a mobile command post. 'A horse, a horse, my kingdom for a horse' cried the last Plantagenet monarch at Bosworth. Not because he contemplated flight but because he could not

Horse in Warfare. The Persian king Darius's war chariot was a mobile headquarters from which he could command his forces.

effectively command his army on foot. In the famous picture of Alexander confronting the Persian King at the Battle of Issus, Darius is driving a chariot which is no longer a fighting vehicle but as much a mobile headquarters as the Duke of Marlborough's (or Napoleon's) coach was. For the same reason, in Anglo-Saxon poetry the saddle is called 'the high king's seat of battle', although right down to the time of Hastings even the best English troops fought on foot in the shield-wall.

The Romans in the days of the Republic and in those of the monarchy before that were not a riding people, and only to a limited extent a chariot-driving people. Their strength lay in infantry, and any but the smallest mounted contingents had to be supplied by their 'allies', which meant either subservient conquered rivals or hired mercenaries called 'auxiliaries'. Great and long-lasting as was the prestige of the infantry legion, the history of the Roman army is a history of 'barbarization' due to shortage of Italian manpower willing to serve under arms, and of increased use of cavalry, which arose primarily out of the nature of enemies encountered. Even at times when the situation in Europe was stable, the Roman army was perpetually standing-to on the eastern front against an enemy (the Persians) whose strength lay on horseback and who could only be countered by cavalry. On the Danube frontier the pressure also came from mounted foes such as the Alans and Sarmatians and Dacae. Last of all on the Rhine frontier the nature of the German opposition changed in the course of four centuries from an almost exclusively unmounted enemy, originally interspersed with charioteers, to an increasingly well-mounted combination of Germans allied to mounted archers such as the Huns.

Incursions of mounted archers had been going on in Europe at least since the Scythian raids in the sixth century B.C. These were the prototype of light cavalry which remained essentially the same down to the twentieth century. The failure of all European armies to learn to use the bow as the Asiatic archers did from the saddle meant that, unable to answer arrow with arrow, they had to sit it out until the Asiatics came to close quarters. It became easier to do this after the invention of chain mail, which, however, added much more to the all-up weight than did the quilted jerkin which was all the armour the Asiatic horseman wore. From perhaps the third century A.D. onwards some of these invaders had been using stirrups in conjunction with wooden-tree saddles quite unlike the glorified pad which was the Roman (indeed the Western) saddle of late Imperial times. Westerners were slow to take up the invention of the stirrup, and not until the time of the Avars, finally expelled from Hungary by Charlemagne, did its use become common in the West.

The armoured spearman, or cataphract, on horseback had been an important element in Byzantine armies since long before this date, but now with his feet in stirrups he could use his spear not only overhand to thrust or throw but under his armpit with the full momentum of the horse behind its point: in fact, as a lance. This combination of armour, lance and stirrup is what makes the medieval knight, and the adoption of increasingly heavy horses was not due primarily, as many suppose, to the weight of armour carried, but in order to bring as much weight behind the spearpoint as possible. Also, the horse itself was regarded as a weapon (only stallions were ridden in battle) to 'bear down' the enemy foot regardless of what arms the rider used; hence the bigger the warhorse the better, and hence the introduction, in the fourteenth century, of armour for horse as well as for rider (see Accoutrements). Horse armour, and plate armour for knights, were an attempt to counter the cloth-yard arrow with its high velocity discharged at a rapid rate from the Anglo-Welsh longbow, and never became entirely successful in this function. But armour and later the cuirass were retained for the protection they afforded against sword cuts in armour-to-armour *melées*, until the seventeenth century when the best cuirass would not stop a pistol ball fired at close range by the opposing horseman.

Weight still counted in cavalry engagements down to this time; not until about 1700 was it finally discounted in favour of mobility. Throughout the seventeenth century the mounted musketeer or dragoon had been steadily gaining ground. He could be, in terms of powder and shot, the counterpart of the old Asiatic mounted archer, and in this role the Hungarian hussars were supreme. More commonly the dragoon fired only at the halt, and often from the ground, not the saddle, so that his chief employment was to ride at best speed to some flanking position whence he could bring the enemy under *enfilade* fire while his own infantry advanced frontally (as at Culloden Moor). By the mid-eighteenth century all English and much European cavalry was called 'dragoon', either 'heavy' or 'light' (the difference in practice was minimal). The employment of 'true' cavalry, with its ability to deliver surprise attacks, which formed up on a start-line out of range and often well out of sight of the enemy, was almost a monopoly of the Prussians under Frederick the Great, although he used units first raised and trained under the eye of his father, Frederick William I. Though these hussars and uhlans might contain in their ranks nothing but German troopers, the technique in using the pistol, the sword and the lance were respectively Hungarian and Polish, and so was the type of horse ridden. Fast light horses of great stamina, bred on the borders of the Turkish and Austrian empires in such terri-

Horse in Warfare. An officer of the French Imperial Guard, *c.* 1812, painted by Théodore Géricault

tories as Wallachia and Moldavia, were hard enough for the Prussians to acquire, but for more westerly powers like France even more expensive. Most European state studs were founded with the object of producing a homebred substitute that would do the same job, at less expense and with a less precarious source of supply. In this field the British army of early Hanoverian times hardly competed: hence there were no British state studs, and royal and other private establishments of the same period were founded in Britain with other purposes in mind.

The new-style cavalry force could only be used with maximum effect if supported by field artillery that marched at the same speed and could bring its guns into action in the short time between the cavalry's forming into line and closing with the enemy. In fact, field artillery, 'ordnance on their carriages', had been a reality since the days of Shakespeare, but some of these 'carriages' had been ox-drawn. During the Thirty Years' War (1618–48) the Swedish armies of Gustavus Adolphus first used light field pieces served by gun-crews who rode on the march. The other role of the horse (or often mule) in the light-artillery field began slightly earlier with pack artillery whose role was to support the infantry attack in mountainous country. In the campaigns of the sixteenth century in Italy cannon that broke down into single loads to go on a pack-saddle were already in use.

'True' cavalry in great masses was used in all the European wars of the nineteenth century, but in the course of the Franco-Prussian war of 1871 the Montigny machine gun first came into service. In 1914 the armies of all the principal belligerents were equipped with some version of the Vickers/Maxim machine gun whose effect on cavalry even in relatively open order at ranges up to 2,000 yd (1·8 km) could be devastating. At the same time all these Maxim-type weapons were water-cooled, a factor which made their adoption by cavalry itself no easier; but even the provision of machine-gun squadrons within the cavalry regiment, armed with such early air-cooled types as the Hotchkiss, did not solve the problems to which the increasing tactical use of barbed wire contributed. On the Western Front, when cavalry played any effective part at all it was as mounted infantry, to which role all British regiments had come within an ace of being converted as a result of experience in the South African War. Only on the Eastern Front did 'real' cavalry engagements in nineteenth-century style occur between German, Austrian and Russian cavalry corps. So also the aftermath of strife between Soviet Russia and the infant Polish state was largely a 'traditional' cavalry war.

Cavalry warfare ended almost where it began, in the steppe. Late in World War II, when the German lines of communication in the East had been stretched beyond endurance, especially in the depths of winter, reserve units of the Wehrmacht suffered heavy losses from Russian cavalry divisions riding across the snow which the frozen-up tanks could not cross, on the same unsightly steppe ponies as the Scythians had ridden, firing machine carbines and throwing hand-grenades from the saddle with the same deadly effect as the Huns had loosed their arrows; and like them, melting away across the horizon before the dazed enemy had time to react. AD

Horse in Warfare. Cavalry continued to be used up to World War II. Cossacks attacking the enemy on the second Ukrainian front in 1943

Warmblood

Apart from the use of the terms 'coldblood' and 'warmblood' to distinguish animals with variable body temperature from those with constant body temperature, in some European countries they are applied to horses to distinguish those with Arab blood from those without. For example, the English Thoroughbred ('thoroughbred' is a literal translation of the Arabic *kuhaylan*) is a direct descendant of one of three Arab stallions (the DARLEY ARABIAN, GODOLPHIN ARABIAN or BYERLEY TURK) and is therefore a 'warmblood'. The HANOVERIAN horses, also 'warmbloods', are derived from English Thoroughbreds and the German Great Horse.

'Coldbloods' include the SHIRE, CLYDESDALE, SUFFOLK PUNCH, PERCHERON and ponies. WSC

Waziri Ponies see India and Pakistan

Weaving

The horse rocks from side to side. As it never gets adequate rest it is unable to do a normal day's work. See Vices. CF

Welfare Associations

Societies concerned with the welfare of the horse and pony proliferate in Britain, and range from the excellent to the not so good. The R.S.P.C.A., perhaps the best known, spreads its net widely from race meetings to horse shows, and its inspectors do splendid work in the wilder regions, ensuring that horses and ponies turned out on moorland

Welfare Associations. An R.S.P.C.A. official keeps a watch on the handling and conditions of ponies at a sale.

Westchester Cup

1886 Great Britain	Newport 10–4, 14–2
1902 Great Britain	Hurlingham 1–2, 6–1, 7–1
1909 United States	Hurlingham 9–5, 8–2
1911 United States	Meadow Brook 4½–3, 4½–3½
1913 United States	Meadow Brook 5½–3, 4½–4¼
1914 Great Britain	Meadow Brook 8½–3, 4–2¾
1921 United States	Hurlingham 11–4, 10–6
1924 United States	Meadow Brook 16–5, 14–5
1927 United States	Meadow Brook 13–3, 8–5
1930 United States	Meadow Brook 10–5, 14–9
1936 United States	Hurlingham 10–9, 8–6
1939 United States	Meadow Brook 11–7, 9–4

receive adequate hay in severe winter conditions. The Horses and Ponies Protection Association has concerned itself very actively with the conditions under which animals are exported to the continent of Europe, and has undoubtedly done a very great deal to alleviate the lot of horses and ponies which are sold for export. 'Ponies of Britain', however, under its indefatigable chairman, Mrs Glenda Spooner, has probably done more for the ordinary cob and pony than any other single body. A stalwart band of knowledgeable inspectors, who work on a voluntary basis, ensure that riding schools and trekking centres are properly conducted, that their animals are well kept and not overworked, and that adequate supervision is available so that they do not suffer from the well-meaning but often disastrous attentions of ignorant people. The approval of 'Ponies of Britain' is only granted to those who genuinely deserve it, and means more than that of any other body in the horse world. The British Horse Society also investigates and examines riding schools, and the Horse and Pony Benefit Fund assists a variety of worthy causes associated with welfare. At the other end of the scale is a considerable collection of privately-run establishments of the 'home of rest' type, where old horses and ponies pass the twilight of their days by courtesy of public subscription. PMM

In the United States, the principal nationwide organizations devoted to the welfare of animals, including horses, are the American Society for the Prevention of Cruelty to Animals (A.S.P.C.A.), based on the British R.S.P.C.A., and the American Humane Association. Vigilant inspectors attend most horse shows, rodeo and circus performances. Successful campaigns have been waged in recent years against severe bitting and the use of painful devices to produce brilliant artificial gaits in certain breeds, notably in the TENNESSEE WALKING HORSE. The American Horse Shows Association now penalizes any exhibitor whose horse shows scars or signs of bleeding of the mouth, muzzle, or feet, and includes in its rules specific restrictions concerning training and showing practices. Violations automatically bar an exhibitor from competing in recognized shows and may lead to fines and further penalties. On American racetracks, state and individual track authorities are constantly alert to detect and penalize the use of stimulating or pain-killing drugs in racehorses. Furthermore, individual philanthropists throughout the country have endowed animal shelters and hospitals. Since retiring from racing, Kelso, one of the greatest American Thoroughbred racehorses of the century, has made numerous public appearances as a fund-raiser for the Grayson Foundation for equine research and the veterinarian hospital of the University of Pennsylvania. MAS

Welsh Cob, Welsh Mountain Pony, Welsh Pony, see Mountain and Moorland Ponies

Westchester Cup

The Westchester Cup, a series of polo matches between the United States and Great Britain, started in 1886 in the United States. The first match, at Newport, Rhode Island, was won by Great Britain; the last, at Meadow Brook, Long Island, in 1939, by the United States. The contests consisted of the best of three matches, a match being eight periods of polo (sometimes seven). The Westchester Cup does not take place at fixed intervals but only when one country challenges and the other accepts. There have been no contests since World War II. HG

Western Horse see U.S.A.

Western Riding

The cowboy of the western United States has been admired ever since it was known that cowboys existed. Novelists made his life seem so noble and romantic that boys dreamed of becoming cowboys and girls dreamed of marrying them. Cinema and television increased the romance and popularity of Western riding.

Western riding today is mostly pleasure riding and is not very different from English riding except for the gear. Buying a horse trained by a Western trainer and riding with Western gear does not, however, immediately make the rider a bronco-buster. He still suffers the aches and pains of the novice horseman and is just as prone to fall from his horse as are his friends who use English tack.

Western riding is, of course, based on the riding cowboys actually do. Cowhorses do sometimes buck, so the saddle should be of such design that a good cowboy can ride a bucking horse in it. The cutting horse is almost as difficult to ride as a bucking horse for the rider must anticipate the cow's moves and the horse's moves to block the cow. If the horse or the man makes a mistake the rider can easily be thrown, so help from a wider fork and a higher cantle is in order.

When gathering cattle in rough country, the rider must throw caution to the winds and be in the right place at the right time. He must jump his horse over logs and dash down mountainous slopes at full gallop, all the while maintaining control over the cattle. Riding bucking horses, roping steers and working cattle at full gallop are all facets of Western riding. Of course, there are times when the cowboy plods along, pushing tired cattle at a snail's pace, a task that could be handled by a novice.

The men who show cutting horses and the men who rope calves and steers in rodeos generally have some ranch background. People who show horses in Western pleasure, trail horse, Western riding and Western equitation classes generally have little or no ranch background though the professionals rising in such events often come from ranches.

The Western horse is generally shown with a loose rein that would be condemned in an English class. This is because cutting horse people ride with a very loose rein to show the judge that they are not handling the horse. For a while, the reins in all Western classes were held ridiculously loose but the tendency is now towards a little contact to show control over the horse at all times. The seat of the Western rider is generally a bit sloppy for the shape of the saddle forces the rider back over the horse's kidneys. He soon rides with all of his weight on the seat with little weight in the stirrups. His back becomes hunched from this position. This sloppy seat is not recommended because a person who rides a horse in such a way could not ride a bad horse. The cowboy of thirty years ago rode his horse in a more alert fashion, straight in the saddle, ready for any sudden movement his horse might make. There is now a welcome trend in the United States toward a 'balanced ride' and towards saddles designed to allow the rider to take a more sensible seat. DJ

Western States Trail Ride see Long-Distance Riding

Western Tack

The gear used on the American Western horse is unique. The Western saddle is derived from the war saddle of the *conquistadores*. The vast land areas of the western and southwestern United States caused the cattle to become wild and the horse gear evolved according to necessity.

The Californians found that some form of rope was required to capture a cow that had become wild. A rawhide lariat was carried on a long pole and the loop was dropped over the cow's head. Finally, throwing the lariat became the favoured method and the cowmen became very proficient at this. The lariat had to be tied to something in order to hold the cow. First, it was fixed to the horse's tail but this proved a bit impractical. Then a sort of button was fashioned on the back of the saddle. This, too, was discarded in favour of the saddle horn. The primary purpose of the saddle horn was (and is) to furnish a post for the lariat to be tied to.

California ranches were large and generally free of brush. The *vaquero* (cowboy) carried a long *reata* (lariat), would catch his his cow and take turns of the lariat (Spanish *dar la vuelta*, to 'give a turn', shortened to 'dallies') around the saddle horn. His braided lariat was not strong so he would lessen the shock by allowing the lariat to slip a bit on impact. He would play his steer or cow as a fisherman plays his trout. Since the lariat was not strong, the saddle did not have to be securely attached to the horse. One *cincha* (girth) was used, rigged from the centre of the saddle or 'centre-fire' rigging, the name derived from gun cartridges where the firing pin strikes the centre of the primer.

The *vaquero*'s horse was beautifully trained. A rawhide noseband called a *jaquima* (HACKAMORE) was used for the initial training since metal for bits was very scarce. A traditional method of training with the hackamore, very similar to basic dressage training, was handed down from father to son. The California horse was fully trained when the hackamore was discarded in favour of the finishing bit, the spade. This bit has a very high port and, when used by an expert, offers a refined means of communication between horse and rider. The bit and headstall were generously adorned with beautifully engraved silver and gold. The reins were made of braided rawhide and the braidwork was and is beautiful.

An entirely different mode of cattle handling evolved in the southwest, namely Texas, New Mexico and Arizona, and spread from the Rio Grande up into Canada. This was brush country where the cowboy had no chance to throw a long lariat. He would have a quick throw where the brush thinned out. If the opportunity was lost, so was the cow. A short rope and a strong saddle were needed. The rope was tied 'hard and fast' to the saddle horn. This method was dangerous but necessary. The saddle rigged with one *cincha* could not stand the strain of heavy roping and it was found that the centre-fire rig was prone to slip, so 'rim-fire' rigging evolved: one cinch was fixed directly below the horn and another was fastened to the back of the saddle. When the cow was caught, she was tied to the saddle.

Horses were not as highly trained as in California. If the horse could run up to a cow in the brush to allow its rider a throw, that was sufficient. The horse had to be jerked around more than its California neighbour so the bit that evolved was a mild one with a low port and short shanks. The bit shank generally bent backwards to allow the horse to graze, hence the name 'grazing bit'. Saddles and bridles were generally plain, for their use was in rough brush that would scar prettier equipment. Reins were long, strong and divided since riders led and tied their mounts by the bridle reins, a thing no self-respecting Californian would do.

The rim-fire (double-rigged) saddle is in almost universal use today. The basic saddle has a seat that slopes back to the cantle. The stirrups hang farther back than in most other saddles. The sloping seat and the position of the stirrups seem uncomfortable until one becomes used to them. Some saddles are being made with a level seat and forward-hung stirrups to make the Western saddle ride like the other saddles of the world. The saddle has a sheepskin lining and several woollen blankets are gener-

Western Tack. A 'balanced ride' saddle. The seat is level and the stirrup strap is hung far forward. This saddle is ridden sitting well forward.

ally used for padding. The saddle lining holds the woollen blankets in place. DJ

Westfalen

There is no Westfalen breed as such; 'Westfalen' designates warmblood horses bred in the German province of Westphalia. Thoroughbred, East Prussian, Oldenburg, Hanoverian and Norman stallions have been used on the local mares to produce a strong, deep, well-built, active saddle/harness and working horse. See also Germany. DMG

West Indies

There were no horses on the islands of the Caribbean Sea before the arrival of Europeans in the late fifteenth century. The Carib and Arawak Indians who had already colonized most of the islands used dugout canoes for transport and did not venture far inland. The Spanish, the first Europeans to take possession of most of the islands, brought with them horses and other animals, including pigs and goats which very soon escaped and lived in a wild state, in the process destroying much of the natural vegetation and wild life. On a few of the islands, notably the Caymans and the Grenadines, the horses ran wild and interbred, eventually producing a distinctive local breed of very small, fine-boned Arabian-type horses. These horses, usually no more than 11 hands (1·12 m) are hardy and in the Grenadines are used for racing over short distances.

The basic stock of horses in the West Indies is the Spanish or Arabian type. On the whole they are small, averaging 14–15 hands (1·42–1·52 m). Many have Arabian features and they are noted for their hardiness and surefootedness. They are often very fast over short distances. Until recent years they were used exclusively for plantation work and for crossing with Thoroughbreds for racing, a popular sport on several islands for well over a hundred years which has encouraged the introduction of a considerable amount of Thoroughbred blood into the local breed. Polo has also been popular, particularly in Jamaica, for many years and this has led to selective breeding, although good plantation cutting horses are often used on the polo field.

In the West Indies in 1971 Jamaica had the most types and probably the finest horses. There are Thoroughbred horse farms which are comparable or superior to any in Central America, four polo clubs and several riding stables, most of which offer trail-type riding through beautiful country. Until the early part of this century quality horses of the Arabian type were regularly imported from Cuba, which, until the break up of the big estates, had several Arabian horse farms.

In Hispaniola, Haiti has a small inbred and rather dejected-looking type of horse which is found mainly on the north coast, where it is used to carry tourists from Cap Haitien to the Citadel. In the Bahamas on New Providence Island, QUARTER HORSES imported from the United States of America are used for racing.

On most islands of any size there are horses, but they are usually not good riding horses, except in Jamaica and to a lesser extent St Croix in the Virgin Islands. There is no hunting or organized jumping, although attempts to start the latter are being made in Jamaica. Horses are still extensively used by overseers and cattlemen on the larger islands. There are also riding stables of greatly varying quality and, in the British tradition, saddles and equipment of English type are used on most of the islands.

With the introduction of Thoroughbred Quarter Horse and Arabian stallions for breeding purposes into several of the islands of the West Indies, a steady improvement can be expected in the years to come. PT

Whistling

Pathologically identical with ROARING, the only difference is the higher-pitched sound. CF

Wild West Show see Rodeo

Windgalls

Synovial distensions which occur in the region of the fetlock joint. Articular windgalls involve the joint capsule and tendinous windgalls arise from the sesamoidean sheath surrounding the flexor tendons. CF

Windsor Greys

Grey coach horses bred at the Royal Stud, Windsor, England; since 1923 they have replaced the Hanoverian Creams (ISABELLAS) in British royal processions. LFB

Windsucking

A VICE similar to CRIB BITING except that the horse succeeds in swallowing air without grasping any object in its teeth. CF

Below: **Windgalls.** Fore leg with windgall (arrowed)

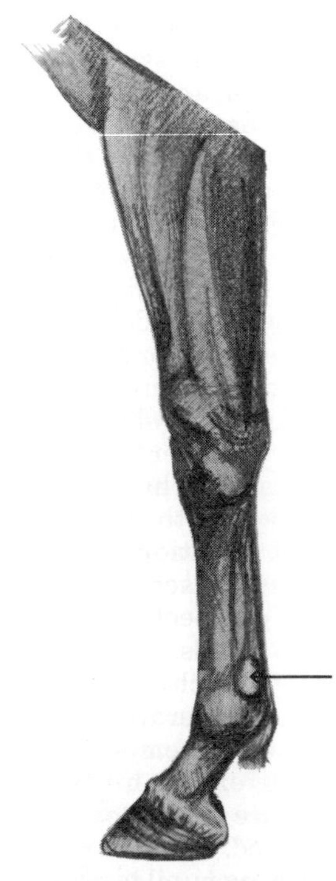

Bottom: **West Indies.** Jamaican sportsmen play polo on the north coast near Montego Bay.

Winkers see Blinkers

Wobbler Disease
Seen in young Thoroughbreds under two years, this is characterized by uncoordinated movement of the hindquarters. The cause has not been fully elucidated but it may be linked with accidents to the spine during foalhood that ultimately cause pressure on the spinal cord. CF

Working Pupils
Working pupil schemes are at best a means by which the pupil can learn his trade without having to pay a large premium for the privilege and at worst a source of cheap labour for the employer.

By definition, a working pupil is one who enters a riding establishment on the basis of working for his or her keep and instruction. He may or may not receive remuneration in addition. If he does, it is usually simply pocket money. He will probably be confined, at least at the outset, to the more menial tasks of mucking out, sweeping up the yard and cleaning tack, and actual riding instruction will not be as frequent as if he were paying fees for his instruction. On the other hand, a conscientious proprietor with a sense of fair play will ensure that his working pupils are given every opportunity available to improve their riding.

It is quite possible to derive just as much benefit from being a working pupil, in a reputable establishment, as the paying pupils, although it may be that the objective takes somewhat longer to attain. Many working pupils are, when qualified, taken on to the strength of the training establishment, or found situations when they leave. The more reputable schools usually have a waiting list of prospective employers for their qualified pupils.

The success of such schemes depends entirely on the cooperation of those involved. It is up to the employer to ensure that he does not exploit his working pupils, and that they are neither overworked nor under-instructed. It is equally incumbent upon the working pupil to render wholehearted service, in the knowledge that he is being given opportunities for which others have to pay. See also Careers. PMM

Württemberg
The chief stud of the Württemberg warmblood horses is Marbach, founded in 1573. As with so many German light breeds, the type of horse required was one suited to the climate, soil and country (about 2,400 ft or 730 m up in the Swabian Alps) to work for farmers of small means, in other words a hardy and hard-working horse. The ARABIAN, which possess these qualities, was crossed into the local warmblood horses. EAST PRUSSIAN mares and ANGLO-NORMAN stallions were also used, following a fundamental rule that to 'fix' a breed only suitable, carefully selected breeding stock should be used. However, the breed did not succeed until the Stud Director, von Hofacker, stopped experiments and set his sights on a warmblood of Anglo-Norman type. The Württemberg developed the characteristics of a useful all-round cob. Because of limited means, the owners of brood mares send weaned filly foals to special farms where the range of grazing is good, while colt foals are raised at the Marbach National Stud. See Germany. DMG

Xenophon
Xenophon, a Greek cavalry officer and historian, was born at Athens *c.* 430 B.C., the son of Gryllus, and died probably later than 355 B.C. He belonged to an equestrian family of knights from the ancient township of Attica who may have been friends of Socrates. As a young man Xenophon fought at Arginusae and was made an officer in the expedition against Artaxerxes II in which he was the leading spirit. After fighting with the Spartans against Athens he eventually settled near Olympia to indulge his taste in sport and literature. He is best known to horsemen by the fact that his essays on horsemanship (*Hippike*) and hunting boar and hare (*Cynogeticus*) are the first of their kind ever to be written on these subjects. His works on horsemanship have been translated into many modern languages. Probably the most complete and the most readable for the modern horseman is Professor Morris-Morgan's *Art of Horsemanship by Xenophon* translated direct from the Greek text and published in 1893. LFB

Yaboo a word of Persian origin meaning 'nag'. The term refers not to a particular breed but to a nondescript horse of any type. See Persian Horse. LF

Yakut see Horse Breeding under U.S.S.R.

Yarimkan a halfbred Arab. See Turkey

Yearling
A horse over one year and under two: yearling colt, yearling filly. CF

Yomud (Iomud, Jomud) see Turkoman

Yorkshire Coach Horse
This tall bay carriage horse, now officially extinct, was popular in London and other capital cities throughout the nineteenth

Yorkshire Coach Horse. Candidate 64, winner of the first prize at the Yorkshire Agricultural Society's show held at Driffield in 1875

Z

century. Produced by what was called the 'one in three' cross between Thoroughbred and Cleveland Bay blood (e.g. by mating a Cleveland Bay mare with a Thoroughbred × Cleveland Bay stallion) it was always a type rather than a pure breed, since it needed constant infusions of both Cleveland and Thoroughbred blood to maintain its quality and vigour. But as a type it was probably the best and most beautiful carriage horse in the world, with the elegance and speed of the Thoroughbred combined with the power, bearing and unvarying colour of the Cleveland. Throughout the century these horses were exported in thousands all over the world, at prices which must have seemed fantastic to the Cleveland farmers, who were not slow to cross their mares with Thoroughbred or part Thoroughbred horses in order to benefit by them. Numbers of the old breed dwindled dangerously, and in spite of the efforts of the Cleveland Bay Horse Society, formed in 1884 and at first working in conjunction with the Yorkshire Coach Horse breeders, this trend continued. Friction between the two sets of breeders arose when the Cleveland Bay Society refused to admit the Coach Horse Candidate to their Stud Book; in 1886 the Yorkshire Coach Horse breeders broke away, formed their own society and produced their own Stud Book. But though they flourished for some years their horses, produced only for carriage work, were driven out of existence by the car. Fifty years after the publication of their first Stud Book the Yorkshire Coach Horse Society was wound up. RK

Yunnan Pony see China

Zabaikal see Horse Breeding under U.S.S.R.

Zebra

At present, there are extant three striped species of the genus *Equus*. The largest is Grévy's zebra (*E. grevyi*), about 13 hands (1·32 m) high. It lives in the open scrub-covered plains of Ethiopia, northern Kenya and Somaliland. The black-and-white stripes are narrow, continuing down the legs, while the belly is off-white in colour. The muzzle is brown as are the tips of the ears and ends of the upright mane.

The mountain zebra (*E. zebra*) which once roamed as far as Cape Province, from S.W. Africa and Angola, is the smallest, the wildest and the most asslike of the three. This zebra has rarely been tamed, although Mrs Hayes, wife of the writer Capt. M. H. Hayes, rode one sidesaddle.

The third species is *Equus burchelli* of which Burchell's or the Chapman zebra is the best known. It has also been domesticated and is nearest to the horse in conformation, although completely striped with bands of dun or brown between the darker stripes, which cover a basically white body. Some members of this species have striped, others white legs. Its habitat is north of the Orange river. The true quagga is now unfortunately extinct, destroyed by Boer colonists in the nineteenth century. Only the forequarters and head were striped, the rest of the body was a dun colour with lighter, almost white legs. It lived on the Great Karroo of Cape Province and in the Orange Free State.

There have been substantiated reports of albino zebras, the stripes so faint as to be scarcely visible, and also of maneless zebras. Zebras are without callosities on the hind legs. DMG

Reference: Capt. W. Cornwallis Harris, *Wild Animals of South Africa*. (n.d.).
W. B. Tegetmeier and C. L. Sutherland, *Horses, Asses, Zebras, Mules and Mule Breeding*, 1895.

Zebra. *Top: Equus zebra* has narrow black-and-white stripes, which continue down the legs.
Centre: Equus burchelli (Burchell's or Chapman zebra) has paler stripes between the darker stripes.
Above: Equus quagga, the true quagga, now extinct, had stripes only on its head and fore quarters.

Zemaituka

There are two strains of this primitive, very ancient native horse of the Baltic states, particularly of western Lithuania: the steppe Tartar pony type with Przevalski blood (see Asiatic Wild Horse) and the Oriental horse brought back by the Crusaders of the Teutonic Order and more recently improved by fresh introductions of Arabian blood. Characteristic colours are dun and mouse dun. DMG

Zhmudky see Lithuanian Heavy Horse